THE DECLINE OF THE WEST

OSWALD SPENGLER
BORN MAY 29, 1880 — DIED MAY 8, 1936

THE DECLINE OF
THE WEST
[DER UNTERGANG DES ABENDLANDES]

VOLUME ONE
FORM AND ACTUALITY
[GESTALT UND WIRKLICHKEIT]

VOLUME TWO
PERSPECTIVES OF WORLD-HISTORY
[WELTHISTORISCHE PERSPEKTIVEN]

LETTERS OF OSWALD SPENGLER
1913-1936
TRANSLATED & EDITED BY ARTHUR HELPS
[BRIEFE 1913-36. EDITED BY MANFRED SCHRÖTER
AND ANTON KOKTENEK]

THESE ARE BORZOI BOOKS PUBLISHED BY
ALFRED A. KNOPF

OSWALD SPENGLER
THE DECLINE OF THE WEST

VOLUME TWO

Perspectives of World-History

AUTHORIZED TRANSLATION WITH NOTES BY

CHARLES FRANCIS ATKINSON

NEW YORK · ALFRED · A · KNOPF · MCMLXXX

THE DECLINE OF THE WEST

TRANSLATOR'S NOTE

In the annotations to this volume I have followed the same course as in the first — namely, that of giving primary references to the *Encyclopædia Britannica* as being the most considerable work of the kind that is really widely distributed in both the English-speaking fields, though occasionally special encyclopædias or other works are referred to. Owing to the more definitely historical character of this volume, as compared with its predecessor, and particularly its stressing of a history that scarcely figures as yet in a regular education — the "Magian" — such references are necessarily more numerous. Even so, more might perhaps have been inserted with advantage. The Translator's notes have no pretension to be critical in themselves, though here and there an argument is pointed with an additional example, or an obvious criticism anticipated. In each domain they will no doubt be resented by an expert, but the same expert will, it is hoped, find them useful for domains not his own.

In the first volume of the English version, references to the second were necessarily given according to the pagination of the German. A comparative table of English and German page numbers has therefore been inserted. A list of corrigenda to Vol. I is also issued with this volume.

London, July 1928   C. F. A.

TABLE OF GERMAN AND ENGLISH PAGES

GERMAN VOL. II	ENGLISH VOL. II	GERMAN VOL. II	ENGLISH VOL. II
334	273	403	327
342	279	421	340
343	280	427	345
345	281	441	355
346	282	482	388
350	286	488	392
354	288	521	416
357	291	529	422
358	292	539	430
359	293	562	449
360	293	577	460
362	295	589	471
363	296	603	481
365	297	607	484
368	299	610	486
369	300	616	490
370	301	618	492
373	303	624	499
376	306	625	500
378	307	626	501
382	310	627	501
385	313	631	504

CONTENTS OF VOLUME II

ix

CONTENTS

CHAPTER I
ORIGIN AND LANDSCAPE
(A)
THE COSMIC AND THE MICROCOSM

ORIGIN AND LANDSCAPE

(A)

THE COSMIC AND THE MICROCOSM

I[1]

REGARD the flowers at eventide as, one after the other, they close in the setting sun. Strange is the feeling that then presses in upon you — a feeling of enigmatic fear in the presence of this blind dreamlike earth-bound existence. The dumb forest, the silent meadows, this bush, that twig, do not stir themselves, it is the wind that plays with them. Only the little gnat is free — he dances still in the evening light, he moves whither he will.

A plant is nothing on its own account. It forms a part of the landscape in which a chance made it take root. The twilight, the chill, the closing of every flower — these are not cause and effect, not danger and willed answer to danger. They are a single process of nature, which is accomplishing itself near, with, and in the plant. The individual is not free to look out for itself, will for itself, or choose for itself.

An animal, on the contrary, can choose. It is emancipated from the servitude of all the rest of the world. This midget swarm that dances on and on, that solitary bird still flying through the evening, the fox approaching furtively the nest — these are *little worlds of their own within another great world*. An animalcule in a drop of water, too tiny to be perceived by the human eye, though it lasts but a second and has but a corner of this drop as its field — nevertheless is *free and independent in the face of the universe*. The giant oak, upon one of whose leaves the droplet hangs, is not.[1]

Servitude and freedom — this is in last and deepest analysis the differentia by which we distinguish vegetable and animal existence. Yet only the plant is wholly and entirely what it is; in the being of the animal there is something dual. A vegetable is only a vegetable; an animal is a vegetable and something more besides. A herd that huddles together trembling in the presence of danger, a child that clings weeping to its mother, a man desperately striving to force a way into his God — all these are seeking to return out of the life of freedom into the vegetal servitude from which they were emancipated into individuality and loneliness.

The seeds of a flowering plant show, under the microscope, two sheath-

---

[1] In what follows I have drawn upon a metaphysical work that I hope shortly to be able to publish.

leaves which form and protect the young plant that is presently to turn towards the light, with its organs of the life-cycle and of reproduction, and in addition a third, which contains the future root and tells us that the plant is destined irrevocably to become once again part of a landscape. In the higher animals, on the contrary, we observe that the fertilized egg forms, in the first hours of its individualized existence, an outer sheath by which the inner containers of the cyclic and reproductive components — i.e., the plant element in the animal body — are enclosed and shut off from the mother body and *all the rest of the world*. This outer sheath symbolizes the essential character of animal existence and distinguishes the two kinds in which the Living has appeared on this earth.

There are noble names for them, found and bequeathed by the Classical world. The plant is something *cosmic*, and the animal is additionally *a microcosm in relation to a macrocosm*. When, and not until, the unit has thus separated itself from the All and can define its position with respect to the All, it becomes thereby a microcosm. Even the planets in their great cycles are in servitude, and it is only these tiny worlds that move freely relative to a great one which appears in their consciousness as their world-around (environment). Only through this individualism of the microcosm does that which the light offers to its eyes — our eyes — acquire meaning as "body," and even to planets we are from some inner motive reluctant to concede the property of bodiliness.

All that is cosmic bears the hall-mark of *periodicity;* it has "beat" (rhythm, tact). All that is microcosmic possesses *polarity;* it possesses "tension."

We speak of tense alertness and tense thought, but all wakeful states are in their essence tensions. Sense and object, I and thou, cause and effect, thing and property — each of these is a tension between discretes, and when the state pregnantly called "*détente*" appears, then at once fatigue, and presently sleep, set in for the microcosmic side of life. A human being asleep, discharged of all tensions, is leading only a plantlike existence.

Cosmic beat, on the other hand, is everything that can be paraphrased in terms like direction, time, rhythm, destiny, longing — from the hoof-beats of a team of thoroughbreds and the deep tread of proud marching soldiers to the silent fellowship of two lovers, the sensed tact that makes the dignity of a social assembly, and that keen quick judgment of a "judge of men" which I have already, earlier in this work,[1] called physiognomic tact.

This beat of cosmic cycles goes on notwithstanding the freedom of microcosmic movement in space, and from time to time breaks down the tension of the waking individual's being into the *one* grand felt harmony. If we have ever followed the flight of a bird in the high air — how, always in the same way, it rises, turns, glides, loses itself in the distance — we must have felt the plantlike certainty of the "it" and the "we" in this ensemble of motion, which needs no bridge of reason to unite your sense of it with mine. This is the meaning

[1] For instance, Vol. I, p. 154. — *Tr.*

of war-dances and love-dances amongst men and beasts. In this wise a regiment mounting to the assault under fire is forged into a unity, in this wise does
the crowd collect at some exciting occasion and become a body, capable of
thinking and acting pitifully, blindly, and strangely for a moment ere it falls
apart again. In such cases the microcosmic wall is obliterated. *It* jostles and
threatens, *it* pushes and pulls, *it* flees, swerves, and sways. Limbs intertwine,
feet rush, *one* cry comes from every mouth, *one* destiny overlies all. Out of a
sum of little single worlds comes suddenly a complete whole.

The perception of cosmic beat we call "feel (*Fühlen*)," that of microcosmic
tensions "feeling (*Empfinden*)." The ambiguity of the word "*Sinnlichkeit*"
has obscured this clear difference between the general and plantlike side and
the specifically animal side of life. If we say for the one race- or sex-life, and
for the other sense-life, a deep connexion reveals itself between them. The
former ever bears the mark of periodicity, beat, even to the extent of harmony
with the great cycles of the stars, of relation between female nature and the
moon, of this life generally to night, spring, warmth. The latter consists in
tensions, polarities of light and object illuminated, of cognition and that which
is cognized, of wound and the weapon that has caused it. Each of these sides of
life has, in the more highly developed genera, taken shape in special organs,
and the higher the development, the clearer the emphasis on each side. We
possess *two cyclic organs of the cosmic existence*, the blood system and the sex-organ,
and two differentiating organs of microcosmic mobility, senses and nerves. We have
to assume that in its origin the *whole* body has been both a cyclic and a tactual
organ.

The blood is for us the symbol of the living. Its course proceeds without
pause, from generation to death, from the mother body in and out of the body of
the child, in the waking state and in sleep, never-ending. The blood of the
ancestors flows through the chain of the generations and binds them in a
great linkage of destiny, beat, and time. Originally this was accomplished
only by a process of division, redivision, and ever new division of the cycles,
until finally a specific organ of sexual generation appeared and made *one moment*
into a symbol of duration. And how thereafter creatures begat and conceived,
how the plantlike in them drove them to reproduce themselves for the maintenance beyond themselves of the eternal cycle, how the *one* great pulse-beat
operates through all the detached souls, filling, driving, checking, and often
destroying — that is the deepest of all life's secrets, the secret that all religious mysteries and all great poems seek to penetrate, the secret whose tragedy
stirred Goethe in his "*Selige Sehnsucht*" and "*Wahlverwandtschaften*," where
the child has to die because, brought into existence out of discordant cycles of
the blood, it is the fruit of a cosmic sin.

To these cosmic organs the microcosm as such adds (in the degree to which
it possesses freedom of movement *vis-à-vis* the macrocosm) the organ "sense,"

which is originally touch-sense and nothing else. Even now, at our own high level of development, we use the word "touch" quite generally of contacts by eye, by ear, and even by the understanding, for it is the simplest expression of the mobility of a living creature that needs constantly to be establishing its relation to its world-around. But to "establish" here means to fix *place*, and thus all senses, however sophisticated and remote from the primitive they may seem, are essentially *positive senses;* there are no others. Sensation of all kinds distinguishes proper and alien. And for the positional definition of the alien with respect to the proper the scent of the hound serves just as much as the hearing of the stag and the eye of the eagle. Colour, brightness, tones, odours, all conceivable modes of sensation, imply detachment, distance, extension.

Like the cosmic cycle of the blood, the differentiating activity of sense is originally a unity. The active sense is always an understanding sense also. In these simple relations seeking and finding are one — that which we most appositely call "touch." It is only later, in a stage wherein considerable demands are made upon developed senses, that sensation and understanding of sensation cease to be identical and the latter begins to detach itself more and more clearly from the former. In the outer sheath the critical organ separates itself from the sense-organ (as the sex-organ does from that of blood-circulation). But our use of words like "keen," "sensitive," "insight," "poking our nose," and "flair," not to mention the terminology of logic, all taken from the visual world, shows well enough that we regard all understanding as derived from sensation, and that even in the case of man the two still work hand in hand.

We see a dog lying indifferent and then in a moment tense, listening, and scenting — what he merely senses he is seeking to understand as well. He is able, too, to reflect — that is a state in which the understanding is almost alone at work and playing upon mat sensations. The older languages very clearly expressed this graduation, sharply distinguishing each degree as an activity of a specific kind by means of a specific label — e.g., hear, listen, listen for (*lauschen*); smell, scent, sniff; see, spy, observe. In such series as these the reason-content becomes more and more important relative to the sensation-content.

Finally, however, a supreme sense develops among the rest. A something in the All, which for ever remains inaccessible to our will-to-understand, evokes for itself a bodily organ. The eye comes into existence — and in and with the eye, as its opposite pole, light. Abstract thinking about light may lead (and has led) to an ideal light representable by an ensemble picture of waves and rays, but the significance of this development in actuality was that thenceforward life was embraced and taken in *through the light-world of the eye.* This is the supreme marvel that makes everything human what it is. Only with this light-world of the eye do distances come into being as colours and brightnesses; only in this world are night and day and things and motions visible in the extension of illumined space, and the universe of infinitely remote stars circling above the earth, and that light-horizon of the individual life which stretches so far beyond the environs of the body.

In the world of this light — not the light which science has deduced indirectly by the aid of mental concepts, themselves derived from visions ("theory" in the Greek sense) — it comes to pass that seeing, human herds wander upon the face of this little earth-star, and that circumstances of light — the full southern flood over Egypt and Mexico, the greyness of the north — contribute to the determination of their entire life. It is for his *eye* that man develops the magic of his architecture, wherein the constructional elements given by touch are restated in relations generated by light. Religion, art, thought, have all arisen for light's sake, and all differentiations reduce to the one point of whether it is the bodily eye or the mind's eye that is addressed.

And with this there emerges in all clarity yet another distinction, which is normally obscured by the use of the ambiguous word "consciousness (*Bewusstsein*)." I distinguish *being* or "being there" (*Dasein*) from *waking-being* or waking-consciousness (*Wachsein*).[1] Being possesses beat and direction, while waking-consciousness is tension and extension. In being a destiny rules, while waking-consciousness distinguishes causes and effects. The prime question is for the one "when and wherefore?" for the other "where and how?"

A plant leads an existence that is without waking-consciousness. In sleep all creatures become plants, the tension of polarity to the world-around is extinguished, and the beat of life goes on. A plant knows only a relation to the when and the wherefore. The upthrust of the first green shoots out of the wintry earth, the swelling of the buds, the whole mighty process of blooming, scent, colour glory, and ripening — all this is desire to fulfil a destiny, constant yearning towards a "when?"

"Where?" on the other hand can have no meaning for a plant existence. It is the question with which awakening man daily orients himself afresh with respect to the world. For it is only the pulse-beat of Being that endures throughout the generations, whereas waking-consciousness begins anew for each microcosm. And herein lies the distinction between procreation and birth, the first being a pledge of duration, the second a beginning. A plant, therefore, is bred, but it is not born. It "is there," but no awakening, no birthday, expands a sense-world around it.

II

With this we are brought face to face with man. In man's waking-consciousness nothing disturbs the now pure lordship of the eye. The sounds of the night, the wind, the panting of beasts, the odour of flowers, all stimulate in him *a "whither" and a "whence" in the world of light*. Of the world of scent, in which even our closest comrade the dog still co-ordinates his visual impressions, we

[1] See Vol. 1, p. 54. — *Tr.*

have no conception whatever. We know nothing of the world of the butterfly, whose crystalline eye projects no synthetic picture, or of those animals which, while certainly not destitute of senses, are blind. *The only space that remains to us is visual space*, and in it places have been found for the relics of other sense-worlds (such as sounds, scents, heat and cold) as *properties and effects of light-things* — it is a seen fire that warmth comes from, it is a seen rose in illumined space that gives off the scent and we speak of a certain tone as violin-tone. As to the stars, our conscious relations with them are limited to seeing them — over our heads they shine, describing their visible path.[1] But of these sense-worlds there is no doubt that animals and even primitive men still have sensations that are wholly different from ours; some of these sensations we are able to figure to ourselves indirectly by the aid of scientific hypotheses, but the rest now escape us altogether.

This impoverishment of the sensual implies, however, an immeasurable deepening. Human waking-consciousness is no longer a mere tension between body and environment. It is now life *in* a self-contained light-world. The body moves *in* the space that is seen. The depth-experience [2] is a mighty out-thrust *into the visible distance* from a light-centre [3] — the point which we call "I." "I" is a light-concept. From this point onward the life of an "I" becomes essentially a life in the sun, and night is akin to death. And out of it, too, there arises a new feeling of fear which absorbs all others within itself — *fear before the invisible*, fear of that which one hears or feels, suspects, or observes in its effects without seeing. Animals indeed experience fear in other forms, but man finds these forms puzzling, and even uneasiness in the presence of stillness to which primitive men and children are subject (and which they seek to dispel by noise and loud talking) is disappearing in the higher types of mankind. It is fear of the invisible that is the essence and hall-mark of human religiousness. Gods are surmised, imagined, envisaged light-actualities, and the idea of an "invisible" god is the highest expression of human transcendence. Where the bounds of the light-world are, there lies the beyond, and salvation is emancipation from the spell of the light-world and its facts.

In precisely this resides the ineffable charm and the very real power of emancipation that music possesses for us men. For music is the only art whose means lie outside the light-world that has so long become coextensive with our total world, and music alone, therefore, can take us right out of this world, break up the steely tyranny of light, and let us fondly imagine that we are on the verge of reaching the soul's final secret — an illusion due to the fact that our waking consciousness is now so dominated by one sense only, so thoroughly adapted

---

[1] Even scientific astronomy, when applied to everyday work, states the movements of the heavenly bodies in terms referred to our perception of them. — *Tr.*

[2] See Vol. I, p. 172. — *Tr.*

[3] A very similar notion of the light-world diffused from the light-centre forms the cardinal point of the philosophy of Robert Grosseteste, Bishop of Lincoln (1175-1273). — *Tr.*

to the eye-world, that it is incapable of forming, out of the impressions it receives, a world of the ear.[1]

Man's thought, then, is visual thought, our concepts are derived from vision, and the whole fabric of our logic is a light-world in the imagination.

This narrowing and consequent deepening, which has led to all our sense-impressions being adapted to and ordered with those of sight, has led also to the replacement of the innumerable methods of thought-communication known to animals by the one single medium of language, which is a bridge *in the light-world* between two persons present to one another's bodily or imaginative eyes. The other modes of speaking of which vestiges remain at all have long been absorbed into language in the form of mimicry, gesture, or emphasis. The difference between purely human speech and general animal utterance is that words and word-linkages constitute a domain of inward light-ideas, which has been built up under the sovereignty of the eyes. Every word-meaning has a light-value, even in the case of words like "melody," "taste," "cold," or of perfectly abstract designations.

Even among the higher animals, the habit of reciprocal understanding by means of a sense-link has brought about a marked difference between *mere* sensation and *understanding* sensation. If we distinguish in this wise *sense-impressions* and *sense-judgments* (e.g., scent-judgment, taste-judgment, or aural-judgment), we find that very often, even in ants and bees, let alone birds of prey, horses, and dogs, the centre of gravity has palpably shifted towards the judgment side of waking-being. But it is only under the influence of language that there is set up within the waking-consciousness a definite *opposition* between sensation and understanding, a tension that in animals is quite unthinkable and even in man can hardly have been at first anything more than a rarely actualized possibility. The development of language, then, brought along with it a determination of fundamental significance — *the emancipation of understanding from sensation.*

More and more often there appears, in lieu of the simple comprehension of the gross intake, a comprehension of the significances of the component sense-impressions, which have hardly been noticed as such before.[2] Finally these impressions themselves are discarded and replaced by the felt connotations of familiar word-sounds. The word, originally the name of a visual thing, changes imperceptibly into the label of a mental thing, the "concept." We are far from being able to fix exact meanings to such names — that we can do only with wholly new names. We never use a word twice with identical connotation, and no one ever understands exactly as another does. But mutual comprehen-

---

[1] The coming of radio broadcasting has in no way altered, but has rather confirmed, the validity of this. The listener either translates his aural impressions into those of the light-world or else yields even more readily than usual to the "illusion" here discussed. — *Tr.*

[2] The original reads: "*An Stelle des völlig einheitlichen verstehenden Empfindens erscheint oft und öfter ein Verstehen der Bedeutung von kaum noch beachteten Sinneseindrücken.*" — *Tr.*

sion is possible, in spite of this, because of the common world-outlook that has been induced in both, with and by the use of a common language; in an ambiance common to the lives and activities of both, mere word-sounds suffice to evoke cognate ideas. It is this mode of comprehending by means of sounds at once derived and detached (abstract) from actual seeing which, however rarely we can find it definitely evidenced at the primitive level, does in fact sharply separate the generic-animal kind of waking-consciousness from the purely human kind which supervenes. Just so, at an earlier stage, the appearance of waking-consciousness as such fixed a frontier between the general plantlike and the specifically animal existence.

Understanding detached from sensation is called thought. Thought has introduced a permanent disunity into the human waking-consciousness. From early times it has rated understanding and sensibility as "higher" and "lower" soul-power. It has created the fateful opposition between the light-world of the eye, described as a figment and an illusion, and the world-imagined ("*vorgestellte,*" "set before" oneself), in which the concepts, with their faint but ineffaceable tinge of light-coloration, live and do business. And henceforth for man, so long as he "thinks," this is the true world, the world-in-itself. At the outset the ego was waking-being as such (in so far, that is, as, having sight, it felt itself as the centre of a light-world); now it becomes "spirit" — namely, pure understanding, which "cognizes" itself as such and very soon comes to regard not only the world *around* itself, but even the remaining component of life, its own body, as qualitatively *below itself*. This is evidenced not only in the upright carriage of man, but in the thoroughly intellectualized formation of his head, in which the eyes, the brow, and the temples become more and more the vehicles of expression.[1]

Clearly, then, thought, when it became independent, discovered a new mode of activity for itself. To the practical thought which is directed upon the constitution of the light-things in the world-around, with reference to this or that practical end, there is added the theoretical, penetrating, subtilizing thought which sets itself to establish the constitution of these things "in themselves," the *natura rerum*. From that which is seen, the light is abstracted, the depth-experience of the eye intensifies itself in a grand and unmistakable course of development into a depth-experience within the tinted realm of word-connotations. Man begins to believe that it is not impossible for his inner eye to see right through into the things that actually are. Concept follows upon concept, and at last there is a mighty thought-architecture made up of buildings that stand out with full clarity under the inner light.

The development of theoretical thought within the human waking-consciousness gives rise to a kind of activity that makes inevitable a fresh conflict —

---

[1] Hence we call that which we observe in the faces of men who have not the habit of thought "animal" — admiringly or contemptuously as the case may be.

that between Being (existence) and Waking-Being (waking-consciousness). The animal microcosm, in which existence and consciousness are joined in a self-evident unity of living, knows of consciousness *only as the servant* of existence. The animal "lives" simply and does not reflect upon life. Owing, however, to the unconditional monarchy of the eye, life is presented as the life of a visible entity in the light; understanding, then, when it becomes interlocked with speech, promptly forms a *concept* of thought and with it a *counter-concept* [1] of life, and in the end it distinguishes life as it is from that which might be. Instead of straight, uncomplicated living, we have the antithesis represented in the phrase "thought and action." That which is not possible at all in the beasts becomes in every man not merely a possibility, but a fact and in the end an alternative. The entire history of mature humanity with all its phenomena has been formed by it, and the higher the form that a Culture takes, the more fully this opposition dominates the significant moments of its conscious being.

The plantlike-cosmic, Being heavy with Destiny, blood, sex, possess an immemorial mastery and keep it. They *are* life. The other only serves life. But this other wills, not to serve, but to rule; moreover, it believes that it does rule, for one of the most determined claims put forward by the human spirit is its claim to possess power over the body, over "nature." But the question is: Is not this very belief a service to life? Why does our thought think just so? Perhaps because the cosmic, the "it," wills that it shall? Thought shows off its power when it calls the body a notion, when it establishes the pitifulness of the body and commands the voices of the blood to be silent. But in truth the blood rules, in that silently it commands the activity of thought to begin and to cease. There, too, is a distinction between speech and life — Being can do without consciousness and the life of understanding, but not vice versa. Thought rules, after all, in spite of all, only in the "realm of thought."

III

It only amounts to a verbal difference whether we say that thought is a creation of man, or higher mankind a creation of thought. But thought itself persistently credits itself with much too high a rank in the ensemble of life, and through its ignorance of, or indifference to, the fact that there are other modes of ascertainment besides itself, forfeits its opportunity of surveying the whole without prejudice. In truth, all professors of thought — and in every Culture they have been almost the only authorized spokesmen — have taken it as self-evident that cold abstract thought is *the* way of approach to "last things." Moreover, they have assumed, also as self-evident, that the "truth" which they reach on this line of advance is the same as the truth which they have set before themselves as an aim, and not, as it really is, a sort of imaginary picture which takes the place of the unknowable secrets.

[1] See Vol. 1, p. 126. — *Tr.*

For, although man is a thinking being, it is very far from the fact that his being consists in thinking. This is a difference that the born subtilizer fails to grasp. The aim of thought is called "truth," and truths are "established" — i.e., brought out of the living impalpability of the light-world into the form of concepts and assigned permanently to places in a system, which means a kind of intellectual space. Truths are absolute and eternal — i.e., they have nothing more to do with life.

But for an animal, not truths, but only facts exist. Here is the difference between practical and theoretical understanding. Facts and truths [1] differ as time and space, destiny and causality. A fact addresses itself to the whole waking-consciousness, for the service of being, and not to that side of the waking-consciousness which imagines it can detach itself from being. Actual life, history, knows only facts; life experience and knowledge of men deal only in facts. The active man who does and wills and fights, daily measuring himself against the power of facts, looks down upon mere truths as unimportant. The real statesman knows only political facts, not political truths. Pilate's famous question is that of every man of fact.

It is one of the greatest achievements of Nietzsche that he confronted science with the problem of the *value* of truth and knowledge — cheap and even blasphemous though this seems to the born thinker and savant, who regards his whole *raison d'être* as impugned by it. Descartes meant to doubt everything, but certainly not the value of his doubting.

It is one thing, however, to pose problems and quite another to believe in solutions of them. The plant lives and knows not that it lives. The animal lives and knows that it lives. Man is astounded by his life and asks questions about it. But even man cannot give an answer to his own questions, he can only *believe* in the correctness of his answer, and in that respect there is no difference between Aristotle and the meanest savage.

Whence comes it, then, that secrets must be unravelled and questions answered? Is it not from that fear which looks out of even a child's eyes, that terrible dowry of human waking-consciousness which compels the understanding, free now from sensation and brooding on images, to probe into every deep for solutions that mean release? Can a desperate faith in knowledge free us from the nightmare of the grand questions?

"Shuddering awe is mankind's noblest part." He to whom that gift has been denied by fate must seek to discover secrets, to attack, dissect, and destroy the awe-inspiring, and to extract a booty of knowledge therefrom. The will-to-system is a will to kill something living, to "establish," stabilize, stiffen it, to bind it in the train of logic. The intellect has *conquered* when it has completed the business of making rigid.

This distinction that is usually drawn between "reason" (*Vernunft*) and

[1] See Vol. I, p. 102. — *Tr.*

"understanding" (*Verstand*) is really that between the divination and flair belonging to our plant side, which merely *makes use* of the language of eye and word, and the understanding proper, belonging to our animal side, which is *deduced from* language. "Reason" in this sense is that which calls ideas into life, "understanding" that which finds truths. Truths are lifeless and can be imparted (*mitgeteilt*); ideas belong to the living self of the author and can only be sympathetically evoked (*mitgefühlt*). Understanding is essentially critical, "reason" essentially creative.[1] The latter begets the object of its activity, the former starts from it. In fact, understanding criticism is first practised and developed in association with ordinary sensations — it is in sensation-judgments that the child learns to comprehend and to differentiate. Then, abstracted from this connexion and henceforward busied with itself, criticism needs a substitute for the sensation-activity that had previously served as its object. And this cannot be given it but by an *already existing* mode of thought, and it is upon this that criticism now works. This, only this, and not something building freely on nothingness, is Thought.

For quite early, before he has begun to think abstractly, primitive man forms for himself a religious world-picture, and this is the object upon which the understanding begins to operate critically. Always science has grown up on a religion and under all the spiritual prepossessions of that religion, and always it signifies nothing more or less than an abstract melioration of these doctrines, considered as false because less abstract. Always it carries along the kernel of a religion in its ensemble of principles, problem-enunciations, and methods. Every new truth that the understanding finds is nothing but a critical judgment upon some other that was already there. The polarity between old and new knowledge involves the consequence that in the world of the understanding there is only the relatively correct — namely, judgments of greater convincingness than other judgments. Critical knowledge rests upon the belief that the understanding of to-day is better than that of yesterday. And that which forces us to this belief, is again, life.

Can criticism then, as criticism, solve the great questions, or can it merely pose them? At the beginning of knowledge we believe the former. But the more we know, the more certain we become of the latter. So long as we hope, we call the secret a problem.

Thus, for mankind aware, there is a double problem, that of Waking-Being and that of Being; or of Space and of Time; or of the world-as-nature[2] and the world as history; or of pulse and tension. The waking consciousnes seeks to understand not only itself, but in addition something that is akin to itself. Though an inner voice may tell one that here all possibilities of knowl-

---

[1] Hence Bayle's profound observation that the understanding is capable only of discovering errors.

[2] See Vol. I, p. 94. — *Tr.*

edge are left behind, yet, in spite of it, fear overpersuades — everyone — and one goes on with the search, preferring even the pretence of a solution to the alternative of looking into nothingness.

IV

Waking-consciousness consists of sensation and understanding, and their common essence is a continuous self-adjustment in relation to the macrocosm. To that extent waking-consciousness is identical with ascertainment (*Feststellen*), whether we consider the touch of an infusorian, or human thinking of the highest order. Feeling, now, for touch with itself in this wise, the waking-consciousness first encounters the epistemological problem. What do we mean by cognition, or by the knowledge of cognition? And what is the relation between the original meanings of these terms and their later formulations in words? Waking and sleep alternate, like day and night, according to the course of the stars, and so, too, cognition alternates with dreams. How do these two differ?

Waking-consciousness, however — whether it be that of sensation or that of understanding — is synonymous with the existence of oppositions, such as that between cognition and the object cognized, or thing and property, or object and event. Wherein consists the essence of these oppositions? And so arises the second problem, that of *causality*. When we give the names "cause" and "effect" to a pair of sensuous elements, or "premiss" and "consequence" to a pair of intellectual elements, we are fixing between them a relation of power and rank — when one is there, the other must be there also. In these relations, observe, time does not figure at all. We are concerned not with facts of destiny, but with causal truths, not with a "When?" but with a law-fixed dependence. Beyond doubt this is the understanding's most promising line of activity. Mankind perhaps owes to discoveries of this order his happiest moments; and thus he proceeds, from these oppositions in the near and present things of everyday life that strike him immediately, forward in an endless series of conclusions to the first and final causes in the structure of nature that he calls God and the meaning of the world. He assembles, orders, and reviews his system, his dogma of law-governed connexions, and he finds in it a refuge from the unforeseen. He who can demonstrate, fears no longer. But wherein consists the essence of causality? Does it lie in knowing, in the known, or in a unity of both?

The world of tensions is necessarily in itself stiff and dead — namely, "eternal truth," something beyond all time, something that is a state. The actual world of waking-consciousness, however, is full of changes. This does not astonish an animal in the least, but it leaves the thought of the thinker powerless, for rest and movement, duration and change, become and becoming,[1]

[1] See Vol. I, pp. 53, et seq. — Tr.

are oppositions denoting something that in its very nature "passeth all under-standing" and *must* therefore (from the point of view of the understanding) contain an absurdity. For is that a fact at all which proves to be incapable of distillation from the sense-world in the form of a truth? On the other hand, though the world is cognized as timeless, a time element nevertheless adheres to it — tensions appear as beat, and direction associates itself with extension. And so all that is problematical for the understanding consciousness somehow gathers itself together in one last and gravest problem, *the problem of motion.* And on that problem free and abstract thought breaks down, and we begin to discern that the microcosmic is after all as dependent as ever upon the cosmic, just as the individualness of a being from its first moment is consti-tuted not by a body, but by the sheath of a body. Life can exist without thought, but thought is only one mode of life. High as may be the objectives that thought sets before itself, in actuality life makes use of thought for *its* ends and gives it a living objective quite apart from the solution of abstract problems. For thought the solutions of problems are correct or erroneous — for life they are valuable or valueless, and if the will-to-know breaks down on the motion problem, it may well be because life's purpose has at that point been achieved. In spite of this, and indeed because of this, the motion problem remains the centre of gravity of all higher thought. All mythology and all natural science has arisen out of man's wonder in the presence of the mystery of motion.

The problem of motion touches, at once and immediately, the secrets of existence, which are alien to the waking-consciousness and yet inexorably press upon it. In posing motion as a problem we affirm our will to compre-hend the incomprehensible, the when and wherefore, Destiny, blood, all that our intuitive processes touch in our depths. Born to see, we strive to set it before our eyes in the light, so that we may in the literal sense grasp it, assure ourselves of it as of something tangible.

For this is the decisive fact, of which the observer is unconscious — his whole effort of seeking is aimed not at life, but at the seeing of life, and not at death, but at the seeing of death. We try to grasp the cosmic as it appears in the macrocosm to the microscosm, *as the life of a body in the light-world* be-tween birth and death, generation and dissolution, and with that differenti-ation of body and soul that follows of deepest necessity from our ability to experience [1] the inward-proper as a sensuous alien.

That we do not merely live but *know* about "living" is a consequence of our bodily existence in the light. But the beast knows only life, not death. Were we pure plantlike beings, we should die unconscious of dying, for to feel death and to die would be identical. But animals, even though they hear the death-cry, see the dead body, and scent putrefaction, behold death with-

[1] Original: "*aus dem Erlebnis.*" — Tr.

out comprehending it. Only when understanding has become, through language, detached from visual awareness and pure, does death appear to man as the great enigma of the light-world about him.

Then, and only then, life becomes the short span of time between birth and death, and it is in relation to death that that other great mystery of generation arises also. Only then does the diffuse animal fear of everything become the definite human fear of death. It is *this* that makes the love of man and woman, the love of mother and child, the tree of the generations, the family, the people, and so at last world-history itself the infinitely deep facts and problems of destiny that they are. To death, as the common lot of every human being born into the light, adhere the ideas of guilt and punishment, of existence as a penance, of a new life beyond the world of this light, and of a salvation that makes an end of the death-fear. In the knowledge of death is originated that world-outlook which we possess as being men and not beasts.

v

There are born destiny-men and causality-men. A whole world separates the purely living man — peasant and warrior, statesman and general, man of the world and man of business, everyone who wills to prosper, to rule, to fight, and to dare, the organizer or entrepreneur, the adventurer or bravo or gambler — from the man who is destined either by the power of his mind or the defect of his blood to be an "intellectual" — the saint, priest, savant, idealist, or ideologue. Being and waking-being, pulse and tension, motives and ideas, cyclic organs and touch-organs — there has rarely been a man of any significance in whom the one side or the other has not markedly predominated. All that motives and urges, the eye for men and situations, the belief in his star which every born man of action possesses and which is something wholly different from belief in the correctness of a standpoint, the voices of the blood that speak in moments of decision, and the immovably quiet conviction that justifies any aim and any means — all these are denied to the critical, meditative man. Even the footfall of the fact-man sounds different from, sounds more planted than, that of the thinker, in whom the pure microcosmic can acquire no firm relation with earth.

Destiny has made the man so or so — subtle and fact-shy, or active and contemptuous of thought. But the man of the active category is a whole man, whereas in the contemplative a single organ can operate without (and even against) the body. All the worse, then, when this organ tries to master actuality as well as its own world, for then we get all those ethico-politico-social reform-projects which demonstrate, unanswerably, how things ought to be and how to set about making them so — theories that without exception rest upon the hypothesis that all men are as rich in ideas and as poor in motives as the author is (or thinks he is). Such theories, even when they have taken the field armed with the full authority of a religion or the prestige of a famous name, have not in one single instance effected the slightest alteration in life. They have merely caused us to *think* otherwise than before about life. And this, precisely, is the doom of the "late" ages of a Culture, the ages of much writing and much reading — that they should perpetually confuse the opposition of life and thought with the opposition between thought-about-life and thought-about-thought. All world-improvers, priests, and philosophers are unanimous in holding that life is a fit object for the nicest meditation, but the life of the world goes its own way and cares not in the least what is said about it. And even when a community succeeds in living " according to rule," all that it achieves is, at best, a note on itself in some future history of the world — if there is space left after the proper and only important subject-matter has been dealt with.

For, in the last resort, only the active man, the man of destiny, lives in the *actual* world, the world of political, military, and economic decisions, in which concepts and systems do not figure or count. Here a shrewd blow is more than a shrewd conclusion, and there is sense in the contempt with which statesmen and soldiers of all times have regarded the "ink-slinger" and the "bookworm" who think that world-history exists for the sake of the intellect or science or even art. Let us say it frankly and without ambiguity: the understanding divorced from sensation is only one, and not the decisive, side of life. A history of Western thought may not contain the name of Napoleon, but in the history of actuality Archimedes, for all his scientific discoveries, was possibly less effective than that soldier who killed him at the storming of Syracuse.

Men of theory commit a huge mistake in believing that their place is at the head and not in the train of great events. They misunderstand completely the rôle played, for example, by the political Sophists in Athens or by Voltaire and Rousseau in France. Often enough a statesman does not "know" what he is doing, but that does not prevent him from following with confidence just the one path that leads to success; the political doctrinaire, on the contrary, always knows what should be done, and yet his activity, once it ceases to be limited to paper, is the least successful and therefore the least valuable in history. These intrusions happen only too frequently in times of uncertainty, like that of the Attic enlightenment, or the French or the German revolutions, when the ideologue of word or pen is eager to be busy with the actual history of the people instead of with systems. He mistakes his place. He belongs with his principles and programs to no history but the history of a literature. Real history passes judgment on him not by controverting the theorist, but by leaving him and all his thoughts to himself. A Plato or a Rousseau — not to mention the smaller intellects — could build up abstract political structures, but for Alexander, Scipio, Cæsar, and Napoleon, with their schemes and battles and settlements, they were entirely without importance. The thinker could discuss destiny if he liked; it was enough for these men to be destiny.

Under all the plurality of microcosmic beings, we are perpetually meeting with the formation of *inspired mass-units*, beings of a higher order, which, whether they develop slowly or come into existence in a moment, contain all the feelings and passions of the individual, enigmatic in their inward character and inaccessible to reasoning — though the connoisseur can see into and reckon upon their reactions well enough. Here too we distinguish the generic animal unities which are sensed, the unities profoundly dependent upon Being and Destiny — like the way of an eagle in the air or the way of the stormers on the breach — from the purely human associations which depend upon the understanding and cohere on the basis of like opinions, like purposes, or like knowledge. Unity of cosmic pulse one has without willing to have it; unity of common ground is acquired at will. One can join or resign from an intellectual association as one pleases, for only one's waking-consciousness is involved. But to a cosmic unity one is *committed*, and committed with one's entire being. Crowds of this order of unity are seized by storms of enthusiasm or, as readily, of panic. They are noisy and ecstatic at Eleusis or Lourdes, or heroically firm like the Spartans of Thermopylæ and the last Goths in the battle of Vesuvius.[1] They form themselves to the music of chorales, marches, and dances, and are sensitive like human and animal thoroughbreds to the effects of bright colours, decoration, costume, and uniform.

These inspired aggregates are born and die. Intellectual associations are mere sums in the mathematical sense, varying by addition and subtraction, unless and until (as sometimes happens) a mere coincidence of opinion strikes so impressively as to reach the blood and so, suddenly, to create out of the sum a Being. In any political turning-point words may become fates and opinions passions. A chance crowd is herded together in the street and has *one* consciousness, *one* sensation, *one* language — until the short-lived soul flickers out and everyone goes his way again. This happened every day in the Paris of 1789, whenever the cry of "*A la lanterne!*" fell upon the ear.

These souls have their special psychology,[2] and the knowledge of this psychology is for the public man an essential. A single soul is the mark of every genuine order or class, be it the chivalry and military orders of the Crusades, the Roman Senate or the Jacobin club, polite society under Louis XIV or the Prussian country "*Adel*," peasantry or guilds, the masses of the big city or the folk of the secluded valley, the peoples and tribes of the migrations or the adherents of Mohammed and generally, of any new-founded religion or sect, the French of the Revolution or the Germans of the Wars of Libera-

---

[1] A.D. 553 (Gibbon, *Decline and Fall*, ch. xliii). — *Tr.*

[2] G. Le Bon's *Psychologie des Foules* (which has been translated into English under the title *The Crowd*) is the pioneer work on this subject, and though unduly coloured perhaps by the author's personal prepossessions, still retains its interest and value. — *Tr.*

tion. The mightiest beings of this kind that we know are the higher Cultures, which are born in great spiritual upheavals, and in a thousand years of existence weld all aggregates of lower degree — nations, classes, towns, generations — into one unit.

All grand events of history are carried by beings of the cosmic order, by peoples, parties, armies, and classes, while the history of the intellect runs its course in loose associations and circles, schools, levels of education, "tendencies" and "isms." And here again it is a question of destiny whether such aggregates at the decisive moments of highest effectiveness find a leader or are driven blindly on, whether the chance headmen are men of the first order or men of no real significance tossed up, like Robespierre or Pompey, by the surge of events. It is the hall-mark of the statesman that he has a sure and penetrating eye for these mass-souls that form and dissolve on the tide of the times, their strength and their duration, their direction and purpose. And even so, it is a question of Incident [1] whether he is one who *can* master them or one who is swept away by them.

[1] See Vol. I., pp. 139, et seq. — *Tr.*

CHAPTER II

ORIGIN AND LANDSCAPE

(B)

THE GROUP OF THE HIGHER CULTURES

ORIGIN AND LANDSCAPE

(B)

THE GROUP OF THE HIGHER CULTURES

I

Now, man — no matter whether it is for life or for thought that he is born into the world — so long as he is acting or is thinking, is awake and therefore *in focus* — i.e., adjusted to the one significance that for the moment his light-world holds for him. Everyone knows that it is almost sharply painful to switch off suddenly in the middle of, say, an experiment in physics, in order to think about some event of the day. I have said earlier that the innumerable settings that take turns in man's waking consciousness fall into two distinct groups — the worlds of destiny and pulsation, and the worlds of causes and tensions. The two pictures I have called *world-as-history* and *world-as-nature*. In the first, life makes use of critical understanding. It has the eye under command, the felt pulsation becomes the inwardly imagined wave-train, and the shattering spiritual experience becomes pictured as the epochal peak. In the second, thought itself rules, and its causal criticism turns life into a rigorous process, the living content of a fact into an abstract truth, and tension into formula.

How is this possible? Each is an eye-picture, but in the one the seer is giving himself up to the never-to-be-repeated facts, and in the other he is striving to catch truths for an ever-valid system. In the history-picture, that in which knowledge is simply an *auxiliary*, the cosmic makes use of the microcosmic. In the picture which we call memory and recollection, things are present to us as bathed in an inner light and swept by the pulsation of our existence. But the chronological element [1] tells us that history, as soon as it becomes *thought* history, is no longer immune from the basic conditions of all waking-consciousness. In the nature- (or science-) picture it is the ever-present subjective that is alien and illusive, but in the history-picture it is the equally ineliminable objective, Number, that leads into error.

When we are working in the domain of Nature (science), our settings and self-adjustments should be and can be up to a certain point impersonal — one "forgets oneself" — but every man, class, nation, or family sees the picture of history *in relation to itself*. The mark of Nature is an extension that is inclusive of everything, but History is that which comes up out of the dark-

---

[1] Meaning here names, dates, numbers — the chronology in the usual extensive sense, and not the intensive or deep sense. See Vol. I, pp. 97, 153 (foot-note). — *Tr.*

ness of the past, presents itself to the *seer*, and from him sweeps onward into the future. He, as the present, is always its middle point, and it is quite impossible for him to order the facts with any meaning if he ignores their direction — which is an element proper to life and nòt to thought. Every time, every land, every living aggregate has its own historical horizon, and it is the mark of the genuine historical thinker that he actualizes the picture of history that his time demands.

Thus Nature and History are distinguishable like pure and impure criticism — meaning by "criticism" the opposite of lived experience. Natural science *is* criticism and nothing else. But in History, criticism can do no more than scientifically prepare the field over which the historian's eye is to sweep. *History is that ranging glance itself*, whatever the direction in which it ranges. He who possesses such an eye can understand every fact and every situation "historically." Nature is a system, and systems can be learnt.

The process of *historical* self-adjustment begins for everyone with the earliest impressions of childhood. Children's eyes are keen, and the facts of the nearest environment, the life of the family and the house and the street, are sensed and felt right down to the core, long before the city and its population come into their visual field, and while the words "people," "country," "state," are still quite destitute of tangible meaning to them. Just so, and so thoroughly, primitive man knows all that is presented to his narrow field of view as history, as living — and above all Life itself, the drama of birth and death, sickness and eld; the history of passionate war and passionate love, as experienced in himself or observed in others; the fate of relatives, of the clan, of the village, their actions and their motives; tales of long enmity, of fights, victory, and revenge. The life-horizon widens, and shows not lives, but Life coming and going. The pageant is not now of villages and clans, but of remote races and countries; not of years, but of centuries. The history that is actually lived with and participated in never reaches over more than a grandfather's span — neither for ancient Germans and present-day Negroes, nor for Pericles and Wallenstein. Here the horizon of living ends, and a new plane begins wherein the picture is based upon hearsay and historical tradition, a plane in which direct sympathies are adapted to a mind-picture that is both distinct and, from long use, stable. The picture so developed shows very different amplitudes for the men of the different Cultures. For us Westerners it is with this secondary picture that genuine history begins, for we live under the aspect of eternity, whereas for the Greeks and Romans it is just then that history ceases. For Thucydides[1] the events of the Persian Wars, for Cæsar those of the Punic Wars, were already devoid of living import.

---

[1] He affirmed, on the first page of his history (about 400 B.C.) that before his time nothing of significance had happened (οὐ μεγάλα νομίζω γενέσθαι οὔτε κατὰ τοὺς πολέμους οὔτε ἐς τα ἄλλα. Thucydides, I, 1.).

And beyond this plane again, other historic unit-pictures rise to the view — pictures of the destinies of the plant world and the animal world, the landscape, the stars — which at the last fuse with the last pictures of natural science into mythic images of the creation and the end of the world.

The nature- (science-) picture of the child and the primitive develops out of the petty technique of every day, which perpetually forces both of them to turn away from the fearful contemplation of wide nature to the critique of the facts and situations of their near environment. Like the young animal, the child discovers its first truths through play. Examining the toy, cutting open the doll, turning the mirror round to see what is behind it, the feeling of triumph in having established something as corrrect for good and all — no nature-research whatsoever has got beyond this. Primitive man applies this critical experience, as he acquires it, to his arms and tools, to the materials for his clothing, food, and housing — i.e., to things *in so far as they are dead*. He applies it to animals as well when suddenly they cease to have meaning for him as living beings whose movements he watches and divines as pursuer or pursued, and are apprehended mechanically instead of vitally, as aggregates of flesh and bone for which he has a definite use — exactly as he is conscious of an event, now as the act of a dæmon and a moment afterwards as a sequence of cause and effect. The mature man of the Culture transposes in exactly the same way, every day and every hour. Here, too, is a "nature"-horizon, and beyond it lies the secondary plane formed of our impressions of rain, lightning, and tempest, summer and winter, moon-phases and star-courses. But at that plane religiousness, trembling with fear and awe, forces upon man criteria of a far higher kind. Just as in the history-picture he sounds the ultimate facts of life, so here he seeks to establish the ultimate truths of nature. What lies beyond any attainable frontier of knowledge he calls God, and all that lies within that frontier he strives to comprehend — as action, creation, and manifestation of God — causally.

Every group of scientifically established elements, therefore, has a dual tendency, inherent and unchanged since primitive ages. The one tendency urges forward the completest possible system of *technical* knowledge, for the service of practical, economical, and warlike ends, which many kinds of animals have developed to a high degree of perfection, and which from them leads, through primitive man and his acquaintance with fire and metals, directly to the machine-technics of our Faustian Culture. The other tendency took shape only with the separation of strictly human thought from physical vision by means of language, and the aim of its effort has been an equally complete *theoretical* knowledge, which we call in the earlier phases of the Culture *religious*, and in the later *scientific*. Fire is for the warrior a weapon, for the craftsman part of his equipment, for the priest a sign from God, and for the scientist a problem. But in all these aspects alike it is proper to the "natural," the scientific, mode of waking-consciousness. In the world-as-history we do not find fire as such, but the conflagration of Carthage and the flames of the faggots heaped around John Hus and Giordano Bruno.

II

I repeat, every being livingly experiences every other being and its destiny *only in relation to itself.* A flock of pigeons is regarded by the farmer on whose fields it settles quite otherwise than by the nature-lover in the street or the hawk in the air. The peasant sees in his son the future and the heritage, but what the neighbour sees in him is a peasant, what the officer sees is a soldier, what the visitor sees is a native. Napoleon experienced men and things very differently as Emperor and as lieutenant. Put a man in a new situation, make the revolutionary a minister, the soldier a general, and at once history and the key men of history become for him something other than what they were. Talleyrand saw through the men of his time because he belonged with them, but had he been suddenly plumped down in the company of Crassus, Cæsar, Catiline, and Cicero, his understanding of their measures and views would have been either null or erroneous. There is no history-in-itself. The history of a family is taken differently by each member of it, that of a country differently by each party, that of the age by each nation. The German looks upon the World War otherwise than the Englishman, the workman upon economic history otherwise than the employer, and the historian of the West has a quite other world-history before his eyes than that of the great Arabian and Chinese historians. The history of an era could be handled objectively only if it were very distant in time, and the historian were radically disinterested; and we find that our best historians cannot judge of or describe even the Peloponnesian Wars and Actium without being in some measure influenced by present interests.

It is not incompatible with, rather it is essential to, a profound knowledge of men that the appraiser should see through glasses of his own colour. This knowledge, indeed, is exactly the component that we discern to be wanting in those generalizations that distort or altogether ignore that all-important fact, the uniqueness of the constituent event in history [1] — the worst example of this being the "materialistic" conception of history, about which we have said almost all there is to say when we have described it as physiognomic barrenness. But both in spite of this and on account of this [2] there is for every man, *because* he belongs to a class and a time and a nation and a Culture, a typical picture of history as it ought to appear in relation to himself, and equally there are typical pictures specific to the time or class or Culture, *qua*

---

[1] Original: "*Alles Bedeutende, nämlich das Einmalige der Geschichte.*" — *Tr.*
[2] I suppose the meaning of these words to be that generalization and flair are not really opposed, but interdependent. — *Tr.*

time or class or Culture. The supreme generalization possible to each Culture as a major being is a primary and, for it, symbolical image of its own world-as-history, and all self-attunements of the individual — or of the group livingly effective as individual — are with reference to that image. Whenever we describe another person's ideas as profound or superficial, original or trivial, mistaken or obsolete, we are unwittingly judging them with reference to a picture which springs up to answer for the value at the moment of a continuous function of our time and our personality.[1]

Obviously, then, every man of the Faustian Culture possesses his own picture of history and, besides, innumerable other pictures from his youth upwards, which fluctuate and alter ceaselessly in response to the experiences of the day and the year. And how different, again, are the typical history-images of men and different eras and classes, the world of Otto the Great and that of Gregory VII, that of a Doge of Venice and that of a poor pilgrim! In what different worlds lived Lorenzo de' Medici, Wallenstein, Cromwell, Marat, and Bismarck, a serf of the Gothic age, a savant of the Baroque, the army officer of the Thirty Years' War, the Seven Years' War, and the Wars of Liberation respectively! Or, to consider our own times alone, a Frisian peasant whose life of actuality is limited to his own countryside and its folk, a high merchant of Hamburg, and a professor of physics! And yet to all of these, irrespective of individual age, status, and period, there is a common basis that differentiates the ensemble of these figures, their prime-image, from that of every other Culture.

But, over and above this, there is a distinction of another kind which separates the Classical and the Indian history-pictures from those of the Chinese, the Arabian, and, most of all, the Western Cultures — the *narrow horizon* of the two first-named. Whatever the Greeks may (and indeed must) have known of ancient Egyptian history, they never allowed it to penetrate into their peculiar history-picture, which for the majority was limited to the field of events that could be related by the oldest surviving participant, and which even for the finer minds stopped at the Trojan War, a frontier beyond which they would not concede that there had been historical life at all.[2]

The Arabian Culture,[3] on the other hand, very early dared the astounding gesture — we see it in the historical thought alike of the Jews and of the Persians from Cyrus's time — of connecting the legend of creation to the present by means of a genuine chronology; the Persians indeed comprised the future as well in the sweep of the gesture, and predated the last judgment and the

---

[1] Original: ("*So geschieht dies stets . . .*) im Hinblick auf das im Augenblick geforderte *Bild als der beständigen Funktion der Zeit und des Menschen.*" — Tr.

[2] Even at the level of the Trojan War the timeless mythological figures of gods and demigods are still involved, intimately and in detail, in the human story. See, on the whole question of the Greek attitude towards time and history, Vol. I, p. 9 and *passim.* — Tr.

[3] See Chapter VIII below. — Tr.

coming of the Messiah. This exact and very narrow definition of human history — the Persian reckoning allows twelve millennia from first to last, the Jewish counts less than six up to the present — is a necessary expression of the Magian world-feeling and fundamentally distinguishes the Judæo-Persian creation-sagas from those of the Babylonian Culture, from which so many of their external traits are derived.

Different, again, are the primary feelings which give historical thought in the Chinese and the Egyptian Cultures its characteristically wide and unbounded horizons, represented by chronologically stated sequences of dynasties which stretch over millennia and finally dissolve into a grey remoteness.

The Faustian picture of world-history, again, prepared in advance by the existence of a Christian chronology,[1] came into being suddenly, with an immense extension and deepening of the Magian picture which the Western Church had taken over, an extension and deepening that was to give Joachim of Floris [2] in the high Gothic the basis of his wonderful interpretation of all world-destinies as a sequence of three æons under the aspects of the Father, the Son, and the Holy Ghost. Parallel with this there was an immense widening of the geographical horizon, which even in Gothic times (thanks to Vikings and Crusaders) came to extend from Iceland to the remotest ends of Asia; [3] and from 1500 onwards, the developed man of the Baroque is able to do what none of his peers in the other Cultures could do and — for the first time in human history — to regard the whole surface of the planet as its field. Thanks to compass and telescope, the savant of that mature age could for the first time not merely posit the sphericity of the earth as a matter of theory, but actually feel that he was living upon a sphere in space. The land-horizon is no more. So, too, time-horizons melt in the double endlessness of the calendar before and after Christ. And to-day, under the influence of this picture, which comprises the whole planet and will eventually embrace all the high Cultures, the old Gothic division of history into "ancient," "mediæval," and modern, long become trite and empty, is visibly dissolving.[4]

In all other Cultures the aspects of world-history and of man-history coincide. The beginning of the world is the beginning of man, and the end of man is the end of the world. But the Faustian infinity-craving for the first time separated the two notions during the Baroque, and now it has made human history, for all its immense and still unknown span, *a mere episode in world-history*, while the Earth — of which other Cultures had seen not even

[1] Introduced in Rome in 522 during the Ostrogoth domination, not until Charlemagne's times did it make headway in the Germanic lands. Then, however, its spread was rapid.

[2] See Vol. I, p. 19. — *Tr.*

[3] On the other hand — and very significantly — the field of the history-picture livingly experienced in the consciousness of the sincere Renaissance classicist markedly contracted.

[4] See Vol. I, p. 16. — *Tr.*

the whole, but only superficial fractions as "the world" — has become a little star amongst millions of solar systems.

The extension of the historical world-picture makes it even more necessary in this Culture than in any other to distinguish between the everyday self-attunements of ordinary people and that extreme self-attunement of which only the highest minds are capable, and which even in them holds only for moments. The difference between the historical view-field of Themistocles and that of an Attic husbandman is probably very small, but this difference is already immense as between Henry VI and a hind of his day,[1] and as the Faustian Culture mounts up and up, the power of self-focusing attains to such heights and depths that the circle of adepts grows ever smaller and smaller. In fact, there is formed a sort of pyramid of possibilities, in which individuals are graded according to their endowments; every individual, according to his constitution, stands at the level which he is capable at his best focus of holding. But it follows from this that between Western men there are limitations to the possibilities of reciprocal understanding of historical life-problems, limitations that do not apply to other Cultures, at any rate in such fateful rigour as they do to ours. Can a workman to-day really understand a peasant? Or a diplomat a craftsman? The historico-geographical horizon that determines for each of them the questions worth asking and the form in which these are asked is so different from the horizons of the others that what they can exchange is not a communication, but passing remarks. It is, of course, the mark of the real appraiser of man that he understands how "the other man" is adjusted and regulates his intercourse with him accordingly (as we all do in talking to children), but the art of appraising in this sense some man of the past (say Henry the Lion or Dante), of living oneself into his history-picture so thoroughly that his thoughts, feelings, and decisions take on a character of self-evidence, is, owing to the vast difference between the one's and the other's waking consciousness, so rare that up to the eighteenth century it was not even seen that the historian ought to attempt it. Only since 1800 has it become a desideratum for the writing of history, and it is one very seldom satisfied at that.

The typically Faustian separation of human history, as such, from the far wider history of the world has had the result that since the end of the Baroque our world-picture has contained several horizons disposed one behind the other in as many planes. For the exploration of these, individual sciences, more or less overtly historical in character, have taken shape. Astronomy, geology, biology, anthropology, one after the other follow up the destinies of the star-world, the earth's crust, life, and man, and only then do we come to the "world"-history — as it is still called even to-day — of the higher Cultures, to which, again, are attached the histories of the several cultural elements, family

[1] The Emperor Henry VI reigned 1190–7. — Tr.

history, and lastly (that highly developed speciality of the West) biography.

Each of these planes demands a particular self-focusing, and the moment the special focus becomes sharp the narrower and the broader planes cease to be live Being and become mere given facts. If we are investigating the battle of the Teutoburger Wald, the growing up of this forest in the plant-world of the North German plain is presupposed. If, on the other hand, we are examining into the history of the German tree-world, the geological stratification of the earth is the presupposition, though it is just a fact whose particular destiny need not be further followed out in this connexion. If, again, our question is the origin of the Cretaceous, the existence of the Earth itself as a planet in the solar system is a datum, not a problem. Or, to express it otherwise, that there is an Earth in the star-world, that the phenomenon "life" occurs in the Earth, that within this "life" there is the form "man," that within the history of man there exists the organic form of the Culture, is in each case an incident in the picture of the next higher plane.

In Goethe, from his Strassburg period to his first Weimar residence, the inclination to attune himself to "world"-history was very strong — as evidenced in his Cæsar, Mohammed, Socrates, Wandering Jew, and Egmont sketches. And after that painful renunciation of the prospect of high political achievement [1] — the pain which calls to us in *Tasso* even through the sober resignedness of its final form — this precisely was the attunement that he chose to cut out of his life; and thereafter he limits himself, almost fiercely, to the picture-planes of plant-history, animal-history, and earth-history (his "living nature") on the one hand and to biography on the other.

All these "pictures," developed in the same man, have the same structure. Even the history of plants and animals, even that of the earth's crust or that of the stars, is a *fable convenue* and mirrors in outward actuality the inward tendency of the ego's being. The student of the animal world or of stratification is a man, living in a period and having a nationality and a social status, and it is no more possible to eliminate his subjective standpoint from his treatment of these things than it would be to obtain a perfectly abstract account of the French Revolution or the World War. The celebrated theories of Kant, Laplace, Cuvier, Lyell, Darwin, have also a politico-economic tinting, and their very power and impressiveness for the lay public show that the mode of outlook upon all these historical planes proceeds from a single source. And what is accomplishing itself to-day is the final achievement of which Faustian history-thinking is capable — the organic linking and disposition of these historical planes in a single vast world-history of uniform physiognomic that

---

[1] During his Italian sojourn of 1786–8 Goethe made up his mind to resign his political offices at Weimar, retaining merely a non-executive seat on the Council and definitely devoting himself to art and science. This resolution he carried into effect on his return to Weimar in 1788; *Tasso* finally appeared in 1790. — *Tr.*

shall enable our glance to range from the life of the individual man without a break to the first and last destinies of the universe. The nineteenth century — in mechanistic (i.e., unhistorical) form — enunciated the problem. It is one of the preordained tasks of the twentieth to solve it.

III

The picture that we possess of the history of the Earth's crust and of life is at present still dominated by the ideas which civilized [1] English thought has developed, since the Age of Enlightenment, out of the English habit of life — Lyell's "phlegmatic" theory of the formation of the geological strata, and Darwin's of the origin of species, are actually but derivatives of the development of England herself. In place of the incalculable catastrophes and metamorphoses such as von Buch and Cuvier [2] admitted, they put a methodical evolution over very long periods of time and recognize as causes only *scientifically calculable* and indeed *mechanical utility-causes.*

This "English" type of causality is not only shallow, but also far too narrow. It limits possible causal connexions, in the first place, to those which work out their *entire* course on the earth's surface; but this immediately excludes all great cosmic relations between earthly life-phenomena and the events of the solar system and the stellar universe, and assumes the impossible postulate that the exterior face of the earth-ball is a completely insulated region of natural phenomena. And, secondly, it assumes that connexions which are not comprehensible by the means at present available to the human consciousness — namely, sensation refined by instruments and thought precised by theory — do not even exist.

It will be the characteristic task of the twentieth century, as compared with the nineteenth, to get rid of this system of superficial causality, whose roots reach back into the rationalism of the Baroque period, and to put in its place a pure physiognomic. We are sceptics in regard to any and every mode of thought which "explains" causally. We let things speak for themselves, and confine ourselves to sensing the Destiny immanent in them and contemplating the form-manifestations that we shall never penetrate. The extreme to which we can attain is the discovery of causeless, purposeless, purely existent forms underlying the changeful picture of nature. For the nineteenth century the word "evolution" meant progress in the sense of increasing fitness of life to purposes. For Leibniz — whose *Protogæa* (1691), a work full of significant thought, outlines, on the basis of studies made in the Harz silver-mines, a picture of the world's infancy that is Goethian through and through — and for Goethe himself it meant fulfilment in the sense of increasing connotation of

---

[1] For the special sense in which the word "Civilization" is used throughout this work see Vol. I, p. 31. Briefly, the Civilization is the outcome of the Culture of which it is in one sense the final phase, but in another the distinct and unlike sequel. — *Tr.*

[2] Christian Leopold von Buch, 1774–1853; Cuvier, 1769–1832. — *Tr.*

the form. The two concepts, Goethe's form-fulfilment and Darwin's evolution, are in as complete opposition as destiny to causality, and (be it added) as German to English thought, and German to English history.

There is no more conclusive refutation of Darwinism than that furnished by palæontology. Simple probability indicates that fossil hoards can only be test samples. Each sample, then, should represent a different stage of evolution, and there ought to be merely "transitional" types, no definition and no species. Instead of this we find perfectly stable and unaltered forms persevering through long ages, forms that have not developed themselves on the fitness principle, but *appear suddenly and at once in their definitive shape;* that do not thereafter evolve towards better adaptation, but become rarer and finally disappear, while quite different forms crop up again. What unfolds itself, in ever-increasing richness of form, is the great classes and kinds of living beings which *exist aboriginally and exist still, without transition types,* in the grouping of to-day. We see how, amongst fish, the Selachians, with their simple form, appear first in the foreground of history and then slowly fade out again, while the Teleostians slowly bring a more perfected fish-type to predominance. The same applies to the plant-world of the ferns and horsetails, of which only the last species now linger in the fully developed kingdom of the flowering plants. But the assumption of utility-causes or other visible causes for these phenomena has no support of actuality.[1] It is a Destiny that evoked into the world life as life, the ever-sharper opposition between plant and animal, each single type, each genus, and each species. And along with this existence there is given also a definite *energy* of the form — by virtue of which in the course of its self-fulfilment it keeps itself pure or, on the contrary, becomes dull and unclear or evasively splits into numerous varieties — and finally a *life-duration of this form,* which (unless, again, incident intervenes to shorten it) leads naturally to a senility of the species and finally to its disappearance.

As for mankind, discoveries of the Diluvial age indicate more and more pointedly that the man-forms existing then correspond to those living now; there is not the slightest trace of evolution towards a race of greater utilitarian "fitness." And the continued failure to find man in the Tertiary discoveries indicates more and more clearly that the human life-form, like every other, originates in a sudden mutation (*Wandlung*) of which the "whence," "how," and "why" remain an impenetrable secret. If, indeed, there were evolution in the English sense of the word, there could be neither defined earth-strata nor specific animal-classes, but only a single geological mass and a chaos of living singular forms which we may suppose to have been left over from the struggle for existence. But all that we see about us impels us to the conviction that again and

---

[1] The first proof that the basic forms of plants and animals did not evolve, but were suddenly there, was given by H. de Vries in his *Mutation Theory* (1886). In the language of Goethe, we see how the "impressed form" [See Vol. I, p. 157. — Tr.] works itself out in the individual samples, but not how the die was cut for *the whole genus.*

again profound and very sudden changes take place in the being of plants and animals, changes which are of a cosmic kind and nowise restricted to the earth s surface, which are beyond the ken of human sense and understanding in respect of causes, if not indeed in all respects.[1] So, too, we observe that swift and deep changes assert themselves in the history of the great Cultures, without assignable causes, influences, or purposes of any kind. The Gothic and the Pyramid styles come into full being as suddenly as do the Chinese imperialism of Shi-hwang-ti and the Roman of Augustus, as Hellenism and Buddhism and Islam. It is exactly the same with the events in the individual life of every person who counts at all, and he who is ignorant of this knows nothing of men and still less of children. Every being, active or contemplative, strides on to its fulfilment by *epochs* and we have to assume just such epochs in the history of solar systems and the world of the fixed stars. The origins of the earth, of life, of the free-moving animal *are* such epochs, and, therefore, mysteries that we can do no more than accept.[2]

IV

That which we know of man divides clearly into two great ages of his being. The first is, as far as our view is concerned, limited on the one side by that profound fugue of planetary Destiny which we call the beginning of the Ice Age — and about which we can (within the picture of world-history) say no more than *that* a cosmic change took place — and on the other by the beginnings of high cultures on Nile and Euphrates, with which the whole meaning of human existence became suddenly different. We discover everywhere the sharp frontier of Tertiary and Diluvial, and on the hither side of it we see man as a completely formed type, familiar with custom, myth, wit, ornament, and technique and endowed with a bodily structure that has not materially altered up to the present day.

We will consider the first age as that of the primitive Culture. The only field in which this Culture endured throughout the second age (though certainly in a very "late" form) and is found alive and fairly intact to-day is north-west Africa. It is the great merit of Leo Frobenius [3] that he recognized this quite clearly, beginning with the assumption that in this field a *whole world* of primitive life (and not merely a greater or less number of primitive tribes) remained remote from the influences of the high Cultures. The ethnolo-

[1] With this it becomes unnecessary to postulate vast periods of time for the original states of man, and we can regard the interval between the oldest man-type hitherto discovered and the beginning of the Egyptian Culture as a span, greater indeed, but certainly not unthinkably greater, than the 5,000 years of recognized cultural history.

[2] It is perhaps not unnecessary to remark that the word "epoch" is used throughout this book in its proper sense of "turning point" or "moment of change" and *not* in the loose sense of "period" which it has acquired. — *Tr.*

[3] *Und Afrika Sprach* (1912); *Paideuma, Umrisse einer Kultur- und Seelenlehre* (1920). Frobenius distinguishes three ages.

gist-psychologist, on the contrary, delights in collecting, from all over the five continents, fragments of peoples who really have nothing in common but the negative fact of living a subordinate existence in the middle of one or another of the high Cultures, without participation in its inner life. The result is a congeries of tribes, some stationary, some inferior, and some decadent, whose respective modes of expression, moreover, are indiscriminately lumped together.

But the primitive Culture is not fragmentary, but something *strong and integral*, something highly vital and effectual. Only, this Culture is so different from everything that we men of a higher Culture possess in the way of spiritual potentialities that we may question whether even those people which have carried the first age very deep into the second are good evidence, in their present modes of being and waking-being, for the condition of the old time.

For some thousands of years now the waking-consciousness of man has had the impression of constant mutual touch between the tribes and peoples as an obvious everyday fact. But in dealing with the first age we must not forget that in it man, cohering in a very few small groups, is completely lost in the immensity of the landscape, the ruling element therein being the mighty masses of the great animal-herds. The rarity of our finds sufficiently proves this. At the time of Aurignacian Man there were perhaps a dozen hordes, each a few hundred strong, wandering in the whole area of France, and such hordes must have regarded it as a deeply impressive and puzzling event when (if ever) they became aware that fellow men existed. Can we imagine even in the least degree what it was to live in a world almost empty of men — we for whom all nature has long since become a background for the human multitude? How man's world-consciousness must have changed when, besides the forests and the herds of beasts, other men "just like himself" began to be met with, more and more frequently, in the country-side. The increase of man's numbers — this, too, doubtless took place very suddenly — made experience of "fellow men" habitual, and replaced the impression of astonishment by the feelings of pleasure or hostility, and these again evoked a whole new world of experiences and of involuntary and inevitable relations. It was for the history of the human soul perhaps the deepest and most pregnant of all events. It was in relation to alien life-forms that man first became conscious of his own, and now the interior organization of the clan was enriched by a wealth of intertribal forms of relation, which thereafter completely dominated primitive life and thought. For it was then that, out of very simple modes of sensuous understanding, the rudiments of verbal language (and, therefore, of abstract thought) came into being, amongst them the particularly fortunate few, which — though we can form no idea of their structure — we may assume as the origins of the later Indogermanic and Semitic language-groups.

Then, out of this general primitive Culture of a humanity linked by intertribal relations, there shot up suddenly (about 3000 b.c.[1]) the Culture of Egypt and Babylonia. Probably for a millennium before that date both these fields had been nursing something that differed radically from every primitive Culture in kind and in intent, something having an inward unity common to all its forms of expression and directional in all its life. To me it seems highly probable that, if not indeed all over the earth's surface, at any rate in man's essence a change was accomplished at that time; and if so, then any primitive Culture worthy of the name that is still found living later, ever dwindling, in the midst of higher Cultures, should itself be something different from the Culture of the first Age. But, with reference to primitive Culture of any sort, that which I call the pre-Culture (and which can be shown to occur as a uniform process in the beginning of every high Culture) is something different in kind, something entirely new.

In all primitive existence the "it," the Cosmic, is at work with such immediacy of force that all microcosmic utterances, whether in myth, custom, technique, or ornament, obey only the pressures of the very instant. For us, there are no ascertainable rules for the duration, tempo, and course of development of these utterances. We observe, say, an ornamental form-language — not to be called a style [2] — ruling over the population of a wide area, spreading, changing, and at last dying out. Alongside this, and perhaps with quite different fields of extension, we may find modes of fashioning and using weapons, tribal organizations, religious practices, each developing in a special way of its own, with epochal points of its own, beginnings and ends of its own, completely influenced by other form-domains. When in some prehistoric stratum we have identified an accurately known type of pottery, we cannot safely argue from it to the customs and religion of the population to which it belonged. And if by chance the same area does hold for a particular form of marriage and, say, a certain type of tattooing, this never signifies a common basic idea such as is indicated, for example, by the discovery of gunpowder and that of perspective in painting. No necessary connexions come to light between ornament and organization by age-classes, or between the cult of a god and the kind of agriculture practised. Development in these cases means always some development of one or another individual aspect or trait of the primitive Culture, never of that Culture itself. This, as I have said before, is essentially chaotic; the primitive Culture is neither an organism nor a sum of organisms.

But with the type of the higher Culture this "it" gives way to a strong and undiffused *tendency*. Within the primitive Culture tribes and clans are the only quickened beings — other than the individual men of course. *Here, however, the Culture itself is such a being.* Everything primitive is a sum — a sum of the

---

[1] This work appeared before the discovery of the Sumerian (or Pre-Sumerian) tombs of Ur. — *Tr.*
[2] See Vol. I, p. 108. — *Tr.*

expression-forms of primitive groupings. The high Culture, on the contrary, is the waking-being of a single huge organism which makes not only custom, myths, technique, and art, but the very peoples and classes incorporated in itself the vessels of one single form-language and one single history. The oldest speech that we know of belongs to the primitive Culture, and has lawless destinies of its own which cannot be deduced from those of, say, Ornament or Marriage. But the history of script belongs integrally with the expression-history of the several higher Cultures. That the Egyptian, Chinese, Babylonian, and Mexican each formed a special script in its pre-Cultural age — that the Indian and the Classical on the other hand did not do so, but took over (and very late) the highly developed writing of a neighbouring Civilization — that in the Arabian, again, every new religion and sect immediately formed its particular script — all these are facts that stand in a deeply intimate relation to the generic form-history of these Cultures and its inner significance.

To these two ages our knowledge of man is restricted, and they certainly do not suffice to justify conclusions of any sort about possible or certain new eras or about their "when" and "how" — quite apart from the fact that in any case the cosmic connexions that govern the history of man as a genus are entirely inaccessible to our measures.

My kind of thought and observation is limited to the physiognomy of the actual. At the point when the experience of the "judge of men" *vis-à-vis* his environment, and that of the "man of action" *vis-à-vis* his facts, become ineffective, there also this insight finds its limit. The existence of these two ages is a *fact of historical experience;* more, our experiencing of the primitive Culture consists not only in surveying, in its relics, a self-contained and closed-off thing, but also in reacting to its deeper meaning by virtue of an inward relation to it which persists in us. But the second age opens to us another and quite different kind of experience. It was an incident, the sense of which cannot now be scrutinized, that the type of the higher Culture appeared suddenly in the field of human history. Quite possibly, indeed, it was some sudden event in the domain of earth-history that brought forth a new and different form into phenomenal existence. But the fact that we have before us eight such Cultures, all of the same build, the same development, and the same duration, justifies us in *looking at them comparatively*, and therefore justifies our treating them as comparable, studying them comparatively, and obtaining from our study a knowledge which we can extend backwards over lost periods and forwards over the future — provided always that a Destiny of a different order does not replace this form-world, suddenly and basically, by another. Our licence to proceed thus comes from general experience of organic being. As in the history of the Raptores or the Coniferæ we cannot prophesy whether and when a new species will arise, so in that of Cultural history we cannot say whether and when a new Culture shall be. But from the moment when a new being is conceived in the womb, or a seed sinks into the earth, we do know *the inner form of this new life-course;* and we know that the quiet course of its development and fulfilment may be disturbed by the pressure of external powers, but never altered.

This experience teaches, further, that the Civilization which at this present time has gripped the earth's whole surface is not a third age, but a stage — a necessary stage — of the Western Culture, distinguished from its analogues only by the forcefulness of its extension-tendency. Here experience ends, and all speculation on what new forms will govern the life of future mankind (or, for that matter, whether there will be any such new forms) all building of majestic card-houses on the foundation of "it should be, it shall be" is mere trifling — far too futile, it seems to me, to justify one single life of any value being expended on it.

The group of the high Cultures is not, as a group, an organic unit. That they have happened in just this number, at just these places and times, is, for the human eye, an incident without deeper intelligibility. The ordering of the individual Cultures, on the contrary, has stood out so distinctly that the historical technique of the Chinese, the Magian, and the Western worlds — often, indeed, the mere common consent of the educated in these Cultures — has been able to fashion a set of names upon which it would be impossible to improve.[1]

Historical thought, therefore, has the double task of dealing comparatively with *the individual life-courses of the Cultures*, and of examining the incidental and irregular relations of the Cultures amongst themselves in respect of their meaning. The necessity of the first of these tasks, obvious enough, has yet been overlooked hitherto. The second has been handled, but only by the lazy and shallow method of imposing causality over the whole tangle and laying it out tidily along the "course" of a hypothetical "world"-history, thereby making it impossible to discover either the psychology of these difficult, but richly suggestive, relations or to discover that of the inner life of any particular Culture. In truth, the condition for solving the first problem is that the second has been solved already. The relations are very different, even under the simple aspect of time and space. The Crusades brought a Springtime face to face with an old and ripe Civilization; in the Cretan-Mycenæan world seed-time and golden autumn are seen together. A Civilization may stream over from immense remoteness, as the Indian streamed into the Arabian from the East, or lie senile and stifling over an infancy, as the Classical lay upon its other side. But there are differences, too, of kind and strength; the Western Culture seeks out relations, the Egyptian tries to avoid them; the former is beaten by them

---

[1] Goethe, in his little essay "*Geistesepochen*," has characterized the four parts of a Culture — its preliminary, early, late, and civilized stages — with such a depth of insight that even today there is nothing to add. See the tables at the end of Vol. I, which agree with this exactly.

again and again in tragic crises, while the Classical gets all it can out of them, without suffering. But all these tendencies have their roots in the spirituality of the Culture itself — and sometimes they tell us more of this Culture than does its own language, which often hides more than it communicates.

v

A glance over the group of the Cultures discloses task after task. The nineteenth century, in which historical research was guided by natural science, and historical thought by the ideas of the Baroque, has simply brought us to a pinnacle whence we see the new world at our feet. Shall we ever take possession of that new world?

Even to-day uniform treatment of these grand life-courses is immensely difficult, because the more remote fields have not been seriously worked up at all. Once more, it is the lordly outlook of the West European — he will only notice that which approaches him from one or another antiquity by the proper and respectful route of a Middle Age, and that which goes its own ways will get but little of his attention. Thus, of the things of the Chinese and the Indian worlds, certain kinds are now beginning to be tackled — art, religion, philosophy — but the political history is dealt with, if at all, "chattily." It does not occur to anyone to treat the great constitutional problems of Chinese history — the Hohenstaufen-destiny of the Li-Wang (842), the first Congress of Princes (659), the struggle of principle between the imperialism (Lien-heng) of the "Roman" state of Tsin and the League-of-Nations idea (Ho-tsung) between 500 and 300, the rise of the Chinese Augustus, Hwang-ti (221) — with anything of the thoroughness that Mommsen devoted to the principate of Augustus. India, again; however completely the Indians themselves have forgotten their state-history, we have after all more available material for Buddha's time than we have for history of the Classical ninth and eighth centuries, and yet even to-day we act as though "the" Indian had lived entirely in his philosophy, just as the Athenians (so our classicists would have us believe) spent their lives in beauty-philosophizing on the banks of the Ilissus. But even Egyptian politics receive little reflective attention. The later Egyptian historian concealed under the name "Hyksos period" the same crisis which the Chinese treat of under the name "Period of the Contending States" — here, too, is something never yet investigated. And interest in the Arabian world has reached to the frontier of the Classical tongues and no further. With what endless assiduity we have described the constitution of Diocletian, and assembled material for the entirely unimportant administrative history of the provinces of Asia Minor — because it is written in Greek. But the Sassanid state, the precedent and in every respect the model of Diocletian's, comes into the picture only occasionally, and then as Rome's *opponent* in war. What about *its own* administrative and juristic history? What is the poor sum-total of material that we have assembled for the law and economics of Egypt, India, and China [1] in comparison with the work that has been done on Greek and Roman law.

About 3000 [2] after a long "Merovingian" period, which is still distinctly perceptible in Egypt, the two oldest Cultures began, in exceedingly limited areas on the lower Nile and the lower Euphrates. In these cases the distinctions between early and late periods have long ago been labelled as Old and Middle Kingdom, Sumer and Akkad. The outcome of the Egyptian feudal period marked by the establishment of a hereditary nobility and the decline (from Dynasty VI) of the older Kingship, presents so astounding a similarity with the course of events in the Chinese springtime from I-Wang (934–909) and that in the Western from the Emperor Henry IV (1056–1106) that a unified comparative study of all three might well be risked. At the beginning of the Babylonian "Baroque" we see the figure of the great Sargon (2500), who pushed out to the Mediterranean coast, conquered Cyprus, and styled himself, like Justinian I and Charles V, "lord of the four parts of the earth." And in due course, about 1800 on the Nile and rather earlier in Sumer-Akkad, we perceive the beginnings of the first Civilizations. Of these the Asiatic displayed immense expansive power. The "achievements of the Babylonian Civilization" (as the books say), many things and notions connected with measuring, numbering, and accounting, travelled probably as far as the North and the Yellow Seas. Many a Babylonian trademark upon a tool may have come to be

[1] Another blank is the history of the countryside or landscape (i.e., of the soil, with its plant-mantle and its weathering) in which man's history has been staged for five thousand years. And yet man has so painfully wrested himself from the history of the landscape, and withal is so held to it still by myriad fibres, that without it life, soul, and thought are inconceivable.

So far as concerns the South-European field, from the end of the Ice Age, a hitherto rank luxuriance gradually gave place in the plant-world to poverty. In the course of the successive Egyptian, Classical, Arabian, and Western Cultures, a climatic change developed all around the Mediterranean, which resulted in the peasant's being compelled to fight no longer *against* the plant-world, but *for* it — first against the primeval forest and then against the desert. In Hannibal's time the Sahara lay very far indeed to the south of Carthage, but today it already penetrates to northern Spain and Italy. Where was it in the days of the pyramid-builders, who depicted sylvan and hunting scenes in their reliefs? When the Spaniards expelled the Moriscos, their countryside of woods and ploughland, already only artificially maintained, lost its character altogether, and the towns became oases in the waste. In the Roman period such a result could not have ensued.

[2] The new method of comparative morphology affords us a safe test of the datings which have been arrived at by other means for the beginnings of past Cultures. The same kind of argument which would prevent us, even in the absence of positive information, from dating Goethe's birth more than a century earlier than the "*Urfaust*," or supposing the career of Alexander the Great to have been that of an elderly man, enables us to demonstrate, from the individual characteristics of their political life and the spirit of their art, thought, and religion, that the Egyptian Culture dawned somewhere about 3000 and the Chinese about 1400. The calculations of French investigators and more recently of Borchardt (*Die Annalen und die zeitliche Festlegung des Alten Reiches*, 1919) are as unsound intrinsically as those of Chinese historians for the legendary Hsia and Shang dynasties. Equally, it is impossible that the Egyptian calendar should have been introduced in 4241 B.C. As in every chronology we have to allow that evolution has been accompanied by radical calendar changes, the attempt to fix the exact starting-date *a posteriori* is objectless.

honoured, out there in the Germanic wild, as a magic symbol, and so may have originated some "Early-German" ornament. But meantime the Babylonian realm itself passed from hand to hand. Kassites, Assyrians, Chaldeans, Medes, Persians, Macedonians — all of these small [1] warrior-hosts under energetic leaders — successively replaced one another in the capital city without any serious resistance on the part of its people.

It is a first example — soon paralleled in Egypt — of the "Roman Empire" style. Under the Kassites rulers were set up and displaced by prætorians; the Assyrians, like the later soldier-emperors of Rome (after Commodus), maintained the old constitutional forms; the Persian Cyrus and the Ostrogoth Theodoric regarded themselves as managers of the Empire, and the warrior bands, Mede and Lombard, as master-peoples in alien surroundings. But these are constitutional rather than factual distinctions; in intent and purpose the legions of Septimius Severus, the African, did not differ from the Visigoths of Alaric, and by the battle of Adrianople [2] "Romans" and "barbarians" have become almost indistinguishable.

After 1500 three new Cultures begin — first, the Indian, in the upper Punjab; then, a hundred years later, the Chinese on the middle Hwang-Ho; and then, about 1100, the Classical, on the Ægean Sea. The Chinese historians speak of the three great dynasties of Hsia, Shang, and Chóu in much the same way as Napoleon regarded himself as a fourth dynasty following the Merovingians, the Carolingians, and the Capetians — in reality, the third coexisted with the Culture right through its course in each case. When in 441 B.C. the titular Emperor of the Chóu dynasty became a state pensioner of the "Eastern Duke" and when in A.D. 1793 "Louis Capet" was executed, the Culture in each case passed into the Civilization. There are some bronzes of very great antiquity preserved from late Chang times, which stand towards the later art in exactly the same relation as Mycenæan to Early Classical pottery and Carolingian to Romanesque art. In the Vedic, Homeric, and Chinese springtimes, with their "*Pfalzen*" and "*Burgen*," their knighthood and feudal rulership, can be seen the whole image of our Gothic, and the "period of the Great Protectors" (Ming-Chu, 685–691) corresponds precisely to the time of Cromwell, Wallenstein, and Richelieu and to the First Tyrannis of the Greek world.

The period 480–230 is called by the Chinese historians the "Period of the Contending States"; it culminated in a century of unbroken warfare between

---

[1] Eduard Meyer (*Gesch. d. Altertums*, III, 97) estimates the Persians, probably too highly, at half a million as against the fifty millions of the Babylonian Empire. The numerical relation between the Germanic peoples and legions of the third-century Roman emperors and the Roman population as a whole, and that of the Ptolemaic and Roman armies to that of the Egyptian people, was of much the same order.

[H. Delbrück, in his well-known *Gesch. der Kriegskunst* (1908), Vol. I, Part I, chapter i, and elsewhere, deals in considerable detail with the strengths of ancient armies. — *Tr.*]

[2] A.D. 378. See C. W. C. Oman, *History of the Art of War: Middle Ages* (1898), ch. i; H. Delbrück, *Gesch. der Kriegskunst*, Vol. II, book I, ch. x, and book II. — *Tr.*

mass-armies with frightful social upheavals, and out of it came the "Roman" state of Tsin as founder of a Chinese Imperium. This phase Egypt experienced between 1780 and 1580, of which the last century was the "Hyksos" time. The Classical experienced it from Chæronea (338), and, at the high pitch of horror, from the Gracchi (133) to Actium (31 B.C.). And it is the destiny of the West-European-American world for the nineteenth and twentieth centuries.

During this period the centre of gravity changes — as from Attica to Latium, so from the Hwang-ho (at Ho-nan-fu) to the Yang-tse (modern province of Hu-pei). The Si-Kiang was as vague for the Chinese savants of those days as the Elbe for the Alexandrian geographer, and of the existence of India they had as yet no notion.

As on the other side of the globe there arose the principes of the Julian-Claudian house, so here in China there arose the mighty figure of Wang-Cheng, who led Tsin through the decisive struggle to sole supremacy and in 221 assumed the title of Shi (literally equivalent to "Augustus") and the Cæsar-name Hwang-ti. He founded the "*Pax Serica*," as we may call it, carried out a grand social reform in the exhausted Empire, and — as promptly as Rome [1] — began to build his "*Limes*," the famous Great Wall, for which in 214 he annexed a part of Mongolia. He was the first, too, to subdue the barbarians south of the Yang-tse, in a series of large-scale campaigns followed and confirmed by military roads, castles, and colonies. But "Roman," too, was his family history — a Tacitean drama with Lui-Shi (Chancellor and stepfather of the Emperor) and Li-Szu, the great statesman (the Agrippa of his day, and unifier of the Chinese script), playing parts, and one that quickly closed in Neronic horrors. Followed then the two Han dynasties (Western, 206 B.C.–A.D. 23; Eastern, A.D. 25–220), under which the frontiers extended more and more, while in the capital eunuch-ministers, generals, and soldiery made and unmade the rulers at their pleasure. At certain rare moments, as under Wu-ti (140–86) and Ming-ti (58–76), the Chinese-Confucian, the Indian–Buddhist, and the Classical-Stoic world-forces approached one another so closely in the region of the Caspian that they might easily have come into actual touch.[2]

Chance decreed that the heavy attacks of the Huns should break themselves in vain upon the Chinese "Limes," which at each crisis found a strong emperor to defend it. The decisive repulse of the Huns took place in 124–119 under the Chinese Trajan, Wu-ti; and it was he, too, who finally incorporated Southern China in the Empire, with the object of obtaining a route into India, and built a grand embattled road to the Tarim. And so the Huns turned westward, and

---

[1] In the case of Rome, the idea of a fixed frontier against the barbarian emerged soon after the defeat of Varus, and the fortifications of the Limes were laid down before the close of the first century of our era. — *Tr.*

[2] For at that time imperialistic tendencies found expression even in India, in the Maurya and Sunga dynasty; these, however, could only be confused and ineffective, Indian nature being what it was.

in due course they appear, impelling a swarm of Germanic tribes, in face of the Limes of the Roman world. This time they succeeded. The Roman Imperium collapsed, and thus two only of the three empires continued, and still continue, as desirable spoil for a succession of different powers. To-day it is the "red-haired barbarian" of the West who is playing before the highly civilized eyes of Brahman and Mandarin the rôle once played by Mogul and Manchu, playing it neither better nor worse than they, and certain like them to be superseded in due course by other actors. But in the colonization-field of foundering Rome, on the other hand, the future Western Culture was ripening underground in the north-west, while in the east the Arabian Culture had flowered already.

The Arabian Culture [1] is a discovery. Its unity was suspected by late Arabians, but it has so entirely escaped Western historical research that not even a satisfactory name can be found for it. Conformably to the dominant languages, the seed-time and the spring might be called the Aramaic and the later time the Arabian, but there is no really effectual name. In this field the Cultures were close to one another, and the extension of the corresponding Civilizations led to much overlaying. The pre-Cultural period of the Arabian, which we can follow out in Persian and Jewish history, lay completely within the area of the old Babylonian world, but the springtime was under the mighty spell of the Classical Civilization, which invaded from the West with all the power of a just-attained maturity, and the Egyptian and Indian Civilizations also made themselves distinctly felt. And then in turn the Arabian spirit — under Late Classical disguises for the most part — cast its spell over the nascent Culture of the West. The Arabian Civilization stratified over a still surviving Classical in the popular soul of south Spain, Provence, and Sicily, and became the model upon which the Gothic soul educated itself. The proper landscape of this Culture is remarkably extended and singularly fragmented. Let one put oneself at Palmyra or Ctesiphon, and, musing, look outwards all round. In the north is Osrhoene; Edessa became the Florence of the Arabian spring. To the west are Syria and Palestine — the home of the New Testament and of the Jewish Mishna, with Alexandria as a standing outpost. To the east Mazdaism experienced a mighty regeneration, which corresponded to the birth of Jesus in Jewry and about which the fragmentary state of Avesta literature enables us to say only *that* it happened.[2] Here, too, were born the Talmud and the religion of Mani. Deep in the south, the future home of Islam, an age of chivalry was able to develop as fully as in the realm of the Sassanids; even to-day there survive, unexplored, the ruins of castles and strongholds whence the decisive wars were waged between the Christian state of Axum and the Jewish state of the Himyarites on the two shores of the Red Sea, with Roman

---

[1] Chapters vii–ix below.
[2] On the history of the Avesta see *Ency. Brit.*, XI ed., articles "Zend-Avesta" and "Zoroaster." — *Tr.*

and Persian diplomacy poking the fire.   In the extreme north was Byzantium, that strange mixture of sere, civilized, Classical, with vernal and chevaleresque which is manifested above all in the bewildering history of the Byzantine army system.   Into this world Islam at last — and far too late — brought a consciousness of unity, and this accounts for the self-evident character of its victorious progress and the almost unresisting adhesion of Christians, Jews, and Persians alike.   Out of Islam in due course arose the Arabian Civilization which was at the peak of its intellectual completeness when the barbarians from the West broke in for a moment, marching on Jerusalem.   How, we may ask ourselves, did this inroad appear in the eyes of cultivated Arabians of the time?   Somewhat like Bolshevism, perhaps?   For the statecraft of the Arabian World the political relations of "Frankistan" were something on a lower plane. Even in our Thirty Years' War — from that point of view a drama of the "Far West" — when an English envoy [1] strove to stir up the Porte against the house of Habsburg, the statesman who handled policy over a field stretching from Morocco to India, evidently judged that the little predatory states on the horizon were of no real interest.   And even when Napoleon landed in Egypt, there were still many without an inkling of the future.

Meantime yet another new Culture developed in Mexico.   This lay so remote from the rest that no word even passed between them.   All the more astonishing, therefore, is the similarity of its development to that of the Classical.   No doubt the archæologist standing before a teocalli would be horrified to think of his Doric temple in such a connexion;   yet it was a thoroughly Classical trait — feebleness of the will-to-power in the matter of technics — that kept the Aztecs ill armed and so made possible their catastrophe.

For, as it happens, this is the one example of a Culture ended by violent death.   It was not starved, suppressed, or thwarted, but murdered in the full glory of its unfolding, destroyed like a sunflower whose head is struck off by one passing.   All these states — including a world-power and more than one federation — with an extent and resources far superior to those of the Greek and Roman states of Hannibal's day;   with a comprehensive policy, a carefully ordered financial system, and a highly developed legislation;   with administrative ideas and economic tradition such as the ministers of Charles V could never have imagined;   with a wealth of literature in several languages, an intellectually brilliant and polite society in great cities to which the West could not show one single parallel — all this was not broken down in some desperate war, but washed out by a handful of bandits in a few years, and so

[1] Sir Thomas Roe, 1620.   A similar mission went to Turkey on the part of Frederick and the Bohemian nobles to ask for assistance and to justify to the Turk their action in deposing the Habsburg King.   The answer they received was what might be expected of a great imperialist power asked to intervene in the affairs of lesser neighbours — namely, material guarantees of the reality of the movement it was asked to support and pledges that no settlement would be made without its agreement. — *Tr.*

entirely that the relics of the population retained not even a memory of it all. Of the giant city Tenochtitlan [1] not a stone remains above ground. The cluster of great Mayan cities in the virgin forests of Yucatan succumbed swiftly to the attack of vegetation, and we do not know the old name of any one of them. Of the literature three books survive, but no one can read them.

The most appalling feature of the tragedy was that it was not in the least a necessity of the Western Culture that it should happen. It was a private affair of adventurers, and at the time no one in Germany, France, or England had any idea of what was taking place. This instance shows, as no other shows, that *the history of humanity has no meaning whatever* and that deep significances reside only in the life-courses of the separate Cultures. Their inter-relations are unimportant and accidental. In this case the accident was so cruelly banal, so supremely absurd, that it would not be tolerated in the wildest farce. A few cannon and handguns began and ended the drama. [2]

A sure knowledge of even the most general history of this world is now for ever impossible. Events as important as our Crusades and Reformation have vanished without leaving a trace. Only in recent years has research managed to settle the outline, at any rate, of the later course of development, and with the help of these data comparative morphology may attempt to widen and deepen the picture by means of those of other Cultures. [3] On this basis the epochal points of this Culture lie about two hundred years later than those of the Arabian and seven hundred years before those of our own. There was a pre-Cultural period which, as in China and Egypt, developed script and calendar, but of this we now know nothing. The time-reckoning began with an initial date which lies far behind the birth of Christ, but it is impossible now to fix it with certainty relative to that event. [4] In any case, it shows an extraordinarily strongly developed history-sense in Mexican mankind.

The springtime of the "Hellenic" Maya states is evidenced by the dated relief-pillars of the old cities of Copan (in the south), Tikal, and somewhat later Chichen Itza (in the north), Naranjo, and Seibal [5] — about 160–450.

---

[1] Mexico City, or, better, the agglomeration of towns and villages in the valley of Mexico. — *Tr.*

[2] According to Prescott, Cortez's force on landing had thirteen hand firearms and fourteen cannon, great and small, altogether. The whole of these were lost in the first defeat at Mexico. Later a pure accident gave Cortez the contents of a supply-ship from Europe. In a military sense horses contributed to the Spanish victories nearly if not quite as much as firearms, but these, too, were in small numbers, sixteen at the outset. — *Tr.*

[3] The following attempt is based upon the data of two American works — L. Spence, *The Civilization of Ancient Mexico* (Cambridge, 1912); and H. J. Spinden, *Maya Art: Its Subject matter and Historical Development* (Cambridge, 1913) — which independently of one another attempt to work out the chronology and which reach a certain measure of agreement.

[4] Since the publication of the German original, Spinden's further researches (*Ancient Civilizations of Mexico*) have placed the historical zero date at 613 B.C. (and the cosmological zero of back-reckoning at 3373 B.C.). This historical zero seems to lie deep in the pre-Cultural period, if later events have the dates given in the text. But compare Author's note on p. 39. — *Tr.*

[5] These are the names of near-by villages serving as labels; the true names are lost.

At the end of this period Chichen Itza was a model of architecture that was followed for centuries. The full glory of Palenque and Piedras Negras (in the west) may correspond to our Late Gothic and Renaissance (450–600 = European 1250–1400?). In the Baroque or Late period Champutun appears as the centre of style-formation, and now the "Italic" Nahua peoples of the high plateau of Anahuac began to come under the cultural influence. Artistically and spiritually these peoples were mere recipients, but in their political instincts they were far superior to the Maya (about 600–960, = Classical 750–400 = Western 1400–1750?). And now Maya entered on the "Hellenistic" phase. About 960 Uxmal was founded, soon to be a cosmopolis of the first rank, an Alexandria or Baghdad, founded like these on the threshold of the Civilization. With it we find a series of brilliant cities like Labna, Mayapan, Chacmultun, and a revived Chichen Itza. These places mark the culminating point of a grandiose architecture, which thereafter produced no new style, but applies the old motives with taste and discrimination to mighty masses. Politically this is the age of the celebrated League of Mayapan, an alliance of three leading states, which appears to have maintained the position successfully — if somewhat artificially and arbitrarily — in spite of great wars and repeated revolutions (960–1165 = Classical 350–150 = Western 1800–2000).

The end of this period was marked by a great revolution, and with it the definitive intervention of the ("Roman") Nahua powers in the Maya affair. With their aid Hunac Ceel brought about a general overthrow and destroyed Mayapan (about 1190 = Classical 150). The sequel was typical of the history of the over-ripened Civilization in which different peoples contend for military lordship. The great Maya cities sink into the same bland contentment as Roman Athens and Alexandria, but out on the horizon of the Nahua lands was developing the last of these peoples, the Aztecs — young, vigorous, barbaric, and filled with an insatiable will-to-power. In 1325 (= the Age of Augustus) they founded Tenochtitlan, which soon became the paramount and capital city of the whole Mexican world. About 1400 military expansion began on the grand scale. Conquered regions were secured by military colonies and a network of military roads, and a superior diplomacy kept the dependent states in check and separated. Imperial Tenochtitlàn grew enormous and housed a cosmopolitan population speaking every tongue of this world-empire.[1] The Nahua provinces were politically and militarily secure, the southward thrust was developing rapidly, and a hand was about to be laid on the Maya states; there is no telling what the course of the next centuries would have been. And suddenly — the end.

[1] And was there an element of *panem et circenses* in the mass-sacrifice of captives? May it be that the acceptance of the Spaniard as the expected manifestation of the god Quetzalcoatl ("*redeunt Saturnia regna*"), and the serious disputations on matters of religion that took place between Montezuma and the Christians, were presages of the phase which Spengler calls the "Second Religiousness" (see below, p. 310) of the Civilization? — *Tr.*

At that date the West was at a level which the Maya had already overpassed by 700; nothing short of the age of Frederick the Great would have been ripe enough to comprehend the politics of the Mayapan League, and what the Aztecs of A.D. 1500 were organizing lies for us well in the future. But that which distinguished Faustian man, even then, from the man of any other Culture was his irrepressible urge into distance. It was this, in the last resort, that killed and even annihilated the Mexican and Peruvian Culture — the unparalleled drive that was ready for service in any and every domain. Certainly the Ionic style was imitated in Carthage and in Persepolis, and Hellenistic taste in the Gandara art of India found admirers. Future investigation will probably find some Chinese in the primitive German wood-architecture. The Mosque style ruled from Farther India to North Russia, to West Africa, and to Spain. But all that amounts to nothing as compared with the expansion-power of the Western Soul. The true style-history of that soul, it need hardly be said, accomplished itself only on the mother soil, but its resultant effects knew no bounds. On the spot where Tenochtitlan had stood, the Spaniards erected a Baroque cathedral adorned with masterpieces of Spanish painting and plastic. Already at that date the Portuguese had got to work in Hither India and Late-Baroque architects from Spain and Italy in the heart of Poland and Russia. The English Rococo, and especially Empire, made for themselves a broad province in the Plantation States of North America, whose wonderful rooms and furniture are far less well known in Germany than they ought to be. Classicism was at work already in Canada and at the Cape, and presently there were no limits at all. It was just the same in every other domain of form; the relation between this forceful young Civilization and the still remaining old ones — is that it covers them, all alike, with ever-thickening layers of West-European-American life-forms under which, slowly, the ancient native form disappears.

VI

In the presence of this picture of the world of man — which is destined to displace the older one of "Ancient-Mediæval-Modern" that is still firmly established even in the best minds — it will become possible, too, to give a new answer (and for our Civilization, I think, a final answer) to the old question: What is History?

Ranke, in the preface of his *World History* says: "History only begins when the monuments become intelligible, and trustworthy written evidences are available." This is the answer of a collector and arranger of data; obviously, it confuses that which has happened with that which happened within the field of view open at the particular time to the particular student. Mardonius was defeated at Platæa — has this ceased to be history if two thousand years later it has somehow dropped out of the ken of the historians? For a fact to be a fact, must it be mentioned in books?

The weightiest historian since Ranke, Eduard Meyer,[1] says: "Historic is that which is, or has been, effective. . . . Only through historical treatment does the individual process, lifted by history from among the infinite mass of contemporary processes, become the historical event." The remark is thoroughly in the manner and spirit of Hegel. Firstly, its starting-point is the fact and not any accidental knowledge or ignorance of the fact, and if there is any mode of picturing history which necessarily imposes such a starting-point, it is that presented in these pages, since it compels us to assume the existence of facts of the first order in majestic sequences, even when we do not (and never will) know them in the scientific sense. We have to learn to handle the unknown in the most comprehensive way. Secondly, truths exist for the mind, facts only in relation to life. Historical treatment — in my terminology, *physiognomic fact* — is decided by the *blood*, the gift of judging men broadened out into past and future, the innate flair for persons and situations, for the event, for that which had to be, must have been. It does *not* consist in bare scientific criticism and knowing of data. The scientific mode of experience is, for every true historian, something additional or subordinate. It addresses to the waking-consciousness, by the way of understanding and imparting, laborious and repetitive proof of that which *one moment* of illumination has already, and instantly, demonstrated to Being.

Just because the force of our Faustian being has by now worked up about us a circumcircle of inner experiences such as no other men and no other time could acquire — just because for us the remotest events become increasingly significant and disclose relationships that no one else, not even the closest contemporaries of these events, could perceive — much has now become history (i.e., life in tune with our life) that centuries ago was not history. Tacitus probably "knew" the data concerning Tiberius Gracchus's revolution, but for him it no longer meant anything effectively, whereas for us it is full of meaning. The history of the Monophysites and their relation to Mohammed's *milieu* signify nothing whatever to the Islamic believer, but for *us* it is recognizably the story of English Puritanism in another setting. For the world-view of a Civilization which has made the whole earth its stage, nothing is in the last resort quite unhistorical. The scheme of ancient-mediæval-modern history, as understood by the nineteenth century, contained only a selection of the more obvious relations. But the influence that old Chinese and Mexican history are beginning to exercise on us to-day is of a subtler and more intellectual kind. There we are sounding the last necessities of life itself. We are learning out of another life-course to know ourselves what we are, what we must be, what we shall be. It is the great school of our future. We who have history still, are making history still, find here on the extreme frontiers of historical humanity what history *is*.

[1] "*Zur Theorie und Methodik der Geschichte*" (*Kleine Schriften*, 1910), which is by far the best piece of historical philosophy ever written by an opponent of all philosophy.

A battle between two Negro tribes in the Sudan, or between the Cherusci and Chatti of Cæsar's time, or — what is substantially the same — between ant-communities, is merely a drama of "living Nature." But when the Cherusci beat the Romans, as in the year 9,[1] or the Aztecs the Tlascalans, it is *history*. Here the "when" is of importance and each decade, or even year, matters, for here one is dealing with the march of a grand life-course, in which every decision takes rank as an epoch. Here there is an object towards which every happening impels, a being that strives to fulfil its predestination, a tempo, an organic duration — and not the disorderly ups and downs of Scythians, Gauls, or Caribs, of which the particular detail is as unimportant as that of doings in a colony of beavers or a steppe-herd of gazelles. These are *zoölogical happenings* and have their place in an altogether different orientation of our outlook, that in which we are concerned not with the destiny of individual peoples or herds, but with that of "man," or "the" gazelle, or "the" ants, *as species*. Primitive man has history only in the biological sense, and all prehistoric study boils down to the investigation of this sense. The increasing familiarity of men with fire, stone tools, and the mechanical laws which make weapons effective, characterizes only the development of the type and of its latent possibilities. The objects for which one tribe employed these weapons against another tribe are of no importance in this plane of history. Stone Age and Baroque are age-grades in the existence of respectively a genus and a Culture — i.e., two organisms belonging to two fundamentally different settings. And here I would protest against two assumptions that have so far vitiated all historical thought: the assertion of an ultimate aim of mankind as a whole and the denial of there being ultimate aims at all. The life *has* an aim. It is the fulfilment of that which was ordained at its conception. But the individual belongs by birth to the particular high Culture on the one hand and to the type Man on the other — there is no third unit of being for him. His destiny must lie either in the zoölogical or in the world-historical field. "Historical" man, as I understand the word and as all great historians have meant it to be taken, is the man of a Culture that is in full march towards self-fulfilment. Before this, after this, outside this, man is *historyless;* and the destinies of the people to which he belongs matter as little as the Earth's destiny matters when the plane of attention is the astronomical and not the geological.

From this there follows a fact of the most decisive importance, and one that has never before been established: that man is not only historyless before the birth of the Culture, but again becomes so as soon as a Civilization has worked itself out fully to the definitive form which betokens the end of the living development of the Culture and the exhaustion of the last potentialities of its significant existence. That which we see in the Egyptian Civilization after Seti I (1300) and in the Chinese, the Indian, the Arabian to this day is —

---

[1] Varus's disaster in the Teutoburger Wald. — *Tr.*

notwithstanding all the cleverness of the religious, philosophical and, especially, political forms in which it is wrapped — just the old zoölogical up-and-down of the primitive age again. Whether the lords sitting in Babylon were wild war-hordes like the Kassites or refined inheritors like the Persians, when, for how long, and with what success they kept their seats, signified nothing from the standpoint of Babylon. The comfort of the population was affected by such things, naturally, but they made no difference either way to the fact that the soul of this world was extinct and its events, therefore, void of any deep meaning. A new dynasty, native or foreign, in Egypt, a revolution or a conquest in China, a new Germanic people in the Roman Empire, were elements in the history of the landscape like a change in the fauna or the migration of a flock of birds.

In the history, the genuine history, of higher men the stake fought for and the basis of the animal struggle to prevail is ever — even when driver and driven are completely unconscious of the symbolic force of their doings, purposes, and fortunes — the actualization of something that is essentially spiritual, the translation of an idea into a living historical form. This applies equally to the struggle of big style-tendencies in art (Gothic and Renaissance), of philosophy (Stoics and Epicureans), of political ideals (Oligarchy and Tyrannis), and of economic forms (Capitalism and Socialism). But the post-history is void of all this. All that remains is the struggle for mere power, for animal advantage *per se*. Whereas previously power, even when to all appearance destitute of any inspiration, was always serving the Idea somehow or other, in the late Civilization even the most convincing illusion of an idea is only the mask for purely zoölogical strivings.

The distinction between Indian philosophy before and after Buddha is that the former is a grand movement towards attaining the aim of Indian thought by and in the Indian soul, and the latter the perpetual turning-up of new facets of a now crystallized and undevelopable thought-stock. The solutions are there, for good, though the fashions of expressing them change. The same is true of Chinese painting before and after the Han dynasties — whether we know it or not — and of Egyptian architecture before and after the beginning of the New Empire. So also with technics. The West's discoveries of the steam-engine and of electricity are accepted by the Chinese to-day in just the same way — and with just the same religious awe — as bronze and the plough were accepted four thousand years ago, and fire in a still remoter age. Both, spiritually, differ *in toto* from the discoveries which the Chinese made for themselves in the Chóu period and which in each instance signified an epoch in their inner history.[1] Before and after that time, centuries play a vastly less

[1] The Japanese belonged formerly to the Chinese Civilization and again belong to a Civilization — the Western — today. A Japanese Culture in the genuine sense there has never been. Japanese Americanism must, therefore, be judged otherwise than as an outgrowth of what never was there.

important rôle than decades and even years within the Culture, *for the spans of time are gradually returning to the biological order.* This it is that confers upon these very Late conditions — which to the people living in them seem almost self-evident — that character of changeless pageantry which the genuine Culture-man — e.g., Herodotus in Egypt and the Western successors of Marco Polo in China — has found so astonishing in comparison with his own vigorous pulse of development. It is the changelessness of non-history.

Is not Classical history at an end with Actium and the *Pax Romana?* There are no more of those great decisions which concentrate the inner meaning of a whole Culture. Unreason, biology, is beginning to dominate, and it is becoming a matter of indifference for the world — though not for the actions of the private individual — whether an event turns out thus or thus. All great political questions are solved, as they are solved sooner or later in every Civilization, inasmuch as questions are no longer felt as questions and are not asked. Yet a little while, and man will cease to understand what problems were really involved in the earlier catastrophes; what is not livingly experienced of oneself cannot be livingly experienced of another. When the later Egyptians speak of the Hyksos time, or the later Chinese of the corresponding period of the "Contending States," they are judging the outward picture according to the criteria of their own ways of life, in which there are no riddles more. They see in these things merely struggles for power, and they do not see that those desperate wars, external and internal, wars in which men stirred up the alien against their own kin, were fought for an idea. To-day we understand what was taking place, in fearful alternations of tension and discharge, round the murder of Tiberius Gracchus and that of Clodius. In 1700 we could not have done so, and in 2200 we shall again be unable to do so. It is just the same with that of Chian, a Napoleonic figure, in whom later Egyptian historians could discover nothing more characterized than a "Hyksos king." Had it not been for the coming of the Germans, Roman historians a thousand years later might have put the Gracchi, Marius, Sulla, and Cicero together as a dynasty which was overthrown by Cæsar.

Compare the death of Tiberius Gracchus with the death of Nero, when Rome received the news of Galba's rising, or the victory of Sulla over the Marian party with that of Septimius Severus over Pescennius Niger. If in these later cases the event had gone otherwise, would the course of the Imperial Age have been altered in any way? The distinction so carefully drawn by Mommsen and Eduard Meyer [1] between the "principate" of Pompey and Augustus and the "monarchy" of Cæsar misses the mark completely. At that stage, the point is merely a constitutional one, though fifty years before it would still have signified an opposition between ideas. When Vindex and Galba in 68 set out to restore "the Republic," they were gambling on a notion in

[1] *Cæsars Monarchie und das Principat des Pompejus* (1918) pp. 501, et seq.

days when notions having genuine symbolic force had ceased to be, and the only question was who should have the plain material power. The struggle for the Cæsar-title became steadily more and more negroid, and might have gone on century after century in increasingly primitive and, therefore, "eternal" forms.

These populations no longer possessed a soul. Consequently they could no longer have a history proper to themselves. At best they might acquire some significance as an object in the history of an alien Culture, and whatever deeper meaning this relation possessed would be derived entirely from the will of the alien Life. Any effective historical happening that does take place on the soil of an old Civilization acquires its consistency as a course of events from elsewhere and never from any part played in it by the man of that soil. And so once again we find ourselves regarding the phenomenon of "world-history" under the two aspects — life-courses of the great Cultures and relations between them.

CHAPTER III
ORIGIN AND LANDSCAPE
(C)
THE RELATIONS BETWEEN THE CULTURES

ORIGIN AND LANDSCAPE

(C)

THE RELATIONS BETWEEN THE CULTURES

I

ALTHOUGH consideration of the Cultures themselves should logically precede that of the relations between them, modern historical thought generally
reverses the order. The less it really knows of the life-courses which together
make up a seeming unity of world-happenings, the more zealously it searches
for life in the web of relations, and the less it understands even of these. What
a wealth of psychology there is in the probings, rejections, choices, trans-
valuations, errors, penetrations, and welcomings! — and not only between
Cultures which immediately touch one another, wonder at one another, fight
one another, but also as between a living Culture and the form-world of a dead
one whose remains still stand visible in the landscape. And how narrow and
poor, on the other hand, are the conceptions which the historians label "influence," "continuity," and "permanent effects"!

This is pure nineteenth century. What is sought is just a chain of causes
and effects. Everything follows and nothing is prime. Since every young
Culture superficially shows form-elements of older Cultures, these elements
are supposed to have had continuing effect (*fortgewirkt*), and when a set of such
effects has been strung together, the historian regards it with satisfaction as
a sound piece of work.

At bottom, this mode of treatment rests upon that idea which inspired the
great Gothics long ago, the idea of a significant singleness in the history of all
mankind. They saw how, on earth, men and peoples changed, but ideas
stayed, and the powerful impressiveness of the picture has not worn itself out
even to-day. Originally it was seen as a plan that God was working out by
means of the human instrument. And it could still be regarded as such at a
far later stage, in fact so long as the spell of the "ancient-mediæval-modern"
scheme lasted and its parade of permanence prevented us from noting that
actuality was ever changing. But meantime our outlook also has altered
and become cooler and wider. Our knowledge has long overpassed the limits
of this chart, and those who are still trying to sail by it are beating about in
vain. It is not products that "influence," but creators that absorb. Being
has been confused with waking-being, life with the means by which it expresses
itself. The critical thought, or even simple waking-consciousness, sees every-

where theoretical units subjected to motion. That is truly dynamic and Faustian, for in no other Culture have men imagined history thus. The Greek, with his thoroughly corporeal understanding of the world, would never have traced "effects" of pure expression-units like "Attic drama" or "Egyptian art."

Originally what happens is that a name is given to a *system of expression-forms* conjuring up in our minds a particular complex of relations. But this does not last long, and soon one is suppositing under the name a being, and under the relation an effect. When we speak to-day of Greek philosophy, or Buddhism, or Scholasticism, we mean something that is somehow living, a power-unit that has grown and grown until it is mighty enough to take possession of men, to subject their waking-consciousness and even their being, and in the end to force them into an active conformity, which prolongs the direction followed by its own "life." It is a whole mythology, and, significantly, it is only men of the Western Culture — the only mankind that lives with and in this picture is the Western — whose myth contains plenty of dæmons of this sort — "electricity" and "positional energy," for example.

In reality these systems only exist in the human waking-consciousness, and they exist as modes of activity. Religion, science, art, are *activities of waking-consciousness* that are based on a being. Faith, meditation, creation, and whatever of visible activity is required as outcome of these invisibles — as sacrifice, prayer, the physical experiment, the carving of a statue, the statement of an experience in communicable words — are activities of the waking-consciousness and nothing else. Other men see only the visible and hear only words. In so doing they experience something in themselves, but they cannot give any account of the relation between this experience and that which the creator lived in himself. We see a form, but we do not know what in the other's soul begat that form; we can only have some belief about the matter, and we believe by putting in our own soul. However definitely and distinctly a religion may express itself in words, they are words, and the hearer puts his own sense into them. However impressive the artist's notes or colours, the beholder sees and hears in them only himself, and if he cannot do so, the work is for him meaningless. (The extremely rare and highly modern gift, possessed by a few intensely historical men, of "putting oneself in the other's place" need not be considered in this connexion.) The German whom Boniface converted did not transfer himself into the missionary's soul. It was a springtide quiver that passed in those days through the whole young world of the North, and what it meant was that each man found suddenly in conversion a language wherein to express his own religiousness. Just so the eyes of a child light up when we tell it the name of the object in its hand.

It is not, then, microcosmic units that move, but cosmic entities that pick amongst them and appropriate them. Were it otherwise — were these systems very beings that could exercise an activity (for "influence" is an organic activity) — the picture of history would be quite other than what it is. Consider how every maturing man and every living Culture is continuously bathed in innumerable potential influences. Out of all these, only some few are *admitted* as such — the great majority are not. Is choice concerned with the works, or with the men?

The historian who is intent upon establishing causal series counts only the influences that are present, and the other side of the reckoning — those that are not — does not appear. With the psychology of the "positive" influences is associated that of the "negative." This is a domain into which no one has yet ventured, but here, if anywhere, there are fruits to be reaped, and it must be tackled unless the answer to the whole question is to be left indeterminate; for if we try to evade it, we are driven into illusory visions of world-historical happening as a continuous process in which everything is properly accounted for. Two Cultures may touch between man and man, or the man of one Culture may be confronted by the dead form-world of another as presented in its communicable relics. In both cases the agent is the man himself. The closed-off act of A can be vivified by B only out of his own being, and *eo ipso* it becomes B's, his inward property, his work, and part of himself. There was no movement of "Buddhism" from India to China, but an acceptance of part of the Indian Buddhists' store of images by Chinese of a certain spiritual tendency, who fashioned out a *new* mode of religious expression having meaning for Chinese, and only Chinese, Buddhists. What matters in all such cases is not the original meanings of the forms, but the forms themselves, as disclosing to the active sensibility and understanding of the observer potential modes of his own creativeness. Connotations are not transferable. Men of two different kinds are parted, each in his own spiritual loneliness, by an impassable gulf. Even though Indians and Chinese in those days both felt as Buddhists, they were spiritually as far apart as ever. The same words, the same rites, the same symbol — but two different souls, each going its own way.

Searching through all Cultures, then, one will always find that the continuation of earlier creations into a later Culture is only apparent, and that in fact the younger *being* has set up a few (very few) relations to the older *being*, always without regard to the original meanings of that which it makes its own. What becomes, then, of the "permanent conquests" of philosophy and science? We are told again and again how much of Greek philosophy still lives on to-day, but this is only a figure of speech without real content, for first Magian and then Faustian humanity, each with the deep wisdom of its unimpaired instincts, rejected that philosophy, or passed unregarding by it, or retained its formulæ under radically new interpretations. The naïve credulity of erudite enthusiasm deceives itself here — Greek philosophic notions would make a long catalogue, and the further it is taken, the more vanishingly small becomes the proportion of the alleged survivals. Our custom is simply to overlook as incidental "errors" such conceptions as Democritus's theory of atomic images,[1] the very corporeal world of Plato's "ideas," and the fifty-two hollow spheres of Aristotle's universe, as though we could presume to know what the dead meant better than they knew themselves! These things are truths and essential — only, not for us. The sum total of the Greek philosophy that we possess, actually and not merely superficially, is practically nil. Let us be honest and take the old philosophers at their word; not one proposition of Heraclitus or Democritus or Plato is true for us unless and until we have accommodated it to ourselves. And how much, after all, have we taken over of the methods, the concepts, the intentions, and the means of Greek science, let alone its basically incomprehensible terms? The Renaissance, men say, was completely under the "influence" of Classical art. But what about the form of the Doric temple, the Ionic column, the relation of column to architrave, the choice of colour, the treatment of background and perspective in painting, the principles of figure-grouping, vase-painting, mosaic, encaustic, the structural element in statuary, the proportions of Lysippus? Why did all this exercise no "influence?"

Because that which one (here, the Renaissance artist) wills to express is in him a priori. Of the stock of dead forms that he had in front of him, he really saw only the few that he wanted to see, and saw them as he wanted them — namely, in line with his own intention and not with the intention of the original creator, for no living art ever seriously considers that. Try to follow, element by element, the "influence" of Egyptian plastic upon early Greek, and you will find in the end that there is none at all, but that the Greek will-to-form took out of the older art-stock some few characteristics that it would in any case have discovered in some shape for itself. All round the Classical landscape there were working, or had worked, Egyptians, Cretans, Babylonians, Assyrians, Hittites, Persians, and Phœnicians, and the works of these peoples — their buildings, ornaments, art-works, cults, state-forms, scripts, and sciences — were known to the Greeks in profusion. But how much out of all this mass did the Classical soul extract as its own means of expression? I repeat, it is only the relations that are accepted that we observe. But what of those that were not accepted? Why, for example, do we fail to find in the former category the pyramid, pylon, and obelisk of Egypt, or hieroglyphic, or cuneiform? What of the stock of Byzantium and of the Moorish East was not accepted by Gothic art and thought in Spain and Sicily? It is impossible to overpraise the wisdom (quite unconscious) that governed the choice and the unhesitating transvaluation of what was chosen. Every relation that was accepted was not only an exception, but also a misunderstanding, and the inner force of a Being is never so clearly evidenced as it is in this art of deliberate misunderstanding. The more enthusiastically we laud the principles of an alien thought, the more fundamentally in

---

[1] I.e., that sensation consists in the absorption of small particles radiated by the object. — Tr.

truth we have denatured it. Only consider the praises addressed by the West to Plato! From Bernard of Chartres and Marsilius Ficinus to Goethe and Schelling! And the more humble our acceptance of an alien religion, the more certain it is that that religion has already assumed the form of the new soul. Truly, someone ought to have written the history of the "three Aristotles" — Greek, Arabian, and Gothic — who had not one concept or thought in common. Or the history of the transformation of Magian Christianity into Faustian! We are told in sermon and book that this religion extended from the old Church into and over the Western field without change of essence. Actually, Magian man evolved out of the deepest depths of his dualistic world-consciousness a language of his own religious awareness that we call "the" Christian religion. So much of this experience as was communicable — words, formulæ, rites — was accepted by the man of the Late-Classical Civilization as a means of expression for his religious need; then it passed from man to man, even to the Germans of the Western pre-Culture, in words always the same and in sense always altering. Men would never have dared to *improve upon* the original meanings of the holy words — it was simply that they did not know these meanings. If this be doubted, let the doubter study "the" idea of Grace, as it appears under the dualistic interpretation of Augustine affecting a substance in man, and under the dynamic interpretaion of Calvin, affecting a will in man. Or that Magian idea, which we can hardly grasp at all, of the consensus (Arabic *ijma*) [1] wherein, as a consequence of the presence in each man of a *pneuma* emanating from the divine *pneuma*, the unanimous opinion of the elect is held to be immediate divine Truth. It was this that gave the decisions of the early Church Councils their authoritative character, and it underlies the scientific methods that rule in the world of Islam to this day. And it was because Western men did not understand this that the Church Councils of later Gothic times amounted, for him, to nothing more than a kind of parliament for limiting the spiritual mobility of the Papacy. This idea of what a Council meant prevailed even in the fifteenth century — think of Constance and Basel, Savonarola and Luther — and in the end it disappeared, as futile and meaningless, before the conception of Papal Infallibility. Or, again, the idea, universal in the Early Arabian world, of the resurrection of the flesh, which again presupposed that of divine and human *pneuma*. Classical man assumed that the soul, as the form and meaning of the body, was somehow co-created herewith, and Greek thought scarcely mentions it. Silence on a matter of such gravity may be due to one or the other of two reasons — the idea's not being there at all, or being so self-evident as not to emerge into consciousness as a problem. With Arabian man it was the latter. But just as self-evident for him was the notion that his *pneuma* was an emanation from God that had taken up residence in his body. Necessarily, therefore, there had to be something from which the

[1] See Ch. VIII below. — *Tr.*

human soul should rise again on the Day of Judgment, and hence resurrection was thought of as ἐκ νεκρῶν, "out of the corpses." This, in its deeper meaning, is utterly incomprehensible for the West. The words of Holy Scripture were not indeed doubted, but unconsciously another meaning was substituted by the finer minds amongst Catholics, this other meaning, unmistakable already in Luther and to-day quite general, is the conception of immortality as the continued existence to all eternity of the soul as a centre of force. Were Paul or Augustine to become acquainted with our ideas of Christianity, they would reject all our dogmas, all our books, and all our concepts as utterly erroneous and heretical.

As the strongest example of a system that to all appearance has travelled unaltered through two millennia, and yet actually has passed through three whole courses of evolution in three Cultures, with completely different meanings in each, we may take *Roman law*.

II

Law, in the Classical world, *is law made by citizens for citizens* and presupposes that the state-form is that of the Polis. It was this basic form of public life that led — and self-evidently — to the notion of the person as identical with the man who, added to others like him, made up the body (σῶμα)[1] of the State. From this formal fact of Classical world-feeling grew up the whole structure of Classical law.

"*Persona*" *then is a specifically Classical notion, possessing meaning and valency only in the Classical Culture.* The individual person is a body which belongs to the stock of the Polis. It is with reference to him that the law of the Polis is ordered, downwards into the law of Things — with, as a marginal case, the slave who was body, but not person — and upward into the law of Gods — with, as a marginal case, the hero who from being person had attained godhead and the legal right to a cult, like Lysander and Alexander in the Greek cities and *Divus Julius* and his successors in Rome. This tendency, becoming more and more definite in the development of Classical jurisprudence, explains also the notion of *capitis deminutio media*, which is so alien to our Western ideas; for we can imagine a person (in our sense of the word) as deprived of certain rights and even of all rights, but the Classical man under this punishment *ceased to be a person* although living on as a body. And the specifically Classical idea of the thing, *res*, is only intelligible in contrast to and as the object of *persona*.

As Classical religion was State religion through and through, there is no distinction made as to the fount of law; real law and divine law were made, like personal law, by the citizen, and the relations of things and of gods to persons were precise and definite. Now, it was a fact of decisive significance

[1] See R. Hirzel, *Die Person* (1914), p. 7.

for the Classical jurisprudence that it was always the product of immediate
public experience — and, moreover, not the professional experience of the
jurists, but the practical everyday experience of men who counted in political
and economic life generally.   The man who followed the public career in Rome
had necessarily to be jurist, general, administrator, and financial manager.
When he gave judgment as prætor, he had behind him a wide experience of
many fields other than law.   A judicial *class*, professionally (let alone theoretically) specialized in law as its sole activity, was entirely unknown to the
Classical.   The whole outlook of the later jurisprudence was determined by
this fact.   The Romans were here neither systematists nor historians nor
theorists, but just splendidly practical.   Their jurisprudence is an *empirical
science of individual cases*, a refined technique, and not in the least a structure of
abstractions.[1]

It would give an incorrect idea to oppose Greek and Roman law to one
another as quantities of the same order.   Roman law in its whole development
is an individual city law, one amongst hundreds of such, and Greek law as a unity
never existed at all.   Although Greek-speaking cities very often had similar
laws, this did not alter the fact that the law of each was its own and no other's.
Never did the idea of a general Doric, still less a general Hellenic, legislation
arise.   Such notions were wholly alien to Classical thought.   The *jus civile*
applied only to Quirites — foreigners, slaves and the whole world outside the
city [2] simply did not count in the eyes of the law, whereas even the *Sachsenspiegel* [3] evidences already our own deep-felt idea that there can only really be one
law.   Until far into Imperial times the strict distinction was maintained between the *jus civile* of citizens and the *jus gentium* for "other people" who came
within the cognizance of Rome's jurisdiction as sojourners.[4]   (It need hardly
be added that this "law of nations" has no sort of resemblance to that which we
call by the same name.)   It was only because Rome as a unit-city attained —
as under other conditions Alexandria might have attained — to "Imperium"
over the Classical world that Roman law became pre-eminent, not because of its
intrinsic superiority, but firstly through Rome's political success and afterwards
because of Rome's monopoly of practical experience on the large scale.   The
formation of a general Classical jurisprudence of Hellenistic cast — if we are
entitled to call by that name an affinity of spirit in a large number of separate
legal systems — falls in a period when Rome was still politically a third-rate
power.   And when Roman law began to assume bigger forms, this was only one

[1] L. Wenger, *Das Recht der Griechen und Römer* (1914), p. 170; R.v. Mayr, *Römische Rechtsgeschichte,*
II, 1, p. 87.
[2] A curious sidelight on this appears in the provisions of the savage law against recalcitrant
debtors, who (after certain delays and formalities) could be put to death and even hewn in pieces
by their creditors, or — "sold as slaves beyond the Tiber." — *Tr.*
[3] A thirteenth-century collection by Eike von Repgow of German customs and customary
law (ed. K. G. Homeyer, 1861). — *Tr.*
[4] And were judged by a different authority, the peregrin prætor. — *Tr.*

aspect of the fact that Roman intellect had subjugated Hellenism. The work of forming later Classical law passed from Hellenism to Rome — i.e., from a sum of city-states, which one and all had been impressively made aware of their individual impotence, to one single city whose whole activity was in the end devoted to the upholding and exploitation of an effective primacy. Thus it came about that Hellenism never formed a jurisprudence in the Greek tongue. When the Classical world entered upon a stage in which it was ripe for this science (the latest of all), there was but *one* lawgiving city that counted in the matter.

In reality, insufficient regard has been paid to the fact that Greek and Roman law are not parallel in time but successive. Roman law is the younger and presupposes the long experience of the elder; [1] it was built up, in fact, late and, with this exemplar before it, very swiftly. It is not without significance that the flowering-time of the Stoic philosophy, which deeply affected juridical ideas, followed that of Greek, but preceded that of Roman, law.

III

This jurisprudence, however, was built up by the mind of an intensely ahistorical species of man. Classical law, consequently, is law *of the day and even the moment;* it was in its very idea occasional legislation for particular cases, and when the case was settled, it ceased to be law. To extend its validity over subsequent cases would have been in contradiction to the Classical sense of the present.

The Roman prætor, at the beginning of his year of office, issued an edict in which he set forth the rules that he intended to follow, but his successor next year was in nowise bound to them. And even this limitation of a year on the validity of the rules did not mean that this was actually the duration of the rules. On the contrary (particularly after the *Lex Æbutia*) the prætor formulated in each individual case the concrete rule of law for the judges [2] to whom he remitted the matter for judgment, which had to be according to this rule and no other. That is, the prætor produced, and indeed generated, a *present* law without duration. [3]

Similar in appearance, but so profoundly different in meaning as to leave no doubt as to the great gap which is set between Classical and Western Law, is that inspired and truly Germanic notion of English jurisprudence, the creative power of the judge who "declares" the law. His business is to apply a law

---

[1] The "dependence" of Classical law upon Egyptian is, as it chances, still traceable. Solon the wholesale merchant introduced into his Attic legislation provisions concerning debt-slavery, contract, work-shyness, and unemployment taken from Egypt. Diodorus, I, 77, 79, 94.

[2] The process is clearly explained in Goudy's article "Roman Law," *Ency. Brit.*, XI ed. Very roughly, the prætor corresponded to the judge, and the judges to the jury, of modern English law, but such a parallel must not be pressed far. — *Tr.*

[3] L. Wenger, *Recht der Griechen und Römer*, pp. 166, et seq.

which in principle possesses eternal validity. Even the application of the existing body of laws he can regulate, according to the situations disclosed in the course of the case, by means of his "rules" (which have nothing in common with the prætor's). And if he should conclude in the presence of a particular set of facts that current law is defective in respect of these, he can *fill the gap at once*, and thus in the very middle of a trial create new law, which (if concurred in by the judicial body in the due forms) *becomes thereafter part and parcel of the permanent stock of law*. This is what makes it so completely un-Classical. In the old jurisprudence, the gradual formation of a stock of rules was due purely to the fact that public life followed a substantially homogeneous course thoughout a particular period, and produced again and again the same situations to be dealt with — rules *not* deliberately invested with validity for the future, but more or less recreated again and again as empirical rulings *ad hoc*. The sum of these rulings — not a system, but a collection — came to constitute "the law" as we find it in the later legislation by prætor's edict, each successive prætor having found it practically convenient to take over substantial portions of his predecessor's work.

Experience, then, means for the ancient lawgiver something different from what it means to us. It means, not the comprehensive outlook over a consistent mass of law that contains implicitly every possible case, associated with practical skill in applying it, but the experimental knowledge that certain jural situations are for ever recurring, so that one can save oneself the trouble of forming new law on every occasion.

The genuine Classical form for the slow accretion of legal material is an almost automatic summation of individual νομοί *leges, edicta*, as we find it in the heyday of the Roman prætor. All the so-called legislations of Solon, Charondas, and the Twelve Tables are nothing but occasional collections of such edicts as had been found to be useful. The Law of Gortyn,[1] which is more or less contemporary with the Twelve, is a supplement to some older collection. A newly-founded city would promptly provide itself with such a collection, and in the process a certain amount of dilettantism would slip in (cf. the lawmakers satirized by Aristophanes in *The Birds*). But there is never system in them, still less any intention of establishing enduring law thereby.

In the West it is conspicuously the other way about. The tendency is from the first to bring the entire living body of law into a general code, ordered for ever and exhaustively complete, containing in advance the decision of every conceivable future problem.[2] All Western law bears the stamp of the future, all Classical the stamp of the moment.

---

[1] See *Ency. Brit.*, XI ed., Vol. XII, p. 502. Fragments of the older collection referred to were found in the vicinity. — *Tr.*

[2] In English legal theory the judge does not *make law* by a new decision, but "*declares*" the law — i.e., makes explicit what has been implicit in the law from the first, though the occasion for its manifestation has not hitherto arisen. — *Tr.*

IV

But this, it may be said, is contradicted by the fact that there actually were Classical law-works compiled by professional jurists for permanent use. Undoubtedly so. But we must remember that we are completely ignorant of Early Classical law (1100–700) and it is pretty certain that the customary law of the country-side and the nascent town was never noted down as that of the Gothic age was set forth in the *Sachsenspiegel* or that of the Early Arabian in the *Syrian Law-book*.[1] The earliest stratification that we can now detect consists of the collections (from 700 B.C.) ascribed to mythical or semi-mythical personages like Lycurgus, Zaleucus, Charondas, and Dracon,[2] and certain Roman kings.[3] That these existed the form of the saga shows, but of their real authors, the actual process of their codification, and their original contents even the Greeks of the Persian War period were ignorant.

A second stratification, corresponding to Justinian's code and to the "Reception" of Roman Law in Germany, is connected with the names of Solon (600), Pittacus (550), and others. Here the laws have already attained to a structure and are inspired by the city; they are described as "politeiai," "nomoi," in contrast to old "thesmai" and "rhetrai."[4] In reality, therefore, we only know the history of *late* Classical law. Now, why these sudden codifications? A mere look at these names shows that at bottom they were not processes of putting down the results of pure experience, but *decisions of political power problems.*

It is a grave error to suppose that a law that surveys all things evenly and without being influenced by political and economic interests can exist at all. Such a state of things can be pictured, and is always being pictured, by those who suppose that the imagining of political possibilities is a political activity. But nothing alters the fact that such a law, born of abstractions, does not exist in real history. Always the law contains in abstract form the world-picture of its author, and every historical world-picture contains a political-economic *tendency* dependent, not upon what this man or that thinks, but upon what is practically intended by the class which in fact commands the power and, with it, the legislation. Every law is established by a class in the name of the generality. Anatole France once said that "our law in majestic equality forbids the rich no less than the poor to steal bread and to beg in the street."[5]

---

[1] See *Ency. Brit.*, XI ed., Vol XXVI, p. 315. — Tr.

[2] See Beloch, *Griechische Geschichte*, I, 1, p. 350.

[3] The background of this is Etruscan law, the primitive form of the Roman. Rome was an Etruscan city.

[4] Busolt, *Griechische Staatskunde*, p. 528.

[5] Compare the famous ironical judgment of Mr. Justice Maule which led to the reform of the divorce laws in England (1857): ". . . It is true that the course which you should legally have taken] would have cost you many hundreds of pounds, whereas probably you have not as many pence. *But the Law knows no distinction between rich and poor.*" — Tr.

A one-sided justice no doubt. But equally the other side will always try to win sole authority for laws derived from *its* outlook upon life. These legislative codes are one and all political acts, and party-political acts at that — in the case of Solon a democratic constitution (πολιτεία) combined with private laws (νομοί) of the same stamp, in that of Dracon and the Decemvirs [1] an oligarchic constitution fortified by private law. It was left to Western historians, accustomed to their own durable law, to undervalue the importance of this connexion; Classical man was under no misapprehension as to what really happened in these cases. The product of the Decemvirs was in Rome the last code of purely patrician character. Tacitus calls it the end of right law (*"finis aequi juris,"* Annals, III, 27). For, just as the fall of the Decemvirs was followed very significantly by the rise of another Ten, the Tribunes, so immediately the *jus* of the Twelve Tables and the constitution on which it was founded began to be attacked by the undermining process of the *lex rogata* (people's law), which set itself with Roman constancy to do what Solon had achieved in one act in the case of Dracon's work, the πατρίος πολιτεία which was the law-ideal of the Attic oligarchy. Thenceforward Dracon and Solon were the "slogans" in the long battle between Oligarchy and Demos, which in Rome meant Senate and Tribunate. The Spartan constitution associated with the name "Lycurgus" not only stood for the ideal of Dracon and the Twelve Tables, but concreted it. We can see, parallel with the closely related course of events in Rome, the tendency of the two Spartan kings to evolve from the condition of Tarquinian tyrants to that of tribunes of the Gracchan kind; the fall of the last Tarquins or the institution of the Decemvirs — a *coup d'état* of one kind or another against the tribunician tendency [2] — corresponds more or less to the fall of Cleomenes (488) and of Pausanias (470); and the revolution of Agis III and Cleomenes III (about 240) aligns itself with the political activity of C. Flaminius, which began only a few years later. But never in Sparta were the kings able to achieve any thorough-going success over the senatorial element represented by the Ephors.

In the period of these struggles, Rome had become a megalopolis of the late-

---

[1] What is important to us, therefore, in the Law of the Twelve Tables is not the supposed contents (of which scarcely an authentic clause survived even in Cicero's day), but the political act of codification itself, the tendency of which corresponded to that of the overthrow of the Tarquinian Tyrannis by senatorial Oligarchy — a success which, now endangered, it was sought to stabilize for the future. The text which schoolboys learned in detail in Cæsar's time must have had the same destiny as the consular lists of the old time, in which had been interpolated names upon names of families whose wealth and influence was of much later origin. In recent years Pais and Lambert have disputed the whole story of the Twelve Tables, and so far as concerns the authenticity of the reputed text, they may well be right — not so, however, as regards the course of political events in the years about 450.

[2] Only half a century separates the traditional dates of these events (509, 451), in spite of the wealth of traditional history afterwards attached to the period. The "coup," in the case of the Decemvirs, was the capture by the patricians of a machine set up for the redress of plebeian grievances. — *Tr.*

Classical type. The rustic instincts were more and more pushed back by the intelligence of the city.[1] Consequently from about 350 we find side by side with the *lex rogata* of the people the *lex data*, the administrative law, of the prætor. With this the Twelve Tables idea drops out of the contest and it is the prætor's edict that becomes the football of the party battle.

It did not take long for the prætor to become the centre of both legislation and judicial practice. And presently, corresponding to the political extension of the city's power, the jurisdiction of the prætor and the field of his *jus civile* — the law of the citizens — begin to diminish in significance and the peregrin prætor with his *jus gentium* — the law of the alien — steps into the foreground. And when finally the whole population of the Classical world, save the small part possessing Roman citizenship, was comprised in the field of this alien law, the *jus peregrinum* of the city of Rome became practically an imperial law. All other cities — and even Alpine tribes and migrant Bedouin clans were *civitates* from the administrative point of view — retained their local laws only as supplements, not alternatives, to the peregrin law of Rome.

It marked the close of Classical law-making, therefore, when Hadrian (about A.D. 130) introduced the *Edictum perpetuum*, which gave final form to the well-established corpus of the annual pronouncements of the prætors and forbade further modifications thereof. It was still, as before, the prætor's duty to publish the "law of his year," but, even though this law had no greater degree of validity than corresponded to his administrative powers and was not the law of the Empire, he was obliged thenceforth to stick to the established text.[2] It is the very symbol of the petrified "Late" Civilization.[3]

With the Hellenistic age began jurisprudence, the *science* of law, the systematic comprehension of the law which men actually apply. Since legal thought presupposes a substance of political and economic relations, in the same way as mathematical thought presupposes physical and technical elements of knowledge,[4] Rome very soon became *the home of Classical jurisprudence*. Similarly in the Mexican world it was the conquering Aztecs whose academies (e.g., Tezcuco) made law the chief subject of study. Classical jurisprudence was the Roman's science, and his only one. At the very moment when the creative mathematic closes off with Archimedes, juristic literature begins with Ælius's *Tripertita*, a commentary on the Twelve (198 B.C.).[5] The first systematic private law was written by M. Scævola about 100. The genuine maturity of Classical law is in the two centuries 200–0 — although we to-day, with quaint perversity, apply

---

[1] Cf. Ch. IV below.

[2] Sohm, *Institutionen* (14) p. 101. [This is the edict of "Julian" (Salvius Julianus, urban prætor). Romanists are not agreed as to how far, if at all, it included material derived from the decisions of the peregrin prætor. See Professor Goudy's article "Roman Law," *Ency. Brit.*, XI ed., p. 563. — Tr.]

[3] Lenel, *Das Edictum perpetuum* (1907); L. Wenger, p. 168.

[4] Even the multiplication table of the children assumes the elements of dynamics in counting.

[5] V. Mayr II, 1, p. 85; Sohm, p. 105.

the time to a period which was really that of Early Arabian law. And from the relics of these two literatures we can measure the greatness of the gap that separates the thought of two Cultures. The Romans treat only of cases and their classification; they never analyse a basic idea such as, for instance, judicial error. They distinguish carefully the sorts of contracts, but they have no conception of Contract as an idea, or of any theories as to invalidity or unsoundness. "Taking everything into account," says Lenel,[1] "it is clear that the Romans cannot possibly be regarded as exemplars of scientific method."

The last phase is that of the schools of the Sabiniani and Proculiani (Augustus to about 160 A.D.). They are scientific schools like the philosophical schools in Athens, and in them, possibly, the expiring stages of the conflict between the senatorial and the tribunician (Cæsarian) conceptions of law were fought, for amongst the best of the Sabiniani were two descendants of Cæsar's slayers and one of the Proculiani was picked upon by Trajan as his potential successor. While the method was to all intents and purposes settled and concluded, the practical fusion of the citizen's statute-law (*jus civile*) and the prætor's edict (*jus honorarium*) was carried out here.

The last landmark of Classical jurisprudence, so far as we know, was the *Institutes* of Gaius (about 161).

Classical law is a law of bodies. In the general stock composing the world it distinguishes bodily Persons and bodily Things and, like a sort of Euclidean mathematic of public life, establishes ratios between them. The affinity between mathematical and legal thought is very close. The intention, in both, is to take the prima facie data, to separate out the sensuous-incidental, and to find the intellectually basic principle — the *pure* form of the object, the *pure* type of the situation, the *pure* connexity of cause and effect. Life, in the Classical, presents itself to the critical waking-consciousness of the Classical man in a form penetrated with Euclidean character, and the image that is generated in the legal mind is one of bodies, of positional relations between bodies, and of reciprocal effects of bodies by contact and reaction — just as with Democritus's atoms. It is juristic statics.[2]

V

The first creation of "Arabian" law was *the concept of the incorporeal person.*

Here is an element entirely absent in Classical law,[3] and appearing quite suddenly in the "Classical" jurists (who were all Aramæans), which cannot be estimated at its full value, or in its symbolic importance as an index of the new

---

[1] *Enzyklopädie der Rechtswissensch.*, I, 357.

[2] Egyptian law of the Hyksos period, and Chinese of the Period of Contending States, in contrast to the Classical and the Indian law of the Dharmasutras, must have been built up on basic ideas quite other than the idea of the corporeality of persons and things. It would be a grand emancipation from the load of Roman "antiquities" if German research were to succeed in establishing these.

[3] Sohm, p. 220.

world-feeling, unless we realize the full extent of the field that this "Arabian" law covered.

The new landscape embraces Syria and northern Mesopotamia, southern Arabia and Byzantium. In all these regions a new law was coming into being, an oral or written customary law of the same "early" type as that met with in the *Sachsenpiegel*. Wonderfully, the *law of individual cities* which is so self-evident on Classical ground is here silently transmuted into a *law of creed-communities*. It is Magian, magic, through and through. Always *one* Pneuma, *one* like spirit, *one* identical knowledge and comprehension of whole and sole truth, welds the believers of the same religion into a unit of will and action, *into one juristic person*. A juristic person is thus a collective entity which has intentions, resolutions, and responsibilities as an entity. In Christianity we see the idea already actual and effective in the primitive community at Jerusalem,[1] and presently it soars to the conception of a triune Godhead of three Persons.[2]

Before Constantine, even, the Late Classical law of imperial decrees (*constitutiones*, *placita*) though the Roman form of city law was strictly kept, was genuinely a law for the *believers of the "Syncretic Church,"*[3] that mass of cults perfused by one single religiousness. In Rome itself, it is true, law was conceived of by a large part of the population as city-state law, but this feeling became weaker and weaker with every step towards the East. The fusion of the faithful into a single *jural community* was effected in express form by the Emperor-cult, which was religious law through and through. In relation to this law Jews and Christians[4] were infidels who ensconced themselves with their own laws in another field of law. When in 212 the Aramæan Caracalla, by the *Constitutio Antoniana*, gave Roman citizenship to all inhabitants except *dediticii* peregrins,[5] the form of his act was purely Classical, and no doubt there were plenty of people who understood it in the Classical spirit — i.e., as literally an incorporation of the citizens of every other city in the city of Rome. But the Emperor himself conceived it quite otherwise. It made everyone subject to the "Ruler of the Faithful," the head of the cult-religion venerated as *Divus*. With

---

[1] Acts XV. Herein lies the germ of the idea of a Church law.

[2] For Islam as a "juristic person" see M. Horten, *Die religiose Gedankenwelt des Volkes im heutigem Islam* (1917), p. xxiv.

[3] See Ch. VII below. We can venture to make the label so positive because the adherents of all the Late Classical cults were bound together in devout consensus, just as the primitive Christian communities were.

[4] The Persian Church came into the Classical field only in the Classical form of Mithraism, which was assimilable in the ensemble of Syncretism.

[5] It is difficult to describe this class in a few words. Roughly, they (and the "Junian Latins," so called, who were excepted with them) represented a stratum of Roman society, largely composed of "undesirables," which was only just not servile. In the older legislation they were necessarily lumped with the outer world as peregrins, but when Caracalla made this outer world "Roman," there were obvious reasons against bringing these people into the fold as well. In somewhat the same way the word "outsider" is used in colloquial English with the dual meaning of a foreigner or non-member, and a socially undesirable person. — *Tr.*

Constantine came the great change; he turned Imperial Caliph law on to the creed-community of Christianity in lieu of that of Syncretism, and thereby *constituted the Christian Nation*. The labels "devout" and "unbeliever" changed places. From Constantine onwards the quiet transformation of "Roman" law into *orthodox Christian law* proceeded more and more decisively, and it was as such that converted Asiatics and Germans received and adopted it. Thus a perfectly new law came into being in old forms. According to the old marriage-law it was impossible for a Roman burgher to marry the daughter of, say, a Capuan burgher if legal community, *connubium*, was not in force between the two cities.[1] But now the question was whether a Christian or a Jew — irrespective of whether he was Roman, Syrian, or Moor — could legally marry an infidel. For in the Magian law-world there was no *connubium* between those of different faiths. There was not the slightest difficulty about an Irishman in Constantinople marrying a Negress if both were Christians, but how could a Monophysite Christian marry a Nestorian maiden who was his neighbour in their Syrian village? Racially they were probably indistinguishable, but they belonged to legally different nations.

This Arabian concept of nationality is a new and wholly decisive fact. The frontiers between "home" and "abroad" lay in the Apollinian world between every two towns, and in the Magian between every two creed-communities. What the "enemy," the peregrin, was to the Roman, the Pagan was to the Christian, the Amhaarez to the Jew. What the acquisition of Roman citizenship meant for the Gaul or the Greek in Cæsar's time, Christian baptism meant for him now — entry into the leading nation of the leading Culture.[2] The Persians of the Sassanid period no longer conceived of themselves, as their predecessors of Achæmenid times had done, as a unit by virtue of origin and speech, but as a unit of Mazdaist believers, *vis-à-vis* unbelievers, irrespective of the fact that the latter might be of pure Persian origin (as indeed the bulk of the Nestorians were). So also with the Jews, and later the Mandæans and Manichæans, and later again the Monophysite and the Nestorian Christians — each body felt itself a nation, a legal community, a juristic person in a new sense.

Thus there arises a group of Early Arabian laws, differentiated according to religions as decisively as Classical laws are differentiated according to cities. In the realm of the Sassanids schools arose for the teaching the Zoroastrian law proper to them; the Jews, who formed an exceedingly large portion of the population from Armenia to Sabæa, created their proper law in the Talmud, which was completed and closed some few years before the *Corpus Juris*. Each one of these Churches had its peculiar jurisdiction, independent of the geo-

---

[1] In the Twelve Tables *connubium* was disallowed even between the patrician and plebian citizens of Rome itself. [The hold of the patricians on this privilege, however, was already exceedingly precarious, and it vanished a few years later in the *lex Canuleia*. — Tr.]

[2] Cf. Ch. VI below.

graphical frontiers of the moment — as in the East to-day — and the judge representing the ground-lord judged only cases between parties of different faiths. The self-jurisdiction of the Jews within the Empire had never been contested by anyone, but the Nestorians and the Monophysites also began, very soon after their separation, to create and to apply laws of their own, and thus by a negative process — i.e., by the gradual withdrawal of all heterodox communities — Roman imperial law came to be the law of the Christians who confessed the same creed as the Emperor. Hence the importance of the Roman-Syrian law-book, which has been preserved in several languages. It was probably [1] pre-Constantinian and written in the chancery of the Patriarch of Antioch; it is quite unmistakably Early Arabian law in Late Classical form, and, as its many translations indicate, it owed its currency to the opposition to the orthodox Imperial Church. It was without doubt the basis of Monophysite law, and it reigned till the coming of Islam over a field far larger than that of the *Corpus Juris*.

The question arises, what in such a tapestry of laws could have been the real practical value of the part of them which was written in Latin? The law historians, with all the one-sidedness of the expert, have hitherto looked at this part alone and therefore have not yet realized that there is a problem here at all. Their texts were "Law" unqualified, the law that descended from Rome to us, and they were concerned only to investigate the history of these texts and not their real significance in the lives of the Eastern peoples. What in reality we have here is the highly civilized law of an aged Culture forced upon the springtime of a young one.[2] It came over as learned literature, and in the train of political developments which were quite other than they would have been had Alexander or Cæsar lived longer or had Antony won at Actium. We must look at Early Arabian law from the standpoint of Ctesiphon and not from that of Rome. The law of the distant West had long before reached inward fulfilment — could it be here more than a mere literature? What part did it play, if any, in the active law-study, law-making, and law-practice of this landscape? And, indeed we must further ask how much of Roman — or for that matter of Classical generally — is contained in this literature itself.[3]

---

[1] Lenel, I, 380.

[2] Here, as in every line of the history of the "Pseudomorphosis," we are reminded of Christ's parable of new wine and old bottles (Matt. ix, 17), an expression not of mere abstract shrewdness, as it seems to us now, but of intense living force and even passion. It is only one short verse, not obligatory in its context, but leaping out of depths. — *Tr.*

[3] As long ago as 1891 Mitteis (*Reichsrecht und Volksrecht*, p. 13) drew attention to the Oriental vein in Constantine's legislation. Collinet (*Études historiques sur le droit de Justinien I*, 1912), chiefly on the basis of German researches, throws an immense amount back on Hellenistic law; but how much, after all, of this "Hellenistic" was really Greek and not merely written in Greek? The results of interpolation-research have proved truly devastating for the "Classical spirit" in Justinian's Digests.

The history of this Latin-written law belongs after 160 to the Arabian East, and it says a great deal that it can be traced in exactly parallel courses into the history of Jewish, Christian, and Persian literature.[1] The "Classical" jurists (160–220), Papinian, Ulpian, and Paul, were Aramæans, and Ulpian described himself with pride as a Phœnician from Tyre. They came, therefore, from the same population as the Tannaim who perfected the Mishnah shortly after 200, and most of the Christian Apologists (Tertullian 160–223). Contemporary with them is the fixation of canon and text for the New Testament by Christian, for the Hebrew Old Testament by Jewish,[2] and for the Avesta by Persian, scholars. It is the high Scholasticism of the Arabian Springtime. The digests and commentaries of these jurists stand towards the petrified legal store of the Classical in exactly the same relation as the Mishnah to the Torah of Moses (and as, much later, the Hadith to the Koran) — they are "Halakhoth"[3] — a new customary law grasped in the forms of an authoritative and traditional law-material. The casuistic method is everywhere the same. The Babylonian Jews possessed a well-developed civil law which was taught in the academies of Sura and Pumbeditha. Everywhere a class of law-men formed itself — the *prudentes* of the Christians, the rabbis of the Jews, later the ulemas (in Perian, mollahs) of the Islamic nation — who enunciated opinions, *responsa* (Arabic, *Fetwa*). If the Ulema was acknowledged by the State, he was called "Mufti" (Byzantine, *ex auctoritate principis*). Everywhere the forms are exactly the same.

About 200 the Apologists pass into the Fathers proper, the Tannaim into the Amoraim, the great casuists of juridical law (*jus*) into the exegetes and codifiers of constitutional law (*lex*). The constitutions of the Emperors, from 200 the sole source of new "Roman" law, are again a new "Halakhah" laid down over that in the jurists' writings, and therefore correspond exactly to the Gemara, which rapidly evolved as an outlier of the Mishnah. The new tendencies reached fulfilment simultaneously in the *Corpus Juris* and the Talmud.

The opposition between *jus* and *lex* in Arabian-Latin usage comes to expression very clearly in the work of Justinian. Institutes and Digests are *jus;* they have essentially the significance of canonical texts. Constitutions and Novels are *leges*, new law in the form of elucidations. The canonical books of the New Testament and the traditions of the Fathers are related to one another in the same way.

As to the Oriental character of the thousands of constitutions, no one now has any doubts. It is pure customary law of the Arabian world that the living

---

[1] See Ch. VII below.

[2] Coupled with the destruction of all other documents.

[3] Fromer, *Der Talmud* (1920), p. 190. [The English student will find a fairly full account of the main groups of Jewish literature in the article "Hebrew Literature" and cognate articles in the *Ency. Brit.*, XI ed. — Tr.]

pressure of evolution forced under the texts of the learned.[1] The innumerable decrees of the Christian rulers of Byzantium, of the Persian of Ctesiphon, of the Jewish (the Resh-Galuta [2]) in Babylonia, and finally of the Caliphs of Islam have all exactly the same significance.

But what significance had the *other* part of pseudo-Classical, the old jurists', law? Here it is not enough to explain texts, and we must know what was the relation between texts, jurisprudence, and court decisions. It can happen that one and the same law-book is, in the waking-consciousness of two groups of peoples, equivalent to two fundamentally different works.

It was not long before it became the habit, not to apply the old laws of the city of Rome to the fact-material of the given case, but to quote the jurists' texts like the Bible.[3] What does this signify? For our Romanists it is a sign of decadence, but looked at from the view-point of the Arabian world, it is just the reverse — a proof that Arabian man did eventually succeed in making an alien and imposed literature inwardly his own, in the form admissible for his own world-feeling. With this the completeness of the opposition between the Classical and the Arabian world-feeling becomes manifest.

VI

Whereas the Classical law was made by burghers on the basis of practical experience, the Arabian came from God, who manifested it through the intellect of chosen and enlightened men. The Roman distinction between *jus* and *fas* (such as it was, for the content even of *fas* had proceeded from human reflection) became meaningless. The law, of whatever kind, spiritual or secular, came into being, as stated in the first words of Justinian's Digests, *Deo auctore*. The authoritativeness of Classical laws rests upon their success, that of the Arabian on the majesty of the name that they bear.[4] But it matters very considerably indeed in a man's feelings whether he regards law as an expression of some fellow man's will or as an element of the divine dispensation. In the one case he either sees for himself that the law is right or else yields to force, but in the other he devoutly acknowledges ("*Islam*" = to commit, devote). The Oriental does not ask to see either the practical object of the law that is applied to him or the logical grounds of its judgments. The relation of the cadi to the people, therefore, has nothing in common with that of the prætor to the citizens. The latter bases his decisions upon an insight trained and tested in high positions, the former upon a spirit that is effective and immanent in him

---

[1] Mitteis (*Röm. Privatrecht bis auf die Zeit Dioklezians* (1908), preface) remarks how, "while the ancient law-forms were retained, the law itself nevertheless became something quite different."

[2] Head of the exilic Jews under Persian overlordship. — *Tr.*

[3] Mayr, IV, pp. 45, et seq.

[4] Hence the fictitious names of authors on innumerable books in every Arabian literature — Dionysius the Areopagite, Pythagoras, Hermes Trismegistus, Hippocrates, Enoch, Baruch, Daniel, Solomon, the Apostle-names attached to the numerous gospels and apocalypses.

and speaks through his mouth. But it follows from this that their respective relations to written law — the prætor's to his edict, the cadi's to the jurists' texts — must be entirely different. It is a quintessence of concentrated experience that the prætor makes his own, but the texts are a sort of oracle that the cadi esoterically questions. It does not matter in the least to the cadi what a passage originally meant or why it was framed. He consults the words — *even the letters* — and he does so not at all for their everyday meanings, but for the *magic* relations in which they must stand towards the case before him. We know this relation of the "spirit" to the "letter" from the Gnosis, from the early-Christian, Jewish, and Persian apocalyptic and mystical literature, from the Neopythagorean philosophy, from the Kabbalah; and there is not the slightest doubt that the Latin codices were used in exactly the same way in the minor judicial practice of the Aramæan world. The conviction that the letters contain secret meanings, penetrated with the Spirit of God, finds imaginative expression in the fact (mentioned above) that all religions of the Arabian world formed scripts of their own, in which the holy books had to be written and which maintained themselves with astounding tenacity as badges of the respective "nations" even after changes of language.[1]

But even in law the basis of determining the truth by a majority of texts is the fact of the consensus of the spiritual elect, the *ijma*.[2] This theory Islamic science worked out to its logical conclusions. We seek to find the truth, each for himself, by personal pondering, but the Arabian savant feels for and ascertains the general conviction of his associates, which cannot err because the mind of God and the mind of the community are the same. If *consensus* is found, truth is established. "*Ijma*" is the key of all Early Christian, Jewish, and Persian Councils, but it is the key, too, of the famous Law of Citations of Valentinian III (426), which the law-men have universally ridiculed without in the least understanding its spiritual foundations. The law limits the number of great jurists whose texts were allowed to be cited to five, and thus set up a canon — in the same sense as the Old and New Testaments, both of which also were summations of texts which might be cited as canonical. If opinions differed, the law of Valentinian laid it down that a majority should prevail, or if the texts were equally divided, the authority of Papinian.[3] The interpolation method, used on a large scale by Tribonian for the Digest of Justinian,

---

[1] For example, Hebrew was supplanted by Aramaic for all ordinary purposes as early as the Maccabees — and to such an extent that in the synagogues the Scriptures had to be translated for the people — but has held its ground as a religious vehicle, and above all as a script, even to this day. (The present use of a *spoken* Hebrew represents a revival in more recent times, after the wider dispersion of the early Middle Ages had broken the connexion with the Aramaic lands.) In the Persian field the older Zend survived alongside the newer Pehlevi. In Egypt somewhat similar influences were contemporaneously determining the evolution of popular Demotic and official Greek into the Coptic language with Greek characters. — Tr.

[2] M. Horten, *D. rel. Gedankenwelt d. Volkes im heut. Islam*, p. xvi. Cf. Chapter VII below.

[3] Mayr, IV, 45, et seq. [*Ency. Brit.*, XI ed., Vol. XXIII, p. 570. — Tr.]

is a product of this same outlook. A canonical text is in its very idea true and incapable of improvement. But the actual needs of the spirit alter, and so there grew up a technique of secret modifications which outwardly kept up the fiction of inalterability and which is employed very freely indeed in all religious writings of the Arabian world, the Bible included.

After Mark Antony, Justinian is the most fateful personality of the Arabian world. Like his "contemporary" Charles V he ruined everything for which he was invoked. Just as in the West the Faustian dream of a resurrection of the Holy Roman Empire runs through all the political romanticism that darkened the sense of fact during and beyond the age of Napoleon — and even that of the princely fools of 1848 — so also Justinian was possessed with a Quixotic urgency to recover the entire Imperium. It was always upon distant Rome instead of upon his proper world, the Eastern, that his eyes were fixed. Even before he ascended the throne, he was already in negotiation with the Pope of Rome, who was still subordinate to the great Patriarch of Christendom and not yet generally recognized even as *primus inter pares*. It was at the Pope's instance that the dual-nature symbol was introduced at Chalcedon,[1] a step which lost the Monophysite countries wholly and for ever. The consequence of Actium was that Christianity in its first two decisive and formative centuries was pulled over into the West, into Classical territories, where the higher intellectual stratum held aloof. Then the Early Christian spirit rose afresh with the Monophysites and Nestorians. But Justinian thrust this revival back upon itself, and the result was that in the realms of Eastern Christianity the reformist movement, when in due course it appeared, was not a Puritanism but the *new religion* of Islam. And in the same way, at the very moment when the Eastern customary law had become ripe for codification, he framed a Latin codex which, for language reasons in the East and for political reasons in the West, was condemned from the first to remain a literary product.

The work itself, like the corresponding codes of Dracon and Solon, came into being at the threshold of a "Late" period, and with political intentions. In the West, where the fiction of a continuing *Imperium Romanum* produced the utterly meaningless campaigns of Belisarius and Narses, Latin codes had been put together (about A.D. 500) by Visigoths, Burgundians and Ostrogoths for subjugated Romans, and so Byzantium must needs get out a genuine Roman code in opposition. In the East the Jewish nation has already settled its code, the Talmud, while, for the immense numbers of people who were subject to the Emperor's law, a code proper for the Emperor's own nation, the Christian, had become a necessity.

For the *Corpus Juris* with its topsy-turviness and its technical faults is, in spite of everything, an Arabic — in other words, a *religious* — creation, as evidenced

---

[1] 471. See *Ency. Brit.*, XI ed., article "Chalcedon, Council of," and references therein. — *Tr.*

in the Christian tendency of many interpolations;[1] in the fact that the constitutions relative to ecclesiastical law, which had been put at the end even in the Theodosian codex, were now placed at the beginning; and very markedly in the preambles of many of the Novels. Yet the book is not a beginning, but an end. Latin, which had long become valueless, now disappears completely from legal life (even the Novels are mostly in Greek), and with it the work so misguidedly written in that language. But the history of the law pursues the way that the Syrian-Roman law-book had indicated to it, and in the eighth century arrives at works in the mode of our eighteenth, such as the Ecloga of the Emperor Leo [2] and the Corpus of the great Persian jurist Archbishop Jesubocht.[3] In that time, too, came the greatest figure of Islamic jurisprudence, Abu Hanifah.

VII

The law-history of the West begins in total independence of Justinian's creation. At that time it was in complete oblivion, so thoroughly unimportant, in fact, that of its main element, the Pandects (Digest), there was but one manuscript, which by accident (an unfortunate one) was discovered about 1050.

The pre-Cultural phase, from about A.D. 500, had thrown up a series of Germanic tribal codes — the Visigothic, Ostrogothic, Burgundian, Frankish, and Lombard — which correspond to those of the Arabian pre-Culture that survives for us only in the Jewish [4] Deuteronomy (c. 621, more or less our Deuteronomy xii–xxvi) and Priestly History (c. 450, now represented by the second, third, and fourth books of the Pentateuch). Both are concerned with the values of basic significance for a primitive existence — family and chattels — and both make use, crudely, yet shrewdly, of an old and civilized law — the Jews (and no doubt the Persians and others) working upon the late Babylonian,[5] and the Germans upon some few relics of Urbs Roma.

The political life of the Gothic springtime, with its peasant, feudal, and simple burgher laws, leads very soon to particular development in three great branches of law which have remained distinct to this day — and there has been no unifying comparative history of law in the West to probe the deep meaning of this development.

The most important by far, owing to the political destinies in which it was involved, was the Norman law, which was borrowed from the Frankish. After the Conquest of England in 1066, this drove out the native Saxon, and since

---

[1] Wenger, p. 180.
[2] Krumbacher, *Byzantinische Literatur-Geschichte*, p. 606.
[3] Sachau, *Syrische Rechtsbücher*, Vol. III.
[4] Bertholet, *Kulturgeschichte Israels*, pp. 200, et seq.
[5] We get a hint of this in the famous code of Hammurabi, though unfortunately we cannot tell in what relation this single work stood, in point of intrinsic importance, to the general level of contemporary jurisprudence in the Babylonian world.

that day in England "the law of the great men has become the law of the whole people." Its purely German spirit has developed it, without a catastrophe, from a feudal régime of unparalleled stringency into the institutions of the present day which have become law in Canada, India, Australia, South Africa, and the United States. Even apart from the extent of its power, it is the most instructive in West Europe. Its development, unlike that of the rest, did *not* lie in the hands of theoretical jurists. The study of Roman law at Oxford was not allowed to touch practice; and at Merton in 1236 the higher nobility expressly rejected it. The Bench itself continued to develop the old law-material by means of creative precedents, and it was these practical decisions ("Reports") that formed the basis of law-books such as that of Bracton.[1] Since then, and to this day, a statute law, kept living and progressive by the court decisions, and a common law, which always vividly underlies the legislation, exist side by side, without its ever becoming necessary for the representatives of the people to make single large efforts at codification.

In the South, the law of the German-Roman codices above mentioned prevailed — in southern France the Visigothic (called the *droit écrit* in contrast to the Frankish *droit coutumier* of the north), and in Italy the Lombard (which was the most important of them, was almost purely Germanic, and held its own till well into the Renaissance). Pavia became a study-centre for German law and produced about 1070 the "*Expositio*," by far the greatest achievement of juridical science in the age, and immediately after it a code, the "*Lombarda*."[2] The legal evolution of the entire South was broken off by Napoleon's *Code Civil*, which took its place. But this in turn has become in all Latin lands and far beyond them the basis for further creative work — and hence, after the English, it is the most important.

In Germany, the movement that set in so powerfully with the Gothic tribal laws (*Sachsenspiegel*, 1230; *Schwabenspiegel*, 1274) frittered itself away to nullity. A host of petty civic and territorial rights went on springing up until indignation with the facts induced an unreal political romanticism in dreamers and enthusiasts, the Emperor Maximilian among them, and law came under attack with the rest. The Diet of Worms in 1495 framed its "*Kammergerichtsordnung*"[3] after an Italian model. Now there was not only the "Holy Roman Empire" on German ground, but "Roman law" as German common-law. The old German procedures were exchanged for Italian. The judges had to study their law beyond the Alps, and obtained their experience not from the ambient life, but from a logic-chopping philology. In this country alone are to be found, later, the ideologues for whom the *Corpus Juris* is an ark to be defended against the profanation of realities.

---

[1] See Professor Maitland's article "English Law" in *Ency. Brit.*, XI ed., Vol. IX. — *Tr.*
[2] Sohm, *Inst.*, p. 156.
[3] See J. Janssen, *Hist. German People at the End of the Middle Ages*, English translation, Book IV, Ch. I-II. — *Tr.*

What, in fact, was it that under the high-sounding name passed into the intellectual keeping of a handful of Gothic men? About 1100, at the University of Bologna, a German, Irnerius, had made that unique manuscript of the Pandects the object of a veritable Scholasticism. He transferred the Lombard method to the new text, "the truth of which, as a *ratio scripta*, was believed in as implicitly as the Bible and Aristotle."[1] Truth! — but the Gothic understanding, tied to the Gothic life-content, was incapable even of distantly guessing at the spirit of these texts, for the principles fixed in them were the principles of a civilized and megalopolitan life. This school of the glossators, like Scholasticism in general, stood under the spell of concept-realism; as they held the genuine real, the substance of the world, to be not in things, but in universal concepts, so they maintained that the law was to be found not in custom and usage as displayed in the despised [2] *Lombarda*, but in the manipulation of abstract notions. Their interest in the book was purely dialectical [3] — never was it in their minds to apply their work to life. It was only after 1300, and then slowly, that their anti-Lombard glosses and summæ made their way into the cities of the Renaissance. The jurists of the Late Gothic, above all Bartolus, had fused canon and Germanic law into one whole with a definitely practical intention, and into it they brought ideas of actuality — here, as in Dracon's code and the Imperial Edicts from Theodosius to Justinian, the actuality of a Culture that is on the threshold of its "Late" stage. It was *the creation of Bartolus that became effective* in Spain and Germany as "Roman law"; only in France did the jurists of the Baroque, after Cujacius and Donellus, get back from the Scholastic to the Byzantine text.

But Bologna witnessed, besides Irnerius's achievement in abstraction, an event of quite other and decisive import — the famous Decretum of Gratian, written about 1140.[4] This created the Western *science of spiritual law*. For by bringing the old-Catholic, Magian, church-law,[5] founded in the Early-Arabian sacrament of baptism,[6] into a system, it provided the very form that the new-Catholic, Faustian Christianity needed for the jural expression of its own being, which reached back to the prime sacrament of an altar and a consecrated priesthood. With the *Liber extra* of 1234 the main body of the *Corpus Juris Canonici* is complete. What the Empire had failed to accomplish — the creation, out of the immense undeveloped profusion of tribal laws, of a general Western "*Corpus Juris Germanici*" — the Papacy achieved. There came into existence a complete private law, with sanctions and processes, produced with German method out of the ecclesiastical and secular law-material of the Gothic. This is the

---

[1] Lenel, I, p. 395.

[2] The punning contrast of Lombard *faex* (excrement) and Roman *lex* is Huguccio's (1200).

[3] W. Goetz, *Arch. für Kulturgeschichte*, 10, 28, et seq.

[4] See the article "Canon Law" in *Ency. Brit.*, XI ed. — Tr.

[5] See Sohm's last work, *Das altkatholische Kirchenrecht und das Dekret Gratians* (1918).

[6] See Ch. VII below.

law called "Roman" which presently, after Bartolus, was infused into all study of the texts of Justinian themselves.   And it shows us, in the domain of jurisprudence as elsewhere, that great dissidence, inherent in the Faustian, which produced the gigantic conflict between the Papacy and the Empire. The destruction between *fas* and *jus*, impossible in the Arabian world, was inevitable in the Western.   They are two expressions of a will-to-power over the infinite, but the will behind "temporal" legislation is rooted in custom and lays hands on the generations of the future, while that of "spiritual" originates in mystical certainty and pronounces a timeless and eternal law.[1] This battle between equally matched opponents has never yet been ended, and it is visible even to-day in our law of marriage, with its opposition of the ecclesiastical and the civil wedding.

With the dawn of the Baroque, life, having by that time assumed urban and money-economic forms, begins to demand a law like that of the Classical city-states after Solon.   The purpose of the prevailing law was now perfectly clear.   But it was a fateful legacy from the Gothic that the creation of "the law inborn in us" was looked upon as the privilege of a learned class, and this privilege no one succeeded in shaking.

Urban rationalism turned, as in the case of the Sophists and the Stoics, to busy itself with the "law of nature," from its foundation by Oldendorp and Bodinus to its destruction by Hegel.   In England the great Coke successfully defended Germanic self-developing practical law against the last attempts of the Tudors to introduce Pandect law.   But on the Continent the systems of the learned evolved in *Roman* forms right down to the state codes of Germany and the schemes of the *Ancien Régime* in France on which the Code Napoléon was based.   And therefore Blackstone's *Commentaries on the Laws of England* (1765) is the one purely Germanic Code, and it appeared when the Faustian Culture had already reached the threshold of its Civilization.

VIII

With this I reach the objective and look around me.   I see three law-histories, connected merely by the elements of verbal and syntactical form, taken over by one from another, voluntarily or perforce, but never revealing to the new user the nature of the alien being which underlay them.   Two of these histories are complete.   The third is that in which we ourselves are standing — standing, too, at a decisive point where we embark in our turn upon the big constructive task that Rome and Islam, each for itself and in its season, have accomplished before us.

What has "Roman" law been for us hitherto?   What has it spoilt?   What can it be for us in the future?

All through our legal history runs, as basic motive, the conflict between

[1] See Ch. X below.

book and life. The Western book is not an oracle or magician's text with Magian under-sense, but *a piece of preserved history.* It is compressed Past that wants to become Future, through us who read it and in whom its content lives anew. Faustian man does not aim, like Classical man, at bringing his life to a self-contained perfection, but at carrying on a life that emerged long before him and will draw to its end long after him. For Gothic man — so far as he reflected about himself at all — the question was not whether he should look for linkages of his being and history, but in what direction to look for them. He required a past in order to find meaning and depth in the present. On the spiritual side the past which presented itself to him was ancient Israel; on the mundane it was ancient Rome, whose relics he saw all about him. What was revered was revered not because it was great, but because it was old and distant. If these men had known Egypt, they would hardly have noticed Rome, and the language of our Culture would have developed differently.

As it was a Culture of books and readers, Classical texts were "received" in any and every field as Roman law was "received" in Germany, and their further development assumed the form of a slow and unwilling self-emancipation. "Reception" of Aristotle, of Euclid, of the *Corpus Juris,* means in this Culture (in the Magian East it was different) discovering a ready-made vessel for our own thought a great deal too soon, with the result of making a historically built kind of man into a slave of concepts. The alien life-feeling, of course, did not and could not enter into his thought, but it was a hindrance to his own life-feeling's development of an unconstrained speech of its own.

Now, legal thought is forced to attach itself to something tangible — there must be something before it can abstract its concepts; it must have something from which to abstract. And it was the misfortune of Western jurisprudence that, instead of quarrying in strong, firm custom of social and economic life, it abstracted prematurely and in a hurry from Latin writings. The Western jurist became a philologist, and practical experience of life was replaced by scholarly experience in the purely logical separation and disposition of legal concepts on self-contained foundations.

Owing to this, we have been completely cut off from touch with the fact that *private law is meant to represent the social and economic existence of its period.* Neither the Code Napoléon nor the Prussian Landrecht, neither Grotius nor Mommsen, was definitely conscious of this fact. Neither in the training of the legal profession nor in its literature do we detect the slightest inkling of this — the genuine — "source" of valid law.

And consequently we possess a private law that rests on the shadowy foundations of *the Late Classical economy.* The intense embitterment which, in these beginnings of our Civilization's economy, opposes the name of Capitalism to the name of Socialism comes very largely from the fact that scholarly jurisprudence, and under its influence educated thought generally, have tied up such all-important notions as person, thing, and property to the conditions and the dispositions of Classical life. The book puts itself between the facts and the perception of them. The learned — meaning thereby the book-learned — weigh up everything to this day in scales that are essentially Classical. The man who is merely active and not trained to judgment feels himself misunderstood. He sees the contradiction between the life of the times and the law's outlook upon it, and calls for the heads of those who — to gain their private ends, as he thinks — have promoted this opposition.

Again the question is: By whom and for whom is Western law made? The Roman prætor was a landowner, a military officer, a man experienced in administrative and financial questions; and it was just this experience that was held to qualify him for the inseparable functions of expounder and maker of the law. The peregrin prætor developed his aliens' law as a law of commercial intercourse adapted to the Late Classical megalopolis — without plan, without tendency, out of the cases that came before him and nothing else.

But the Faustian will-to-duration demands a book, something valid "for evermore," [1] a system that is intended to provide in advance for every possible case, and this book, a work of learning, necessarily called for a scholarly class of jurists and judges — the doctors of the faculties, the old German legal families, and the French "noblesse de robe." The English judges, who number hardly over a hundred,[2] are drawn indeed from an upper class of advocates (the "barristers"), but they actually rank above many members of the Government.

A scholar-class is alien to the world, and despises experience that does not originate in thought. Inevitably conflict arises between the "state of knowledge" as the scholar will accept it and the flowing custom of practical life. That manuscript of the Pandect of Irnerius became, and for centuries remained, the "world" in which learned jurists lived. Even in England, where there are no law faculties (in the European sense), it was exclusively the legal profession that controlled further growth, so that even here the development of legal ideas diverged from the development of general life.

Thus what we have hitherto called juristic science is in fact either the philology of law-language, or the scholarship of law-ideas. It is now the only science that still continues to deduce the meaning of life from "eternally valid" principles. "The German jurisprudence of to-day," says Sohm,[3] "represents very largely indeed an inheritance from mediæval Scholasticism. We have not yet begun to consider in deep earnest the bearing of the basic values of the *actual* life about us upon legal theory. We do not even yet know what these values are."

---

[1] The permanently valid element in English law is the constant *form* of an incessant *development* by the courts.

[2] If the higher courts alone are meant, the number is well below fifty for England and Wales. Scots law is independent of English and has its own jurisprudence. — *Tr.*

[3] *Inst.*, p. 170.

Here, then, is the task that German thought of the future has to perform. From the practical life of the present it has to develop the deepest principles of that life and elevate them into basic law-ideas. If our great arts lie behind us, our great jurisprudence is yet to come.

For the work of the nineteenth century — however creative that century believed itself to be — was merely preparatory. *It freed us from the book of Justinian, but not from the concepts.* The ideologues of Roman law among scholars no longer count, but scholarship of the old cast remains. It is another kind of jurisprudence that is needed now to free us from the schematism of these concepts. Philological expertness must give place to social and economic.

A glance at German civil and penal law will make the position clear. They are systems ringed with a chaplet of minor laws — it was impossible to embody the material of these in the main law. Conceptually, and therefore syntactically, that which could not be understood in terms of the Classical scheme separates itself from that which can be so understood.

How was it that in 1900 the theft of electric power — after grotesque discussions as to whether the matter in dispute was a corporeal thing [1] — had to be dealt with under an *ad hoc* statute? Why was it impossible to work the substance of patent law into the ensemble of the law about things? Why was copyright law unable conceptually to differentiate the intellectual creation, its communicable form the manuscript, and the objective product in print? Why, in contradiction with the law of things, had the artistic and the material property in a picture to be distinguished by separating acquisition of the original from acquisition of the right to reproduce it? Why is the misappropriation of a business idea or a scheme of organization unpunishable, and theft of the piece of paper on which it is set forth punishable? Because even to-day we are dominated by the Classical idea of the material thing.[2] We *live* otherwise. Our instinctive experience is subject to *functional* concepts, such as working power, inventiveness, enterprise, such as intellectual and bodily, artistic and organizing, energies and capacities and talents. In our physics (of which the theory, advanced though it is, is but a copy of our present mode of life) the old idea of a body has in principle ceased to exist — as in this very instance of electrical power. Why is our law conceptually helpless in the presence of the great facts of modern economics? Because *persons, too,* are known to it *only as bodies.*[3]

If the Western jurisprudence took over ancient words, yet only the most superficial elements of the ancient meanings still adhered to them. The consistency of the text disclosed only the *logical* use of the words, not the life that underlay them. No practice can reawaken the silent metaphysic of old jural

[1] Similar problems are now (1927) arising in connexion with radio broadcasting. — *Tr.*

[2] *Bürgerliches Gesetzbuch,* § 90.

[3] As evidenced in terms of French law like "*Société anonyme*," "*raison sociale*," "*personne juridique*." — *Tr.*

ideas. No laws in the world make this last and deepest element explicit, because — just because — it is self-evident. In all of them the essential is tacitly presupposed; in application it is not only the formula but also, and primarily, the inexpressible element beneath it that the people inwardly understands and can practise. Every law is, to the extent that it would be impossible to exaggerate, customary law. Let the statute define the words; it is life that explains them.

If, however, a scholars' law-language of alien origin and alien scheme tries to bind the native and proper law, the ideas remain void and the life remains dumb. Law becomes, not a tool, but a burden, and actuality marches on, not with, but apart from legal history.

And thus it is that the law-material that our Civilization needs fits only in externals, or even not at all, with the Classical scheme of the law-books, and for the purposes of our proper jurisprudence and our educated thought generally is still formless and therefore unavailable.

Are persons and things, in the sense of present-day legislation, law-*concepts* at all? No! They merely serve to draw the ordinary distinction, the zoölogical distinction, so to say, between man and the rest. But of old the whole metaphysic of Classical being adhered to the notion of "*persona*." The distinction between man and deity, the essence of the Polis, of the hero, of the slave, the Cosmos of stuff and form, the life-ideal of Ataraxia, were the self-evident premises, and these premises have for us completely perished. In our thought the word "property" is tied up with the Classical *static* definition, and consequently, in every application to the dynamism of our way of living it falsifies. We leave such definitions to the world-shy abstract professors of ethics, jurists, and philosophers and to the unintelligent debate of political doctrinaires — and this although the *whole* understanding of the economic history of this day *rests upon the metaphysic of this one notion.*

It must be emphasized then — and with all rigour — that Classical law was a law of *bodies*, while ours is a law of *functions*. The Romans created a juristic statics; our task is juristic dynamics. For us persons are not bodies, but units of force and will; and things are not bodies, but aims, means, and creations of these units. The Classical relation between bodies was positional, but the relation between forces is called action. For a Roman the slave was a thing which produced new things. A writer like Cicero could never have conceived of "intellectual property," let alone property in a practical notion or in the potentialities of talent; for us, on the contrary, the organizer or inventor or promoter is *a generative force which works upon other, executive, forces,* by giving direction, aim, and means to their action.[1] Both belong to economic life, not as possessors of things, but as carriers of energies.

---

[1] Note, in this connexion, the remarkable development in modern American industry of a professional managerial class, distinct from the capitalist, the technician, and the "worker." — *Tr.*

The future will be called upon to transpose our entire legal thought into alignment with our higher physics and mathematics. Our whole social, economic, and technical life is waiting to be understood, at long last, in this wise. We shall need a century and more of keenest and deepest thought to arrive at the goal. And the prerequisite is a wholly new kind of preparatory training in the jurist. It demands:

    1. An immediate, extended, and practical experience in the economic life of the present.

    2. An exact knowledge of the legal history of the West, with constant comparison of German, English, and "Roman" development.

    3. Knowledge of Classical jurisprudence, not as a model for principles of present-day validity, but as a brilliant example of how a law can develop strong and pure out of the *practical life* of its time.

Roman law has ceased to be our source for principles of eternal validity. But the relation between Roman existence and Roman law-ideas gives it a renewed value for us. We can learn from it how we have to build up *our* law out of *our* experiences.

CHAPTER IV

CITIES AND PEOPLES

(A)

THE SOUL OF THE CITY

CITIES AND PEOPLES

(A)

THE SOUL OF THE CITY

ABOUT the middle of the second millennium before Christ, two worlds lay over against one another on the Ægean Sea. The one, darkly groping, big with hopes, drowsy with the intoxication of deeds and sufferings, ripening quietly towards its future, was the Mycenæan. The other, gay and satisfied, snugly ensconced in the treasures of an ancient Culture, elegant, light, with all its great problems far behind it, was the Minoan of Crete.

We shall never really comprehend this phenomenon, which in these days is becoming the centre of research-interest, unless we appreciate the abyss of opposition that separates the two souls. The man of those days must have felt it deeply, but hardly "cognised" it. I see it before me: the humility of the inhabitant of Tiryns and Mycenæ before the unattainable *esprit* of life in Cnossus, the contempt of the well-bred of Cnossus for the petty chiefs and their followers, and withal a secret feeling of superiority in the healthy barbarians, like that of the German soldier in the presence of the elderly Roman dignitary.

How are we in a position to know this? There are several such moments in which the men of two Cultures have looked into one another's eyes. We know more than one "Inter-Culture" in which some of the most significant tendencies of the human soul have disclosed themselves.

As it was (we may confidently say) between Cnossus and Mycenæ, so it was between the Byzantine court and the German chieftains who, like Otto II, married into it — undisguised wonder on the part of the knights and counts, answered by the contemptuous astonishment of a refined, somewhat pale and tired Civilization at that bearish morning vigour of the German lands which Scheffel has described in *Ekkehard*.[1]

In Charlemagne the mixture of a primitive human spirituality, on the threshold of its awakening, with a superposed Late intellectuality, becomes manifest. Certain characteristics of his rulership would lead us to name him the Caliph of Frankistan, but on his other side he is but the chief of a Germanic tribe; and it is the mingling of the two that makes him symbolic, in the same way as the form of the Aachen palace-chapel — no longer mosque, not yet cathedral. The Germanic-Western pre-Culture meanwhile is moving on, but slowly and underground, for that sudden illumination which we most ineptly call the Carolingian Renaissance is a ray from Baghdad. It must not be

---

[1] Published 1857. English translation, 1872. — *Tr.*

overlooked that the period of Charles the Great is an episode of the surface, ending, as accidentals do end, without issue. After 900, after a new deep depression, there begins something really new, something having the telling force of a Destiny and the depth that promises duration. But in 800 it was the sun of the Arabian Civilization passing on from the world-cities of the East to the countryside of the West. Even so the sunshine of Hellenism had spread to the distant Indus.[1]

That which stands on the hills of Tiryns and Mycenæ is *Pfalz* and *Burg* of root-Germanic type. The palaces of Crete — which are not kings' castles, but huge cult-buildings for a crowd of priests and priestesses — are equipped with megalopolitan — nay, Late-Roman — luxury. At the foot of those hills were crowded the huts of yeoman and vassals, but in Crete (Gournia, Hagia Triada) the excavation of towns and villas has shown that the requirements were those of high civilization, and the building-technique that of a long experience, accustomed to catering for the most pampered taste in furniture and wall-decoration, and familiar with lighting, water-circulation, staircases, and suchlike problems.[2] In the one, the plan of the house is a strict life-symbol; in the other, the expression of a refined utilitarianism. Compare the Kamares vases and the frescoes of smooth stucco with everything that is genuinely Mycenæan — they are, through and through, the product of an industrial art, clever and empty, and not of any grand and deep art of heavy, clumsy, but forceful symbolism like that which in Mycenæ was ripening towards the geometric style. It is, in a word, not a style but a taste.[3] In Mycenæ was housed a primitive race which chose its sites according to soil-value and facilities for defence, whereas the Minoan population settled in business foci, as may be observed very clearly in the case of Philakopi on Melos which was established for the export trade in obsidian. A Mycenæan palace is a promise, a Minoan something that is ending. But it was just the same in the West about 800 — the Frankish and Visigothic farms and manor-houses stretched from the Loire to the Ebro, while south of them lay the Moorish castles, villas, and mosques of Cordova and Granada.

It is surely no accident that the peak of this Minoan luxury coincides with the period of the great Egyptian revolution, and particularly the Hyksos time (1780–1580 B.C.).[4] The Egyptian craftsmen may well have fled in those days to the peaceful islands and even as far as the strongholds of the mainland, as in a later instance the Byzantine scholars fled to Italy. For it is axiomatic that the Minoan Culture is a part of the Egyptian, and we should be able to realize

---

[1] Without Alexander, and even before him, for Alexander neither kindled nor spread that light; he did not lead, but followed its path to the East.

[2] See G. Glotz's recent work *La Civilisation égéenne*, 1923 (English translation, 1927). — *Tr.*

[3] This is now recognized by art-research; cf. Salis, *Die Kunst der Griechen* (1919), pp. 3, et seq.; H. Th. Bosser, *Alt-Kreta* (1921), introduction.

[4] D. Fimmen, *Die kretisch-mykenische Kultur* (1921), p. 210.

this more fully were it not that the part of Egypt's art-store which would have been decisive in this connexion — viz.: what was produced in the Western Delta — has perished from damp. We only know the Egyptian Culture in so far as it flourished on the dry soil of the south, but it has long been admitted as certain that the centre of gravity of its evolution lay elsewhere.

It is not possible to draw a strict frontier between the late Minoan and the young Mycenæan art. Throughout the Egyptian-Cretan world we can observe a highly modern fad for these alien and primitive things, and vice versa the war-band kings of the mainland strongholds stole or bought Cretan *objets d'art* wherever and however they could come by them, admiring and imitating — even as the style of the Migrations, once supposed to be, and prized as, proto-German, borrows the whole of its form-language from the East.[1] They had their palaces and tombs built and decorated by captive or invited craftsmen. The "Treasure-house" (Tomb) of Atreus in Mycenæ, therefore, is exactly analogous to the tomb of Theoderich at Ravenna.

In this regard Byzantium itself is a marvel. Here layer after layer has to be carefully separated. In 326 Constantine, rebuilding on the ruins of the great city destroyed by Septimus Severus, created a *Late Classical cosmopolis* of the first rank, into which presently streamed hoary Apollinism from the West and youthful Magism from the East. And long afterwards again, in 1096, it is a *Late Magian* cosmopolis, confronted in its last autumn days with spring in the shape of Godfrey of Bouillon's crusaders, whom that clever royal lady Anna Comnena [2] portrays with contempt. As the easternmost of the Classical West, this city bewitched the Goths; then, a millennium later, as the northernmost of the Arabian world, it enchanted the Russians. And the amazing Vasili Blazheny in Moscow (1554), the herald of the Russian pre-Culture, stands "between styles," just as, two thousand years before, Solomon's Temple had stood between Babylon the Cosmopolis and early Christianity.

II

Primeval man is a *ranging* animal, a being whose waking-consciousness restlessly feels its way through life, all microcosm, under no servitude of place or home, keen and anxious in its senses, ever alert to drive off some element of hostile Nature. A deep transformation sets in first with agriculture — for that is something *artificial*, with which hunter and shepherd have no touch. He who digs and ploughs is seeking not to plunder, but to *alter* Nature. To plant implies, not to take something, but to produce something. *But with this, man himself becomes plant* — namely, as peasant. He roots in the earth that he tends, the soul of man discovers a soul in the countryside, and a new earth-boundness of being, a new feeling, pronounces itself. Hostile Nature becomes

---

[1] Dehio, *Gesch. d. deutsch. Kunst* (1919), pp. 16, et seq.
[2] Dieterich, *Byzant. Charakterköpfe*, pp. 136, et seq.

the friend; earth becomes *Mother* Earth. Between sowing and begetting, harvest and death, the child and the grain, a profound affinity is set up. A new devoutness addresses itself in chthonian cults to the fruitful earth that grows up along with man. And as completed expression of this life-feeling, we find everywhere the *symbolic shape of the farmhouse*, which in the disposition of the rooms and in every line of external form tells us about the blood of its inhabitants. The peasant's dwelling is the great symbol of settledness. It is itself plant, thrusts its roots deep into its "own" soil.[1] It is *property* in the most sacred sense of the word. The kindly spirits of hearth and door, floor and chamber—Vesta, Janus, Lares and Penates—are as firmly fixed in it as the man himself.

This is the condition precedent of every Culture, which itself in turn grows up out of a mother-landscape and renews and intensifies the intimacy of man and soil. What his cottage is to the peasant, that the town is to the Culture-man. As each individual house has its kindly spirits, so each town has its tutelary god or saint. The town, too, is a plantlike being, as far removed as a peasantry is from nomadism and the purely microcosmic. Hence the development of a high form-language is linked always to a landscape. Neither an art nor a religion can alter the site of its growth; only in the Civilization with its giant cities do we come again to despise and disengage ourselves from these roots. Man as civilized, as *intellectual nomad*, is again wholly microcosmic, wholly homeless, as free *intellectually* as hunter and herdsman were free sensually. "*Ubi bene, ibi patria*" is valid *before* as well as *after* a Culture. In the not-yet-spring of the Migrations it was a Germanic yearning — virginal, yet already maternal — that searched the South for a home in which to nest its future Culture. To-day, at the end of this Culture, the rootless intellect ranges over all landscapes and all possibilities of thought. But between these limits lies the time in which a man held a bit of soil to be something *worth dying for*.

It is a conclusive fact — yet one hitherto never appreciated — that all great Cultures are town-Cultures. Higher man of the Second Age is a town-tied animal. Here is the real criterion of "world-history" that differentiates it with utter sharpness from man's history — *world-history is the history of civic man*. Peoples, states, politics, religion, all arts, and all sciences rest upon *one* prime phenomenon of human being, the town. As all thinkers of all Cultures themselves live in the town (even though they may reside bodily in the country), they are perfectly unaware of what a bizarre thing a town is. To feel this we have to put ourselves unreservedly in the place of the wonder-struck primitive who for the first time sees this mass of stone and wood set in the landscape, with its stone-enclosed streets and its stone-paved squares — a domicile, truly, of strange form and strangely teeming with men!

But the real miracle is the birth of the *soul* of a town. A mass-soul of a wholly new kind — whose last foundations will remain hidden from us for

---

[1] Even admitting within itself the animals of its fields. — *Tr.*

ever — suddenly buds off from the general spirituality of its Culture. As soon as it is awake, it forms for itself a visible body. Out of the rustic group of farms and cottages, each of which has its own history, arises a *totality*. And the whole lives, breathes, grows, and acquires a face and an inner form and history. Thenceforward, in addition to the individual house, the temple, the cathedral, and the palace, the town-figure itself becomes a unit objectively expressing the form-language and style-history that accompanies the Culture throughout its life-course.

It goes without saying that what distinguishes a town from a village is not size, but the presence of a soul. Not only in primitive conditions, such as those of central Africa, but in Late conditions too — China, India, and industrialized Europe and America — we find very large settlements that are nevertheless not to be called cities. They are centres of landscape; they do not inwardly form worlds in themselves. They have no soul. Every primitive population lives wholly as peasant and son of the soil — the being "City" does not exist for it. That which in externals develops from the village is not the city, but the market, a mere meeting-point of rural life-interests. Here there can be no question of a separate existence. The inhabitant of a market may be a craftsman or a tradesman, but he lives and thinks as a peasant. We have to go back and sense accurately what it means when out of a primitive Egyptian or Chinese or Germanic village — a little spot in a wide land — a city comes into being. It is quite possibly not differentiated in any outward feature, but spiritually it is *a place from which the countryside is henceforth regarded, felt, and experienced as "environs,"* as something different and subordinate. From now on there are two lives, that of the inside and that of the outside, and the peasant understands this just as clearly as the townsman. The village smith and the smith in the city, the village headman and the burgomaster, live in two different worlds. The man of the land and the man of the city are different essences. First of all they feel the difference, then they are dominated by it, and at last they cease to understand each other at all. To-day a Brandenburg peasant is closer to a Sicilian peasant than he is to a Berliner. From the moment of this specific attunement, the City comes into being, and it is this attunement which underlies, as something that goes without saying, the entire waking-consciousness of every Culture.

Every springtime of a Culture is *ipso facto* the springtime of a new city-type and civism. The men of the pre-Culture are filled with a deep uneasiness in the presence of these types, with which they cannot get into any inward relation. On the Rhine and the Danube the Germans frequently, as at Strassburg, settled down at the gates of Roman cities that remained uninhabited.[1] In Crete the conquerors built, on the ruins of the burnt-out cities like Gournia and Cnossus — villages. The Orders of the Western pre-Culture, the Benedictines, and

[1] Dehio, *Gesch. d. deutschen Kunst* (1919), pp. 13, et seq.

particularly the Cluniacs and Premonstratensians, settled like the knights on free land; it was the Franciscans and Dominicans who began to build in the Early Gothic city. There the new soul had just awakened. But even there a tender melancholy still adheres to the architecture, as to Franciscan art as a whole — an almost mystical fear of the individual in presence of the new and bright and conscious, which as yet was only dully accepted by the generality. Man hardly yet dared to cease to be peasant; the first to live with the ripe and considered alertness of genuine megalopolitans are the Jesuits. It is a sign that the countryside is still unconditionally supreme, and does not yet recognize the city, when the ruler shifts his court every spring from palace to palace. In the Egyptian Old Kingdom the thickly-populated centre of the administration was at the "White Wall" (Memphis), but the residences of the Pharaohs changed incessantly as in Sumerian Babylon and the Carolingian Empire.[1] The Early Chinese rulers of the Chóu dynasty had their court as a rule at Lo-Yang (the present Ho-nan-fu) from about 1160, but it was not until 770 — corresponding to our sixteenth century — that the locality was promoted to be the permanent royal residence.[2]

Never has the feeling of earth-boundness, of the plantwise-cosmic, expressed itself so powerfully as it did in the architecture of the petty early towns, which consisted of hardly more than a few streets about a market-place or a castle or a place of worship. Here, if anywhere, it is manifest that every grand style is itself plantlike. The Doric column, the Egyptian pyramid, the Gothic cathedral, *grow out of* the ground, earnest, big with destiny, Being without waking-consciousness. The Ionic column, the buildings of the Middle Kingdom and those of the Baroque, calmly aware and conscious of themselves, free and sure, *stand on* the ground. There, separated from the power of the land — cut off from it, even, by the pavement underfoot — Being becomes more and more languid, sensation and reason more and more powerful. Man becomes intellect, "free" like the nomads, whom he comes to resemble, but narrower and colder than they. "Intellect," "*Geist,*" "*esprit,*" is the specific urban form of the understanding waking-consciousness. All art, all religion and science, become slowly intellectualized, alien to the land, incomprehensible to the peasant of the soil. With the Civilization sets in the climacteric. The immemorially old roots of Being are dried up in the stone-masses of its cities. And the free intellect — fateful word! — appears like a flame, mounts splendid into the air, and pitiably dies.

III

The new Soul of the City speaks a new language, which soon comes to be tantamount to the language of the Culture itself. The open land with its

---

[1] Eduard Meyer, *Gesch. d. Altertums*, I, p. 188.
[2] The English parallel is Winchester. — *Tr.*

village-mankind is wounded; it no longer understands that language, it is
nonplussed and dumb. All genuine style-history is played out in the cities.
It is exclusively the city's destiny and the life-experience of urban men that
speaks to the eye in the logic of visible forms. The very earliest Gothic was
still a growth of the soil and laid hold of the farmhouse with its inhabitants
and its contents. But the Renaissance style flourished only in the Renaissance
city, the Baroque only in the Baroque *city* — not to mention the wholly megalopolitan Corinthian column or Rococo. There was perhaps some quiet
infiltration from these into the landscape; but the land itself was no longer
capable of the smallest creative effort — only of dumb aversion. The peasant
and his dwelling remained in all essentials Gothic, and Gothic it is to this day.
The Hellenic *countryside* preserved the geometric style, the Egyptian village
the cast of the Old Kingdom.

It is, above all, the expression of the city's "visage" that has a history.
The play of this facial expression, indeed, is almost the spiritual history of the
Culture itself. First we have the little proto-cities of the Gothic and other
Early Cultures, which almost efface themselves in the landscape, which are
still genuine peasant-houses crowded under the shadow of a stronghold or a
sanctuary, and without inward change become town-houses merely in the sense
that they have neighbour-houses instead of fields and meadows around them.
The peoples of the Early Culture gradually became town-peoples, and accordingly there are not only specifically Chinese, Indian, Apollinian, and Faustian
town-forms, but, moreover, Armenian and Syrian, Ionian and Etruscan, German and French and English town-physiognomies. There is a city of Phidias,
a city of Rembrandt, a city of Luther. These designations, and the mere names
of Granada, Venice, and Nürnberg conjure up at once quite definite images,
for all that the Culture produces in religion, art, and knowledge has been
produced in such cities. While it was still the spirit of knights' castles and
rural monasteries that evoked the Crusades, the Reformation is urban and belongs to narrow streets and steep-gabled houses. The great Epic, which speaks
and sings of the blood, belongs to *Pfalz* and *Burg*, but the Drama, in which
awakened life tests itself, is city-poetry, and the great Novel, the survey of all
things human by the *emancipated* intellect, presupposes the world-city. Apart
from really genuine folk-song, the only lyrism is of the city. Apart from the
"eternal" peasant-art, there is only urban painting and architecture, with a
swift and soon-ended history.

And these stone visages that have incorporated in their light-world the
humanness of the citizen himself and, like him, are all eye and intellect — how
distinct the language of form that they talk, how different from the rustic
drawl of the landscape! The silhouette of the great city, its roofs and chimneys, the towers and domes on the horizon! What a language is imparted
to us through *one* look at Nürnberg or Florence, Damascus or Moscow, Peking

or Benares. What do we know of the Classical cities, seeing that we do not know the lines that they presented under the Southern noon, under clouds in the morning, in the starry night? The courses of the streets, straight or crooked, broad or narrow; the houses, low or tall, bright or dark, that in all Western cities turn their façades, *their faces*, and in all Eastern cities turn their backs, blank wall and railing, towards the street; the spirit of squares and corners, impasses and prospects, fountains and monuments, churches or temples or mosques, amphitheatres and railway stations, bazaars and town-halls! The suburbs, too, of neat garden-villas or of jumbled blocks of flats, rubbish-heaps and allotments; the fashionable quarter and the slum area, the Subura of Classical Rome and the Faubourg Saint-Germain of Paris, ancient Baiæ and modern Nice, the little town-picture like Bruges and Rothenburg and the sea of houses like Babylon, Tenochtitlan, Rome, and London! All this has history and *is* history. One major political event — and the visage of the town falls into different folds. Napoleon gave to Bourbon Paris, Bismarck gave to worthy little Berlin, a new mien. But the Country stands by, uninfluenced, suspicious and irritated.

In the earliest time the *landscape-figure alone* dominates man's eyes. It gives form to his soul and vibrates in tune therewith. Feelings and woodland rustlings beat together; the meadows and the copses adapt themselves to its shape, to its course, even to its dress. The village, with its quiet hillocky roofs, its evening smoke, its wells, its hedges, and its beasts, lies completely fused and embedded in the landscape. The country town *confirms* the country, is an intensification of the picture of the country. It is the Late city that first defies the land, contradicts Nature in the lines of its silhouette, *denies* all Nature. It wants to be something different from and higher than Nature. These high-pitched gables, these Baroque cupolas, spires, and pinnacles, neither are, nor desire to be, related with anything in Nature. And then begins the gigantic megalopolis, the *city-as-world*, which suffers nothing beside itself and sets about *annihilating* the country picture. The town that once upon a time humbly accommodated itself to that picture now insists that it shall be the same as itself. *Extra muros*, chaussées and woods and pastures become a park, mountains become tourists' view-points; and *intra muros* arises an imitation Nature, fountains in lieu of springs, flower-beds, formal pools, and clipped hedges in lieu of meadows and ponds and bushes. In a village the thatched roof is still hill-like and the street is of the same nature as the baulk of earth between fields. But here the picture is of deep, long gorges between high, stony houses filled with coloured dust and strange uproar, and men dwell in these houses, the like of which no nature-being has ever conceived. Costumes, even faces, are adjusted to a background of stone. By day there is a street traffic of strange colours and tones, and by night a new light that outshines the moon. And the yokel stands helpless on the pavement, understanding nothing and understood by nobody, tolerated as a useful type in farce and provider of this world's daily bread.

It follows, however — and this is the most essential point of any — that we cannot comprehend political and economic history at all unless we realize that the city, with its gradual detachment from and final bankrupting of the country, is the determinative form to which the course and sense of higher history generally conforms. *World history is city history.*

An obvious case in point is, of course, the Classical world, in which the Euclidean feeling of existence connected the city-idea with its need of minimizing extension and thus, with ever-increasing emphasis, identified the State with the stone body of the individual Polis. But, quite apart from this instance, we find in every Culture (and very soon) the type of the *capital city*. This, as its name pointedly indicates, is that city whose spirit, with its methods, aims, and decisions of policy and economics, dominates the land. The land with its people is for this controlling spirit a tool and an object. The land does not understand what is going on, and is not even asked. In all countries of all Late Cultures, the great parties, the revolutions, the Cæsarisms, the democracies, the parliaments, are the form in which the spirit of the capital tells the country what it is expected to desire and, if called upon, to die for. The Classical forum, the Western press, are, essentially, intellectual engines of the ruling City. Any country-dweller who really understands the meaning of politics in such periods, and feels himself on their level, moves into the City, not perhaps in the body, but certainly in the spirit.[1] The sentiment and public opinion of the peasant's country-side — so far as it can be said to exist — is prescribed and guided by the print and speech of the city. Egypt is Thebes, the *orbis terrarum* is Rome, Islam is Baghdad, France is Paris. The history of every springtime phase is played out in the many small centres of many separate districts. The Egyptian nomes, the Greek peoples of Homer, the Gothic counties and free cities, were the makers of history of old. But gradually Policy gathers itself up into a very few capitals, and everything else retains but a shadow of political existence. Even in the Classical world, the atomizing tendency towards city-states did not hold out against the major movement. As early as the Peloponnesian War it was only Athens and Sparta that were really handling policy, the remaining cities of the Ægean being merely elements within the hegemony of the one or the other; of policies of *their own* there is no

[1] The phenomenon is perhaps too well known in our days to need exemplification. But it is worth while recalling that the usual form of disgrace for a minister or courtier of the seventeenth or eighteenth century was to be commanded to "retire to his estates," and that a student expelled from the universities is said to be "rusticated." Since this volume was written, a remarkable proof of the reality of this spiritual indrawing by the Megalopolis has been given by the swift spread of radio broadcasting over the West-European and American world. For the country-dweller, radio reception means intimate touch with the news, the thought, and the entertainment of the great city, and relieves the *grievance* of "isolation" that the older countryfolk would never have felt as a grievance at all. — *Tr.*

longer any question. Finally it is the Forum of the City of Rome alone that is the scene of Classical history. Cæsar might campaign in Gaul, his slayers in Macedonia, Antony in Egypt, but, whatever happened in these fields, *it was from their relation to Rome that events acquired meaning.*

IV

All effectual history begins with the primary classes, nobility and priest-hood, forming themselves and elevating themselves above the peasantry as such. The opposition of greater and lesser nobility, between king and vassal, between worldly and spiritual power, is the basic form of all primitive politics, Homeric, Chinese, or Gothic, until with the coming of the City, the burgher, the *Tiers État*, history changes its style. But it is exclusively in these classes as such, in their class-consciousness, that the whole meaning of history inheres. *The peasant is historyless.* The village stands outside world-history, and all evolution from the "Trojan" to the Mithridatic War, from the Saxon emperors to the World War of 1914, passes by these little points on the landscape, occa-sionally destroying them and wasting their blood, but never in the least touch-ing their inwardness.

The peasant is the eternal man, independent of every Culture that ensconces itself in the cities. He precedes it, he outlives it, a dumb creature propagating himself from generation to generation, limited to soil-bound callings and aptitudes, a mystical soul, a dry, shrewd understanding that sticks to practical matters, the origin and the ever-flowing source of the blood that makes world-history in the cities.

Whatever the Culture up there in the city conceives in the way of state-forms, economic customs, articles of faith, implements, knowledge, art, he receives mistrustfully and hesitatingly; though in the end he may accept these things, never is he altered in kind thereby. Thus the West-European peasant outwardly took in all the dogmas of the Councils from the great Lateran to that of Trent, just as he took in the products of mechanical engineering and those of the French Revolution — but he remains what he was, what he already was in Charlemagne's day. The present-day piety of the peasant is older than Christianity; his gods are more ancient than those of any higher religion. Remove from him the pressure of the great cities and he will revert to the state of nature without feeling that he is losing anything. His real ethic, his real metaphysic, which no scholar of the city has yet thought it worth while to discover, lie outside all religious and spiritual history, have in fact no history at all.

The city is intellect. The Megalopolis is "free" intellect. It is in resistance to the "feudal" powers of blood and tradition that the burgherdom or bour-geoisie, the intellectual class, begins to be conscious of its own separate exist-ence. It upsets thrones and limits old rights in the name of reason and above all in the name of "the People," which henceforward means exclusively the people of the city. Democracy is the political form in which the townsman's outlook upon the world is demanded of the peasantry also. The urban intellect reforms the great religion of the springtime and sets up by the side of the old religion of noble and priest, the new religion of the Tiers État, *liberal science*. The city assumes the lead and control of economic history in replacing the primitive values of the land, which are for ever inseparable from the life and thought of the rustic, by the *absolute idea of money* as distinct from goods. The immemorial country word for exchange of goods is "barter"; even when one of the things exchanged is precious metal, the underlying idea of the process is not yet *monetary* — i.e., it does not involve the abstraction of value from things and its fixation in metallic or fictitious quantities intended to *measure* things qua "commodities." Caravan expeditions and Viking voyages in the springtime are made between land-settlements and imply barter or booty, whereas in the Late period they are made between cities and mean "money." This is the distinction between the Normans before and the Hansa and Venetians after the Crusades,[1] and between the seafarers of Mycenæan times and those of the later colonization period in Greece. The City means not only intellect, but also money.[2]

Presently there arrived an epoch when the development of the city had reached such a point of power that it had no longer to defend itself against country and chivalry, but on the contrary had become a despotism against which the land and its basic orders of society were fighting a hopeless defensive battle — in the spiritual domain against nationalism, in the political against democracy, in the economic against money. At this period the number of cities that really counted as historically dominant had already become very small. And with this there arose the profound distinction — which was above all a spiritual distinction — between the great city and the little city or town. The latter, very significantly called the country-town, was a part of the no longer co-efficient countryside. It was not that the difference between townsman and rustic had become lessened in such towns, but that this difference had become negligible as compared with the new difference between them and the great city. The sly-shrewdness of the country and the intelligence of the megalopolis are two forms of waking-consciousness between which reciprocal understanding is scarcely possible. Here again it is evident that what counts is not the number of inhabitants, but the spirit. It is evident, moreover, that in all great cities nooks remained in which relics of an almost rural mankind lived in their byeways much as if they were on the land, and the people on the two sides of the street were almost in the relation of two villages. In fact, a

---

[1] In the case of the Venetians the money-outlook was already potent during the earlier Crusades. But the fact that their financial exploitation of the great religious adventure was regarded as scandalous indicates sufficiently that the rural world of the West was not yet face to face with the money-idea. — *Tr.*

[2] See Ch. XIII below.

pyramid of mounting civism, of decreasing number and increasing field of view, leads up from such quasi-rural elements, in ever-narrowing layers, to the small number of genuine megalopolitans at the top, who are at home wherever their spiritual postulates are satisfied.

With this the notion of money attains to full abstractness. It no longer merely *serves* for the understanding of economic intercourse, but *subjects* the exchange of goods to *its own* evolution. It values things, no longer as between each other, but *with reference to itself*. Its relation to the soil and to the man of the soil has so completely vanished, that in the economic thought of the leading cities — the "money-markets" — it is ignored. Money has now become a power, and, moreover, a power that is wholly intellectual and merely figured in the metal it uses, a power the reality of which resides in the waking-consciousness of the upper stratum of an economically active population, a power that makes those concerned with it just as dependent upon itself as the peasant was dependent upon the soil. There is monetary thought, just as there is mathematical or juristic.

But the earth is actual and natural, and money is abstract and artificial, a mere "category" — like "virtue" in the imagination of the Age of Enlightenment. And therefore every primary, pre-civic economy is dependent upon and held in bondage by the cosmic powers, the soil, the climate, the type of man, whereas money, as the pure form of economic intercourse within the waking-consciousness, is no more limited in potential scope by actuality than are the quantities of the mathematical and the logical world. Just as no view of facts hinders us from constructing as many non-Euclidean geometries as we please, so in the developed megalopolitan economics there is no longer any inherent objection to increasing "money" or to thinking, so to say, in other money-dimensions. This has nothing to do with the availability of gold or with any values in actuality at all. There is no standard and no sort of goods in which the value of the talent in the Persian Wars can be compared with its value in the Egyptian booty of Pompey. Money has become, for man as an economic animal, a form of the activity of waking-consciousness, having no longer any roots in Being. This is the basis of its monstrous power over every beginning Civilization, which is always an unconditional *dictatorship of money*, though taking different forms in different Cultures. But this is the reason, too, for the want of solidity, which eventually leads to its losing its power and its meaning, so that at the last, as in Diocletian's time, it disappears from the thought of the closing Civilization, and the primary values of the soil return anew to take its place.

Finally, there arises the monstrous symbol and vessel of the completely emancipated intellect, the world-city, the centre in which the course of a world-history ends by winding itself up. A handful of gigantic places in each Civilization disfranchises and disvalues the entire motherland of its own Culture under the contemptuous name of "the provinces." The "provinces" are now everything whatsoever — land, town, *and* city — except these two or three points. There are no longer noblesse and bourgeoisie, freemen and slaves, Hellenes and Barbarians, believers and unbelievers, *but only cosmopolitans and provincials*. All other contrasts pale before this one, which dominates all events, all habits of life, all views of the world.

The earliest of all world-cities were Babylon and the Thebes of the New Empire — the Minoan world of Crete, for all its splendour, belonged to the Egyptian "provinces." In the Classical the first example is Alexandria, which reduced old Greece at one stroke to the provincial level, and which even Rome, even the resettled Carthage, even Byzantium, could not suppress. In India the giant cities of Ujjaina, Kanauj, and above all Pataliputra were renowned even in China and Java, and everyone knows the fairy-tale reputation of Baghdad and Granada in the West. In the Mexican world, it seems, Uxmal (founded in 950) was the first world-city of the Maya realms, which, however, with the rise of the Toltec world-cities Tezcuco and Tenochtitlan sank to the level of the provinces.

It should not be forgotten that the word "province" first appears as a constitutional designation given by the Romans to Sicily; the subjugation of Sicily, in fact, is the first example of a once pre-eminent Culture-landscape sinking so far as to be purely and simply an object. Syracuse, the first real great-city of the Classical world, had flourished when Rome was still an unimportant country town, but thenceforward, *vis-à-vis* Rome, it becomes a provincial city. In just the same way Habsburg Madrid and Papal Rome, leading cities in the Europe of the seventeenth century, were from the outset of the eighteenth depressed to the provincial level by the world-cities of Paris and London. And the rise of New York to the position of world-city during the Civil War of 1861-5 may perhaps prove to have been the most pregnant event of the nineteenth century.

v

The stone Colossus "Cosmopolis" stands at the end of the life's course of every great Culture. The Culture-man whom the land has spiritually formed is seized and possessed by his own creation, the City, and is made into its creature, its executive organ, and finally its victim. This stony mass is the *absolute* city. Its image, as it appears with all its grandiose beauty in the light-world of the human eye, contains the whole noble death-symbolism of the definitive thing-become. The spirit-pervaded stone of Gothic buildings, after a millennium of style-evolution, has become the soulless material of this dæmonic stone-desert.

These final cities are *wholly* intellect. Their houses are no longer, as those of the Ionic and the Baroque were, derivatives of the old peasant's house, whence the Culture took its spring into history. They are, generally speaking, no longer houses in which Vesta and Janus, Lares and Penates, have any sort of footing, but mere premises which have been fashioned, not by blood but by requirements, not by feeling but by the spirit of commercial enterprise. So long as the hearth has a pious meaning as the actual and genuine centre of a family, the old relation to the land is not wholly extinct. But when *that*, too, follows the rest into oblivion, and the mass of tenants and bed-occupiers in the sea of houses leads a vagrant existence from shelter to shelter like the hunters and pastors of the "pre-" time, then the intellectual nomad is completely developed. This city is a world, is *the* world. Only as a whole, as a human dwelling-place, has it meaning, the houses being merely the stones of which it is assembled.

Now the old mature cities with their Gothic nucleus of cathedral, town-halls, and high-gabled streets, with their old walls, towers, and gates, ringed about by the Baroque growth of brighter and more elegant patricians' houses, palaces, and hall-churches, begin to overflow in all directions in formless masses, to eat into the decaying country-side with their multiplied barrack-tenements and utility buildings, and to destroy the noble aspect of the old time by clearances and rebuildings. Looking down from one of the old towers upon the sea of houses, we perceive in this petrification of a historic being the exact epoch that marks the end of organic growth and the beginning of an inorganic and therefore unrestrained process of massing without limit. And now, too, appears that artificial, mathematical, utterly land-alien product of a pure intellectual satisfaction in the appropriate, the city of the city-architect. In all Civilizations alike, these cities aim at the chessboard form, which is the symbol of soullessness. Regular rectangle-blocks astounded Herodotus in Babylon and Cortez in Tenochtitlan. In the Classical world the series of "abstract" cities begins with Thurii, which was "planned" by Hippodamus of Miletus in 441. Priene, whose chessboard scheme entirely ignores the ups and downs of the site, Rhodes, and Alexandria follow, and become in turn models for innumerable provincial cities of the Imperial Age. The Islamic architects laid out Baghdad from 762, and the giant city of Samarra a century later, according to plan.[1]   In the West-European and American world the lay-out of Washington in 1791 is the first big example.[2] There can be no doubt

[1] Samarra exhibits, like the Imperial Fora of Rome and the ruins of Luxor, truly American proportions. The city stretches for 33 km. [20 miles] along the Tigris. The Balkuwara Palace, which the Caliph Mutawakil built for one of his sons, forms a square of 1250 m. [say, three-quarters of a mile] on each side. One of the giant mosques measures in plan 260 × 180 m. [858 × 594 ft.]. Schwarz, *Die Abbasidenresidenz Samarra* (1910); Herzfeld, *Ausgrabungen von Samarra* (1912). Pataliputra, in the days of Chandragupta and Asoka, measured *intra muros* 10 miles × 2 miles (equal to Manhattan Island or London along the Thames from Greenwich to Richmond. — Tr.

[2] Karlsruhe, with its fan-scheme, and Mannheim, with its rectangles, are earlier than Washington. But both are small places. The one is a sort of extension of the prince's Rococo park and centred on his *point de vue;* the other, though its block-numbering, unique in Europe, seems to

that the world-cities of the Han period in China and the Maurya dynasty in India possessed this same geometrical pattern. Even now the world-cities of the Western Civilization are far from having reached the peak of their development. I see, long after A.D. 2000, cities laid out for ten to twenty million inhabitants, spread over enormous areas of country-side, with buildings that will dwarf the biggest of to-day's and notions of traffic and communication that we should regard as fantastic to the point of madness.[1]

Even in this final shape of his being, the Classical man's form-ideal remains the corporeal point. Whereas the giant cities of our present confess our ir-resistible tendency towards the infinite — our suburbs and garden cities, invading the wide country-side, our vast and comprehensive network of roads, and within the thickly built areas a controlled fast traffic on, below, and above straight, broad streets — the genuine Classical world-city ever strove, not to expand, but to thicken — the streets narrow and cramped, impossible for fast traffic (although this was fully developed on the great Roman roads), entire unwillingness to live in suburbs or even to make suburbs possible.[2] Even at that stage the city must needs be a body, thick and round, $\sigma\hat{\omega}\mu\alpha$ in the strictest sense. The synœcism that in the early Classical had gradually drawn the land-folk into the cities, and so created the type of the Polis, repeated itself at the last in absurd form; everyone wanted to live in the middle of the city, in its densest nucleus, for otherwise he could not feel himself to be the urban man that he was. All these cities are only *cités*, inner towns. The new synœcism formed, instead of suburban zones, *the world of the upper floors*. In the year 74 Rome, in spite of its immense population, had the ridiculously small perimeter of nineteen and a half kilometres [twelve miles].[3] Consequently these city-bodies extended in general not in breadth, but more and more upward. The block-tenements of Rome such as the famous Insula Feliculæ, rose, with a street breadth of only three to five metres [ten to seventeen feet][4] to heights that have never been seen in Western Europe and are

---

relate it to the American city, was really planned as a self-contained military capital, rectangular only within its oval enceinte, whereas the American rectangles are meant to be added to. The lay-out of Petersburg by Peter the Great (which has been adhered to to this day and is still incompletely filled in in detail) is a much more forcible example of the arbitrary planning of a megalopolis. Though outside the "European" world, it is of it, for it was the visible symbol of Peter's will to force Europe upon Russia. It is contemporary with Mannheim and Karlsruhe (early eighteenth century), but its creator conceived of it as a city *of the future*. — *Tr.*

[1] In the case of Canada, not merely great regions, but the *whole country* has been picketed out in equal rectangles for future development. — *Tr.*

[2] It has been left to the *Western* Civilization of present-day Rome to build the garden suburbs that the Classical Civilization could have built. — *Tr.*

[3] Friedländer, *Sittengeschichte Roms*, I, p. 5. Compare this with Samarra, which had nothing like this population. The "Late Classical city on Arabian soil was un-Classical in this respect as in others. The garden suburb of Antioch was renowned throughout the East."

[4] The city which the Egyptian "Julian the Apostate," Amenophis IV (Akhenaton) built himself in Tell-el-Amarna had streets up to 45 m. [149 ft.] wide.

seen in only a few cities in America. Near the Capitol, the roofs already reached to the level of the hill-saddle.[1] But always the splendid mass-cities harbour lamentable poverty and degraded habits, and the attics and mansards, the cellars and back courts are breeding a new type of raw man — in Baghdad and in Babylon, just as in Tenochtitlan and to-day in London and Berlin. Diodorus tells of a deposed Egyptian king who was reduced to living in one of these wretched upper-floor tenements of Rome.

But no wretchedness, no compulsion, not even a clear vision of the madness of this development, avails to neutralize the attractive force of these dæmonic creations. The wheel of Destiny rolls on to its end; the birth of the City entails its death. Beginning and end, a peasant cottage and a tenement-block are related to one another as soul and intellect, as blood and stone. But "Time" is no abstract phrase, but a name for the actuality of Irreversibility. Here there is only forward, never back. Long, long ago the country bore the country-town and nourished it with her best blood. Now the giant city sucks the country dry, insatiably and incessantly demanding and devouring fresh streams of men, till it wearies and dies in the midst of an almost uninhabited waste of country. Once the full sinful beauty of this last marvel of all history has captured a victim, it never lets him go. Primitive folk can loose themselves from the soil and wander, but the intellectual nomad never. Homesickness for the great city is keener than any other nostalgia. Home is for him any one of these giant cities, but even the nearest village is alien territory. He would sooner die upon the pavement than go "back" to the land. Even disgust at this pretentiousness, weariness of the thousand-hued glitter, the *tædium vitæ* that in the end overcomes many, does not set them free. They take the City with them into the mountains or on the sea. They have lost the country within themselves and will never regain it outside.

What makes the man of the world-cities incapable of living on any but this artificial footing is that the cosmic beat in his being is ever decreasing, while the tensions of his waking-consciousness become more and more dangerous. It must be remembered that in a microcosm the animal, waking side supervenes upon the vegetable side, that of being, and not vice versa. Beat and tension, blood and intellect, Destiny and Causality are to one another as the country-side in bloom is to the city of stone, as something existing *per se* to something existing dependently. Tension without cosmic pulsation to animate it is the transition to nothingness. But Civilization is nothing but tension. The head, in all the outstanding men of the Civilizations, is dominated exclusively by an expression of extreme tension. Intelligence is only the capacity for understanding at high tension, and in every Culture these heads are the types of its final men — one has only to compare them with the peasant heads, when such happen to emerge in the swirl of the great city's street-

[1] Pöhlmann, *Aus Altertum und Gegenwart* (1910), pp. 211, et seq.

life. The advance, too, from peasant wisdom — "slimness," mother wit, instinct, based as in other animals upon the sensed beat of life — through the city-spirit to the cosmopolitan intelligence — the very word with its sharp ring betraying the disappearance of the old cosmic foundation — can be described as a steady diminution of the Destiny-feeling and an unrestrained augmentation of needs according to the operation of a Causality. Intelligence is the replacement of unconscious living by exercise in thought, masterly, but bloodless and jejune. The intelligent visage is similar in all races — what is recessive in them is, precisely, race. The weaker the feeling for the necessity and self-evidence of Being, the more the habit of "elucidation" grows, the more the fear in the waking-consciousness comes to be stilled by causal methods. Hence the assimilation of knowledge with demonstrability, and the substitution of scientific theory, the causal myth, for the religious. Hence, too, money-in-the-abstract as the pure causality of economic life, in contrast to rustic barter, which is pulsation and not a system of tensions.

Tension, when it has become intellectual, knows no form of recreation but that which is specific to the world-city — namely, *détente*, relaxation, distraction. Genuine play, *joie de vivre*, pleasure, inebriation, are products of the cosmic beat and as such no longer comprehensible in their essence. But the relief of hard, intensive brain-work by its opposite — conscious and practised fooling — of intellectual tension by the bodily tension of sport, of bodily tension by the sensual straining after "pleasure" and the spiritual straining after the "excitements" of betting and competitions, of the pure logic of the day's work by a consciously enjoyed mysticism — all this is common to the world-cities of all the Civilizations. Cinema, Expressionism, Theosophy, boxing contests, nigger dances, poker, and racing — one can find it all in Rome. Indeed, the connoisseur might extend his researches to the Indian, Chinese, and Arabian world-cities as well. To name but one example, if one reads the Kama-sutram one understands how it was that Buddhism *also* appealed to men's tastes, and then the bullfighting scenes in the Palace of Cnossus will be looked at with quite different eyes. A cult, no doubt, underlay them, but there was a savour over it all, as over Rome's fashionable Isis-cult in the neighbourhood of the Circus Maximus.

And then, when Being is sufficiently uprooted and Waking-Being sufficiently strained, there suddenly emerges into the bright light of history a phenomenon that has long been preparing itself underground and now steps forward to make an end of the drama — the *sterility of civilized man*. This is not something that can be grasped as a plain matter of Causality (as modern science naturally enough has tried to grasp it); it is to be understood as an essentially *metaphysical* turn towards death. The last man of the world-city no longer *wants* to live — he may cling to life as an individual, but as a type, as an aggregate, no, for it is a characteristic of this collective existence that it eliminates the terror of death. That which strikes the true peasant with a deep and inexplicable fear, the notion that the family and the name may be extinguished, has now lost its meaning. The continuance of the blood-relation in the visible world is no longer a duty of the blood, and the destiny of being the last of the line is no longer felt as a doom. Children do not happen, not because children have become impossible, but principally because intelligence at the peak of intensity can no longer find any reason for their existence. Let the reader try to merge himself in the soul of the peasant. He has sat on his glebe from primeval times,[1] or has fastened his clutch in it, to adhere to it with his blood. He is rooted in it as the descendant of his forbears and as the forbear of future descendants. *His* house, *his* property, means, here, not the temporary connexion of person and thing for a brief span of years, but an enduring and inward union of *eternal* land and *eternal* blood. It is only from this mystical conviction of settlement that the great epochs of the cycle — procreation, birth, and death — derive that metaphysical element of wonder which condenses in the symbolism of custom and religion that all landbound people possess. For the "last men" all this is past and gone. Intelligence and sterility are allied in old families, old peoples, and old Cultures, not merely because in each microcosm the overstrained and fettered animal-element is eating up the plant element, but also because the waking-consciousness assumes that being is normally regulated by causality. That which the man of intelligence, most significantly and characteristically, labels as "natural impulse" or "life-force," he not only knows, but also values, causally, giving it the place amongst his other needs that his judgment assigns to it. When the ordinary thought of a highly cultivated people begins to regard "having children" as a question of *pro's* and *con's*, the great turning-point has come. For Nature knows nothing of *pro* and *con*. Everywhere, wherever life is actual, reigns an inward organic logic, an "it," a drive, that is utterly independent of waking-being, with its causal linkages, and indeed not even observed by it. The abundant proliferation of primitive peoples is a *natural phenomenon*, which is not even thought about, still less judged as to its utility or the reverse. When reasons have to be put forward at all in a question of life, life itself has become questionable. At that point begins prudent limitation of the number of births. In the Classical world the practice was deplored by Polybius as the ruin of Greece, and yet even at his date it had long been established in the great cities; in subsequent Roman times it became appallingly general. At first explained by the economic misery of the times, very soon it ceased to explain itself at all. And at that point, too, in Buddhist India as in Babylon, in Rome as in our own cities, a man's choice of the woman who is to be, not mother of his children as amongst peasants and primitives, but

---

[1] Some years ago a French peasant was brought to notice whose family had occupied its glebe since the ninth century. — *Tr.*

his own "companion for life," becomes a problem of mentalities. The Ibsen marriage appears, the "higher spiritual affinity" in which both parties are "free" — free, that is, as intelligences, free from the plantlike urge of the blood to continue itself, and it becomes possible for a Shaw to say "that unless Woman repudiates her womanliness, her duty to her husband, to her children, to society, to the law, and to everyone but herself, she cannot emancipate herself." [1] The primary woman, the peasant woman, is *mother*. The whole vocation towards which she has yearned from childhood is included in that one word. But now emerges the Ibsen woman, the comrade, the heroine of a whole megalopolitan literature from Northern drama to Parisian novel. Instead of children, she has soul-conflicts; marriage is a craft-art for the achievement of "mutual understanding." It is all the same whether the case against children is the American lady's who would not miss a season for anything, or the Parisienne's who fears that her lover would leave her, or an Ibsen heroine's who "belongs to herself" — they all belong to themselves and they are all unfruitful. The same fact, in conjunction with the same arguments, is to be found in the Alexandrian, in the Roman, and, as a matter of course, in every other civilized society — and conspicuously in that in which Buddha grew up. And in Hellenism and in the nineteenth century, as in the times of Lao-Tzu and the Charvaka doctrine,[2] there is an ethic for childless intelligences, and a literature about the inner conflicts of Nora and Nana. The "quiverful," which was still an honourable enough spectacle in the days of Werther, becomes something rather provincial. The father of many children is for the great city a subject for caricature; Ibsen did not fail to note it, and presented it in his *Love's Comedy*.

At this level all Civilizations enter upon a stage, which lasts for centuries, of appalling depopulation. The whole pyramid of cultural man vanishes. It crumbles from the summit, first the world-cities, then the provincial forms, and finally the land itself, whose best blood has incontinently poured into the towns, merely to bolster them up awhile. At the last, only the primitive blood remains, alive, but robbed of its strongest and most promising elements. This residue is the *Fellah type*.

If anything has demonstrated the fact that Causality has nothing to do with history, it is the familiar "decline" of the Classical, which accomplished itself long before the irruption of Germanic migrants.[3] The Imperium enjoyed the completest peace; it was rich and highly developed; it was well organized; and it possessed in its emperors from Nerva to Marcus Aurelius a series of rulers such as the Cæsarism of no other Civilization can show. And yet the population dwindled, quickly and wholesale. The desperate marriage-and-children

[1] Shaw, *The Quintessence of Ibsen*.
[2] An ancient Hindu materialism. — *Tr.*
[3] For what follows see Eduard Meyer, *Kl. Schriften* (1910), pp. 145, et seq.

laws of Augustus — amongst them the *Lex de maritandis ordinibus*, which dismayed Roman society more than the destruction of Varus's legions — the wholesale adoptions, the incessant plantation of soldiers of barbarian origin to fill the depleted country-side, the immense food-charities of Nerva and Trajan for the children of poor parents — nothing availed to check the process. Italy, then North Africa and Gaul, and finally Spain, which under the early Cæsars had been one of the most densely populated parts of the Empire, become empty and desolate. The famous saying of Pliny — so often and so significantly quoted to-day in connexion with national economics — "*Latifundia perdidere Italiam, jam, vero et provincias,*"[1] inverts the order of the process; the large estates would never have got to this point if the peasantry had not already been sucked into the towns and, if not openly, at any rate inwardly, surrendered their soil. The terrible truth came out at last in the edict of Pertinax, A.D. 193, by which anyone in Italy or the provinces was permitted to take possession of untended land, and if he brought it under cultivation, to hold it as his legal property. The historical student has only to turn his attention seriously to other Civilizations to find the same phenomenon everywhere. Depopulation can be distinctly traced in the background of the Egyptian New Empire, especially from the XIX dynasty onwards. Street widths like those to Amenophis IV at Tell-el-Amarna — of fifty yards — would have been unthinkable with the denser population of the old days. The onset of the "Sea-peoples," too, was only barely repulsed — their chances of obtaining possession of the realm were certainly not less promising than those of the Germans of the fourth century *vis-à-vis* the Roman world. And finally the incessant infiltration of Libyans into the Delta culminated when one of their leaders seized the power, in 945 B.C. — precisely as Odoacer seized it in A.D. 476. But the same tendency can be felt in the history of political Buddhism after the Cæsar Asoka.[2] If the Maya population literally vanished within a very short time after the Spanish conquest, and their great empty cities were reabsorbed by the jungle, this does not prove merely the brutality of the conqueror — which in this regard would have been helpless before the self-renewing power of a young and fruitful Culture-mankind — but an extinction from within that no doubt had long been in progress. And if we turn to our own civilization, we find that the old families of the French noblesse were not, in the great majority of cases, eradicated in the Revolution, but have died out since 1815, and their sterility has spread to the bourgeoisie and, since 1870, to the peasantry which that very Revolution almost re-created. In England, and still more in the United States — particularly in the east, the very states where the stock is best and oldest — the process of "race suicide" denounced by Roosevelt set in long ago on the largest scale.

[1] *Hist. Nat.*, XVIII, 7. — Tr.

[2] We know of measures to promote increase of population in China in the third century B.C., precisely the Augustan Age of Chinese evolution. See Rosthorn, *Das soziale Leben der Chinesen* (1919), p. 6.

Consequently we find everywhere in these Civilizations that the provincial cities at an early stage, and the giant cities in turn at the end of the evolution, stand empty, harbouring in their stone masses a small population of fellaheen who shelter in them as the men of the Stone Age sheltered in caves and pile-dwellings.[1] Samarra was abandoned by the tenth century; Pataliputra, Asoka's capital, was an immense and completely uninhabited waste of houses when the Chinese traveller Hsinan-tang visited it about A.D. 635, and many of the great Maya cities must have been in that condition even in Cortez's time. In a long series of Classical writers from Polybius onward [2] we read of old, renowned cities in which the streets have become lines of empty, crumbling shells, where the cattle browse in forum and gymnasium, and the amphitheatre is a sown field,[3] dotted with emergent statues and herms. Rome had in the fifth century of our era the population of a village, but its Imperial palaces were still habitable.

This, then, is the conclusion of the city's history; growing from primitive barter-centre to Culture-city and at last to world-city, it sacrifices first the blood and soul of its creators to the needs of its majestic evolution, and then the last flower of that growth to the spirit of Civilization — and so, doomed, moves on to final self-destruction.

VI

If the Early period is characterized by the birth of the City out of the country, and the Late by the battle between city and country, the period of Civilization is that of the victory of city over country, whereby it frees itself from the grip of the ground, but to its own ultimate ruin. Rootless, dead to the cosmic, irrevocably committed to stone and to intellectualism, it develops a form-language that reproduces every trait of its essence — not the language of a becoming and growth, but that of a becomeness and completion, capable of alteration certainly, but not of evolution. Not now Destiny, but Causality, not now living Direction, but Extension, rules. It follows from this that whereas every form-language of a Culture, together with the history of its evolution, adheres to the original spot, civilized forms are at home anywhere and capable, therefore, of unlimited extension as soon as they appear. It is quite true that the Hanse Towns in their north-Russian staples built Gothically, and the Spaniards in South America in the Baroque style, but that even the smallest chapter of Gothic style-*history* should *evolve* outside the limits of

---

[1] The *amphitheatres* of Nîmes and Arles were filled up by mean townlets that used the outer wall as their fortifications. — *Tr.*

[2] Strabo, Pausanias, Dio Chrysostom, Avienus, etc. See E. Meyer, *Kl. Schriften*, pp. 164, et seq.

[3] The Colosseum of Rome itself in due course fell into this decay and we read in the guide-books that "its flora were once famous " — 420 wild species lived in its ruins. If this could happen in Rome, we need not be surprised at the quick, almost catastrophic, conquest of the Maya cities by tropical vegetation. — *Tr.*

West Europe was impossible, as impossible as that Attic or English drama, or the art of fugue, or the Lutheran or the Orphic religion should be propagated, or even inwardly assimilated, by men of alien Cultures. But the essence of Alexandrinism and of our Romanticism is something which belongs to all urban men without distinction. Romanticism marks the beginning of that which Goethe, with his wide vision, called world-literature — the literature of the leading world-*city*, against which a provincial literature, native to the soil but negligible, struggles everywhere with difficulty to maintain itself. The state of Venice, or that of Frederick the Great, or the English Parliament (as an effective reality), cannot be reproduced, but "modern constitutions" can be "introduced" into any African or Asiatic state as Classical Poleis could be set up amongst Numidians and ancient Britons. In Egypt the writing that came into common use was not the hieroglyphic, but the letter-script, which was without doubt a technical discovery of the Civilization Age.[1] And so in general — it is not true Culture-languages like the Greek of Sophocles or the German of Luther, but world-languages like the Greek Koine and Arabic and Babylonian and English, the outcome of daily practical usage in a world-city, which are capable of being acquired by anybody and everybody. Consequently, in all Civilizations the "modern" cities assume a more and more uniform type. Go where we may, there are Berlin, London, and New York for us, just as the Roman traveller would find his columnar architecture, his fora with their statuary, and his temples in Palmyra or Trier or Timgad or the Hellenistic cities that extended out to the Indus and the Aral. But that which was thus disseminated was no longer a style, but a taste, not genuine custom but mannerism, not national costume but the fashion. This, of course, makes it possible for remote peoples not only to accept the "permanent" gains of a Civilization, but even to re-radiate them in an independent form. Such regions of "moonlight" civilization are south China and especially Japan (which were first Sinized at the close of the Han period, about A.D. 220); Java as a relay of the Brahman Civilization; and Carthage, which obtained its forms from Babylon.

All these are forms of a waking-consciousness now acute to excess, mitigated or limited by no cosmic force, purely intellectual and extensive, but on that very account capable of so powerful an output that their last flickering rays reach out and superpose effects over almost the whole earth. Fragments of the forms of Chinese Civilization are probably to be found in Scandinavian wood-architecture, Babylonian measures probably in the South Seas, Classical coins in South Africa, Egyptian and Indian influences probably in the land of the Incas.

But while this process of extension was overpassing all frontiers, the

---

[1] According to the researches of K. Sethe. Cf. Robert Eisler, *Die kenitischen Weihinschriften der Hyksoszeit*, etc. (1919).

development of inner form of the Civilization was fulfilling itself with impressive consistency. Three stages are clearly to be distinguished — the release from the Culture, the production of the thoroughbred Civilization-form, and the final hardening. For us this development has now set in, and, as I see it, it is Germany that is destined, as the last nation of the West, to crown the mighty edifice. In this stage all questions of the life — the Apollinian, Magian, or Faustian life — have been thought upon to the limit, and brought to a final clear condition of knowledge and not-knowledge. For or about ideas men fight no more. The last idea — that of the Civilization itself — is formulated in outline, and technics and economics are, as *problems*, enunciated and prepared for handling. But this is only the beginning of a vast task; the postulates have to be unfolded and these forms applied to the whole existence of the earth. Only when this has been accomplished and the Civilization has become definitely established not only in shape, but in mass, does the hardening of the form set in. Style, in the Cultures, has been the *rhythm of the process of self-implementing*. But the Civilized style (if we may use the word at all) arises as the *expression of the state of completeness*. It attains — in Egypt and China especially — to a splendid perfection, and imparts this perfection to all the utterances of a life that is now inwardly unalterable, to its ceremonial and mien as to the superfine and studied forms of its art-practice. Of history, in the sense of an urge towards a form-ideal, there can now be no question, but there is an unfailing and easy superficial adaptiveness which again and again manages to coax fresh little art-problems and solutions out of the now basically stable language. Of this kind is the whole "history" of Chinese-Japanese painting (as we know it) and of Indian architecture. And just as the real history of the Gothic style differs from this pseudo-history, so the Knight of the Crusades differs from the Chinese Mandarin — *the becoming state from the finished*. The one *is* history; the other has long ago overcome history. "Long ago," I say; for the history of these Civilizations is merely apparent, like their great cities, which constantly change in face, but never become other than what they are. In these cities there is no Soul. They are land in petrified form.

What is it that perishes here? And what that survives? It is a mere incident that German peoples, under pressure from the Huns, take possession of the Roman landscape and so prevent the Classical from prolonging itself in a "Chinese" end-state. The movement of the "Sea-peoples" (similar to the Germanic, even down to the details) which set in against the Egyptian Civilization from 1400 B.C. succeeded only as regards the Cretan island-realm — their mighty expeditions against the Libyan and Phœnician coasts, with the accompaniment of Viking fleets, failed, as those of the Huns failed against China. And thus the Classical is our one example of a Civilization broken off in the moment of full splendour. Yet the Germans only destroyed the upper layer of the forms and replaced it by the life of their own pre-Culture. The "eternal" layer was never reached. It remains, hidden and completely shrouded by a new form-language, in the underground of the whole following history, and to this day in southern France, southern Italy, and northern Spain tangible relics of it endure. In these countries the popular Catholicism is tinged from beneath with a Late Classical colouring, that sets it off quite distinctly from the Church Catholicism of the West-European layer above it. South Italian Church-festivals disclose Classical (and even pre-Classical) cults, and generally in this field there are to be found deities (saints) in whose worship the Classical constitution is visible behind the Catholic names.

Here, however, another element comes into the picture, an element with a significance of its own. We stand before the problem of Race.

CHAPTER V

CITIES AND PEOPLES

(B)

PEOPLES, RACES, TONGUES

CITIES AND PEOPLES

(B)

PEOPLES, RACES, TONGUES

I

THROUGHOUT the nineteenth century the scientific picture of history was vitiated by a notion that was either derived from, or at any rate brought to a point by, Romanticism — the idea of the "People" in the moral-enthusiastic sense of the word. If, here and there, in earlier time a new religion, a new ornamentation, a new architecture, or a new script appeared, the question that it raised presented itself to the investigator thus — What was the name of the *people* who produced the phenomenon? This enunciation of the problem is peculiar to the Western spirit and the present-day cast of that spirit; but it is so false at every point that the picture that it evokes of the course of events must necessarily be erroneous. "The people" as the absolute basic form in which men are historically effective, the original home, the original settlement, the migrations of "the" peoples — all this is a reflection of the vibrant idea expressed in the "*Nation*" of 1789, of the "*Volk*" of 1813, both of which, in last analysis, are derived from the self-assuredness of England and Puritanism. But the very intensity of passion that the idea contains has protected it only too well from criticism. Even acute investigators have unwittingly made it cover a multitude of utterly dissimilar things, with the result that "peoples" have developed into definite and supposedly well-understood unit-quantities by which all history is *made*. For us, to-day, world-history means — what it cannot be asserted to mean self-evidently, or to mean for, e.g., the Greeks and the Chinese — the history of Peoples. Everything else, Culture, speech, wit, religion, is created by the peoples. The State is the form of a people.

The purpose of this chapter is to demolish this romantic conception. What has inhabited the earth since the Ice Age is man, not "peoples." In the first instance, their Destiny is determined by the fact that the bodily succession of parents and children, the bond of the blood, forms natural groups, which disclose a definite tendency to take root in a landscape. Even nomadic tribes confine their movements within a limited field. Thereby the cosmic-plantlike side of life, of Being, is invested with a character of duration. This I call *race*. Tribes, septs, clans, families — all these are designations for the fact of a blood which circles, carried on by procreation, in a narrow or a wide landscape.

But these human beings possess also the microcosmic-animal side of life, in waking-consciousness and receptivity and reason. And the form in which the waking-consciousness of one man gets into relation with that of another I call *language*, which begins by being a mere unconscious living expression that is received as a sensation, but gradually develops into a conscious *technique of communication* that depends upon a common sense of the meanings attaching to signs.

In the limit, every race is a single great body, and every language [1] the efficient form of *one* great waking-consciousness that connects many individual beings. And we shall never reach the ultimate discoveries about either unless they are treated together and constantly brought into comparison with one another.

But, further, we shall never understand man's higher history if we ignore the fact that man, as constituent of a race and as possessor of a language, as derivative of a blood-unit and as member of an understanding-unit, has different Destinies, that of his being and that of his waking-being. That is, the origin, development, and duration of his race side and the origin, development, and duration of his language side are *completely independent of one another*. Race is *something cosmic and psychic (Seelenhaft)*, periodic in some obscure way, and in its inner nature partly conditioned by major astronomical relations.

Languages, on the other hand, are causal forms, and operate through the polarity of their means. We speak of race-instincts and of the spirit of a language. But they are two distinct *worlds*. To Race belong the deepest meanings of the words "time" and "yearning"; to language those of the words "space" and "fear." But all this has been hidden from us, hitherto, by the overlying idea of "peoples."

There are, then, *currents of being* and *linkages of waking-being*. The former have physiognomy, the latter are based on system. Race, as seen in the picture of the world-around, is the aggregate of all bodily characters so far as these exist for the sense-perceptions of conscious creatures. Here we have to remember that a body develops and fulfils from childhood to old age the specific inner form that was assigned to it at the moment of its conception, while at the same time that which the body is (considered apart from its form) is perpetually being renewed. Consequently nothing of the body actually remains in the man except the living meaning of his existence, and of this all that we know is so much as presents itself in the world of waking-consciousness. Man of the higher sort is limited, as to the impression of race that he can receive, almost wholly to what appears in the light-world of his eye, so that for him race is essentially a sum of *visible* characters. But even for him there are not

---

[1] Henceforward, and indeed throughout this work, the word "language" is not to be regarded as limited to spoken and written language. As the above definition indicates, it includes all modes of intelligible conscious-expression — " affective language " in the widest sense. — *Tr.*

inconsiderable relics of the power to observe non-optical characters such as smell, the cries of animals, and, above all, the modalities of human speech. In the other higher animals, on the contrary, the capacity to receive the impression of race is decidedly *not* dominated by sight. Scent is stronger, and, besides, the animals have modes of sensation that entirely elude human understanding. It is, however, only men and animals that can *receive the impression of race*, and not the plants, and yet these too *have* race, as every nurseryman knows. It is, to me, a sight of deep pathos to see how the spring flowers, craving to fertilize and be fertilized, cannot for all their bright splendour attract one another, or even see one another, but must have recourse to animals, for whom alone these colours and these scents exist.

"Language" I call the entire free activity of the waking microcosm in so far as it brings something to expression *for others*. Plants have no waking-being, no capacity of being moved, and therefore no language. The waking-consciousness of animal existences, on the contrary, is through and through a speaking, whether individual acts are intended to tell or not, and even if the conscious or the unconscious purpose of the doing lies in a quite other direction. A peacock is indubitably speaking when he spreads his tail, but a kitten playing with a cotton-reel also speaks to us, unconsciously, through the quaint charm of its movements. Everyone knows the difference there is in one's movements according as one is conscious or unconscious of being observed; one suddenly begins to speak, consciously, in all one's actions.

This, however, leads at once to the very significant distinction between two genera of language — the language which is only an *expression for the world*, an inward necessity springing from the longing inherent in all life to actualize itself before witnesses, to display its own presence to itself, and the language that is meant to be *understood by definite beings*. There are, therefore, *expression-languages* and *communication-languages*. The former assume only a state of waking-being, the latter a connexion of waking-beings. To understand means to respond to the stimulus of a signal with one's own feeling of its significance. To understand one another, to hold "conversation," to speak to a "thou," supposes, therefore, a sense of meanings in the other that corresponds to that in oneself. Expression-language before witnesses merely proves the presence of an "I," but communication-language postulates a "thou." The "I" is that which speaks, and the "thou" that which is meant to understand the speech of the "I." For primitives a tree, a stone, or a cloud can be a "thou." Every deity is a "thou." In fairy-tales there is nothing that cannot hold converse with men, and we need only look at our own selves in moments of furious irritation or of poetic excitement to realize that anything can become a "thou" for us even to-day. And it is by some "thou" that we first came to the knowledge of an "I." "I," therefore, is a designation for the fact that a bridge exists to some other being.

It is impossible, however, to delimit an exact frontier between religious and artistic expression-languages and pure communication-languages. This is true also (and indeed specially) of the higher Cultures with the separate development of their form-domains. For, on the one hand, no one can speak without putting into his mode of speech some significant trait of emphasis that has nothing to do with the needs of communication as such; and, on the other hand, we all know the drama in which the poet wants to "say" something that he could have said equally well or better in an exhortation, and the painting whose contents are meant to instruct, warn, or improve — the picture-series in any Greek Orthodox church, which conforms to a strict canon and has the avowed purpose of making the truths of religion clear to a beholder to whom the book says nothing; or Hogarth's substitute for sermons; or, for that matter, even prayer, the direct address to God, which also can be replaced by the performance before one's eyes of cult-ritual that speaks to one intelligibly. The theoretical controversy concerning the purpose of art rests upon the postulate that an artistic expression-language should in no wise be a communication-language, and the phenomenon of priesthood is based upon the persuasion that the priest alone knows the language in which man can communicate with God.

All currents of Being bear a historical, and all linkages of Waking-Being a religious, stamp. What we know to be inherent in every genuine religious or artistic form-language, and particularly in the history of every script (for writing is verbal language for the eye), holds good without doubt for the origin of human articulate speech in general — indeed the prime words (of the structure of which we now know nothing whatever) must also certainly have had a cult-colouring. But there is a corresponding linkage on the other side between Race and everything that we call life (as struggle for power), History (as Destiny), or, to-day, politics. It is perhaps too fantastic to argue something of political instinct in the search of a climbing plant for points of attachment that shall enable it to encircle, overpower, and choke the tree in order finally to rear itself high in the air above the tree-top — or something of religious world-feeling in the song of the mounting lark. But it is certain that from such things as these the utterances of being and of waking-being, of pulse and tension, form an uninterrupted series up to the perfected political and religious forms of every modern Civilization.

And here at last is the key to those two strange words which were discovered by the ethnologists in two entirely different parts of the world in rather limited applications, but have since been quietly moving up into the foreground of research — "*totem*" and "*taboo*." The more enigmatic and indefinable these words became, the more it was felt that in them we were touching upon an ultimate life-basis which was not that of merely primitive man. And now, as the result of the above inquiry, we have clear meanings for both before us.

Totem and Taboo describe the ultimate meanings of Being and Waking-Being, Destiny and Causality, Race and Language, Time and Space, yearning and fear, pulse and tension, politics and religion. The Totem side of life is plant-like and inheres in all being, while the Taboo side is animal and presupposes the free movement of a being in a world. Our Totem organs are those of the blood-circulation and of reproduction, our Taboo organs those of the senses and the nerves. All that is of Totem has physiognomy, all that is of Taboo has system. In the Totemistic resides the common feeling of beings that belong to the same stream of existence. It cannot be acquired and cannot be got rid of; it is a fact, *the* fact of all facts. That which is of Taboo, on the other hand, is the characteristic of linkages of waking-consciousness, it is learnable and acquirable, and on that very account guarded as a secret by cult-communities, philosophers' schools, and artists' guilds — each of which possesses a sort of cryptic language of its own.[1]

But Being can be thought of without waking-consciousness, whereas the reverse is not the case — i.e., there are race-beings without language, but no languages without race. All that is of race, therefore, possesses its proper expression, independent of any kind of waking-consciousness and common to plant and animal. This expression — not to be confounded with the ex-pression-*language* which consists in an *active alteration* of the expression — is not meant for witnesses, but is simply there; it is physiognomy. Not that it stops at the plant; in every living language, too (and how significant the word "living"!) we can detect, besides the Taboo side that is learnable, an entirely untransferable quality of race that the old vessels of the language cannot pass on to alien successors; it lies in melody, rhythm, stress; in colour, ring, and tempo of the expression; in idiom, in accompanying gesture. On this account it is necessary to distinguish between language and speaking, the first being in itself a dead stock of signs, and the second the activity that operates with the signs.[2] When we cease to be able to hear and see directly how a language is spoken, thenceforward it is only its ossature and not its flesh that we can know. This is so with Sumerian, Gothic, Sanskrit, and all other languages that we have merely deciphered from texts and inscriptions, and we are right in calling these languages dead, for the human communities that were formed by them have vanished. We know the Egyptian tongue, but not the tongues of the Egyptians. Of Augustan Latin we know approximately the sound-values of the letters and the meaning of the words, but we do not know how the oration

---

[1] Obviously, Totemistic facts, so far as they come under the observation of the waking-consciousness, obtain a significance of the Taboo kind also; much in man's sexual life, for example, is performed with a profound sense of fear, because his will-to-understand is baffled by it.

[2] W. von Humboldt (*Über die Verschiedenheit des menschlichen Sprachbaues*) was the first to empha-size the fact that a language is not a thing, but an activity. "If we would be quite precise, we can certainly say *there is no such thing as ' language*,' just as there is no such thing as ' intellect'; but man does speak, and does act intellectually."

of Cicero sounded from the rostra and still less how Hesiod and Sappho spoke their verses, or what a conversation in the Athenian market-place was really like. If in the Gothic age Latin came into actual speech again, it was as a new language; this Gothic Latin did not take long to pass from the formation of rhythms and sounds characteristic of itself (but which our imagination to-day cannot recapture, any more than those of old Latin) to encroachments upon the word-meanings and the syntax as well. But the anti-Gothic Latin of the Humanists, too, which was meant to be Ciceronian, was anything but a revival. The whole significance of the race-element in language can be measured by comparing the German of Nietzsche and of Mommsen, the French of Diderot and of Napoleon, and observing that in idiom Voltaire and Lessing are much closer together than Lessing and Hölderlin.

It is the same with the most telling of all the expression-languages, art. The Taboo side — namely, the stock of forms, the rules of convention, and style in so far as it means an armoury of established expedients (like vocabulary and syntax in verbal language) — stands for the language itself, which can be learned. And it is learned and transmitted in the tradition of the great schools of painting, the cottage-building tradition, and generally in the strict craft-discipline which every genuine art possesses as a matter of course and which in all ages has been meant to give the sure command of the idiom that at a particular time is quite definitely living idiom of that time. For in this domain, too, there are living and dead languages. The form-language of an art can only be called living, when the artist corps as a whole employs it like a mother tongue, which one uses without even thinking about its structure. In this sense Gothic in the sixteenth century and Rococo in 1800 were both dead languages. Contrast the unqualified sureness with which architects and musicians of the seventeenth and eighteenth centuries expressed themselves with the hesitations of Beethoven, the painfully acquired, almost self-taught, *philological* art of Schinkel and Schadow,[1] the manglings of the Pre-Raphaelites and the Neo-Gothics, and the baffled experimentalism of present-day artists.

In an artistic form-language, as presented to us by its products, the voice of the Totem side, the race, makes itself heard, and not less so in individual artists than in whole generations of artists. The creators of the Doric temples of South Italy and Sicily, and those of the brick Gothic of North Germany were emphatically race-men, and so too the German musicians from Heinrich Schütz to Johann Sebastian Bach. To the Totem side belong the influences of the cosmic cycles — the importance of which in the structure of art-history has hardly been suspected, let alone established — and the creative times of spring and love-stirrings which (apart altogether from the executive sureness in

---

[1] Hans Friedrich Schinkel (1781–1841), architect of the Opera House, the Altes Museum, and the Königswache of Berlin. Gottfried Schadow (1764–1850), sculptor (statues of Frederick II, Zieten, etc.; Quadriga of Brandenburger Tor), a classicist *malgré lui* (not to be confused with two other artists of the same name, quasi-contemporaries). — *Tr.*

imparting form) determine the force of the forms and the depth of the conceptions. The formalists are explained by depth of world-fear or by defect of
"race," and the great formless ones by plethora of blood or defect of discipline.
We comprehend that there is a difference between the history of artists and that
of styles, and that the language of an art may be carried from country to country,
but mastery in speaking it, never.

A race has roots. Race and landscape belong together. Where a plant takes
root, there it dies also. There is certainly a sense in which we can, without
absurdity, work backwards from a race to its "home," but it is much more
important to realize that the race adheres permanently to this home with some
of its most essential characters of body and soul. If in that home the race
cannot now be found, this means that the race has ceased to exist. A race does
not migrate. Men migrate, and their successive generations are born in ever-
changing landscapes; but the landscape exercises a secret force upon the plant-
nature in them, and eventually the race-expression is completely transformed by
the extinction of the old and the appearance of a new one. Englishmen and
Germans did not migrate to America, but human beings migrated thither *as*
Englishmen and Germans, and their descendants are there *as* Americans. It
has long been obvious that the soil of the Indians has made its mark upon them
— generation by generation they become more and more like the people they
eradicated. Gould and Baxter have shown that Whites of all races, Indians,
and Negroes have come to the same average in size of body and time of maturity
— and that so rapidly that Irish immigrants, arriving young and developing
very slowly, come under this power of the landscape within the same generation.
Boas has shown that the American-born children of long-headed Sicilian and
short-headed German Jews at once conform to the same head-type. This is not a
special case, but a general phenomenon, and it should serve to make us very
cautious in dealing with those migrations of history about which we know
nothing more than some names of vagrant tribes and relics of languages (e.g.,
Danai, Etruscans, Pelasgi, Achæans, and Dorians). As to the race of these
"peoples" we can conclude nothing whatever. That which flowed into the
lands of southern Europe under the diverse names of Goths, Lombards, and
Vandals was without doubt a race in itself. But already by Renaissance times
it had completely grown itself into the root characters of the Provençal, Cas-
tilian, and Tuscan soil.

Not so with language. The home of a language means merely the accidental
place of its formation, and this has no relation to its inner form. Languages
migrate in that they spread by carriage from tribe to tribe. Above all, they
are capable of being, and are, exchanged — indeed, in studying the early history
of races we need not, and should not, feel the slightest hesitation about postu-
lating such speech-changes. It is, I repeat, the form-content and not the
speaking of a language that is taken over, and it is taken over (as primitives

are for ever taking over ornament-motives) in order to be used with perfect sureness as elements of their own form-language. In early times the fact that a people has shown itself the stronger, or the feeling that its language possesses superior efficacy, is enough to induce others to give up their own language and — with genuinely religious awe — to take its language to themselves. Follow out the speech-changes of the Normans, whom we find in Normandy, England, Sicily, and Constantinople with different languages in each place, and ever ready to exchange one for another. Piety towards the mother tongue — the very term testifies to deep ethical forces, and accounts for the bitterness of our ever-recurring language-battles — is a trait of the *Late* Western soul, almost unknowable for the men of other Cultures and entirely so for the primitive. Unfortunately, our historians not only are sensible of this, but tacitly extend it as a postulate over their entire field, which leads to a multitude of fallacious conclusions as to the bearing of linguistic discoveries upon the fortunes of "peoples" — think of the reconstruction of the "Dorian migration," argued from the distribution of later Greek dialects. It is impossible, therefore, to draw conclusions as to the fortunes of the race side of peoples from mere place-names, personal names, inscriptions, and dialects. Never do we know *a priori*, whether a folkname stands for a language-body, or a race-part, or both, or neither — besides which, folk-names themselves, and even land-names, have, as such, Destinies of their own.

II

Of all expressions of race, the purest is the House. From the moment when man, becoming sedentary, ceases to be content with mere shelter and builds himself a dwelling, this expression makes its appearance and marks off, within the race "man" (which is the element of the *biological* world-picture [1]) the human races of world-history proper, which are streams of being of far greater spiritual significance. The prime form of the house is everywhere a product of feeling and of growth, never at all of knowledge. Like the shell of the nautilus, the hive of the bee, the nest of the bird, it has an innate self-evidentness, and every trait of original custom and form of being, of marriage, of family life, and of tribal order is reflected in the place and in the room-organization of parterre, hall, wigwam, atrium, court, chamber, and gynæceum. One need only compare the lay-out of the old Saxon and that of the Roman house to feel that the soul of the men and the soul of the house were in each case identical.

This domain art-history ought never to have laid its hands on. It was an error to treat the building of the dwelling-house as a branch of the art of architecture. It is a form that arises in the obscure courses of being and not for the eye that looks for forms in the light; no room-scheme of the boor's hovel was ever thought out by an architect as the scheme of a cathedral was thought out.

[1] See p. 29 above.

This significant frontier line has escaped the observation of art-research — although Dehio [1] in one place remarks that the old German wooden house has nothing to do with the later great architecture, which arose quite independently — and the result has been a perpetual perplexity in method, of which the art-savant is sensible enough, but which he cannot understand. His science gathers, indiscriminately in all the "pre-" and "primitive" periods, all sorts of gear, arms, pottery, fabrics, funerary monuments, and houses, and considers them from the point of view of form as well as that of decoration; and, proceeding thus, it is not until he comes to the *organic* history of painting, sculpture, and architecture (i.e., the self-contained and differentiated arts) that he finds himself on firm ground. But, unknowing, he has stepped over a frontier between two worlds, that of soul-*expression* and that of visual expression-*language*. The house, and like it the completely unstudied basic (i.e., customary) forms of pots, weapons, clothing, and gear, belong to the Totem side. They characterize, not a taste, but a way of fighting, of dwelling, of working. Every primitive seat is the offset of a racial mode of body-posing, every jar-handle an extension of the supple arm. Domestic painting and dressmaking, the garment as ornament, the decoration of weapons and implements, belong, on the contrary, to the Taboo side of life, and indeed for primitive man the patterns and motives on these things possess even magical properties.[2] We all know the Germanic sword-blades of the Migrations with their Oriental ornamentation, and the Mycenæan strongholds with their Minoan artistry. It is the distinction between blood and sense, race and speech, *politics and religion*.

There is, in fact, as yet no world-history of the House and its Races, and to give us such a history should be one of the most urgent tasks of the researcher. But we must work with means quite other than those of art-history. The peasant dwelling is, as compared with the tempo of all *art*-history, something constant and "eternal" like the peasant himself. It stands outside the Culture and therefore outside the higher history of man; it recognizes neither the temporal nor the spacial limits of this history and it maintains itself, unaltered ideally, throughout all the changes of architecture, which it witnesses, but in which it does not participate. The round hut of ancient Italy is still found in Imperial times.[3] The form of the Roman rectangular house, the existence-mark of a second race, is found in Pompeii and even in the Imperial palaces. Every sort of ornament and style was borrowed from the Orient, but no Roman would ever think of imitating the Syrian house,[4] any more than the

---

[1] *Gesch. d. Deutsch. Kunst* (1919), pp. 14, et seq.

[2] This practice of inscription survives till deep into the Civilization. Even in 1914 the guns of the German Army, true products of the advanced machine-shop though they were, carried a Latin threat to the foe. From the magic rune of the blade it is a step to the motto on the shield, and then to the motto alone as unity-charm of the regiment or the Order. — *Tr.*

[3] W. Altmann, *Die ital. Rundbauten* (1906).

[4] A striking case in point is the Roman military camp. See Vol. I (English edition), p. 185, foot-note. — *Tr.*

Hellenistic city-architect tampered with the megaron form of Mycenæ and Tiryns and the old Greek peasant-house described by Galen. The Saxon and Franconian peasant-house kept its essential nucleus unimpaired right from the country farm, through the burgher-house of the old Free Cities, up to the patrician buildings of the eighteenth century, while Gothic, Renaissance, Baroque, and Empire styles glided over it one after the other, clothing it from cellar to garret with *their* essences, but never perverting the Soul of the House. And the same is true of the furniture-forms, in which we have to distinguish carefully the psychological from the artistic treatment. In particular, the evolution of the Northern seat-furniture is, right up to the club arm-chair, a piece of race-history and not of what is called style-history. Every other character can deceive us as to the fortunes of race — the Etruscan names amongst the "Sea-folk" defeated by Rameses III, the enigmatic inscription of Lemnos, the wall-paintings in the tombs of Etruria, afford no sure evidences of the bodily connexion of these men. Although towards the end of the Stone Age a telling ornamentation arose and continued in the vast region east of the Carpathians, it is perfectly possible that race superseded race there. If we possessed in western Europe only pottery remains for the centuries between Trojan and Chlodwig, we should not have the least inkling of the event that we know as the "great Migrations." But the presence of an oval house in the Ægean region [1] and of another and very striking example of it in Rhodesia,[2] and the much-discussed concordance of the Saxon peasant-house with that of the Libyan Kabyle disclose a piece of race-history. Ornaments spread when a people incorporates them in its form-language, but a house-type is only transplanted along with its race. The disappearance of an ornament means no more than a change of language, *but when a house-type vanishes it means that race is extinguished.*

It follows that art-history, besides taking care to begin properly with the Culture, must not neglect even in its course to separate the race side carefully from the language proper. At the outset of a Culture two well-defined forms of a higher order rise up over the peasant village, as expressions of being and language of waking-being. They are the *castle* and the *cathedral*.[3] In them the distinction between Totem and Taboo, longing and fear, blood and intellect, rises to a grand symbolism. The ancient Egyptian, the ancient Chinese, the Classical, the South-Arabian, and the Western castle stands, as the home of continuing generations, very near to the peasant cottage, and both, as copies of the realities of living, breeding, and dying, lie outside all art-history. The history of the German *Burgen* is a piece of race-history throughout. On them both, early ornament does indeed venture to spread itself, beautifying here

---

[1] Bulle, *Orchomenos*, pp. 26, et seq.; Noack, *Ovalhaus und Palast in Kreta*, pp. 53, et seq. The house-plans still traceable in Latin times in the Ægean and Asia Minor may perhaps allow us to order our notions of human conditions in the pre-Classical period; but the linguistic remains, never.

[2] *Medieval Rhodesia* (London, 1906).

[3] Cf. Ch. X.

the beams, there the door, and there again the staircase, but it can be so, or so, at choice, or omitted altogether, for there is no inward bond between the structure and the ornament. The cathedral, on the other hand, is not ornamented, but *is itself ornament*. Its history is coincident with that of the Gothic style, and the same is true of the Doric temple and all other Early Culture buildings. So complete is the congruence, in the Western and every other Culture whose art we know at all, that it has never occurred to anyone to be astonished at the fact that strict architecture (which is simply the highest form of pure ornament) is entirely confined to religious building. All the beauty of architecture that there is in Gelnhausen, Goslar, and the Wartburg has been *taken over* from cathedral art; it is decoration and not essence. A castle or a sword or a pitcher can do without this decoration altogether without losing its meaning or even its form.[1] But in a Cathedral, or an Egyptian pyramid-temple, such a distinction between essence and art is simply inconceivable.

We distinguish, then, the building that *has a style* and the building *in which* men have a style. Whereas in monastery and cathedral it is the stone that possesses form and communicates it to the men who are in its service, in farmhouse and feudal stronghold it is the full strength of the countryman's and the knight's life that forms the building forth from itself. Here the man and not the stone comes first, and here, too, there is an ornamentation; it is an ornament which is proper to man and consists in the strict nature and stable form *of manners and customs*. We might call this living, as distinct from rigid, style. But, just as the power of this living form lays hands on the priesthood also, creating in Gothic and in Vedic times the type of the knightly priest, so the Romanesque-Gothic *sacred* form-language seizes upon everything pertaining to this secular life — costume, arms, rooms, implements, and so forth — and stylizes their surface. But art-history must not let itself lose its bearings in this alien world — it is only the surface.

In the early cities it is the same; nothing new supervenes. Amongst the race-made houses, which now form streets, there are scattered the handful of cult-buildings that *have* style. And, as having it, they are the seats of art-history and the sources whence its forms radiate out on to squares, façades, and house-rooms. Even though the castle develops into the urban palace and patrician residence, and the *palatium* and the men's hall, into guild-house and town-hall, one and all they receive and carry a style, they do not *have* it. True, at the stage of real burgherdom the metaphysical creativeness of the early religion has been lost. It develops the ornament further, *but not the building as ornament*, and from this point art-history splits up into the histories of the separate arts. The picture, the statue, the house, become particular objects

---

[1] Though magic or prestige may of course be involved in their ornamentation, these are supervening and not radical virtues. — *Tr.*

to which the style is to be applied. Even the church itself is now such a house.
A Gothic cathedral *is* ornament, but a Baroque hall-church is a building clothed
with ornament. The process begun in the Ionic style and the sixteenth century is
completed in the Corinthian and Rococo, wherein the house and its ornament
are separated for good and all, so completely that even the master-works
amongst eighteenth-century churches and monasteries cannot mislead us —
we know that all this art of theirs is secular, is adornment. With Empire
the style transforms itself into a "taste," and with the end of this mode architecture turns into a craft-art. And that is the end of the ornamental expression-
language, and of art-history with it. But the peasant-house, with its unaltered
race-form, lives on.

III

The practical importance of the house as race-expression begins to be appreciated as and when one realizes the immense difficulty of approaching the
kernel of race. I do not refer to its inner essence, its soul — as to that, feeling
speaks to us clearly enough and we all know a man of race, a "thoroughbred,"
when we see one. But what are the hall-marks for our sense, and above all
for our eye, by which we recognize and distinguish races? This is a matter
that belongs to the domain of Physiognomic just as surely as the classification
of tongues belongs to that of Systematic. But how immense and how varied
the material that would be required! How much of it is irretrievably lost by
destruction, and how much more by corruption! In the most favourable cases,
what we have of prehistoric men is their skeletons, and how much does a
skeleton *not* tell us! Very nearly everything. Prehistoric research in its naïve
zeal is ready to deduce the incredible from a jaw-bone or an arm-bone. But
think of one of those mass-graves of the War in northern France, in which we
know that men of all races, white and coloured, peasants and townsmen, youths
and men lie together. If the future had no collateral evidence as to their nature, it would certainly not be enlightened by anthropological research. In
other words, immense dramas of race can pass over a land without the investigator of its grave-skeletons obtaining the least hint of the fact. It is the *living*
body that carries nine-tenths of the expression — not the articulation of the
parts, but their articulate motions; not the bone of the face, but its mien.
And, for that matter, how much potentially interpretable race-expression is
actually observed even by the keenest-sensed contemporary? How much we
fail to see and to hear! What is it for which — unlike many species of beasts
— we lack a sense-organ?

The science of the Darwinian age met this question with an easy assurance.
How superficial, how glib, how mechanistic the conception with which it
worked! In the first place, this conception groups an aggregate of such grossly
palpable characters as are observable in the anatomy of the discoveries —

that is, characters that even a corpse displays. As to observing the body qua living thing, there is no question of it. Secondly, it investigates only those signs which very little perspicacity is needed to detect, and investigates them only in so far as they are measurable and countable. The microscope and not the pulse-sense determines. When language is used as a differentia, it is to classify races, not according to their *way of speaking*, but according to the grammatical *structure of the speech*, which is just anatomy and system of another sort. No one as yet has perceived that the investigation of these *speech-races* is one of the most important tasks that research can possibly set itself. In the actuality of daily experience we all know perfectly well that the way of speaking is one of the most distinctive traits in present-day man — examples are legion; each of us knows any number of them. In Alexandria the same Greek was spoken in the most dissimilar race-modes, as we can see even to-day from the script of the texts. In North America the native-born speak exactly alike, whether in English, in German, or for that matter in Indian. What in the speech of East-European Jews is a race-trait of the land, and present therefore in Russian also, and what is a race-trait of the blood common to all Jews, independent of their habitat and their hosts, in their speaking of any of the European "mother"-tongues? What in detail are the relations of the sound-formations, the accentuations, the placing of words?

But science has completely failed to note that race is not the same for rooted plants as it is for mobile animals, that with the microcosmic side of life a fresh group of characters appears, and that for the animal world it is decisive. Nor again has it perceived that a completely different significance must be attached to "races" when the word denotes subdivisions *within the integral race "Man."* With its talk of adaptation and of inheritance it sets up a soulless causal concatenation of superficial characters, and blots out the fact that here the blood and there the power of the land over the blood are expressing themselves — secrets that cannot be inspected and measured, but only livingly experienced and felt from eye to eye.

Nor are the scientists at one as to the relative rank of these superficial characters amongst themselves. Blumenbach classified the races of man according to skull-forms, Friedrich Müller (as a true German) by hair and language-structure, Topinard (as a true Frenchman) by skin-colour and shape of nose, and Huxley (as a true Englishman) by, so to say, sport characteristics. This last is undoubtedly in itself a very suitable criterion, but any judge of horses would tell him that breed-characteristics cannot be hit off by scientific terminology. These "descriptions" of races are without exception as worthless as the descriptions of "wanted" men on which policemen exercise their theoretical knowledge of men.

Obviously, the *chaotic* in the total expression of the human body is not in the least realized. Quite apart from smell (which for the Chinese, for example, is a most characteristic mark of race) and sound (the sound of speech, song, and, above all, laughter, which enables us accurately to sense deep differences inaccessible to scientific method) the profusion of images before the eye is so embarrassingly rich in details, either actually visible or sensible to the inner vision, that the possibility of marshalling them under a few aspects is simply unthinkable. And all these sides to the picture, all these traits composing it, are independent of one another and have each their individual history. There are cases in which the bony structure (and particularly the skull-form) completely alter without the expression of the fleshy parts — i.e., the face — becoming different. The brothers and sisters of the same family·may all present almost every differentia posited by Blumenbach, Müller, and Huxley, and yet the identity of their living race-expression may be patent to anyone who looks at them. Still more frequent is similarity of bodily build accompanied by thorough diversity of living expression — I need only mention the immeasurable difference between genuine peasant-stock, like the Frisians or the Bretons, and genuine city-stock.[1] But besides the energy of the blood — which coins the same living features ("family" traits) over and over again for centuries — and the power of the soil — evidenced in its stamp of man — there is that mysterious cosmic force of the syntony of close human connexions. What is called the "*Versehen*" of a pregnant woman [2] is only a particular and not very important instance of the workings of a very deep and powerful formative principle inherent in all that is of the race side. It is a matter of common observation that elderly married people become strangely like one another, although probably Science with its measuring instruments would "prove" the exact opposite. It is impossible to exaggerate the formative power of this living pulse, this strong inward feeling for the perfection of one's own type. The feeling for race-beauty — so opposite to the conscious taste of ripe urbans for intellectual-individual traits of beauty — is immensely strong in primitive men, and for that very reason never emerges into their consciousness. But such a feeling is race-forming. It undoubtedly moulded the warrior- and hero-type of a nomad tribe more and more definitely on *one bodily ideal*, so that it would have been quite unambiguous to speak of the race-figure of Romans or Ostrogoths. The same is true of any ancient nobility — filled with a strong and deep sense of its own unity, it achieves the formation of a bodily ideal. Comradeship breeds races. French *noblesse* and Prussian *Landadel* are genuine race-denotations. But it is just this, too, that has bred the types of the Euro-

---

[1] In this connexion it ought to be someone's business to undertake physiognomic studies upon the massy, thoroughly peasantish, Roman busts; the portraits of Early Gothic; those of the Renaissance, already visibly urban; and, most of all, the polite English portraiture from the late-eighteenth century onward. The great galleries of "ancestors" contain an endless wealth of material.

[2] The sudden fear of some animal or object seen, believed to result in her child's bearing the mark of it. Cf. Jacob and the speckled cattle (Genesis xxx, 37). The attitude of biologists to this question is not negative, but non-committal. — *Tr.*

pean Jew, with his immense race-energy and his thousand years of ghetto life; and it always will forge a population into a race whenever it has stood for long together spiritually firm and united in the presence of its Destiny. Where a race-ideal exists, as it does, supremely, in the Early period of the Culture — the Vedic, the Homeric, the knightly times of the Hohenstaufen — the yearning of a ruling class towards this ideal, its will to be just *so* and not otherwise, operates (quite independently of the choosing of wives) towards actualizing this ideal and eventually achieves it. Further, there is a statistical aspect of the matter which has received far less attention than it should. For every human being alive to-day there were a million ancestors even in A.D. 1300 and ten million in A.D. 1000. This means that every German now living, without exception, is a blood-relative of every European of the age of the Crusades and that the relationship becomes a hundred and a thousand times more intensely close as we narrow the limits of its field, so that within twenty generations or less the population of a land grows together into *one single family;* and this, together with the choice and voice of the blood that courses through the generations, ever driving congeners into one another's arms, dissolving and breaking marriages, evading or forcing all obstacles of custom, leads to innumerable procreations that in utter unconsciousness fulfil the *will of the race.*

Primarily, this applies to the vegetal race-traits, the "physiognomy of position," as apart from movement of the mobile — i.e., everything which does *not* differ in the living and in the dead animal-body and cannot but express itself even in stiffened members. There is undoubtedly something cognate in the growth of an ilex or a Lombardy poplar and that of a man — "thickset," "slim," "drooping," and so forth. Similarly, the outline of the back of a dromedary, or the striping of a tiger- or zebra-skin is a vegetal race-mark. And so, too, are the motion-actions of nature *upon and with a creature* — a birch-tree or a delicately built child, which both sway in the wind, an oak with its splintered crown, the steady circles or frightened flutterings of birds in the storm, all belong to the plant side of race. But on which side of the line do such characters stand when *blood and soil contend for the inner form of the "transplanted" species,* human or animal? And how much of the constitution of the soul, the social code, the house, is of this kind?

It is quite another picture that presents itself when we attune ourselves to receive the impressions of the purely animal. The difference between plant-wise being and animalwise waking-being (to recall what has been said earlier) is such that we are here concerned, not simply with waking-being itself and its language, but with the combination of cosmic and microcosmic to form a freely moving body, a microcosm *vis-à-vis* a macrocosm, whose independent life-activity possesses an expression peculiar to itself, which makes use in part of the organs of waking-consciousness and which — as the corals show — is mostly lost again with the cessation of mobility.

If the race-expression of the plant consists predominantly in the physiognomy of position, the animal-expression resides in *a physiognomy of movement* — namely, in the form as having motion, in the motion itself, and in the set of the limbs as figuring the motion.   Of this race-expression not very much is revealed in the sleeping animal, and far less still in the dead animal, whose parts the scientist explores; we have practically nothing to learn now about the skeleton of the vertebrate.   Hence it is that in vertebrates the limbs are more expressive than the bones.   Hence it is that the limb-masses are the true seat of expressiveness in contrast to the ribs and skull-bones — the jaw being an exception in that its structure discloses the character of the animal's food, whereas the plant's nutrition is a mere *process of nature*.   Hence it is, again, that the insect's skeleton, which clothes its body, is fuller of expression than the bird's, which is clothed by its body.   It is pre-eminently the organs of the outer sheath that more and more forcefully gather the race-expression to themselves — the eye, not as a thing of form and colour, but as *glance* and expressive *visage;* the mouth, which becomes through the usage of speech the expression of understanding; and the head (not the skull), with its lineaments formed by the flesh, which has become the very throne of the non-vegetable side of life. Consider how, on the one hand, we breed orchids and roses and, on the other, we breed horses and dogs — and would like human beings to be bred, too. But it is not, I repeat, the mathematical form of the visible parts, but exclusively the expression of the movement, that displays this physiognomy. When we seize at a glance the race-expression of a motionless man, it is because our experienced eye sees the appropriate motion already potentially in the limbs.   The real race-appearance of a bison, a trout, a golden eagle, is not to be reproduced by any reckoning of the creature's plane or solid dimensions; and the deep attractiveness that they possess for the creative artist comes precisely from the fact that the secret of race can reveal itself in the picture *by way of the soul* and not by any mere imitation of the visible.   One has to see and, seeing, to feel how the immense energy of this life concentrates upon head and neck, how it speaks in the bloodshot eye, in the short compact horn, in the "aquiline" beak and profile of the bird of prey — to mention one or two only of the innumerable points that cannot be communicated by words and are only expressible, by me for you, in the language of an art.

But with such hall-marks as those quoted, characterizing the noblest sorts of animals, we come very near to the concept of race which enables us to perceive within the type "mankind" differences of a higher sort than either the vegetable or the animal — differences that are spiritual rather, and *eo ipso* less accessible to scientific methods.   The coarse characters of the skeletal structure have ceased to possess independent importance.   Already Retzius (d. 1860) had put an end to the belief of Blumenbach that race and skull-formation are coincident, and J. Ranke summarizes his tenets in these words: [1] "What in point of variety of skull-formation is displayed by mankind in general is displayed also on the smaller scale by every tribe (*Volksstamm*) and even by many fair-sized communities — a union of the different skull-forms with the extremes led up to through finely graduated intermediate forms." No one would deny that it is reasonable to seek for ideal basic forms, but the researcher ought not to lose sight of the fact that these are ideals and that, for all the objectivity of his measurements, it is his taste that really fixes his limits and his classification. Much more important than any attempts to discover an ordering principle is the fact that within the unit " humanity" all these forms occur and have occurred from the earliest ice-times, that they have never markedly varied, and that they are found indiscriminately even within the same families. The one certain result of science is that observed by Ranke, that when skull-forms are arranged serially with respect to transitions, certain averages emerge which are characteristic not of "race," but of the land.

In reality, the race-expression of a human head can associate itself with any conceivable skull-form, the decisive element being not the bone, but the flesh, the look, the play of feature. Since the days of Romanticism we have spoken of an "Indogermanic" race. But is there such a thing as an Aryan or a Semitic skull? Can we distinguish Celtic and Frankish skulls, or even Boer and Kaffir? And if not, what may not the earth have witnessed in the way of history unknown to us, for which not the slightest evidences, but only bones, remain! How unimportant these are for that which we call race in higher mankind can be shown by a drastic experiment. Take a set of men with every conceivable race-difference, and, while mentally picturing "race," observe them in an X-ray apparatus. The result is simply comic. As soon as light is let through it, "race" vanishes suddenly and completely.

It cannot be too often repeated, moreover, that the little that is really illustrative in skeletal structure is a growth of the landscape and never a function of the blood. Elliot Smith in Egypt and von Luschen in Crete have examined an immense material yielded by graves ranging from the Stone Age to the present day. From the "Sea-peoples" of the middle of the second millennium B.C. to the Arabs and the Turks one human stream after another has passed over this region, but the average bone-structure has remained unaltered. It would be true, in a measure, to say that "race" has travelled as flesh over the fixed skeleton-form of the land.[2] The Alpine region to-day contains "peoples"

---

[1] J. Ranke, *Der Mensch* (1912), II, p. 205.

[2] This suggestive sentence should, of course, be read with its reservation. The cranial evidences of Crete are highly illustrative in this connexion; they would not indeed be trusted by a modern historian without weighty collateral evidence, but here this evidence exists. Up to the latter part of Middle Minoan, the "long" head predominated heavily, not only from the outset, but increasingly as the Culture rose, until it included two-thirds of the whole, intermediates forming a quarter and "short" heads a mere handful. But from about the time of the catastrophic fall of

of the most diverse origins — Teuton, Latin, Slav — and we need only glance backward to discover Etruscans and Huns there also. Tribe follows tribe. But the skeletal structure in the mankind of the region in general is ever the same, and only on the edges, towards the plains, does it gradually disappear in favour of other forms, which are themselves likewise fixed. As to race, therefore, and the race-wanderings of primitive men, the famous finds of prehistoric bones, Neanderthal to Aurignacian, prove nothing. Apart from some conclusions from the jaw-bone as to the kinds of food eaten, they merely indicate the basic land-form that is found there to this day.

Once more, it is the mysterious power of the soil, demonstrable at once in every living being as soon as we discover a criterion independent of the heavy hand of the Darwinian age. The Romans brought the vine from the South to the Rhine, and there it has certainly not visibly — i.e., botanically — changed. But in this instance "race" can be determined in other ways. There is a soil-born difference not merely between Southern and Northern, between Rhine and Moselle wines, but even between the products of every different site on every different hill-side; and the same holds good for every other high-grade vegetable "race," such as tea and tobacco. Aroma, a genuine growth of the country-side, is one of the hall-marks (all the more significant because they cannot be measured) of true race. But noble races of men are differentiated in just the same intellectual way as noble wines. There is a like element, only sensible to the finest perceptions, a faint aroma in every form, that underneath all higher Culture connects the Etruscans and the Renaissance in Tuscany,[1] and the Sumerians, the Persians of 500 B.C., and the Persians of Islam on the Tigris.

None of this is accessible to a science that measures and weighs. It exists for the feelings — with a plain certainty and at the first glance — but not for the savant's treatment. And the conclusion to which I come is that Race, like Time and Destiny, is a decisive element in every question of life, something which everyone knows clearly and definitely so long as he does not try to set himself to comprehend it by way of rational — i.e., soulless — dissection and ordering. Race, Time, and Destiny belong together. But the moment scientific thought approaches them, the word "Time" acquires the significance

Late Minoan II, the long heads fall to a startlingly low figure, while intermediates account for half, and short heads for more than a third. It marks the end of Minoan Civilization and the coming of the Achæans. But just as the Minoan skull held its own throughout the Minoan Age, so now, after its fall, the short head maintained itself, as stated in the text, through all subsequent vicissitudes, from the "Sea-peoples" through Roman, Arab, and Turk, to this day. Thus the Cretan landscape has had two skull-types successively; but the change from one to the other occurred in connexion with an immense cataclysm, nothing less than the collapse of a Civilization. The rough deduction that seems to emerge from this case is that a great Culture holds its skull, no doubt in the course of its striving towards ideal physical type of its own (see p. 127), but that where that major organism does not exist, the skull endures as the land endures and the peasant endures. This applies also to the Alpine region, which has received the deposit of migrations, but has never been the centre of a high Culture. — Tr.

[1] Cf. D. Randall-MacIver, The Etruscans (1928), Ch. I. — Tr.

of a dimension, the word "Destiny" that of causal connexion, while Race, for which even at that stage of scientific *askesis* we still retain a very sure feeling, becomes an incomprehensible chaos of unconnected and heterogeneous characters that (under headings of land, period, culture, stock) interpenetrate without end and without law. Some adhere toughly and permanently to a stock and are transmissible; others glide over a population like mere cloud-shadows; and many are, as it were, dæmons of the land, which possess everyone who inhabits it for as long as he stays in it. Some expel one another, some seek one another. A strict classification of races — the ambition of all ethnology — is impossible. The attempt is foredoomed from the start, as it contradicts this very essence of the racial, and every systematic lay-out always has been and will be, inevitably, a falsification and misapprehension of the nature of its subject. Race, in contrast to speech, is unsystematic through and through. In the last resort every individual man and every individual moment of his existence have their own race. And therefore the only mode of approach to the Totem side is, not classification, but physiognomic fact.

IV

He who would penetrate into the essence of language should begin by putting aside all the philologist's apparatus and observe how a hunter speaks to his dog. The dog follows the outstretched finger. He listens, tense, to the sound of the word, but shakes his head — this kind of man-speech he does not understand. Then he makes one or two sentences to indicate *his* idea; he stands still and barks, which in his language is a sentence containing the question: "Is that what Master means?" Then, still in dog language, he expresses his pleasure at finding that he was right. In just the same way two men who do not really possess a single word in common seek to understand one another. When a country parson explains something to a peasant-woman, he looks at her keenly, and, unconsciously, he puts into his look the essence that she would certainly never be able to understand from a parsonic mode of expression. The locutions of to-day, without exception, are capable of comprehension only in association with other modes of speech — adequate by themselves they are not, and never have been.

If the dog, now, wants something, he wags his tail; impatient of Master's stupidity in not understanding this perfectly distinct and expressive speech, he adds a vocal expression — he barks — and finally an expression of attitude — he mimes or makes signs. Here the man is the obtuse one who has not yet learned to talk.

Finally something very remarkable happens. When the dog has exhausted every other device to comprehend the various speeches of his master, he suddenly plants himself squarely, and his eye bores into the eye of the human. Something deeply mysterious is happening here — the immediate contact of Ego and Tu.   The look emancipates from the limitations of waking-consciousness.   Being understands itself without signs.   Here the dog has become a "judge" of men, looking his opposite straight in the eye and grasping, behind the speech, the speaker.

Languages of these kinds we habitually use without being conscious of the fact.   The infant speaks long before it has learned its first word, and the grown-up talks with it without even thinking of the ordinary meanings of the words he or she is using — that is, the sound-forms in this case subserve a language that is quite other than that of words.   Such languages also have their groups and dialects; they, too, can be learned, mastered, and misunderstood, and they are so indispensable to us that verbal language would mutiny if we were to attempt to make it do all the work without assistance from tone- and gesture-language.   Even our script, which is verbal language for the eye, would be almost incomprehensible but for the aid that it gets from gesture-language in the form of punctuation.

It is the fundamental mistake of linguistic science that it confuses language in general with human word-language — and that not merely theoretically, but habitually in the practical conduct of all its investigations.   As a result, it has remained immensely ignorant of the vast profusion of speech-modes of different kinds that are in common use amongst beasts and men.   The domain of speech, taken as a whole, is far wider, and verbal speech, with its incapacity to stand alone (an incapacity not wholly shaken off, even now) has really a much more modest part in it, than its students have observed.   As to the "origin of human speech," the very phrase implies a wrong enunciation of the problem.   Verbal speech — for that is what is meant — never had origins at all in the sense here postulated.   It is not primary, and it is not unitary.   The vast importance to which it has attained, since a certain stage in man's history, must not deceive us as to its position in the history of free-moving entity.   An investigation into speech certainly ought not to begin with man.

But the idea of a beginning for animal language, too, is erroneous.   Speaking is so closely bound up with the living being of the animal (in contradiction to the mere being of the plant) that not even unicellular creatures devoid of all sense-organs can be conceived of as speechless.   To be a microcosm in the macrocosm is one and the same thing as having a power to communicate oneself to another.   To speak of a beginning of speech in animal history is meaningless.   For that microcosmic existences are *in plurality* is a matter of simple self-evidence.   To speculate on other possibilities is mere waste of time.   Granted that Darwinian fancies about an original generation and first pairs of ancestors belong with the Victorian rearguard and should be left there, still the fact remains that swarms also are awake and aware, inwardly and livingly sensible, of a "we," and reaching out to one another for linkages of waking-consciousness.

Waking-being is activity in the extended; and, further, is willed activity. This is the distinction between the movements of a microcosm and the mechanical mobility of the plant, the animal, or the man in the plant-state — i.e., asleep. Consider the animal activity of nutrition, procreation, defence, attack — one side of it regularly consists in getting into touch with the macrocosm by means of the senses, whether it be the undifferentiated sensitivity of the unicellular creature or the vision of a highly developed eye that is in question. Here there is a definite *will to receive impression;* this we call orientation. But, besides, there exists from the beginning a *will to produce impression in the other* — what we call expression — and with that, at once, we have *speaking as an activity of the animal waking-consciousness.* Since then nothing fundamentally new has supervened. The world-languages of high Civilizations are nothing but exceedingly refined expositions of potentialities that were all implicitly contained in the fact of willed impressions of unicellular creatures upon one another.

But the foundations of this fact lie in the primary feeling of fear. The waking-consciousness makes a cleft in the cosmic, projects a space between particulars, and alienates them. To feel oneself alone is one's first impression in the daily awakening, and hence the primitive impulse to crowd together in the midst of this alien world, to assure oneself sensibly of the proximity of the other, to seek a conscious connexion with him. The "thou" is deliverance from the fear of the being-alone. *The discovery of the Thou,* the sense of another self resolved organically and spiritually out of the world of the alien, is the grand moment in the early history of the animal. Thereupon animals *are.* One has only to look long and carefully into the tiny world of a water-droplet under the microscope to be convinced that the discovery of the Thou, and *with it that of the I* has been taking place here in its simplest imaginable form. These tiny creatures know not only the Other, but also the Others; they possess not merely waking-consciousness but also relations of waking-consciousness, and therewith not only expression, but the elements of an expression-*speech.*

It is well to recall here the distinction between the two great speech-groups. Expression-speech treats the Other as witness, and aims purely at effects upon him, while communication-speech regards him as a collocutor and expects him to answer. To understand means to receive impressions with one's own feeling of their significance, and it is on this that the effect of the highest form of human expression-speech, art, depends.[1] To come to an understanding, to hold a conversation, postulates that the Other's feeling of significances is the same as one's own. The elementary unit of an expression-speech before witnesses is called the Motive. Command of the motive is the basis of all

---

[1] Art is fully developed in the animals. So far as man can get at it by way of analogy, it consists for them in rhythmic movement ("dance") and sound-formation ("song"). But this is by no means the limit of artistic impression *on* the animal itself.

expression-technique.   On the other hand, the impression produced for the purpose of an understanding is called the Sign, and is the elementary unit of all communication-technique — including, therefore, at the highest level, human speech.

Of the extensiveness of both these speech-worlds in the waking-consciousness of man we to-day can scarcely form an idea. Expression-speech, which appears in the earliest times with all the religious seriousness of the Taboo, includes not only weighty and strict ornament — which in the beginning coincides completely with the idea of art and makes every stiff, inert thing into a vehicle of the expression — but also the solemn ceremonial — whose web of formulæ spreads over the whole of public life, and even over that of the family [1] — and the language of costume, which is contained in clothing, tattooing, and personal adornment, all of which have a *uniform* significance. The investigators of the nineteenth century vainly attempted to trace the origin of clothing to the feeling of shame or to utilitarian motives.   It is in fact intelligible only as the means of an expression-speech, and as such it is developed to a grandiose level in all the high Civilizations, including our own of to-day. We need only think of the dominant part played by the "mode" in our whole public life and doings, the regulation attire for important occasions, the nuances of wear for this and that social function, the wedding-dress, mourning; of the military uniform, the priest's robes, orders and decorations, mitre and tonsure, periwig and queue, powder, rings, styles of hairdressing; of all the significant displays and concealments of person, the costume of the mandarin and the senator, the odalisque and the nun; of the court-state of Nero, Saladin and Montezuma — not to mention the details of peasant costumes, the language of flowers, colours, and precious stones.   As for the language of religion, it is superfluous to mention it, for all this *is* religion.

The communication-languages, in which every kind of sense-impression that it is possible to conceive more or less participates, have gradually evolved (so far as the peoples of the higher Cultures are concerned) three outstanding signs — picture, sound, and gesture, which in the script-speech of the Western Civilization have crystallized into a unit of letter, word, and punctuation mark.

In the course of this long evolution there comes about at the last the *detachment of speaking from speech*.   Of all processes in the history of language, none has a wider bearing than this.   Originally all motives and signs are unquestionably the product of the moment and meant only for a single individual act of the active waking-consciousness.   Their actual and their felt and willed significances are one and the same.   But this is no longer so when a *definite stock of signs offers itself* for the living act of giving the sign, for with that not only

[1] Jesus says to the Seventy whom he is sending out on mission: "And salute no man on the way" (Luke x, 4). The ceremonial of greeting on the high-road is so complicated that people in a hurry have to omit it. A. Bertholet, *Kulturgeschichte Israels* (1919), p. 162.

is the activity differentiated from its means, but the means are differentiated *from their significance*. The unity of the two not only ceases to be a matter of self-evidence, it ceases even to be a possibility. The feeling of significance is a living feeling and, like everything else belonging with Time and Destiny, it is uniquely occurring and non-recurring. No sign, however well known and habitually used, is ever repeated with exactly the same connotation; and hence it is that originally no sign ever recurred in the same form. The domain of the rigid sign is unconditionally one of things-become of the pure extended; it is *not an organism, but a system*, which possesses its own *causal* logic and brings the irreconcilable opposition of space and time, intellect and mood, also into the waking connexions of two beings.

This fixed stock of signs and motives, with its ostensibly fixed meanings, must be acquired by learning and practice if one wishes to belong to the community of waking-consciousness with which it is associated. *The necessary concomitant of speech divorced from speaking is the notion of the school.* This is fully developed in the higher animals; and in every self-contained religion, every art, every society, it is presupposed as the background of the believer, the artist, the "well-brought-up" human being. And from this point each community has its sharply defined frontier; to be a member one must know its language — i.e., its articles of faith, its ethics, its rules. In counterpoint and Catholicism alike, bliss is not to be compassed by mere feeling and goodwill. Culture means a hitherto unimagined intensification of the depth and strictness of the form-language in every department; for each individual belonging to it, it consists — as his *personal* Culture, religious, ethical, social, artistic — in a lifelong process of education and training *for* this life. And consequently in all great arts, in the great Churches, mysteries and orders, there is reached such a command of form as astonishes the human being himself, and ends by breaking itself under the stress of its own exigences — whereupon, in every Culture alike, there is set up (expressly or tacitly) the slogan of a "return to nature." This *maestria* extends also to verbal language. Side by side with the social polish of the period of the Tyrannis or of the troubadours, with the fugues of Bach and the vase-paintings of Exekias,[1] we have the art of Attic oratory and that of French conversation, both presupposing, like any other art, a strict and carefully matured convention and a long and exacting training of the individual.

Metaphysically the significance of this separating-off of a set language can hardly be over-estimated. The daily practice of intercourse in settled forms, and the command of the entire waking-consciousness through such forms — of which there is no longer a sensed process of formation *ad hoc*, but which are

[1] Exekias — represented in the British Museum by his "Achilles and Penthesilea" (*Ency. Brit.*, XI ed., article "Ceramics," Plate I) — stands at the end of Black Figure as the master of the possibilities of refinement in it — on the verge of the style-change to Red Figure, yet apart from it. Sebastian Bach is his "contemporary." — *Tr.*

just simply there, and require understanding in the strictest sense of the word — lead to an ever-sharper distinction between understanding and feeling within the waking-consciousness. An incipient language is felt understandingly; the practice of speaking requires one, first, to feel the *known* speech-medium and, secondly, to understand the intention put into it on *this* occasion. Consequently the kernel of all schooling lies in the acquisition of elements of knowledge. Every Church proclaims unhesitatingly that not feeling but knowledge leads into its ways of salvation; all true artistry rests on the sure knowledge of forms that the individual has not to discover, but to learn. "Understanding" is knowledge conceived of as a being. It is that which is completely alien to blood, race, time; from the opposition of rigid speech to coursing blood and developing history come the *negative* ideals of the absolute, the eternal, the universally valid — the ideals of Church and School.

But just this, in the last analysis, makes languages incomplete and leads to the eternal contradiction between what is in fact spoken and what was willed or meant by the speaking. We might indeed say that lies came into the world with the separation of speech from speaking. The signs are fixed, but not so their meaning — from the outset we feel that this is so, then we know it, and finally we turn our knowledge to account. It is an old, old, experience that when one wills to say something, the words "fail" one (*versagen*, mis-say); that one does not "express oneself aright" and in fact says something other than what was meant; that one may speak accurately and be understood inaccurately. And so finally we get to the art — which is widespread even amongst animals (e.g., cats) — of "using words to conceal thoughts." One says not everything, one says something quite different, one speaks formally about nothing, one talks briskly to cover the fact that one has said something. Or one imitates the speech of another. The red-backed shrike (*Lanius collurio*) imitates the strophes of small song-birds in order to lure them. This is a well-known hunter's dodge, but here again established motives and signs are precedent for it, just as much as they are a condition for the faking in antiques or the forgery of a signature. And all these traits, met with in attitude and mien as in handwriting and verbal utterance, reappear in the language of every religion, every art, every society — we need only refer to the ideas expressed by the words "hypocrite," "orthodox," "heretic," the English "cant," the secondary senses of "diplomat," "Jesuit," "actor," the masks and warinesses of polite society, and the painting of to-day, in which nothing is honest more and which in every gallery offers the eye untruth in every imaginable form.

In a language that one stammers, one cannot be a diplomat. But in the real command of a language there is the danger that the relation between the means and the meaning may be made into a new means. There arises an intellectual art of *playing* with expression, practised by the Alexandrines and the

Romantics — by Theocritus and Brentano in lyric poetry, by Reger in music, by Kierkegaard in religion.

Finally, speech and truth exclude one another.[1] And in fact this is just what brings up, in the age of fixed language, the typical "judge of men," who is all race and knows how to take the being that is speaking. To look a man keenly in the eyes, to size up the speaker behind the stump speech or the philosophical discourse, to know behind the prayer the heart, and behind the common good-tone the more intimate levels of social importance — and that instantaneously, immediately, and with the self-evident certainty that characterizes everything cosmic — that is what is lacking to the real Taboo-man, for whom *one* language at any rate carries conviction. A priest who is also a diplomat cannot be genuinely a priest. An ethical philosopher of the Kant stamp is never a "judge of men."

The man who lies in his verbal utterances betrays himself, without observing it, in his demeanour. One who uses demeanour to dissimulate with betrays himself in his tone. It is precisely because rigid speech separates means and intent that it never carries it off with the keen appraiser. The adept reads between the lines and understands a man as soon as he sees his walk or his handwriting. The deeper and more intimate a spiritual communion, the more readily it dispenses with signs and linkages through waking-consciousness. A real comradeship makes itself understood with few words, a real faith is silent altogether. The purest symbol of an understanding that has again got beyond language is the old peasant couple sitting in the evening in front of their cottage and entertaining one another without a word's being passed, each knowing what the other is thinking and feeling. Words would only disturb the harmony. From such a state of reciprocal understanding something or other reaches back, far beyond the collective existence of the higher animal-world, deep in the primeval history of free-moving life. Here deliverance from the waking-consciousness is, at moments, very nearly achieved.

V

Of all the signs that have come to be fixed, none has led to greater consequences than that which in its present state we call "word." It belongs, no doubt, to the purely human history of speech, but nevertheless the idea, or at any rate the conventional idea, of an "origin" of verbal language is as meaningless and barren as that of a zero-point for speech generally. A precise beginning is inconceivable for the latter because it is compresent with and contained in the essence of the microcosm, and for the former because it presup-

---

[1] "All forms, even those that are most felt, contain an element of untruth" (Goethe). In systematic philosophy the intent of the thinker coincides neither with the written words nor with the understanding of his readers, as it consists in his thinking meanings into words in the course of using the words themselves (*da es ein Denken in Wortbedeutungen ist, im Verlauf der Darstellung mit sich selbst*).

poses many fully developed kinds of communication-speech and constitutes only one element — though in the end the dominant element — of a slow and quiet evolution. It is a fundamental error in all theories (however diametrically opposed to each other) like those of Wundt and of Jespersen [1] that they investigate speaking in words as if it were something new and self-contained, which inevitably leads them into a radically false psychology. In reality verbal language is a very late phenomenon, not a young shoot, but the last blossom borne by one of the ramifications of the parent stem of all vocal speeches.

In actuality a pure word-speech does not exist. No one speaks without employing, in addition to the set vocabulary, quite other modes of speech, such as emphasis, rhythm, and facial play, which are much more primary than the language of the word, and with which, moreover, it has become completely intertwined. It is highly necessary, therefore, to avoid regarding the ensemble of present-day word-languages, with its extreme structural intricacy, as an inner unity with a homogeneous history. Every word-language known to us has very different sides, and each of these sides has its own Destiny within the history of the whole. There is not one sense-perception that would be wholly irrelevant to an adequate history of the use of words. Further, we must distinguish very strictly between vocal and verbal languages; the former is familiar even to the simpler genera of animals, the latter is in certain characters — individual characters, it is true, but all the more significant for that — a radically different thing. For every animal voice-language, further, expression-motives (a roar of anger) and communication-signs (a cry of warning) can be clearly distinguished, and doubtless the same may be said of the earliest words. But was it, then, as an expression- or as a communication-language that verbal language *arose*? Was it in quite primitive conditions, independent, more or less, of any and every visual language such as picture and gesture? To such questions we have no answer, since we have no inkling of what the pre-forms of the "word," properly so called, were. Naïve indeed is the philology which uses what we of to-day call "primitive" languages (in reality, incomplete pictures of very *late* language-conditions) as premisses for conclusions as to the origin of words and the Word. The word is in them an already established, highly developed, and self-evident means — i.e., precisely what anything "originally" is *not*.

There can be no doubt that the sign which made it possible for the future word-language to detach itself from the general vocal speech of the animal world was that which I call "name" — a vocal image serving to denote a Something in the world-around, which was felt as a being, and by the act of naming became a numen.[2] It is unnecessary to speculate as to how the first names came

---

[1] Jespersen deduces language trom poesy, dance, and particularly courtship. *Progress in Language* (1894), p. 357.
[2] See Vol. I, p. 80. — *Tr.*

to be — no human speech accessible to us at this time of day gives us the least *point d'appui* here. But, contrary to the view of modern research, I consider that the decisive turn came not from a change of the throat-formation or from a peculiarity of sound-formation or from any other physiological factor — if any such changes ever took place at all, it would be the race side that they would affect — not even an increased capacity for self-expression by existing means, like, say, the transition from word to sentence (H. Paul [1]), but *a profound spiritual change*. With the Name comes a new world-outlook. And if speech in general is the child of fear, of the unfathomable terror that wells up when the waking-consciousness is presented with the facts, that impels all creatures together in the longing to prove each other's reality and proximity — then the first word, the Name, is a mighty leap upward. The Name grazes the *meaning* of consciousness and the *source* of fear alike. The world is not merely existent, a secret is felt in it. Above and apart from the more ordinary objects of expression- and communication-language, man names *that which is enigmatic*. It is the beast that knows no enigmas. Man cannot think too solemnly, reverently, of this first name-giving. It was not well always to speak the name, it should be kept secret, a dangerous power dwelt in it. *With the name the step is taken from the everyday physical of the beast to the metaphysical of man.* It was the greatest turning-point in the history of the human soul. Our epistemology is accustomed to set speech and thought side by side, and it is quite right, if we take into consideration only the languages that are still accessible at the present day. But I believe that we can go much deeper than this and say that with the Name religion in the proper sense, *definite* religion in the midst of formless quasi-religious awe, came into being. Religion in this sense means religious *thought*. It is the new conception of the creative understanding emancipated from sensation. We say, in a very significant idiom, that we "reflect on," "think *over*," something. With the understanding of things-named the formation of a *higher* world, *above* all sensational existence, is begun — "higher" both according to obvious symbolism and in reference to the position of the head which man guesses (often with painful distinctness) to be the home of his thoughts. It gives to the primary feeling of fear both an object and a glimpse of liberation. On this religious first thought all the philosophical, scholarly, scientific thought of later times has been and remains dependent for its very deepest foundations.

These first names we have to think of as quite separate and individual elements in the stock of signs of a highly developed sound- and gesture-language, the richness of which we can no longer imagine, since these other means have come to be subordinate to the word-languages, and their further developments

---

[1] Sentence-like complexes of sound are known also to the dog. When the Australian dingo reverted from domestication to the wild state, he reverted also from the house-dog's bark to the wolf's howl — a phenomenon that indicates a transition to very much simpler sound-signs, but has nothing to do with "words."

have been in dependent connexion therewith.[1] One thing, however, was assured when the name inaugurated the transformation and spiritualization of communication-technique — the pre-eminence of the eye over the other sense-organs. Man's awakeness and awareness was in an illuminated space, his depth-experience [2] was a radiation outward towards light-sources and light-resistances, and he conceived of his ego as a middle point in the light. "Visible" or "invisible" was the alternative which governed the state of understanding in which the first names arose. Were the first *numina*, perhaps, things of the light-world that were felt, heard, observed in their effects, *but not seen?* No doubt the group of names, like everything else that marks a turning-point in the course of world-happenings, must have developed both rapidly and powerfully. The entire light-world, in which everything possesses the properties of position and duration in space, was — in the midst of what tensions of cause and effect, thing and property, object and subject! — very soon listed with innumerable names, and so anchored in the memory, for what we now call "memory" is the capacity of storing for the understanding, by means of the name, *the named.* Over the realm of understood visuals (*Sehdinge*) supervenes a more intellectual realm of namings, which shares with it the logical property of being purely extensive, disposed in polarity, and ruled by the causal principle. All word-types like cases and pronouns and prepositions (which arise, of course, much later) have a causal or local meaning in respect of named units; adjectives, and verbs also, have frequently come into existence in pairs of opposites; often (as in the E'we languages of West Africa investigated by Westermann) the same word is pronounced low or high to denote for example great and small, far and near, passive and active.[3] Later these relics of gesture-language pass completely into the word-form,[4] as we see clearly, for example, in the Greek μακρός and μικρός and the *u*-sounds of Egyptian designations of

[1] The gesture-languages of to-day (Delbrück, *Grundfragen d. Sprachforsch.*, pp. 49, et seq., with reference to the work of Jorio on the gestures of the Neapolitans) without exception presuppose word-language and are completely dependent upon its intellectual systematism. Examples: the mimicry of the actor, and the language which the American Indians have formed for themselves for the purpose of mutually understanding one another in spite of extreme differences and fluidity in the verbal languages of the various tribes. Wundt (*Völkerpsychologie*, I, p. 212) quotes the following to show how complicated sentences can be handled in this language: "White soldiers, led by an officer of high rank, but little intelligence, took the Mescalero Indians prisoners."

[2] See Vol. I, p. 172. — *Tr.*

[3] The case of voice-differentiations of the same word in Chinese is not analogous. It arose only out of scholars' work in the later phases of the Chinese Civilization as understood in this work. And it is a mechanical expedient and not a structural character — i.e., it lacks the *polarity* mentioned in the text. Voice-management distinguishes, not "great" from "small," but "pig" from "God," "bamboo" from "to dwell." English students will find a clear and understandable account of this and other Chinese differential devices in Karlgren's little book: *Sound and Symbol in Chinese* (English translation, 1923). — *Tr.*

[4] Possibly connected with this is the *emphatic antithesis* characterizing many of our proverbs and everyday idioms — e.g., "up hill and down dale" ("*par monts et vaux*," "*bergauf bergab*"), meaning hardly more than "everywhere." — *Tr.*

suffering. It is the form of thinking in opposites which, starting from these antithetical word-pairs, constitutes the foundation of all inorganic logic, and turns every scientific discovery of truths into a movement of conceptual contraries, of which the most universal instance is that of an old view and a new one being contrasted as "error" and "truth."

The second great turning-point was the use of *grammar*. Besides the name there was now the sentence, besides the verbal designation the verbal relation, and thereupon reflection — which is a thinking in word-relations that follows from the perception of things for which word-labels exist — became the decisive characteristic of man's waking-consciousness. The question whether the communication-languages already contained effective "sentences" before the appearance of the genuine "name" is a difficult one. The sentence, in the *present* acceptation of the word, has indeed developed within these languages according to its own conditions and with its own phases, but nevertheless it postulates the *prior* existence of the name. Sentences as conceptual relations become possible only with the intellectual change that accompanied their birth. And we must assume further that within the highly developed wordless languages one character or trait after another, in the course of continuous practical use, was transformed into verbal form and as such fell into its place in an increasingly solid structure, the prime form of our present-day languages. Thus the inner build of all verbal languages rests upon foundations of far older construction, and for its further development is *not* dependent upon the stock of words and its destiny.

It is in fact just the reverse. For with syntax the original group of individual *names* was transformed into a system of words, whose character was given, not by their proper, but by their grammatical significance. The name made its appearance as something novel and entirely self-contained. But word-species arose as elements of the sentence, and thereafter the contents of waking-consciousness streamed in overflowing profusion into this world of words, demanding to be labelled and represented in it, until finally even "all" became, in one shape or another, a word and available for the thought-process.

Thenceforward the sentence is the decisive element — we speak in sentences and not words. Attempts to define the two have been frequent, but never successful. According to F. N. Finck, word-formation is an analytical and sentence-formation a synthetical activity of the mind, the first preceding the second. It is demonstrable that the same actuality received as impression is variously understood, and words, therefore, are definable from very different points of view.[1] But according to the usual definition, a sentence is the verbal expression of a *thought*, a symbol (says H. Paul) for the connexion of several *ideas* in the soul of the speaker. It seems to me quite impossible to settle the nature of the sentence from its contents. The fact is simply that we call the

[1] *Die Haupttypen des Sprachbaus*, 1910.

relatively largest mechanical units employed "sentences" and the relatively smallest "words." Over this range extends the validity of grammatical *laws*. But as soon as we pass from theory to practice, we see that language as currently used is no longer such a mechanism; it obeys not laws, but *pulse*. Thus a race-character is involved, *a priori*, in the way in which the matter to be communicated is set in sentences. Sentences are not the same for Tacitus and Napoleon as for Cicero and Nietzsche. The Englishman orders his material syntactically in a different way from the German. Not the ideas and thoughts, but the thinking, the kind of life, *the blood*, determine in the primitive, Classical, Chinese, and Western speech-communities the type of the sentence-unit, and with it the *mechanical* relation of the word to the sentence. The boundary between grammar and syntax should be placed at the point where the mechanical of speech ceases and the organic of speaking begins — usages, custom, the *physiognomy* of the way that a man employs to express himself. The other boundary lies where the mechanical structure of the word passes into the organic factors of sound-formation and expression. Even the children of immigrants can often be recognized by the way in which the English "*th*" is pronounced — a race-trait of the land. Only that which lies between these limits is the "language," properly so called, which has system, is a technical instrument, and can be invented, improved, changed, and worn out; enunciation and expression, on the contrary, adhere to the *race*. We recognize a person known to us, without seeing him, by his pronunciation, and not only that, but we can recognize a member of an alien race even if he speaks perfectly correct German. The great sound-modifications, like the Old High German in Carolingian times and the Middle High German in the Late Gothic, have territorial frontiers and affect only the speaking of the language, not the inner form of sentence and word.

Words, I have just said, are the relatively smallest mechanical units in the sentence. There is probably nothing that is so characteristic of the thinking of a human species as the way in which these units are acquired by it. For the Bantu Negro a thing that he sees belongs first of all to a very large number of categories of comprehension. Correspondingly the word for it consists of a kernel or root and a number of monosyllabic prefixes. When he speaks of a woman in a field, his word is something like this: "living, one, big, old, female, outside, *human*"; this makes seven syllables, but it denotes a single, clear-headed, and to us quite alien act of comprehension.[1] There are languages in which the word is almost coextensive with the sentence.

The gradual replacement of bodily or sonic by grammatical gestures is thus the decisive factor in the formation of sentences, but it has never been completed. There are no purely verbal languages. The activity of speaking, in words, as it emerges more and more precise, consists in this, that through word-

---

[1] See the article "Bantu Languages," by Sir H. H. Johnston, *Ency. Brit.*, XI ed. — *Tr.*

sounds we awaken significance-feelings, which in turn through the sound of the word-connexions evoke further relation-feelings. Our schooling in speech trains us to understand in this abbreviated and indicative form not only light-things and light-relations, but also thought-things and thought-relations. Words are only named, not used definitively, and the hearer has to feel what the speaker means. This and this alone amounts to speech, and hence mien and tone play a much greater part than is generally admitted in the understanding of modern speech. Substantive signs may conceivably exist for many of the animals even, but verb-signs never.

The last grand event in this history, which brings the formation of verbal speech more or less to a close, is the coming of the verb. This assumes at the outset a very high order of abstraction. For substantives are words whereby things sense-defined in illuminated space [1] become evocable also in after-thought, while verbs describe *types* of change, which are not seen, but are extracted from the unendingly protean light-world, by noting the special characters of the individual cases, and generating concepts from them. "Falling stone" is originally a unit impression, but we first separate movement and thing moved and then isolate falling as one *kind* of movement from innumerable other sorts and shades thereof — sinking, tottering, stumbling, slipping. We do not "see" the distinction, we "know" it. The difference between fleeing and running, or between flying and being wafted, altogether transcends the visual impression they produce and is only apprehensible by a word-trained consciousness. But now, with this verb-thinking, even life itself has become accessible to reflection. Out of the living impress made on the waking-consciousness, out of the ambiance of the becoming (which gesture-speech, being merely imitative, leaves unquestioned and unprobed) that which is life itself — namely, singularity of occurrence — is unconsciously eliminated, and the rest, as effect of a cause (the wind wafts, lightning flashes, the peasant ploughs), is put, under purely extensive descriptions, into suitable places in the sign-system. One has to bury oneself completely in the solid definiteness of subject and predicate, active and passive, present and perfect, to perceive how entirely the understanding here masters the senses and unsouls actuality. In substantives one can still regard the mental thing (the idea) as a copy of the visual thing, but in the verb *something inorganic has been put in place of something organic*. The fact that we live — namely, that we at this instant perceive something — becomes eventually a *property* of the something perceived. In terms of word-thought, the perceived endures — "is." Thus, finally, are formed the categories of thought, graded according to what is and what is not natural to it; thus Time appears as a dimension, Destiny as a cause, the living as chemical or psychical mechanism. It is in this wise that the style of mathematical, judicial, and dogmatic thought arises.

[1] Even calling something "invisible" is a definition of it under the light-aspect.

And in this wise, too, arises that disunity which seems to us inseparable from the essence of man, but is really only the expression of the dominance of word-language in his waking-consciousness. This instrument of communication between Ego and Tu has, by reason of its perfection, fashioned out of the animal understanding of sensation, a thinking-in-words which stands proxy for sensation. Subtle thinking — "splitting hairs," as it is called — is conversing with oneself in word-significances. It is the activity that no kind of language but the language of words can subserve, and it becomes, with the perfection of the language, distinctive of the life-habit of whole classes of human beings. The divorce of speech, rigid and devitalized, from speaking, which makes it impossible to include the whole truth in a verbal utterance, has particularly far-reaching consequences in the sign-system of words. Abstract thinking consists in the use of a finite word-framework into which it is sought to squeeze the whole infinite content of life. Concepts kill Being and falsify Waking-Being. Long ago in the springtime of language-history, while understanding had still to struggle in order to hold its own with sensation, this mechanization was without importance for life. But now, from a being who occasionally thought, man has become a thinking being, and it is the ideal of every thought-system to subject life, once and for all, to the domination of intellect. This is achieved in theory by according validity only to the known and branding the actual as a sham and a delusion. It is achieved in practice by forcing the voices of the blood to be silent in the presence of universal ethical principles.[1]

Both, logic and ethics alike, are systems of absolute and eternal truths for the intellect, and correspondingly untruths for history. However completely the inner eye may triumph over the outer in the domain of thought, in the realm of facts the belief in eternal truths is a petty and absurd stage-play that exists only in the heads of individuals. A true system of thoughts emphatically cannot exist, for no sign can replace actuality. Profound and honest thinkers are always brought to the conclusion that all cognition is conditioned *a priori* by its own form and can never reach that which the words mean — apart, again, from the case of technics, in which the concepts are instruments and not aims in themselves. And this *ignorabimus* is in conformity also with the intuition of every true sage, that abstract principles of life are acceptable only as figures of speech, trite maxims of daily use underneath which life flows, as it has always flowed, onward. Race, in the end, is stronger than languages, and thus it is that, under all the great names, it has been thinkers — who are personalities — and not systems — which are mutable — that have taken effect upon life.

[1] Only technics are entirely true, for here the words are merely the key to actuality, and the sentences are continually modified until they are, not "truth," but actuality. A hypothesis claims, not rightness, but usefulness.

VI

So far, then, the inner history of word-languages shows three stages. In the first there appears, within highly developed but wordless communication-languages, the first names — units in a new sort of understanding. The world awakens *as a secret*, and religious thought begins. In the second stage, a complete communication-speech is gradually transformed into grammatical values. The gesture becomes the sentence, and the sentence transforms the names into words. Further, the sentence becomes the great school of understanding *vis-à-vis* sensation, and an increasingly subtle significance-feeling for abstract relations within the mechanism of the sentence evokes an immense profusion of inflexions, which attach themselves especially to the substantive and the verb, the space-word and the time-word. This is the blossoming time of grammar, the period of which we may probably (though under all reserves) take as the two millennia preceding the birth of the Egyptian and Babylonian Culture. The third stage is marked by a rapid decay of inflexions and a simultaneous replacement of grammar by syntax. The intellectualization of man's waking-consciousness has now proceeded so far that he no longer needs the sense-props of inflexion and, discarding the old luxuriance of word-forms, communicates freely and surely by means of the faintest nuances of idiom (particles, position of words, rhythm). By dint of speaking in words, the understanding has attained supremacy over the waking-consciousness, and to-day it is in process of liberating itself from the restrictions of sensible-verbal machinery and working towards pure mechanics of the intellect. Minds and not senses are making the contact.

In this third stage of linguistic history, which as such takes place in the biological plane [1] and therefore belongs to *man as a type*, the history of the higher Cultures now intervenes with an entirely new speech, the speech of the distance — writing — an invention of such inward forcefulness that again there is a sudden decisive turn in the destinies of the word-languages.

The written language of Egypt is already by 3000 in a state of rapid grammatical decomposition; likewise the Sumerian literary languages called *eme-sal* (women's language). The written language of China — which *vis-à-vis* the vernaculars of the Chinese world has long formed a language apart — is, even in the oldest known texts, so entirely inflexionless that only recent research has established that it ever had inflexions at all.[2] The Indogermanic system is known to us only in a state of complete break-down. Of the Case in Old Vedic (about 1500 B.C.) the Classical languages a thousand years later retained only fragments.[3] From Alexander the Great's time the dual disappeared from

[1] See pp. 29, et seq.
[2] The English reader may refer to Karlgren's *Sound and Symbol in Chinese*, already mentioned, for details. — *Tr.*
[3] See the article "Indo-European Languages," *Ency. Brit.*, XI ed. — *Tr.*

the declension of ordinary Hellenistic Greek, and the passive vanished from the conjugation entirely. The Western languages, although of the most miscellaneous provenance imaginable — the Germanic from primitive and the Romanic from highly civilized stock — modify in the same direction, the Romanic cases having become reduced to one, and the English, after the Reformation, to zero. Ordinary German definitely shed the genitive at the beginning of the nineteenth century and is now in process of abolishing the dative. Only after trying to translate a piece of difficult and pregnant prose — say of Tacitus or Mommsen — "back" [1] into some very ancient language rich in inflexions does one realize how meantime the technique of signs has vaporized into a technique of thoughts, which now only needs to employ the signs — abbreviated, but replete with meaning — merely as the counters in a game that only the initiates of the particular speech-communion understand. This is why to a west-European, the sacred Chinese texts must always be in the fullest sense a sealed book; but the same holds good also for the primary words of every other Culture-language — the Greek λογός and ἀρχή, the Sanskrit *Atman* and *Braman* — indications of the world-outlook of their respective Cultures that no one not bred in the Culture can comprehend.

The external history of languages is as good as lost to us in just its most important parts. Its springtime lies deep in the primitive era, in which (to repeat what has been said earlier), we have to imagine "humanity" in the form of scattered and quite small troops, lost in the wide spaces of the earth. A spiritual change came when reciprocal contacts became habitual (and eventually natural) to them, but correspondingly there can be no doubt that this contact was first sought for and then regulated, or fended off, by means of speech, and that it was the impression of an earth filled with men that first brought the waking-consciousness to the point of tense intelligent shrewdness, forcing verbal language under pressure to the surface. So that, perhaps, the birth of grammar is connected with the race hall-mark of the grand Number.

Since then, no other grammatical system has ever come into existence, but only novel derivatives of what was already there. Of these *authentic* primitive languages and their structure and sound we know nothing. As far as our backward look takes us, we see only complete and developed linguistic systems, used by everyone, learned by every child, as something perfectly natural. And we find it more than difficult to imagine that once upon a time things may have been different, that perhaps a shudder of fear accompanied the hearing of such strange and enigmatic language — an awe like that which in historic times has been and still is excited by script. And yet we have to reckon with the possibility that at one time, in a world of wordless communication, verbal language constituted an aristocratic privilege, a jealously preserved class-secret. We have a thousand examples — the diplomats with their French, the scholars

---

[1] Translation, it must be remembered, is normally from older into younger linguistic conditions.

with their Latin, the priests with their Sanskrit — to suggest that there may have been such a tendency. It is part of the thoroughbred's pride to be able to speak to one another in a way that outsiders cannot understand — a language for everybody is a vernacular. To be "on conversational terms with" someone is a privilege or a pretension. So, too, the use of literary language in talking with educated people, and contempt for dialect, mark the true bourgeois pride. It is only we who live in a Civilization wherein it is just as normal for children to learn to write as to learn to walk — in all earlier Cultures it was a rare accomplishment, to which few could aspire. And I am convinced that it was just so once with verbal language.

The tempo of linguistic history is immensely rapid; here a mere century signifies a great deal. I may refer again to the gesture-language of the North Indians,[1] which became necessary because the rapidity of changes in the tribal dialects made intertribal understanding impossible otherwise. Compare, too, the Latin of the recently discovered Forum inscription [2] (about 500) with the Latin of Plautus (about 200) and this again with the Latin of Cicero (about 50). If we assume that the oldest Vedic texts have preserved the linguistic state of 1200 B.C., then even that of 2000 may have differed from it far more completely than any Indogermanic philologists working by *a posteriori* methods can even surmise.[3] But *allegro* changes to *lento* in the moment when script, the language of duration, intervenes and ties down and immobilizes the systems at entirely different age-levels. This is what makes this evolution so opaque to research; all that we possess is remains of written languages. Of the Egyptian and Babylonian linguistic world we do possess originals from as far back as 3000, but the oldest Indogermanic relics are *copies*, of which the linguistic state is much younger than the contents.

Very various, under all these determinants, have been the destinies of the different grammars and vocabularies. The first attaches to the intellect, the second to things and places. Only grammatical systems are subject to natural inward change. The use of words, on the contrary, psychologically presupposes that, although the expression may change, inner mechanical structure is maintained (and all the more firmly) as being the basis on which denomination essentially rests. *The great linguistic families are purely grammatical families.* The words in them are more or less homeless and wander from one to another. It is a fundamental error in philological (especially Indogermanic) research that grammar and vocabulary are treated as a unit. All specialist vocabularies — the jargon of hunter, soldier, sportsman, seaman, savant — are in reality *only stocks of words*, and can be used within any and every grammatical system. The semi-Classical vocabulary of chemistry, the French of diplomacy, and the

[1] See p. 140 above. — *Tr.*
[2] See *Ency. Brit.*, XI. ed., Vol. XVI, p. 251b. — *Tr.*
[3] See the articles "Sanskrit" and "Indo-European Languages," *Ency. Brit.*, XI ed — *Tr.*

English of the racecourse have become naturalized in all modern languages alike. We may talk of "alien" words, but the same could have been said at some time or other of most of the "roots," so-called, in all the old languages. All names adhere to the things that they denote, and share their history. In Greek the names for metals are of alien provenance; words like ταῦρος, χιτῶν, οἶνος are Semitic. Indian numerals are found in the Hittite texts of Boghaz Keüi,[1] and the contexts in which they occur are technical expressions which came into the country with horse-breeding. Latin administrative terms invaded the Greek East,[2] German invaded Petrine Russia in multitudes, Arabic words permeate the vocabulary of Western mathematics, chemistry, and astronomy. The Normans, themselves Germanic, inundated English with French words. Banking, in German-speaking regions, is full of Italian expressions,[3] and similarly and to a far greater extent masses of designations relating to agriculture and cattle-breeding, to metals and weapons, and in general to all transactions of handicraft, barter, and intertribal law, must have migrated from one language to another, just as geographical nomenclature always passed into the proper vocabulary of the dominant language, with the result that Greek contains numerous Carian and German Celtic place-names. It is no exaggeration to say that the more widely an Indogermanic word is distributed, the *younger* it is, the more likely it is to be an "alien" word. It is precisely the very oldest names that are hoarded as private possessions. Latin and Greek have only quite young words in common. Or do "telephone," "gas," "automobile," belong to the word-stock of the "primitive" people? Suppose, for the sake of argument that three-fourths of the Aryan "primitive" words came from the Egyptian or the Babylonian vocabularies of the third millennium; we should not find a trace of the fact in Sanskrit after a thousand years of unwritten development, for even in German thousands of Latin loan-words have long ago become completely unrecognizable. The ending "-ette" in "Henriette" is Etruscan — how many genuine Aryan and genuine Semitic endings, notwithstanding their thoroughly alien origin, defy us to prove them intruders? What is the explanation of the astounding similarity of many words in the Australian and the Indogermanic languages?

The Indogermanic system is certainly the youngest, and therefore the most intellectual. The languages derived from it rule the earth to-day, but did it really exist at all in 2000 as a specific grammatical edifice? As is well known, a single initial form for Aryan, Semitic, and Hamitic is nowadays assumed as probable. The oldest Indian texts preserve the linguistic conditions of (probably) before 1200, the oldest Greek those of (probably) 700. But Indian personal and divine names occur in Syria and Palestine,[4] simultaneously with the

---

[1] P. Jensen, *Sitz. Preuss. Akademie* (1919), pp. 367, et seq.
[2] L. Hahn, *Rom und Romanismus im griech-röm. Osten* (1906).
[3] See the article "Book-keeping" in *Ency. Brit.*, XI ed. — *Tr.*
[4] Ed. Meyer, *Gesch. des Alt.*, I, §§ 455, 465.

horse, at a much later date, the bearers of these names being apparently first soldiers of fortune and afterwards potentates.[1] May it be that about 1600 these land-Vikings, these first *Reiter* — men grown up inseparable from their horses, the terrifying originals of the Centaur-legend — established themselves more or less everywhere in the Northern plains as adventurer-chiefs, bringing with them the speech and divinities of the Indian feudal age? And the same with the Aryan aristocratic ideals of breed and conduct. According to what has been said above on race, this would explain the race-ideal of Aryan-speaking regions without any necessity for "migrations" of a "primitive" folk. After all, it was in this way that the knightly Crusaders founded their states in the East — and in exactly the same locality as the heroes with Mitanni names had done so twenty-five hundred years before.

Or was this system of about 3000 merely an unimportant dialect of a language that is lost? The Romanic language-family about A.D. 1600 dominated all the seas. About 400 B.C. the "original" language on the Tiber possessed a domain of little more than a thousand square miles. It is certain that the geographical picture of the grammatical families at about 4000 was still very variegated. The Semitic-Hamitic-Aryan group (*if* it ever did form a unit) can hardly have been of much importance at that time. We stumble at every turn upon the relics of old speech-families — Etruscan, Basque, Sumerian, Ligurian, the ancient tongues of Asia Minor, and others — that in their day must have belonged to very extensive systems. In the archives of Boghaz-Keüi eight new languages have so far been identified, all of them in use about the year 1000. With the then prevailing tempo of modification, Aryan may in 2000 have formed a unit with languages that we should never dream of associating with it.

VII

Writing is an entirely new kind of language, and implies a complete change in the relations of man's waking-consciousness, in that it *liberates it from the tyranny of the present*. Picture-languages which portray objects are far older, older probably than any words; but here the picture is no longer an immediate denotation of some sight-object, but primarily the sign of a word — i.e., something already abstract from sensation. It is the first and only example of a language that demands, without itself providing, the necessary preparatory training.

Script, therefore, presupposes a fully developed grammar, since the activity of writing and reading is infinitely more abstract than that of speaking and hearing. Reading consists in scanning a script-image *with a feeling of the significances of corresponding word-sounds;* what script contains is not signs for things, but signs for other signs. The grammatical sense must be enlarged by instantaneous comprehension.

[1] See below.

The word is a possession of man generally, whereas writing belongs exclusively to Culture-men. In contrast to verbal language it is conditioned, not merely partially, but entirely, by the political and religious Destinies of world-history. All scripts come into being in the *individual* Cultures and are to be reckoned amongst their profoundest symbols. But hitherto a comprehensive history of script has never been produced, and a psychology of its forms and their modifications has never even been attempted. *Writing is the grand symbol of the Far*, meaning not only extension-distance, but also, and above all, duration and future and the will-to-eternity. Speaking and listening take place only in proximity and the present,[1] but through script one speaks to men whom one has never seen, who may not even have been born yet; the voice of a man is heard centuries after he has passed away. It is one of the first distinguishing marks of the *historical* endowment. But for that very reason nothing is more characteristic of a Culture than its inward relation to writing. If we know as little as we do about Indogermanic, it is because the two earliest Cultures whose people made use of this system — the Indian and the Classical — were so *a-historic* in disposition that they not only formed no script of their own, but even fought off alien scripts until well into the Late period of their course. Actually, the whole art of Classical prose is designed immediately for the ear. One read it as if one were speaking, whereas we, by comparison, speak everything as though we were reading it — with the result that in the eternal seesaw between script-image and word-sound we have never attained to a prose style that is perfect in the Attic sense. In the Arabian Culture, on the other hand, each religion developed its own script and kept it even through changes of verbal language; the duration of the sacred books and teachings and the script as symbol of duration belong together. The oldest evidences of alphabetical script are found in southern Arabia in the Minæan and Sabæan scripts — differentiated, without doubt, according to sect — which probably go back to the tenth century before Christ.[2] The Jews, Mandæans, and Manichæans in Babylonia spoke Eastern Aramaic, but all of them had scripts of their own. From the Abbassid period onward Arabic ruled, but Christians and Jews wrote it in their own characters. [3] Islam spread the Arabic script universally amongst its adherents, irrespective of whether their spoken language was Semitic, Mongolian, Aryan, or a Negro tongue.[4] The growth of the writing habit brings with it, everywhere and inevitably, the distinction between the written and the colloquial languages. The written language brings the symbolism

[1] Radio broadcasting does not controvert this. Its characteristic quality is not (as is often supposed) dissemination to vast numbers irrespective of physical distance, but a special intimacy of address to the listening individual. — *Tr.*

[2] See the article "Semitic Language," *Ency. Brit.*, XI ed. — *Tr.*

[3] Similarly the modern Jews of the Dispersion write Yiddish, which is a modified German, in Hebrew characters. — *Tr.*

[4] See Lidzbarski, *Sitz. Berl. Akad.* (1916), p 1218. There is plentiful material in M. Miese, *Die Gesetze der Schriftgeschichte* (1919).

of duration to bear upon its own grammatical condition, which itself yields only slowly and reluctantly to the progressive modifications of the colloquial language — the latter, therefore, always representing at any given moment a younger condition. There is not one Hellenic κοινή, but two,[1] and the immense distance between the written and the living Latin of Imperial times is sufficiently evidenced in the structure of the early Romance languages.[2] The older a Civilization becomes, the more abrupt is the distinction, until we have the gap that to-day separates written Chinese from Kuan-Chua, the spoken language of educated North Chinese — a matter no longer of two dialects but of two reciprocally alien languages.

Here, it should be observed, we have direct expression of the fact that writing is above everything a matter of status, and more particularly an ancient privilege of priesthood. The peasantry is without history *and therefore without writing*. But, even apart from this, there is in Race an unmistakable antipathy to script. It is, I think, a fact of the highest importance to graphology that the more the writer has race (breed), the more cavalierly he treats the ornamental structure of the letters, and the more ready he is to replace this by personal line-pictures. Only the Taboo-man evidences a certain respect for the proper forms of the letters and ever, if unconsciously, tries to reproduce them. It is the distinction between the man of action, who makes history, and the scholar, who merely puts it down on paper, "eternalizes" it. In all Cultures the script is in the keeping of the priesthood, in which class we have to count also the poet and the scholars. The nobility despises writing; it has people to write for it. From the remotest times this activity has had something intellectual-sacerdotal about it. Timeless truths came to be such, not at all through speech, but only when there came to be script for them. It is the opposition of castle and cathedral over again: which shall endure, deed or truth? The archivist's "sources" preserve facts, the holy scripture, truths. What chronicles and documents mean in the first-named, exegesis and library mean in the second. And thus there is something besides cult-architecture that is not decorated with ornament, but *is* ornament [3] — the *book*. The art-history of all Cultural springtimes ought to begin with the script, and the cursive script even before the monumental. Here we can observe the essence of the Gothic style, or of the Magian, at its purest. No other ornament possesses the inwardness of a letter-shape or a manuscript page; nowhere else is arabesque as perfect as it is in the Koran texts on the walls of a mosque. And, then, the great art of initials, the architecture of the marginal picture, the plastic of the covers! In a Koran in the Kufi script every page has the effect of a piece of tapestry. A Gothic book of the Gospels is, as it were, a little cathedral. As for Classical art, it is very sig-

[1] P. Kretschmer, in Gercke-Norden, *Einl. i. d. Altertumswissenschaft*, I, p. 551.
[2] See the articles "Romance Languages" and "Latin Language," *Ency. Brit.*, XI ed. — Tr.
[3] Cf. p. 122.

nificant that the one thing that it did not beautify with its touch was the script and the book-roll — an exception founded in its steady hatred of that which endures, the contempt for a technique which insists on being more than a technique. Neither in Hellas nor in India do we find an art of monumental inscription as in Egypt. It does not seem to have occurred to anybody that a sheet of handwriting of Plato was a relic, or that a fine edition of the dramas of Sophocles ought to be treasured up in the Acropolis.

As the city lifted up its head over the countryside, as the burgher joined the noble and the priest and the urban spirit aspired to supremacy, writing, from being a herald of nobles' fame and of eternal truths, became a means of commercial and scientific intercourse. The Indian and the Classical Cultures rejected the pretension and met the working requirement by importation from abroad; it was as a humble tool of everyday use that alphabetical script slowly won their acceptance. With this event rank, as contemporaneous and like in significance, the introduction into China of the phonetic script about 800, and the discovery of book-printing in the West in the fifteenth century; the symbol of duration and distance was reinforced in the highest degree by making it accessible to the large number. Finally the Civilizations took the last step and brought their scripts into utilitarian form. As we have seen, the discovery of alphabetical script in the Egyptian Civilization, about 2000, was a purely technical innovation. In the same way Li Si, Chancellor to the Chinese Augustus, introduced the Chinese standard script in 227. And lastly, amongst ourselves — though as yet few of us have appreciated the real significance of the fact — a new kind of writing has appeared. That Egyptian alphabetic script is in no wise a final and perfected thing is proved by the discovery of its fellow, our *stenography*, which means no mere shortening of writing, but *the overcoming of the alphabetic script by a new and highly abstract mode of communication*. It is not impossible, indeed, that in the course of the next centuries script-forms of the shorthand kind may displace letters completely.

VIII

May the attempt be made, thus early, to write a morphology of the Culture-languages? Certainly, science has not as yet even discovered that there is such a task. Culture-languages are languages of *historical* men. Their Destiny accomplishes itself not in biological spaces of time, but in step with the organic evolution of strictly limited lifetimes. *Culture languages are historical languages*, which means, primarily, that there is no historical event and no political institution that will not have been determined in part by the spirit of the language employed in it and, conversely, that will not have its influence upon the spiritual form of that language. The build of the Latin sentence is yet another consequence of Rome's battles, which in giving her conquests compelled the nation as a whole to think administratively; German prose bears traces even to-day of the Thirty Years' War in its want of established norms, and early Christian dogma would have acquired a different shape if the oldest Scriptures, instead of being one and all written in Greek, and been set down in Syriac form like those of the Mandæans. But secondarily it means that world-history is dependent — to a degree that students have hitherto scarcely imagined — *upon the existence of script as the essentially historical means of communication.* The State (in the higher sense of the word) presupposes intercourse by writing; the style of all politics is determined absolutely by the significance that the politico-historical thought of the nation attaches in each instance to charters and archives, to signatures, to the products of the publicist; the battle of legislation is a fight for or against a written law; constitutions replace material force by the composition of paragraphs and elevate a piece of writing to the dignity of a weapon. Speech belongs with the present, and writing with duration, but equally, oral understanding pairs with practical experience, and writing with theoretical thought. The bulk of the inner political history of all Late periods can be traced back to this opposition. The ever-varying facts resist the "letter," while *truths demand it* — that is the world-historical opposition of two parties that in one form or another is met with in the great crises of all Cultures. The one lives in actuality, the other flourishes a text in its face; all great revolutions presuppose a literature.

The group of Western Culture-languages appeared in the tenth century. The available bodies of language — namely, the Germanic and Romance dialects (monkish Latin included) — were developed into script-languages under a single spiritual influence. It is *impossible* that there should not be a common character in the development of German, English, Italian, French, and Spanish from 900 to 1900, as also in the history of the Hellenic and Italic (Etruscan included) between 1100 and the Empire. But what is it that, irrespective of the area of extension of language-families or races, acquires specific unity from the landscape-limit of the Culture alone? What modifications have Hellenistic and Latin in common after 300 — in pronunciation and idiom, metrically, grammatically, and stylistically? What is present in German and Italian after 1000, but not in Italian and Rumanian? These and similar questions have never yet been systematically investigated.

Every Culture at its awakening finds itself in the presence of *peasant-languages*, speeches of the cityless countryside, "everlasting," and almost unconcerned with the great events of history, which have gone on through late Culture and Civilization as unwritten dialects and slowly undergone imperceptible changes. On the top of this now the language of the two primary Estates raises itself as the first manifestation of a waking relation that *has* Culture, that *is* Culture. Here, in the ring of nobility and priesthood, languages become Culture-languages, and, more particularly, *talk belongs with the castle, and speech to the cathedral.* And thus on the very threshold of evolution the plantlike separates itself from the animal, the destiny of the living from the destiny of the dead, that of the organic side from that of the mechanical side of understanding. For the Totem side affirms and the Taboo side denies, blood and Time. Everywhere we meet, and very early indeed, rigid cult-languages whose sanctity is guaranteed by their inalterability, systems long dead, or alien to life and artificially fettered, which have the strict vocabulary that the formulation of eternal truths requires. Old Vedic stiffened as a religious language, and with it Sanskrit as a savant-language. The Egyptian of the Old Kingdom was perpetuated as priests' language, so that in the New Empire sacred formulæ were no more understandable than the *Carmen Saliare* and the hymn of the Fratres Arvales in Augustan times.[1] In the Arabian pre-Cultural period Babylonian, Hebrew, and Avestan simultaneously went out of use as workaday languages — probably in the second century before Christ — indeed on that very account Jews and Persians used them in their Scriptures as in opposition to Aramaic and Pehlevi. The same significance attached to Gothic Latin for the Church, Humanists' Latin for the learning of the Baroque, Church Slavonic in Russia, and no doubt Sumerian in Babylonia.

In contrast with this, the nursery of talk is in the early castles and palaces of assize. Here the *living* Culture-languages have been formed. Talk is the custom of speech, its manners — "good form" in the intonation and idiom, fine tact in choice of words and mode of expression. All these things are a mark of *race;* they are learned not in the monastery cell or the scholar's study, but in polite intercourse and from living examples. In noble society, and as a hall-mark of nobility, the language of Homer,[2] as also the old French of the Crusades and the Middle High German of the Hohenstaufen, were erected out of the ordinary talk of the country-side. When we speak of the great epic poets, the Skalds, the Troubadours, as creators of language, we must not forget that they began by being trained for their task, *in language as in other things*, by moving in noble circles. The great art by which the Culture finds its tongue is the achievement of a race and not that of a craft.

The clerical language on the other hand starts from concepts and conclusions. It labours to improve the dialectical capacities of the words and sentence-forms to the maximum. There sets in, consequently, an ever-increasing differentiation of scholastic and courtly, of the idiom of intellectual from that of social intercourse. Beyond all divisions of language-families there is a component common to the expression of Plotinus and Thomas Aquinas, of Veda and Mishna. Here we have the starting-point of all the ripe scholar-languages of the West — which, German and English and French alike, bear

---

[1] For this reason I am one of those who believe that, even quite late, Etruscan still played a very important part in the colleges of the Roman priesthood.

[2] Precisely for this reason it has to be recognized that the Homeric poems, which were first fixed in the colonization period, can only give us an urban literary language and not the courtly conversation-language in which they were originally declaimed.

to this day the unmistakable signs of their origin in scholars' Latin — and, therefore, the starting point of all the apparatus of technical expression and logical sentence-form. This opposition between the modes of understanding of "Society" and of Science renews itself again and again till far into the Late period. The centre of gravity in the history of French was decisively on the side of race; i.e., of talk. At the Court of Versailles, in the salons of Paris, the *esprit précieux* of the Arthurian romances evolves into the "conversation," the classical art of talk, whose dictature the whole West acknowledges. The fact that Ionic-Attic, too, was fashioned entirely in the halls of the tyrants and in symposia created great difficulties for Greek philosophy: for later on, it was almost impossible to discuss the syllogism in the language of Alcibiades. On the other hand, German prose, in the decisive phase of Baroque, had no central point on which it could rise to excellence, and so even to-day it oscillates in point of style between French and Latin — courtly and scholarly — according as the author's intuition is to express himself well or accurately. Our Classical writers, thanks to their linguistic origin in office or study and their stay as tutors in the castles and the little courts, arrived indeed at personal styles, and others are able to imitate these styles, but a specifically German prose, standard for all, they were unable to create.

To these two class-languages the rise of the city added a third, the language of the bourgeoisie, which is the true script-speech, reasoned and utilitarian, prose in the strictest sense of the word. It swings gently between the expression-modes of elegant society and of learning, in the one direction thinking for ever of new turns and words *à la mode*, in the other keeping sturdy hold on its existing stock of ideas. But in its inner essence it is of a *mercantile* nature. It feels itself frankly as a class badge *vis-à-vis* the historyless-changeless phrasing of the "people" which Luther and others employed, to the great scandal of their superficial contemporaries. With the final victory of the city the urban speech absorbs into itself that of elegance and that of learning. There arises in the upper strata of megalopolitan populations the uniform, keenly intelligent, practical κοινή, the child and symbol of its Civilization, equally averse from dialect and poetry — something perfectly mechanical, precise, cold, leaving as little as possible to gesture. These final homeless and rootless languages can be learned by every trader and porter — Hellenistic in Carthage and on the Oxus, Chinese in Java, English in Shanghai — and for their comprehension talk has no importance or meaning. And if we inquire what really created these languages, we find not the spirit of a race or of a religion, but the spirit of economics.

CHAPTER VI

CITIES AND PEOPLES

(C)

PRIMITIVES, CULTURE–PEOPLES, FELLAHEEN

CITIES AND PEOPLES

(C)

PRIMITIVES, CULTURE–PEOPLES, FELLAHEEN

I

Now at last it is possible to approach — if with extreme precaution — the conception "people," and to bring order into that chaos of people-forms that the historical research of the present day has only succeeded in making worse confounded than before. There is no word that has been used more freely and more utterly uncritically, yet none that calls for a stricter critique, than this. Very careful historians, even, after going to much trouble to clear their theoretical basis (up to a point) slide back thereafter into treating peoples, race-parts, and speech-communities as completely equivalent. If they find the name of a people, it counts without more ado as the designation of a language as well. If they discover an inscription of three words, they believe they have established a racial connexion. If a few "roots" correspond, the curtain rises at once on a primitive people with a primitive habitat in the background. And the modern nationalist spirit has only enhanced this "thinking in terms of peoples."

But is it the Hellenes, the Dorians, or the Spartans that are a people? If the Romans were a people, what are we to say about the Latins? And what kind of a unit within the population of Italy at *c.* 400 do we mean by the name "Etruscan?" Has not their "nationality," like that of Basques and Thracians, been made actually to depend upon the build of their language? What ethnic idea underlies the words "American," "Swiss," "Jew," "Boer"? Blood, speech, faith, State, landscape — what in all these is determinative in the formation of a people? In general, relationships of blood and language are determined only by way of scholarship, and the ordinary individual is perfectly unconscious of them. "Indogermanic" is purely and simply a scientific, more particularly a philological, concept. The attempt of Alexander the Great to fuse Greeks and Persians together was a complete failure, and we have recently had experience of the real strength of Anglo-German community of feeling. But "people" is a linkage of which one is *conscious*. In ordinary usage, one designates as one's "people" — and with feeling — that community, out of the many to which one belongs, which inwardly stands nearest to one.[1] And then he extends the use of this concept, which is really quite particular and derived from personal experience, to collectivities of the most varied kinds. For Cæsar the Arverni were a "*civitas*"; for us the Chinese are a "nation." On this basis, it was the Athenians and not the Greeks who constituted a nation, and in fact there were only a few individuals who, like Isocrates, felt themselves *primarily* as Hellenes. On this basis, one of two brothers may call himself a Swiss and the other, with equal right, a German. These are not philosophical concepts, but historical facts. A people is an aggregate of men which feels itself a unit. The Spartiates [2] felt themselves a people in *this* sense; the "Dorians" of 1100, too, probably, but those of 400 certainly not. The Crusaders became genuinely a people in taking the oath of Clermont; the Mormons in their expulsion from Missouri, in 1839; [3] the Mamertines [4] by their need of winning for themselves a stronghold of refuge.[5] Was the formative principle very different with the Jacobins and Hyksos? How many peoples may have originated in a chief's following or a band of fugitives? Such a group can change race, like the Osmanli, who appeared in Asia Minor as Mongols; or language, like the Sicilian Normans; or name, like Achæans and Danaoi. So long as the common feeling is there, the people as such is there.

We have to distinguish the destiny of a people from its name. The latter is often the only thing about which information remains to us; but can we fairly conclude from a name anything about the history, the descent, the language, or even merely the identity of those who bore it? Here again the historical researcher is to blame, in that, whatever his theory may have been, he has in practice treated the relation between name and bearer as simply as he would treat, say, the personal names of to-day. Have we any conception of the number of unexplored possibilities in this field? To begin with, the very act of name-giving is of enormous importance in early associations. For with a name the human group consciously sets itself up with a sort of sacral dignity. But, here, cult- and war-names may exist side by side; others the land or the heritage may provide; the tribal name may be exchanged for that of an eponymous hero, as with the Osmanli; [6] lastly, an unlimited number of alien names can be applied along the frontiers of a group without more than a part of the community ever hearing them at all. If only such names as these be handed

---

[1] So much so that the workers of the great cities call themselves *the* People, thereby excluding the bourgeoisie, with which no community feeling conjoins them. The bourgeoisie of 1789 did exactly the same.

[2] The dominant nucleus within the Spartan ensemble. — *Tr.*

[3] Ed. Meyer, *Ursprung und Geschichte der Mormonen* (1912), pp. 128, et seq. [An extended summary of Mormon history will be found in the article "Mormons," *Ency. Brit.*, XI ed. — *Tr.*]

[4] Ex-mercenaries of Agathocles, tyrant of Syracuse, who seized and settled in Messina. The questions arising out of this act precipitated the First Punic War. — *Tr.*

[5] A still more celebrated case is the "ambulatory Polis" formed by Xenophon's Ten Thousand. — *Tr.*

[6] And in numerous Classical instances. — *Tr.*

down, it becomes practically inevitable that conclusions about the bearers of them will be wrong. The indubitably sacral names of Franks, Alemanni, and Saxons have superseded a host of names of the period of the Varus battle — but if we did not happen to know this, we should long ago have been convinced that an expulsion or annihilation of old tribes by new intruders had taken place here. The names "Romans" and "Quirites," "Spartans" and "Lacedæmonians," "Carthaginian" and "Punic" have endured side by side — here again there was a risk of supposing two peoples instead of one. In what relation the names "Pelasgi," "Achæans," "Danai," stand to one another we shall never learn, and had we nothing more than these names, the scholar would long ago have assigned to each a separate people, complete with language and racial affinities. Has it not been attempted to draw from the regional designation "Doric" conclusions as to the course of the Dorian migration? How often may a people have adopted a land-name and taken it along with them? This is the case with the modern Prussians, but also with the modern Parsees, Jews, and Turks, while the opposite is the case in Burgundy and Normandy. The name "Hellenes" arose about 650, and, therefore, cannot be connected with any movement of population. Lorraine (Lothringen) received the name of a perfectly unimportant prince, and that, in connexion with the decision of a heritage and not a folk-migration. Paris called the Germans Allemands in 1814, Prussians in 1870, Boches in 1914 — in other circumstances three distinct peoples might have been supposed to be covered by these names. The West-European is called in the East a Frank, the Jew a Spaniole — the fact is readily explained by historical circumstances, but what would a philologist have produced from the *words alone?*

It is not to be imagined at what results the scholars of A.D. 3000 might arrive if they worked by present-day methods on names, linguistic remains, and the notion of original homes and migration. For example, the Teutonic Knights about 1300 drove out the heathen "Prussians," and in 1870 these people suddenly appear on their wanderings at the gates of Paris! The Romans, pressed by the Goths, emigrate from the Tiber to the lower Danube! Or a part of them perhaps settled in Poland, where Latin was spoken? Charlemagne on the Weser defeated the Saxons, who thereupon emigrated to the neighbourhood of Dresden, their places being taken by the Hanoverians, whose original settlement, according to the dynasty-name, was on the Thames! The historian who writes down the history of names instead of that of peoples, forgets that names, too, have their destinies. So also languages, which, with their migrations, modifications, victories, and defeats, are inconclusive even as to the existence of peoples associated with them. This is the basic error of Indo-Germanic research in particular. If in historic times the names "Pfalz" and "Calabria" have moved about, if Hebrew has been driven from Palestine to Warsaw, and Persian from the Tigris to India, what conclusions can be drawn from the history of the Etruscan name and the alleged "Tyrsenian" inscription at Lemnos? [1] Or did the French and the Haytian Negroes, as shown by their common language, once form a single primitive people? In the region between Budapest and Constantinople to-day two Mongolian, one Semitic, two Classical, and three Slavonic languages are spoken, and these speech-communities all feel themselves essentially as peoples. [2] If we were to build up a migration-story here, the error of the method would be manifested in some singular results. "Doric" is a dialect designation — that we know, and that is all we know. No doubt some few dialects of this group spread rapidly, but that is no proof of the spread or even of the existence of a human stock belonging with it. [3]

II

Thus we come to the pet idea of modern historical thought. If a historian meets a people that has achieved something, he feels that he owes it to these people to answer the question: Whence did it come? It is a matter of dignity for a people to have come from somewhere and to have an original home. The notion that it is at home in the place where we find it is almost an insulting assumption. Wandering is a cherished saga-motive of primitive mankind, but its employment in serious research also has become a sheer mania. *Whether* the Chinese invaded China or the Egyptians Egypt no one inquires, the question being always *when* and *whence* they did so. It would be less of an effort to originate the Semites in Scandinavia or the Aryans in Canaan than to abandon the notion of an original home.

Now, the fact that all early populations were highly mobile is unquestionable. In it, for example, lies the secret of the Libyan problem. The Libyans or their predecessors spoke Hamitic, but, as shown even by old Egyptian reliefs, they were all blond and blue-eyed and, therefore, doubtless of North-European provenance. [4] In Asia Minor at least three migration-strata since 1300 have been determined, which are related probably to the attacks of the "Sea-peoples" in Egypt, and something similar has been shown in the Mexican Culture. But as to the nature of these movements we know nothing at all. In any case, there can be no question of migrations such as modern historians like to picture

[1] See *Ency. Brit.*, XI ed., Vol. IX, p. 860. — *Tr.*

[2] In Macedonia, in the nineteenth century, Serbs, Bulgars, and Greeks all founded schools for the anti-Turkish population. If it happens that a village has been taught Serb, even the next generation consists of fanatical Serbs. The present strength of the "nations" is thus merely a consequence of previous school-policy.

[3] For Beloch's scepticism concerning the reputed Dorian migration see his *Griechische Geschichte*, I, 2, Section VIII. [A brief account of the question, by J. L. Myres, is in *Ency. Brit.*, XI ed., article "Dorians." — *Tr.*]

[4] C. Mehlis, *Die Berberfrage* (*Archiv für Anthropologie* 39, pp. 249, et seq.) where relations between North German and Mauretanian ceramics, and even resemblances of toponymy (rivers, mountains) are dealt with. The old pyramid buildings of West Africa are closely related, on the one hand, to the Nordic dolmens (*Hünengräber*) of Holstein and, on the other, to the graves of the Old Kingdom (some illustrations in L. Frobenius, *Der kleinafrikanische Grabbau*, 1916).

— movements of close-pressed peoples traversing the lands in great masses, pushing and being pushed till finally they come to rest somewhere or other. It is not the alterations in themselves, but the conceptions we have formed about them, that have spoilt our outlook upon the nature of the peoples. Peoples in the modern sense of the word do not wander, and that which of old *did* wander needs to be very carefully examined before it is labelled, as the label will not always stand for the same thing. The motive, too, that is ever-lastingly assigned to these migrations is colourless and worthy of the century that invented it — material necessity. Hunger would normally lead to efforts of quite a different sort, and it has certainly been only the last of the motives that drove men of race out of their nests — although it is understandable that it would very frequently make itself felt when such bands suddenly en-countered a military obstacle. It was doubtless, in this simple and strong kind of man, the primary microcosmic urgency to move in free space which sprang up out of the depths of his soul as love of adventure, daring, liking for power and booty; as a blazing desire, to us almost incomprehensible, for deeds, for joy of carnage, for the death of the hero. Often, too, no doubt, domestic strife or fear of the revenge of the stronger, was the motive, but again a strong and manly one. Motives like these are infectious — the "man who stays at home" is a coward. Was it common bodily hunger, again, that induced the Crusades, or the expeditions of Cortez and Pizarro, or in our time the ven-tures of "wild west" pioneers? Where, in history, we find the little handful invading wide lands, it is ever the voices of the blood, the longing for high destinies, that drive them.

Further, we have to consider the position in the country traversed by the invaders. Its characteristics are always modified more or less, but the modi-fications are due not merely to the influence of the immigrants, but more and more to the nature of the settled population, which in the end becomes numeri-cally overwhelming.

Obviously, in spaces almost empty of men it is easy for the weaker simply to evade the onslaught, and as a rule he was able to do so. But in later and denser conditions, the inroad spelt dispossession for the weaker, who must either defend himself successfully or else win new lands for old. Already there is the out-thrust into space. No tribe lives without constant contacts on all sides and a mistrustful readiness to stand to arms. The hard necessity of war breeds men. Peoples grow by, and against, other peoples to inward greatness. Weapons become weapons against men and not beasts. And finally we have the only migration-form that counts in historic times — warrior bands sweep through thoroughly populated countries, whose inhabitants remain, undisturbed and upstanding, as an essential part of the spoils of victory. And then, the victors being in a minority, completely new situations arise. Peoples of strong inward form spread themselves on top of much larger but formless populations, and the further transformations of peoples, languages, and races depend upon very complicated factors of detail. Since the decisive investigations of Beloch [1] and Delbrück [2] we know that all migrant peoples — and the Persians of Cyrus, the Mamertines and the Crusaders, the Ostrogoths and the "Sea-peoples" of the Egyptian inscriptions were all peoples in this sense — were, in comparison with the inhabitants of the regions they occupied, very small in numbers, just a few thousand warriors, superior to the natives only in respect of their determination to *be* a Destiny and not to submit to one. It was not inhabitable, but inhabited, land of which they took possession, and thus the relation between the two peoples became a question of status, the migration turned into the campaign, and the process of settling down became a political process. And here again, in presence of the fact that at a historic distance of time the successes of a small war-band, with the consequent spread of the victor's names and language, may all too easily be taken for a "migration of peoples," it is necessary to repeat our question, what, in fact, the men, things, and factors are that *can* migrate.

Here are some of the answers — the name of a district or that of a collectivity (or of a hero, adopted by his followers), in that it spreads, becomes extinct here and is taken by or given to a totally different population there: in that it may pass from land to people and travel with the latter or vice versa — the language of the conqueror or that of the conquered, or even a third language, adopted for reciprocal understanding — the war-band of a chief which subdues whole countries and propagates itself through captive women, or some accidental group of heterogeneous adventurers, or a tribe with its women and children, like the Philistines of 1200, who quite in the Germanic fashion trekked with their ox-wagons along the Phœnician coast to Egypt.[3] In such conditions, we may again ask, can conclusions be drawn from the destinies of names and languages as to those of peoples and races? There is only one possible answer, a decided negative.

Amongst the "Sea-peoples" that repeatedly attacked Egypt in the thirteenth century appear the *names* of Danai and Achæans — but in Homer both are almost mythical designations — the *name* of the Lukka — which adhered later to Lycia, though the inhabitants of that country called themselves Tramilæ — and the *names* of the Etruscans, the Sards, the Siculi — but this in no wise proved that these "Tursha" spoke the later Etruscan, nor that there was the slightest physical connexion with the like-named inhabitants of Italy or anything else entitling us to speak of "one and the same people." Assuming that the Lemnos inscription is Etruscan, and Etruscan an Indogermanic language, much could be deduced therefrom in the domain of linguis-

---

[1] *Die Bevölkerung der griechisch-römischen Welt* (1886).

[2] *Geschichte der Kriegskunst* (from 1900).

[3] Rameses III, who defeated them, portrayed their expedition in the relief of Medinet Habet. W. M. Müller, *Asien und Europa*, p. 366.

tic history, but in that of racial history nothing whatever. Rome was an Etruscan city, but is not the fact completely without bearing upon the *soul* of the Roman people? Are the Romans Indogermanic because they happen to speak a Latin dialect? The ethnologists recognize a Mediterranean Race and an Alpine Race, and north and south of these an astonishing physical resemblance between North-Germans and Libyans; but the philologists know that the Basques are in virtue of their speech a "pre-Indogermanic" — Iberian — population. The two views are mutually exclusive. Were the builders of Mycenæ and Tiryns "Hellenes"? — it would be as pertinent to ask were the Ostrogoths Germans. I confess that I do not comprehend why such questions are formulated at all.

For me, the "people" is a *unit of the soul*. The great events of history were not really achieved by peoples; *they themselves created the peoples*. Every act alters the soul of the doer. Even when the event is preceded by some grouping around or under a famous name, the fact that there is a people and not merely a band behind the prestige of that name is not a condition, but a result of the event. It was the fortunes of their migrations that made the Ostrogoths and the Osmanli what they afterwards were. The "Americans" did *not* immigrate from Europe; the name of the Florentine geographer Amerigo Vespucci designates to-day not only a continent, but also a people in the true sense of the word, whose specific character was born in the spiritual upheavals of 1775 and, above all, 1861–5.

This is the one and only connotation of the word "people." Neither unity of speech nor physical descent is decisive. That which distinguishes the people from the population, raises it up out of the population, and will one day let it find its level again in the population is always the inwardly lived experience of the "we." The deeper this feeling is, the stronger is the *vis viva* of the people. There are energetic and tame, ephemeral and indestructible, forms of peoples. They can change speech, name, race, and land, but so long as their soul lasts, they can gather to themselves and transform human material of any and every provenance. The Roman name in Hannibal's day meant a people, in Trajan's time nothing more than a population.

Of course, it is often quite justifiable to align peoples with races, but "race" in this connexion must not be interpreted in the present-day Darwinian sense of the word. It cannot be accepted, surely, that a people was ever held together by the mere unity of physical origin, or, if it were, could maintain that unity even for ten generations. It cannot be too often reiterated that this physiological provenance has no existence except for science — never for folk-consciousness — and that no people was ever yet stirred to enthusiasm for *this* ideal of blood-purity. In race there is nothing material, but something cosmic and directional, the felt harmony of a Destiny, the single cadence of the march of historical Being. It is inco-ordination of this (wholly metaphysical) beat that produces race-hatred, which is just as strong between Germans and Frenchmen as it is between Germans and Jews, and it is resonance on this beat that makes the true love — so akin to hate — between man and wife. He who has not race knows nothing of this perilous love. If a part of the human multitude that now speaks Indogermanic languages, cherishes a certain race-ideal, what is evidenced thereby is not the existence of the prototype-people so dear to the scholar, but the metaphysical force and power of the ideal. It is highly significant that this ideal is expressed, never in the whole population, but mainly in its warrior-element and pre-eminently in its genuine nobility — that is, in men who live entirely in a world of facts, under the spell of historical becoming, destiny-men who will and dare — and it was precisely in the early times (another significant point) that a born alien of quality and dignity could without particular difficulty gain admittance to the ruling class, and wives in particular were chosen for their "breed" and not their descent. Correspondingly, the impress of race-traits is weakest (as may be observed even to-day) in the true priestly and scholarly natures,[1] even though these often do stand in close blood-relationship to the others. A strong spirit trains up the body into a product of art. The Romans formed, in the midst of the confused and even heteroclite tribes of Italy, a race of the firmest and strictest inward unity that was neither Etruscan nor Latin nor merely "Classical," but quite specifically Roman.[2] Nowhere is the force that cements a people set before us more plainly than in Roman busts of the late Republican period.

I will cite yet another example, than which none more clearly exhibits the errors that these scholars' notions of people, language, and race inevitably entail, and in which lies the ultimate, perhaps the determining reason why the Arabian Culture has never yet been recognized as an organism. It is that of the Persians. Persian is an Aryan language, hence "the Persians" are an "Indogermanic people," and hence Persian history and religion are the affair of "Iranian" philology.

To begin with, is Persian a language of equal rank with the Indian, derived from a common ancestor, *or is it merely an Indian dialect?* Seven centuries of linguistic development, scriptless and therefore very rapid, lie between the Old Vedic of the Indian texts and the Behistun Inscription [3] of Darius. It is almost as great a gap as that between the Latin of Tacitus and the French of the Strassburg Oath of 842.[4] Now the Tell-el-Amarna letters and the archives

---

[1] Which, therefore, have discovered for themselves the nonsensical designation "aristocracy of intellect" (*Geistesadel*).

[2] Although — or should we say "thus"? — Rome accorded citizenship to freedmen, who in general were of wholly alien blood, and sons of ex-slaves were admitted to the Senate even by Appius Claudius the Censor in 310. One of them, Flavius, had already been curule ædile.

[3] See articles "Persia (history: ancient)," "Behistun," "Cuneiform," in *Ency. Brit.*, XI ed., or indeed almost any work upon Babylonian and Persian antiquities. — *Tr.*

[4] Sworn by Louis the German and Charles the Bald in both languages. The manuscript of the oath, however, is later — say, 950. — *Tr.*

of Boghaz Keüi tell us many "Aryan" names of persons and gods of the middle of the second millennium B.C. — that is, the Vedic Age of Chivalry. It is Palestine and Syria that furnish these names. Nevertheless, Eduard Meyer observes [1] that they are Indian and not Persian, and the same holds good for the numerals that have now been discovered.[2] There is not a unit of Persians, or of any other "people" in the sense of our historical writers. They were Indian heroes, who rode westward and with their precious weapon the war-horse and their own ardent energy made themselves felt as a power far and wide in the ageing Babylonian Empire.

About 600 there appears in the middle of this world Persis, a little district with a politically united population of peasant barbarians. Herodotus says that of its tribes only three were of genuine Persian nationality. Had the language of these knights of old lived on in the hills, and is "Persians" really a land-name that passed to a people? The Medes, who were very similar, bear only the name of a land where an upper warrior-stratum had learned through great political successes to feel itself as a unit. In the Assyrian archives of Sargon and his successors (about 700) are found, along with the non-Aryan place-names, numerous "Aryan" names of persons, all leading figures, but Tiglath-Pileser IV (745–727) calls the people black-haired.[3] It can only have been later that the "Persian people" of Cyrus and Darius was formed, out of men of varied provenance, but forged to a strong inner unity of lived experience. But when, scarce two centuries later, the Macedonians put an end to their lordship — was it that the Persians in this form were *no longer in existence?* (Was there still a Lombard people at all in Italy in A.D. 900?) It is certain that the very wide diffusion of the empire-language of Persia, and the distribution of the few thousands of adult males from Persia over the immense system of military and administrative business, must long ago have led to the dissolution of the Persian nation and set up in its place, as carriers of the Persian name in upper-class conscious of itself as a *political* unit, of whose members very few could have claimed descent from the invaders from Persia.[4] There is, indeed, not even a country that can be considered as the theatre of Persian history. The events of the period from Darius to Alexander took place partly in northern Mesopotamia (that is, in the midst of an Aramaic-speaking population), partly lower down in old Sinear, anywhere but in Persis, where the handsome buildings begun by Xerxes were never carried out. The Parthians of the succeeding Achæmenid period were a Mongol tribe which had adopted a Persian dialect and in the midst of this people sought to embody the Persian national feeling in themselves.

[1] "*Die ältesten datierten Zeugnisse der iranischen Sprache*" (*Zeitschr. f. vgl. Sprachf.* 42, p. 26.)
[2] See above, p. 145.
[3] Ed. Meyer, op. cit., pp. 1, et seq.
[4] Compare the absorption of the Norman conquerors into England and the subsequent development of an English aristocracy. — *Tr.*

Here the Persian religion emerges as a problem no less difficult than those of race and language.[1] Scholarship has associated it with these as though the association were self-evident, and has, therefore, treated it always with reference to India. But the religion of these land-Vikings was not related to, it was identical with the Vedic, as shown by the divine pairs Mitra-Varuna and Indra-Nasatya of the Boghaz Keüi texts. And within this religion which held up its head in the middle of the Babylonian world Zarathustra now appeared, from out of the lower ranks of the people, as reformer. It is known that he was not a Persian. That which he created (as I hope to show) was a transfer of *Vedic* religion into the forms of the *Aramæan* world-contemplation, in which already there were the faint beginnings of the Magian religiousness. The *dævas*, the gods of the old Indian beliefs, grew to be the demons of the Semitic and the jinn of the Arabian. Yahweh and Beelzebub are related to one another precisely as Ahuramazda and Ahriman in this peasant-religion, which was essentially Aramæan and, therefore, founded in an ethical-dualistic world-feeling. Eduard Meyer [2] has correctly established the difference between the Indian and the Iranian view of the world, but, owing to his erroneous premises, has not recognized its origin. *Zarathustra is a travelling-companion of the prophets of Israel,* who like him, and at the same time, transformed the old (Mosaic-Canaanitish) beliefs of the people. It is significant that the whole eschatology is a common possession of the Persian and Jewish religions, and that the Avesta texts were originally written in Aramaic (in Parthian times) and only afterwards translated into Pehlevi.[3]

But already in Parthian times there occurred amongst both Persians and Jews that profoundly intimate change which makes no longer tribal attachment but orthodoxy the hall-mark of nationality.[4] A Jew who went over to the Mazda faith *became thereby a Persian;* a Persian who became a Christian belonged to the Nestorian "people." The very dense population of northern Mesopotamia — the motherland of the Arabian Culture — is partly of Jewish and partly of Persian nationality in this sense of the word, which is not at all concerned with race and very little with language. Even before the birth of Christ, "Infidel" designates the non-Persian as it designates the non-Jew.

This nation is the "Persian people" of the Sassanid empire, and, connected with the fact, we find that Pehlevi and Hebrew die out simultaneously, Aramaic becoming the mother tongue of both communities. If we speak in terms of Aryans and Semites, the Persians in the time of the Tell-el-Amarna Corre-

---

[1] For what follows, cf. Ch. VII — IX.

[2] *Geschichte des Altertums*, I, § 590, et seq.

[3] Andreas and Wackernagel, *Nachrichten der Göttingischen Gesellschaft der Wissenschaften* (1911), p. 1, et seq. [On the subject generally, see articles by K. Geldner, "Zend-Avesta" and "Zoroaster," and by Ed. Meyer, "Parthia," in *Ency. Brit.*, XI ed. — *Tr.*]

[4] See, further, below.

spondence were Aryans, but no "people": in that of Darius a people, but without race: in Sassanid times a community of believers, but of Semitic origin. There is no proto-Persian "people" branched off from the Aryan, nor a general history of the Persians, and for the three special histories, which are held together only by certain linguistic relations, there is not even a common historical theatre.

III

With this are laid, at last, the foundations for a *morphology of peoples*. Directly its essence is seen, we see also an inward order in the historical stream of the peoples. They are neither linguistic nor political nor zoölogical, but spiritual, units. And this leads at once to the further distinction between *peoples before, within, and after a Culture*. It is a fact that has been profoundly felt in all ages that Culture-peoples are *more distinct* in character than the rest. Their predecessors I will call primitive peoples. These are the fugitive and heterogeneous associations that form and dissolve without ascertainable rule, till at last, in the presentiment of a still unborn Culture (as, for example, in the pre-Homeric, the pre-Christian, and the Germanic periods), phase by phase, becoming ever more definite in type, they assemble the human material of a population into groups, though all the time little or no alteration has been occurring in the stamp of man. Such a superposition of phases leads from the Cimbri and Teutones through the Marcomanni and Goths to the Franks, Lombards, and Saxons. Instances of primitive peoples are the Jews and Persians of the Seleucid age, the "Sea-peoples," the Egyptian Nomes of Menes's time.[1] And that which follows a Culture we may call — from its best-known example, the Egyptians of post-Roman times — fellah-peoples.

In the tenth century of our era the Faustian soul suddenly awoke and manifested itself in innumerable shapes. Amongst these, side by side with the architecture and the ornament, there appears a distinctly characterized form of "people." Out of the people-shapes of the Carolingian Empire — the Saxons, Swabians, Franks, Visigoths, Lombards — arise suddenly the German, the French, the Spaniards, the Italians. Hitherto (consciously and deliberately or not) historical research has uniformly regarded these Culture-peoples as something in being, as primaries, and have treated the Culture itself as secondary, as their product. The creative units of history, accordingly, were simply the Indians, the Greeks, the Romans, the Germans, and so on. As the Greek Culture was the work of the Hellenes, they must have been in existence as such far earlier; therefore they must have been immigrants. Any other idea of creator and creation seemed inconceivable.

I regard it, therefore, as a discovery of decisive importance that the facts here set forth lead to the reverse conclusion. It will be established in all rigour

---

[1] Dynasty I. — *Tr.*

that the great Cultures are entities, primary or original, that arise out of the deepest foundations of spirituality, and that the peoples under the spell of a Culture are, alike in their inward form and in their whole manifestation, its products and not its authors. These shapes in which humanity is seized and moulded possess style and style-history no less than kinds of art and modes of thought. The people of Athens is a symbol not less than the Doric temple, the Englishman not less than modern physics. There are peoples of Apollinian, Magian, Faustian cast. The Arabian Culture was *not* created by "the Arabs" — quite the contrary; for the Magian Culture begins in the time of Christ, and the Arabian people represents its last great creation of that kind, a community bonded by Islam as the Jewish and Persian communities before it had been bonded by their religions. World-history is the history of the great Cultures, and peoples are but the symbolic forms and vessels in which the men of these Cultures fulfil their Destinies.

In each of these Cultures, Mexican and Chinese, Indian and Egyptian, there is — whether our science is aware of it or not — *a group of great peoples of identical style*, which arises at the beginning of the springtime, forming states and carrying history, and throughout the course of its evolution bears its fundamental form onward to the goal. They are in the highest degree unlike amongst themselves — it is scarcely possible to conceive of a sharper contrast than that between Athenians and Spartans, Germans and Frenchmen, Tsin and Tsu — and all military history shows national hatred as the loftiest method of inducting historic decisions. But the moment that a people alien to the Culture makes an appearance in the field of history, there awakens everywhere an overpowering feeling of spiritual relationship, and the notion of the barbarian — meaning the man who inwardly does *not* belong to the Culture — is as clear-cut in the peoples of the Egyptian settlements and the Chinese world of states as it is in the Classical. The energy of the form is so high that it grasps and recasts neighbouring peoples, witness the Carthaginians of Roman times with their half-Classical style, and the Russians who have figured as a people of Western style from Catherine the Great to the fall of Petrine Tsardom.

Peoples in the style of their Culture we will call *Nations*, the word itself distinguishing them from the forms that precede and that follow them. It is not merely a strong feeling of "we" that forges the inward unity of its most significant of all major associations; *underlying the nation there is an Idea*. This stream of a collective being possesses a very deep relation to Destiny, to Time, and to History, a relation that is different in each instance and one, too, that determines the relation of the human material to race, language, land, state, and religion. As the styles of the Old Chinese and the Classical peoples differ, so also the styles of their histories.

Life as experienced by primitive and by fellaheen peoples is just the zoological up-and-down, a planless happening without goal or cadenced march in time, wherein occurrences are many, but, in the last analysis, devoid of significance. The only historical peoples, the peoples whose existence *is world-history*, are the nations. Let us be perfectly clear as to what is meant by this. The Ostrogoths suffered a great destiny, and therefore, inwardly, they have no history. Their battles and settlements were not necessary and therefore were episodic; their end was insignificant. In 1500 B.C. that which lived about Mycenæ and Tiryns was not *as yet* a nation, and that which lived in Minoan Crete was *no longer* a nation. Tiberius was the last ruler who tried to lead a Roman nation further on the road of history, who sought to *retrieve* it for history. By Marcus Aurelius there was only a Romanic population to be defended — a field for occurrences, but no longer for history. How many free pre-generations of Mede or Achæan or Hun folk there were, in what sort of social groups their predecessors and their descendants lived, cannot be determined and depends upon no rule. But of a nation the life-period *is* determinate, and so are the pace and the rhythm in which its history moves to fulfilment. From the beginning of the Chóu period to the rulership of Shih-Hwang-ti, from the events on which the Troy legend was founded to Augustus, and from Thinite times to the XVIII Dynasty, the numbers of generations are more or less the same. The "Late" period of the Culture, from Solon to Alexander, from Luther to Napoleon, embraces no more than about ten generations. Within such limits the destiny of the genuine Culture-people, and with it that of world-history in general, reach fulfilment. The Romans, the Arabs, the Prussians, are late-born nations. How many generations of Fabii and Junii had already come and gone *as Romans* by the time Cannæ was fought?

Further, nations are *the true city-building peoples*. In the strongholds they arose, with the cities they ripen to the full height of their world-consciousness, and in the world-cities they dissolve. Every town-formation that has character has also *national* character. The village, which is wholly a thing of race, does not yet possess it; the megalopolis possesses it no longer. Of this essential, which so characteristically colours the nation's public life that its slightest manifestation identifies it, we cannot exaggerate — we can scarcely imagine — the force, the self-sufficingness, and the *loneliness*. If between the souls of two Cultures the screen is impenetrable, if no Western may ever hope completely to understand the Indian or the Chinese, this is equally so, even more so, as between well-developed nations. Nations understand one another as little as individuals do so. Each understands merely a self-created picture of the other, and individuals with the insight to penetrate deeper are few and far between. *Vis-à-vis* the Egyptians, all the Classical peoples necessarily felt themselves as relatives in one whole, but as between themselves they never understood each other. What sharper contrast is there than that between the Athenian and the Spartan spirit? German, French, and English modes of philosophical thinking are distinct, not merely in Bacon, Descartes, and Leibniz, but already in the age of Scholasticism; [1] and even now, in modern physics and chemistry, the scientific method, the choice and type of experiments and hypotheses, their inter-relations, and their relative importance for the course and aim of the investigation are markedly different in every nation. German and French piety, English and Spanish social ethics, German and English habits of life, stand so far apart that for the average man, and, therefore, for the public opinion of his community, the real inwardness of every foreign nation remains a deep secret and a source of continual and pregnant error. In the Roman Empire men began generally to understand one another, but this was precisely because there had ceased to be anything worth understanding in the Classical city. With the advent of mutual comprehension this particular humanity ceased to live in nations, *and ipso facto ceased to be historic.*[2]

Owing to the very depth of these experiences, it is not possible for a whole people to be *uniformly and throughout* a Culture-people, a nation. Amongst primitives each individual man has the same feeling of group-obligations, but the awakening of a nation into self-consciousness invariably takes place in gradations — that is, pre-eminently in the particular class that is strongest of soul and holds the others spellbound by a power derived from what it has experienced. *Every nation is represented in history by a minority.* At the beginning of the springtime it is the nobility,[3] which in that period of its first appearance is the fine flowering of the people, the vessel in which the national character — unconscious, but felt all the more strongly in its cosmic pulse — receives its destined Style. The "we" is the knightly class, in the Egyptian feudal period of 2700 not less than in the Indian and the Chinese of 1200. The Homeric heroes *are* the Danai; the Norman barons *are* England. Centuries later, Saint-Simon — the embodiment, it is true, of an older France — used to say that "all France" was assembled in the King's ante-room, and there was a time in which Rome and the Senate were actually identical. With the advent of the town the burgher becomes the vessel of nationality, and (as we should expect from the growth of intellectuality) of a national *consciousness* that it gets from the nobility and carries through to its fulfilment. Always it is particular circles, graduated in fine shades, that *in the name of* the people live, feel, act, and know how to die, but these circles become larger and larger. In the eighteenth century arose the Western *concept* of the Nation which sets up (and on occasion energetically insists upon) the claim to be championed by everybody without exception; but in reality, as we know, the *émigrés* were just as convinced as the Jacobins that they were *the* people, *the* representatives of the French nation. A Culture-people which is coincident with "all" does not exist — this is possible only in primitive and fellaheen peoples, only in a mere joint being with-

---

[1] Albertus Magnus; St. Thomas Aquinas; Grosseteste, and Roger Bacon. — *Tr.*
[2] Cf. p. 105.
[3] Cf. Ch. X.

out depth or historical dignity. So long as a people is a nation and works out the Destiny of a nation, there is in it a minority which in the name of all represents and fulfils its history.

IV

The Classical nations, in accordance with the static-Euclidean soul of their Culture, were corporeal units of the smallest imaginable size. It was not Hellenes or Ionians that were nations, but in each city the Demos, a union of adult men, legally and *by the same token nationally* defined between the type of the hero as upper limit and the slave as lower.[1] Synœcism, that mysterious process of early periods in which the inhabitants of a countryside give up their villages and assemble themselves as a town, marks the moment at which, having arrived at self-consciousness, the Classical nation constitutes itself as such. We can still trace the way in which this form of the nation steadily makes good from Homeric times [2] to the epoch of the great colonizations. It responds exactly to the Classical prime-symbol: each folk was a body, visible and surveyable, a $\sigma\tilde{\omega}\mu\alpha$, the express negation of the idea of geographical space.

It is of no importance to Classical history whether or not the Etruscans in Italy were identical physically or linguistically with the bearers of this name amongst the "Sea-peoples," or what the relation was between the pre-Homeric units of the Pelasgi or Danai and the later bearers of the Doric or the Hellenic name. If, about 1100, there are Doric and Etruscan primitive peoples (as is probable), nevertheless *a Doric or an Etruscan nation never existed.* In Tuscany as in the Peloponnese there were only City-states, *national points* which in the period of colonization *could only multiply, never expand.* The Etruscan wars of Rome were always waged against one or more cities,[3] and the nations that the Persians and the Carthaginians confronted were of this same type. To speak of "the Greeks and the Romans" as the eighteenth century did (and as we still do) is completely erroneous. A Greek "nation" in our sense is a misconception — the Greeks themselves never knew such an idea at all. The name of "Hellenes," which arose about 500, did not denote a people, but the aggregate of Classical Culture-men, the *sum* of their nations,[4] in contradistinction to the "Barbarian" world. And the Romans, a true urban people, could not conceive of their

---

[1] See p. 60 above. The slave did not belong to the nation. On this account the enrolment of non-citizens in the army of a city, which on occasions of dire crisis was inevitable, was always felt as a profound blow to the national idea.

[2] Even in the Iliad we can perceive the tendency to the nation-feeling in the small, and even the smallest, aggregates.

[3] And she had rarely to deal with anything more formidable than a loose partial confederacy. Often Etruscan cities were in alliance with Rome against other Etruscan cities. — *Tr.*

[4] It is not to be overlooked that both Plato and Aristotle in their political writings were unable to conceive of the ideal people otherwise than in the Polis form. But it was equally natural for the eighteenth-century thinkers to regard "the Ancients" as nations after the fashion of Shaftesbury and Montesquieu — it is *we* their successors who ought not to have stayed on that note.

Empire otherwise than in the form of innumerable nation-points, the *civitates* into which, juridically as in other respects, they dissolved all the primitive peoples of their Imperium.[1] When national feeling in *this* shape is extinguished, there is an end to Classical history.

It will be the task — one of the heaviest tasks of historians — to trace, generation by generation, the quiet fading-out of the Classical nations in the eastern Mediterranean during the "Late Classical" age, and the ever stronger inflow of a new nation-spirit, the Magian.

A nation of the Magian type is the community of co-believers, the group of all who know the right way to salvation and are inwardly linked to one another by the *ijma* [2] of this belief. Men belonged to a Classical nation by virtue of the possession of citizenship, but to a Magian nation by virtue of a sacramental act — circumcision for the Jews, specific forms of baptism for the Mandæans or the Christians. An unbeliever was for a Magian folk what an alien was for a Classical — no intercourse with him, no *connubium* — and this national separation went so far that in Palestine a Jewish-Aramaic and a Christian-Aramaic dialect formed themselves side by side.[3] The Faustian nation, though necessarily bound up with a particular religiousness, is not so with a particular confession; the Classical nation is by type non-exclusive in its relations to different cults; but *the Magian nation comprises neither more nor less than is covered by the idea of one or another of the Magian Churches.* Inwardly the Classical nation is linked with the city, and the Western with a landscape, but the Arabian knows neither fatherland nor mother tongue. Outwardly its specific world-outlook is only expressed by the distinctive script which each such nation develops as soon as it is born. But for that very reason the inwardness and hidden force — the magic, in fact — of a Magian nation-feeling impresses us Faustians, who notice the absence of the home-idea, as something entirely enigmatic and uncanny. This tacit, self-secure cohesion (that of the Jews, for example, in the homes of the Western peoples) is what entered "Roman Law" (called by a Classical label *but worked out by Aramæans*) as the concept of the "juridical person,"[4] which is nothing but the Magian notion of a community. Post-exilic Judaism was a juridical person long before anyone had discovered the concept itself.

The primitives who preceded this evolution were predominantly tribal associations, among them the South-Arabian Minæans,[5] who appear about the beginning of the first millennium, and whose name vanishes in the first century

---

[1] Mommsen described the Roman Empire as a "universal Empire founded upon municipal autonomy." And even Alexander's empire was originally conceived, and to a great extent actually organized, in this spirit. See P. Jouguet, *L'Impérialisme macédonien* (1926), Ch. IV. — *Tr.*

[2] See p. 67.

[3] F. N. Finck, *Die Sprachstämme des Erdkreises* (1915), pp. 29, et seq.

[4] About the end of the second century of our era.

[5] See foot-note, p. 197, et seq. — *Tr.*

before Christ; the Aramaic-speaking Chaldeans, who, likewise about 1000 B.C., sprang up as clan-groups and from 659 to 539 ruled the Babylonian world; the Israelites before the Exile; [1] and the Persians of Cyrus. [2] So strongly already the populations felt this form that the priesthoods which developed here, there, and everywhere after the time of Alexander received the names of foundered or fictitious tribes. Amongst the Jews and the South-Arabian Sabæans they were called Levites; amongst the Medes and Persians, Magi (after an extinct Indian tribe); and amongst the adherents of the new Babylonian religion Chaldeans (also after a disintegrated clan-grouping). [3] But here, as in all other Cultures, the energy of the national *consensus* completely overrode the old tribal arrangements of the primitives. Just as the *Populus Romanus* unquestionably contained folk-elements of very varied provenance, and as the nation of the French took in Salian Franks and Romanic and Old Celtic natives alike, so the Magian nation also ceased to regard origin as a distinguishing mark. The process, of course, was an exceedingly long one. The tribe still counts for much with the Jews of the Maccabean period and even with the Arabs of the first Caliphs; but for the inwardly ripened Culture-peoples of this world, such as the Jews of the Talmudic period, it no longer possessed any meaning. He who belongs to the Faith belongs to the Nation — it would have been blasphemy even to admit any other distinction. In early Christian times the Prince of Adiabene [4] went over to Judaism with his people in a body, and they were all *ipso facto* incorporated in the Jewish nation. The same applies to the nobility of Armenia and even the Caucasian tribes (which at that period must have Judaized on a large scale) and, in the opposite direction, to the Beduins of Arabia, right down to the extreme south, and beyond them again to African tribes as far afield as Lake Chad. [5] Here evidently is a national common feeling proof even against such race-distinctions as these. It is stated that even to-day Jews can amongst themselves distinguish very different races at the first glance, and that in the ghettos of eastern Europe the "tribes" (in the Old Testament sense) are clearly recognized. But none of this constitutes a difference of *nation*. According to von Erckert [6] the West-European Jew-type is universally distributed within the non-Jewish Caucasian peoples, whereas according to Weissenberg [7] it does not occur at all amongst the long-headed Jews of southern Arabia, where the

---

[1] A loose group of Edomite tribes which, with Moabites, Amalekites, Ishmaelites, and others, thus constituted a fairly uniform Hebrew-speaking population.

[2] See p. 167.

[3] Aristotle says that "philosophers are called Calani among the Indians, and Jews among the Syrians." Exactly the same is stated by Megasthenes, the Seleucid ambassador at Pataliputra, of Brahmins and Jews. — *Tr.*

[4] The district south of Lake Van, of which the capital was Arbela, the old home of the goddess Ishtar.

[5] As evidenced by the Falasha, the black Jews of Abyssinia.

[6] *Arch. f. Anthrop.*, Vol. XIX.

[7] *Zeitschr. f. Ethnol.* (1919).

Sabæan tomb-sculptures show a human type that might almost claim to be Roman or Germanic and is the ancestor of these Jews who were converted by missionary effort at least by the birth of Christ.

But this resolution of the tribal primitives into the Magian nations of Persians, Jews, Mandæans, Christians, and the rest must have occurred quite generally and on an immense scale. I have already drawn attention to the decisive fact that long before the beginning of our era the Persians represented simply a religious community, and it is certain that their numbers were indefinitely increased by accessions to the Mazdaist faith. The Babylonian religion vanished at that time — which means that its adherents became in part Jews and in part Persians — but emerging from it there is a *new* religion, inwardly alien to both Jewish and Persian, an astral religion, which bears the name of the Chaldees and whose adherents constituted a genuine Aramaic-speaking nation. From this Aramæan population of Chaldean-Jewish-Persian nationality came, firstly the Babylonian Talmud, the Gnosis, and the religion of Mani, and secondly, in Islamic times, Sufism and the Shia.

Moreover, as seen from Edessa, the inhabitants of the Classical world, they also, appear as nations in the Magian style. "The Greeks" in the Eastern idiom means the aggregate of all who adhered to the Syncretic cults and were bound together by the *ijma* of the Late Classical religiousness. The Hellenistic city-nations are no longer in the picture, which shows only *one* community of believers, the "worshippers of the mysteries," who under the names of Helios, Jupiter, Mithras, θεός ὕψιστος, worshipped a kind of Yahweh or Allah. Throughout the East, Greekness is a definite *religious* notion, and for that matter one completely concordant with the facts as they then were. The feeling of the Polis is almost extinct, and a Magian nation needs neither home nor community of origin. Even the Hellenism of the Seleucid Empire, which made converts in Turkestan and on the Indus, was related in inward form to Persian and post-exilic Judaism. Later, the Aramæan Porphyry, the pupil of Plotinus, attempted to organize this Greekness as a cult-Church on the model of the Christian and the Persian, and the Emperor Julian raised it to the dignity of being the State Church — an act not merely religious, but also and above all national. When a Jew sacrificed to Sol or to Apollo, he thereby became a Greek. So, for example Ammonius Saccas (d. 242), the teacher of Plotinus and probably also of Origen, went over "from the Christians to the Greeks"; so also Porphyry, born Malchus and (like the "Roman" jurist Ulpian) [1] a Phœnician of Tyre.[2] In these cases we see jurists and State officials taking Latin, and philosophers Greek, names — and for the philological spirit of modern and religious research, this is quite historical enough to justify these men's being regarded

[1] *Digesta*, 50, 15.
[2] Geffcken, *Der Ausgang des griech.-röm. Heidentum* (1920), p. 57 [English readers may refer to the article "Neoplatonism" and shorter articles under the personal names, in *Ency. Brit.*, XI ed. — *Tr.*]

as Roman and Greek in the Classical city-national sense! But how many of the great Alexandrines may have been Greeks only in the Magian sense of the term? In point of birth were not Plotinus and Diophantus[1] perhaps Jews or Chaldeans?

Now, the Christians also felt themselves from the outset as a nation of the Magian cast, and, moreover, the others, Greeks ("heathen") and Jews alike, regarded them as such. Quite logically the latter considered their secession from Judaism as high treason, and the former their missionary infiltration into the Classical cities as an invasion and conquest, while the Christians, on their side, designated people of other faiths as τὰ ἔθνη.[2] When the Monophysites and the Nestorians separated themselves from the Orthodox, new nations came into being as well as new Churches. The Nestorians since 1450 have been governed by the Mar Shimun,[3] who was at once prince and patriarch of his people and, vis-à-vis the Sultan, occupied exactly the same position as, long before, the Jewish Resh Galutha had occupied in the Persian Empire.[4] This nation-consciousness, derived from particular and defined world-feeling and therefore self-evident with an *a priori* sureness, cannot be ignored if we are to understand the later persecutions of the Christians. The Magian State is inseparably bound up with the concept of orthodoxy. Caliphate, nation, and Church form an intimate unit. It was as *states* that Adiabene went over to Judaism, Osrhoene about 200 (so soon!) from Greekdom to Christendom, Armenia in the sixth century from the Greek to the Monophysite Church. Each of these events expresses the fact that the State was identical with the orthodox community as a juridical person.[5] If Christians lived in the Islamic State, Nestorians in the Persian, Jews in the Byzantine, they did not and could not as unbelievers belong to it, and consequently were thrown back upon their own jurisdictions.[6] If by reason of their numbers or their missionary spirit they became a threat to the continuance

[1] See Vol. I, pp. 63, 71. — *Tr.*

[2] Which we translate by "Gentiles," but which literally means "the nations" or "peoples." — *Tr.*

[3] See the article "Nestorians," *Ency. Brit.*, XI ed. — *Tr.*

[4] See the articles "Jews" (§ 43), "Exilarch," and "Gaon," *Ency. Brit.*, XI. ed. In Europe, too, far into the Dispersion, there are rabbis recognized by the State as governors of their communities, such as the famous Rabbi Löw of Prague (1513-1609). — *Tr.*

[5] It may not be at all fanciful to connect the Reception of "Roman" law in Germany and the rise of the doctrine of *cujus regio, ejus religio* which played so great a part in the religious wars and treaties of our sixteenth and seventeenth centuries. At any rate, "practical politics" so-called provides an inadequate motive by itself to account for the latter. Considering it in contrast to the notion of Mortmain, and having regard to the intensity of religious belief in many of the princes who applied it, the idea appears as something much more positive than a mere formula of compromise. — *Tr.*

[6] See p. 70. The "capitulations" under which until recently Europeans were exempt from the jurisdiction of Turkish courts are regarded nowadays as a right enforced by more civilized powers to protect their subjects from the laws of a less civilized state, and their abolition is a symbol of the rise of the latter to the rank of a civilized power. But originally it was quite the reverse. The first "capitulation" was sued for by France in an hour of danger when Turkish aid was essential to her. See *Ency. Brit.*, XI ed., article "Capitulations." — *Tr.*

of the identity of state and creed-community, persecution became a national duty. It was on this account that first the "orthodox" (or "Greek") and then the Nestorian Christians suffered in the Persian Empire. Diocletian also, who as "Caliph" [1] (*Dominus et Deus*) had linked the Imperium with the pagan cult-Churches and saw himself in all sincerity as Commander of *these* Faithful, could not evade the duty of suppressing the second Church. Constantine changed the "true" Church *and in that act changed the nationality* of the Byzantine Empire. From that point on, the Greek name slowly passed over to the Christian nation, and specifically to that Christian nation which the Emperor as Head of the Faithful recognized and allowed to sit in the Great Councils. Hence the uncertain lines of the picture of Byzantine history — in 290 the organization that of a Classical Imperium, but the substance already a Magian national state; in 312 a change of nationality without change of name. Under this name of "Greeks," first Paganism as a nation fought the Christians, and then Christianity as a nation fought Islam. And in the latter fight, Islam itself being a nation also (the Arabian), nationality stamped itself more and more deeply upon events. Hence the present-day Greeks are a creation of the Magian Culture, developed first by the Christian Church, then by the sacred language of this Church, and finally by the name of this Church. Islam brought with it from the home of Mohammed the Arab name as the badge of its nationality. It is a mistake to equate these "Arabs" with the Beduin tribes of the desert. What created the new nation, with its passionate and strongly characteristic soul, was the *consensus* of the new faith. Its unity is no more derived from race and home than that of the Christian, Jewish, or Persian, and therefore it did not "migrate"; rather it owes its immense expansion to the incorporation within itself of the greater part of the early Magian nations. With the end of the first millennium of our era these nations one and all pass over into the form of fellah-peoples, and it is as fellaheen that the Christian peoples of the Balkans under Turkish rule, the Parsees in India, and the Jews in Western Europe have lived ever since. [2]

In the West, nations of Faustian style emerge, more and more distinctly, from the time of Otto the Great (936–973), and in them the primitive peoples of the Carolingian period are swiftly dissolved. [3] Already by A.D. 1000 the men who

---

[1] See Vol. I., p. 212.

[2] The author's meaning may perhaps be precised thus: so much of the old Magian nations as was not Arabized became fellah peoples, either outside the Magian sphere (as in Europe and India) or within it, under the Turkish (Mongol) domination, but even the old Arab-element itself was largely ripe for the change into the fellah condition when the Turks came. — *Tr.*

[3] I am convinced that the nations of China which sprang up in members in the middle, Hwang-Ho region at the beginning of the Chóu dynasty, as also the regional peoples of the Egyptian Old Kingdom (which had each its own capital and its own religion, and as late as Roman times fought each other in definitely religious wars), were in their inward form more closely akin to the peoples of the West than to those of the Classical and the Arabian worlds. However, research into such fields has hitherto been conspicuous by its absence.

"mattered most" were everywhere beginning to sense themselves as Germans, Italians, Spaniards, Frenchmen; whereas hardly six generations earlier their ancestors had been to the depths of their souls Franks, Lombards, and Visigoths.

The people-form of this Culture is founded, like its Gothic architecture and its Infinitesimal Calculus upon a tendency to the Infinite, in the spatial as well as the temporal sense. The nation-feeling comprises, to begin with, a geographical horizon that, considering the period and its means of communication, can only be called vast, and is not paralleled in any other Culture. The fatherland as *extent*, as a region whose boundaries the individual has scarcely, if ever, seen and which nevertheless he will defend and die for, is something that in its symbolic depth and force men of other Cultures can never comprehend. The Magian nation does not as such possess an earthly home; the Classical possesses it only as a point-focus. The actuality that, even in Gothic times, united men from the banks of the Adige with men in the Order-castles of Lithuania in an association of feeling would have been inconceivable even in ancient China and ancient Egypt, and stands in the sharpest opposition to the actuality of Rome and Athens, where every member of the Demos had the rest constantly in sight.

Still stronger is the sensitivity to distance *in time*. Before the fatherland-idea (which is a *consequence* of the existence of the nation) emerged at all, this passion evolved another idea to which the Faustian nations owe that existence — the *dynastic* idea. Faustian peoples are historical peoples, communities that feel themselves bound together not by place or consensus, but by history; and the eminent symbol and vessel of the common Destiny is the ruling "house." For Egyptian and for Chinese mankind the dynasty is a symbol of quite other meaning. Here what it signifies, as a will and an activity, *is Time*. All that we have been, all that we would be, is manifested in the being of the one generation; and our sense of this is much too profound to be upset by the worthlessness of a regent. What matters is not the person, but the idea, and it is for the sake of the idea that thousands have so often marched to their deaths with conviction in a genealogical quarrel. Classical history was for Classical eyes only a chain of incidents leading from moment to moment; Magian history was for its members the progressive actualization in and through mankind of a world-plan laid down by God and accomplished between a creation and a cataclysm; but Faustian history is in our eyes a single grand willing of conscious logic, in the accomplishment of which nations are led and represented by their rulers. It is a trait of race. Rational foundations it has not and cannot have — it has simply been felt so, and because it has been felt so, the companion-trust of the Germanic migration-time developed on into the feudal troth of the Gothic, the loyalty of the Baroque, and the merely seemingly undynastic patriotism of the nineteenth century. We must not misjudge the depth and dignity of this feeling because there is an endless catalogue of perjured vassals and peoples [1] and an eternal comedy in the cringing of courtiers and the abjectness of the vulgar. All great symbols are spiritual and can be comprehended only in their highest forms. The private life of a pope bears no relation to the idea of the Papacy. Henry the Lion's very defection [2] shows how fully in a time of nation-forming a real ruler feels the destiny of "his" people incorporated in himself. He represents that destiny in the face of history, and at times it costs him his honour to do so.

All nations of the West are of dynastic origins. In the Romanesque and even in Early Gothic architecture the soul of the Carolingian primitives still quivers through. There is no French or German Gothic, but Salian, Rhenish, and Suabian, as there is Visigothic (northern Spain, southern France) and Lombard and Saxon Romanesque. But over it all there spreads soon the minority, composed of men of race, that feels membership in a nation as a great historical vocation. From it proceed the Crusades, and in them there truly were French and German chivalries. It is the hall-mark of Faustian peoples that they are conscious of the direction of their history. But this direction attaches to the sequence of the generations, and so the nature of the race-ideal is *genealogical* through and through — Darwinism, even, with its theories of descent and inheritance is a sort of caricature of Gothic heraldry — and the world-as-history, when every individual lives in the plane of it, contains not only the tree of the individual family, ruling or other, but also the tree of the people as the basic form of all its happenings.[3] It needs very exact observation to perceive that this Faustian-genealogical principle, with its eminently historical notions of "*Ebenbürtigkeit*" (equivalence by virtue of birth) and of purity of blood, is just as alien to the Egyptians and Chinese, for all their historical disposition, as it is to the Roman nobility and the Byzantine Empire. On the other hand, neither our peasantry nor the patriciate of the cities is conceivable without it. The scientific conception of the people, which I have dissected above, is derived essentially from the genealogical sense of the Gothic period. The notion that the peoples have their trees has made the Italians proud to be the heirs of Rome, and the Germans proud to recall their Teuton forefathers, and that is something quite different from the Classical belief in timeless descent from heroes and gods.

[1] That the dynasts themselves have contributed heavily to the catalogue of perjury and bad faith only reinforces the argument. — *Tr.*

[2] His desertion of the emperor Frederick Barbarossa in the Lombard war, 1176. The details of the long struggle between Frederick and Henry will be found in any fairly full history of Europe or in the respective articles devoted to them in the *Ency. Brit.*, XI ed. While Frederick stood — and with real hopes as well as ideals — for the inclusive Empire, Henry through all his vicissitudes stood for Germany's eastern expansion, the colonization of the Slavonic north-east, and the development of the Baltic. — *Tr.*

[3] In mediæval hymns the cross is symbolically regarded as a tree bearing Christ as its last and grandest fruit; it is identified, indeed, with the Tree of Knowledge. (See Yrjo Hirn, *The Sacred Shrine.*) — *Tr.*

And eventually, when after 1789 the notion of mother tongue came to be fitted on to the dynastic principle, the once merely scientific fancy of a primitive Indogermanic people transformed itself into a deeply felt genealogy of "the Aryan race," and in the process the word "race" became almost a designation for Destiny.

But the "races" of the West are not the creators of the great nations, but *their result*. Not one of them had yet come into existence in Carolingian times. It was the class-ideal of chivalry that worked creatively in different ways upon Germany, England, France, and Spain and impressed upon an immense area that which within the individual nations is felt and experienced as race. On this rest (as I have said before) the nations — so *historical*, so alien to the Classical — of equivalence by birth (*peer-age, Ebenbürtigkeit*) and blood-purity. It was because the blood of the ruling family incorporated the destiny, the being, of the whole nation, that the state-system of the Baroque was of genealogical structure and that most of the grand crises assumed the form of wars of dynastic succession. Even the catastrophic ruin of Napoleon, which settled the world's political organization for a century, took its shape from the fact than an adventurer dared to drive out with his blood that of the old dynasties, and that his attack upon a symbol made it historically a sacred duty to resist him. For all these peoples were the *consequence* of dynastic destinies. That there is a Portuguese people, and a Portuguese Brazil in the midst of Spanish America, is the result of the marriage of Count Henry of Burgundy in 1095. That there are Swiss and Hollanders is the result of a reaction against the House of Habsburg. That Lorraine is the name of a land and not of a people is a consequence of the childlessness of Lothar II.

It was the Kaiser-idea that welded the disjunct primitives of Charlemagne's time into the German nation. Germany and Empire are inseparable ideas. The fall of the Hohenstaufens meant the replacement of one great dynasty by a handful of small and tiny ones; and the German nation of Gothic style was inwardly shattered even before the beginning of the Baroque — that is, at the very time when the nation-idea was being raised to higher levels of intellect in leader-cities like Paris, Madrid, London, and Vienna. The Thirty Years' War, so conventional history says, destroyed Germany in its flower. Not so; the fact that it could occur at all in this wretched form simply confirmed and showed up a long-completed decadence — it was the final consequence of the fall of the Hohenstaufens. There could hardly be a more convincing proof that Faustian nations are dynastic units. But then again, the Salians and the Hohenstaufens created also — at least in idea — an Italian nation out of Romans, Lombards, and Normans. Only the Empire made it possible for them to stretch a hand back to the age of Rome. Even though alien power evoked the hostility of the townsmen, and split the two primary orders, the nobles to the Emperor, the priests to the Pope; even though in these conflicts of Guelph and Ghibelline the nobility soon lost its importance and the Papacy rose through the anti-dynastic cities to political supremacy; even though at the last there was but a tangle of predatory states whose "Renaissance"-politics opposed the soaring world-policy of the Gothic Empire, as Milan of old had defied the will of Frederick Barbarossa — yet the ideal of *Una Italia*, the ideal for which Dante sacrificed the peace of his life, was a pure dynastic creation of the great Germany emperors. The Renaissance, whose historical horizon was that of the urban patriciate, led the nation as far out of the path of self-fulfilment as it is possible to imagine. All through the Baroque and Rococo the land was depressed to the state of being a mere pawn in the power-politics of alien houses. And not until after 1800 did Romanticism arise and reawaken the Gothic feeling with an intensity that made of it a political power.

The French people was forged out of Franks and Visigoths by its kings. It learned to feel itself as a whole for the first time at Bouvines in 1214.[1] Still more significant is the creation of the House of Habsburg, which, out of a population linked neither by speech nor folk-feeling nor tradition caused to arise the Austrian nation, which proved its nationhood in defending Maria Theresa and in resisting Napoleon — its first tests, and its last. The political history of the Baroque age is in essentials the history of the Houses of Bourbon and Habsburg. The rise of the House of Wettin in place of that of Welf is the reason why "Saxony" was on the Weser in 800, and is on the Elbe to-day. Dynastic events, and finally the intervention of Napoleon, brought it about that half of Bavaria has shared in the history of Austria and that the Bavarian State consists for the most part of Franconia and Suabia.

The latest nation of the West is the Prussian, a creation of the Hohenzollerns as the Roman was the last creation of the Classical Polis-feeling, and the Arabian the last product of a religious *consensus*. At Fehbellin [2] the young nation gained its recognition; at Rossbach [3] it won for Germany. It was Goethe who with his infallible eye for historic turning-points described the then new "Minna von Barnhelm" as the first German poetry of specifically national content. It is one more example, and a deeply significant one, to show how dynastically the Western nations defined themselves, that Germany thus at one stroke re-discovered her poetic language. The collapse of the Hohenstaufen rule had been accompanied by that of Germany's Gothic literature also. What did emerge here and there in the following centuries — the golden age of all the Western literatures — was undeserving of the name. But with the victories of Frederick the Great a new poesy began. "From Lessing to Hebbel" means the same as "from Rossbach to Sedan." The attempts that were made to restore the lost connexion by consciously leaning upon, first the French, and then Shakespeare,

[1] And every English schoolboy knows the meaning of the "Early Plantagenets." — *Tr.*
[2] Against the Swedes, 1675. — *Tr.*
[3] Against the French and their German dependent allies, 1757. — *Tr.*

upon the Volkslied, and finally (in Romanticism) upon the poetry of the age of chivalry, produced at least the unique phenomenon of an art-history which, though it never really attained one aim, was constituted, for the greater part, of flashes of genius.

The end of the eighteenth century witnessed the accomplishment of that remarkable turn with which national consciousness sought to emancipate itself from the dynastic principle. To all appearance this had happened in England long before; In this connexion Magna Charta (1215) will occur to most readers, but some will not have failed to observe that on the contrary, the very recognition of the nation involved in the recognition of its representatives gave the dynastic feeling a fresh-enforced depth and refinement to which the peoples of the Continent remained almost utter strangers. If the modern Englishman is (without appearing so) the most conservative human being in the world, and if in consequence his political management solves its problems so much by word-less harmony of national pulse instead of express discussion, and therefore has been the most successful up to now, the underlying cause is the *early emancipation of the dynastic feeling* from its expression in monarchical power.

The French Revolution, on the contrary, was in this regard only a victory of Rationalism. It set free not so much the nation as the concept of the nation. The dynastic has penetrated into the blood of the Western races, and on that very account it is a vexation to their intellect. For a dynasty represents history, it is the history-become-flesh of a land, and intellect is timeless and unhistorical. The ideas of the Revolution were all "eternal" and "true." Universal human rights, freedom, and equality are literature and abstraction and not facts. Call all this republican if you will, in reality it was one more case of a minority striving in the name of all to introduce the new ideal into the world of fact. It became a power, but at the cost of the ideal, and all it did was to replace the old felt adherence by the reasoned patriotism of the nineteenth century; by a civilized nationalism, only possible in our Culture, which in France itself and even to-day is unconsciously dynastic; and by the concept of the *fatherland as dynastic unit* which emerged first in the Spanish and Prussian uprisings against Napoleon and then in the German and Italian wars of *dynastic* unification. Out of the opposition of race and speech, blood and intellect, a new and specifically Western ideal arose to confront the genealogical ideal — that of the mother tongue. Enthusiasts there were in both countries who thought to replace the unifying force of the Emperor- and King-idea by the linking of republic and poetry — something of the "return to nature" in this, but a return of history to nature. In place of the wars of succession came language-struggles, in which one nation sought to force its language and therewith its nationality upon the fragments of another. But no one will fail to observe that even the rationalistic conception of a nation as a linguistic unit can at best ignore, never abolish, the dynastic feeling, any more than a Hellenistic Greek could inwardly overcome his Polis-consciousness or a modern Jew the national *ijma*. The mother tongue does not arise out of nothing, but is itself a product of dynastic history. Without the Capetian line there would have been no French language, but a Romance-Frankish in the north and a Provençal in the south. The Italian written-language is to be credited to the German Emperors and above all to Frederick II. The modern nations are primarily the populations of an old dynastic history. Yet in the nineteenth century the second concept of the nation as a unit of written language has annihilated the Austrian, and probably created the American. Thenceforward there have been in all countries two parties representing the nation in two opposed aspects, as dynastic-historical unit and as intellectual unit — the race party and the language party — but these are reflections that evoke too soon problems of politics that must await a later chapter.

v

At first, when the land was still without cities, it was the nobility that represented, in the highest sense of the word, the nation. The peasantry, "everlasting" and historyless, was a people *before* the dawn of the Culture, and in very fundamental characters it continued to be the primitive people, surviving when the form of the nation had passed away again. "The nation," like every other grand symbol of the Culture, is intimately the cherished possession of a few; those who have it are born to it as men are born to art or philosophy, and the distinctions of creator, critic, and layman, or something like them, hold for it also — alike in a classical Polis, a Jewish consensus, and a Western people. When a nation rises up ardent to fight for its freedom and honour, it is always a minority that really fires the multitude. The people "awakens" — it is more than a figure of speech, for only thus and then does the waking-consciousness of the whole become manifested. All these individuals whose "we"-feeling yesterday went content with a horizon of family and job and perhaps home-town are suddenly to-day men of nothing less than the People. Their thought and feeling, their Ego, and therewith the "it" in them have been transformed to the very depths. It has become *historic*. And then even the unhistorical peasant becomes a member of the nation, and a day dawns for him in which he experiences history and not merely lets it pass him by.

But in the world-cities, besides a minority which has history and livingly experiences, feels, and seeks to lead the nation, there arises another minority of timeless a-historic, literary men, men not of destiny, but of reasons and causes, men who are inwardly detached from the pulse of blood and being, wide-awake thinking consciousnesses, that can no longer find any "reasonable" connotation for the nation-idea. Cosmopolitanism is a mere waking-conscious association of intelligentsias. In it there is hatred of Destiny, and above all of history as the expression of Destiny. Everything national belongs to race —

so much so that it is incapable of finding language for itself, clumsy in all that demands thought, and shiftless to the point of fatalism. *Cosmopolitanism is literature* and remains literature, very strong in reasons, very weak in defending them otherwise than with more reasons, in defending them with the blood.

All the more, then, this minority of far superior intellect chooses the intellectual weapon, and all the more is it able to do so as the world cities are pure intellect, rootless, and by very hypothesis the common property of the civilization. The born world-citizens, world-pacifists, and world-reconcilers — alike in the China of the "Contending States," in Buddhist India, in the Hellenistic age, and in the Western world to-day — are the *spiritual leaders of fellaheen.* "*Panem et circenses*" *is only another formula for pacifism.* In the history of all Cultures there is an anti-national element, whether we have evidences of it or not. Pure self-directed thinking was ever alien to life, and therefore alien to history, unwarlike, raceless. Consider our Humanism and Classicism, the Sophists of Athens, Buddha and Lao-tze — not to mention the passionate contempt of all nationalisms displayed by the great champions of the ecclesiastical and the philosophical world-view. However the cases differ amongst themselves otherwise, they are alike in this, that the world-feeling of race; the political (and therefore national) instinct for fact ("my country, right or wrong!"); the resolve to be the subject and not the object of evolution (for one or the other it has to be) — in a word, the *will*-to-power — has to retreat and make room for a tendency of which the standard-bearers are most often men without original impulse, but all the more set upon their logic; men at home in a world of truths, ideals, and Utopias; bookmen who believe that they can replace the actual by the logical, the might of facts by an abstract justice, Destiny by Reason. It begins with the everlastingly fearful who withdraw themselves out of actuality into cells and study-chambers and spiritual communities, and proclaim the nullity of the world's doings, and it ends in every Culture with the apostles of world-peace. Every people has such (historically speaking) wasteproducts. Even their heads constitute physiognomically a group by themselves. In the "history of intellect" they stand high — and many illustrious names are numbered amongst them — but regarded from the point of view of actual history, they are inefficients.

The Destiny of a nation plunged in the events of its world depends upon how far its race-quality is successful in making these events historically ineffective against it. It could perhaps be demonstrated even now that in the Chinese world of states the realm of Tsin won through (250 B.C.) because it alone had kept itself free from Taoist sentiments. Be this as it may, the Roman people prevailed over the rest of the Classical world because it was able to insulate its conduct of policy from the fellah-instincts of Hellenism.

A nation is humanity brought into living form. The practical result of world-improving theories is consistently a *formless and therefore historyless mass.*

All world-improvers and world-citizens stand for fellaheen ideals, whether they know it or not. *Their success means the historical abdication of the nation in favour, not of everlasting peace, but of another nation.* World-peace is always a one-sided resolve. The *Pax Romana* had for the later soldier-emperors and Germanic band-kings only the one practical significance that it made a formless population of a hundred millions a mere object for the will-to-power of small warrior-groups. This peace cost the peaceful sacrifices beside which the losses of Cannæ seem vanishingly small. The Babylonian, Chinese, Indian, Egyptian worlds pass from one conqueror's hands to another's, and it is their own blood that pays for the contest. That is their — peace. When in 1401 the Mongols conquered Mesopotamia, they built a victory memorial out of the skulls of a hundred thousand inhabitants of Baghdad, which had not defended itself. From the intellectual point of view, no doubt, the extinction of the nations puts a fellaheen-world above history, civilized at last and for ever. But in the realm of facts it reverts to a state of nature, in which it alternates between long submissiveness and brief angers that for all the bloodshed — world-peace never diminishes that — alter nothing. Of old they shed their blood for themselves; now they must shed it for others, often enough for the mere entertainment of others — that is the difference. A resolute leader who collects ten thousand adventurers about him can do as he pleases. Were the whole world a single Imperium, it would thereby become merely the maximum conceivable field for the exploits of such conquering heroes.

"*Lever doodt als Sklav* (better dead than slave)" is an old Frisian peasant-saying. The reverse has been the choice of every Late Civilization, and every Late Civilization has had to experience how much that choice costs it.

CHAPTER VII
PROBLEMS OF THE ARABIAN CULTURE

(A)
HISTORIC PSEUDOMORPHOSES

PROBLEMS OF THE ARABIAN CULTURE

(A)

HISTORIC PSEUDOMORPHOSES

I

In a rock-stratum are embedded crystals of a mineral. Clefts and cracks occur, water filters in, and the crystals are gradually washed out so that in due course only their hollow mould remains. Then come volcanic outbursts which explode the mountain; molten masses pour in, stiffen, and crystallize out in their turn. But these are not free to do so in their own special forms. They must fill up the spaces that they find available. Thus there arise distorted forms, crystals whose inner structure contradicts their external shape, stones of one kind presenting the appearance of stones of another kind. The mineralogists call this phenomenon *Pseudomorphosis*.

By the term "historical pseudomorphosis" I propose to designate those cases in which an older alien Culture lies so massively over the land that a young Culture, born in this land, cannot get its breath and fails not only to achieve pure and specific expression-forms, but even to develop fully its own self-consciousness. All that wells up from the depths of the young soul is cast in the old moulds, young feelings stiffen in senile works, and instead of rearing itself up in its own creative power, it can only hate the distant power with a hate that grows to be monstrous.

This is the case of the Arabian Culture. Its pre-history lies entirely within the ambit of the ancient Babylonian Civilization,[1] which for two thousand years had been the prey of successive conquerors. Its "Merovingian period" is marked by the dictatorship of a small [2] Persian clan, primitive as the Ostrogoths, whose domination of two hundred years, scarcely challenged, was founded on the infinite weariness of a fellah-world. But from 300 B.C. onwards there begins and spreads a great awakening in the young Aramaic-speaking [3] peoples between Sinai and the Zagros range. As at the epoch of the Trojan War and at that of the Saxon emperors, a new relation of man to God, a wholly new world-feeling, penetrated all the current religions, whether these bore the name of Ahuramazda, Baal, or Yahweh, impelling everywhere to a great effort of creation. But precisely at this juncture there came the Macedonians —

[1] See pp. 166, et seq., and 174, et seq.
[2] Less than one per cent of the population.
[3] It is to be noted that the home of the Babylonian Culture, the ancient Sinear, plays no part of any importance in the coming events. For the Arabian Culture only the region north of Babylon, not that to south, comes into question.

so appositely that some inner connexion is not altogether impossible, for the Persian power had rested on spiritual postulates, and it was precisely these that had disappeared. To Babylon these Macedonians appeared as yet another swarm of adventurers like the rest. They laid down a thin sheet of Classical Civilization over the lands as far as Turkestan and India. The kingdoms of the Diadochi might indeed have become, insensibly, states of pre-Arabian spirit — the Seleucid Empire, which actually coincided geographically with the region of Aramaic speech, was in fact such a state by 200 B.C. But from the battle of Pydna [1] onwards it was, in its western part, more and more embodied in the Classical Imperium and so subjected to the powerful workings of a spirit which had its centre of gravity in a distant region. And thus was prepared the Pseudomorphosis.

The Magian Culture, geographically and historically, is the midmost of the group of higher Cultures — the only one which, in point both of space and of time, was in touch with practically all others. The structure of its history as a whole in our world-picture depends, therefore, entirely on our recognizing the true inner form which the outer moulds distorted. Unhappily, that is just what we do not yet know, thanks to theological and philological prepossessions, and even more to the modern tendency of over-specialization which has unreasonably subdivided Western research into a number of separate branches — each distinguished from the others not merely by its materials and its methods, but by its very way of thinking — and so prevented the big problems from being even seen. In this instance the consequences of specialization have been graver perhaps than in any other. The historians proper stayed within the domain of Classical philology and made the Classical language-frontier their eastern horizon; hence they entirely failed to perceive the deep unity of development on both sides of their frontier, which spiritually had no existence. The result is a perspective of "Ancient," "Mediæval," and "Modern" history, ordered and defined by the use of the Greek and Latin languages. For the experts of the old languages, with their "texts," Axum, Saba, and even the realm of the Sassanids were unattackable, and the consequence is that in "history" these scarcely exist at all. The literature-researcher (he also a philologist) confuses the spirit of the language with the spirit of the work. Products of the Aramæan region, if they happen to be written in Greek or even merely preserved in Greek, he embodies in his "Late Greek literature" and proceeds to classify as a special period of that literature. The cognate texts in other languages are outside his department and have been brought into other groups of literature in the same artificial way. And yet here was the strongest of all proofs that the history of a literature never coincides with the history of a language.[2] Here, in reality, was a self-

---

[1] The victory of L. Æmilius Paullus over Perseus, 168 B.C. — Tr.

[2] This has an important bearing also in the histories of the Western literatures. The German is written in part in Latin, and English in French.

contained ensemble of Magian national literature, single in spirit, but written in several languages — the Classical amongst others. For a nation of Magian type has no mother tongue. There are Talmudic, Manichæan, Nestorian, Jewish, or even Neopythagorean national literatures, but *not* Hellenistic or Hebrew.

Theological research, in its turn, broke up its domain into subdivisions according to the different West-European confessions, and so the "philological" frontier between West and East came into force, and still is in force, for Christian theology also. The Persian world fell to the student of Iranian philology, and as the Avesta texts were disseminated, though not composed, in an Aryan dialect, their immense problem [1] came to be regarded as a minor branch of the Indologist's work and so disappeared absolutely from the field of vision of Christian theology. And lastly the history of Talmudic Judaism, since Hebrew philology became bound up in one specialism with Old Testament research, not only never obtained separate treatment, but has been *completely forgotten* by all the major histories of religions with which I am acquainted, although these find room for every Indian sect (since folk-lore, too, ranks as a specialism) and every primitive Negro religion to boot. Such is the preparation of scholarship for the greatest task that historical research has to face to-day.

II

The Roman world of the Imperial period had a good idea of its own state. The later writers are full of complaints concerning the depopulation and spiritual emptiness of Africa, Spain, Gaul, and, above all, the mother countries Italy and Greece. But those provinces which belong to the Magian world are consistently excepted in these mournful surveys. Syria in particular is densely peopled and, like Parthian Mesopotamia, flourishes in blood and spirit.

The preponderance of the young East, palpable to all, had sooner or later to find political expression also. Viewing the scene from this standpoint, we see behind the epic and pageant of Marius and Sulla, Cæsar and Pompey, Antony and Octavian, this East striving ever more intensely to free itself from the historically dying West, the fellah-world waking up. The transfer of the capital to Byzantium was a great symbol. Diocletian had selected Nicodemia; Cæsar had had thoughts of Alexandria or Troy. A better choice than any would have been Antioch. But the act came too late by three centuries, and these had been the decisive period of the Magian Springtime.

The Pseudomorphosis began with Actium; there *it should have been Antony who won*. It was not the struggle of Rome and Greece that came there to an issue — that struggle had been fought out at Cannæ and Zama, where it was the tragic fate of Hannibal to stand as champion not for his own land, but for Hellenism. At Actium it was the unborn Arabian Culture that was opposed to

---

[1] See Professor Geldner's article "Zend-Avesta," *Ency. Brit.*, XI ed. — *Tr.*

iron-grey Classical Civilization; the issue lay between Principate and Caliphate. Antony's victory would have freed the Magian soul; his defeat drew over its lands the hard sheet of Roman *Imperium*. A comparable event in the history of the West is the battle between Tours and Poitiers, A.D. 732. Had the Arabs won it and made "Frankistan" into a caliphate of the North-east, Arabic speech, religion, and customs would have become familiar to the ruling classes, giant cities like Granada and Kairawan would have arisen on the Loire and the Rhine, the Gothic feeling would have been forced to find expression in the long-stiffened forms of Mosque and Arabesque, and instead of the German mysticism we should have had a sort of Sufism. That the equivalent of these things actually happened to the Arabian world was due to the fact that the Syro-Persian peoples produced no Charles Martel to battle along with Mithradates or Brutus and Cassius or Antony (or for that matter without them) against Rome.

A second pseudomorphosis is presented to our eyes to-day in Russia. The Russian hero-tales of the Bylini culminated in the epic cycle of Prince Vladimir of Kiev (*c.* A.D. 1000), with his Round Table, and in the popular hero Ilya Muromyets.[1] The whole immense difference between the Russian and the Faustian soul is already revealed in the contrast of these with the "contemporary" Arthur, Ermanarich, and Nibelungen sagas of the Migration-period in the form of the *Hildebrandslied* and the *Waltharilied*.[2] The Russian "Merovingian" period begins with the overthrow of the Tatar domination by Ivan III (1480) and passes, by the last princes of the House of Rurik and the first of the Romanovs, to Peter the Great (1689–1725). It corresponds exactly to the period between Clovis (481–511) and the battle of Testry (687), which effectively gave the Carolingians their supremacy. I advise all readers to read the Frankish history of Gregory of Tours (to 591) in parallel with the corresponding parts of Karamzin's patriachal narrative, especially those dealing with Ivan the Terrible, and with Boris Godunov and Vassili Shuiski.[3] There could hardly be a closer parallel. This Muscovite period of the great Boyar families and Patriarchs, in which a constant element is the resistance of an Old Russia party to the friends of Western Culture, is followed, from the founding of Petersburg in 1703, by the pseudomorphosis which forced the primitive Russian soul into the alien mould, first of full Baroque, then of the Enlightenment, and then of the nineteenth century. The fate-figure in Russian history is Peter the Great, with whom we may compare the Charlemagne who deliberately and

---

[1] See Wollner, *Untersuchungen über die Volksepik des Grossrussen* (1879). [A convenient edition of the Kiev Stories is Mary Gill, *Les Légendes slaves* (Paris, 1912). — *Tr.*]

[2] The former is dated about 800, the latter about 930. — *Tr.*

[3] These two figures — the one an authorized Mayor of the Palace before he was Tsar, the other a crude usurper — dominate the period of Russian history called the "Period of Troubles" — i.e., that between the death of Ivan the Terrible in 1584 and the election of Michael Romanov in 1613. — *Tr.*

with all his might strove to impose the very thing which Charles Martel had just prevented, the rule of the Moorish-Byzantine spirit. The possibility was there of treating the Russian world in the manner of a Carolingian or that of Seleucid — that is, of choosing between Old Russian and "Western" ways, and the Romanovs chose the latter. The Seleucids liked to see Hellenes and not Aramæans about them. The primitive tsarism of Moscow is the only form which is even to-day appropriate to the Russian world, but in Petersburg it was distorted to the dynastic form of western Europe. The pull of the sacred South — of Byzantium and Jerusalem — strong in every Orthodox soul, was twisted by the worldly diplomacy which set its face to the West. The burning of Moscow, that mighty symbolic act of a primitive people, that expression of Maccabæan hatred of the foreigner and heretic, was followed by the entry of Alexander I into Paris, the Holy Alliance, and the concert of the Great Powers of the West. And thus a nationality whose destiny should have been to live without a history for some generations still was forced into a false and artificial history that the soul of Old Russia was simply incapable of understanding. Late-period arts and sciences, enlightenment, social ethics, the materialism of world-cities, were introduced, although in this pre-cultural time religion was the only language in which man understood himself and the world. In the townless land with its primitive peasantry, cities of alien type fixed themselves like ulcers — false, unnatural, unconvincing. "Petersburg," says Dostoyevski, "is the most abstract and artificial city in the world." Born in it though he was, he had the feeling that one day it might vanish with the morning mist. Just so ghostly, so incredible, were the Hellenistic artifact-cities scattered in the Aramaic peasant-lands. Jesus in his Galilee knew this. St. Peter must have felt it when he set eyes on Imperial Rome.

After this everything that arose around it was felt by the true Russdom as lies and poison. A truly apocalyptic hatred was directed on Europe, and "Europe" was all that was not Russia, including Athens and Rome, just as for the Magian world in its time Old Egypt and Babylon had been antique, pagan, devilish. "The first condition of emancipation for the Russian soul," wrote Aksakov in 1863 to Dostoyevski, "is that it should hate Petersburg with all its might and all its soul." Moscow is holy, Petersburg Satanic. A widespread popular legend presents Peter the Great as Antichrist. Just so the Aramaic Pseudomorphosis cries out in all the Apocalypses from Daniel and Enoch in Maccabæan times to John, Baruch, and Ezra IV after the destruction of Jerusalem, against Antiochus the Antichrist, against Rome the Whore of Babylon, against the cities of the West with their refinement and their splendour, against the whole Classical Culture. All its works are untrue and unclean; the polite society, the clever artistry, the classes, the alien state with its civilized diplomacy, justice, and administration. The contrast between Russian and Western, Jew-Christian and Late-Classical nihilisms is extreme —

the one kind is hatred of the alien that is poisoning the unborn Culture in the womb of the land, the other a surfeited disgust of one's own proper overgrowths. Depths of religious feeling, flashes of revelation, shuddering fear of the great awakening, metaphysical dreaming and yearning, belong to the beginning, as the pain of spiritual clarity belongs to the end of a history. In these pseudomorphoses they are mingled. Says Dostoyevski: "Everyone in street and market-place now speculates about the nature of Faith." So might it have been said of Edessa or Jerusalem. Those young Russians of the days before 1914 — dirty, pale, exalted, moping in corners, ever absorbed in metaphysics, seeing all things with an eye of faith even when the ostensible topic is the franchise, chemistry, or women's education — are the Jews and early Christians of the Hellenistic cities, whom the Romans regarded with a mixture of surly amusement and secret fear. In Tsarist Russia there was no bourgeoisie and, in general, no true class-system, but merely, as in the Frankish dominions, lord and peasant. There were no Russian towns. Moscow consisted of a fortified residency (the Kreml) round which was spread a gigantic market. The imitation city that grew up and ringed it in, like every other city on the soil of Mother Russia, is there for the satisfaction and utilities of the Court, the administration, the traders, but that which lives in it is, on the top, an embodiment of fiction, an Intelligentsia bent on discovering problems and conflicts, and below, an uprooted peasantry, with all the metaphysical gloom, anxiety, and misery of their own Dostoyevski, perpetually homesick for the open land and bitterly hating the stony grey world into which Antichrist has tempted them. Moscow had no proper soul. The spirit of the upper classes was Western, and the lower had brought in with them the soul of the countryside. Between the two worlds there was no reciprocal comprehension, no communication, no charity. To understand the two spokesmen and victims of the pseudomorphosis, it is enough that Dostoyevski is the peasant, and Tolstoi the man of Western society. The one could never in his soul get away from the land; the other, in spite of his desperate efforts, could never get near it.

Tolstoi is the former Russia, Dostoyevski the coming Russia. The inner Tolstoi is tied to the West. He is the great spokesman of Petrinism even when he is denying it. The West is never without a negative — the guillotine, too, was a true daughter of Versailles — and rage as he might against Europe, Tolstoi could never shake it off. Hating it, he hates himself and so becomes the father of Bolshevism. The utter powerlessness of this spirit, and "its" 1917 revolution, stands confessed in his posthumously published *A Light Shines in the Darkness*. This hatred Dostoyevski does not know. His passionate power of living is comprehensive enough to embrace all things Western as well — "I have two fatherlands, Russia and Europe." He has passed beyond both Petrinism and revolution, and from *his* future he looks back over them as from afar. His soul is apocalyptic, yearning, desperate, but of this future *certain.* "I will go to Europe," says Ivan Karamazov to his brother, Alyosha; "I know well enough that I shall be going only to a churchyard, but I know too that that churchyard is dear, very dear to me. Beloved dead lie buried there, every stone over them tells of a life so ardently lived, so passionate a belief in its own achievements, its own truth, its own battle, its own knowledge, that I know — even now I know — I shall fall down and kiss these stones and weep over them." Tolstoi, on the contrary, is essentially a great understanding, "enlightened" and "socially minded." All that he sees about him takes the Late-period, megalopolitan, and Western form of a *problem*, whereas Dostoyevski does not even know what a problem is. Tolstoi is an event within and of Western Civilization. He stands midway between Peter and Bolshevism, and neither he nor these managed to get within sight of Russian earth. The thing they are fighting against reappears, recognizable, in the very form in which they fight. Their kind of opposition is not apocalyptic but intellectual. Tolstoi's hatred of property is an economist's, his hatred of society a social reformer's, his hatred of the State a political theorist's. Hence his immense effect upon the West — he belongs, in one respect as in another, to the band of Marx, Ibsen, and Zola.

Dostoyevski, on the contrary, belongs to no band, unless it be the band of the Apostles of primitive Christianity. His "Dæmons" were denounced by the Russian Intelligentsia as reactionaries. But he himself was quite unconscious of such conflicts — "conservative" and "revolutionary" were terms of the West that left him indifferent. Such a soul as his can look beyond everything that we call social, for the things of this world seem to it so unimportant as not to be worth improving. No genuine religion aims at improving the world of facts, and Dostoyevski, like every primitive Russian, is fundamentally unaware of that world and lives in a second, metaphysical world beyond. What has the agony of a soul to do with Communism? A religion that has got as far as taking social problems in hand has ceased to be a religion. But the reality in which Dostoyevski lives, even during this life, is a religious creation directly present to him. His Alyosha has defied all literary criticism, even Russian. His life of Christ, had he written it — as he always intended to do — would have been a genuine gospel like the Gospels of primitive Christianity, which stand completely outside Classical and Jewish literary forms. Tolstoi, on the other hand, is a master of the Western novel — *Anna Karenina* distances every rival — and even in his peasant's garb remains a man of polite society.

Here we have beginning and end clashing together. Dostoyevski is a saint, Tolstoi only a revolutionary. From Tolstoi, the true successor of Peter, and from him only, proceeds Bolshevism, which is not the contrary, but the final issue of Petrinism, the last dishonouring of the metaphysical by the social, and *ipso facto* a new form of the Pseudomorphosis. If the building of

Petersburg was the first act of Antichrist, the self-destruction of the society formed of that Petersburg is the second, and so the peasant soul must feel it. For the Bolshevists are not the nation, or even a part of it, but the lowest stratum of this Petrine society, alien and western like the other strata, yet not recognized by these and consequently filled with the hate of the downtrodden. It is all megalopolitan and "Civilized" — the social politics, the Intelligentsia, the literature that first in the romantic and then in the economic jargon champions freedoms and reforms, before an audience that itself belongs to the society. The real Russian is a disciple of Dostoyevski. Although he may not have read Dostoyevski or anyone else, nay, perhaps *because* he cannot read, he is himself Dostoyevski in substance; and if the Bolshevists, who see in Christ a mere social revolutionist like themselves, were not intellectually so narrowed, it would be in Dostoyevski that they would recognize their prime enemy. What gave this revolution its momentum was not the intelligentsia's hatred. It was the people itself, which, *without hatred*, urged only by the need of throwing off a disease, destroyed the old Westernism in one effort of upheaval, and will send the new after it in another. For what this townless people yearns for is its own life-form, its own religion, its own history. Tolstoi's Christianity was a misunderstanding. He spoke of Christ and he meant Marx. But to Dostoyevski's Christianity the next thousand years will belong.

III

Outside the Pseudomorphosis, and the more vigorously in proportion as the Classical influence is weaker over the country, there spring up all the forms of a genuine feudal age. Scholasticism, mysticism, feudal fealty, minstrelsy, the crusade spirit, all existed in the first centuries of the Arabian Culture and will be found in it as soon as we know how to look for them. The legion existed in name even after Septimius Severus, but in the East, legions look for all the world like ducal retinues. Officials are nominated, but what nomination amounts to in reality is the investiture of a count with his fief. While in the West the Cæsar-title fell into the hands of chieftains, the East transformed itself into an early Caliphate amazingly like the feudal state of mature Gothic. In the Sassanid Empire,[1] in Hauran,[2] in southern Arabia, there dawned a pure feudal period. The exploits of a king of Saba,[3] Shamir Juharish, are immortalized like those of a Roland or an Arthur, in the Arabic saga which tells of his advance through Persia as far as China.[4] The Kingdom of Ma'in[5] existed side by

---

[1] Covering, before its later extensions, Persia and Iraq to the Euphrates. — *Tr.*
[2] The region south of Damascus and east of the Sea of Galilee. — *Tr.*
[3] Saba (Sheba) is, roughly, the modern Yemen, though the centre of gravity of the Sabæan Kingdom may earlier have been in northern Arabia. See Dr. D. H. Müller's article "Sabaeans" in *Ency. Brit.*, XI ed. — *Tr.*
[4] Schiele, *Die Religion in Geschichte und Gegenwart*, I, 647.
[5] The "Minæan" and the Sabæan kingdoms were the two outstanding hegemonies of early

side with the realm of Israel during the millennium before Christ, and its remains (which suggest comparisons with Mycenæ and Tiryns) extend deeply
into Africa.[1] But now the feudal age flowered throughout Arabia and even in
the mountains of Abyssinia.[2] In Axum there arose during early Christian times
mighty castles and kings' tombs with the largest monoliths in the world.[3]
Behind the kings stands a feudal nobility of counts (*kail*) and wardens (*kabir*),
vassals of often questionable loyalty whose great possessions more and more
narrowed the power of the king and his household. The endless Christian-
Jewish wars between south Arabia and the kingdom of Axum [4] have essentially
the character of chivalry-warfare, frequently degenerating into baronial feuds
based on the castles. In Saba ruled the Hamdanids — who later became
Christian. Behind them stood the Christian realm of Axum, in alliance with
Rome, which about A.D. 300 stretched from the White Nile to the Somali
coast and the Persian Gulf, and in 525 overthrew the Jewish-Himaryites.[5]
In 542 there was a diet of princes at Marib [6] to which both the Roman and the
Sassanid Empires sent ambassadors. Even to-day the country is full of innumerable relics of mighty castles, which in Islamic times were popularly
attributed to supernatural builders. The stronghold of Gomdan is a work of
twenty tiers.[7]

In the Sassanid Empire ruled the Dikhans, or local lords, while the brilliant
court of these early-Eastern "Hohenstaufen" was in every respect a model for
that of the Byzantines who followed Diocletian. Even much later the Abbassids in their new capital of Baghdad could think of nothing better than to
imitate, on a grand scale, the Sassanid ideal of court life. In northern Arabia,

---

Arabian history. Ma'in, in southern Arabia, should not be confused with the Ma'an which lies
north-east of the Gulf of Akaba. — *Tr.*

[1] Bent, *The Sacred City of the Ethiopians* (London 1893), pp. 134, et seq., deals with the remains
of Jeha, the inscriptions of which are dated by Glaser between the seventh and fifth centuries before
Christ. See D. H. Müller, *Burgen and Schlösser Südarabiens.*

[2] Grimme, *Mohammed*, pp. 26, et seq.

[3] German Axum Expedition record (1913), Vol. II.

[4] An ancient trade-route from Persia crossed the straits of Ormus and of Bab-el-Mandeb, traversing South Arabia and terminating in Abyssinia and the Nile region. It is historically more
important than the northern route over the Isthmus of Suez.

[5] So little is known as to these events by British (or any other) students that a brief record may
be useful. The original Himaryites or Homerites, a people of the south-west angle of Arabia, had
displaced the Sabæans in control of South Arabia in the second century B.C. The Himaryite hegemony was overthrown by invaders from Axum over the water about A.D. 300, and the Axumite
rulers were, *inter alia*, kings of Hadramaut — hence the mention in the text of the Persian Gulf.
But a Himaryite opposition continued, and, adopting Judaism as a counter-religion, it succeeded
for a time in throwing off the Abyssinian rule. Axum, however (aided, as a Christian state, by
Rome), reasserted her dominion in 525 and held it for fifty years, till an attack of Sassanid Persians
displaced them again. Thereafter southern Arabia fell into the swaying chaos in which the coming of Mohammed found it. — *Tr.*

[6] The capital of Saba. — *Tr.*

[7] Grimme, p. 43. Illustrations of these immense ruins of Gomdan, ibid., p. 81, and reconstruc-
tions in the German Axum report.

at the courts of the Ghassanids [1] and at those of the Lakhmids, [2] there sprang up a genuine troubadour and *Minne* poetry; and knightly poets, in the days of the Early Fathers, fought out their duels with "word, lance, and sword." One of them was the Jew Samuel, lord of the castle of Al Alblaq, who stood a famous siege by the King of Hira for the sake of five precious suits of armour.[3] In relation to this lyric poetry, the Late-Arabic which flourished, especially in Spain, from 800 stands as Uhland and Eichendorff stand to Walter von der Vogelweide.

For this young world of the first centuries of our era our antiquarians and theologians have had no eyes. Busied as they are with the state of Late Republican and Imperial Rome, the conditions of the Middle East seem to them merely primitive and void of all significance. But the Parthian bands that again and again rode at the legions of Rome were a chivalry exalted by Mazdaism; in their armies there was the spirit of crusade. So, too, might it have been with Christianity if it had not been wholly bound under the power of the pseudomorphosis. The spirit was there — Tertullian spoke of the "*militia Christi*," and the sacrament was the soldier's oath of fidelity.[4] But it was only later that Christ became the hero for whom his vassals went out against the heathen; for the time being, the hither side of the Roman frontier knew not Christian lords and knights, but only Roman legates; not the castle, but the *castra;* not tournaments, but executions. Yet in spite of all this it was not, strictly speaking, a Parthian war, but a true crusade of Jewry that blazed out in 115 when Trajan marched into the East, and it was as a reprisal for the destruction of Jerusalem that the whole infidel ("Greek") population of Cyprus — traditionally 240,000 souls — was massacred.[5] Nisibis, defended by Jews, made an illustrious resistance. Warlike Adiabene (the upper Tigris plain) was a Jewish state. In all the Parthian and Persian wars against Rome the gentry and peasantry, the feudal levy, of Jewish Mesopotamia fought in the front line.

Byzantium, even, was not able entirely to evade the influence of the Arabian feudal age, and, under a crust of Late Classical administrative forms, the fief system (especially in the interior of Asia Minor) came into existence. There there were powerful families whose loyalty was doubtful and whose ambition was to possess the Imperial throne. "Originally tied to the capital, which they

---

[1] The country of Ghassan extends east of the Jordan, parallel to and inland of Palestine and Syria, approximately from Petra to the middle Euphrates. — *Tr.*

[2] The Lakhmids were the ruling dynasty, from the third to the sixth century after Christ, of the realm of Hira, which ran in a strip between the Euphrates and the present Nejd coast on the one hand and the desert of Arabia on the other. — *Tr.*

[3] Brockelmann, *Geschichte der arabischen Literatur*, p. 34.

[4] The whole structure of Mithraism (so far as we know it) presents strong analogies with that of a military order. — *Tr.*

[5] As well as it is said 220,000 at Cyrene. At Alexandria, too, there were *émeutes* and counter-*émeutes*. — *Tr.*

were not allowed to leave without the Emperor's permission, this nobility settled down later on its broad estates in the provinces. From the fourth century onwards this provincial nobility was *de facto* an 'Estate of the realm,' and in course of time it claimed a certain independence of Imperial control." [1]

The "Roman Army" in the East, meanwhile, was transformed in less than two centuries from an army of modern type to one of the feudal order. The Roman legion disappeared in the reorganization of the age of Severus,[2] about A.D. 200. While in the West the army degenerated into hordes, in the East there arose, in the fourth century a genuine, if belated, knighthood — a fact that Mommsen long ago pointed out, without, however, seeing the significance of it.[3] The young noble received a thorough education in single combat, horsemanship, use of bow and lance. About A.D. 260 the Emperor Gallienus — the friend of Plotinus and the builder of the Porta Nigra of Trier, one of the most striking and most unfortunate figures of the period of the soldier-emperors — formed, from Germans and Moors, a new type of mounted force, the personal military suite.[4] A significant light is thrown upon the changes by the fact that the old city-gods give way, in the religion of the army, to the German gods of personal heroism, under the labels of Mars and Hercules.[5] Diocletian's *palatini* are not a substitute for the prætorians abolished by Septimius Severus, but a small, well-disciplined knight-army, while the *comitatenses*, the general levy, are organized in "*numeri*" or companies. The tactics are those of every Early period, with its pride of personal courage. The attack takes the Germanic form of the so-called "boar's head" — the deep mass technically called the *Gevierthaufe*.[6] Under Justinian we find, fully developed, a system corresponding precisely to the *Landsknecht* system of Charles V, in which condottieri [7] of the Frundsberg type [8] raise professional forces on a territorial basis. The expedition

---

[1] Roth, *Sozial- und Kulturgeschichte des Byzantinischen Reiches*, p. 15.

[2] Delbrück *Geschichte der Kriegskunst*, II, p. 222. [For British students C. W. C. Oman's *Art of War: Middle Ages* will be more readily available, although Oman treats the subject more as a matter of formal military organization than does Delbrück. Neither writer deals with any special features of the change as it worked itself out in the East, both being concerned almost entirely with its Western aspects and phases. The origin of the late-Byzantine army system, as military historians are aware, is an obscure and difficult subject. By what stages, after the decadence of the legion, was the "*Landsknecht*" army of Justinian reached? Like other elements of middle-East history in the epoch of the Arabian Culture, it still awaits the full investigation that the West has already had. — *Tr.*

[3] *Gesammelte Schriften*, IV, 532.

[4] *Gefolgstreuen* in German. The choice of an equivalent mediæval term in English is difficult, since any one that may be selected carries with it certain implications for students of feudal origins. — *Tr.*

[5] Domaszewski, *Die Religion der römischen Heeres*, p. 49.

[6] The typical form, for instance, of the Swiss in their independence-battles, and of Western infantry generally in the fifteenth and sixteenth centuries, during the transition from hand-arm to fire-arm warfare. — *Tr.*

[7] *Buccellarii;* see Delbrück, op. cit., II, 354.

[8] Georg von Frundsberg (1473–1528). Short article in *Ency. Brit.*, XI ed. — *Tr.*

of Narses is described by Procopius [1] just as one might describe the great re-
cruiting-operations of Wallenstein.

But there appeared also in these early centuries a brilliant Scholasticism
and Mysticism of Magian type, domesticated in the renowned schools of the
Aramæan region — the Persian schools of Ctesiphon, Resaina, Gundisapora,
the Jewish of Sura, Nehardea, Kinnesrin.[2] These are flourishing headquarters
of astronomy, philosophy, chemistry, medicine. But towards the west these
grand manifestations, too, become falsified by the Pseudomorphosis. The
characteristically Magian elements of this knowledge assume at Alexandria the
forms of Greek philosophy and at Beyrout those of Roman jurisprudence; they
are committed to writing in the Classical languages, squeezed into alien and
long-petrified literary forms, and perverted by the hoary logic of a Civilization of
quite other structure. It is in this, and not in the Islamic, time that Arabian
science began. Yet, as our philologists only unearthed what had been put in
Late Classical dress at Alexandria and Antioch, and had not an inkling either of
the immense wealth of the Arabian spring or of the real pivots of its researches
and ideas, there arose the preposterous notion that the Arabs were spiritual
epigoni of the Classical. In reality, practically everything that was produced on
the "other" side — from Edessa's point of view — of the philologist's frontier,
though seeming to the Western eye an offspring of a "Late Classical" spirit, is
nothing but a reflection of Early Arabian inwardness. And so we come to consider what the Pseudomorphosis did for the Arabian religion.

IV

The Classical religion lived in its vast number of *separate cults*, which in this
form were natural and self-evident to Apollinian man, essentially inaccessible
to any alien. As soon as cults of this kind arise, we have a Classical Culture,
and when their essence changes, in later Roman times, then the soul of this
Culture is at an end. Outside the Classical landscape they have never been
genuine and living. The divinity is always *bound to and bounded by one locality*,
in conformity with the static and Euclidean world-feeling. Correspondingly
the relation of man to the divinity takes the shape of a local cult, in which
the significances lie in the *form* of its ritual procedure and not in a dogma underlying them. Just as the population was scattered geographically in innumerable
points, so spiritually its religion was subdivided into these petty cults, each of
which was entirely independent of the rest. *Only their number, and not their*

---

[1] *Gothic War*, IV, 26. [The same holds good for Belisarius's armies. — *Tr.*]

[2] Nisibis and Edessa in the up-country between Euphrates and Tigris are represented to-day
by Nasibin (Nezib) and Urfa respectively; just to the west of them, east of the Euphrates above
Sura, were the three Jewish academies, in which Talmudic Judaism took shape after the Dispersion.
Kinnesrin lay just south of Aleppo. Ctesiphon is, of course, the classical city on the Tigris, still
dominant under the Sassanids, and Resaina lies in the up-country south-west of Nisibis. Gundisapora is Gunder-Shapur (Jundaisapur), near the site of the old Elamite capital Susa in Arabistan.
— *Tr.*

scope, was capable of increase. Within the Classical religion multiplication was the only form of growth, and missionary effort of any sort was excluded, for men could practise these cults without *belonging* to them. There were no communities of fellow believers. Though the later thought of Athens reached somewhat more general ideas of God and his service, it was philosophy and not religion that it achieved; it appealed to only a few thinkers and had not the slightest effect on the feeling of the nation — that is, the Polis.

In the sharpest contrast to this stands the visible form of the Magian religion — the Church, the brotherhood of the faithful, which has no home and knows no earthly frontier, which believes the words of Jesus, "when two or three are gathered together in My name, there am I in the midst of them." It is self-evident that every such believer must believe that only one good and true God can be, and that the gods of the others are evil and false.[1] The relation between this God and man rests, not in expression or profession, but in the secret force, the magic, of certain symbolic performances, which if they are to be effective must be exactly known in form and significance and practised accordingly. The knowledge of this significance belongs to the Church — in fact, it is the Church itself, qua community of the instructed. And, therefore, the centre of gravity of every Magian religion lies not in a cult, but in a doctrine, in *the creed*.

As long as the Classical remained spiritually strong, pseudomorphosis of all the Churches of the East into the style of the West continued. This is a most important aspect of Syncretism. The Persian religion enters in the shape of the Mithras cult, the Chaldean-Syrian element as the cults of the star-gods and Baals (Jupiter Dolichenus, Sabazius, Sol Invictus, Atargatis), the Jewish religion in the form of a Yahweh-cult (for no other name can be applied to the Egyptian communities of the Ptolemaic period [2]), and primitive Early-Christianity too — as the Pauline Epistles and the Catacombs of Rome clearly show — took substance as a Jesus-cult. And however loudly each of these various religions (which from about Hadrian's time drove the genuine old Classical deities completely into the background) might proclaim itself as the revelation of the one true faith — Isis styled herself *deorum dearumque facies uniformis* — in reality they carry, one and all, marks of the Classical separatism — that is, they multiply to infinity; every community stands for itself and is local; all the temples, catacombs, Mithræa, house chapels, are holy places to which (in

[1] Not "non-existent." It would be a misconception of the Magian world-feeling to attach a Faustian-dynamic meaning to the phrase "true God." In combating the worship of godlings, the reality of godlings and dæmons is presupposed. The Israelite prophets never dreamed of denying the Baals, and similarly Isis and Mithras for the Early Christians, Jehovah for the Christian Marcion, Jesus for the Manichæans, are devilish, but perfectly real, powers. *Disbelieving in them* would have had no meaning for the Magian soul — what was required was that one should not *turn to them.* To use an expression now long current, it is "Henotheism" and not Monotheism.

[2] Schürer, *Geschichte des jüdischen Volkes im Zeitalter Jesu Christi*, III, 499; Wendland, *Die hellenistisch-römische Kultur*, p. 192.

feeling, even though not in formal expression) the deity is considered to be attached.[1] Nevertheless, there is Magian feeling even in this piety. Classical cults are *practised*, and one may practise as many of them as one pleases, but of these newer, *a man belongs to one and one alone*. In the old, propaganda is unthinkable; in the new it goes without saying, and the purport of religious exercises tends more and more to the doctrinal side.

From the second century onwards, with the fading of the Apollinian and the flowering of the Magian soul, the relations are reversed. The consequences of the Pseudomorphosis continue, *but it is now cults of the West which tend to become a new Church of the East* — that is, from the sum of separate cults there evolves a community of those who believe in these gods and their rituals — and so there arises, by processes like those of the Early Persian and the Early Judaic, a Magian Greek nationality. Out of the rigorously established forms of detail-procedure in sacrifices and mysteries grows a sort of dogma concerning the inner significance of these acts. The cults can now represent each other, and men no longer practise or perform them in the old way, but become "adherents" of them. And the little god *of* the place becomes — without the gravity of the change being noticed by anyone — the great God really present in the place.

Carefully as Syncretism has been examined in recent years, the clue to its development — the transformation of Eastern Churches into Western cults, and then the reverse process of transformation of Western cults into Eastern Churches — has been missed.[2] Yet without this key it is quite impossible to understand the religious history of Early Christianity. The battle that in Rome was between Christ and Mithras as cult-deities took the form, east of Antioch, of a contest between the Persian and the Christian Churches. But the heaviest battle that Christianity had to fight, after it came itself under the influence of the Pseudomorphosis and began to develop spiritually with its face to the West, was not that against the true Classical deities. With these it was never face to face, for the public city-cults had long been inwardly dead and possessed no hold whatever on men's souls. The formidable enemy was Paganism, or Hellenism, emerging as *a powerful new Church* and born of the selfsame spirit as Christianity itself. In the end there were in the east of the Roman Empire not one cult-Church, but two, and if one of these comprised exclusively the followers of Christ, the other, too, was made up of communities which, under a thousand different labels, consciously worshipped one and the same divine principle.

[1] Contrast with this the exactly opposite process in Jewry before the Pseudomorphosis had begun to affect it, — to wit, the battle against the local "high places" and the concentration of sanctity in Jerusalem. — Tr.

[2] With the result that Syncretism is presented as a mere hotchpotch of every conceivable religion. Nothing is further from the truth. The process of taking shape moved first from East to West and then from West to East.

Much has been written on the Classical toleration. The nature of a religion may perhaps be most clearly seen in the limits of its tolerance, and there were such limits in Classical religions as in others. It was, indeed, one essential character of these religions that they were numerous, and another that they were religions of pure performance; for them, therefore, the question of toleration, as the word is usually understood, did not arise. But respect for the cult-formalities as such was postulated and required, and many a philosopher, even many an unwitting stranger, who infringed this law by word or deed, was made to realize the limits of Classical toleration. The reciprocal persecutions of the Magian Churches are something different from this; there it was the duty of the henotheist to his own faith that forbade him to recognize false tenets. Classical *cults* would have tolerated the Jesus-cult as one of their own number. But the cult-*Church* was bound to attack the Jesus-Church. All the great persecutions of Christians (corresponding therein exactly to the later persecutions of Paganism) came, not from the "Roman" State, but from this cult-Church, and they were only political inasmuch as the cult-Church was both nation and fatherland. It will be observed that the mask of Cæsar-worship covered *two* religious usages. In the Classical cities of the West, Rome above all, the special cult of the *Divus* arose as a last expression of that Euclidean feeling which required that there should be legal and therefore sacral means of communication between the body-unit man and the body-unit God. In the East, on the other hand, the product was a creed of Cæsar as Saviour, God-man, Messiah of all Syncretists, which this Church brought to expression in a supremely national form. The sacrifice for the Emperor was the most important *sacrament* of the Church — exactly corresponding to the baptism of the Christians — and it is easy, therefore, to understand the symbolic significance in the days of persecution of the command and the refusal to do these acts. *All* these Churches had their sacraments: holy meals like the Haoma-drinking of the Persians,[1] the Passover of the Jews, the Lord's Supper of the Christians, similar rites for Attis and Mithras, and baptismal ceremonies amongst the Mandæans, the Christians, and the worshippers of Isis and Cybele. Indeed, the individual cults of the Pagan Church might be regarded almost as sects and orders — a view which would lead to a much better understanding of their reciprocal propaganda.

All true Classical mysteries, such as those of Eleusis and those founded by the Pythagoreans in the South-Italian cities about 500 B.C., had been place-bound,[2] and had consisted in some symbolical act or process. Within the field of the Pseudomorphosis these freed themselves from their localities; they could

---

[1] The Haoma plant symbolized the Tree of Life (Gaokerena) like the Soma plant of Brahmanism. — *Tr.*

[2] Hence the expression "profaning" the mysteries, which meant, not revealing them, but bringing them outside their fane. — *Tr.*

be performed wherever initiates were gathered, and had now as their object the Magian ecstasy and the ascetic change of life. The visitors to the holy place had transformed themselves into practising Orders. The community of the Neopythagoreans, formed about 50 B.C. and closely related to the Jewish Essenes, is anything but a Classical "school of philosophy"; it is a pure monastic order, and it is not the only such order in the Syncretic movement that anticipated the ideals of the Christian hermits and the Mohammedan dervishes. These Pagan Churches had their anchorites, saints, prophets, miraculous conversions, scriptures, and revelations.[1] In the significance of images there came about a very remarkable transformation, which still awaits research. The greatest of Plotinus's followers, Iamblichus, finally, about A.D. 300, evolved a mighty system of orthodox theology, ordered hierarchy, and rigid ritual for the Pagan Church, and his disciple Julian devoted, and finally sacrificed, his life to the attempt to establish this Church for all eternity.[2] He sought even to create cloisters for meditating men and women and to introduce ecclesiastical penance. This great work was supported by a great enthusiasm which rose to the height of martyrdom and endured long after the Emperor's death. Inscriptions exist which can hardly be translated but by the formula: "There is but one god and Julian is his Prophet."[3] Ten years more, and this Church would have become a historic, permanent fact. In the end not only its power, but also in important details its very form and content were inherited by Christianity. It is often stated that the Roman Church adapted itself to the structure of the Roman State; this is not quite correct. The latter structure was itself by hypothesis a Church. There was a period when the two were in touch — Constantine the Great acted simultaneously as convener of the Council of Nicæa and as Pontifex Maximus, and his sons, zealous Christians as they were, made him *Divus* and paid to him the prescribed rites. St. Augustine dared to assert that the true religion had existed before the coming of Christianity in the form of the Classical.[4]

v

For the understanding of Judaism as a whole between Cyrus and Titus it is necessary constantly to bear in mind three facts, of which scholarship is quite aware, but which, owing to philological and theological *parti pris*, it refuses to admit as factors in its discussions. First, the Jews are a "nation without a land," a *consensus*, and in the midst, moreover, of a world of pure nations of the same type. Secondly, Jerusalem is indeed a Mecca, a holy centre, but it is

---

[1] J. Geffcken, *Der Ausgang des griechisch-römischen Heidentums* (1920), pp. 197, et seq.
[2] Geffcken, op. cit., pp. 131, et seq.
[3] Geffcken, op. cit., p. 292, note 149.
[4] "*Res ipsa, quæ nunc religio Christiana nuncupatur, erat apud antiquos nec defecit ab initio generis humani, quousque Christus veniret in carnem. Unde vera religio, quæ jam erat coepit appellari Christiana*" (*Retractationes*, I, 13).

neither the home nor the spiritual focus of the people. Lastly, the Jews are a peculiar phenomenon in world-history only so long as we insist on treating them as such.

It is true that the post-exilic Jews, in contradistinction to the pre-exilic Israelites are — as Hugo Winckler was the first to recognize — a people of quite new type. But they are not the only representatives of the type. The Aramæan world began in those days to arrange itself in a great number of such peoples, including Persians and Chaldeans,[1] all living in the same district, yet in stringent aloofness from each other, and even then practising the truly Arabian way of life that we call the ghetto.

The first heralds of the new soul were the *prophetic religions*, with their magnificent inwardness, which began to arise about 700 B.C. and challenged the primeval practices of the people and their rulers. They, too, are an essentially Aramæan phenomenon. The more I ponder Amos, Isaiah, and Jeremiah on the one hand, Zarathustra on the other, the more closely related they appear to me to be. What seems to separate them is not their new beliefs, but the objects of their attack. The first battled with that savage old-Israel religion, which in fact is a whole bundle of religious elements [2] — belief in holy stones and trees, innumerable place-gods (Dan, Bethel, Hebron, Shechem, Beersheba, Gilgal), a single Yahweh (or Elohim), whose name covers a multitude of most heterogeneous numina, ancestor-worship and human sacrifices, dervish-dancing and sacral prostitution — intermixed with indistinct traditions of Moses and Abraham and many customs and sagas of the Late Babylonian world, now after long establishment in Canaan degenerated and hardened into peasant forms. The second combated the old Vedic beliefs of heroes and Vikings, similarly coarsened, no doubt, and certainly needing to be recalled to actuality, time and again, by glorifications of the sacred cattle and of the care thereof. Zarathustra lived about 600 B.C., often in want, persecuted and misunderstood, and met his end as an old man in war against the unbelievers [3] — a worthy contemporary of the unfortunate Jeremiah, who for his prophesying was hated by his countrymen, imprisoned by his king, and after the catastrophe carried off by the fugitives to Egypt and there put to death. And it is my belief that this great epoch brought forth yet a third prophet-religion, the Chaldean.

This, with its penetrating astronomy and its ever-amazing inwardness, was, I venture to guess, evolved at that time and by creative personalities of the Isaiah stature from relics of the old Babylonian religion.[4] About 1000, the Chaldeans

[1] The name Chaldean signifies, before the Persian epoch, a tribe; later, a religious society. See p. 175 above.

[2] A. Bertholet, *Kulturgeschichte Israels* (1919), pp. 253, et seq. [Clear and useful English manuals are G. Moore, *Literature of the Old Testament*; R. H. Charles, *Between the Old and the New Testaments*. See also the article "Hebrew Religion" in *Ency. Brit.*, XI ed. — *Tr.*]

[3] According to Williams Jackson's *Zoroaster* (1901).

[4] Research has treated the Chaldean, like the Talmudic, as a stepchild. The investigator's whole attention has been concentrated on the religion of the Babylonian Culture, and the Chaldean

were a group of Aramaic-speaking tribes like the Israelites, and lived in the south of Sinear — the mother tongue of Jesus is still sometimes called Chaldean. In Seleucid times the name was applied to a widespread religious community, and especially to its priests. The Chaldean religion was an astral religion, which before Hammurabi the Babylonian was *not*. It is the deepest of all interpretations of the Magian universe, the World-Cavern [1] and Kismet working therein, and consequently it remained the fundamental of Islamic and Jewish speculation to their very latest phases. It was by it, and not by the Babylonian Culture, that after the seventh century there was formed an astronomy worthy to be called an exact science — that is, a priestly technique of observation of marvellous acuteness.[2] It replaced the Babylonian moon-week by the planet-week. Ishtar, the most popular figure of the old religion, the goddess of life and fruitfulness, now became a planet, and Tammuz, the ever-dying and ever-revived god of vegetation, a fixed star. Finally, the henotheistic feeling announced itself; for Nebuchadnezzar the Great Marduk [3] was the one true god, the god of mercy, and Nebo, the old god of Borsippa, was his son and envoy to mankind. For a century (625–539) Chaldean kings were world-rulers, but they were also the heralds of the new religion. When temples were being built, they themselves carried bricks. The accession-prayer of Nebuchadnezzar, the contemporary of Jeremiah, to Marduk is still extant, and in depth and purity it is in nowise surpassed by the finest passages of Israelite prophecy. The Chaldean penitential psalms, closely related in rhythm and inner structure to those of the Jews, know the sin of which man is unconscious and the suffering that contrite avowal before the incensed god can avert. It is the same trust in the mercy of the Deity that finds a truly Christian expression in the inscriptions of the Bel temple of Palmyra.[4]

The kernel of the prophetic teachings is already Magian. There is *one* god — be he called Yahweh, Ahuramazda or Marduk-Baal — who is the principle of good, and all other deities are either impotent or evil. To this doctrine there attached itself the hope of a Messiah, very clear in Isaiah, but also bursting out everywhere during the next centuries, under pressure of an inner necessity. It

---

has been regarded as its dying echo. Such a view inevitably excludes any real understanding of it. The material is not even separated out, but is dispersed in all the books on Assyrian-Babylonian religion. (H. Zimmern, *Die Keilinschriften und das alte Testament* II; Gunkel, *Schöpfung und Chaos;* M. Jastrow, C. Bezold, etc.) On the other hand the subject is assumed by some (e.g., Bousset, *Hauptprobleme der Gnosis,* 1907) to have been exhausted.

[1] See Vol. I., p. 184. — *Tr.*

[2] The fact that Chaldean science was, in comparison with Babylonian empiricism, a new thing has been clearly recognized by Bezold (*Astronomie, Himmelsschau und Astrallehre bei den Babyloniern,* 1911, pp. 17, et seq.). Its data were taken and developed by different Classical savants according to their own way of reasoning — that is, as a matter of applied mathematics, and to the exclusion of all feeling for distance.

[3] See Jastrow's articles "Babylonian and Assyrian Religion" and "Marduk" in *Ency. Brit.,* XI ed. — *Tr.*

[4] J. Hehn, *Hymnen und Gebete an Marduk* (1905).

is the basic idea of Magian religion, for it contains implicitly the conception of the world-historical struggle between Good and Evil, with the power of Evil prevailing in the middle period, and the Good finally triumphant on the Day of Judgment. This moralization of history is common to Persians, Chaldees, and Jews. But with its coming, the idea of the localized people *ipso facto* vanished and the genesis of Magian nations without earthly homes and boundaries was at hand. The idea of the Chosen People emerged.[1] But it is easy to understand that men of strong blood, and in particular the great families, found these too spiritual ideas repugnant to their natures and harked back to the stout old tribal faiths. According to Cumont's researches the religion of the Persian kings was polytheistic and did not possess the Haoma sacrament — that is, it was not wholly Zoroastrian. The same is true of most of the kings of Israel, and in all probability also of the last Chaldean Nabu-Nabid (Nabonidus), whose overthrow by Cyrus and his own subjects was in fact made possible by his rejection of the Marduk faith. And it was in the Captivity that circumcision and the (Chaldean) Sabbath were first acquired, as rites, by the Jews.

The Babylonian exile, however, did set up an important difference between the Jews and the Persians, in respect, not of the ultimate truths of conscious piety, but of all the facts of actuality and consequently men's inward attitude to these facts. It was the Yahweh believers who *were permitted* to go home and the adherents of Ahuramazda who *allowed* them to do so. Of two small tribes that two hundred years before had probably possessed equal numbers of fighting men, the one had taken possession of a world — while Darius crossed the Danube in the north, his power extended in the south through eastern Arabia to the island of Sokotra on the Somali coast [2] — and the other had become an entirely unimportant pawn of alien policy.

This is what made one religion so lordly, the other so humble. Let the student read, in contrast to Jeremiah, the great Behistun inscription [3] of Darius — what a splendid pride of the King in his victorious god! And how despairing are the arguments with which the Israelite prophets sought to preserve intact

[1] For Chaldeans and Persians there was no need to trouble here about proof — they had by their God conquered the world. But the Jews had only their literature to cling to, and this accordingly turned to theoretical proof in the absence of positive. In the last analysis, this unique national treasure owes its origin to the constant need of reacting against self-depreciation. [For example, the repeated restatement of the *date* of the Messiah's advent in the successive works of the age of the prophets. — Tr.]

[2] Glaser, *Die Abessinier in Arabien und in Afrika* (1895), p. 124. Glaser is convinced that Abyssinian, Pehlevi, and Persian cuneiform inscriptions of the highest importance await discovery there.

[3] The inscription and sculptures of Behistun (on an almost inaccessible cliff in the Zagros range on the Baghdad-Hamadan road) were reinvestigated by a British Museum expedition in 1904; see *The Inscription of Darius the Great at Behistun* (London, 1907). "Thus saith Darius the King. That what I have done I have done altogether by the grace of Ahuramazda. Ahuramazda and the other gods that be, brought aid to me. For this reason did Ahuramazda and the other gods that be bring aid to me because I was not hostile nor a liar nor a wrongdoer, neither I nor my family, but according to Rectitude have I ruled" (A. V. Williams Jackson, *Persia Past and Present*). — Tr.

the image of their god. Here, in exile, with every Jewish eye turned by the Persian victory to the Zoroastrian doctrine, the pure Judaic prophecy (Amos, Hosea, Isaiah, Jeremiah) passes into *Apocalypse* (Deutero-Isaiah,[1] Ezekiel, Zechariah). All the new visions of the Son of Man, of Satan, of archangels, of the seven heavens, of the last judgment, are *Persian presentations of the common world-feeling*. In Isaiah xli appears Cyrus himself, hailed as Messiah. Did the great composer of Deutero-Isaiah draw his enlightenment from a Zoroastrian disciple? Is it possible that the Persians released the Jews out of a feeling of the inward relationship of their two teachings? It is certain at any rate that both shared one popular idea as to last things, and felt and expressed a common hatred of the old Babylonian and Classical religions, of unbelievers generally, which they did not feel towards one another.

We must not, however, forget to look at the "return from captivity" also from the point of view of Babylon. The great mass, strong in race-force, was in reality far removed from these ideas, or regarded them as mere visions and dreams; and the solid peasantry, the artisans, and no doubt the nascent land-aristocracy quietly remained in its holdings *under a prince of their own*, the Resh Galutha, whose capital was Nehardea.[2] Those who returned "home" were the small minority, the stubborn, the zealots. They numbered with their wives and children forty thousand, a figure which cannot be one-tenth or even one-twentieth of the total, and anyone who confuses these settlers and their destiny with Jewry as a whole [3] must necessarily fail to read the inner meaning of all following events. The *little world of Judaism lived a spiritually separate life*, and the nation as a whole, while regarding this life with respect, certainly did not share in it. In the East apocalyptic literature, the heiress of prophecy, blossomed richly. It was a genuine native poetry of the people, of which we still have the masterpiece, the Book of Job — a work in character Islamic and decidedly un-Jewish [4] — while a multitude of its other tales and sagas, such as Judith, Tobit, Achikar,[5] are spread as motives over all the literatures of the "Arabian" world. In Judea only the Law flourished; the Talmudic spirit appears first in Ezekiel (chs. xl, et seq.) and after 450 is made flesh in the scribes (Sopherim) headed by Ezra. From 300 B.C. to A.D. 200 the Tannaim ("Teachers") expounded the Torah and developed the Mishnah. Neither the coming of Jesus nor the destruction of the Temple interrupted this abstract

---

[1] Isaiah xl–lxvi. For the critical questions arising on Deutero-Isaiah see Dr. T. K. Cheyne's article "Isaiah" in the *Encyclopædia Biblica*, the same scholar's summary in *Ency. Brit.*, XI ed., article "Isaiah," or G. Moore's summary, *Literature of the Old Testament*, Ch. XVI. — *Tr.*

[2] This "King of the Banishment" (Exilarch) was long a conspicuous and politically important figure in the Persian Empire. He was only removed by Islam.

[3] As Christian and Jewish theology both do — the only difference between these is in their respective interpretations of the later development of Israelite literature (recast in Judea as the literature of Judaism), the one inflecting it towards Evangelism, the others towards Talmudism.

[4] Later it occurred to some Pharisee mind to Judaize it by interpolating chs. xxxii–xxxvii.

[5] See the articles "Tobit," etc., in *Jewish Encyclopædia* and *Ency. Biblica.* — *Tr.*

scholarship. Jerusalem became for the rigid believer a Mecca, and his Koran was a Code of laws to which was gradually added a whole primitive history compounded of Chaldeo-Persian motives reset according to Pharisaic ideas.[1] But in this atmosphere there was no room for a worldly art, poetry, or learning. All that the Talmud contains of astronomical, medical, and juristic knowledge is exclusively of Mesopotamian origin.[2] It is probable, too, that it was in Mesopotamia, and *before* the end of the Captivity, that there began that Chaldean-Persian-Jewish formation of sects which developed into the formation of great religions at the beginning of the Magian Culture, and reached its climax in the teaching of Mani. "The Law and the Prophets" — *these two nouns practically define the difference between Judea and Mesopotamia.* In the late Persian and in every other Magian theology both tendencies are united; it is only in the case here considered that they were separated in space. The decisions of Jerusalem were recognized everywhere, but it is a question how widely they were obeyed. Even as near as Galilee the Pharisees were the object of suspicion, while in Babylonia no Rabbi could be consecrated. For the great Gamaliel, Paul's teacher, it was a title to fame that his rulings were followed by the Jews "even abroad." How independent was the life of the Jews in Egypt is shown by the recently discovered documents of Elephantine and Assuan.[3] About 170, Onias asked the King for permission to build a temple "according to the measurements of the Temple in Jerusalem," on the ground that the numerous non-conforming temples that existed were the cause of eternal bickerings amongst the communities.

One other subject must be considered. Jewry, like Persia, had since the Exile increased enormously beyond the old small clan-limits; this was owing to conversions and secessions — *the only form of conquest open to a landless nation and, therefore, natural and obvious to the Magian religions.* In the north it very early drove, through the Jew State of Adiabene, to the Caucasus; in the south (probably along the Persian Gulf) it penetrated to Saba; in the west it was dominant in Alexandria, Cyrene, and Cyprus. The administration of Egypt and the policy of the Parthian Empire were largely in Jewish hands.

But this movement *came out of Mesopotamia alone,* and the spirit in it was the Apocalyptic and not the Talmudic. Jerusalem was occupied in creating yet more legal barriers against the unbeliever. It was not enough even to abandon the practice of making converts. A Pharisee permitted himself to summon the universally beloved King Hyrcanus (135–106) to lay down the office of High Priest because his mother had once been in the power of the infidels.[4] This is

---

[1] If the assumption of a Chaldean prophecy corresponding to Isaiah and Zarathustra be correct, it is to this young, inwardly cognate, and contemporary astral religion (and not to the Babylonian) that Genesis owes its amazingly profound cosmogony, just as it owes to the Persian religion its visions of the end of the world.

[2] S. Funk, *Die Entstehung des Talmuds* (1919), p. 106.

[3] E. Sachau, *Aramäische Papyros und Ostraka aus Elephantine* (1911).

[4] Josephus, *Antiq.*, 13, 10.

the same narrowness which in the primitive Christian brotherhood of Judea took the form of opposing the preaching of the Gospel to the heathen. In the East it would simply never have occurred to anyone to draw such barriers, which were contrary to the whole idea of the Magian nation. But in that very fact was based *the spiritual superiority* of the wide East. The Synedrion in Jerusalem might possess unchallenged religious authority, but politically, and therefore historically, the power of the Resh Galutha was a very different matter. Christian and Jewish research alike have failed to perceive these things. So far as I am aware, no one has noticed the important fact that the persecution of Antiochus Epiphanes was directed not against "Jewry" but against Judea. And this brings us to another fact, of still greater importance.

The destruction of Jerusalem hits only a very small part of the nation, one moreover that was spiritually and politically by far the least important. It is not true that the Jewish people has lived "in the Dispersion" since that day, for it had lived for centuries (and so too had the Persian and others) in a form which was independent of country. On the other hand, we realize equally little the impression made by this war upon the real Jewry which Judea thought of and treated as an adjunct. The victory of the heathen and the ruin of the Sanctuary was felt in the inmost soul,[1] and in the crusade of 115 [2] a bitter revenge was taken for it; but the ideal outraged and vindicated was the ideal of Jewry and not that of Judaism. Zionism then, as in Cyrus's day and in ours, was a reality only for a quite small and spiritually narrow minority. If the calamity had been really felt in the sense of a "loss of home" (as we figure it to ourselves with the Western mind), a hundred opportunities after Marcus Aurelius's time could have been seized to win the city back. But that would have contradicted the Magian sense of the nation, whose ideal organic form was the synagogue, the pure *consensus* — like the early Catholic "visible Church" and like Islam — and it was precisely the annihilation of Judea and the clan spirit of Judea that *for the first time completely actualized this ideal.*

For Vespasian's War, directed against Judea, was a liberation of Jewry. In the first place, it ended both the claim of the people of this petty district to be the genuine nation, and the pretensions of their bald spirituality to equivalence with the soul-life of the whole. The research, the scholasticism, and the mysticism of the Oriental academies entered into possession of their rights; so, for instance, the judge Karna — the contemporary, more or less, of Ulpian and Papinian — formulated at the academy of Nehardea the first code of civil law.[3] In the second place, it rescued this religion from the dangers of that pseudomorphosis to which Christianity in that same period was succumbing. Since 200 B.C. there had existed a half-Hellenistic Jewish literature. The

---

[1] Much as, say, the destruction of the Vatican would be felt by the Catholic Church.
[2] See p. 198. — *Tr.*
[3] Cf. p. 69.

"Preacher" (Ecclesiastes, Koheleth) contains Pyrrhonic ideas.[1] The Wisdom of Solomon, 2 Maccabees, Theodotion, the Aristeas Letter, etc., follow; there are things like the Menander collection of Maxims, as to which it is impossible to say whether they ought to be regarded as Jewish or as Greek.   There were, about 160, high priests who were so Hellenistic in spirit that they combated the Jewish religion, and later there were rulers like Hyrcanus and Herod who did the same by political methods. This danger came to an end instantly and for good in A.D.70.

In the time of Jesus there were in Jerusalem three tendencies which can be described as generally Aramæan, represented respectively by the Pharisees, the Sadducees, and the Essenes. Although the connotations of these names varied, and although both in Christian and in Jewish research most diverse views are held about them, it may at any rate be said that the first of these tendencies is found in greatest purity in Judaism, the second in Chaldeanism, the third in Hellenism.[2] Essene is the rise of the cult (almost the Order) of Mithras in the east of Asia Minor. The Sadducees, although in Jerusalem they appear as a small and distinguished group — Josephus compares them with the Epicureans — are thoroughly Aramæan in their apocalyptic and eschatological views, in virtue of a certain element which makes them, so to say, the Dostoyevskis of this Early period. They stand to the Pharisees in the relation of mysticism to scholasticism, of John to Paul, of Bundahish to Vendidad[3] in the Persian world. The Apocalyptic is popular, and many of its traits are spiritually common property throughout the Aramæan world; the Talmudic and Avestan Pharisaism is exclusive and tries to rule out every other religion with uncompromising rigour.

The Essenes appear in Jerusalem as a monastic order like the Neopythagoreans. They possessed secret texts.[4] In the broad sense they are representative of the Pseudomorphosis, and in consequence they disappear from Jewry completely after A.D. 70, while precisely in this period Christian literature was becoming purely Greek — not in the least of the causes of this being that the Hellenized Western Jews left Judaism to retreat into its East, and gradually adopted Christianity.

But also Apocalyptic, which is an expression-form of townless and town-fearing mankind, soon came to an end within the Synagogue, after a last wonderful reaction to the stimulus of the great catastrophe.[5] When it had become evident that the teaching of Jesus would lead not to a reform of Judaism,

---

[1] Pyrrho himself had studied under Magian priests. See, for Pyrrhonism, *Ency. Brit.*, XI ed., articles "Scepticism," "Megarian School," "Pyrrho." — *Tr.*

[2] Schiele (*Die Religion in Geschichte und Gegenwart*, III, 812) reverses the two latter names; this, however, does not affect the phenomenon in any way.

[3] The Cosmogony and the Law, in the Zoroastrian Scriptures. — *Tr.*

[4] Bousset, *Rel. d. Jud.*, p. 532.

[5] Baruch, Ezra IV (2 Esdras), the original text of John's Revelation.

but to a new religion, and when, about A.D. 100, the daily imprecation-formula against the Jew-Christians was introduced, Apocalyptic for the short remainder of its existence resided in the young Church.

VI

The incomparable thing which lifted the infant Christianity out above all religions of this rich Springtime is the figure of Jesus. In all the great creations of those years there is nothing which can be set beside it. Tame and empty all the legends and holy adventures of Mithras, Attis, and Osiris must have seemed to any man reading or listening to the still recent story of Jesus's sufferings — the last journey to Jerusalem, the last anxious supper, the hours of despair in Gethsemane, and the death on the cross.

Here was no matter of philosophy. Jesus's utterances, which stayed in the memory of many of the devoted, even in old age, are those of a child in the midst of an alien, aged, and sick world. They are not sociological observations, problems, debatings. Like a quiet island of bliss was the life of these fishermen and craftsmen by the Lake of Gennesareth in the midst of the age of the great Tiberius, far from all world-history and innocent of all the doings of actuality, while round them glittered the Hellenistic towns with their theatres and temples, their refined Western society, their noisy mob-diversions, their Roman cohorts, their Greek philosophy. When the friends and disciples of the sufferer had grown grey and his brother was president of their group in Jerusalem, they put together, from the sayings and narratives generally current in their small communities, a biography so arresting in its inward appeal that it evolved a presentation-form of its own, of which neither the Classical nor the Arabian Culture has any example — the Gospel. Christianity is the one religion in the history of the world in which the fate of a man of the immediate present has become the emblem and the central point of the whole creation.

A strange excitement, like that which the Germanic world experienced about A.D. 1000, ran in those days through the whole Aramæan land. The Magian soul was awakened. That element which lay in the prophetic religions like a presentiment, and expressed itself in Alexander's time in metaphysical outlines, came now to the state of fulfilment. And this fulfilment awakened, in indescribable strength, the primitive feeling of Fear. The birth of the Ego, and of the world-anxiety with which it is identical, is one of the final secrets of humanity and of mobile life generally. In front of the Microcosm there stands up a Macrocosm wide and overpowering, an abyss of alien, dazzling existence and activity that frightens the small lonely ego back into itself. Even in the blackest hours of life no adult experiences fear like the fear which sometimes overpowers a child in the crisis of awakening. Over the dawn of the new Culture likewise lay this deathly anxiety. In this early morning of Magian world-feeling, timorous and hesitant and ignorant of itself, young

eyes saw the end of the world at hand — it is the first thought in which every
Culture to this day has come to knowledge of itself.   All but the shallower
souls trembled before revelations, miracles, glimpses into the very fundament of
things.   Men now lived and thought only in apocalyptic images.   Actuality
became appearance.   Strange and terrifying visions were told mysteriously by
one to another, read out from fantastic veiled texts, and seized at once with an
immediate inward certainty.   These writings travelled from community to
community, village to village, and it is quite impossible to assign them to any
one particular religion.[1]   Their colouring is Persian, Chaldean, Jewish, but they
have absorbed all that was circulating in men's minds.   Whereas the canonical
books are national, the apocalyptic literature is international in the literal
sense of the word.   It is there, and no one seems to have composed it.   Its
content is fluid — to-day it reads thus and to-morrow otherwise.   But this
does not mean that it is a "poetry" — it is not.[2]   These creations resemble the
terrible figures of the Romanesque cathedral-porches in France, which also are
not "art," but fear turned into stone.   Everyone knows those angels and devils,
the ascent to heaven and descent to hell of divine Essence, the Second Adam,
the Envoy of God, the Redeemer of the last days, the Son of Man, the eternal
city, and the last judgment.[3]   In the alien cities and the high positions of strict
Judaic and Persian priesthoods the different doctrines might be tangibly
defined and argued about, but below in the mass of the people there was practically no specific religion, but a general Magian religiousness which filled all
souls and attached itself to glimpses and visions of every conceivable origin.
The Last Day was at hand.   Men expected it and knew that on that day "He"
of whom all these revelations spoke would appear.   Prophets arose.   More and
more new communities and groups gathered, believing themselves to have
found either a better understanding of the traditional religion, or the true
religion itself.   In this time of amazing, ever-increasing tension, and in the
very years around Jesus's birth-year, there arose, besides endless communities
and sects, another redemption-religion, the Mandæan, as to which we know

[1] For instance, the Book of Naasenes (P. Wendland, *Hellenistisch-römische Kultur*, pp. 177, et seq.);
the "Mithras Liturgy" (ed. A. Dieterich); the Hermetic Pœmander (ed. Reitzenstein), the Psalms
of Solomon, the Gospels of Thomas and Peter, the Pistis-Sophia, etc. [Information as to these will
be found in the articles "Ophites," "Mithras," "Hermes Trismegistus," "Apocalyptic Literature,"
"Apocryphal Literature," "Gnosticism," in the *Ency. Brit.*, XI ed. — *Tr.*]

[2] Any more than Dostoyevski's "*Dream of a Ridiculous Person*" is so.

[3] Our definitive ideas of this early Magian vision-world we owe to the manuscripts of Turfan,
which have reached Berlin since 1903. It was these which at last freed our knowledge and, above all,
our criteria from the deformations due to the preponderance of Western-Hellenistic material — a
preponderance that had been augmented by Egyptian papyrus finds — and radically transformed all
our existing views. Now at last the pure, almost unknown, East is seen operative in all the apocalypses, hymns, liturgies, and books of edification of the Persians, Mandæans, Manichæans, and
countless other sects; and primitive Christianity for the first time really takes its place in the movement to which it owes its spiritual origins (see H. Lüders, *Sitzungen der Berliner Akademie*, 1914,
and R. Reitzenstein, *Das iranische Erlösungsmysterium* (1921).

nothing of founder or origins. In spite of its hatred of the Judaism of Jerusalem and its definite preference for the Persian idea of redemption, the Mandæan religion seems to have stood very close to the popular beliefs of Syrian Jewry. One after another, pieces of its wonderful documents are becoming available, and they consistently show us a "Him," a Son of Man, a Redeemer who is sent down into the depths, who himself must be redeemed and is the goal of man's expectations. In the Book of John, the Father high upraised in the House of Fulfilment, bathed in light, says to his only begotten Son: "My Son, be to me an ambassador; go into the world of darkness, where no ray of light is." And the Son calls up to him: "Father, in what have I sinned that thou hast sent me into the darkness?" And finally: "Without sin did I ascend and there was no sin and defect in me."[1]

All the characters of the great prophetic religions and of the whole store of profound glimpses and visions later collected into apocalypses are seen here as foundations. Of Classical thought and feeling not a breath reached this Magian underworld. No doubt the beginnings of the new religion are lost irrevocably. But *one* historical figure of Mandæanism stands forth with startling distinctness, as tragic in his purpose and his downfall as Jesus himself—John the Baptist.[2] He, almost emancipated from Judaism, and filled with as mighty a hatred of the Jerusalem spirit as that of primitive Russia for Petersburg, preached the end of the world and the coming of the Barnasha, the Son of Man, *who is no longer the longed-for national Messiah of the Jews*, but the bringer of the world-conflagration.[3] To him came Jesus and was his disciple.[4] He was thirty years old when the awakening came over him. Thenceforth the apocalyptic, and in particular the Mandæan, thought-world filled his whole being. The other world of historical actuality lying round him was to him as something sham, alien, void of significance. That "He" would now come and make an end

[1] Lidzbarski, *Das Johannesbuch der Mandäer*, Ch. LXVI. Also W. Bousset, *Hauptprobleme der Gnosis* (1907) and Reitzenstein, *Das Mandäische Buch der Herrn der Grösse* (1919), an apocalypse approximately contemporary with the oldest Gospels. On the Messiah texts, the Descent-into-Hell texts, and the Songs of the Dead see Lidzbarski, *Mandäische Liturgien* (1920); also the Book of the Dead (especially the second and third books of the left Genza) in Reitzenstein's *Das iranische Erlösungsmysterium* (especially pp. 43, et seq.). [The Mandæan religion survives to-day in the region of the Shatt-el-Arab and the Karun valley or Khuzistan. — Tr.]

[2] See Reitzenstein, pp. 124, et seq., and references there quoted.

[3] In the New Testament, of which the final redaction lies entirely in the sphere of Western-Classical thought, the Mandæan religion and the sects belonging thereto are no longer understood, and indeed everything Oriental seems to have dropped out. Acts xviii–xix, however, discloses a perceptible hostility between the then widespread John-communities and the Primitive Christians (see Dibelius *Die Urchristliche Überlieferungen von Johannes dem Täufer*). The Mandæans later rejected Christianity as flatly as they had rejected Judaism. Jesus was for them a false Messiah. In their Apocalypse of the Lord of Greatness the apparition of Enosh was also announced.

[4] According to Reitzenstein (*Das Buch von Herrn der Grösse*) Jesus was condemned at Jerusalem as a John-disciple. According to Lidzbarski (*Mand. Lit.*, 1920, XVI and Zimmern (*Ztschr. d. D. Morg. Gesellschaft*, 1920, p. 429), the expression "Jesus the Nazarene" or "Nasorene," which was later by the Christian communities referred to Nazareth (Matthew ii, 23, with a doubtful citation), really indicates the membership in a Mandæan Order.

of this unreal reality was his magnificent certainty, and like his master John, he stepped forth as its herald. Even now we can see, in the oldest Gospels that were embodied into the New Testament, gleams of this period in which he was, in his consciousness, nothing but a prophet.[1]

But there was a moment in his life when an inkling, and then high certainty, came over him — "Thou art thyself It!" It was a secret that he at first hardly admitted to himself, and only later imparted to his nearest friends and companions, who thereafter shared with him, in all stillness, the blessed mission, till finally they dared to reveal the truths before all the world by the momentous journey to Jerusalem. If there is anything at all that clouds the complete purity and honour of his thought, it is that doubt as to whether he has deceived himself which from time to time seizes him, and of which, later, his disciples told quite frankly. He comes to his home. The village crowds to him, recognizes the former carpenter who left his work, is angered. The family — mother and all the brothers and sisters — are ashamed of him and would have arrested him. And with all these familiar eyes upon him he was confused and felt the magic power depart from him (Mark vi). In Gethsemane doubts of his mission [2] mingled themselves in the terrible fear of coming things, and even on the cross men heard the anguished cry that God had forsaken him.

Even in these last hours he lived entirely in the form of his own apocalyptic world, which alone was ever real to him. What to the Roman sentries standing below him was reality was for him an object of helpless wonder, an illusion that might at any moment without warning vanish into nothingness. He possessed the pure and unadulterated soul of the townless land. The life of the cities and their spirit were to him utterly alien. Did he really see the semi-Classical Jerusalem, into which he rode as the Son of Man, and understand its historical nature? This is what thrills us in the last days — and the collision of facts with truths, of two worlds that will never understand one another, and his entire incomprehension of what was happening about him.

So he went, proclaiming his message without reservation, through his country. But this country was Palestine. He was born in the Classical Empire and lived under the eyes of the Judaism of Jerusalem, and when his soul, fresh from the awful revelation of its mission, looked about, it was confronted by the actuality of the Roman State and that of Pharisaism. His repugnance for the stiff and selfish ideal of the latter, which he shared with all Mandæanism and doubtless with the peasant Jewry of the wide East, is the hall-mark of all his discourses from first to last. It angered him that this wilderness of cold-hearted formulæ was reputed to be the only way to salvation. Still, thus far it was only

[1] E.g., Mark vi; and then the great change, Mark viii, 27, et seq. There is no religion which has given us more honestly the tale of its birth.

[2] Similarly in Mark i, 38, et seq., when he arose in the night and sought a lonely place in order to fortify himself by prayer.

another kind of piety that his conviction was asserting against Rabbinical logic. Thus far it is only the Law versus the Prophets.

But when Jesus was taken before Pilate, then *the world of facts and the world of truths were face to face in immediate and implacable hostility.* It is a scene appallingly distinct and overwhelming in its symbolism, such as the world's history had never before and has never since looked at. The discord that lies at the root of all mobile life from its beginning, in virtue of its very *being,* of its having both existence *and* awareness, took here the highest form that can possibly be conceived of human tragedy. In the famous question of the Roman Procurator: "What is truth?" — the one word that is race-pure in the whole Greek Testament — lies *the entire meaning of history,* the exclusive validity of the deed, the prestige of the State and war and blood, the all-powerfulness of success and the pride of eminent fitness. Not indeed the mouth, but the silent feeling of Jesus answers this question by that other which is decisive in all things of religion — *What is actuality?* For Pilate actuality was all; for him nothing. Were it anything, indeed, pure religiousness could never stand up against history and the powers of history, or sit in judgment on active life; or if it does, it ceases to be religion and is subjected itself to the spirit of history.

My kingdom is not of this world. This is the final word which admits of no gloss and on which each must check the course wherein birth and nature have set him. A being that makes use of a waking-consciousness, or a waking-consciousness which subjects being to itself; pulsation or tension, blood or intellect, history or nature, politics or religion — here it is one or the other, there is no honest way of compromise. A statesman can be deeply religious, a pious man can die for his country — but they must, both, know on which side they are really standing. The born politician despises the inward thought-processes of the ideologue and ethical philosopher in a world of fact — and rightly. For the believer, all ambition and succession of the historical world are sinful and without lasting value — he, too, is right. A ruler who wishes to improve religion in the direction of political, practical purposes is a fool. A sociologist-preacher who tries to bring truth, righteousness, peace, and forgiveness into the world of actuality is a fool also. No faith yet has altered the world, and no fact can ever rebut a faith. There is no bridge between directional Time and timeless Eternity, between the *course* of history and the *existence* of a divine world-order, in the structure of which the word "providence" or "dispensation" denotes the form of causality. *This is the final meaning of the moment in which Jesus and Pilate confronted one another.* In the one world, the historical, the Roman caused the Galilean to be crucified — that was his Destiny. In the other world, Rome was cast for perdition and the Cross became the pledge of Redemption — that was the "will of God." [1]

---

[1] The method of the present work is historical. It therefore recognizes the anti-historical as well as the historical as a *fact.* The religious method, on the contrary, necessarily looks upon itself as the *true* and the opposite as *false.* This difference is quite insuperable.

Religion is metaphysic and nothing else — *"Credo quia absurdum"* — and this metaphysic is not the metaphysic of knowledge, argument, proof (which is mere philosophy or learnedness), but *lived and experienced* metaphysic — that is, the unthinkable as a certainty, the supernatural as a fact, life as existence in a world that is non-actual, but true. Jesus never lived one moment in any other world but this. He was no moralizer, and to see in moralizing the final aim of religion is to be ignorant of what religion is. Moralizing is nineteenth-century Enlightenment, humane Philistinism. To ascribe social purposes to Jesus is a blasphemy. His occasional utterances of a social kind, so far as they are authentic and not merely attributed sayings, tend merely to edification. They contain nothing whatever of new doctrine, and they include proverbs of the sort then in general currency. His *teaching* was the proclamation, nothing but the proclamation, of those Last Things with whose images he was constantly filled, the dawn of the New Age, the advent of heavenly envoys, the last judgment, a new heaven and a new earth.[1] Any other conception of religion was never in Jesus, nor in any truly deep-feeling period of history. *Religion is, first and last, metaphysic*, other-worldliness (*Jenseitigkeit*), awareness in a world of which the evidence of the senses merely lights the foreground. It is life in and with the supersensible. And where the capacity for this awareness, or even the capacity for believing in its existence, is wanting, real religion is at an end. "My kingdom is *not* of this world," and only he who can look into the depths that this flash illumines can comprehend the voices that come out of them. It is the Late, city periods that, no longer capable of seeing into depths, have turned the remnants of religiousness upon the external world and replaced religion by humanities, and metaphysic by moralization and social ethics.

In Jesus we have the direct opposite. "Give unto Cæsar the things that are Cæsar's" means: "Fit yourselves to the powers of the fact-world, be patient, suffer, and ask it not whether they are 'just.'" What alone matters is the salvation of the soul. "Consider the lilies" means: "Give no heed to riches *and poverty*, for both fetter the soul to cares of this world." "Man cannot serve both God and Mammon" — by Mammon is meant the *whole* of actuality. It is shallow, and it is cowardly, to argue away the grand significance of this demand. Between working for the increase of one's own riches, and working for the social ease of everyone, he would have felt no difference whatever. When wealth affrighted him, when the primitive community in Jerusalem —

---

[1] Hence Mark xiii, taken from an older document, is perhaps the purest example of his usual daily discourse. Paul (1 Thess. iv, 15–17) quotes another, which is missing in the Gospels. With these, we have the priceless — but, by commentators dominated by the Gospel tone, misunderstood — contributions of Papias, who about 100 was still in a position to collect much oral tradition. The little that we have of his work suffices amply to show us the apocalyptic character of Jesus's daily discourses. It is Mark xiii and not the Sermon on the Mount that reproduces the real note of them. But as *his* teaching became modified into a teaching *of Him*, this material likewise was transformed and the record of his utterances became the narrative of his manifestation. In this one respect the picture given by the Gospels is inevitably false.

which was a strict Order and not a socialist club — rejected ownership, it was the most direct opposite of "social" sentiment that moved them. Their conviction was, not that the visible state of things was all, but that it was nothing: that it rested not on appreciation of comfort in this world, but on unreserved contempt of it. Something, it is true, must always exist to be set against and to nullify worldly fortune, and so we come back to the contrast of Tolstoi and Dostoyevski. Tolstoi, the townsman and Westerner, saw in Jesus only a social reformer, and in his metaphysical impotence — like the whole civilized West, which can only think about *distributing*, never *renouncing* — elevated primitive Christianity to the rank of a social revolution. Dostoyevski, who was poor, but in certain hours almost a saint, never thought about social ameliorations — of what profit would it have been to a man's *soul* to abolish *property*?

VII

Amongst Jesus's friends and disciples, stunned as they were by the appalling outcome of the journey to Jerusalem, there spread after a few days the news of his resurrection and reappearance. The impression of this news on such souls and in such a time can never be more than partially echoed in the sensibilities of a Late mankind. It meant the actual fulfilment of all the Apocalyptic of that Magian Springtime — the end of the present æon marked by the ascension of the redeemed Redeemer, the second Adam, the Saoshyant, Enosh, Barnasha, or whatever other name man attached to "Him," into the light-realm of the Father. And therewith the foretold future, the new world-æon, "the Kingdom of Heaven," became immediately present. They felt themselves at the decisive point in the history of redemption.

This certainty completely transformed the world-outlook of the little circles. "His" teachings, as they had flowed from his mild and noble nature — his inner feeling of the relation between God and man and of the high meaning of the times, and were exhaustively comprised in and defined by the word "love" — fell into the background, and their place was taken by the *teaching of Him*. As the Arisen he became for his disciples a new figure, in and of the Apocalyptic, and (what was more) its most important and final figure. But therewith their image of the future took form as an image of memory. Now, this was something of quite decisive importance, unheard-of in the world of Magian thought — the transference of an actuality, lived and experienced, on to the plane of the high story itself. The Jews (amongst them the young Paul) and the Mandæans (amongst them the disciples of John the Baptist) fought against it with passion and made of Jesus a "False Messiah" such as had been spoken of in the earliest Persian texts.[1] For them "He" was still to come from afar; for the little community "He" had already been — had they not seen him and lived with him? We have to enter into this conception unreservedly

[1] Jesus himself was aware of this (Matt. xxiv, 5, 11).

if we are to appreciate the enormous superiority it had in those times. Instead of an uncertain glimpse into the distance,[1] a compelling present; instead of fearful waiting for a liberating certainty, instead of a saga, a lived and shared human destiny — truly they were "glad tidings" that were proclaimed.

But to whom? Even in the first days the question arose which decided the whole Destiny of the new revelation. Jesus and his friends were Jews by birth, but they did not belong to the land of Judea. Here in Jerusalem men looked for the Messiah of their old sacred books, a Messiah who was to appear for the "Jewish people," in the old tribal sense, and only for them. But all the rest of the Aramæan world waited upon the Saviour of the *world*, the Redeemer and Son of Man, the figure of all apocalyptic literature, whether written out in Jewish, Persian, Chaldean, or Mandæan terms.[2] In the one view the death and resurrection of Jesus were merely local events; in the other they betokened a world-change. For, while everywhere else the Jews were a Magian nation without home or unity of birth, Jerusalem held firmly to the tribal idea. The conflict was not one between "preaching to the Jews" and "preaching to the Gentiles" — it went far deeper. The word "mission" had essentially here a twofold meaning. In the Judaic view there was essentially no need for re-cruiting — quite the reverse, as it was a contradiction to the Messiah-idea. The words "tribe" and "mission" are reciprocally exclusive. The members of the Chosen People, and in particular the priesthood, had merely to convince *themselves* that their longing was now fulfilled. But to the Magian nation, based on *consensus* or community of feeling, what the Resurrection conveyed was a full and definitive truth, and consensus in the matter of this truth gave the *principle of the true nation*, which must necessarily expand till it had taken in all older and conceptually incomplete principles. "A Shepherd and his sheep" was the formula of the new world-nation. The nation of the Redeemer was identical with mankind. When, therefore, we survey the early history of this Culture, we see that the controversy in the Apostles' Council [3] had been already decided, five hundred years before, by facts. Post-exilic Jewry (with the sole exception of self-contained Judea) had, like the Persians, Chaldeans, and others, recruited widely amongst the heathen, from Turkestan to inner Africa, regardless of home and origin. As to this there is now no controversy. It never at any time entered the heads of this community to be anything but

---

[1] Made more uncertain perhaps by the failure of previous prophecies that had been so confidently dated — e.g., Jeremiah xxv, 11; xxiv, 5–6; reinterpreted in Daniel vii, ix; 1 Enoch lxxxiii–xc; and again to be reinterpreted in 2 Baruch xxxvi–xl and 4 Ezra x–xii. — *Tr.*

[2] The designation "Messiah (Christ)" was old-Jewish, those of "Lord" ($\kappa\upsilon\rho\iota\acute{o}s$, *divus*) and "Saviour" ($\sigma\hat{\omega}\tau\eta\rho$, *Asklepios*) were east-Aramæan in origin. In the course of the pseudomorphosis "Christ" became the *name* of Jesus, and "Saviour" the *title;* but already "Lord" and "Saviour" were titles current in the Hellenistic Emperor- worship; and in this was implicit the whole destiny of westward-looking Christianity (compare here Reitzenstein, *Das iranische Erlösungsmysterium*, p. 132, note).

[3] Acts xv; Gal. ii.

what it really was. It was itself already the result of *a national existence in dispersion.* In utter contrast to the old-Jewish texts — which were a carefully preserved treasure, and of which the right interpretation, the Halakha, was reserved by the Rabbis to themselves — the apocalyptic literature was written so that it could reach all the souls to be wakened, and interpreted so that it might strike home in everyone.

It is easy to see which of these conceptions was that of Jesus's oldest friends, for they established themselves as a community of the Last Days in Jerusalem and frequented the Temple. For these simple folk — amongst them his brothers, who erstwhile had openly rejected him, and his mother, who now believed in her executed Son [1] — the power of the Judaic tradition was even stronger than the spirit of Apocalypse. In their object of convincing the Jews they failed (although at first even Pharisees came over to them) and so they remained as one of the numerous sects within Judaism, and their product, the "Confession of Peter," may fairly be characterized as an express assertion that they themselves were the true Jewry and the Synedrion the false. [2]

The final destiny of this circle [3] was to fall into oblivion when, as very soon happened, the whole world of Magian thought and feeling responded to the new apocalyptic teaching. Amongst the later disciples of Jesus were many who were definitely and purely Magian, and wholly free from the Pharisaic spirit. Long before Paul, they had tacitly settled the mission question. Not to preach, for them, was not to live at all, and presently they had assembled, everywhere from the Tigris to the Tiber, small circles in which the figure of Jesus, in every conceivable presentation, merged with the mass of prior visions. [4] Out of this, a new discord arose, as between mission to the heathen and mission to the Jews, and this was far more important than the conflict between Judea and the world on issues already decided. Jesus had lived in Galilee. Was his teaching to look west or east? Was it to be a Jesus-cult or an Order of the Saviour? Was it to seek intimacy with the Persian or with the Syncretic Church, both of which were in process of formation?

This was the question decided by Paul — the first great personality in the new movement, and the first who had the sense not only of truths, but of facts.

[1] Acts i, 14; cf. Mark vi.

[2] As against Luke, Matthew is the representative of this conception. His is the only Gospel in which the word "*Ecclesia*" is used, and it denotes the true Jews, in contradistinction to the masses that refuse to listen to Jesus. This is not the missionary idea, any more than Isaiah was a missionary. Community, in this connexion, means an Order within Judaism. The prescriptions of Matt. xviii, 15-20 are wholly incompatible with any general dissemination.

[3] It fell apart later into sects, amongst which were the Ebionites and the Elkazites (the latter having a strange sacred book, the Elxai; see Bousset, *Hauptprobleme der Gnosis*, p. 154). [See the articles "Ebionites" and "Sabians" in *Ency. Brit.*, XI ed. — Tr.]

[4] Such sects were attacked in the Acts of the Apostles and in all Paul's Epistles, and indeed there was hardly a Late Classical or Aramæan religion or philosophy which did not give rise to some sort of Jesus-sect. The danger was indeed real of the Passion story becoming, not the nucleus of a new religion, but an integrating element of all existing ones.

As a young rabbi from the West, and a pupil of one of the most famous of the Tannaim, he had persecuted the Christians qua Jewish sectaries. Then, after an awakening of the sort that often happened in those days, he turned to the numerous small cult-communities of the West and forged out of them a Church of *his own* modelling: so that thenceforward, the Pagan and the Christian cult-Churches evolved in parallel, and with constant reciprocal action, up to Iamblichus and Athanasius (about A.D. 330). In the presence of this great ideal, Paul had for the Jesus-communities of Jerusalem a scarcely veiled contempt. There is nothing in the New Testament more express and exact than the beginning of the Epistle to the Galatians; his activity is a self-assumed task; he has taught how it pleased him and he has built how it pleased him. Finally, after fourteen years, he goes to Jerusalem in order, by force of his superior mentality, his success, and his effective independence of the old comrades of Jesus, to compel them there to agree that his, Paul's, creation contained the true doctrine. Peter and his people, alien to actualities, failed to seize and appreciate the far-reaching significance of the discussion. And from that moment the primitive community was superfluous.

Paul was a rabbi in intellect and an apocalyptic in feeling. He recognized Judaism, but as a *preliminary* development. And thus there came to be two Magian religions with the same Scriptures (namely, the Old Testament), but a double Halakha, the one setting towards the Talmud — developed by the Tannaim at Jerusalem from 300 B.C. onwards — and the other, founded by Paul and completed by the Fathers, in the direction of the Gospel. But, further, Paul drew together the whole fullness of Apocalypse and salvation-yearning then circulating in these fields [1] into a salvation-*certainty*, the certainty immediately revealed to him and to him *alone* near Damascus. "*Jesus is the Redeemer and Paul is his Prophet*" — this is the whole content of his message. The analogy with Mohammed could scarcely be closer. They differed neither in the nature of the awakening, nor in prophetic self-assuredness, nor in the consequent assertion of sole authority and unconditional truth for their respective expositions.

With Paul, urban man and his "intelligence" come on the scene. The others, though they might know Jerusalem or Antioch, never grasped the essence of these cities. They lived soil-bound, rural, wholly soul and feeling. But now there appeared a spirit that had grown up in the great cities of Classical cast, that could only live in cities, that neither understood nor respected the peasant's countryside. An understanding was possible with Philo, but with

---

[1] Of this he was fully aware. Many of his deepest intuitions are unimaginable without Persian and Mandæan influences (e.g., Romans vii, 22–24; 1 Corinthians xv, 26; Ephesians v, 6, et seq., with a quotation of Persian origin. See Reitzenstein, *Das iran. Erlös.-Myst.*, pp. 6, 133, et seq.). But this does not prove familiarity with Persian-Mandæan literature. The stories were spread in these days as sagas and folk-tales were amongst us. One heard about them in childhood as things of daily hearsay, but without being in the least aware of how deeply one was under their spell.

Peter never. Paul was the first by whom the Resurrection-experience was *seen as a problem;* the ecstatic awe of the young countryman changed in his brain into a conflict of spiritual principles. For what a contrast! — the struggle of Gethsemane, and the hour of Damascus: Child and Man, soul-anguish and intellectual decision, self-devotion to death and resolve to change sides! Paul had begun by seeing in the new Jewish sect a danger to the Pharisaism of Jerusalem; now, suddenly, he comprehended that the Nazarenes "were right" — a phrase that is inconceivable on the lips of Jesus — and took up their cause against Judaism, thereby setting up as an *intellectual quantity* that which had previously consisted in the knowledge of an experience. An intellectual quantity — but in making his cause into this he unwittingly drove it close to the other intellectual powers, *the cities of the West.* In the ambiance of pure Apocalyptic there is no "intellect." For the old comrades it was simply not possible to understand him in the least — and mournfully and doubtfully they must have looked at him while he was addressing them. Their living image of Jesus (whom Paul had never seen) paled in this bright, hard light of concepts and propositions. Thenceforward the holy memory faded into a Scholastic system. But Paul had a perfectly exact feeling for the true home of his ideas. His missionary journeys were all directed westward, and the East he ignored. *He never left the domain of the Classical city.* Why did he go to Rome, to Corinth, and not to Edessa or Ctesiphon? And why was it that he worked *only in the cities, and never from village to village?*

That things developed thus was due to Paul *alone.* In the face of his practical energy the feelings of all the rest counted for nothing, and so the young Church took the urban and Western tendency decisively, so decisively that later it could describe the remaining heathen as "*pagani,*" country-folk. Thus arose an immense danger that only youth and vernal force enabled the growing Church to repel; the fellah-world of the Classical cities grasped at it with both hands, and the marks of that grasp are visible to-day. But — how remote already from the essence of Jesus, whose entire life had been bound to country and the country-folk! The Pseudomorphosis in which he was born he had simply not noticed; his soul contained not the smallest trace of its influence — and now, a generation after him, probably within the lifetime of his mother, that which had grown up out of his death had already become a centre of formative purpose for that Pseudomorphosis. The Classical City was soon the only theatre of ritual and dogmatic evolution. Eastward the community extended only furtively and unobtrusively.[1] About A.D. 100 there were already Christians beyond the Tigris, but as far as the development of the Church was concerned they and their beliefs might almost have been non-existent.

[1] The early missionary effort in the East has scarcely been investigated and is still very difficult to establish in detail. Sachau, *Chronik von Arbela* (1915) and "*Die Ausbreitung der Christentums in Asien*" in *Abh. Pr. Akad. d. Wiss.* (1919); Harnack, *Mission und Ausbreitung des Christentums,* II, 117, et seq.

It was a second creation, then, that came out of Paul's immediate entourage, and it was this creation that, essentially, defined the form of the new Church. The personality and the story of Jesus cried aloud to be put into poetic form, and yet it is due to one man alone, Mark, that Gospels came into existence at all.[1] What Paul and Mark had before them was a firm tradition in the community, *the* "Gospel," a continued and propagated hearsay, supported by formless and insignificant notes in Aramaic and Greek, but in no way set out. In any case, of course, serious documents would have come into existence some time or another, but their natural form as products of the spirit of those who had *lived* with Jesus (and of the spirit of the East generally) would have been a canonical collection of his sayings, amplified, conclusively defined, and provided with an exegesis by the Councils and pivoting upon the Second Advent. But any tentatives in this direction were completely broken off by the Gospel of Mark, which was written down about A.D. 65, at the same time as the last Pauline Epistles, and, like them, in Greek. The writer had no suspicion, perhaps, of the significance of his little work, but it made him one of the supremely important personalities not only of Christianity, but of the Arabian Culture generally. All older attempts vanished, leaving writings in Gospel-form as the sole sources concerning Jesus. (So much so that "*Evangelium*," from signifying the content of glad tidings, came to mean the form itself.) The work was the outcome of the wishes of Pauline, literate, circles that had never heard any one of Jesus's companions discourse about him. It is *an apocalyptic life-picture from a distance;* lived experience is replaced by narrative, and narrative so plain and straightforward that the apocalyptic tendency passes quite unperceived.[2] And yet Apocalyptic is its condition precedent. It is not the words of Jesus, but the doctrine of Jesus in the Pauline form, that constitutes the substance of Mark. The first Christian book emanates from the Pauline creation. But very soon the latter itself becomes unthinkable without the book and its successors.

For presently there arose something which Paul, the born schoolman, had never intended, but which nevertheless had been made inevitable by the tendency of his work — the *cult-church of Christian nationality.* While the Syncretic creed-community, in proportion as it attained to consciousness of itself, drew the innumerable old city-cults and the new Magian together and by means of a supreme cult endowed the structure with henotheistic form, the Jesus-cult of the oldest Western communities was so long dissected and enriched that it also came to consist of just such another mass of cults.[3] Around the

---

[1] The researchers who argue with such over-learnedness about a proto-Mark, Source Q, the "Twelve"-source, and so on, overlook the essential novelty of Mark, which is *the first* "*Book*" *of Christendom*, plan-uniform and entire. Work of this sort is never the natural product of an evolution, but the merit of an individual man, and it marks, here if anywhere, a historical turning-point.

[2] Mark is generally *the* Gospel; after him the partisan writings (Matthew, Luke) begin; the tone of narrative passes into that of legend and ends, beyond the Hebrew and John gospels, in Jesus-romances like the gospels of Peter and James.

[3] If the word "catholic" be used in its oldest sense (*Ignatius ad Smyrn.*, 8) — namely, to signify

birth of Jesus, of which the Disciples knew nothing, grew up a story of his childhood. In the Mark Gospel it has not yet come into existence. Already in the old Persian apocalyptic, indeed, the Saoshyant as Saviour of the Last Day was said to be born of a virgin. But the new western myth was of quite other significance and had incalculable consequences. For within the Pseudo-morphosis-region there arose presently beside Jesus a figure to which he was Son, which transcended his figure — that of the Mother of God. She, like her Son, was a simple human destiny of such arresting and attractive force that she towered above all the hundred and one Virgins and Mothers of Syncretism — Isis, Tanit, Cybele, Demeter — and all the mysteries of birth and pain, and finally drew them into herself. For Irenæus she is the Eve of a new mankind. Origen champions her continued virginity. By giving birth to Redeemer-God it is *she* really who has redeemed the world. Mary the "Theotokos" (she who bare God) was the great stumbling-block for the Christians outside the Classical frontier, and it was the doctrinal developments of this idea that led Monophysites and Nestorians to break away and re-establish the pure Jesus-religion.[1] But the Faustian Culture, again, when it awoke and needed a symbol whereby to express its primary feeling for Infinity in time and to manifest its sense of the succession of generations, *set up the "Mater Dolorosa" and not the suffering Redeemer* as the pivot of the German-Catholic Christianity of the Gothic age; and for whole centuries of bright fruitful inwardness this woman-figure was the very synthesis of Faustian world-feeling and the object of all art, poetry, and piety. Even to-day in the ritual and the prayers of the Roman Catholic Church, and above all in the thoughts of its people, Jesus takes second place after the Madonna.[2]

Along with the Mary-cult there arose the innumerable cults of the saints, which certainly exceeded in number those of the antique place-gods; when the Pagan Church finally expired, the Christian had been able to absorb the whole store of local cults in the form of the veneration of saints.

Paul and Mark were decisive in yet another matter of inestimably wide import. It was a result of Paul's mission that, contrary to all the initial probabilities, Greek became the language of the Church and — following the lead of the first Gospel — of a sacred *Greek* literature. Let the reader consider what this meant, in one way and another. The Jesus Church was artificially separated from its spiritual origins and attached to an alien and scholarly element. Touch with the folk-spirit of the Aramæan motherland was lost. Thenceforward both the cult-Churches possessed the same language, the same conceptual

the *sum* of the cult-communities, *both* the Churches were Catholic. In the East the word had no meaning. The Nestorian Church was no more a sum than was the Persian: it was a Magian unit.

[1] A brief survey of the Mary doctrine is given in article "Mary,"*Ency. Brit.*, XI ed. The symbolism involved in the details of the story of Mary, as told in writing and in art, is very fully gone into in Yrjo Hirn, *The Sacred Shrine.* — *Tr.*

[2] Ed. Meyer, *Ursprung und Anfänge des Christentums* (1921), pp. 77, et seq.

traditions, the same book-literature from the same schools. The far less sophisticated Aramaic literatures of the East — the truly Magian, written and thought in the language of Jesus and his companions — were cut off from cooperating in the life of the Church. They could not be read, they dropped out of sight, and finally they were forgotten altogether. After all, notwithstanding that the Persian Scriptures were set down in Avestan and the Jewish in Hebrew, the language of their authors and exegetes; the language of the whole Apocalyptic from which the teachings of Jesus, and secondarily the teachings about Jesus, sprang; the language, lastly, of the scholars of all the Mesopotamian universities — was Aramaic. All this vanished from the field of view, to be replaced by Plato and Aristotle, both of whom were taken up, worked upon in common, and misunderstood in common by the Schoolmen of the two cult-Churches.

A final step in this direction was attempted by a man who was the equal of Paul in organizing talent and greatly his superior in intellectual creativeness, but who was inferior to him in the feeling for possibilities and actualities, and consequently failed to achieve his grandly conceived schemes — Marcion.[1] He saw in Paul's creation and its consequences only the basis on which to found the true religion of salvation. He was sensible of the absurdity of two religions that were unreservedly at war with one another possessing the same Holy Writ — namely, the *Jewish* canon. To us to-day it seems almost inconceivable that this should have been, but in fact it was so, for a century — but we have to remember what a sacred text meant in every kind of Magian religiousness. In these texts Marcion saw the real "conspiracy against the truth" and the most urgent danger for the doctrines intended by Jesus and, in his view, not yet actualized. Paul the prophet had declared the Old Testament as fulfilled and concluded — Marcion the founder pronounced it defeated and cancelled. He strove to cut out everything Jewish, down to the last detail. From end to end he was fighting nothing but Judaism. Like every true founder, like every religiously creative period, like Zarathustra, the prophets of Israel, like the Homeric Greeks, and like the Germans converted to Christianity, he transformed the old gods into defeated powers.[2] Jehovah as the Creator-God, the Demiurge, is the "Just" *and therefore the Evil:* Jesus as the incarnation of the Saviour-God in this evil creation is the "alien" — that is, the good Principle.[3] The foundation of Magian, and in particular Persian, feeling is perfectly unmistakable here. Marcion came from Sinope, the old capital of that Mithra-

[1] C. 85–155. See the recent work of Harnack, *Marcion: Das Evangelium vom fremden Gott* (1921). [Harnack's article "Marcion" in *Ency. Brit.*, XI ed., is dated 1910. — Tr.]

[2] Harnack, op. cit., pp. 136, et seq.; N. Bonwetsch, *Grundr. d. Dogmengesch.* (1919), p. 45, et seq.

[3] This is one of the profoundest ideas in all religious history, and one that must for ever remain inaccessible to the pious average man. Marcion's identification of the "Just" with the Evil enables him in this sense to oppose the Law of the Old Testament to the Evangel of the New.

datic Empire whose religion is indicated in the very name of its kings. Here
of old, too, the Mithras cult had originated.

But to the new doctrine properly belonged new Scriptures. The "Law and
Prophets" which had hitherto been canonical for the whole of Christendom
was the *Bible of the Jewish God*, and in fact it had just been given final shape as
such by the Synedrion at Jabna. Thus, it was a Devil's book that the Christian
had in his hands, and Marcion, therefore, now set up against it the Bible of the
Redeemer-God — likewise an assemblage and ordering of writings that had
hitherto been current in the community [1] as simple edification-books without
canonical claims. In place of the Torah he puts the — *one and true* — Gospel,
which he builds up uniformly out of various separate, and, in his view, corrupted and falsified, Gospels. In place of the Israelite prophets he sets up the
Epistles of the *one prophet of Jesus*, who was Paul.

Thus Marcion became the real creator of the New Testament. But for that
reason it is impossible to ignore the mysterious personage, closely related to
him, who not long before had written the Gospel "according to John." The
intention of this writer was neither to amplify nor to supersede the Gospels
proper; what he did — and, unlike Mark, consciously did — was to create
something quite new, *the first sacred book* of Christianity, the Koran of the new
religion.[2] The book proves that this religion was already conceived of as something complete and enduring. The idea of the immediately impending end of
the world, with which Jesus was filled through and through and which even
Paul and Mark in a measure shared, lies far behind "John" and Marcion.
Apocalyptic is at an end, and Mysticism is beginning. Their content is not
the teaching of Jesus, nor even the Pauline teaching about Jesus, but the enigma
of the universe, the World-Cavern. There is here no question of a Gospel;
not the figure of the Redeemer, but the principle of the Logos, is the meaning
and the means of happening. The childhood story is rejected again; a god is
not "born," he is "there," and wanders in human form over the earth. And
this god is a Trinity — God, the Spirit of God, the Word of God. This sacred
book of earliest Christianity contains, for the first time, the Magian problem
of "Substance," which dominated the following centuries to the exclusion of
everything else and finally led to the religion's splitting up into three churches.
And — what is significant in more respects than one — the solution of that
problem to which "John" stands closest is that which the Nestorian East
stood for as the true one. It is, in virtue of the Logos idea (Greek though

---

[1] About A.D. 150. See Harnack, op. cit., pp. 32, et seq.

[2] For the notions of Koran and Logos, see below. Again as in the case of Mark, the really
important question is, not what the material before him was, but how this entirely novel idea
for such a book, which anticipated and indeed made possible Marcion's plan for a Christian Bible,
could arise. The book presupposes a great spiritual movement (in eastern Asia Minor?) that knew
scarcely anything of Jewish Christianity and was yet remote from the Pauline, westerly thought-
world. But of the region and type of this movement we know nothing whatever.

the word happens to be) the "easternmost" of the Gospels, and presents Jesus, emphatically not as the bringer of the final and total revelation, but as the second envoy, who is to be *followed by a third* (the Comforter, Paraclete, of John xiv, 16, 26; xv, 26). This is the astounding doctrine that Jesus himself proclaims, and the decisive note of this enigmatic book. Here is unveiled, quite suddenly, the faith of the Magian East. If the Logos does not go, the Paraclete [1] cannot come (John xvi, 7), but between them lies the last Æon, the rule of Ahriman (xiv, 30). The Church of the Pseudomorphosis, ruled by Pauline intellect, fought long against the John Gospel and gave it recognition only when the offensive, darkly hinted doctrine had been covered over by a Pauline interpretation. The real state of affairs is disclosed in the Montanist movement (Asia Minor, 160) which harked back to oral tradition and proclaimed in Montanus the manifested Paraclete and the end of the world. Its popularity was immense. Tertullian went over to it at Carthage in 207. About 245 Mani,[2] who was intimately in touch with the currents of Eastern Christianity,[3] cast out the Pauline, human Jesus as a demon and confessed the Johannine Logos as the true Jesus, but announced himself as the Paraclete of the fourth Gospel. In Carthage, Augustine became a Manichæan, and it is a highly suggestive fact that both movements finally fused with Marcionism.

To return to Marcion himself, it was he who carried through the idea of "John" and created a Christian Bible. And then, verging on old age, when the communities of the extreme west recoiled from him in horror,[4] he set out to build the masterly structure of his own Redeemer-Church.[5] From 156 to 190 this was a power, and it was only in the following century that the older Church succeeded in degrading the Marcionites to the rank of heretics. Even so, in the broad East and as far out as Turkestan, it was still important at a much later date, and it ended, in a way deeply significant of its essential feeling, by fusing with the Manichæans.[6]

Nevertheless, though in the fullness of his conscious superiority he had underestimated the *vis inertiæ* of existing conditions, his grand effort was not in vain. He was, like Paul before him and Athanasius after him, the deliverer of Christianity at a moment when it threatened to break up, and the grandeur of his idea is in no wise diminished by the fact that union came about in opposition to, instead of through, him. The early Catholic Church — that is, the *Church of the Pseudomorphosis* — arose in its greatness only about 190, and then

---

[1] Vohu Mano, the Spirit of Truth, in the shape of the Saoshyant.

[2] See the article by Harnack and Conybeare "Manichæism," *Ency. Brit.*, XI ed. — *Tr.*

[3] Bardesanes, too, and the system of the "Acts of Thomas" are very near to him and to "John." [See the articles "Bardaisan," "Thomas," and "Gnosticism," *Ency. Brit.*, XI ed. — *Tr.*]

[4] Harnack, p. 24. The break with the established Church occurred at Rome, in 144.

[5] Harnack, pp. 181, et seq.

[6] It had, like each of the other Magian religions, a script of its own, and this script steadily came to resemble the Manichæan more and more closely.

it was in self-defence against the Church of Marcion and with the aid of an organization taken from that Church. Further, it replaced Marcion's Bible by another of similar structure — Gospels and apostolic Epistles — which it then proceeded to combine with the Law and the Prophets in one unit. And finally, this act of linking the two Testaments having in itself settled the Church's attitude towards Judaism, it proceeded to combat Marcion's third creation, his Redeemer-doctrine, by making a start with a theology of its own on the basis of *his* enunciation of the problem.

This development, however, took place on Classical soil, and, therefore, even the Church that arose in opposition to Marcion and his anti-Judaism was looked upon by Talmudic Jewry (whose centre of gravity lay entirely in Mesopotamia and its universities) as a mere piece of Hellenistic paganism. The destruction of Jerusalem was a conclusive event that in the world of fact no spiritual power could nullify. Such is the intimacy of inward relationship between waking-consciousness, religion, and speech that the complete severance after 70 of the Greek Pseudomorphosis and the Aramaic (that is, the truly Arabian) region was bound to result in the formation of two distinct domains of Magian religious development. On the Western margin of the young Culture the Pagan cult-Church, the Jesus-Church (removed thither by Paul), and the Greek-speaking Judaism of the Philo stamp were in point of language and literature so interlocked that the last-named fell into Christianity even in the first century, and Christianity and Hellenism combined to form a *common* early philosophy. In the Aramaic-speaking world from the Orontes to the Tigris, on the other hand, Judaism and Persism interacted constantly and intimately, each creating in this period its own strict theology and scholastic in the Talmud and the Avesta; and from the fourth century both these theologies exercised *the most potent influence upon the Aramaic-speaking Christendom that resisted the Pseudomorphosis,* so that finally it broke away in the form of the Nestorian Church.

Here in the East the difference, inherent in every human waking-consciousness, between sense-understanding and word-understanding — and, therefore between eye and letter — led up to purely Arabian methods of mysticism and scholasticism. The apocalyptic certainty, "Gnosis" in the first-century sense, that Jesus intended to confer,[1] the divining contemplation and emotion, is that of the Israelite prophets, the Gathas, Sufism, and we have it recognizable still in Spinoza, in the Polish Messiah Baal Shem [2] and in Mirza Ali Mohammed, the enthusiast-founder of Bahaism, who was executed in Teheran in 1850. The other way, "Paradosis," is the characteristically Talmudic method of word-exegesis, of which Paul was a master;[3] it pervades all later Avestan works, the Nestorian dialectic,[4] the entire theology of Islam alike.

[1] Matthew xi, 25, et seq., on which see Eduard Meyer, *Urspr. u. Anf. d. Christ.*, pp. 286, et seq.; here it is the old and Eastern (i.e., the genuine) form of gnosis that is described.
[2] See further, below, p. 321.
[3] As a drastic instance, Galatians iv, 24–26.
[4] Loofs, *Nestoriana* (1905), pp. 176, et seq.

On the other side, the Pseudomorphosis is single and whole both in its Magian believing acceptance (Pistis) and its metaphysical introversion (Gnosis).[1] The Magian belief in its Westerly shape was formulated for the Christians by Irenæus and, above all, by Tertullian, whose famous aphorism "*Credo quia absurdum*" is the very summation of this certainty in belief. The Pagan counterpart is Plotinus in his Enneads and even more so Porphyry in his treatise *On the Return of the Soul to God*.[2] But for the great schoolmen of the Pagan Church too, there were Father (Nus), Son, and the middle Being, just as already for Philo the Logos had been first-born Son and second God. Doctrines concerning ecstasy, angels and demons, and the dual substance of soul were freely current amongst them, and we see in Plotinus and Origen, both pupils of the same master, that the scholasticism of the Pseudomorphosis consisted in the development of Magian concepts and thoughts, by systematic transvaluation of the texts of Plato and Aristotle.

The characteristic *central idea of the whole thought of the Pseudomorphosis is the Logos*,[3] in use and development its faithful image. There is no possibility here of any "Greek," in the sense of Classical, influence; there was not a man alive in those days whose spiritual disposition could have accommodated the smallest trace of the Logos of Heraclitus and the Stoa. But, equally, the theologies that lived side by side in Alexandria were never able to develop in full purity the Logos-notion as they meant it, whereas both in Persian and Chaldean imaginings — as Spirit or Word of God — and in Jewish doctrine — as Ruach and Memra — it played a decisive part. What the Logos-teaching in the West did was to develop a Classical formula, by way of Philo and the John Gospel (the enduring effect of which on the West was its mark upon the schoolmen) not only into an element of Christian mysticism, but, eventually, into a dogma.[4] This was inevitable. This dogma which *both* the Western Churches held, corresponded, on the side of knowledge, to that which, on the side of faith, was represented *both by* the syncretic cults and the cults of Mary and the Saints. And against the whole thing, dogma and cult, the feeling of the East revolted from the 4th century on.

For the eye the history of these thoughts and feelings is repeated in the history of Magian architecture.[5] *The basic form of the Pseudomorphosis is the Basilica*, which was known to the Jews of the West and to the Hellenistic sects of the Chaldeans even before the time of Christ. As the Logos of the John Gospel is a Magian fundamental in Classical shape, so the Basilica is a Magian

[1] The best exposition of the mass of thought common to both Churches is Windelband's *Geschichte der Philosophie* (1900), pp. 177, et seq.; for the dogmatic history of the Christian Chruch see Harnack, *Dogmengeschichte* (1914), while — unconsciously — Geffcken (*Der Ausgang des griechisch-römischen Heidentums*, 1920) gives the corresponding "dogmatic history of the Pagan Church."

[2] Geffcken, op. cit., p. 69 [article "Neoplatonism" in *Ency. Brit.*, XI ed. — *Tr.*].

[3] See the following chapter.

[4] Harnack, *Dogmengeschichte*, p. 165.

[5] See Vol. I, p. 209.

room whose inner walls correspond to the outer surfaces of the old Classical temple, the cult-building introverted. The architectural form of the pure East is the *cupola building, the Mosque,* which without doubt existed long before the oldest Christian Churches in the temples of the Persians and Chaldeans, the synagogues of Mesopotamia, and probably the temples of Saba as well. The attempts to reconcile East and West in the Church Councils of the Byzantine period were finally symbolized in the mixed form of the domed basilica. For this item of the history of ecclesiastical architecture is really another expression of the great change that set in with Athanasius and Constantine, the last great champions of Christianity. The one created the firm western dogma and also Monasticism, into whose hands dogma gradually passed from those of the ageing schools. The other founded the State of Christian nationality, to which likewise the name of "Greek" passed in the end. And of this transition the domed basilica is the symbol.

CHAPTER VIII
PROBLEMS OF THE ARABIAN CULTURE

(B)
THE MAGIAN SOUL

PROBLEMS OF THE ARABIAN CULTURE

(B)

THE MAGIAN SOUL

I

THE world, as spread out for the Magian waking-consciousness, possesses a kind of extension that may be called cavern-like,[1] though it is difficult for Western man to pick upon any word in his vocabulary that can convey anything more than a hint of the meaning of Magian "space." For "space" has essentially unlike meanings for the perceptions of the two Cultures. The world-as-cavern is just as different from the world-as-extent of the passionate, far-thrusting Faustian as it is from the Classical world-as-sum-of-bodily-things. The Copernican system, in which the earth, as it were, loses itself, must necessarily seem crazy and frivolous to Arabian thought. The Church of the West was perfectly right when it resisted an idea so incompatible with the world-feeling of Jesus, and the Chaldean *cavern-astronomy*, which was wholly natural and convincing for Persians, Jews, peoples of the Pseudomorphosis, and Islam, became accessible to the few genuine Greeks who knew of it at all only after a process of transvaluing its basic notions of space.

The tension between Macrocosm and Microcosm (which is identical with the waking-consciousness) leads, in the world-picture of every Culture, to further oppositions of symbolic importance. All a man's sensations or understanding, faith or knowledge, receive their shape from a primary opposition which makes them not only activities of the individual, but also expressions of the totality. In the Classical the opposition that universally dominates the waking-consciousness is the opposition of matter and form; in the West it is that of force and mass. In the former the tension loses itself in the small and particular, and in the latter it discharges itself in the character of work. In the World-Cavern, on the other hand, it persists in traversing and swaying to and fro in unsure strugglings, and so becomes that "Semitic" primary-dualism which, ever the same under its thousand forms, fills the Magian world. The light shines through the cavern and battles against the darkness (John i, 5). Both are Magian substances. Up and down, heaven and earth become powers that have entity and contend with one another. But these polarities in the most primary sensations mingle with those of the refined and critical under-

---

[1] The expression is Leo Frobenius's (Paideuma, 1920, p. 92). [See Vol. I, p. 184. — *Tr.*]

standing, like good and evil, God and Satan. Death, for the author of the John Gospel as for the strict Moslem, is not the end of life, but a Something, a death-force, that contends with a life-force for the possession of man.

But still more important than all this is the opposition of Spirit and Soul (Hebrew *Ruach* and *nephesh*, Persian *ahu* and *urvan*, Mandæan *monuhmed* and *gyan*, Greek *pneuma* and *psyche*) which first comes out in the basic feeling of the prophetic religions, then pervades the whole of Apocalyptic, and finally forms and guides the world-contemplations of the awakened Culture — Philo, Paul and Plotinus, Gnostics and Mandæans, Augustine and the Avesta, Islam and the Kabbalah. *Ruach* means originally "wind" and *nephesh* "breath." [1] The *nephesh* is always in one way or another related to the bodily and earthly, to the below, the evil, the darkness. Its effort is the "upward." The *ruach* belongs to the divine, to the above, to the light. Its effects in man when it descends are the heroism of a Samson, the holy wrath of an Elijah, the enlightenment of the judge (the Solomon passing judgment,[2]) and all kinds of divination and ecstasy. It is poured out.[3] From Isaiah xi, 2, the Messiah becomes the incarnation of the *ruach*. Philo and the Islamic theology divide mankind into born Psychics and born Pneumatics (the "elect," a concept thoroughly proper to the world-cavern and Kismet). All the sons of Jacob are pneumatics. For Paul (1 Cor. xv) the meaning of the Resurrection lies in the opposition of a psychic and a pneumatic body, which alike for him and Philo and the author of the Baruch apocalypse coincides with the opposition of heaven and earth, light and darkness.[4] For Paul, the Saviour is the heavenly Pneuma.[5] In the John Gospel he fuses as Logos with the Light; in Neoplatonism he appears as *Nus* or, in the Classical terminology, the All-One opposed to *Physis*.[6] Paul and Philo, with their "Classical" (that is, western) conceptual criteria, equated soul and body with good and bad respectively, Augustine, as a Manichæan [7] with Persian-Eastern bases of distinction, lumps soul and body together as the naturally bad, in contrast to God as the sole Good, and finds in this opposition the source of his doctrine of Grace, which developed also, in the same form (though quite independently of him) in Islam.

But souls are at bottom discrete entities, whereas the Pneuma is one and

---

[1] The soul-stones on Jewish, Sabæan, and Islamic tombs are also called *nephesh*. They are unmistakable symbols of the "upward." With them belong the huge storeyed stelæ of Axum which belong to the first to third centuries of our era — i.e., the great period of the early Magian religions. The giant stele, long overthrown, is the largest monolith known to art-history, larger than any Egyptian obelisk (German Axum Expedition report, Vol. II, pp. 28, et seq.).

[2] On this rests the whole theory and practice of Magian law (see p. 72 above).

[3] Isaiah xxxii, 15; 4 Ezra xiv, 39; Acts ii.

[4] Reitzenstein *Das iran. Erlösungsmysterium*, pp. 108, et seq.

[5] Bousset, *Kyrios Christos*, p. 142.

[6] Windelband, *Gesch. d. Phil.* (1900), pp. 189, et seq.; Windelband-Bonhöffer, *Gesch. d. antiken Phil.* (1912), pp. 328, et seq.; Geffcken, *Der Ausgang des griech.-röm. Heidentums* (1920), pp. 51, et seq.

[7] Jodl, *Geschichte der Ethik*, I, p. 58.

ever the same. The man *possesses* a soul, but he only *participates* in the spirit
of the Light and the Good; the divine descends into him, thus binding all the
individuals of the Below together with the one in the Above. This primary
feeling, which dominates the beliefs and opinions of all Magian men, is something perfectly singular, and not only characterizes their world-view, but
marks off the essence and kernel of their religiousness in all its forms from that
of every other kind of man. This Culture, as has been shown, was characteristically the Culture of the middle. It could have borrowed forms and ideas
from most of the others, and the fact that it did not do so, that in the face of all
pressure and temptation it remained so profoundly mistress of its own inward
form, attests an unbridgeable gulf of difference. Of all the wealth of Babylonian
and Egyptian religion it admitted hardly more than a few names; the Classical
and the Indian Cultures, or rather the Civilizations heir to them — Hellenism
and Buddhism — distorted its expression to the point of pseudomorphosis, but
its essence they never touched. All religions of the Magian Culture, from the
creations of Isaiah and Zarathustra to Islam, constitute a complete inward
unit of world-feeling; and, just as in the Avestan beliefs there is not to be found
one trait of Brahmanism nor in early Christianity one breath of Classical feeling,
but merely names and figures and outward forms, so also not a trace of this
Jesus-religion could be absorbed by the Germanic-Catholic Christianity of the
West, even though the stock of tenets and observances was taken over in its
entirety.

Whereas the Faustian man is an "I" that in the last resort draws its own
conclusions about the Infinite; whereas the Apollinian man, as one *soma* among
many, represents only himself; the Magian man, with his spiritual kind of
being, is only a *part of a pneumatic "We"* that, descending from above, is one
and the same in all believers. As body and soul he belongs to himself alone,
but something else, something alien and higher, dwells in him, making him
with all his glimpses and convictions just a member of a consensus which, as
the emanation of God, excludes error, but excludes also all possibility of the
self-asserting Ego. Truth is for him something other than for us. All our
epistemological methods, resting upon the *individual* judgment, are for him
madness and infatuation, and its scientific results a work of the Evil One,
who has confused and deceived the spirit as to its true dispositions and purposes.
Herein lies the ultimate, for us unapproachable, secret of Magian thought in its
cavern-world — the impossibility of a thinking, believing, and knowing Ego
is the presupposition inherent in all the fundamentals of all these religions.
While Classical man stood before his gods as one body before another; whereas
the Faustian willing "I" in its wide world feels itself confronted by deity, also
Faustian, also willing, effective everywhere; the Magian deity is the indefinite,
enigmatic Power on high that pours out its Wrath or its Grace, descends itself
into the dark or raises the soul into the light as it sees fit. The idea of individual

wills is simply meaningless, for "will" and "thought" in man are not prime, but already effects of the deity upon him. Out of this unshakable root-feeling, which is merely re-expressed, never essentially altered, by any conversions, illumination or subtilizing in the world — there emerges of necessity the idea of the Divine Mediator, of one who transforms this state from a torment into a bliss. All Magian religions are by this idea bound together, and separated from those of all other Cultures.

The Logos-idea in its broadest sense, an abstraction of the Magian light-sensation of the Cavern, is the exact correlative of this sensation in Magian thought. It meant that from the unattainable Godhead its Spirit, its "Word," is released as carrier of the light and bringer of the good, and enters into relation with human being to uplift, pervade, and redeem it. This distinctness of three substances, which does not contradict their oneness in religious thought, was known already to the prophetic religions. Ahuramazda's light-gleaming soul is the Word (Yasht 13, 31), and in one of the earliest Gathas his Holy Spirit (*spenta mainyu*) converses with the Evil Spirit (*angra mainyu*, Yasna 45, 2). The same idea penetrates the whole of the old Jewish literature. The thought which the Chaldeans built up on the separation of God and His Word and the opposition of Marduk and Nabu, which breaks forth with power in the whole Aramæan Apocalyptic remained permanently active and creative; by Philo and John, Marcion and Mani, it entered into the Talmudic teachings and thence into the Kabbalistic books Yesirah and Sohar, into the Church Councils and the works of the Fathers, into the later Avesta, and finally into Islam, in which a Mohammed gradually became the Logos and, as the mystically respent, *living* Mohammed of the popular religion, fused into the figure of Christ.[1] This conception is for Magian man so self-evident that it was able to break through even the strictly monotheistic structure of the original Islam and to appear with Allah as the Word of God (*kalimah*), the Holy Spirit (*ruh*), and the "light of Mohammed."

For, for the popular religion, the first light that comes forth from the world-creation is that of Mohammed, in the shape of a peacock [2] "formed of white pearls" and walled about by veilings. But the peacock is the Envoy of God and the prime soul [3] as early as the Mandæans, and it is the emblem of immortality on Early Christian sarcophagi. The light-diffusing pearl that illumines the dark house of the body is the Spirit entered into man, and thought of as substance, for the Mandæans as in the Acts of Thomas.[3] The Jezidi [4]

---

[1] M. Horten, *Die religiöse Gedankenwelt der Volkes im heutigen Islam* (1917), pp. 381, et seq. By the Shiites the Logos-idea was transferred to Ali.

[2] Wolff, *Muhammedanische Eschatologie*, 3, 2, et seq.

[3] Mandæan Book of John, Ch. LXXV.

[3] Usener, *Vortr. u. Aufs.*, p. 217.

[4] The "devil-worshippers" in Armenia; M. Horten in *Der neue Orient* (March 1918). The name arose from the fact that they did not recognize Satan as a being, and accordingly derived the Evil,

reverence the Logos as peacock and light; next to the Druses they have preserved most purely the old Persian conception of the substantial Trinity.

Thus again and again we find the Logos-idea getting back to the light-
sensation from which the Magian understanding derived it. *The world of Magian
mankind is filled with a fairy-tale feeling.*[1] Devils and evil spirits threaten man;
angels and fairies protect him. There are amulets and talismans, mysterious
lands, cities, buildings, and beings, secret letters, Solomon's Seal, the Philosophers' Stone. And over all this is poured the quivering cavern-light that the
spectral darkness ever threatens to swallow up. If this profusion of figures
astonishes the reader, let him remember that Jesus lived in it, and Jesus's teachings are only to be understood from it. Apocalyptic is only a vision of fable
intensified to an extreme of tragic power. Already in the Book of Enoch we
have the crystal palace of God, the mountains of precious stone, and the im-
prisonment of the apostate stars. Fantastic, too, are the whole overpowering
idea-world of the Mandæans, that of the Gnostics and the Manichæans, the
system of Origen, and the figures of the Persian "Bundahish"; and when the
time of the great visions was over, these ideas passed into a legend-poesy and
into the innumerable religious romances of which we have Christian specimens
in the gospels concerning Jesus's childhood, the Acts of Thomas and the anti-
Pauline Pseudo-Clementines. One such story is that of Abraham's having
minted the thirty pieces of silver of Judas. Another is the tale of the "treasure-
cave" in which, deep under the hill of Golgotha, are stored the golden treasure
of paradise and the bones of Adam.[2] Dante's poetic material was after all poetic,
but this was sheer actuality, the only world in which these people lived continuously. Such sensations are unapproachably remote from men who live in
and with a dynamical world-picture. If we would obtain some inkling of how
alien to us all the inner life of Jesus is — a painful realization for the Christian
of the West, who would be glad indeed if he could make that inner life the
point of contact for his own inward piety — if we would discover why nowadays only a pious Moslem has the capacity livingly to experience it, we should
sink ourselves in this wonder-element of a world-image that was Jesus's world-
image. And then, and only then, shall we perceive how little Faustian Christianity has taken over from the wealth of the Church of the Pseudomorphosis
— of its world-feeling nothing, of its inward form little, and of its concepts
and figures much.

---

by a very complicated set of ideas, from the Logos itself. Under old Persian influences the Jews
also busied themselves with the same problem — observe the difference between 2 Samuel xxiv, 1,
and 1 Chron. xxi, 1.

[1] M. Horten, op. cit., p. xxi. This book is the best introduction to the actually existing popular religion of Islam, which deviates considerably from the official doctrines.

[2] Baumstark, *Die christl. Literaturen des Orients*, I, p. 64.

II

The When, for the Magian Soul, issues from the Where. Here too, is no Apollinian clinging to pointlike Present, nor Faustian thrust and drive towards an infinitely distant goal. Here Being has a different pulse, and consequently Waking-being has another sense of time, which is the counter-concept to Magian space. The prime thing that the humanity of this Culture, from poor slaves and porters to the prophets and the caliphs themselves, feels as the Kismet above him is not a limitless flight of the ages that never lets a lost moment recur, but a Beginning and an End of "This Day," which is irrevocably ordained and in which the human existence takes the place assigned to it from creation itself. Not only world-space, but world-time also is cavern-like. Hence comes the thoroughly Magian certainty that *everything has "a" time*, from the origins of the Saviour, whose hour stood written in ancient texts, to the smallest detail of the everyday, in which Faustian hurry would be meaningless and unimaginable. Here, too, is the basis of the Early Magian (and in particular the Chaldean) astrology, which likewise presupposes that all things are written down in the stars and that the scientifically calculable course of the planets authorized conclusions as to the course of earthly things.[1] The Classical oracle answered the only question that could perturb Apollinian man — the form, the "How?" of coming things. But the question of the Cavern is "When?" The whole of Apocalyptic, the spiritual life of Jesus, the agony of Gethsemane, and the grand movement that arose out of his death are unintelligible if we have not grasped this primary question of Magian being and the presuppositions lying behind it. It is an infallible sign of the extinction of the Classical Soul that astrology in its westward advance drove the oracle step by step before it. Nowhere is the stage of transition more clearly visible than in Tacitus, whose entire history is dominated by the confusion and dislocation of his world-picture. First of all, as a true Roman, he brings in the power of the old city-deities; then, as an intelligent cosmopolitan, he regards this very belief in their intervention as a superstition; and finally, as a Stoic (by that time the spiritual outlook of the Stoa had become *Magian*), he speaks of the power of the seven planets that rule the fortunes of men. And thus it comes about that in the following centuries Time itself as vessel of fate — namely, the Vault of Time, limited each way and therefore capable of being grasped as an entity by the inner eye — is by Persian mysticism set above the light of God as Zrvan, and rules the world-conflict of Good and Evil. Zrvanism was the State religion of Persia in 438–457.

---

[1] Cf. p. 205. The Babylonian view of the heavens had not definitely distinguished between astronomical and atmospheric elements; e.g., the covering of the moon by clouds was regarded as a kind of eclipse. For this soothsaying the momentary *figure* of the heavens served only the same purpose as the inspection of the victim's liver. But the Chaldeans' intention was to forecast the *actual* course of the stars; here, therefore, astrology presupposed a genuine astronomy.

Fundamentally, too, it is this belief that all stands written in the stars, that makes the Arabian Culture characteristically that of "eras" — that is, of time-reckonings that begin at some event felt as a peculiarly significant act of Providence. The first and most important is the generic Aramæan era, which begins about 300 B.C. with the growth of apocalyptic tension and is the "Seleucid era." It was followed by many others, amongst them the Sabæan (about 115 B.C.), the starting-point of which is not exactly known to us; that of Diocletian; the Jewish era, beginning with the Creation, which was introduced by the Synedrion in 346; [1] the Persian, from the accession of the last Sassanid Jezdegerd in 632; and the Hijra, by which at last the Seleucid was displaced in Syria and Mesopotamia. Outside this land-field there is mere imitation for practical ends, like Varro's "*ab urbe condita*"; that of the Marcionites, beginning with Marcion's breach with the Church in 144; and that of the Christians, introduced shortly after 500 and beginning with the birth of Jesus.

World-history is the picture of the living world into which man sees himself woven by birth, ancestry, and progeny, and which he strives to comprehend from out of his world-feeling. The historical picture of Classical man concentrates itself upon the pure Present. Its content is no true Becoming, but a foreground Being with a conclusive background of timeless myth, rationalized as "the Golden Age." This Being, however, was a variegated swarming of ups and downs, good and ill fortune, a blind "thereabouts," an eternal alteration, yet ever in its changes the same, without direction, goal, or "Time." The cavern-feeling, on the contrary, requires a surveyable history consisting in a beginning and an end to the world *that is also the beginning and the end of man* — acts of God of mighty magic — and between these turns, spellbound to the limits of the Cavern and the ordained period, the battle of light and darkness, of the angels and Jazatas with Ahriman, Satan, and Eblis, in which Man, his Soul, and his Spirit are involved. The present Cavern God can destroy and replace by a new creation. The Persian-Chaldean apocalyptic offers to the gaze a whole series of such æons, and Jesus, along with his time, stood in expectation of the end of the existing one. [2] The consequence of this is a historic outlook like that which is natural to Islam even to-day — the view over a given time. "The world-view of the people falls naturally into three major parts — world-beginning, world-development, and world-catastrophe. For the Moslem who feels so deeply ethically, the chief essentials in world-development are the salvation-story and the ethical way of life, knit into one as the "life" of man.

---

[1] B. Cohn, "*Die Anfangsepoche der jüd. Kalenders*" (*Sitz. Pr. Akad.*, 1914). The date of the first day of Creation was on this occasion fixed by calculation from a total eclipse of the sun — of course with the aid of Chaldean astronomy. [See, in general, the articles "Chronology," "Calendar," in *Ency. Brit.*, XI ed. — *Tr.*]

[2] The Persian notion of total time is 12,000 years. The Parsees of to-day consider A.D. 1920 as the 11,550th.

This debouches into the world-catastrophe, which contains the sanction of the moral history of humanity." [1]

But, further, for the Magian human-existence, the issue of the feeling of *this* sort of Time and the view of *this* sort of space is a quite peculiar type of piety, which likewise we may put under the sign of the Cavern — a *will-less* resignation, to which the spiritual "I" is unknown, and which feels the spiritual "We" that has entered into the quickened body as simply a reflection of the divine Light. The Arab word for this is Islam (= submission) but this Islam was equally Jesus's normal mode of feeling and that of every other personality of religious genius that appeared in this Culture. Classical piety is something perfectly different,[2] while, as for that of our own Culture, if we could mentally abstract from the piety of St. Theresa and Luther and Pascal their Ego — that Ego which wills to maintain itself against, to submit to, or even to be extinguished by the Divine Infinite — there would be nothing left. The Faustian prime-sacrament of Contrition presupposes the strong and free will that can overcome itself. But it is precisely the *impossibility of an Ego as a free power* in the face of the divine that constitutes "Islam." Every attempt to meet the operations of God with a personal purpose or even a personal opinion is "*masiga*," — that is, not an evil willing, but an evidence that the powers of darkness and evil have taken possession of a man and expelled the divine from him. The Magian waking-consciousness is merely the *theatre* of a battle between these two powers and not, so to say, a power in itself. Moreover, in this kind of world-happening there is no place for individual causes and effects, let alone any universally effective dynamic concatenation thereof, and consequently there is no *necessary* connexion between sin and punishment, no *claim* to reward, no old-Israelitish "righteousness." Things of this order the true piety of this Culture regards as far beneath it. The laws of nature are not something settled for ever that God can alter only by the method of miracle — they are (so to put it) the ordinary state of an autocratic divine will, not possessing in themselves anything of the logical necessity that they have for Faustian souls. In the entire world-cavern there is but *one* Cause, which lies *immediately* behind all visible workings, and this is the Godhead, which, as itself, acts without causes. Even to speculate upon causes in connexion with God is sinful.

From this basic feeling proceeds the Magian idea of Grace. This underlies all sacraments of this Culture (especially the Magian proto-sacrament of Baptism) and forms a contrast of the deepest intensity with the Faustian idea of Contrition. Contrition presupposes the will of an Ego, but Grace knows of no such thing. It was Augustine's high achievement to develop this essentially Islamic thought with an inexorable logic, and with a penetration so thorough

---

[1] M. Horten, *Die religiöse Gedankenwelt des Volkes im heutigen Islam*, p. xxvi.

[2] It shows a great gap in our research that although we possess a whole library of works on Classical religion and particularly its gods and cults, we have not one about Classical religiousness and its history.

that since Pelagius the Faustian Soul has tried by any and every route to circumvent this certainty — which for *it* constitutes an imminent danger of self-destruction — and in using Augustinian propositions to express its own proper consciousness of God has ever misunderstood and transvalued them. Actually, Augustine was the last great thinker of Early Arabian Scholasticism, anything but a Western intellect.[1] Not only was he at times a Manichæan, but he remained so even as a Christian in some important characteristics, and his closest relations are to be found amongst the Persian theologians of the later Avesta, with their doctrines of the Store of Grace of the Holy and of absolute guilt. For him grace is the substantial inflowing of something divine into the human Pneuma, itself also substantial.[2] The Godhead radiates it; man receives it, but does not acquire it. From Augustine, as from Spinoza so many centuries later,[3] the notion of force is absent, and for both the problem of freedom refers not to the Ego and its Will, but to the part of the universal Pneuma that is infused into a man and its relation to the rest of him. Magian waking-being is the *theatre* of a conflict between the two world-substances of light and darkness. The Early Faustian thinkers such as Duns Scotus and William of Occam, on the contrary, see a contest inherent in dynamic waking-consciousness *itself*, a contest of the two forces of the Ego — namely, will and reason,[4] and so imperceptibly the question posed by Augustine changes into another, which he himself would have been incapable of understanding — are willing and thinking free forces, or are they not? Answer this question as we may, one thing at any rate is certain, that the individual ego has *to wage* this war and not to suffer it. The Faustian Grace refers to the success of the Will and not to the species of a substance. Says the

[1] "He is in truth the conclusion and completion of the Christian Classical, its last and greatest thinker, its intellectual practitioner and tribune. This is the starting-point from which he must be understood. What later ages have made of him is another affair. His own real mind, the synthesizer of Classical Culture, ecclesiastical and episcopal authority, and intimate mysticism, could not possibly have been handed on by those who, environed by different conditions, have to deal with different tasks" (E. Troeltsch, *Augustin, die christliche Antike und das Mittelalter*, 1915, p. 7). His power, like Tertullian's, rested also on the fact that his writings were not translated into Latin, but *thought* in this language, the *sacred* language of the Western Church; it was precisely this that excluded both from the field of Aramæan thought. Cf. p. 224 above.

[2] "*Inspiratio bonæ voluntatis*" (*De corr. et grat.*, 3). His "good will" and "ill will" are, quite dualistically, a pair of opposite substances. For Pelagius, on the contrary, will is an *activity* without moral quality as such; only that which is willed has the *property* of being good or evil, and the Grace of God consists in the "*possibilitas utriusque partis*," the freedom to will this or that. Gregory I transmuted Augustinian doctrines into Faustian when he taught that God rejected individuals because he foreknew their evil will.

[3] All the elements of the Magian metaphysic are to be found in Spinoza, hard as he tried to replace the Arabian-Jewish conceptual world of his Spanish masters (and above all Moses Maimonides) by the Western of early Baroque. The individual human mind is for him not an ego, but only a mode of the one divine attribute, the "*cogitatio*" — which is just the Pneuma. He protests against notions like "God's Will." His God is *pure substance* and in lieu of the dynamic causality of the Faustian universe he discovers simply the logic of the divine *cogitatio*. All this is already in Porphyry, in the Talmud, in Islam; and to Faustian thinkers like Leibniz and Goethe it is as alien as anything can possibly be. (*Allgem. Gesch. d. Philos.* in *Kultur der Gegenwart*, I, v, p. 484, Windelband.)

[4] Here, therefore, "good" is an evaluation and not a substance.

Westminster Confession of the Presbyterians (1646): "The rest of Mankind, God was pleased, according to the unsearchable Counsel of his own Will, whereby he extendeth, or withholdeth Mercy, as he pleaseth, for the Glory of his Sovereign Power over his Creatures, to pass by; and to ordain them to Dishonour and Wrath, for their Sin, to the Praise of his glorious Justice." The other conception, that the idea of Grace excludes every individual will and every cause but the One, that it is sinful even to question why man suffers, finds an expression in one of the most powerful poems known to world-history, a poem that came into being in the midst of the Arabian pre-Culture and is in inward grandeur unparalleled by any product of that Culture itself — the Book of Job.[1] It is not Job, but his friends who look for a sin as the cause of his troubles. They — like the bulk of mankind in this and every other Culture, present-day readers and critics of the work, therefore, included — lack the metaphysical depth to get near the ultimate meaning of suffering within the world-cavern. Only the Hero himself fights through the fulfilment, to pure Islam, and he becomes thereby the only possible figure of tragedy that Magian feeling can set up by the side of our Faust.[2]

III

The waking-consciousness of every Culture allows of two ways of inwardness, that in which contemplative feeling spreads into understanding, and that in which the reverse takes place. The Magian contemplation is called by Spinoza "intellectual love of God," and by his Sufist contemporaries in Asia "extinction in God" (*mahw*); it may be intensified to the Magian ecstasy that was vouchsafed to Plotinus several times, and to his pupil Porphyry once in old age. The other side, the rabbinical dialectic, appears in Spinoza as geometrical method and in the Arabian-Jewish "Late" philosophy in general as Kalaam. Both, however, rest upon the fact that there in Magian there is no individual-ego, but a single Pneuma present simultaneously in each and all of the elect, which is likewise Truth. It cannot be too strongly emphasized that the resultant root-idea of the *ijma* is much more than a concept or notion, that it can be a lived experience of even overwhelming force, and that all community of the Magian kind rests upon it and, as doing so, is removed from community in any other Culture. "The mystic Community of Islam extends from the here into the beyond; it reaches beyond the grave, in that it comprises the dead Moslems of earlier generations, nay, even the righteous of the times before Islam. The Moslem feels himself bound up in one unity with them all. They help him, and he, too, can in turn increase their beatitude by the application of his own

---

[1] The period at which it was written corresponds to our Carolingian. Whether the latter really brought forth any poetry of like rank we do not know, but that it may possibly have done so is shown by creations like the Voluspa, Muspilli, the Heliand, and the universe conceived by John Scotus Erigena.

[2] See, for example, Bertholet *Kulturgesch. Israels*, p. 242.

merit." [1] The same, precisely, was what the Christians and the Syncretists of the Pseudomorphosis meant when they used the words *Polis* and *Civitas* — these words, which had formerly implied a sum of bodies, now denoted a consensus of fellow believers. Augustine's famous *Civitas Dei* was neither a Classical Polis nor a Western Church, but a unity of believers, blessed, and angels, exactly as were the communes of Mithras, of Islam, of Manichæism, and of Persia. As the community was based upon consensus, it was in spiritual things infallible. "My people," said Mohammed, "can never agree in an error," and the same is premised in Augustine's State of God. With him there was not and could not be any question of an infallible Papal ego or of any other sort of authority to settle dogmatic truths; that would completely destroy the Magian concept of the Consensus. And the same applied in this Culture generally — not only to dogma, but also to law [2] and to the State. The Islamic community, like that of Porphyry and that of Augustine, embraces the *whole* of the world-cavern, the here and the beyond, the orthodox and the good angels and spirits, and within this community the State only formed a *smaller unit of the visible side*, a unit, therefore, of which the operations were governed by the major whole. In the Magian world, consequently, the separation of politics and religion is theoretically impossible and nonsensical, whereas in the Faustian Culture the battle of Church and State is inherent in the very conceptions — logical, necessary, unending. In the Magian, civil and ecclesiastical law are simply identical. Side by side with the Emperor of Constantinople stood the Patriarch, by the Shah was the Zarathustratema, by the Exilarch the Gaon, by the Caliph the Sheikh-ul-Islam, at once superiors and subjects. There is not in this the slightest affinity to the Gothic relation of Emperor and Pope; equally, all such ideas were alien to the Classical world. In the constitution of Diocletian this Magian embedding of the State in the community of the faithful was for the first time actualized, and by Constantine it was carried into full effect. It has been shown already that State, Church, and Nation formed a spiritual unit — namely, that part of the orthodox consensus which manifested itself in the living man. And hence for the Emperor, as ruler of the Faithful — that is, of that portion of the Magian community which God had entrusted to him — it was a self-evident duty to conduct the Councils so as to bring about the consensus of the elect.

IV

But besides the consensus there is another sort of revelation of Truth — namely, the "Word of God," in a perfectly definite and purely Magian sense of the phrase, which is equally remote from Classical and from Western thought, and has, in consequence, been the source of innumerable misunderstandings. The sacred book in which it has become visibly evident, in which it has been captured by the spell of a sacred script, is part of the stock of every Magian

[1] Horten, op. cit., p. xii.   [2] See p. 67 above.

religion.[1] In this conception three Magian notions are interwoven — each of which, even by itself, presents extreme difficulties for us, while their simultaneous separateness and oneness is simply inaccessible to our religious thought, often though that thought has managed to persuade itself to the contrary. These ideas are: God, the Spirit of God, the Word of God. That which is written in the prologue of the John Gospel — "In the beginning was the Word, and the Word was with God, and the Word was God" — had long before come to perfectly natural expression as something self-evident in the Persian ideas of Spenta Mainyu,[2] and Vohu Mano, [3] and in corresponding Jewish and Chaldean conceptions. And it was the kernel for which the conflicts of the fourth and fifth centuries concerning the substance of Christ were fought. But, for Magian thought, truth is itself a substance,[4] and lie (or error) second substance — again the same dualism that opposes light and darkness, life and death, good and evil. As substance, truth is identical now with God, now with the Spirit of God, now with the Word. Only in the light of this can we comprehend sayings like "I am the truth and the life" and "My word is the truth," sayings to be understood, as they were meant, with reference to substance. Only so, too, can we realize with what eyes the religious man of this Culture looked upon his sacred book: in it the invisible truth has entered into a visible kind of existence, or, in the words of John i, 14: "The Word became flesh and dwelt among us." According to the Yasna the Avesta was sent down from heaven, and according to the Talmud Moses received the Torah volume by volume from God. A Magian revelation is a mystical process in which the eternal and unformed word of God — or the Godhead as Word — enters into a man in order to assume through him the manifest, sensible form of sounds and especially of letters. "*Koran*" *means* "*reading.*" Mohammed in a vision saw in the heaven treasured rolls of scripture that he (although he had never learned how to read) was able to decipher "in the name of the Lord." [5] This is a form of revelation that in the Magian Culture is the rule and in other Cultures is not even the exception,[6] but

---

[1] It is almost unnecessary to say that in all religions of the Germanic West the Bible stands in a quite other relationship to the faith — namely, in that of a *source* in the strictly historical sense, irrespective of whether it is taken as inspired and immune from textual criticism or not. The relation of Chinese thought to the canonical books is similar.

[2] The Holy Spirit, different from Ahuramazda and yet one with him, opposed to the Evil (Angra Mainyu).

[3] Identified by Mani with the Johannine Logos. Compare also Yasht 13, 31. Ahuramazda's shining soul is the Word.

[4] *Aletheia* (Truth) is generally employed in this way in the John Gospel, and *drug* (= lie) is used for Ahriman in Persian cosmology. Ahriman is often shown as though a servant of the *drug*.

[5] Sura 96; cf. 80, 11 and 85, 21, where in connexion with another vision it is said: "This is a noble Koran on a treasured tablet." The best commentary on all this is Eduard Meyer's (*Geschichte der Mormonen*, pp. 70, et seq.).

[6] Classical man receives, in states of extreme bodily excitation, the power of unconsciously predicting future events. But these visions are completely unliterary. The Classical Sibylline books (which have no connexion with the later Christian works bearing that name) are meant to be nothing more than a collection of oracles.

it was only from the time of Cyrus that it began to take shape. The old Israel-itish prophets, and no doubt Zarathustra also, see and hear in ecstasy things that afterwards they spread abroad. The Deuteronomic code (621) was given out as having been "found in the Temple," which meant that it was to be taken as the wisdom of the Father. The first (and a very deliberate) example of a "Koran" is the book of Ezekiel, which the author received in a thought-out vision from God and "swallowed" (iii, 1–3). Here, expressed in the crudest imaginable form, is the basis on which later the idea and shape of all apocalyptic writing was founded. But by degrees this *substantial* form of reception came to be one of the requisites for any book to be canonical. It was in post-Exilic times that the idea arose of the Tables of the Law received by Moses on Sinai; later such an origin came to be assumed for the whole Torah, and about the Macca-bæan period for the bulk of the Old Testament. From the Council of Jabna (about 90 B.C.) the whole word was regarded as inspired and delivered in the most literal sense. But the same evolution took place in the Persian religion up to the sanctification of the Avesta in the third century, and the same idea of a literal delivery appears in the second vision of Hermas, in the Apocalypses, and in the Chaldean and Gnostic and Mandæan writings; lastly, it underlies, as a tacit natural basis, all the ideas that the Neo-Pythagoreans and the Neo-Pla-tonists formed of the writings of their old masters. "Canon" is the technical expression for the totality of writings that are accepted by a religion as de-livered. It was as canons in this sense that the Hermetic collection and the corpus of Chaldean oracles came into being from 200 — the latter a sacred book of the Neoplatonists which alone was admitted by Proclus, the "Father" of this Church, to stand with Plato's *Timæus*.

Originally, the young Jesus-religion, like Jesus himself, recognized the Jewish canon. The first Gospels set up no sort of claim to be the Word made visible. *The John Gospel is the first Christian writing of which the evident purpose is that of a Koran*, and its unknown author is the originator of the idea that there could be and must be a Christian Koran. The grave and difficult decision whether the new religion should break with that which Jesus had believed in clothed itself of deep necessity in the question whether the Jewish scriptures might still be regarded as incarnations of the one truth. The answer of the John Gospel was tacitly, and that of Marcion openly, no, but that of the Fathers was, quite illogically, yes.

It followed from this metaphysical conception of the essence of a sacred book that the expressions "God speaks" and "the Scripture says" were, in a manner wholly alien to our thought, completely identical. To us it is suggestive of the Arabian Nights that God himself should be spellbound in these words and letters and could be unsealed and compelled to reveal the truth by the adepts of this magic. Exegesis no less than inspiration and delivery is a process of mystical under-meaning (Mark i, 22). Hence the reverence — in diametrical opposition to the Classical feeling — with which these precious manuscripts were cared for, their ornamentation by every means known to the young Magian art, and the appearance again and again of new scripts which, in the eyes of their users, alone possessed the power of capturing the truth sent down.

But such a Koran is by its very nature unconditionally right, and therefore unalterable and incapable of improvement.[1] There arose, in consequence, the habit of secret interpretations meant to bring the text into harmony with the convictions of the time. A masterpiece of this kind is Justinian's Digests, but the same applies not only to every book of the Bible, but also (we need not doubt) to the Gathas of the Avesta and even to the then current manuscripts of Plato, Aristotle, and other authorities of the Pagan theology. More important still is the assumption, traceable in every Magian religion, of a secret revelation, or a secret meaning of the Scriptures, preserved not by being written down, but in the memory of adepts and propagated orally. According to Jewish notions, Moses received at Sinai not only the written, but *also a secret oral Torah*,[2] which it was forbidden to commit to writing. "God foresaw," says the Talmud, "that one day a time would come when the Heathen would possess themselves of the Torah and would say to Israel: 'We, too, are sons of God.' Then will the Lord say: 'Only he who knows my secrets is my son.' And what are the secrets of God? The oral teachings." [3] The Talmud, then, in the form in which it is generally accessible, contains only a part of the religious material, and it is the same with Christian texts of the early period. It has often been observed [4] that Mark speaks of the Visitation and of the Resurrection only in hints, and that John only touches upon the doctrine of the Paraclete and omits the institution of the Lord's Supper entirely. The initiates understood what was meant, and the unbeliever ought not to know it. Later there was a whole "secret discipline" which bound Christians to observe silence in the presence of unbelievers concerning the baptismal confession and other matters. With the Chaldeans, Neopythagoreans, Cynics, Gnostics, and especially the sects from Jewish to Islamic, this tendency went to such lengths that the greater part of their secret doctrines is unknown to us. Concerning the Word thus preserved only in the minds there was a *consensus of silence*, the more so as each believer was certain that the other "knew." We ourselves, as it is upon the most important things that we are most emphatic and forthright, run the risk of ministerpreting Magian doctrines through taking the part that was expressed for the whole that existed, and the profane literal meaning of words for their real significance. Gothic Christianity had no secrets and hence it doubly mistrusted the Talmud, which it rightly regarded as being only the foreground of Jewish doctrine.

---

[1] See p. 73.
[2] IV Ezra xiv; S. Funk, *Die Entstehung des Talmuds*, p. 17; Hirsch's commentary on Exodus xxi, 2.
[3] Funk, op. cit., p. 86.
[4] For example, Ed. Meyer, *Urspr. u. Anf. d. Christ.*, p. 95.

Pure Magian, too, is the Kabbalah, which out of numbers, letter-forms, points, and strokes, unfolds secret significances, and therefore cannot but be as old as the Word itself that was sent down as Substance. The secret dogma of the creation of the world out of the two-and-twenty letters of the Hebrew alphabet, and that of the throne-chariot of Ezekiel's Vision, are already traceable in Maccabæan times. Closely related to this is the allegorical exegesis of the sacred texts. All the tractates of the Mishnah, all the Fathers, all the Alexandrian philosophers are full of it; in Alexandria the whole Classical mythology and even Plato were treated in this way and brought into analogy (Moses = Musæus) with the Jewish prophets.

The only strictly *scientific* method that an unalterable Koran leaves open for progressive opinion is that of commentary. As by hypothesis the "word" of an authority cannot be improved upon, the only resource is reinterpretation. No one in Alexandria would ever have asserted that Plato was in "error"; instead, he was glossed upon. It was done in the strictly constructed forms of the Halakha, and the fixation of this exegesis in writing takes the commentary shape that dominates all religious, philosophical, and savant literatures of this Culture. Following the procedure of the Gnostics, the Fathers compiled written commentaries upon the Bible, and similarly the Pehlevi commentary of the Zend appeared by the side of the Avesta, and the Midrash by the side of the Jewish canon. But the "Roman" jurists of about A.D. 200 and the "Late Classical" philosophers — that is, the Schoolmen of the growing cult-Church — went just the same way; the Apocalypse of this Church, commented over and over again after Posidonius, was the *Timæus* of Plato. The Mishnah is one vast commentary upon the Torah. And when the oldest exegetes had become themselves authorities and their writings Korans, commentaries were written upon commentaries, as by Simplicius, the last Platonist, in the West, by the Amoraim, who added the Gemara to the Mishnah in the East, and by the jurists who compiled the Imperial Constitutions into the Digests at Byzantium.

This method, which fictitiously refers back every saying to an immediate inspired delivery, was brought to its keenest edge in the Talmudic and the Islamic theologies. A new Halakha or a Hadith is only valid when it can be referred through an unbroken chain of guarantors back to Moses or Mohammed.[1] The solemn formula for this in Jerusalem was "Let it come over me! So have I heard it from my teacher."[2] In the Zend the citation of the chain of warranty is the rule, and Irenæus justifies his theology by the fact that a chain goes back from him through Polycarp to the primitive Community. Into the Early Christian literature this Halakha-form entered so self-evidently that no

[1] In the West, Plato, Aristotle, and above all Pythagoras were regarded as prophets in this sense. What could be referred back to them, was valid. For this reason the succession of the heads of the schools became more and more important, and often more work was done in establishing — or inventing — them than was done upon the history of the doctrine itself.

[2] Fromer, *Der Talmud*, p. 190.

one remarked it for what it was. Apart altogether from the constant references to the Law and the Prophets, it appears in the superscription of the four Gospels ("*according to*" Mark), each of which had thus to present its warrant if authority was to be claimed for the words of the Lord that it presented.[1] This established the chain back to the Truth that was incarnate in Jesus, and it is impossible to exaggerate the intense reality of this in the world-idea of an Augustine or a Jerome. This is the basis of the practice, which spread even more widely from the time of Alexander onwards, of providing religious and philosophical writings with names,[2] like Enoch, Solomon, Ezra, Hermes, Pythagoras — guarantors and vessels of divine wisdom, in whom, therefore, the Word had been made Flesh of old. We still possess a number of Apocalypses bearing the name of Baruch, who was then compared with Zarathustra, and we can scarcely form an idea of what in the way of literature circulated under the names of Aristotle and Pythagoras. The "Theology of Aristotle" was one of the most influential works of Neoplatonism. And, lastly, this the metaphysical presupposition for the style and the deeper meaning of *citation*, which was employed by Fathers, Rabbis, "Greek" philosophers, and "Roman" jurists, and eventuated on the one hand in the Law of Valentinian III,[3] and on the other in the elimination from the Jewish and Christian canons of apocryphal writings — a fundamental notion, which differentiated the literary stock according to difference of *substance*.

v

With such researches to build upon, it will become possible in the future to write a history of the *Magian group of religions*. It forms an inseparable unit of spirit and evolution, and let no one imagine that any individual one of them can be really comprehended without reference to the rest. Their birth, unfolding, and inward confirmation occupy the period 0–500. It corresponds exactly to the rise of the Western religion from the Cluniac movement to the Reformation. A mutual give-and-take, a confusingly rich blossoming, ripening, transformation — overlayings, migrations, adaptations, rejections — fill these centuries, without any sort of dependence of one system upon the others being demonstrable. But only the forms and the structures change; in the depths it is one and the same spirituality, and in all the languages of this world of religions it is always itself that it brings to expression.

[1] We to-day confuse *authorship* and *authority*. Arabian thought knew not the idea of "intellectual property." Such would have been absurd and sinful, for it is the *one* divine Pneuma that selects the individual as vessel and mouthpiece. Only to that extent is he the "author," and it does not matter even whether he or another actually writes down the material. "The Gospel *according to* Mark" means that Mark *vouches for* the truth of this evangel.

[2] On the pseudonyma and anonyma of Biblical apocryphal literature the English reader will find much of interest in three small books (already referred to) of the "Home University" series: Moore, *Literature of the Old Testament;* Charles, *Between the Old and the New Testaments;* and Bacon, *The Making of the New Testament.* — *Tr.*

[3] See p. 73. — *Tr.*

In the wide realm of old-Babylonian fellahdom young peoples lived. There everything was making ready. The first premonitions of the future awoke about 700 B.C. in the prophetic religions of the Persians, Jews, and Chaldeans. An image of creation of the same kind that later was to be the preface of the Torah showed itself in clear outlines, and with that an orientation, a direction, a goal of desire, was set. Something was descried in the far future, indefinitely and darkly still, but with a profound certainty that it would come. From that time on men lived with the vision of this, with the feeling of a mission.

The second wave swelled up steeply in the Apocalyptic currents after 300. Here it was the Magian waking-consciousness that arose and built itself a metaphysic of Last Things, based already upon the prime-symbol of the coming Culture, the Cavern. Ideas of an awful End of the World, of the Last Judgment, of Resurrection, Paradise, and Hell, and with them the grand thought of a process of salvation in which earth's destiny and man's were one, burst forth everywhere — we cannot say what land or people it was that created them — mantled in wondrous scenes and figures and names. The Messiah-figure presents itself, complete at one stroke. Satan's temptation of the Saviour [1] is told as a tale. But simultaneously there welled up a deep and ever-increasing fear before this certainty of an implacable — and imminent — limit of all happening, before the moment in which there would be only Past. Magian Time, the "hour," directedness under the Cavern, imparted a new pulse to life and a new import to the word "Destiny." Man's attitude before the Deity suddenly became completely different. In the dedicatory inscription of the great basilica of Palmyra (which was long thought to be Christian) Baal was called the good, the compassionate, the mild; and this feeling penetrated, with the worship of Rahman, right to southern Arabia. It fills the psalms of the Chaldeans and the teachings *about* the God-sent Zarathustra that took the place of his teachings. And it stirred the Jewry of Maccabean time — most of the psalms were written then — and all the other communities, long forgotten now, that lay between the Classical and the Indian worlds.

The third upheaval came in the time of Cæsar and brought to birth the great religions of Salvation. And with this the Culture rose to bright day, and what followed continuously throughout one or two centuries was an intensity of religious experience, both unsurpassable and at long last unbearable. Such a tension bordering upon the breaking point the Gothic, the Vedic, and every other Culture-soul has known, once and once only, in its young morning.

Now arose in the Persian, the Mandæan, the Jewish, the Christian, circles of belief, and in that of the Western Pseudomorphosis as well — just as in the Indian, the Classical, and the Western ages of Chivalry — the Grand Myth. In this Arabian Culture religious and national heroism are no more distinctly

---

[1] Vendidad 19, 1; here it is Zarathustra who is tempted.

separable than nation, church, and state, or sacred and secular law. The prophet merges with the fighter, and the story of a great Sufferer rises to the rank of a national epic. The powers of light and darkness, fabulous beings, angels and devils, Satan and the good spirits wrestle together; all nature is a battle-ground from the beginning of the world to its annihilation. Down below in the world of mankind are enacted the adventures and sufferings of the heralds, the heroes, and the martyrs of religion. Every nation, in the sense of the word attaching to this Culture, possessed its heroic saga. In the East the life of the Persian prophet inspired an epic poetry of grand outlines. At his birth the Zarathustra-laughter pealed through the heavens, and all nature echoed it. In the West the suffering of Jesus, ever broadening and developing, became *the veritable epic of the Christian nation*, and by its side there grew up a chain of legends of his childhood which in the end fructified a whole genre of poetry. The figure of the Mother of God and the deeds of the Apostles became, like the stories of the Western Crusade-heroes, the centre of extended romances (Acts of Thomas, Pseudo-Clementines) which in the second century sprang up everywhere from the Nile to the Tigris. In the Jewish Haggada and in the Targums is brought together a rich measure of legends about Saul, David, the Patriarchs, and the great Tannaim, like Schuda and Akiba,[1] and the insatiable fancy of the age seized also upon what it could reach of the Late-Classical cult-legends and founder-stories (lives of Pythagoras, Hermes, Apollonius of Tyana).

With the end of the second century the sounds of this exaltation die away. The flowering of epic poetry is past, and the mystical penetration and dogmatic analysis of the religious material begin. The doctrines of the new Churches are brought into theological systems. Heroism yields to Scholastism, poetry to thought, the seer and seeker to the priest. The early Scholasticism which ends about 200 (as the Western about 1200) comprises the whole Gnosis — in the very broadest sense, the great Contemplation — the author of the John Gospel, Valentinus, Bardesanes, and Marcion, the Apologists and the early Fathers, up to Irenæus and Tertullian, the last Tannaim up to Rabbi Jehuda, the completer of the Mishna, the Neopythagoreans and Hermetics of Alexandria. All this corresponds with, in the West, the School of Chartres, Anselm, Joachim of Floris, Bernard of Clairvaux, Hugo de St. Victor. Full Scholasticism begins with Neoplatonism, with Clement and Origen, the first Amoraim, and the creators of the newer Avesta under Ardeshir (226–241) and Sapor I, the Mazdaist high-priest Tanvasar above all. Simultaneously a higher religiousness begins to separate from the peasant's piety of the countryside, which still lingered in the apocalyptic disposition, and thenceforth maintained itself almost unaltered under various names right into the fellahdom of the Turkish age, while in the urban and more intellectual upper world the Persian, Jewish, and Christian community was absorbed by that of Islam.

[1] M. J. ben Gorion, *Die Sagen der Juden* (1913).

Slowly and steadily now the great Churches moved to fulfilment. It had been decided — the most important religious result of the second century — that the outcome of the teaching of Jesus was not to be a transformation of Judaism, but a new Church, which took its way westward while Judaism, without loss of inward strength, turned itself to the East. To the third century belong the great mental structures of theology. A *modus vivendi* with historical actuality had been reached, the end of the world had receded into the distance, and a new dogmatic grew up to explain the new world-picture. The arrival of mature Scholasticism presupposes faith in the duration of the doctrines that it sets itself to establish.

Viewing the results of their efforts, we find that the Aramæan motherland developed its forms in three directions. In the East, out of the Zoroastrian religion of Achæmenid times and the remains of its sacred literature, there formed itself the Mazdaist Church, with a strict hierarchy and laborious ritual, with sacraments, mass, and confession (*patet*). As mentioned above, Tanvasar made a beginning with the collection and ordering of the *new* Avesta; under Sapor I (as contemporaneously in the Talmud) the profane texts of medicine, law, and astronomy were added; and the rounding-off was the work of the Church magnate Mahraspand under Sapor II (309–379). The immediate accretion of a commentary in Pehlevi was only what was to be expected in the Magian Culture. The new Avesta, like the Jewish and the Christian Bibles, was a canon of separate writings, and we learn that amongst the Nasks (originally twenty-one) now lost there was a gospel of Zarathustra, the conversion-story of Vishtaspa, a Genesis, a law-book, and a genealogical book with trees from the Creation to the Persian kings, while the Vendidad, which Geldner calls the Leviticus of the Persians, was — most significantly — preserved complete.

A new religious founder appeared in 242, in the reign of Sapor I. This was Mani, who, rejecting "redeemerless" Judaism and Hellenism, knit together the whole mass of Magian religions in one of the most powerful theological creations of all times — for which in 276 the Mazdaist priesthood crucified him. Equipped by his father (who quite late in life abandoned his family to enter a Mandæan order) with all the knowledge of the period, he unified the basic ideas of the Chaldeans and Persians with those of Johannine, Eastern, Christianity — a task which had been attempted before in the Christian-Persian Gnosis of Bardesanes, but without any idea of founding a new church.[1] He

---

[1] It is reasonable to suppose that he must through oral tradition have had a very accurate knowledge of the fundamental doctrines of the John Gospel. Even Bardesanes (d. 254), and the "Acts of St. Thomas" that originated in his circle, are very far removed indeed from Pauline doctrines, an alienation that in Mani rose to downright hostility and to the historical Jesus's being described as an evil demon. We obtain here a glimpse into the essence of the almost subterranean Christianity of the East, which was ignored by the Greek-writing churches of the Pseudomorphosis and for that reason has hitherto escaped the attention of Church history. But Marcion and Montanus also came from eastern Asia Minor; here originated the Naasene book, basically Per-

conceived of the mystical figures of the Johannine Logos (for him identical with the Persian Vohu Mano), the Zarathustra of the Avesta legends, and the Buddha of the late texts as divine Emanations, and himself he proclaimed to be the Paraclete of the John Gospel and the Saoshyant of the Persians. As we now know, thanks to the Turfan discoveries which included parts of Mani's works (till then completely lost), the Church-language of the Mazdaists, Manichæans, and Nestorians was — independently of the current languages — Pehlevi.

In the West the two cult-Churches developed (in Greek [1]) a theology that was not only cognate with this, but to a great extent identical with it. In the time of Mani began the theological fusion of the Aramæan-Chaldean sun-religion and the Aramæan-Persian Mithras cult into one system, whose first great "Father" was Iamblichus (c. 300) — the contemporary of Athanasius, but also of Diocletian, the Emperor who in 295 made Mithras the God of a henotheistic State-religion. Spiritually, at any rate, its priests were in nowise distinguishable from those of Christianity. Proclus (he, too, a true "Father") received in dreams elucidations of a difficult text-passage; to him the *Timæus* and the Chaldean oracles were canonical, and he would gladly have seen all other writings of the philosophers destroyed. His hymns, tokens of the lacerations of a true eremite, implore Helios and other helpers to protect him against evil spirits. Hierocles wrote a moral breviary for the believers of the Neopythagorean community, which it needs a keen eye to distinguish from Christian work. Bishop Synesius was a prince-prelate of Neoplatonism before becoming one of Christianity — and the change did not involve an act of conversion; he kept his theology and only altered its names. It was possible for the Neoplatonist Asclepiades to write a great work on the likeness of all theologies. We possess Pagan gospels and hagiologies as well as Christian. Apollonius wrote the life of Pythagoras, Marinus that of Proclus, Damascius that of Isidore; and there is not the slightest difference between these works, which begin and end with prayers, and the Christian Acts of the Martyrs. Porphyry describes faith, love, hope, and truth as the four divine elements.

Between these Churches of the East and the West we see, looking south from Edessa, the Talmudic Church (the "Synagogue") with Aramaic as its written language. Against these great and firm foundations Jewish-Christians (such as Ebionites and Elkazites), Mandæans, and likewise Chaldeans (unless we regard Manichæism as a reconstruction of that religion) were unable to hold their own. Breaking down into numberless sects, they either faded out

---

sian, but overlaid first with Judaism and then with Christianity; and further east, probably in the Matthew monastery of Mosul, Aphrahat wrote, about 340, those strange epistles whose Christianity the Western development from Irenæus to Athanasius left wholly unaffected. The history of Nestorian Christianity, in fact, was already beginning in the second century.

[1] For the later writings of (for example) Tertullian and Augustine remained wholly without effect save in so far as they were translated. In Rome itself even, Greek was the true language of the Church.

in the shadow of the great Churches or were absorbed in their structure as the last Marcionites and Montanists were absorbed into Manichæism. By about 300, outside the Pagan, Christian, Persian, Jewish, and Manichæan Churches no important Magian religions remained in being.

VI

Along with this ripe Scholasticism, there set in also, from 200, the effort to identify the *visible* community, as its organization became ever stricter, with the organism of the State. This followed of necessity from the world-feeling of Magian man, and in turn it led to the transformation of the rulers into caliphs — lords of a creed-society far more than of domains — to the idea of orthodoxy as the premiss of real citizenship; to the duty of persecuting false religions (the "Holy War" of Islam is as old as the Culture itself, and the first centuries were full of it); and to a special régime within the State of unbelievers — just tolerated and under laws and governance of their own [1] (for the law God had given was not for heretics) — and, with it, the ghetto manner of living.

First, Osrhoene, in the centre of the Aramæan landscape, adopted Christianity as the State religion about 200. Then Mazdaism assumed the same position in the Sassanid Empire (226) while under Aurelian (d. 275) and above all Diocletian (295) Syncretism as a compound of the Divus, Sol, and Mithras cults became the state religion of the Roman Imperium. Constantine in 312, King Trdat of Armenia about 321, and King Mirian of Georgia a few years later, went over to Christianity. In the far South, Saba must already have become Christian in the third century, Axum in the fourth; on the other hand, simultaneously with these, the Himaryite State became Jewish, and there was one more effort, that of Julian, to bring back the Pagan Church to supremacy.

In opposition to this — likewise in all the religions of this Culture — we find the spread of Monasticism, with its radical aversion from State, history, and actuality in general. For after all the conflict of being and waking-being — that is, of politics and religion, of history and nature — could not be completely mastered by the form of the Magian Church and its identification with State and nation. Race breaks forth into life in these mind-creations and overpowers the divine, precisely because the latter has absorbed the worldly into itself. But here there was no conflict of Church and State as in the Gothic age, and consequently the split in the nation was between the worldly-pious and the ascetics. A Magian religion relates exclusively to the divine spark, the Pneuma, in the man, that which he shares with the invisible community of the faithful and blessed spirits. The rest of the man belongs to Evil and Darkness. But in the man it is the divine that must rule, overcoming, suppressing, destroying the other. In this Culture the askete is not only the veritable priest — the secular priest, as to-day in Russia, is never really respected, and mostly he is

[1] See p. 177. — *Tr.*

allowed to marry — but, what is more, he is the true man of piety. Outside monasticism it was simply not possible to fulfil the demands of religion, and consequently communities of repentance, monasteries, and convents assume quite early a position that, for metaphysical reasons, they could never have had in India or China — let alone in the West, where the Orders were working and fighting — that is, dynamic — units.[1] Consequently, we must not regard the people of the Magian world as divided into the "world" and the "cloister" as two definitely separate modes of life, with equal possibilities of fulfilling all the demands of religion. Every pious person *was* a monk in some sort.[2] Between world and cloister there was no opposition, but only a difference of *degree*. Magian churches and orders are homogeneous communities which are only to be distinguished from one another by extent. The community of Peter was an Order, that of Paul a Church, while the Mithras religion is at once almost too wide for the one designation and too narrow for the other.

Every Magian Church is itself an Order and it was only in respect of human weakness that there were stages and grades of askesis, and these not ordered, but only permitted, as among the Marcionites and the Manichæans (*electi, auditores*). And, in truth, a Magian nation is nothing but the sum, *the order of all the orders*, which, constituted in smaller and smaller, stricter and stricter groups, come out finally in the eremites, dervishes, and stylites, in whom nothing more is of the world, whose waking-consciousness now belongs only to the Pneuma. Setting aside the prophetic religions — out of which, and between which, the excitation of Apocalypse generated numerous order-like communities — the two cult-Churches of the West produced unnumbered monks, friars, and orders, distinguishable from one another in the end only by the name of the Deity upon whom they called. All observed fasting, prayer, celibacy, poverty. It is very doubtful which of the two Churches in 300 was the more ascetic in its tendency. The Neoplatonist monk Sarapion went into the desert in order to devote himself entirely to studying the hymns of Orpheus. Damascius, guided by a dream, withdrew into a noisome cave in order to pray continuously to Cybele.[3] The schools of philosophy were nothing but ascetic orders; the Neopythagoreans stood close to the Jewish Essenes; the Mithras cult, a true order, admitted only men to its communion and its fraternities; the Emperor Julian had the intention of endowing pagan monasteries. The Mandæan religion seems to have been a group of order-communities of varying rigour; amongst them was that of John the Baptist. Christian monasticism did not begin with Pachomius (320); he was merely the builder of

---

[1] The Faustian monk represses his evil will, the Magian the evil substance in himself. Only the latter is dualistic.

[2] The purity- and food-laws of the Talmud and the Avesta cut far deeper into everyday life than, for example, the Benedictine rule.

[3] Asmus, "Damaskios" (*Philos. Bibl.*, 125 (1911). Christian anchoritism is *later* than pagan: Reitzenstein, "Des Athanasius Werk über das Leben des Antonius" (*Sitz. Heid. Ak.* (1914), VIII, 12).

the first cloister. The movement began with the original community in Jerusalem itself. The Gospel of Matthew and almost all "Acts of the Apostles" testify to rigorously ascetic sentiment.[1] The Persian and Nestorian Churches developed the monastic idea further, and finally Islam assimilated it to the full. To this day Oriental piety is dominated by the Moslem Orders and Brotherhoods. And Jewry followed the same line of evolution, from the Karæi [2] (Qaraites) of the eighth century to the Polish Hasidim of the eighteenth.[3]

Christianity, which even in the second century was hardly more than an extended Order, and whose public influence was out of all proportion to the number of its adherents, grew suddenly vast about the year 250. This is the epochal moment in which the last city-cults of the Classical effaced themselves before, *not Christianity, but the new-born Pagan Church*. The records of the Fratres Arvales in Rome break off in 241, and the last cult-inscriptions at Olympia are of 265. At the same time, the cumulation of the most diverse priestly characters in one man became customary,[4] implying that these usages were felt no longer as specific, but as usages of one single religion. And this religion set out to *convert*, spreading itself far and wide over the lands of the Hellenistic-Roman stock. The Christian religion, on the other hand, was alone in spreading (c. 300) over the great Arabian field. And for that very reason it was inevitable that inner contradiction should now be set up in it. Due, not now to the spiritual dispositions of particular men, but to the spirit of the particular landscapes, these contradictions led to the break-up of Christianity into several religions — and for ever.

The *controversy concerning the nature of Christ* was the issue on which this conflict came up for decision. The matter in dispute was just those problems of substance which in the same form and with the same tendency fill the thoughts of all other Magian theologies. Neoplatonic Scholasticism, Porphyry, Iamblichus, and above all Proclus treated it in a Western formulation, by modes of thought closely akin to Philo's and even to Paul's. The relation between the Primary One, Nus, Logos, the Father, and the Mediator was considered with reference to the substantial. Was the process thereof one of emanation, of partition, or of pervasion? Was one contained in the other, are they identical, or mutually exclusive? Was the Triad at the same time a Monad? In the East a different constitution of the problem is evidenced already in the premisses of the John Gospel and the Bardesanian Gnosis: the relation of Ahuramazda to the Holy Spirit (Spenta Mainyu) and the nature of Vohu Mano gave plenty of

---

[1] Even to the point indicated in Matt. xix, 12, which Origen followed to the letter.

[2] See *Ency. Brit.*, XI ed., article "Qaraites." The outlook of these Protestants so resembled that of the Western Protestants that their name was used as a term of contempt for the latter by the Catholics, and not greatly resented. It is significant also that this movement in Jewry almost coincided in date with the vaster Reformation of Islam. — *Tr.*

[3] The followers of Baal Shem above mentioned (p. 228) not to be confused with the Hasidim or Assideans of the second century. — *Tr.*

[4] Wissowa, *Religion und Kulturs der Römer*, p. 493; Geffcken pp. 4, 144.

occupation to the Avestan "fathers"; and it was just at the time of the decisive Councils of Ephesus and Chalcedon that we find the temporary triumph of Zrvanism (438-457), with its primacy of the divine world-course (Zrvan as historic Time) over the divine substances marking a peak of dogmatic battle. Later, Islam took up the whole subject over again and sought to solve it in relation to the nature (*Wesenheit*) of Mohammed and the Koran. The problem had been there, ever since a Magian mankind had come into being — very much as the specifically Western will-problem, our counterpart to the substance-problem, was posed in the beginnings of Faustian thought. There is no need to look for these problems; they are there as soon as the Culture thinks, they are the fundamental form of its thought, and come to the front, uncalled-for and sometimes not even perceived, in all its studies.

But the three Christian solutions predetermined by the three landscapes of East, West, and South were all present from the first, implicit already in the main tendencies of Gnosticism, which we may indicate by the names of Bardesanes, Basilides, and Valentinus. Their meeting-point was Edessa, where the streets rang with the battle-cries of the Nestorians against the victors of Ephesus and, anon, with the εἷς θεός shout of the Monophysites, demanding that Bishop Ibas should be thrown to the wild beasts of the circus.

The great question was formulated by Athanasius, whose intellectual origins lay in the Pseudomorphosis and who had many affinities with his Pagan contemporary Iamblichus. Against Arius, who saw in Christ a demigod, merely *like* in substance to the Father, he maintained that Father and Son were of *the same* substance (θεότης) which in Christ had assumed a human σῶμα. "The Word became Flesh" — this formula of the West depends upon visible facts of the cult-Churches, and the understanding of the Word upon constant contemplation of the picturable. Here in the iconodule West, where in these very times Iamblichus wrote his book concerning God-statues in which the divine was substantially present and worked miracles,[1] the abstraction of the Triunity was always effectively accompanied by the sensuous-human relation of Mother and Son, and it is the latter which it is impossible to eliminate from the thought-processes of Athanasius.

With the recognition of the homoousia of Father and Son the real problem was for the first time posed — namely, the attitude of the Magian dualism to the historical phenomenon of the Son himself. In the world-cavern there was divine and human substance, in man a part in divine Pneuma and the individual soul somehow related to the "flesh." But what of Christ?

It was a decisive factor — one of the results of Actium — that the contest was fought out in the Greek tongue and in the territory of the Pseudomorphosis — that is, under the full influence of the "Caliph" of the Western Church.

---

[1] This is the metaphysical basis also of the Christian image-worship, which presently set in and of the appearance of wonder-working pictures of Mary and the Saints.

Constantine had even been the convener and president of the Council of Nicæa, where the doctrine of Athanasius carried the day. In the East, with its Aramaic speech and thought, these doings were (as we know from the letters of Aphrahat) hardly followed at all; there men saw no cause to quarrel about what, so far as they were concerned, had long ago been settled. The breach between East and West, a consequence of the Council of Ephesus (431) separated two Christian *nations*, that of the "Persian Church" and that of the Greek Church, but this was no more than the manifestation of a difference, inherent from the first, between *modes of thought* proper to the two different landscapes. Nestorius and the whole East saw in Christ the Second Adam, the Divine Envoy of the last æon. Mary had borne a *man*-child in whose human and created substance (*physis*) the godly, uncreated element *dwelt*. The West, on the contrary, saw in Mary the Mother of a *God:* the divine and the human substance formed in his body (*persona*, in the Classical idiom [1]) a unity, named by Cyril ἕνωσις.[2] When the Council of Ephesus had recognized the mother of God, her who gave birth to God, the city of Diana's old renown burst into a truly Classical orgy of celebration.[3]

But long ere this the Syrian Apollinaris[4] had heralded the "Southern" idea of the matter — that in the living Christ there was not merely a substance, but a single substance. The divine had transmuted itself into, not mingled itself with, a human substance (no κρᾶσις, as Gregory Nazianzen maintained in opposition; significantly enough, the best way of expressing the Monophysite idea is through concepts of Spinoza — the *one* substance in another mode). The Monophysites called the Christ of the Council of Chalcedon (451, where the West once more prevailed) "the idol with the two faces." They not only fell away from the Church, they broke out in fierce risings in Palestine and Egypt; and when in Justinian's time the troops of Persia — that is, of Mazdaism — penetrated to the Nile, they were hailed by the Monophysites as liberators.

The fundamental meaning of this desperate conflict which raged for a

---

[1] See p. 60.

[2] The Nestorians protested against Mary *Theotokos* (she who bore God), opposing to her the concept of Christ the *Theophorus* (he who carried God in him). The deep difference between an image-loving and an image-hating religiousness is here clearly manifested.

[3] Note the "Western" outlook on the substance-questions in the contemporary writings of Proclus — his double Zeus, his triad of πατήρ, δύναμις, νόησις or νοητόν, and so forth (Zeller, *Philosophie der Griechen*, V, pp. 857, et seq.). Proclus's beautiful "Hymn to Athene" is a veritable Ave Maria:

"But when an evil lapse of my being puts me into bondage
(And, ah, I know indeed how I am tossed about by many unholy deeds that in my
    blindness I have done),
Be thou gracious to me, thou gentle one, thou blessing of mankind,
And let me not lie upon the earth as prey to fearful punishments,
For I am, and I remain, thy chattel."
                                (Hymn VII, Eudociæ Aug. rel. A. Ludwich, 1897.)

[4] See *Ency. Brit.*, XI ed., article "Apollinaris, the Younger." — *Tr.*

century — not over scholarly concepts, but over the soul of a landscape that sought to be set free *in its people* — was the *reversal of the work of Paul*. If we can transport ourselves into the inmost soul of the two new-born nations, making no reservations and ignoring all minor points of dogmatics, then we see how the direction of Christianity towards the Greek West and its intellectual affinity with the Pagan Church culminated in the position that the Ruler of the West was the Head of Christianity in general. In the mind of Constantine it was self-evident that the Pauline foundation *within* the Pseudomorphosis was synonymous with Christianity. The Jewish Christians of Petrine tendency were to him a heretical sect, and the Eastern Christians of "Johannine" type he never even noticed. When the spirit of the Pseudomorphosis had, in the three determining councils of Nicæa, Ephesus, and Chalcedon, put *its* seal upon dogma, once and for all, the real Arabian world rose up with the force of nature and set up a barrier against it. With the end of the Arabian Springtime, Christianity fell apart for good into three religions, which can be symbolized by the names of Paul, Peter, and John, and of which none can henceforth claim to be regarded by the historically and doctrinally unprejudiced eye as *the* true and proper Christianity. These three religions are at the same time three nations, living in the old race-areas of Greeks, Jews, and Persians, and the tongues that they used were the Church-languages borrowed from them — namely, Greek, Aramaic, and Pehlevi.

VII

The Eastern Church, since the Council of Nicæa, had organized itself with an episcopal constitution, at the head of which stood the Katholikos of Ctesiphon, and with councils, liturgy, and law of its own. In 486 the Nestorian doctrine was accepted as binding, and the tie with Constantinople was thus broken. From that point on, Mazdaists, Manichæans, and Nestorians have a common destiny, of which the seed was sown in the Gnosis of Bardesanes. In the Monophysite Churches of the South, the spirit of the primitive Community emerged again and spread itself further; with its uncompromising monotheism and its hatred of images its closest affinity was with Talmudic Judaism, and its old battle-cry of εἶς θεός had already marked it to be, with that Judaism, the starting-point of Islam ("Allah il Allah"). The Western Church continued to be bound up with the fate of the Roman Empire — that is, the cult-Church became the State. Gradually it absorbed into itself the adherents of the Pagan Church, and thenceforth its importance lay not so much in itself — for Islam almost annihilated it — but in the accident that it was *from it* that the young peoples of the Western Culture received the Christian system as the basis for a new creation,[1] receiving it, moreover, in the Latin guise of the extreme West — which for the Greek Church itself was unmeaning, since Rome was now a

---

[1] And Russia, too, though hitherto Russia has kept it as a buried treasure.

Greek city, and the Latin language was far more truly at home in Africa and Gaul.

The essential and elemental concept of the Magian nation, a being that consists in extension, had been from the beginning active in extending itself. All these Churches were, deliberately, forcefully, and successfully, missionary Churches. But it was not until men had at last ceased to think of the end of the world as imminent, and dogma appropriate to prolonged existence in this World's Cavern had been built up, and the Magian religions had taken up their standpoint towards the problem of substance, that the extending of the Culture took up that swift, passionate tempo that distinguished it from all others and found in Islam its most impressive, its last, but by no means its only example. Of these mighty facts Western theologians and historians give an entirely false picture. All that their gaze, riveted upon the Mediterranean lands, observes is the Western direction that fits in with their "Ancient-Mediæval-Modern" schema, and even within these limits, accepting the ostensible unity of Christianity, they regard it as passing at a certain period from a Greek into a Latin form, whereby the Greek residue is lost sight of altogether.

But even before Christianity — and this is a fact of which the immense significance has never been observed, which has not even been correctly interpreted as *mission* effort — the Pagan Church had won for the Syncretic Cult the greater part of the population of North Africa, Spain, Gaul, Britain, and the Rhine and Danube frontiers. Of the Druidism that Cæsar had found in Gaul, little remained extant by the time of Constantine. The assimilation of indigenous local gods under the names of the great Magian divinities of the Cult-Church (and especially Mithras-Sol-Jupiter) from the second century on, was essentially a process of conquest, and the same is true of the later emperor-worship.[1] The missionary efforts of Christianity here would have been less successful than they were if the other cult-Church — its near relative — had not preceded it. But the latter's propaganda was by no means limited to barbarian fields; even in the fifth century the missionary Asclepiodotus converted Aphrodisias, a Carian city, from Christianity to Paganism.

The Jews, as has been shown already, directed missionary effort on a large scale towards the East and the South. Through southern Arabia they drove into the heart of Africa, possibly even before the birth of Christ, while on the side of the East their presence in China is demonstrable, even in the second century. To the north the realm of the Khazars[2] and its capital, Astrakhan, later went over to Judaism. From this area came the Mongols of Jewish religion who advanced into the heart of Germany and were defeated, along with the Hungarians, in the battle of the Lechfeld in 955. Jewish scholars of the Span-

[1] The Christian missionary efforts of the West very generally followed the same method, maintaining the local places of prayer, and merely substituting crucifixes or relics for the idols. Gregory the Great even sanctioned the sacrifice of animals in Britain. — *Tr.*

[2] See *Ency. Brit.*, XI ed., art. "Khazars." — *Tr.*

ish-Moorish universities petitioned the Byzantine Emperor (in A.D. 1000) for safe-conduct for an embassy that was to ask the Khazars whether they were the Lost Tribes of Israel.

From the Tigris, Mazdaists and Manichæans penetrated the empires on either hand, Roman and Chinese, to their utmost frontiers. Persian, as the Mithras cult, invaded Britain; Manichæism had by 400 become a danger to Greek Christianity, and there were Manichæan sects in southern France as late as the Crusades[1]; but the two religions drove eastwards as well, along the Great Wall of China (where the great polyglot inscription of Kara Balgassun testifies to the introduction of the Manichæan faith in the Oigur realm) and even to Shantung. Persian fire-temples arose in the interior of China, and from 700 Persian expressions are found in Chinese astrological writings.

The three Christian Churches everywhere followed up the blazed trails. When the Western Church converted the Frankish King Chlodwig in 496, the missionaries of the Eastern Church had already reached Ceylon and the westernmost Chinese garrisons of the Great Wall, and those of the Southern were in the Empire of Axum. At the same time as, after Boniface (718), Germany became converted, the Nestorian missionaries were within an ace of winning China itself. They had entered Shantung in 638. The Emperor Gao-dsung (651–84) permitted churches to be built in all provinces of the Empire, in 750 Christianity was preached in the Imperial palace itself, and in 781, according to the Aramaic and Chinese inscriptions upon a memorial column in Singafu which has been preserved, "all China was covered with the palaces of Concord." But it is in the highest degree significant that the Confucians, who cannot be called inexpert in religious matters, regarded the Nestorians, Mazdaists, and Manichæans as adherents of a single "Persian" religion,[2] just as the population of the Western Roman provinces were unable to discriminate between Mithras and Christ.

Islam, therefore, is to be regarded as the Puritanism of the whole group of Early Magian religions, emerging as a religion only formally new, and in the domain of the Southern Church and Talmudic Judaism. It is this deeper significance, and not merely the force of its warlike onslaught, that gives the key to its fabulous successes. Although on political grounds it practised an astounding toleration — John Damascenus, the last great dogmatist of the Greek Church, was, under the name of Al Manzor, treasurer to the Caliph — Judaism, Mazdaism, and the Southern and Eastern churches of Christianity were swiftly and almost completely dissolved in it. The Katholikos of Seleucia, Jesujabh III, complains that tens of thousands of Christians went over to it as soon as it came on the scene, and in North Africa — the home of Augustine — the entire population fell away to Islam at once. Mohammed died in 632. In 641 the whole domain of the Monophysites and the Nestorians (and, therefore, of the

---

[1] The Albigensian movement of the twelfth century. — Tr.
[2] Hermann, *Chines. Geschichte* (1912), p. 77.

Talmud and the Avesta) were in the possession of Islam. In 717 it stood before Constantinople, and the Greek Church was in peril of extinction. Already in 628 a relative of the prophet had brought presents to the Chinese Emperor Tai-dsung and obtained leave to institute a mission. From 700 there were mosques in Shantung, and in 720 Damascus sent instructions to the Arabs long established in southern France to conquer the realm of the Franks. Two centuries later, when in the West a new religious world was arising out of the remains of the old Western Church, Islam was in the Sudan and in Java.

For all this, Islam is significant only as a piece of *outward* religious history. The inner history of the Magian religion ends with Justinian's time, as truly as that of the Faustian ends with Charles V and the Council of Trent. Any book on religious history shows *"the"* Christian religion as having had *two ages of grand thought-movements* — 0-500 in the East and 1000-1500 in the West.[1] *But these are two springtimes of two Cultures,* and in them are comprised also the non-Christian forms which belong to each religious development. The closing of the University of Athens by Justinian in 529 was not, as is always stated, the end of Classical philosophy — there had been no Classical philosophy for centuries. What he did, forty years before the birth of Mohammed, was to end the theology of the Pagan Church by closing this school and — as the historians forget to add — *to end the Christian theology also* by closing those of Antioch and Alexandria. Dogma was complete, finished — just as it was in the West with the Council of Trent (1564) and the Confession of Augsburg (1540), for with the city and intellectualism religious creative force comes to an end. So also in Jewry and in Persia, the Talmud was concluded about 500, and when Chosroës Nushirvan in 529 bloodily suppressed the Reformation of Mazdak — which was not unlike our Anabaptism in its rejection of marriage and worldly property, and had been supported by King Kobad I as counteracting the power of Church and nobility — Avestan dogma similarly passed into fixity.

---

[1] A third, "contemporary," movement should follow in the Russian world in the first half of the coming millennium.

CHAPTER IX

PROBLEMS OF THE ARABIAN CULTURE

(C)

PYTHAGORAS, MOHAMMED, CROMWELL

CHAPTER IX

PROBLEMS OF THE ARABIAN CULTURE

(C)

PYTHAGORAS, MOHAMMED, CROMWELL

I[1]

RELIGION may be described as the Waking-Being of a living creature in the moments when it overcomes, masters, denies, and even destroys Being. Race-life and the pulse of its drive dwindle as the eyes gaze into an extended, tense, and light-filled world, and *Time yields to Space*. The plantlike desire for fulfilment goes out, and from primary depths there wells up the animal fear of the fulfilment, of the ceasing of direction, of death. Not hate and love, but fear and love are the basic feelings of religion. Hate and fear differ as Time and Space, blood and eye, pulse and tension, heroism and saintliness. And love in the race-sense differs from love in the religious sense in the same way.

All religion is turned to light. The extended itself becomes religious as a world of the eye comprehended from the ego as centre of light. Hearing and touch are adjusted to what is seen and the *Invisible*, whose workings are sensed, becomes the sum of the dæmonic. All that we designate by the words "deity," "revelation," "salvation," "dispensation," is in one way and another an element of illumined actuality. Death, for man, is something that he sees, and knows by seeing, and in relation to death birth is *the other* secret. They are the two visible limits of the sensible cosmic that is incarnate in a live body in lighted space.

There are two sorts of deeper fear — one is fear (known even to the animals) *in presence of* microcosmic freedom in space, before space itself and its powers, before death; the other is fear *for* the cosmic current of being, for life, for directional time. The first awakens a dark feeling that freedom in the extended is just a new and deeper sort of dependence than that which rules the vegetable world, and it leads the individual being, sensible of its weakness, to seek the propinquity and alliance of others. Anxiety produces speech, and our sort of speech is religion — every religion. Out of the fear of Space arise the numina of the *world-as-nature* and the *cults of gods;* out of the fear for time arise the numina of *life*, of sex and breed, of the State, centring on *ancestor-worship*. That is the difference between Taboo and Totem [1] — for the totemistic, too, always appears in religious form, out of holy awe of that which passeth all understanding and is for ever alien.

[1] Cf. pp. 3, et seq. and foot-note p. 3.   [1] See p. 116.

The higher religion requires tense alertness against the powers of blood and being that ever lurk in the depths ready to recapture their primeval rights over the *younger* side of life. "*Watch* and pray, that ye fall not into temptation." Nevertheless, "liberation" is a fundamental word in every religion and an eternal wish of every waking-being. In this general, almost prereligious, sense, it means the desire for freedom from the anxieties and anguishes of waking-consciousness; for relaxation of the tensions of fear-born thought and search; for the obliteration and removal of the consciousness of the Ego's loneliness in the universe, the rigid conditionedness of nature, the prospect of the immovable boundary of all Being in eld and death.

Sleep, too, liberates — "Death and his brother Sleep." And holy wine, intoxication, breaks the rigour of the spirit's tension, and dancing, the Dionysus art, and every other form of stupefaction and ecstasy. These are modes of slipping out of awareness by the aid of being, the cosmic, the "it," *the escape out of space into time*. But higher than all these stands the genuinely religious overcoming of fear *by means of the understanding itself*. The tension between microcosm and macrocosm becomes something that we can love, something in which we can wholly immerse ourselves.[1] We call this *faith*, and it is the beginning of all man's intellectual life.

Understanding is causal only, whether deductive or inductive, whether derived from sensation or not. It is wholly impossible to distinguish being-understood from being-caused — both express the same thing. When something is "actual" for us, we see it and think it in causal (*ursächlich*) form, just as we feel and know ourselves and our activities as things originating, causes (*Ursache*). The assignment of causes is, however, different from case to case, not only in the religious, but also generally in the inorganic logic of man. A fact is thought of at one moment as having such-and-such, at another moment as having something else, as its cause. Every kind of thinking has for every one of its domains of application a proper "system." In everyday life a causal connexion in thought is never exactly repeated. Even in modern physics working hypotheses — that is, causal systems — which partially exclude one another are in use side by side; for instance, the ideas of electrodynamics and those of thermodynamics. The significance of the thought is not thereby nullified, for during a continuous spell of waking-consciousness we "understand" always in the form of single acts of which each has its own causal inception. The viewing of the entire world-as-nature in relation to the individual consciousness as a single causally-ordered concatenation is something perfectly unrealizable by our thought, inasmuch as our thinking proceeds always by unit acts. It remains a belief. It is indeed Faith itself, for it is the basis of religious understanding of the world, which, wherever something is observed, postulates numina as a necessity of thought — ephemeral numina for

[1] "He who loves God with inmost soul, transforms himself into God" (Bernard of Clairvaux).

incidental events which are not again thought of, and enduring numina as place-definite indwellers (of springs, trees, stones, hills, stars, and so forth) or as universals (like the gods of Heaven, of War, of Wisdom) which can be present anywhere. These numina are limited only in virtue of the individualness of each separate act of thought. That which to-day is a property of the god is to-morrow itself the god. Others are now a plurality, now a unity, now a vague Ent. There are invisibles (shapes) and incomprehensibles (principles), which, to those to whom it is vouchsafed, may become phenomenal or comprehensible. Fate [1] in the Classical ($\epsilon i\mu\alpha\rho\mu\acute{e}\nu\eta$) and in the Indian ($rta$) is something which stands as origin-thing (Ur-$Sache$) above the picturable divinities; Magian Destiny, on the contrary, is the operation of the one and formless supreme God. Religious thought ever lets itself graduate values and rank within the causal succession, and leads up to supreme beings or principles, as very first and "governing" causes; "dispensation" is the word used for the most comprehensive of all systems based upon valuation. Science, on the contrary, is a mode of understanding which fundamentally abhors distinctions of rank amongst causes; what it finds is not dispensation, but law.

The understanding of causes sets free. Belief in the linkages discovered compels the world-fear to retreat. God is man's refuge from the Destiny which he can feel and livingly experience, but not think on, or figure, or name, and which sinks into abeyance for so long — only for so long — as the "critical" (literally, the *separating*) fear-born understanding can establish causes behind causes comprehensibly; that is, in order visible to the outer or inner eye. It is the desperate dilemma of the higher grade of man that his powerful will to understand is in constant contradiction with his being. It has ceased to serve his life, but is unable to rule it, and consequently in all important conjunctures there remains an insoluble element. "One has merely to declare oneself free, and one feels the moment to be conditioned. But if one has the courage to declare oneself conditioned, then one has the feeling of being free" (Goethe).

We name a causal linkage within the world-as-nature, as to which we are convinced that no further reflection can alter it — Truth. Truths are established, and they are timeless — "absolute" means detached from Destiny and history, but detached also from the facts of our own living and dying — and they are an inward liberation, consolation, and salvation, in that they disvalue and overcome the incalculable happenings of the world of facts. Or, as it mirrors itself in the mind, men may go, but truth remains.

In the world-around something is established — that is, fixed, spellbound.

---

[1] For religious *thought* Destiny is always a causal quantity. Epistemology knows it, therefore, only as an indistinct word for causality. Only so long as we *do not* think upon it do we really know it.

Understanding man has the secret in the hands, whether this be, as of old, some potent charm or, as nowadays, a mathematical formula. A feeling of triumph, even to-day, accompanies every experimental step in the realm of Nature which determines something — about the purposes and powers of the god of heaven or the storm-spirits of the ground-dæmons; or about the numina of natural science (atom-nuclei, the velocity of light, gravitation); or even about the abstract numina that thought conceives in contemplating its own image (concept, category, reason) — and, in determining, fixes it in the prison of an unalterable system of causal relations. Experience in this inorganic, killing, preserving sense, which is something quite different from life-experience and knowledge of men, takes place in two modes — *theory and technique,*[1] or, in religious language, *myth and cult* — according as the believer's intention is to open up or to confine the secrets of the world-around. Both demand a high development of human understanding. *Both may be born of either fear or love.* There is a mythology of fear, like the Mosaic and the primitive generally, and a mythology of love, like that of early Christianity and Gothic mysticism. Similarly there is a technique of defensive, and another technique of postulant, magic, and this, no doubt the most fundamental, distinction between sacrifice and prayer [2] distinguishes also primitive and mature mankind. Religiousness is a trait of soul, but religion is a talent. "Theory" demands the gift of vision that few possess to the extent of luminous insight and many possess not at all. It is world-view, "*Weltanschauung*" in the most primary sense, whether what one sees in that world is the hand and the loom of powers, or (in a colder urban spirit, not fearing or loving, but inquisitive) the theatre of law-conform forces. The secrets of Taboo and Totem are beheld in god-faiths and soul-faiths, and calculated in theoretical physics and biology. "Technique" presupposes the intellectual gift of binding and conjuring. The theorist is the critical seer, the technician is the priest, the discoverer is the prophet.

The means, however, in which the whole force of intellect concentrates itself is the *form* of the actual, which is abstracted from vision by speech, and of which not every waking-consciousness can discern the quintessence — the conceptual circumscription, the communicable law, name, number. Hence every conjuration of the deity is based on the knowledge of its real name and the use of rites and sacraments, known and available only to the initiated, of which the form must be exact and the words correct. This applies not merely to primitive magic, but just as much to our physical (and particularly our medical) technique. It is for this reason that mathematics have a character of sanctity and are regularly the product of a religious milieu (Pythagoras, Descartes, Pascal); that there is a mysticism of sacred numbers (3, 7, 12) in

---

[1] See p. 25.

[2] The distinction between the two is one of *inner* form. A sacrifice made by Socrates is at bottom a prayer; and generally the Classical sacrifice is to be looked upon as a *prayer in bodily form.* The ejaculated prayer of the criminal, on the contrary, is a sacrifice to which fear drives him.

every religion,[1] and that Ornament (of which cult-architecture is the highest form) is essentially number felt as shape. It is rigid, compelling forms, expression-motives and communication-signs [2] that the microcosm employs in the world of waking-consciousness to get into touch with the macrocosm. In sacerdotal technique they are called precepts, and in scientific, laws — but both are really name and number, and primitive man would discover no difference between the magic wherewith the priests of his villages command the dæmons and that wherewith the civilized technician commands his machines.

The first, and perhaps the only, outcome of man's will-to-understanding is *faith*. "I believe" is the great word against metaphysical fear, and at the same time it is an avowal of love. Even though one's researches or accumulation of knowledge may culminate in sudden illumination or conclusive calculation, yet all one's own sense and comprehension would be meaningless unless there were set up along with it an inward certainty of a "something" which as other and alien *is* — and is, moreover, exactly under the ascertained shape — in the concatenation of cause and effect. The highest intellectual possession, therefore, known to man as a being of speech-deduced thought, is the firm and hard-won belief in this something, withdrawn from the courses of time and destiny, which he has separated out by contemplation and labelled by name and number. But *what* that something is remains in the last analysis obscure. Was it the something of secret logic of the universe that was touched, or only a silhouette? And all the struggle and passion starts afresh, and anxious investigation directs itself upon this new doubt, which may well turn to despair. He needs in his intellectual boring of belief a *final* something attainable by thought, an end of dissection that leaves no remainder of mystery. The corners and pockets of his world of contemplation must all be illuminated — nothing less will give him his release.

Here belief passes over into the knowledge evoked by mistrust, or, more accurately, becomes belief in that knowledge. For the latter form of the understanding is radically dependent upon the former; it is posterior, more artificial, more questionable. Further, religious theory — that is, the contemplation of the believer — *leads to* priestly practice, but scientific theory, on the contrary, *liberates itself* by contemplation *from* the technical knowledge of every day life.[3] The firm belief that is bred by illuminations, revelations, sudden deep glimpses, can dispense with critical work. But critical knowledge presupposes the belief that its methods will lead to just that which is desired — that is, not to fresh imaginings, but to the "actual." History, however, teaches that doubt as to belief leads to knowledge, and doubt as to knowledge (after a period of critical optimism) back again to belief. As theoretical knowledge

---

[1] And herein philosophy differs not in the least from soil-sprung folk-belief. Think of Kant's category-table with its 3×4 units, of Hegel's method, of Iamblichus's triads.

[2] See p. 133.

[3] Cf. p. 24.

frees itself from confiding acceptance, it is marching to self-destruction, after which what remains is simply and solely technical experience.

Belief, in its primitive, unclear condition, acknowledges superior sources of wisdom by which things that man's own subtlety could never unravel are more or less manifest — such as prophetic words, dreams, oracles, sacred scriptures, the voice of the deity. The critical spirit, on the contrary, wants, and believes itself able, to look into everything for itself. It not only mistrusts alien truths, but even denies their possibility. Truth, for it, is only knowledge that it has proved for itself. But if pure criticism creates its means out of itself solely, it did not long go unperceived that this position assumed the reality of the result. *De omnibus dubitandum* is a proposition that is incapable of being actualized. It is apt to be forgotten that critical activity must rest upon a *method*, and the possibility of obtaining this method in turn by the way of criticism is only apparent. For, in reality, it follows from the momentary disposition of the thought.[1] That is, the results of criticism themselves are determined by the basic method, but this in turn is determined by the stream of being which carries and perfuses the waking-consciousness. The belief in a knowledge that needs no postulates is merely a mark of the immense naïveté of rationalist periods. A theory of natural science is nothing but a historically older dogma in another shape. And the only profit from it is that which life obtains, in the shape of a successful technique, to which theory has provided the key. It has already been said that the value of a working hypothesis resides not in its "correctness" but in its usableness. But discoveries of another sort, findings of insight, "Truths" in the optimistic sense, cannot be the outcome of purely scientific understanding, since this always presupposes an existing view upon which its critical, dissecting activity can operate; the natural science of the Baroque is one continuous dissection of the religious world-picture of the Gothic.

The aim of faith and science, fear and curiosity, is not to experience life, but to know the world-as-nature. Of world-as-history they are the express negation. But the secret of waking-consciousness is a twofold one; two fear-born, causally ordered pictures arise for the inner eye — the "outer world" and as its counter-image the "inner world." In both are true problems, and the waking-consciousness is not only a look-out, but is very busy within its own domains as well. The Numen out there is called God; in here Soul. By the critical understanding the deities of the believer's vision are transmuted in thought into mechanical magnitudes referable to its world, but their essence and kernel remain the same — Classical matter and form, Magian light and darkness, Faustian force and mass — and its mode is ever the same dissection

---

[1] And even so the thought has a different disposition according as it is primitive or cultured; Chinese, Indian, Classical, Magian, or Western; and even German, English, or French. In the last resort, there are not even two individuals with exactly the same method.

of the primitive soul-belief, and its end is ever the same, a *predetermined* result. The physics of the within is called systematic psychology and it discovers in man, if it is Classical science, thing-like soul-*parts* (νοῦς, θυμός, ἐπιθυμία); if Magian, soul-*substance* (ruach, nephesh); if Faustian, soul-*forces* (thinking, feeling, willing). These are the shapes that religious meditation, in fear and in love, then follows up in the causal relations of guilt, sin, pardon, conscience, reward, and punishment.

Being is a mystery that, as soon as faith and science turn their attention to it, illudes them into fateful error. Instead of the cosmic itself being reached (which is completely outside the possibilities of the active waking-consciousness) the sensible mobility of body in the field of the eye, and the conceptual image of a mechanical-causal chain abstracted therefrom, are subjected to analysis. But real life *is led*, not cognised. *Only the Timeless is true.* Truths lie beyond history and life, and vice versa life is something beyond all causes, effects, and truths. Criticism in both cases, critique of waking-consciousness and critique of being, are contrary to happening and alien to life. But in the first case the application of a critique is entirely justified by the critical intention and the inner logic of the object that is referred to; in the second case it is not. It follows that the distinction between faith and knowledge, or fear and curiosity, or revelation and criticism, is not, after all, the ultimate distinction. Knowledge is only a late form of belief. But *belief and life*, love springing from the secret fear of the world, and love springing from the secret hate of the sexes, knowledge of inorganic and sense of organic logic, Causes and Destinies — *this* is the deepest opposition of all. And here we distinguish men, not according to what their modes of thinking are — religious or critical — nor according to the objects of their thought, but according to whether they are thinkers (no matter about what) *or doers.*

In the realm of doing the waking-consciousness takes charge only when it becomes *technique.* Religious knowledge, too, is power — man is not only ascertaining causations, but handling them. He who knows the secret relationship between microcosm and macrocosm commands it also, whether the knowledge has come to him by revelation or by eavesdropping. Thus the magician and conjuror is truly the Taboo-man. He compels the deity through sacrifice and prayer; he practises the true rites and sacraments because they are causes of inevitable results, and whosoever knows them, him they must serve. He reads in the stars and in the sacred books; in his power lies, timeless and immune from all accident, the *causal* relation of sin and propitiation, repentance and absolutions, sacrifice and grace. His chain of sacred origins and results makes him himself a vessel of mysterious power and, therefore, a cause of new effects, in which one must have faith before one may have them imparted.

From this starting-point we can understand (what the European-American world of to-day has wellnigh forgotten) the ultimate meaning of religious ethics, *Moral.* It is, wherever true and strong, a relation that has the full import of *ritual act and practice;* it is (to use Loyola's phrase) "*exercitium spirituale,*" performed before the deity,[1] who is to be softened and conjured thereby. "What shall I do to be saved?" This "what?" is the key to the understanding of all real moral. In its deeps there is ever a "wherefore" and a "why," even in the case of those few sublime philosophers who have imagined a moral that is "for its own sake" — confessing in the very phrase that deep down they feel a "wherefore," even though but a sympathetic few of their own kind can appreciate it. *There is only causal moral* — that is, *ethical technique* — on the background of a convinced metaphysic.

Moral is a conscious and planned causality of the conduct, apart from all particulars of actual life and character, something eternal and universally valid, not only without time, but hostile to time and for that very reason "true." Even if mankind did not exist, moral would be true and valid — this is no mere conceit, but an expression of the ethical inorganic logic of the world conceived as system that has actually been used. Never would the philosopher concede that it could have a historical evolution and fulfilment. Space denies Time; true moral is absolute, eternally complete and the same. In the depths of it there is ever a negation of life, a refraining and renunciation carried to the point of askesis and death itself. Negation is expressed in its very phrases — religious moral contains prohibitions, not precepts. Taboo, even where it ostensibly affirms, is a list of disclaimers. To liberate oneself from the world of fact, to evade the possibilities of Destiny, always to look upon the race in oneself as the lurking enemy — nothing but hard system, doctrine, and exercise will give that. No action must be causal or impulsive — that is, left to the blood — everything must be considered according to motives and results and "carried out" according to orders. Extreme tension of awareness is required lest we fall into sin. First of all things, continence in what pertains to the blood, love, marriage. Love and hate in mankind are cosmic and evil; the love of the sexes is the very polar opposite of timeless love and fear of God, and therefore it is the prime sin, for which Adam was cast forth from paradise and burdened man with the heritage of guilt. Conception and death define the life of the body in space, and the fact that it is the *body* that is in question makes the former sin and the latter punishment. Σῶμα σῆμα (the Classical body a grave!) was the confession of the Orphic religion. Æschylus and Pindar comprehended Being as a reproach, and the saints of all Cultures feel it as an impiety that has to be killed off by askesis or (what is nearly related thereto) orgiastic squandering. Action, the field of history, the deed, heroism, delight in battle and victory and spoil, are evil. For in them the pulse of cosmic being knocks on the door too loudly and disturbingly for contemplativeness and thought.

---

[1] Anatole France's story *Le Jongleur de Notre Dame* is something deeper than a beautiful fancy. — *Tr.*

The whole world — meaning the world-as-history — is infamous. It fights instead of renouncing; it does not possess the idea of sacrifice. It prevails over truth by means of facts. As it follows impulse, it baffles thought about cause and effect. And therefore the highest sacrifice that intellectual man can offer is to make a personal present of it to the powers of nature. *Every moral action is a piece of this sacrifice*, and an ethical life-course is an unbroken chain of such sacrifices. Above all, the offering of sympathy, com-passion, in which the inwardly strong gives up his superiority to the powerless. The compassionate man kills something within himself. But we must not confuse this sympathy in the grand religious sense with the vague sentimentality of the everyday man, who cannot command himself, still less with the *race-feeling of chivalry* that is not a moral of reasons and rules at all, but an upstanding and self-evident *custom* bred of the unconscious pulsations of a keyed-up life. That which in civilized times is called social ethics has nothing to do with religion, and its presence only goes to show the weakness and emptiness of the religiousness of the day, which has lost that force of metaphysical sureness that is the condition precedent of strong, convinced, and self-denying moral. Think for instance of the difference between Pascal and Mill. Social ethic is nothing but practical politics. It is a very Late product of *the same* historical world whose Springtime (in all Cultures alike) has witnessed the flowering of an ethic of high courage and knightliness in a strong stock that does not wince under the life of history and fate; an ethic of natural and acquired reactions that polite society to-day would call "the instincts of a gentleman"; an ethic of which vulgarity and not sin is the antithesis. Once again it is the Castle versus the Cathedral. The castle character does not ask about precepts and reasons. In fact, it does not ask questions at all. Its code lies in the blood — which is pulse — and its fear is not of punishment or requital, but of contempt and especially self-contempt. It is not selfless; on the contrary, it springs from the very fullness of a strong self. But Compassion likewise demands inward greatness of soul, and so it is those selfsame Springtimes that produce the most saintly servants of pity, the Francis of Assisi, the Bernard of Clairvaux, in whom renunciation was a pervading fragrance, to whom self-offering was bliss, whose *caritas* was ethereal, bloodless, timeless, historyless, in whom fear of the universe had dissolved itself into pure, flawless love, a summit of causal moral of which Late periods are simply no longer capable.

To constrain one's blood, one must have blood. Consequently it is only in knightly warrior-times that we find a monasticism of the great style, and the highest symbol for the complete victory of Space over Time is the warrior become ascetic — not the born dreamer and weakling, who belongs by nature to the cloister, nor again the scholar, who works at a moral system in the study. Putting cant aside, that which is called moral to-day — a proper affection for one's nearest, or the exercise of worthy inclinations, or the practice of *caritas* with an *arrière-pensée* of acquiring political power by that means — is not honour-moral, or even a low grade of it, according to Springtime standards. To repeat: there is grand moral only with reference to death, and its sources are a fear, pervading the whole waking-consciousness, of metaphysical causes and consequences, a love that overcomes life, a consciousness that one is under the inexorable magic of a causal system of sacred laws and purposes, which are honoured as truths and which one must either wholly belong to or wholly renounce. Constant tension, self-watching, self-testing, accompany the exercise of this moral, which is an art, and in the presence of which the world-as-history sinks to nothingness. Let a man be either a hero or a saint. In between lies, not wisdom, but banality.

II

If there were truths independent of the currents of being, there could be no history of truths. If there were one single eternally right religion, religious history would be an inconceivable idea. But, however highly developed the microcosmic side of an individual's life may be, it is nevertheless something stretched like a membrane over the developing life, perfused by the pulsing blood, ever betraying the hidden drive of cosmic directedness. Race dominates and forms all apprehension. It is the destiny of each moment of awareness to be a cast of Time's net over Space.

Not that "eternal truths" do not exist. Every man possesses them — plenty of them — to the extent that he exists and exercises the understanding faculty in a world of thoughts, in the connected ensemble of which they are, in and for the instant of thought, unalterable fixtures — ironbound as cause-effect combinations in hoops of premisses and conclusions. Nothing in this disposition can become displaced, he believes. But in reality it is just *one* surge of life that is lifting his waking self and its world together. Its unity remains integral, but *as* a unit, a whole, *a fact*, it has a history. Absolute and relative are to one another as transverse and longitudinal sections of a succession of generations, the latter ignoring Space, and the former Time. The systematic thinker stays in the causal order of a moment; only the physiognomist who reviews the sequence of positions realizes the constant alteration of that which "is" true.

Alles Vergängliche ist nur ein Gleichnis holds good for the eternal truths also, as soon as we follow their course in the stream of history, and watch them move on as elements in the world-picture of the generations that live and die. For each man, during the short space of his existence, the *one* religion is eternal and true which Destiny, through the time and place of his birth, has ordained for him. With it he feels, out of it he forms, the views and convictions of his days. To its words and forms he holds fast, although what he means by them is constantly changing. In the world-as-nature there are eternal truths; in the world-as-history there is an eternally changing trueness.

A morphology of religious history, therefore, is a task that the Faustian spirit alone could ever formulate, and one that it is only now, at this present stage of its development, fit to deal with.   The problem is enunciated, and we must dare the effort of getting completely away from our own convictions and seeing before us everything indifferently as equally alien.   And how hard it is! He who undertakes the task must possess the strength not merely to imagine himself in an illusory detachment from the truths of his world-understanding — illusory even to one for whom truths are just a set of concepts and methods — but actually to penetrate his own system physiognomically to its very last cells. And even then is it possible, in a single language, which structurally and spiritually carries the whole metaphysical content of its own Culture, to capture transmissible ideas of the truths of other-tongued men?

There is, to begin with, over the thousands of years of the first age,[1] the colourless throng of primitive populations, which stand fearfully agape in the presence of the chaotic environment, whose enigmas continually weigh upon them, for no man amongst them is able logically to master it.   Lucky in comparison with them is the animal, who is awake and yet not thinking.   An animal knows fear only from case to case, whereas early man trembles before the whole world.   Everything inside and outside him is dark and unresolved.   The everyday and the dæmonic are tangled together without clue and without rule. The day is filled with a frightened and painful religiousness, in which it is rare to find even the suggestion of a religion of confidence — for from this elementary form of the world-fear no way leads to the understanding love.   Every stone on which a man stumbles, every tool that he takes in his hand, every insect buzzing past him, food, house, weather, all can be dæmonic; but the man believes in the powers that lurk in them only so long as he is frightened or so long *as he uses them* — there are quite enough of them even so.   But one can love something only if one believes in its *continued* existence.   Love presupposes the thought of a world-order that has acquired stability.   Western research has been at great pains, not only to set in order individual observations gathered from all parts of the world, but to arrange them according to assumed gradations that "lead up" from animism (or other beginnings, as you please) to the beliefs that it holds itself.   Unfortunately, it is one particular religion that has provided the values of the scheme, and Chinese or Greeks would have built it quite differently.   In reality no such gradation, leading a general human evolution up to one goal, exists.   Primitive man's chaotic world-around, born of his discontinuous understanding of separate moments and yet full of impressive meaning, is always something grown-up, self-complete, and closed off, often with chasms and terrors of deep metaphysical premonition.   Always it contains a system, and it matters little whether this is partially abstracted from the contemplation of the light-world or remains wholly within it.   Such

[1] See p. 33.

a world-picture does not "progress"; nor is it a fixed sum of particulars from which this one and that one ought to be (though usually they are) picked out for comparison irrespective of time, land, and people. In reality they form a *world of organic religions*, which, all over the world, possessed (and, where they linger, still possess) proper and very significant modes of originating, growing, expanding, and fading out, and a well-established specific character in point of structure, style, tempo, and duration. The religions of the high Cultures are not developed from these, but different. They lie clearer and more intellectual in the light, they know what understanding love means, they have problems and ideas, theories and techniques, of strict intellect, but the religious symbolism of everyday light they know no more. The primitive religiousness penetrates everything; the later and individualized religions are self-contained form-worlds of their own.

All the more enigmatic, therefore, are the "pre-" periods of the grand Cultures, still primitive through and through, and yet more and more distinctly anticipating and pointing in a definite direction. It is just these periods, of some centuries' duration, that ought to have been accurately examined and compared amongst themselves and for themselves. In what shape does the coming phenomenon prepare itself? In the case of the Magian religions the threshold period, as we have seen, produced the type of the Prophetic religion, which led up to the Apocalyptic. How comes it that this particular form is more deeply grounded in the essence of this particular Culture? Or why is it that the Mycenæan prelude of the Classical is filled from one end to the other with imaginings of beast-formed deities? [1] They are not the gods of the warriors up in the megaron of the Mycenæan castle, where soul- and ancestor-worship was practised with a high and noble piety evidenced still in the monuments, but the gods of down below, the powers believed in in the peasant's hut. The great menlike gods of the Apollinian religion, which must have arisen about 1100 out of a mighty religious upheaval, bear traces of their dark past on all sides. Hardly one of these figures is without some cognomen, attribute, or telltale transformation-myth indicative of its origin. To Homer Hera is invariably the cow-eyed; Zeus appears as a bull, and the Poseidon of the Thelpusan

[1] Was it that highly civilized Crete, the outpost of Egyptian modes of thought, afforded a pattern (see p. 87)? But, after all, the numerous local and tribal gods of the primitive Thinite time (before 3000), which represented the numina of particular beast-*genera*, were essentially different in meaning. The more powerful the Egyptian deity of this preliminary period is, the more particular individual spirits (*ka*) and individual souls (*bai*) he possesses, and these hide and lurk in the various animals — Bastet in the cat, Sechmet in the lion, Hathor in the cow, Mut in the vulture (hence the human-formed *ka* that figures behind the beast-head in the figures of the gods) — making of this earliest world-picture a very abortion of monstrous fear, filling it with powers which rage against man even after his death and which only the greatest sacrifices avail to placate. The union of the North and the South lands was represented by the common veneration of the Horus-falcon, whose first *ka* resided in the Pharaoh of the time. Cf. Eduard Meyer, *Gesch. d. Alt.*, I, §§ 182, et seq. [See also Moret and Davy: *Des clans aux empires* and Moret: *Le Nil et la civilisation égyptienne* (available in English translations). — *Tr.*]

legend as a horse. Apollo comes to be the name for countless primitive numina; now he was wolf (Lycæus) like the Roman Mars, now dolphin (Delphinius), and now serpent (the Pythian Apollo of Delphi). A serpent, too, is the form of Zeus Meilichios on Attic grave-reliefs and of Asclepios, and of the Furies even in Æschylus; [1] and the sacred snake kept on the Acropolis was interpreted as Erichthonios. In Arcadia the horse-headed figure of Demeter in the temple of Phigalia was still to be seen by Pausanias; the Arcadian Artemis-Callisto appears as a she-bear, but in Athens too the priestesses of Artemis Brauronia were called "*arktoi*" (bears).[2] Dionysus — now a bull, now a stag — and Pan retained a certain beast-element to the end. Psyche (like the Egyptian corporal-soul, *bai*) is the soul-bird. And upon all this supervened the innumerable semi-animal figures like sirens and centaurs that completely fill up the Early Classical nature-picture.[3]

But what are the features, now, of the primitive religion of Merovingian times that foreshadow the mighty uprising of the Gothic that was at hand? That both are *ostensibly* the same religion, Christianity, proves nothing when we consider the entire difference in their deeps. For (we must be quite clear in our own mind on this) the primitive character of a religion does not lie in its stock of doctrines and usages, but in the specific spirituality of the mankind that adopts them and feels, speaks, and thinks with them. The student has to familiarize himself with the fact that primitive Christianity (more exactly, the early Christianity of the Western Church) has twice subsequently become the expression-vehicle of a primitive piety, and therefore itself a primitive religion — namely, in the Celtic-Germanic West between 500 and 900, and in Russia up to this day. Now, how did the world mirror itself to these "converted" minds? Leaving out of account some few clerics of, say, Byzantine education, what did one actually think and imagine about these ceremonies and dogmas. Bishop Gregory of Tours, who, we must remember, represents the highest intellectual outlook of his generation, once lauded the powder rubbed from a saint's tombstone in these words: "O divine purgative, superior to all doctors' recipes, which cleanses the belly like scammony and washes away all stains from our conscience!" For him the death of Jesus was a crime which filled him with indignation, but no more; the Resurrection, on the contrary, which hovered before him vaguely, he felt deep down as an athletic *tour de force* that stamped the Messiah as the grand wizard and so legitimated him as the true Saviour. Of any mystic meaning in the story of the Passion he has not an inkling.[4]

[1] *Eumenides*, 126.

[2] Moreover, in the full maturity of Athens, every little girl of the upper classes was consecrated as a bear to this Artemis. — Tr.

[3] For further information the reader may consult the articles "Demeter," etc., in the *Ency. Brit.*, XI ed.; and, for a suggestive introduction in the fewest possible words, Dr. Jane Harrison's pamphlet, *Myths of Greece and Rome*. — Tr.

[4] Bernoulli, *Die Heiligen der Merowinger* (1900) — a good account of this primitive religion.

In Russia the conclusions of the "Synod of a Hundred Chapters," of 1551, evidence a wholly primitive order of belief. Shaving of the beard and wrong handling of the cross both figure here as deadly sins — they were affronts to the dæmons. The "Synod of Antichrist," of 1667, led to the vast secession of the Raskol movement, because thenceforward the sign of the cross was to be made with three fingers instead of two, and the name "Jesus" was to be pronounced "Yissus" instead of "Issus" — whereby, for the strict believer, the power of this magic over the dæmons would be lost.[1] But this effect of fear is, after all, not the only one nor even the most potent. Why is it that the Merovingian period shows not the slightest trace of that glowing inwardness and longing to sink into the metaphysical that suffuses the Magian seed-time of Apocalyptic and the closely analogous period of the Holy Synod (1721–1917) in Russia? What was it that from Peter the Great's time on led all those martyr-sects of the Raskolniki to celibacy, poverty, pilgrimage, self-mutilation, and asceticism in its most fearful forms, and in the seventeenth century had driven thousands, in religious frenzy, to throw themselves *en masse* into the flames? The doctrines of the Chlysti, with their "Russian Christs" (of whom seven are counted so far); the Dukhobors with their Book of Life, which they use as their Bible and hold to contain psalms of Jesus orally transmitted; the Skoptsi with their ghastly mutilation-precepts — manifestations, one and all, of something without which Tolstoi, Nihilism, and the political revolutions are incomprehensible [2] — how is it that in comparison the Frankish period seems so dull and shallow? Is it that only Aramæans and Russians possess religious genius — and, if so, what have we to expect of the Russia that is to come, now that (just in the decisive centuries) the obstacle of scholarly orthodoxy has been destroyed?

III

Primitive religions have something homeless about them, like the clouds and the wind. The mass-souls of the proto-peoples have accidentally and fugitively condensed into *one* being, and accidental, therefore, is and remains the "where" — which is an "anywhere" — of the linkages of waking-consciousness arising from the fear and defensiveness that spread over them. Whether they stay or move on, whether they alter or not, is immaterial so far as concerns their inward significance.

From life of this order the high Cultures are separated by a deep soil-boundness. Here there is a mother-landscape behind all expression-forms, and just as the State, as temple and pyramid and cathedral, *must* fulfil their history *there* where their idea originated, so too the great religion of every Springtime is

---

[1] For an account of Russian sectarian movements see A. P. Stanley, *Hist. of the Eastern Church;* for a summary, *Ency. Brit.*, XI ed., Vol. XXIII, p. 886. — *Tr.*

[2] Kattenbusch, *Lehrb. d. vgl. Konfessionsk.*, I (1892), pp. 234, et seq.; N. P. Milyukov, *Skizz. russ. Kulturg.* (1901) II, pp. 104, et seq.

bound by all the roots of its being to the land over which its world-image has risen. Sacral practices and dogmas may be carried far and wide, but their inner evolution stays spellbound in the place of their birth. It is simply an impossibility that the slightest trace of evolution of Classical city-cults should be found in Gaul, or a dogmatic advance of Faustian Christianity in America. Whatever disconnects itself from the land becomes rigid and hard.

It begins, in every case, like a great cry. The dull confusedness of terror and defence suddenly passes into a pure awakening of inwardness that blossoms up, wholly plantwise, from mother earth, and sees and comprehends the depth of the light-world with *one* outlook. Wherever introspectiveness exists as a living sense, this change is felt and welcomed as an inward rebirth. In this moment — never earlier, and never (at least with the same deep intensity) later — it traverses the chosen spirits of the time like a grand light, which dissolves all fear in blissful love and lets the invisible appear, all suddenly, in a metaphysical radiance.

Every Culture actualizes here its prime symbol. Each has its own sort of love — we may call it heavenly or metaphysical as we choose — with which it contemplates, comprehends, and takes into itself its godhead, and which remains to every other Culture inaccessible or unmeaning. Whether the world be something set under a domed light-cavern, as it was for Jesus and his companions, or just a vanishingly small bit of a star-filled infinity, as Giordano Bruno felt it; whether the Orphics take their bodily god into themselves, or the spirit of Plotinus, soaring in ecstasy, fuses in henosis with the spirit of God, or St. Bernard in his "mystic union" becomes one with the operation of infinite deity — the deep urge of the soul is governed always by the prime symbol of the particular Culture and of no other.

In the Vth Dynasty of Egypt (2680–2540), which followed that of the great pyramid-builders, the cult of the Horus-falcon, whose *ka* dwelt in the reigning monarch, faded. The old local cults and even the profound Thot religion of Hermopolis fell into the background. The sun-religion of Re appears. Out from his palace westward every king erects a Re-sanctuary by his tomb-temple, the latter a symbol of a life directional from birth to sarcophagus-chamber, the former a symbol of grand and eternal nature. Time and Space, being and waking-being, Destiny and sacred Causality are set face to face in this mighty twin-creation as in no other architecture in the world. To both a covered way leads up; that to the Re is accompanied by reliefs figuring the power of the sun-god over the plant and animal worlds and the changings of seasons. No god-image, no temple, but only an altar of alabaster adorns the mighty terrace on which at day-break, high above the land, the Pharaoh advances out of the darkness to greet the great god who is rising up in the East.[1]

---

[1] Borchardt, *Reheiligtum des Newoserrê*, I (1905). The Pharaoh is no longer an incarnation of godhead, and not yet, as the theology of the Middle Kingdom was to make him, the son of Re; notwithstanding all earthly greatness, he is small, a servant, as he stands before the god.

This youthful inwardness proceeds always out of a townless country-side, out of villages, hovels, sactuaries, solitary cloisters, and hermitages. Here is formed the community of high awareness, of the spiritual elect, which inwardly is separated by a whole world from the great being-currents of the heroic and the knightly. The two prime estates, priesthood and nobility — contemplation in the cathedral and deeds before the castles, askesis and *Minne*, ecstasy and high-bred custom — begin their special histories from this point. Though the Caliph was also worldly ruler of the faithful, though the Pharaoh sacrificed in both holy places, though the German King built his family vault under the cathedral, nothing gets rid of the abyssal opposition of Time and Space that is reflected in the contrast of these two social orders. Religious history and political history, the histories of truths and facts, stand opposed and irreconcilable. Their opposition begins in cathedral and castle, it propagates itself in the ever-growing towns as the opposition of wisdom and business, and in the last stages of historical capacity it closes as a wrestle of intellect and power.

But both these movements take place on the *heights* of humanity. Peasantdom remains historyless under it all, comprehending politics as little as it understands dogmatics. Out of the strong young religion of saintly groups, scholasticism and mysticism develop in the early towns; reformation, philosophy, and worldly learning in the increasing tumult of streets and squares; enlightenment and irreligion in the stone masses of the late megalopolis. The beliefs of the peasant outside remain "eternal" and always the same. The Egyptian hind understood nothing of this Re. He heard the name, but while a grand chapter of religious history was passing over his head in the cities, he went on worshipping the old Thinite beast-gods, until with the XXVIth Dynasty and its fellah-religion they regained supremacy. The Italian peasant prayed in Augustus's time just as he had done long before Homer and as he does to-day. Names and dogmas of big religions, blossoming and dying in turn, have penetrated to him from the towns and have altered the sounds of his words — but the meaning remains ever the same. The French peasant lives still in the Merovingian Age. Freya or Mary, Druids or Dominicans, Rome or Geneva — nothing touches the innermost kernel of his beliefs.

But even in the towns one stratum hangs back, historically, relatively to another. Over the primitive religion of the country-side there is another popular religion, that of the small people in the underground of the towns and in the provinces. The higher a Culture rises — Middle Kingdom, Brahman period, Pre-Socratics, Pre-Confucians, Baroque — the narrower becomes the circle of those who possess the final truths of their time as reality and not as mere name and sound. How many of those who lived with Socrates, Augustine, and Pascal understood them? In religion as otherwise the human pyramid rises with increasing sharpness, till at the end of the Culture it is complete — thereafter, bit by bit, to crumble.

About 3000 in Egypt and Babylon two great religions began their life-courses. In Egypt the "reformation" period at the end of the Old Kingdom saw solar monotheism firmly founded as the religion of priests and educated persons. All other gods and goddesses — whom the peasantry and the humble people continued to worship in their fomer meaning — are now only in-carnations or servants of the one Re. Even the particular religion of Hermop-olis, with its cosmology, was adapted to the grand system, and a theological negotiation brought even the Ptah of Memphis into harmony with dogma as an abstract prime-principle of creation.[1] Exactly as in the times of Justinian and Charles V, the city-spirit asserted mastery over the soul of the land; the formative power of the Springtime had come to an end; the dogma was es-sentially complete, and its subsequent treatment by rational processes took down more of the structure than it improved. Philosophy began. In respect of dogma, the Middle Kingdom was as unimportant as the Baroque.

From 1500 three new religious histories begin — first the Vedic in the Punjab, then the Early Chinese in the Hwang-ho, and lastly the Classical on the north of the Ægean Sea. Distinctly as the Classical man's world-picture and his prime symbol of the unit body is presented to us, it is difficult even to guess the details of the great Early Classical religion. For this lacuna we have to thank the Homeric poems, which hinder rather than help us in compre-hending it. The new notion of godhead that was the special ideal of this Culture is the human-formed body in the light, the hero as mediator between man and god — so much, at any rate, the Iliad evidences. This body might be light-transfigured by Apollo or disjected to the winds by Dionysus, but in every case it was the basic form of Being. The σῶμα as ideal of the extended, the cosmos as sum of these unit bodies, "Being" and "the one" as the extended-in-itself and "Logos"[2] as the order thereof in the light — all this came up before the eyes of priest-men, grandly visible and having the full force of a new religion.

But the Homeric poetry is purely aristocratic. Of the two worlds — that of the noble and that of the priest, that of Totem and that of Taboo, that of heroism and that of sanctity — only the one is here living. It not only does not understand, but actually despises, the other. As in the Edda, so in Homer, it is the greatest glory of an immortal to know the way and code of nobility. The thinkers of the Classical Baroque, from Xenophanes to Plato, regarded these scenes of god-life as impudent and trivial, and they were right; they felt exactly as the theology and philosophy of the later West felt about the Germanic hero-sagas and even about Gottfried of Strassburg, Wolfram, and Walther. If the Homeric epics did not vanish as the hero-songs collected by Charlemagne vanished, it was only because there was no fully formed Classical

---

[1] Erman, "*Ein Denkmal memphitsiche Theologie,*" *Ber. Berl. Ak.* (1911), pp. 916, et seq.

[2] Not, of course, to be connected in any profound sense with that which emerged under the name in the Magian Culture. — *Tr.*

priesthood, with the result that the Classical cities, when they arose, were intellectually dominated by a knightly and not a religious literature. The original doctrines of this religion, which out of opposition to Homer linked themselves with the (probably) still older name of Orpheus, were never written down.

All the same, they existed. Who knows what and how much is hidden behind the figures of Calchas and Tiresias? A mighty upheaval there must have been at the beginning of this Culture, as at that of others — an upheaval extending from the Ægean Sea as far as Etruria — but the Iliad shows as few signs of it as the lays of the Nibelungs and of Roland show of the inwardness and mysticism of Joachim of Floris, St. Francis, and the Crusades, or of the inner fire of that *Dies Iræ* of Thomas of Celano, which would probably have excited mirth at a thirteenth-century court of love. Great personalities there must have been to give a mystical-metaphysical form to the new world-outlook, but we know nothing of them and it is only the gay, bright, easy side of it that passed into the song of knightly halls. Was the "Trojan War" a feud, or was it also a Crusade? What is the meaning of Helen? Even the Fall of Jerusalem has been looked at from a worldly point of view as well as from a spiritual.

In the nobles' poetry of Homer, Dionysus and Demeter, as priests' gods, are unhonoured.[1] But even in Hesiod, the herdsman of Ascra, the enthusiast-searcher inspired by his folk-beliefs, the ideas of the great early time are not to be found pure, any more than in Jakob Böhme the cobbler.[2] That is the second difficulty. *The great early religions, too, were the possession of a class*, and neither accessible to nor understandable by the generality; the mysticism of earliest Gothic, too, was confined to small elect circles, sealed by Latin and the difficulty of its concepts and figures, and neither nobility nor peasantry had any distinct idea of its existence. And excavation, therefore, important as it is in respect of the Classical country-faiths, can tell us as little about the Early Classical *religion* as a village church can tell us about Abelard or Bonaventura.

But Æschylus and Pindar, at any rate, were under the spell of a great priestly tradition, and before them there were the Pythagoreans, who made the Demeter-cult their centre (thereby indicating where the kernel of that mythology is to be sought), and earlier still were the Eleusinian Mysteries and the Orphic reformation of the seventh century; and, finally, there are the fragments of Pherecydes and Epimenides, who were not the first *but the last* dogmatists of a theology in reality ancient. The idea that impiety was a heritable sin, visited upon the children and the children's children, was known to Hesiod and Solon, as well as the doctrine (Apollinian also) of "Hybris."[3] Plato, however, as an

---

[1] And because they were the gods of the eternal peasant, they outlived the Olympians.

[2] Even though Hesiod is two centuries nearer to the source of his Culture than the German mystic is to that of our own. See the article "Boehme," *Ency. Brit.*, XI ed. — *Tr.*

[3] Insolent prosperity tempting Nemesis. — *Tr.*

Orphic opponent of the Homeric conception of life, sets forth very ancient doctrines of hell and the judgment of the dead in his *Phædo*. We know the tremendous formula of Orphism, the Nay of the mysteries that answered the Yea of the agon, which arose, certainly by 1100 at latest, as a protest of Waking-Consciousness against Being — σῶμα σῆμα, that splendid Classical body a grave! Here man is no longer *feeling* himself as a thing of breeding, strength, and movement; he *knows* himself and is terrified by what he knows.   Here begins the Classical askesis, which by strictest rites and expiations, even by voluntary suicide, seeks deliverance from this Euclidean body-being.   It is an entirely erroneous interpretation of the Pre-Socratics to suppose that it was from the view-point of enlightenment that they spoke against Homer.   It was as *ascetics* that they did so.   These "contemporaries" of Descartes and Leibniz were brought up in the strict traditions of the old great Orphism, which were as faithfully preserved in the almost claustral meditation-schools — old and famous holy places — as Gothic Scholasticism was treasured in the wholly intellectual universities of the Baroque.   From the self-immolation of Empedocles the line runs straight forward to the suicide of the Roman Stoic, and straight back to "Orpheus."

Out of these last surviving traces, however, an outline of the Early Classical religion emerges bright and distinct.   Just as all Gothic inwardness directed itself upon Mary, Queen of Heaven and Virgin and Mother, so in that moment of the Classical World there arose a garland of myths, images, and figures around Demeter, the bearing mother, around Gaia and Persephone, and also Dionysus the begetter, chthonian [1] and phallic cults, festivals and mysteries of birth and death.   All this, too, was characteristically Classical, conceived under the aspect of present corporeality.   The Apollinian religion venerated body, the Orphic rejected it, that of Demeter celebrated the moments of fertilization and birth, in which body acquired being.   There was a mysticism that reverently honoured the secret of life, in doctrine, symbol, and mime, but side by side with it there was orgiasm too, for the squandering of the body is as deeply and closely akin to asceticism as sacred prostitution is to celibacy — both, all, are negations of time.   It is the reverse of the Apollinian "halt!" that checks on the threshold of Hybris; detachment is not kept, but flung away.   He who has experienced these things in his soul has "from being a mortal become a god." In those days there must have been great saints and seers who towered as far above the figures of Heraclitus and Empedocles as the latter above the itinerant teachers of Cynicism and Stoicism — things of this order do not happen name-lessly and impersonally.   As the songs of Achilles and Odysseus were dying down everywhere, a grand, strict doctrine arose at the famous old cult-places, a mysticism and scholasticism with developed educational methods and a secret

---

[1] The work of J. J. Bachofen in this field has recently been assembled in concentrated form under the title *Mythus von Occident und Orient* (1926). — *Tr.*

oral tradition, as in India. But all that is buried, and the relics of the later times barely suffice to prove that it once existed.

By putting the knightly poetry and folk-cults quite aside, then, we can even now determine something more of this (*the*) Classical religion. But in doing so there is a third pitfall to be avoided — the opposing of Greek religion to Roman religion. For in reality there was no such opposition.

Rome is only *one* of innumerable city-states that arose during the great epoch of colonization. It was built by Etruscans. From the religious point of view it was re-created under the Etruscan dynasty of the sixth century, and it is possible indeed that the Capitoline group of deities, Jupiter, Juno, Minerva — which at that time replaced the ancient trinity, Jupiter, Mars, Quirinus, of the "Numa" religion — was in some way connected with the family cult of the Tarquins, in which case Minerva, as goddess of the city, is unmistakably a copy of Athene Polias.[1] The cults of this single city are properly comparable only with those of *individual* Greek-speaking cities of the same degree of maturity, say Sparta or Thebes, which were in nowise more colourful. The little that in these latter discloses itself as generally Hellenic will also prove to be generally Italian. And as for the claim that the "Roman" religion is distinguished from that of the Greek city-states by the absence of myth — what is the basis of our knowledge on the point? We should know nothing at all of the great god-sagas of the Springtime if we had only the festival-calendar and the public cults of the Greek city-states to go upon, just as we should learn nothing of Jesus's piety from the proceedings of the Council of Ephesus or of that of St. Francis from a church constitution of the Reformation. Menelaus and Helen were for the Laconian state-cult tree-deities and nothing more. The Classical myth derives from a period when the Poleis with their festivals and sacral constitutions were not yet in existence, when there was not only no Rome, but no Athens. With the religious duties and notions of the cities — which were eminently rational — it has no connexion at all. Indeed, myth and cult are even less in touch with one another in the Classical Culture than in others. The myth, moreover, is in no way a creation of the Hellenic culture-field as a whole — it is not "Greek" — but originated (like the stories of Jesus's childhood and the Grail legend) in this and that group, quite local, under pressure of deep inward stirrings. For instance, the idea of Olympus arose in Thessaly and thence, as a common property of *all* educated persons, spread out to Cyprus and to Etruria, thus, of course, involving Rome. Etruscan painting presupposes it as a thing of common knowledge, and therefore the Tarquins and their

---

[1] Wissowa, *Religion und Kultus der Römer*, p. 41. What has been said above (p. 191) concerning the Talmudic religion applies also to the Etruscan religion by which all Italy — i.e., no less than half of the Classical field — was so deeply influenced. It lies outside the province of both the conventional "Classical" philologies and in consequence has been practically ignored, as compared with the Achæan and Doric religions. In reality (as its tombs, temples, and myths prove), it forms with them a single unit of spirit and evolution.

court must have been familiar with it. We may attach any implications we please to "belief" (whatever that may mean) in this myth; the point is that they will be as valid for Romans of the period of the Kings as for the inhabitants of Tegea or Corcyra.

That the pictures of Greek and Roman mythology that modern research has developed are quite different from this is the result not of the facts, but of the *methods*. In the case of Rome (Mommsen) the festal calendar and the State cults, in that of Greece the poetic literature, were taken as the starting-points. Apply the "Latin" method which has led up to Wissowa's picture to the Greek cities, and the result is a wholly similar picture, as, for example, in Nilsson's *Griechische Festen.*

When this is taken into consideration, the Classical religion is seen to be a whole possessing an inner unity. The grand god-legends of the eleventh century, which have the dew of Spring upon them, and in their tragic holiness remind us of Gethsemane, Balder's death, and Francis, are the purest essence of "theoria," contemplation, a world-picture before the inner eye, and born of the common inward awakening of a group of chosen souls from the world of chivalry.[1] But the much later city-religions are wholly *technique*, formal worship, and as such represent only one side (and a different side) of piety. They are as far from the great myth as they are from the folk-belief. They are concerned neither with metaphysic nor with ethic, but only with the fulfilment of sacral acts. And, finally, the choice of cults by the several cities very often originated, not, like the myth, from a single world-view, but from the accidental ancestor- and family-cults of great houses, which (precisely as in the Gothic) made their sacred figures the tutelary deities of the city and at the same time reserved to themselves the rights of celebrating and worshipping them. In Rome, for example, the Lupercalia in honour of the field-god Faunus were a privilege of the Quinctii and Fabii.

The Chinese religion, of which the great "Gothic" period lies between 1300 and 1100 and covers the rise of the Chóu dynasty, must be treated with extreme care. In presence of the superficial profundity and pedantic enthusiasm of Chinese thinkers of the Confucius and Lao-tse type — who were all born in the *ancien régime* period of their state-world — it seems very hazardous to try to determine anything at all as to high mysticism and grand legends in the beginning. Nevertheless, such a mysticism and such legends must once have existed. But it is not from these over-rationalized philosophies of the great cities that we shall learn anything about them — as little as Homer can give us in the Classical parallel, though for another reason. What should we know

[1] It is immaterial whether or not Dionysus was "borrowed" from Thrace, Apollo from Asia Minor, Aphrodite from Phœnicia. It is the fact that out of the thousands of alien motives these particular few were chosen and combined in so splendid a unity that implies the fundamental newness of the creation — just as does the Mary-cult of the Gothic, although in that case the whole form-material was taken over from the East.

about Gothic piety if all its works had undergone the censorship of Puritans and Retioralists like Locke, Rousseau, and Wolff! And yet we treat the Confucian *close* of Chinese inwardness as its beginning — if, indeed, we do not go farther and describe the syncretism of Han times as "the" religion of China.[1]

We know nowadays that, contrary to the usual assumption, there was a powerful old-Chinese priesthood.[2] We know that in the text of the Shu-Ching, relics of the ancient hero-sagas and god-myths were worked over rationalistically, and were thus able to survive, and similarly the Hou-li, Ngi-li, and Shi-King[3] would still reveal a good deal more if only they were attacked with the conviction that there was in them something far deeper than Confucius and his like were capable of comprehending. We hear of chthonian and phallic cults in early Chóu times; of orgiastic rites in which the service of the gods was accompanied by ecstatic mass-dances; of mimic representations and dialogues between god and priestess, out of which probably (as in Greece) the Chinese drama evolved.[4] And we obtain an inkling finally of why the luxuriant growth of early Chinese god-figures and myths was necessarily swallowed up in an emperor-mythology. For not only all saga-emperors, but also most of the figures of the Hia and Shang dynasties before 1400 are — all dates and chronicles notwithstanding — nothing but nature transformed into history. The origins of such a process lie deep in the possibilities of every young Culture.[5] Ancestor-worship ever seeks to gain power over the nature-dæmons. All Homeric heroes, and Minos and Theseus and Romulus, are gods become kings. In the *Heliand*,[6] Christ is about to become so. Mary is the crowned Queen of Heaven. It is the supreme (and perfectly unconscious) mode which enables men of breeding to venerate something — that is, for them, what is great must have breeding, race, must be mighty and lordly, the ancestor of whole families. A strong priesthood is able to make short work of this mythology of Time, but it won through partially in the Classical and completely in China — exactly in proportion to the disappearance of the priestly element. The old gods are now emperors, princes, ministers, and retainers; natural events have become acts of rulers, and onsets of peoples social enterprises. Nothing could have suited the Confucians better. Here was a myth which could absorb social-ethical tendencies to an indefinite ex-

---

[1] As in De Groot's *Universismus* (1918), where, in fact, the systems of Taoists, Confucians, and Buddhists are handled without a qualm as *the* religions of China. This amounts to the same as saying that the Classical religion dates from Caracalla.

[2] Conrady, in Wassiljew, *Die Erschliessung Chinas* (1909), p. 232; B. Schindler, *Das Priestertum im alten China*, I (1919).

[3] The Shu-Ching or Canon of History is a collection of ancient annals, the Shi-King a canonical anthology of rhymed tales made by Confucius. — *Tr.*

[4] Conrady, *China*, p. 516.

[5] Of which an outstanding example is the Edda. — *Tr.*

[6] See article "Heliand" in *Ency. Brit.*, XI edit., and works there referred to. A handy edition of the text is included in the "Reclam" series. — *Tr.*

tent, and all that was necessary was to expunge the traces of the original nature-myth.

To the Chinese waking-consciousness heaven and earth were halves of the macrocosm, without opposition, each a mirror-image of the other. In this picture there was neither Magian dualism nor Faustian unity of active force. Becoming appears in the unconstrained reciprocal working of two principles, the *yang* and the *yin*, which were conceived rather as periodic than as polar. Accordingly, there are two souls in man, the *kwei* which corresponded with the *yin*, the earthly, the dark, the cold, and disintegrated with the body; and the *sen*, which is higher, light, and permanent.[1] But, further, there are in-numerable multitudes of souls of both kinds outside man. Troops of spirits fill the air and the water and the earth — all is peopled and moved by *kweis* and *sens*. The life of nature and that of man are in reality made out of the play of such units. Wisdom, will, force, and virtue depend on their relationship. Asceticism and orgiasm; the knightly custom of *hiao*, which requires the noble to revenge an impiety towards an ancestor even after centuries, and commands him never to survive defeat;[2] and the reasoning moral of the *yen*, which, according to the judgment of rationalism, followed from knowledge — all proceed from conceptions of the forces and possibilities of the *kwei* and the *sen*.

All this is concentrated in the basic word "*tao*." The conflict between the *yang* and the *yin* in man is the *tao* of his life; the warp and woof of the spirit-swarms outside him are the *tao* of Nature. The world possesses *tao* inasmuch as it possesses beat, rhythm, and periodicity. It possesses *li*, tension, inasmuch as man knows it and abstracts from it fixed relationships for future use. Time, Destiny, Direction, Race, History — all this, contemplated with the great world-embracing vision of the early Chóu times, lies in this one word. The path of the Pharaoh through the dark alley to his shrine is related to it, and so is the Faustian passion of the third dimension, but *tao* is nevertheless far re-moved from any idea of the technical conquest of Nature. The Chinese park avoids energetic perspective. It lays horizon behind horizon and, instead of pointing to a goal, tempts to wander. The Chinese "cathedral" of the early time, the Pi-Yung, with its paths that lead through gates and thickets, stairs and bridges and courts, has never the inexorable march of Egypt or the drive into depth of the Gothic.

When Alexander appeared on the Indus, the piety of these three Cultures — Chinese, Indian, Classical — had long been moulded into the historyless forms of a broad Taoism, Buddhism, and Stoicism. But it was not long before the group of Magian religions arose in the region intermediate between the Classical and the Indian field, and it must have been at about the same time that the

---

[1] This idea differs essentially from that of the Egyptian duality of the spiritual *ka* and the soul-bird *bai*, and still more so from the Magian duality of soul-substances.

[2] O. Franke, *Studien für d. Gesch. der Konfuzianischen Dogmas* (1920), p. 202.

religious history of the Maya and Inca, now hopelessly lost to us, began. A thousand years later, when here also all was inwardly fulfilled and done with, there appeared on the unpromising soil of France, sudden and swiftly mounting, Germanic-Catholic Christianity. It was in this case as in every other; whether the whole stock of names and practices came from the East, or whether thousands of particular details were derived from primeval Germanic and Celtic feelings, the Gothic religion is something so new and unheard-of, something of which the final depths are so completely incomprehensible by anyone outside its faith, that to contrive linkages for them on the historical surface is meaningless jugglery.

The mythic world that thereupon formed itself around this young soul, an integer of force, will, and direction seen under the symbol of Infinity, a stupendous action-into-distance, chasms of terror and of bliss suddenly opening up — it was all, for the elect of this early religiousness, something so entirely natural that they could not even detach themselves sufficiently to "know" it as a unit. They lived in it. To us, on the contrary, who are separated from these ancestors by thirty generations, this world seems so alien and overpowering that we always seek to grasp it in detail, and so misunderstand its wholeness and undividedness.

The father-godhead men felt as Force itself, eternal, grand, and ever-present activity, sacred causality, which could scarcely assume any form comprehensible by human eyes. But the whole longing of the young breed, the whole desire of this strongly coursing blood, to bow itself in humility before the *meaning of the blood* found its expression in the figure of the Virgin and Mother Mary, whose crowning in the heavens was one of the earliest motives of the Gothic art. She is a light-figure, in white, blue, and gold, surrounded by the heavenly hosts. She leans over the new-born Child; she fells the sword in her heart; she stands at the foot of the cross; she holds the corpse of the dead Son. From the turn of the tenth century on, Petrus Damiani and Bernard of Clairvaux developed her cult; there arose the Ave Maria and the angelic greeting and later, among the Dominicans, the crown of roses. Countless legends gathered round her figure.[1] She is the guardian of the Church's store of Grace, the Great Intercessor. Among the Franciscans arose the festival of the Visitation, amongst the English Benedictines (even before 1100) that of the Immaculate Conception, which elevated her completely above mortal humanity into the world of light.

But this world of purity, light, and utter beauty of soul would have been unimaginable without the counter-idea, inseparable from it, an idea that constitutes one of the maxima of Gothic, one of its unfathomable creations — one that the present day forgets, and *deliberately* forgets. While she there sits enthroned, smiling in her beauty and tenderness, there lies in the background another world that throughout nature and throughout mankind weaves and

---

[1] Reference may again be made to Yrjo Hirn, *The Sacred Shrine.* — Tr.

breeds ill, pierces, destroys, seduces — namely, the realm of the Devil. It penetrates the whole of Creation, it lies ambushed everywhere. All around is an army of goblins, night-spirits, witches, werewolves, all in human shape. No man knows whether or not his neighbour has signed himself away to the Evil One. No one can say of an unfolding child that it is not already a devil's temptress. An appalling fear, such as is perhaps only paralleled in the early spring of Egypt, weighs upon man. Every moment he may stumble into the abyss. There were black magic, and devils' masses and witches' sabbaths, night feasts on mountain-tops, magic draughts and charm-formulæ. The Prince of Hell, with his relatives — mother and grandmother, for as his very existence denies and scorns the sacrament of marriage, he may not have wife or child — his fallen angels and his uncanny henchmen, is one of the most tremendous creations in all religious history. The Germanic Loki is hardly more than a preliminary hint of him. Their grotesque figures, with horns, claws, and horses' hoofs, were already fully formed in the mystery plays of the eleventh century; everywhere the artist's fancy abounded in them, and, right up to Dürer and Grünewald, Gothic painting is unthinkable without them. The Devil is sly, malignant, malicious, but yet in the end the powers of light dupe him. He and his brood, bad-tempered, coarse, fiendishly inventive, are of a monstrous imaginativeness, incarnations of hellish laughter opposed to the illumined smile of the Queen of Heaven, but incarnations, too, of Faustian world-humour [1] opposed to the panic of the sinner's contrition.

It is not possible to exaggerate either the grandeur of this forceful, insistent picture or the depth of sincerity with which it was believed in. The Mary-myths and the Devil-myth formed themselves side by side, neither possible without the other. Disbelief in either of them was deadly sin. There was a Mary-cult of prayer, and a Devil-cult of spells and exorcisms. Man walked continuously on the thin crust of the bottomless pit. Life in this world is a ceaseless and desperate contest with the Devil, into which every individual plunges as a member of the Church Militant, to do battle for himself and to win his knight's spurs. The Church Triumphant of angels and saints in their glory looks down from on high, and heavenly Grace is the warrior's shield in the battle. Mary is the protectress to whose bosom he can fly to be comforted, and the high lady who awards the prizes of valour. Both worlds have their legends, their art, their scholasticism, and their mysticism — for the Devil, too, can work miracles. Characteristic of this alone among the religious Springtimes is the symbolism of *colour* — to the Madonna belong white and blue, to the Devil black, sulphur-yellow, and red. The saints and angels float in the æther, but the devils leap and crouch and the witches rustle through the night. It is the two together, light and night, which fill Gothic art with its indescrib-

---

[1] Consider, for example, the fantastic paintings of Hieronymus Bosch. Breughel's similar humour, too, is unthinkable without the tradition of a rank-and-file of evil creatures. — *Tr.*

able inwardness — that, and not any "artistic" fancifulness. Every man knew the world to be peopled with angel and devil troops. The light-encircled angels of Fra Angelico and the early Rhenish masters, and the grimacing things on the portals of the great cathedrals, *really* filled the air. Men saw them, felt their presence everywhere. To-day we simply no longer know what a myth is; for it is no mere æsthetically pleasing mode of representing something to oneself, but a piece of the most lively actuality that mines every corner of the waking-consciousness and shakes the innermost structure of being. These creatures were about one all the time. They were glimpsed without being seen. They were believed in with a faith that felt the very thought of proof as a desecration. What we call myth nowadays, our littérateur's and connoisseur's taste for Gothic colour, is nothing but Alexandrinism. In the old days men did not "enjoy" it — behind it stood Death.[1]

For the Devil gained possession of human souls and seduced them into heresy, lechery, and black arts. It was war that was waged against him on earth,[2] and waged with fire and sword upon those who had given themselves up to him. It is easy enough for us to-day to think ourselves out of such notions, but if we eliminate this appalling reality from Gothic, all that remains is mere romanticism. It was not only the love-glowing hymns to Mary, but the cries of countless pyres as well that rose up to heaven. Hard by the Cathedral were the gallows and the wheel. Every man lived in those days in the consciousness of an immense danger, and it was hell, not the hangman, that he feared. Un-numbered thousands of witches genuinely imagined themselves to be so; they denounced themselves, prayed for absolution, and in pure love of truth confessed their night rides and bargains with the Evil One. Inquisitors, in tears and compassion for the fallen wretches, doomed them to the rack in order to save their souls. That is the Gothic myth, out of which came the cathedral, the crusader, the deep and spiritual painting, the mysticism. In its shadow flowered that profound Gothic blissfulness of which to-day we cannot even form an idea.

In Carolingian times, all this was still strange and far. Charlemagne in the first Saxon Capitulary (787) put a ban on the ancient Germanic belief in were-wolves and night-gangers (*striga*), and as late as 1120 it was condemned as an error in the decree of Burkard of Worms. But twenty years later it was only in a dilute form that the anathema reappeared in the *Decretum Gratiani*. Cæsarius of Heisterbach, already, was familiar with the whole devil-legend and in the *Legenda Aurea* it is just as actual and as effective as the Mary-legends. In 1233, when the Cathedrals of Mainz and Speyer were being vaulted, appeared the bull *Vox in Rama*, by which the belief in Devil and witch was made canonical.

[1] So also in the Classical, the Homeric figures were for educated people of Hellenistic times nothing but literature, representation, artistic motive. Even for Plato's period they were little more than this. But in 1100 B.C., Demeter and Dionysus were a fearful actuality before which men collapsed.

[2] The stern object of Roger Bacon's science; see p. 502, foot-note. — *Tr.*

St. Francis's "Hymn to the Sun" had not long been written, and the Franciscans were kneeling in intimate prayer before Mary and spreading her cult afar, when the Dominicans armed themselves for battle with the Devil by setting up the Inquisition. Heavenly love found its focus in the Mary-image, and *eo ipso* earthly love became akin to the Devil. Woman is Sin — so the great ascetics felt, as their fellows of the Classical, of China, and of India had felt. The Devil rules only through woman. The witch is the propagator of deadly sin. It was Thomas Aquinas who evolved the repulsive theory of Incubus and Succuba. Inward mystics like Bonaventura, Albertus Magnus, Duns Scotus, developed a full metaphysic of the devilish.

The Renaissance had ever the strong faith of the Gothic at the back of its world-outlook. When Vasari eulogized Cimabue and Giotto for returning to Nature as their teacher, it was this Gothic nature that he had in mind, a nature influenced in every nook by the encircling troops of angels and devils that stood there, ever threatening, in the light. "Imitation" of Nature meant imitation of its soul, not of its surface. Let us be rid at last of the fable of a renewal of Classical "Antiquity." Renaissance, *Rinascita*, meant then the Gothic uplift from A.D. 1000 onward,[1] the new *Faustian* world-feeling, the new personal experience of *the Ego in the Infinite*. For some individual spirits, no doubt, it meant a sentimental enthusiasm for the Classical (or what was thought to be the Classical), but that was a manifestation of taste, nothing more.[2] The Classical myth was entertainment-material, an allegorical play, through the thin veil of which men saw, no less definitely than before, the old Gothic actuality. When Savonarola stood up, the antique trappings vanished from the surface of Florentine life in an instant. It was all for the church that the Florentines laboured, and with conviction. Raphael was the most deeply intimate of all Madonna-painters. A firm belief in the realm of Satan, and in deliverance from it through the saints, lay at the root of all this art and literature; and every one of them, painters, architects, and humanists — however often the names of Cicero and Virgil, Venus and Apollo were on their lips — looked upon the burning of witches as something entirely natural and wore amulets against the devil. The writings of Marsilius Ficinus are full of learned disquisitions on devils and witches. Francesco della Mirandola wrote (in elegant Latin) his dialogue "The Witch" in order to warn the fine intellects of his circle against a danger.[3] When Leonardo da Vinci, at the summit of the Renaissance,

[1] This is the real conclusion that emerges from Burdach's *Reformation, Renaissance, Humanismus* (1918).

[2] In this connexion, it is important to observe that the education-movement of Humanism took into its field modern Italian, Hebrew, etc., as well as the Classical knowledge. A Dante professorship was founded in Florence in 1373. As for the Classical itself, side by side with all the enthusiasm we find a significant note in Boccaccio, who thanks Jesus Christ for a victory over unbelief that has delivered up the *enemy's camp* to the victor's enjoyment. Burkhardt, *Renaissance*, Vol. I, p. 262 (Reclam edition). — *Tr.*

[3] Bezold, *Hist. Zeitschr.*, 45, p. 208.

was working upon his "Anna Selbdritt,"[1] the "Witches' Hammer" was being written in Rome (1487) in the finest Humanistic Latin. It was *these* that constitute the real myth of the Renaissance, and without them we shall never understand the glorious and truly Gothic force of this anti-Gothic movement.[2] Men who did not feel the Devil very near at hand could not have created the *Divina Commedia* or the frescoes of Orvieto[3] or the ceiling of the Sistine Chapel.

It was the tremendous background of this myth that awakened in the Faustian soul a feeling of what it was. An Ego lost in Infinity, an Ego that was all force, but a force negligibly weak in an infinity of greater forces;[4] that was all will, but a will full of fear for its freedom. Never has the problem of Free-will been meditated upon more deeply or more painfully. Other Cultures have simply not known it. But precisely because here Magian resignation was totally impossible — because that which thought was not an "it" or particle of an all-soul, but an individual, fighting Ego, seeking to maintain itself — every limitation upon freedom was felt as a chain that had to be dragged along through life, and life in turn was felt as a living death. And if so — why? For *what?*

The result of this in-looking was that immense sense of guilt which runs throughout these centuries like one long, desperate lament. The cathedrals rose ever more supplicatingly to heaven, the Gothic vaulting became a joining of hands in prayer, and little comfort of light shone through the high windows into the night of the long naves. The choking parallel-sequences of the church chants, the Latin hymns, tell of bruised knees and flagellations in the nocturnal cell. For Magian man the world-cavern had been close and the heaven impending, but for Gothic man heaven was infinitely far. No hand seemed to reach down from these spaces, and all about the lone Ego the mocking Devil's world lay in leaguer. And, therefore, the great longing of Mysticism was to lose created form (as Heinrich Seuse said), to be rid of self and all things (Meister Eckart), to abandon selfness (*Theologie deutsch*).[5] And out of these longings there grew up an unending dogged subtilizing on notions which were ever more and more finely dissected to get at the "why," and finally a universal cry for Grace — not the Magian Grace coming down as substance, but the Faustian Grace that unbinds the Will.

To be able to will freely is, at the very bottom, the one gift that the Faustian soul asks of heaven. The seven sacraments of the Gothic, felt as one by Peter Lombard, elevated into dogma by the Lateran Council of 1215, and grounded

---

[1] Italian, "Anna Metterza." The reference is to the St. Anne of the Louvre and the Royal Academy Diploma Gallery, London. — *Tr.*

[2] Cf. Vol. I, p. 232. — *Tr.*

[3] Fra Angelico and Luca Signorelli. — *Tr.*

[4] The sense of such a relativity led to a mathematic (the calculus) which is literally based on the ignoring of second- and third-order magnitudes. — *Tr.*

[5] See article "Mysticism" in *Ency. Brit.*, XI ed. — *Tr.*

in mystical foundations by Thomas Aquinas, mean this and only this. They accompany the unit soul from birth to death and protect it against the diabolical powers that seek to nest themselves in its will. For to sell oneself to the Devil means to deliver up *one's will* to him. The Church Militant on earth is the visible community of those who are enabled, by enjoyment of the sacraments, to will. This certainty of free being is held to be guaranteed in the altar-sacrament, which accordingly suffers a complete change of meaning. The miracle of the holy tranformation which takes place daily under the hands of the priest — the consecrated Host in the high altar of the cathedral, wherein the believer sensed the presence of him who of old sacrificed himself to secure for his own the *freedom to will* — called forth a sigh of relief of such depth and sincerity as we moderns can hardly imagine. It was in thanksgiving, therefore, that the chief feast of the Catholic Church, Corpus Christi, was founded in 1264.[1]

But more important still — and by far — was the essentially Faustian prime-sacrament of Contrition. This ranks with the Mary-myth and the Devil-myth as the third great creation of the Gothic. And, indeed, it is from this third that the other two derive depth and meaning; it discloses the last secrets of this Culture's soul, and so sets it apart from all other Cultures. The effect of the Magian baptism was to incorporate a man in the great *consensus* — the *one* great "it" of the divine spirit took up its abode in him as in the others, and thereafter resignation to all that should happen became his duty. But in the Faustian contrition the *idea of personality* was implicit. It is not true that the Renaissance discovered personality[2]; what it did was to bring personality up to a brilliant surface, whereby it suddenly became visible to everyone. Its birth is in Gothic; it is the most intimate and peculiar property of Gothic; it is one and the same with Gothic soul. For this contrition is something that each one accomplishes for himself alone. He alone can search his own conscience. He alone stands rueful in the presence of the Infinite. He alone can and must in confession understand and put into words his own past. And even the absolution that frees his Ego for new responsible action is personal to himself. Baptism is wholly impersonal — one receives it because one is *a* man, not because one is *this* man — but the idea of contrition presupposes that the value of every act depends uniquely upon the man who does it. This is what differentiates the Western drama from the Classical, the Chinese, and the Indian. This is what directs our legislation more and more with reference to the doer rather than to the deed,

---

[1] After its confirmation in 1311, the character of this festival as one of popular joy became still more marked by its association with the nascent drama (see *Ency. Brit.*, XI ed., articles "Corpus Christi," "Drama"; and Y. Hirn, op. cit., pp. 144–5. — *Tr.*

[2] Or even rediscovered it. For Classical man as a spirit-filled body is one amongst many quite independent units, while Faustian man is a centre in the universe, which with its soul embraces *the whole*. But personality (individuality) means, not something separate (*einzelnes*), but something single (*einziges*).

and bases our primary ethical conceptions on individual doing and not typical behaviour. Faustian responsiblity instead of Magian resignedness, the individual instead of the *consensus*; relief from, instead of submissiveness under, burdens — that is the difference between the most active and the most passive of all sacraments, and at the back of it again lies the difference between the world-cavern and infinity-dynamics. Baptism is something done upon one, Contrition something done by oneself within oneself. And, moreover, this conscientious searching of one's own past is both the earliest evidence of, and the finest training for, the *historical sense* of Faustian mankind. There is no other Culture in which the personal life of the living man, the conscientious tracing of each feature, has been so important, for this alone has required the accounts to be rendered in words. If historical research and biography are characteristic of the spirit of the West from its beginnings; if both in the last resort are self-examination and confession; if our lives are led with an assuredness and conscious reference to the historic background that nowhere else has been even imagined as possible or tolerable; if, lastly, we habitually look at history in terms of millennia, not rhapsodically or decoratively as in the Classical World and in China, but directionally and with the almost sacramental formula "*Tout comprendre, c'est tout pardonner*" ever in our minds — we have this sacrament of the Gothic Church, this continual unburdening of the Ego by *historical* test and justification to thank for it. Every confession is an autobiography. This peculiar liberation of the will is to us so necessary that the refusal of absolution drives to despair, even to destruction. Only he who senses the bliss of such an inward acquittal can comprehend the old name of the *sacramentum resurgentium*, the sacrament of those who are risen again.[1]

When in this heaviest of decisions the soul is left to its own resources, something unresolved remains hanging over it like a perpetual cloud. It may be said, therefore, that perhaps no institution in any religion has brought so much happiness into the world as this. The whole inwardness and heavenly love of the Gothic rests upon the certainty of full absolution through the power invested in the priest. In the insecurity that ensued from the decline of this sacrament, both Gothic joy of life and the Mary-world of the light faded out. Only the Devil's world, with its grim all-presentness, remained. And then, in place of the blissfulness irrecoverably lost, came the Protestant, and especially

---

[1] Hence it is that this sacrament has conferred a position of such immense power upon the Western priest. He receives the personal confession, and speaks personally, in the name of the Infinite, the absolution, without which life would be unbearable.

The notion of confession as a *duty*, which was finally established in 1215, first arose in England, whence came also the first confession-books (Penitentials). In England, too, originated, the idea of the Immaculate Conception, and even the *idea* of the Papacy — at a time when Rome itself thought of it as a question of power and precedence. It is evidence of the independence of Faustian Christianity from Magian that its decisive ideas grew up in those remote parts of its field which lay beyond the Frankish Empire.

Puritan, heroism, which could fight on, even hopeless, in a lost position. "Auricular confession," said Goethe once, "ought never to have been taken from mankind." Over the lands in which it had died out, a heavy earnestness spread itself. Ethic and costume, art and thought, took on the night-colour of the only myth that remained outstanding. Nothing is less sunlit than the doctrines of Kant. "Every man his own priest" is a conviction to which men could win through, but only as to that part of priesthood that involves duties, *not as to that which possesses powers*. No man confesses himself with the inward certainty of absolution. And as the need of the soul to be relieved of its past and to be redirected remained urgent as ever, all the higher forms of communication were transmuted, and in Protestant countries music and painting, letter-writing and memoirs, from being modes of description became modes of self-denunciation, penance, and unbounded confession. Even in Catholic regions too — in Paris above all — art as psychology set in as doubt in the sacrament of Contrition and Absolution grew. Outlook on the world was lost in ceaseless mine-warfare within the self. In lieu of the Infinite, contemporaries and descendants were called in to be priests and judges. Personal art, in the sense that distinguishes Goethe from Dante, and Rembrandt from Michelangelo, was a substitute for the sacrament of confession. It was, also, the sign that this Culture was already in the condition of a Late period.[1]

IV

In all Cultures, Reformation has the same meaning — the bringing back of the religion to the purity of its original idea as this manifested itself in the great

---

[1] The immeasurable difference between the Faustian and the Russian souls is disclosed in certain word-sounds. The Russian word for heaven is "*nyebo*," which contains in its *n* a negative element. Western man looks up, the Russian looks horizontally into the broad plain. The death-impulse, too, of the respective souls is distinguishable, in that for the West it is the passion of drive all-ways into infinite space, whereas for Russians it is an expressing and expanding of self (*Sichentäussern*), till "it" in the man becomes identical with the boundless plain itself. It is thus that a Russian understands the words "man" and "brother." He sees even mankind as a plane. The idea of a Russian's being an astronomer! He does not see the stars at all, he sees only the horizon. Instead of the vault he sees the down-hang of the heavens — something that somewhere combines with the plain to form the horizon. For him the Copernican system, be it never so mathematical, is spiritually contemptible.

While our German "*Schicksal*" rings like a trumpet call, "*Sud'bá*" is a genuflection. There is no room for the upstanding "I" beneath this almost flat-roofed heaven. That "*All are responsible for all*" — the "it" for the "it" in this boundlessly extended plain — is the metaphysical fundament of all Dostoyevski's creation. That is why Ivan Karamasov must name himself murderer although another had done the murder. The criminal is the "unfortunate," the "wretch" — it is the utter negation of Faustian personal responsibility. Russian mysticism has nothing of that upstriving inwardness of Gothic, of Rembrandt, of Beethoven, which can swell up to a heaven-storming jubilation — its god is not the azure depth up above. Mystical Russian love is love of the plain, the love of brothers under equal pressure all along the earth, ever along and along; the love of the poor tortured beasts that wander on it, the love of plants — never of birds and clouds and stars. The Russian "*volya*," our "will," means principally non-compulsion, freedom not *for* something but *from* something, and particularly freedom from compulsion to personal doing. Free-will is

centuries of the beginning. In no Culture is this movement missing, whether we know about it, as in the case of Egypt, or not, as in that of China. It means, further, that the city and with it the city-spirit are gradually freeing themselves from the soul of the country-side, setting up in opposition to the latter's all-power and reconsidering the feelings and thoughts of the primitive pre-urban time with reference to its present self. It was Destiny and not intellectual necessities of thought that led, in the Magian and Faustian worlds, to the budding-off of new religions at this point. We know to-day that, under Charles V, Luther was within an ace of becoming the reformer of the whole undivided Church.

For Luther, like all reformers in all Cultures, was not the first, but *the last of a grand succession* which led from the great ascetics of the open land to the city-priest. Reformation is *Gothic*, the accomplishment and the testament thereof. Luther's chorale "*Ein' feste Burg*" does *not* belong to the spiritual lyrism of the Baroque. There rumbles in it still the splendid Latin of the *Dies iræ*. It is the Church Militant's last mighty Satan-song.[1] Luther, like every reformer that had arisen since the year 1000, fought the Church not because it demanded too much, but because it demanded too little. The great stream flows on from Cluny: through Arnold of Brescia, who preached return to Apostolic simplicity and was burned in 1155; through Joachim of Floris, who was the first to use the world "*reformare;*" the spirituals of the Franciscan Order; Jacopone da Todi, revolutionary and singer of the *Stabat Mater*, the knight whom the death of a young wife turned into an ascetic and who tried to overthrow Boniface VIII for governing the Church too slackly; through Wyclif and Hus and Savonarola; to Luther, Karlstadt, Zwingli, Calvin, and — Loyola. The intention of these men, one and all, was not to overcome the Christianity of the Gothic, but to bring it to inward fulfilment. So also with Marcion, Athanasius, the Monophysites, and the Nestorians, who sought in the Councils of Ephesus and Chalcedon to purify the faith and lead it back to its origins.[2] But so also the Orphics of the Classical seventh century were the last and not the first of a series that must have begun even before 1000 B.C. So with the establishment of the Re religion in Egypt at the close of the Old Kingdom, the Egyptian Gothic. It is an ending, not a new beginning, that these

---

seen as a condition in which no one else can command "it," and in which, therefore, one may give way to one's own disposition. "*Geist*," "*esprit*," "spirit," go thus: ⌐; the Russian "*duch*" goes thus: ⌐. What sort of a Christianity will come forth one day from this world-feeling?

[1] "*Und wenn die Welt voll Teufel wär'*
     Und wollten uns verschlingen
     So fürchten wir uns nimmermehr
     Es soll uns doch gelingen."

[2] And, as the secession of a reformed Church necessarily transforms the parent Church, there was a *Magian counter-reformation* also. In the *Decretum Gelasii* (c. 500, Rome) even Clement of Alexandria, Tertullian, and Lactantius, and in the Synod of Byzantium (543) Origen, were declared heretical.

signify. Just so, again, a reform-fulfilment happened in the Vedic religion about the tenth century and was followed by the setting-in of late Brahmanism. And in the ninth century a corresponding epochal point must have occurred in the religious history of China.

However widely the Reformations of the various Cultures may differ amongst themselves, the purpose is the same for all — to bring the faith, which had strayed all too far into the world-as-history and time-secularism ("*Zeitlichkeit*"), back into the realm of Nature, clean waking-consciousness, and pure cause-controlled and cause-pervaded Space; out of the world of economics ("wealth") into that of science ("poverty"), out of patrician and cavalier society (which was also that of Renaissance and Humanism) into that of spirituals and ascetics; and lastly (as significant as it is impossible) out of the political ambitions of vestmented human thoroughbreds into the realm of holy Causality that is not of this world.

In those times the West — and the situation was the same in the other Cultures — divided the *Corpus Christianorum* of the population into the three classes of *status policticus, ecclesiasticus, and œconomicus* (that is, urban), but as the outlook was that of the city and no longer that of the castle and the village, officials and judges belonged to the first-named class, men of learning to the second — and the peasant was forgotten. This is the key to the opposition of the Renaissance and Reformation, which was an opposition of class and not a difference in world-feeling like that of Renaissance and Gothic. Castle-taste and cloister-soul moved into town, and remained there, as before, in opposition — as in Florence the Medici to Savonarola, and as in old Greece the noble families of the cities — with their Homer now finally written down — to the last Orphics — these, too, writers. The Renaissance artists and Humanists are the legitimate successors of the Troubadours and Minnesingers, and just as there is a line from Arnold of Brescia to Luther, so there is a line from Bertrand de Born and Peire Cardinal, through Petrarch, to Ariosto. The castle has become the town-house, the knight the patrician. The whole movement adhered to palaces, as courts; it limits itself to those fields of expression that affect and interest polite society; it is bright and gay, like Homer, because it is courtly — an atmosphere where problems were bad taste, where Dante and Michelangelo cannot but have felt themselves out of place — and it spread over the Alps to the courts of the North, not as a new world-outlook, but as a new taste. The "Northern" Renaissance of the mercantile and capital cities consisted simply in the fact that the *bon ton* of the Italian patriciate replaced that of the French chivalry.

But the last reformers, too, the Luthers and Savonarolas, were *urban* monks, and this differentiates them profoundly from the Joachims and the Bernards. Their intellectual and urban askesis is the stepping-stone from the hermitages of quiet valleys to the scholar's study of the Baroque. The mystic experience of Luther which gave birth to his doctrine of justification is the experience, not of a St. Bernard in the presence of woods and hills and clouds and stars, but of a man who looks through narrow windows on the streets and house walls and gables. Broad God-perfused nature is remote, outside the city wall; and the free intellect, detached from the soil, is inside it. Within the urban, stone-walled waking-consciousness sense and reason part company and become enemies, and the city-mysticism of the last reformers is thus a mysticism of pure reason through and through, and not one of the eye — an illumination of concepts, in presence of which the brightly coloured figures of the old myth fade into paleness.

Necessarily, therefore, it was, in its real depths, a thing of the few. Nothing was left of that sensible content that formerly had offered even to the poorest something to grip. The mighty act of Luther was a purely intellectual decision. Not for nothing has he been regarded as the last great Schoolman of the line of Occam.[1] He completely liberated the Faustian personality — the inter-mediate person of the priest, which had formerly stood between it and the Infinite, was removed. And now it was wholly alone, self-oriented, its own priest and its own judge. But the common people could only feel, not understand, the element of liberation in it all. They welcomed, enthusiastically, indeed, the tearing-up of visible duties, but they did not come to realize that these had been replaced by intellectual duties that were still stricter. Francis of Assisi had given much and taken little, but the urban Reformation took much and, as far as the majority of people were concerned, gave little.

The holy Causality of the Contrition-sacrament Luther replaced by the mystic experience of inward absolution "by faith alone." He came very near to Bernard of Clairvaux in this concept of contrition as lifelong, as a continu-ous intellectual askesis in contrast to the askesis of outward and visible works. Both of them understood absolution as a divine miracle: in so far as the man changes himself, it is God changing him. But what no purely intellectual mysticism can replace is the "Tu" outside, in free nature. The one and the other preached: "Thou must believe that God has forgiven thee," but for Bernard belief was through the powers of the priest elevated to knowledge, whereas for Luther it sank to doubt and desperate insistence. This little "I," detached from the cosmos, nailed up in an individual being and (in the most terrific sense of the word) alone, needed the proximity of a powerful "Thou," and the weaker the intellect, the more urgent the need. Herein lies the ultimate meaning of the Western priest, who from 1215 was elevated above the rest of mankind by the sacrament of ordination and its *character indelebilis:* he was a hand with which even the poorest wretch could grasp God. This *visible* link with the Infinite, Protestantism destroyed. Strong souls could and did win it back for themselves, but for the weaker it was gradually lost. Bernard, al-though for him the inward miracle was successful of itself, would not deprive

---

[1] Boehmer, *Luther im Lichte der neueren Forschung* (1918), pp. 54, et seq.

others of the gentler way, for the very illumination of his soul showed him the Mary-world of living nature, all-pervading, ever near, and ever helpful. Luther, who knew himself only and not men, set postulated heroism in place of actual weakness. For him life was desperate battle against the Devil, and that battle he called upon everyone to fight. And everyone who fought it fought alone.

The Reformation abolished the whole bright and consoling side of the Gothic myth — the cult of Mary, the veneration of the saints, the relics, the pilgrimages, the mass. But the myth of devildom and witchcraft remained, for it was the embodiment and cause of the inner torture, and now that torture at last rose to its supreme horror.[1] Baptism was, for Luther at least, an exorcism, the veritable sacrament of devil-banning. There grew up a large, purely Protestant literature about the Devil.[2] Out of the Gothic wealth of colour, there remained black; of its arts, music, in particular organ-music. But in the place of the mythic light-world, whose helpful nearness the faith of the common people could not, after all, forgo, there rose again out of long-buried depths an element of ancient German myth. It came so stealthily that even to-day its true significance is not yet realized. The expressions "folk-tale" and "popular custom" are inadequate: it is a true Myth that inheres in the firm belief in dwarfs, bogies, nixies, house-sprites, and sweeping clouds of the disembodied, and a true Cult that is seen in the rites, offerings, and conjurings that are still practised with a pious awe. In Germany, at any rate, the Saga took the place, unperceived, of the Mary-myth: Mary was now called Frau Holde, and where once the saints had stood, appeared the faithful Eckart. In the English people what arose was something that has long been designated "Bible-fetishism."

What Luther lacked — and it is an eternal fatality for Germany — was the eye for facts and the power of practical organization. He did not bring his doctrines to a clear system, nor did he lead the great movement and choose its aim. The one and the other were the work of his great successor Calvin. While the Lutheran movement advanced leaderless in central Europe, he viewed his rule in Geneva as the starting-point of a systematic subjection of the world under a Protantism unfalteringly thought out to its logical conclusion. Therefore he, and he alone, became a world-power; therefore it was the decisive struggle between the spirit of Calvin and the spirit of Loyola that dominated, from the Spanish Armada on, the world-politics of the Baroque

---

[1] See, for instance, H. T. Buckle, *Hist. Civilization in England*, Vol. III, ch. iv, for the Scottish outlook, which at times attributed all this horror, not even to an anti-God, but to God himself. "Consider, who is the contriver of these torments. There have been some very exquisite torments contrived by the wit of men . . . but all these fall as far short of the torments ye are to endure as the wisdom of man falls short of that of God. . . . Infinite wisdom has contrived that evil " (*The Great Concern of Salvation*, by T. Halyburton, 1722). — Tr.

[2] M. Osborn, *Die Teufelsliteratur des 16. Jahrh.* (1893).

and the struggle for sea-supremacy. While in mid-Europe Reformation and Counter-Reformation struggled for some small imperial city or a few poor Swiss cantons, Canada, the mouth of the Ganges, the Cape, the Mississippi, were the scenes of great decisions fought to an issue by France and Spain, England and Holland. And in these decisions the two grand organizers of the Late religion of the West were ever present, ever opposed.

V

Intellectual creativeness of the Late period begins, not with, but after, the Reformation. Its most typical creation is free science. Even for Luther learning was still essentially the "handmaid of theology," and Calvin had the free-thinking doctor Servet burnt. The thought of the Springtimes — Faustian like Egyptian, Vedic, and Orphic — had felt its vocation to be the justification of faith by criticism. If criticism did not succeed, the critical method must be wrong. Knowledge was faith justified, not faith controverted.

Now, however, the critical powers of the city intellect have become so great that it is no longer content to affirm, but must test. The stock of believed probables, and especially that part of it which was received by the understanding and not the heart, was the first obvious target for dissecting activities. This distinguishes the Springtime Scholasticism from the actuality-philosophy of the Baroque — as it distinguishes Neoplatonist from Islamic, Vedic from Brahmanic, Orphic from Pre-Socratic, thought. The (shall we say) profane Causality of human life, the world-around, the process and meaning of cognition, become a problem. The Egyptian philosophy of the Middle Kingdom measured up the value of life in *this* sense; and akin to it, in all probability, was the late pre-Confucian philosophy of China from 800 to 500 B.C. Only the book ascribed to Kwan-tse (d. 645) remains to give us some dim idea of this philosophy, but the indications, slight though they be, are that epistemological and biological problems occupied the centre of the one genuine philosophy of China, now utterly lost.

Within Baroque philosophy, Western natural-science stands by itself. No other Culture possesses anything like it, and assuredly it must have been from its beginnings, not a "handmaid of theology," but *the servant of the technical Will-to-Power*, oriented to that end both mathematically and experimentally — from its very foundations a practical *mechanics*. And as it is firstly technique and only secondly theory, it must be as old as Faustian man himself. Accordingly, we find technical works of an astounding energy of combination even by 1000.[1] As early as the thirteenth century Robert Grosseteste [2] was treating space as a function of light. Petrus Peregrinus in 1289 wrote the best experimentally

---

[1] Clocks being an outstanding example. See Vol. I., p. 15, foot-note. — *Tr.*

[2] The famous Bishop of Lincoln (1175–1253), scholar and philosopher, scientist and statesman — the British Oresme. — *Tr.*

based treatise on magnetism that appeared before Gilbert (1600). And Roger
Bacon, the disciple of both, developed a natural-scientific theory of knowledge
to serve as basis for his technical investigations.[1] But boldness in the discovery
of dynamic interlinkages went further still. The Copernican system was hinted
at in a manuscript of 1322 and a few decades later was mathematically developed
by the Paris Occamists, Buridan, Albert of Saxony, and Oresme.[2] Let us not deceive ourselves as to the fundamental motive-power of these explorations. Pure
contemplative philosophy could have dispensed with experiment for ever, but
not so the Faustian symbol of the *machine*, which urged us to mechanical con-
structions even in the twelfth century and made "*Perpetuum mobile*" the
Prometheus-idea of the Western intellect. For us the first thing is ever the
working hypothesis — the very kind of thought-product that is meaningless to
other Cultures. It is an astounding fact (to which, however, we must accustom
ourselves) that the idea of immediately exploiting in practice any knowledge of
natural relations that may be acquired is alien to every sort of mankind except
the Faustian (and those who, like Japanese, Jews, and Russians, have to-day
come under the intellectual spell of its Civilization). The very notion of the
working hypothesis implicitly contains a dynamic lay-out of the universe.
Theoria, contemplative vision of actuality, was for those subtly inquiring
monks only secondary, and, being itself the outcome of the technical passion,
it presently led them, quite imperceptibly, to the typically Faustian conception
of God as the Grand Master of the machine, who could accomplish everything
that they themselves in their impotence only dared to wish. Insensibly the
world of God became, century by century, more and more like the *Perpetuum
mobile*. And, imperceptibly also, as the scanning of nature became sharper and
sharper in the school of experiment and technique, and the Gothic myth became more and more shadowy, the concepts of monkish working hypotheses
developed, from Galileo onwards, into the critically illuminated numina of
modern science, the collisions and the fields, gravitation, the velocity of light,
and the "electricity" which in our electrodynamic world-picture has absorbed
into itself the other forms of energy and thereby attained to a sort of physical
monotheism. They are the concepts that are set up behind the formulæ, to
endow them with a mythic visibility for the inner eye. The numbers themselves
are technical elements, levers and screws, overhearings of the world's secrets.
The Classical Nature-thought — and that of others also — required no numbers,
for it strove for no powers. The *pure* mathematic of Pythagoras and Plato had
no relation whatever to the nature-views of Democritus and Aristotle.

[1] A clear summary of Grosseteste's, Pierre de Maricourt's, and Roger Bacon's work and outlook will be found in Ch. ix of E. Gilson's short manual, *La Philosophie du Moyen Age* (Paris, 1925).
Ency. Brit., XI ed., may also be consulted for Roger Bacon, but the article "Grosseteste" deals almost entirely with the bishop's political and ecclesiastical career. — *Tr.*

[2] M. Baumgartner, *Gesch. der Philos. des Mittelalters* (1915), pp. 425, 571, 620, et seq. [Brief
account in Ch. xi (3) of Gilson's manual above cited. — *Tr.*]

Just as the Classical mind felt Prometheus's defiance of the gods as "hybris," so our Baroque felt the machine as diabolical.[1] The spirit of Hell had betrayed to man the secret of mastering the world-mechanism and even of himself enacting the part of God. And hence it is that all purely priestly natures, that live wholly in the world of the spirit and expect nothing of "this world" — and notably the idealist philosophers, the Classicists, the Humanists, and even Nietzsche — have for technique nothing but silent hostility.

Every Late philosophy contains this critical protest against the uncritical intuitiveness of the Spring. But this criticism of the intellect that is sure of its own superiority affects also faith itself and evokes the one great creation in the field of religion that is the peculiarity of the Late period — every Late period — namely, Puritanism.

Puritanism manifests itself in the army of Cromwell and his Independents, iron, Bible-firm, psalm-singing as they rode into battle; in the ranks of the Pythagoreans, who in the bitter earnest of their gospel of duty wrecked gay Sybaris and branded it for ever as the city without morals; in the armies of the early Caliphs, which subdued not only states, but souls. Milton's *Paradise Lost*, many surahs of the Koran, the little that we know of Pythagorean teachings — all come to the same thing. They are enthusiasms of a sober spirit, cold intensities, dry mysticism, pedantic ecstasy. And yet, even so, a wild piety flickers up once more in them. All the transcendent inwardness that the City can produce after attaining to unconditional mastery over the soul of the Land is here concentrated, with a sort of terror lest it should prove unreal and evanescent, and is correspondingly impatient, pitiless, and unforgiving. Puritanism — not in the West only, but in all Cultures — lacks the smile that had illumined the religion of the Spring — every Spring — the moments of profound joy in life, the humour of life. Nothing of the quiet blissfulness that in the Magian Springtime flashes up so often in the stories of Jesus's childhood, or in Gregory Nazianzen, is to be found in the Koran, nothing in the palpable blitheness of St. Francis's songs in Milton. Deadly earnest broods over the Jansenist mind of Port Royal, over the meetings of the black-clothed Roundheads, by whom Shakespeare's "Merry England" — *Sybaris over again* — was annihilated in a few years. Now for the first time the battle against the Devil, whose bodily nearness they all felt, was fought with a dark and bitter fury. In the seventeenth century more than a million witches were burnt — alike in the Protestant North, the Catholic South, and even the communities in America and India. Joyless and sour are the duty-doctrines of Islam (*fikh*), with its hard intellectuality, and the Westminster Catechisms of 1643, and the Jansenist ethics (Jansen's *Augustinus*, 1640) as well — for in the realm of Loyola, too, there was of inward necessity a Puritan movement. Religion is livingly experienced metaphysic, but the company of the "godly," as the Independents called themselves,

[1] See Ch. XIV below. — *Tr.*

and the Pythagoreans, and the disciples of Mohammed, all alike experienced it, not with the senses, but primarily as a concept. Parshva, who about 600 B.C. founded the sect of the "Unfettered" [1] on the Ganges, taught, like the other Puritans of his time, that salvation came, not from sacrifices and rights, but only from knowledge of the identity of Atman and Brahman. In all Puritan poetry the place of the old Gothic visions is taken by an unbridled, yet withal jejune, spirit of allegory. In the waking-consciousness of these ascetics the concept is the only real power. Pascal's wrestlings were about concepts and not, like Meister Eckart's, about shapes. Witches were burnt because they were proved, and not because they were seen in the air o' nights; the Protestant jurists employed the witches' hammer of the Dominicans because it was built on concepts. The Madonnas of the early Gothic had appeared to their suppliants, but those of Bernini no man ever saw. They exist because they are proved — and there came to be a positive enthusiasm for existence of this sort. Milton, Cromwell's great secretary of state, clothed concepts with shapes, and Bunyan brings a whole mythology of concepts into ethical-allegorical activity. From that it is but a step to Kant, in whose conceptual ethics the Devil assumes his final shape as the Radically Evil.

We have to emancipate ourselves from the surfaces of history — and, especially, to thrust aside the artificial fences in which the methodology of Western sciences has paddocked it — before we can see that Pythagoras, Mohammed, and Cromwell embody one and the same movement in three Cultures.

Pythagoras was not a philosopher. According to all statements of the Pre-Socratics, he was a saint, prophet and founder of a fanatically religious society that forced its truths upon the people around it by every political and military means. The destruction of Sybaris by Croton — an event which, we may be sure, has survived in historical memory only because it was the climax of a wild religious war — was an explosion of the same hate that saw in Charles I and his gay Cavaliers not merely doctrinal error, but also worldly disposition as something that must be destroyed root and branch. A myth purified and conceptually fortified, combined with rigorous ethical precepts, imbued the Pythagoreans with the conviction that they would attain salvation before all other men. The gold tablets found in Thurii and Petelia, which were put into the hand of the dead initiate, carried the assurance of the god: "Happy and blessed one, thou shalt be no more a mortal, but a god." It is the same certainty that the Koran gave to all believers who fought in the holy war against the infidel — "The monasticism of Islam is the religious war," says a hadith of the Prophet — the same which filled Cromwell's Ironsides when they scattered the King's "Philistines" and "Amalekites" at Marston Moor and Naseby.

Islam was no more a religion of the desert in particular than Zwingli's

[1] Nigantha. See *Ency. Brit.*, XI ed., article "Jains." — *Tr.*

faith was a religion of the high mountains in particular. It is incident, and no more, that the Puritan movement for which the Magian world was ripe proceeded from a man of Mecca and not from a Monophysite or a Jew. For in the northern Arabian desert there were the Christian states of the Ghassanids and Lakhmids, and in the Sabæan South there were religious wars waged between Christians and Jews that involved the world of states from Assuan to the Sassanid Empire. The Congress of Princes at Marib [1] was attended by hardly a single pagan, and shortly after this date South Arabia came under Persian — that is, Mazdaist — government. Mecca was a little island of ancient Arabian paganism in the midst of a world of Jews and Christians, a mere relic that had long been mined by the ideas of the great Magian religions. The little of this paganism that filtered into the Koran was later explained away by the Commentary of the Sunna and its Syro-Mesopotamian intellect. At most Islam was a new religion only to the same extent as Lutheranism was one.[2] Actually, it was the prolongation of the great early religions. Equally, its expansion was not (as is even now imagined) a "migration of peoples" proceeding from the Arabian Peninsula, but an onslaught of enthusiastic believers, which like an avalanche bore along with it Christians, Jews, and Mazdaists and set them at once in its front rank as fanatical Moslems. It was Berbers from the homeland of St. Augustine who conquered Spain, and Persians from Irak who drove on to the Oxus. The enemy of yesterday became the front-rank comrade of to-morrow. Most of the "Arabs" who in 717 attacked Constantinople for the first time, had been born Christians. About 650 Byzantine literature [3] quite suddenly vanished, and the deeper meaning of the fact has so far never been noticed — it was just that the Arabian literature took up the tale. The soul of the Magian Culture found at last its true expression in Islam, and therewith became truly the "Arabian," free thenceforth from all bondage to the Pseudo-morphosis. The Iconoclastic movement, led by Islam, but long prepared by Monophysites and Jews, advanced to and even beyond Byzantium, where the Syrian Leo III (717–41) raised this Puritan movement of Islamic-Christian sects — the Paulicians about 650 and the Bogomils later [4] — to predominance.

The great figures of Mohammed's entourage, such as Abu Bekr and Omar, are the near relatives of the Pyms and Hampdens of the English Revolution, and we should see this relationship to be nearer still if we knew more than we do about the Hanifs, the Arabian Puritans before and about the Prophet. All of them had won out of Predestination the guarantee that they were God's

---

[1] 542. See p. 197.

[2] "Mahommedanism must be regarded as an eccentric heretical form of Eastern Christianity. This in fact was the ancient mode of regarding Mahommet. He was considered, not in the light of the founder of a new religion, but rather as one of the chief heresiarchs of the Church. Among them he is placed by Dante in the "Inferno." Dean Stanley, *Eastern Church* (1861), Lecture VIII. — *Tr.*

[3] Krumbacher, *Byzant. Literaturgesch.*, p. 12.

[4] See *Ency. Brit.*, XI ed., under these names. — *Tr.*

elect. The grand Old Testament exaltation of Parliament and the camps of Independency — which left behind it, in many an English family, even to the nineteenth century,[1] the belief that the English are the descendants of the ten Lost Tribes of Israel, a nation of saints predestined to govern the world — dominated also the emigration to America which began with the Pilgrim Fathers of 1620. It formed that which may be called the American religion of to-day, and bred and fostered the trait which gives the Englishman even now his particular political insouciance, an assurance that is essentially religious and has its roots in predestination. The Pythagoreans themselves, too (an unheard-of thing in the religious history of the Classical world) assumed political power for the furtherance of religious ends and sought to advance their puritanism from Polis to Polis. Everywhere else unit cults reigned in unit states, each of which left the other unconcernedly to its own religious duties; here and here only do we find a community of saints, and their practical energy as far surpassed that of the old Orphics as fighting Independency surpassed the spirit of the Reformation wars.

But in Puritanism there is hidden already the seed of Rationalism, and after a few enthusiastic generations have passed, this bursts forth everywhere and makes itself supreme. This is the step from Cromwell to Hume. Not cities in general, not even the great cities, but a few particular cities now become the theatre of intellectual history — Socratic Athens, Abbassid Baghdad, eighteenth-century London and Paris.[2] "Enlightenment" is the cliché of that time. The sun bursts forth — but what is it that clears off the heavens of the critical consciousness to make way for that sun?

Rationalism signifies the belief in the data of critical understanding (that is, of the "reason") *alone*. In the Springtime men could say "*Credo quia absurdum*," because they were certain that the comprehensible and the incomprehensible were *both* necessary constituents of the world — the nature which Giotto painted, in which the Mystics immersed themselves, and into which reason can penetrate, but only so far as the deity permits it to penetrate. But now a secret jealousy breeds the notion of the Irrational — that which, as incomprehensible, is *therefore* valueless. It may be scorned openly as superstition, or privily as metaphysic. Only critically-established understanding possesses value. And secrets are merely evidences of ignorance. The new *secretless* religion is in its highest potentialities called wisdom ($\sigma o \phi \iota a$), its priests philosophers, and its adherents "educated" people. According to Aristotle, the old religion is indispensable only to the uneducated,[3] and his view is Confucius's and Gotama Buddha's, Lessing's and Voltaire's. Men go away from Culture "back to nature," but this nature is not something livingly ex-

---

[1] Not to say the twentieth. — *Tr.*

[2] To which may be added Edinburgh. — *Tr.*

[3] ηρὸς τὴν πειβὼ τῶν ηολλῶν, *Metaphysics* XI, 8, p. 1074 (Bekker) 13. — *Tr.*

perienced, but something proved, something born of, and accessible only to, the intellect — a Nature that has no existence at all for a peasantry, a Nature by which one is not in the least overawed but merely put into a condition of sensibility. Natural religion, rational religion, Deism — all this is not lived metaphysics, but a comprehended mechanics, called by Confucius the "Laws of Heaven" and by Hellenism τυχή. Formerly philosophy was the handmaid of transcendent religiousness, but now comes sensibility, and philosophy must therefore become scientific as epistemology and critique of nature and critique of values. No doubt there was a feeling that this philosophy was, even so, nothing but a diluted dogmatism, for the idea that pure knowledge was *possible* itself involved a belief. Systems were woven out of phenomenally guaranteed beginnings, but in the long run the result was merely to say "Force" instead of "God," and "Conservation of Energy" instead of "Eternity." Under all Classical rationalism is to be found Olympus, under all Western the dogma of the sacraments. And so our Western philosophy swings to and fro between religion and technical science, and is defined thus, or thus, according as the author of the definition is a man with some relic of priesthood still in him, or is a pure expert and technician of thought.

"*Weltansschauung*" is the characteristic expression for an enlightened waking-consciousness that, under the guidance of the critical understanding, looks about it in a godless light-world and, when sense-perceptions are found not to square with sound human reason, treats sense as a "lying jade." That which was once myth — the actualest of the actual — is now subjected to the methods of what is called Euhemerism. The learned Euhemerus, about 300 B.C., "explained" the Classical divinities to the public that they had formerly served so well, and the process occurs under one form or another in every "age of enlightenment." We have our Euhemeristic interpretations of Hell as a guilty conscience, the Devil as evil desire, and God as the beauty of nature, and it is the same tendency that declares itself when Attic tomb-inscriptions of about 400 invoke, not the city-goddess Athene, but a goddess "Demos" — a near relation, by the way, of the Jacobins' Goddess of Reason — and where the δαιμόνιον for Socrates, νοῦς for other philosophers, take the place of Zeus. Confucius says "heaven" instead of "Shang-ti," which means that he believes only in laws of nature. The "collection" and "ordering" of the canonical writings of China by the Confucians was a colossal act of Euhemerism, in which actually almost all the old religious works were literally destroyed and the residue subjected to rationalist falsification. Had it been possible, the enlighteners of our eighteenth century would no doubt have served the Gothic heritage in the same way.[1] Confucius belongs to the Chinese

---

[1] Caliphs like Al Maimun (813–33) and the last Ommayads would have entirely approved of similar measures in Islam. In those times there was a club in Baghdad in which Christians, Jews, Moslems, and Atheists debated, and appeals to the authority of Bible or Koran were "out of order."

"eighteenth century" through and through. Lao-tse (who despised him) stands at a midpoint in the Taoist movement, which manifested traits of Protestantism, Puritanism, and Pietism in turn, and both finally propagated a practical world-tone based upon a wholly mechanistic world-view. The word "*tao*" underwent in the Late period of China just the same continuous alteration of its fundamental content, and in the same mechanistic direction, as the word "Logos" in the history of Classical thought from Heraclitus to Posidonius, and as the word "Force" between Galileo's day and ours. That which once had been grandly moulded myth and cult is called, in this "religion of educated people," *Nature* and *Virtue* — but this Nature is a reasonable mechanism, and this Virtue is knowledge.[1] Confucius and Buddha, Socrates and Rousseau are at one in this. Confucius contains little of prayer or of meditation upon the life after death, and nothing at all of revelation. To busy oneself overmuch with sacrifices and rites stamps one as uneducated and unreasoning. Gotama Buddha and his contemporary Mahavira, the founder of Jainism [2] — both of whom came from the political world of the lower Ganges, east of the old Brahmanic Culture-field — recognized, as everyone knows, neither the idea of God nor myth and cult. Of the real teaching of Buddha little can now be ascertained — for it all appears in the colours of the later fellah-religion baptized by his name — but one of the unquestionably authentic ideas concerning "conditioned arising" [3] is the derivation of suffering *from ignorance* — ignorance, namely, of the "Four Noble Truths." This is true rationalism. Nirvana, for them, is a purely intellectual release and corresponds exactly with the "Autarkeia" and "Eudaimonia" of the Stoics. It is that condition of the understanding and waking-consciousness for which Being no longer is.

The great ideal of the educated of such periods is the Sage. The sage goes back to Nature — to Ferney or Ermenonville, to Attic gardens or Indian groves — which is the most intellectual way of being a megalopolitan. The sage is the man of the Golden Mean. His askesis consists in a judicious depreciation of the world in favour of meditation. The wisdom of the enlightenment never interferes with comfort. Moral with the great Myth to back it is always a sacrifice, a cult, even to extremes of asceticism, even to death; but Virtue with Wisdom at its back is a sort of secret enjoyment, a superfine intellectual egoism. And so the ethical teacher who is outside real religion becomes the Philistine. Buddha, Confucius, Rousseau, are arch-Philistines, for all the nobility of their

[1] Whereas "*virtù*" in Dante always carries a connotation of vital force, as also does the older English use of the word; e.g., in Chaucer's "of which vertue engendred is the flour," (*Canterbury Tales*, Prol. 4) and in the Bible (Mark v, 30). In Mediæval Latin "*virtutes*" is used for miracles. — *Tr.*

[2] See *Ency. Brit.*, XI ed., article "Jains." — *Tr.*

[3] E.g., "Given eye and visible object, visual consciousness arises; the conjunction of the three is contact; whereby conditioned, arises feeling; whereby conditioned, arises perception. . . ." Majjima Nikhaya, I, 111 (quoted by Mrs. Rhys Davids, *Buddhism*). — *Tr.*

ordered ideas, and the pedantry of the Socratic life-wisdom is insurmountable.

Along with this (shall we call it) scholasticism of sane reason, there must of inner necessity be a rationalistic mysticism of the educated. The Western Enlightenment is of English origin and Puritan parentage. The rationalism of the Continent comes wholly from Locke. In opposition to it there arose in Germany the Pietists (Herrnhut, 1700, Spener and Francke, and in Württemberg Oetinger) and in England the Methodists (Wesley "awakened" by Herrnhut, 1738). It was Luther and Calvin over again — the English at once organized themselves for a world-movement and the Germans lost themselves in mid-European conventicles. The Pietists of Islam are to be found in *Sufism,* which is not of "Persian" but of common Aramæan origin and in the eighth century spread all over the Arabian world. Pietists or Methodists, too, are the Indian lay preachers, who shortly before Buddha's time were teaching release from the cycle of life (*sansara*) through immersion in the identity of Atman and Brahman. But Pietists or Methodists, too, are Lao-tse and his disciples and — notwithstanding their rationalism — the Cynic mendicants and itinerant preachers and the Stoic tutors, domestic chaplains, and confessors of early Hellenism.[1] And Pietism may ascend even to the peak of rationalist vision, of which Swedenborg is the great example, which created for Stoics and Sufists whole worlds of fancy, and by which Buddhism was prepared for its reconstruction as Mahayana. The expansion of Buddhism and that of Taoism in their original significations are closely analogous to the Methodist expansion in America, and it is no accident that they both reached their full maturity in those regions (lower Ganges and south of the Yang-tse-kiang) which had cradled the respective Cultures.

VI

Two centuries after Puritanism the mechanistic conception of the world stands at its zenith. It is the effective religion of the time. Even those who still thought themselves to be religious in the old sense, to be "believers in God," were only mistaking the world in which their waking-consciousness was mirroring itself. Religious truths were always in their understanding mechanistic truths, and in general it was only the habit of traditional words that imparted a colour-wash of myth to a Nature that was in reality regarded scientifically. Culture is ever synonymous with religious creativeness. Every great Culture begins with a mighty theme that rises out of the pre-urban country-side, is carried through in the cities of art and intellect, and closes with a finale of materialism in the world-cities. But even the last chords are strictly in the key of the whole. There are Chinese, Indian, Classical, Arabian, Western materialisms, and each is nothing but the original stock of myth-shapes, cleared

---

[1] Gercke-Norden, *Einleit. in die Altertumswiss.*, II, 210.

of the elements of experience and contemplative vision and viewed mechanistically.

Confucianism as reasoned out by Yang-Chu concluded in this sense. The system of Lakayata was the prolongation of the contempt for a de-souled world which had been the common characteristic of Gotama Buddha, Mahavira, and the contemporary Pietists, and which they in turn had derived from Sankhya atheism. Socrates is alike the heir of the Sophists and the ancestor of the Cynic itinerants and of Pyrrhonian skepsis. All are manifestations of the superiority of the megalopolitan intellect that has done with the irrational for good and all and despises any waking-consciousness that still knows or acknowledges mysteries. Gothic men shrank at every step before the fathomless, more awe-inspiring still as presented in dogmatic truths. But to-day even the Catholic has arrived at the point of feeling these dogmas as a successful systematic exposition of the riddle of the universe. The miracle is regarded as a physical occurrence of a higher order, and an English bishop professes his belief in the possibility of electric power and the power of prayer both originating in one homogeneous nature-system.[1] The belief is belief in force and matter, even if the words used be "God" and "world," "Providence" and "man."

Unique and self-contained, again, is the Faustian materialism, in the narrower sense of the word. In it the technical outlook upon the world reached fulfilment. The whole world a dynamic system, exact, mathematically disposed, capable down to its first causes of being experimentally probed and numerically fixed so that man can dominate it — this is what distinguishes our particular "return to Nature" from all others. That "Knowledge is Virtue" Confucius also believed, and Buddha, and Socrates, but "Knowledge is Power" is a phrase that possesses meaning only within the European-American Civilization. "Return to nature" here means the elimination of all forces that stand between the practical intelligence and nature — everywhere else materialism has contented itself with establishing (by way of contemplation or logic, as the case may be) supposedly simple units whose causal play accounts for everything without any residue of secrets, the supernatural being put down to want of knowledge. But the grand intellectual myth of Energy and Mass is at the same time a vast *working hypothesis*. It draws the picture of nature in such a way that men can *use* it. The Destiny element is mechanized as evolution, development, progress, and put into the centre of the system; the Will is an albumen-process; and all these doctrines of Monism, Darwinism, Positivism, and what not are elevated into the fitness-moral which is the beacon of American business men, British politicians, and German progress-Philistines alike — and turns out, in the last analysis, to be nothing but an intellectualist caricature of the old justification by faith.

[1] Compare the renewed controversy as to Transubstantiation in the English Church, 1926–8, in which a bishop actually proposed that physical tests could be applied to the altar-miracle. — *Tr.*

Materialism would not be complete without the need of now and again easing the intellectual tension, by giving way to moods of myth, by performing rites of some sort, or by enjoying with an inward light-heartedness the charms of the irrational, the unnatural, the repulsive, and even, if need be, the merely silly.   This tendency, which is visible enough, even to us, in the times of Meng-tse (372–289) and in those of the first Buddhist brotherhoods, is present also (and with the same significance) in Hellenism, of which indeed it is a leading characteristic.   About 312 poetical scholars of the Callimachus type in Alexandria invented the Serapis-cult and provided it with an elaborate legend.   The Isis-cult in Republican Rome was something very different both from the emperor-worship that succeeded it and from the deeply earnest Isis-religion of Egypt; it was a religious pastime of high society, which at times provoked public ridicule and at times led to public scandal and the closing of the cult-centres.[1]   The Chaldean astrology was in those days a *fashion*,[2] very far removed from the genuine Classical belief in oracles and from the Magian faith in the might of the hour.   It was "relaxation," a "let's pretend."   And, over and above this, there were the numberless charlatans and fake prophets who toured the towns and sought with their pretentious rites to persuade the half-educated into a renewed interest in religion.   Correspondingly, we have in the European-American world of to-day the occultist and theosophist fraud, the American Christian Science, the untrue Buddhism of drawing-rooms, the religious arts-and-crafts business (brisker in Germany than even in England) that caters for groups and cults of Gothic or Late Classical or Taoist sentiment.   Everywhere it is just a toying with myths that no one really believes, a tasting of cults that it is hoped might fill the inner void.   The real belief is always the belief in atoms and numbers, but it requires this highbrow hocus-pocus to make it bearable in the long run.   Materialism is shallow and honest, mock-religion shallow and dishonest.   But the fact that the latter is possible at all foreshadows a new and genuine spirit of seeking that declares itself, first quietly, but soon emphatically and openly, in the civilized waking-consciousness.

This next phase I call the *Second Religiousness*.   It appears in all Civilizations as soon as they have fully formed themselves as such and are beginning to pass, slowly and imperceptibly, into the non-historical state in which time-periods cease to mean anything.   (So far as the Western Civilization is concerned, therefore, we are still many generations short of that point.)   The Second Religiousness is the necessary counterpart of Cæsarism, which is the final *political* constitution of Late Civilizations; it becomes visible, therefore, in the Augustan Age of the Classical and about the time of Shi-hwang-ti's time in China.   In both phenomena the creative young strength of the Early Culture is lacking. But both have their greatness nevertheless.   That of the Second Religiousness

---

[1] Which was ordered no less than four times in the decade 58–49.
[2] Horace's fine lady, Leuconoë. — *Tr.*

consists in a deep piety that fills the waking-consciousness — the piety that impressed Herodotus in the (Late) Egyptians and impresses West-Europeans in China, India, and Islam — and that of Cæsarism consists in its unchained might of colossal facts.   But neither in the creations of this piety nor in the form of the Roman Imperium is there anything primary and spontaneous.   Nothing is built up, no idea unfolds itself — it is only as if a mist cleared off the land and revealed the old forms, uncertainly at first, but presently with increasing distinctness.   The material of the Second Religiousness is simply that of the first, genuine, young religiousness — only otherwise experienced and expressed. It starts with Rationalism's fading out in helplessness, then the forms of the Springtime become visible, and finally the whole world of the primitive religion, which had receded before the grand forms of the early faith, returns to the foreground, powerful, in the guise of the popular syncretism that is to be found in every Culture at this phase.

Every "Age of Enlightenment" proceeds from an unlimited optimism of the reason — always associated with the type of the megalopolitan — to an equally unqualified scepticism.   The sovereign waking-consciousness, cut off by walls and artificialities from living nature and the land about it and under it, cognises nothing outside itself.   It applies criticism to its imaginary world, which it has cleared of everyday sense-experience, and continues to do so till it has found the last and subtlest result, the form of the form — itself: namely, nothing.   With this the possibilities of physics as a critical mode of world-understanding are exhausted, and the hunger for metaphysics presents itself afresh.   But it is not the religious pastimes of educated and literature-soaked cliques, still less is it the intellect, that gives rise to the Second Religiousness. Its source is the naïve belief that arises, unremarked but spontaneous, among the masses that there is some sort of mystic constitution of actuality (as to which formal proofs are presently regarded as barren and tiresome word-jugglery), and an equally naïve heart-need reverently responding to the myth with a cult.   The forms of neither can be foreseen, still less chosen — they appear of themselves, and as far as we are ourselves concerned, we are as yet far distant from them.[1]   But already the opinions of Comte and Spencer, the Materialism and the Monism and the Darwinism, which stirred the best minds of the nineteenth century to such passion, have become the world-view proper to country cousins.

The Classical philosophy had exhausted its ground by about 250 B.C.   From that time on, "knowledge" was no longer a continually tested and augmented stock, but a belief therein, due basically to force of habit, but still able to convince, thanks to an old and well-tried methodology.   In the time of Socrates

[1] It is perhaps possible for us to make some guess already as to these forms, which (it is self-evident) must lead back to certain elements of Gothic Christianity.   But be this as it may, what is quite certain is that they will not be the product of any literary taste for Late-Indian or Late-Chinese speculation, but something of the type, for example, of Adventism and suchlike sects.

there had been Rationalism as the religion of educated men, with, above it, the scholar-philosophy and, below it, the "superstition" of the masses. Now, philosophy developed towards an intellectual, and the popular syncretism towards a tangible, religiousness. The tendency was the same in both, and myth-belief and piety spread, not downwards, but upwards. Philosophy had much to receive and little to give. The Stoa had begun in the materialism of the Sophists and Cynics, and had explained the whole mythology on allegorical lines, but the prayer to Zeus at table — one of the most beautiful relics of the Classical Second Religiousness [1] — dates from as early as Cleanthes (d. 232). In Sulla's time there was an upper-class Stoicism that was religious through and through, and a popular syncretism which combined Phrygian, Syrian, and Egyptian cults with numberless Classical mysteries that had become almost forgotten — corresponding exactly to the development of Buddha's enlightened wisdom into Hinayana for the learned and Mahayana for the masses, and to the relation between learned Confucianism and Taoism as the vessel of Chinese syncretism which it soon became.

Contemporary with the "Positivist" Meng-tse (372–289) there suddenly began a powerful movement towards alchemy, astrology, and occultism. It has long been a favourite topic of dispute whether this was something new or a recrudescence of old Chinese myth-feeling — but a glance at Hellenism supplies the answer. This syncretism appears "simultaneously" in the Classical, in India and China, and in popular Islam. It starts always on rationalist doctrines — the Stoa, Lao-tse, Buddha — and carries these through with peasant and springtime and exotic motives of every conceivable sort. From about 200 B.C. the Classical Syncretism — which must not be confused with that of the later Magian Pseudomorphosis [2] — raked in motives from Orphism, from Egypt, from Syria; from 67 B.C. the Chinese brought in Indian Buddhism in the popular Mahayana form, and the potency of the holy writings as charms, and the Buddha-figures as fetishes, was thought to be all the greater for their alien origin. The original doctrine of Lao-tse disappeared very quickly. At the beginning of Han times (c. A.D. 200) the troops of the Sen had ceased to be "moral representations" and become kindly beings. The wind-, cloud-, thunder-, and rain-gods came back. Crowds of cults which purported to drive out the evil spirits by the aid of the gods acquired a footing. It was in that time that there arose — doubtless out of some basic principle of pre-Confucian philosophy — the myth of Pan-ku, the prime principle from which the series of mythical emperors descended. As we know, the Logos-idea followed a similar line of development.[3]

[1] Arnim, *Stoic. vet. fragm.*, 537.
[2] See p. 202.
[3] The Lü-shi Chun-tsiu of Lü-pu-Wei (d. 237 B.C., Chinese Augustan Age) is the first monument of this syncretism, of which the final deposit was the ritual work *Li-ki* of the Han period (B. Schindler, *Das Priestertum im alten China*, I, 93).

The theory and practice of the conduct of life that Buddha taught were the outcome of world-weariness and intellectual disgusts, and were wholly unrelated to religious questions. And yet at the very beginning of the Indian "Imperial" period (250 B.C.) he himself had already become a seated god-figure; and the Nirvana-theories, comprehensible only to the learned, were giving place more and more to solid and tangible doctrines of heaven, hell, and salvation, which were probably borrowed, as in other syncretisms, from an alien source — namely, Persian Apocalyptic. Already in Asoka's time there were eighteen Buddhist sects. The salvation-doctrine of Mahayana found its first great herald in the poet-scholar Asvagosha (c. 50 B.C.) and its fulfilment proper in Naganjuna (c. A.D. 150). But side by side with such teaching, the whole mass of proto-Indian mythology came back into circulation. The Vishnu- and Shiva-religions were already in 300 B.C. in definite shape, and, moreover, in syncretic form, so that the Krishna and the Rama legends were now transferred to Vishnu. We have the same spectacle in the Egyptian New Empire, where Amen of Thebes formed the centre of a vast syncretism, and again in the Arabian world of the Abbassids, where the folk-religion, with its images of Purgatory, Hell, Last Judgment, the heavenly Kaaba, Logos-Mohammed, fairies, saints, and spooks drove pristine Islam entirely into the background.[1]

There are still in such times a few high intellects like Nero's tutor Seneca and his antitype Psellus [2] the philosopher, royal tutor and politician of Byzantium's Cæsarism-phase; like Marcus Aurelius the Stoic and Asoka the Buddhist, who were themselves the Cæsars; [3] like the Pharaoh Amenhotep IV (Akhenaton), whose deeply significant experiment was treated as heresy and brought to naught by the powerful Amen-priesthood — a risk that Asoka, too, had, no doubt, to face from the Brahmins.

But Cæsarism itself, in the Chinese as in the Roman Empire, gave birth to an emperor-cult, and thereby concentrated Syncretism. It is an absurd notion that the veneration of the Chinese for the living emperor is a relic of ancient religion. During the whole course of the Chinese Culture there were no emperors at all. The rulers of the States were called Wang (that is, kings), and scarcely a century before the final victory of the Chinese Augustus Meng-tse wrote — in the vein of our nineteenth century — "The people is the most important element in the country; next come the useful gods of the soil and the crops, and least in importance comes the ruler." The mythology of the pristine emperors was without doubt put together by Confucius and his contemporaries,

---

[1] M. Horten, *Die religiöse Gedankenwelt des Volkes im heutigen Islam* (1917).

[2] 1018–78; cf. Dieterich, *Byzant. Charakterköpfe* (1909), p. 63. [Or *Ency. Brit.*, XI ed., article "Psellus." — *Tr.*]

[3] It was only in old age and after long and heavy warring that both these Cæsars gave themselves up to a mild and weary piety, and both of them held aloof from the more definite religions. From the point of view of dogma, Asoka was no Buddhist; what he did was to understand the currents and take them under his protection (Hillebrandt, *Altindien*, p. 143). [Asoka's life is dealt with in several of the works of Rhys Davids; for example, Ch. xv of his *Buddhist India*. — *Tr.*]

its constitutional and social-ethical form was dictated by their rationalist aims, and from this myth the first Chinese Cæsar borrowed both title and cult-idea. The elevation of men to divinity is the full-cycle return to the springtime in which gods were converted into heroes — exactly like these very emperors and the figures of Homer — and it is a distinguishing trait of almost all religions of this second degree. Confucius himself was deified in A.D. 57, with an official cult, and Buddha had been so long before. Al Ghazali (*c.* 1050), who helped to bring about the "Second Religiousness" of the Islamic world, is now, in the popular belief, a divine being and is beloved as a saint and helper. In the philosophy-schools of the Classical there was a cult of Plato, and of Epicurus, and Alexander's claim to descent from Heracles and Cæsar's to descent from Venus lead directly to the cult of the *Divus*, in which immemorial Orphic imaginings and family religions crop up afresh, just as the cult of Hwang-ti contains traits of the most ancient mythology of China.

But with the coming of the emperor-cults there begins at once, in each of the two, an attempt to bring the Second Religiousness into fixed organizations, which, however named — sects, orders, Churches — are always stiff re-constructions of what had been living forms of the Springtime, and bear the same relation to these as "caste" bears to "status."

There are signs of the tendency even in the Augustan reforms, with their artificial revival of long-dead city-cults, such as the rites of the Fratres Arvales, but it is only with the Hellenistic mystery-religions, or even with Mithraism,[1] that community or Church organization proper begins, and its development is broken off in the ensuing downfall of the Classical. The corresponding feature in Egypt is the theocratic state set up by the priest-kings of Thebes in the eleventh century. The Chinese analogue is the Tao churches of the Han period and especially that founded by Chang-lu, which gave rise to the fearful insurrection of the Yellow Turbans (recalling the religious provincial rebellions of the Roman Empire), which devastated whole regions and brought about the fall of the Han dynasty.[2] And the very counterpart of these ascetic Churches of Taoism, with their rigidity and wild mythology, is to be found in the late Byzantine monk-states such as Studion and the autonomous group of monasteries on Athos, founded in 1100, which are as suggestive of Buddhism as anything could well be.

In the end Second Religiousness issues in the *fellah-religions*. Here the opposition between cosmopolitan and provincial piety has vanished again, as completely as that between primitive and higher Culture. What this means the conception of the fellah people, discussed in an earlier chapter,[3] tells us. Religion becomes entirely historyless; where formerly decades constituted an

[1] In so far as it is permissible to reckon Mithraism as Classical at all — for it is really a religion of the Magian Spring.

[2] De Groot, *Universismus* (1918), p. 134.

[3] P. 169.

epoch, now whole centuries pass unimportantly, and the ups and downs of superficial changes only serve to show the unalterable finality of the inner state. It matters nothing that "Chufucianism" appeared in China (1200) as a variant of the Confucian state-doctrine, when it appeared, and whether or not it succeded. Equally, it signifies nothing that Indian Buddhism, long become a polytheistic religion of the people, went down before Neo-Brahmanism (whose great divine, Sankhara, lived about 800), nor is it of importance to know the date at which the latter passed over into the Hinduism of Brahma, Vishnu, and Shiva. There always are and always will be a handful of superlatively intellectual, thoughtful, and perfectly self-sufficing people, like the Brahmins in India, the Mandarins in China, and the Egyptian priests who amazed Herodotus. But the fellah-religion itself is once more primitive through and through — the animal-cults of the Egyptian XXVIth dynasty; the composite of Buddhism, Confucianism, and Taoism that constitutes the state religion of China; the Islam of the present-day East. The religion of the Aztecs was very likely another case in point, for, as Cortez found it, it seems remote indeed from the intensely intellectualized religion of the Mayas.

VII

The religion of Jewry, too, is a fellah-religion since the time of Jehuda ben Halevi who (like his Islamic teacher, Al Ghazali) regarded scientific philosophy with an unqualified scepticism, and in the *Kuzari* (1140) refused to it any rôle save that of handmaid of the orthodox theology. This corresponds exactly to the transition from Middle Stoicism to the later form of the Imperial period, and to the extinction of Chinese speculation under the Western Han Dynasty. Still more significant is the figure of Moses Maimonides,[1] who in 1175 collected the entire dogmatic material of Judaism, as something fixed and complete, in a great work of the type of the Chinese *Li-ki*, entirely regardless of whether the particular items still retained any meaning or not.[2] Neither in this period nor in any other is Judaism unique in religious history, though from the view-point that the Western Culture has taken up on its own ground, it may seem so. Nor is it peculiar to Jewry that, unperceived by those who bear it, its name is for ever changing in meaning, for the same has happened, step by step, in the Persian story.

In their "Merovingian" period — approximately the last five centuries before the birth of Christ — both Jewry and Persia evolve from tribal groups into nations of Magian cast, without land, without unity of origin, and (even so soon) with the characteristic ghetto mode of life that endures unchanged to-day for the Jews of Brooklyn and the Parsees of Bombay alike.

[1] See the article "Maimonides" in *Ency. Brit.*, XI ed. — *Tr.*

[2] Fromer, *Der Talmud*, p. 217. The "red cow" and the ritual of anointing a Jewish king were treated in this work with the same seriousness as the most important provisions of private law. [See J. and J. Tharaud, *Petite Histoire des Juifs*, Ch. I, (1927). — *Tr.*]

In the Springtime (first five centuries of the Christian era) this landless Consensus spread geographically from Spain to Shantung. This was the Jewish Age of Chivalry and its "Gothic" blossoming-time of religious creative-force. The later Apocalyptic, the Mishnah, and also primitive Christianity (which was not cast off till after Trajan's and Hadrian's time) are creations of this nation. It is well known that in those days the Jews were peasants, artisans, and dwellers in little towns, and "big business" was in the hands of Egyptians, Greeks, and Romans — that is, members of the Classical world.

About 500 [1] begins the Jewish Baroque, which Western observers are accustomed to regard, very one-sidedly, as part of the picture of Spain's age of glory. The Jewish Consensus, like the Persian, Islamic, and Byzantine, now advances to an urban and intellectual awareness, and thenceforward it is master of the forms of city-economics and city-science. Tarragona, Toledo, and Granada are predominantly Jewish cities. Jews constitute an essential element in Moorish high society. Their finished forms, their *esprit*, their knightliness, amazed the Gothic nobility of the Crusades, which tried to imitate them; but the diplomacy also, and the war-management and the administration of the Moorish cities would all have been unthinkable without the Jewish aristocracy, which was every whit as thoroughbred as the Islamic. As once in Arabia there had been a Jewish *Minnesang*, so now here there was a high literature of enlightened science. It was under the guidance of the Rabbi Isaac Hassan, and by the hand of Jewish and Islamic as well as Christian savants, that Alfonso X's new work on the planets was prepared (*c.* 1250); [2] in other words, it was an achievement of Magian and not of Faustian world-thought. [3] But Spain and Morocco after all contained but a very small fraction of the Jewish Consensus, and even this Consensus itself had not merely a worldly but also (and predominantly) a spiritual significance. In it, too, there occurred a Puritan movement, which rejected the Talmud and tried to get back to the pure Torah. The community of the Qaraites, preceded by many a forerunner, arose about 760 in northern Syria, the selfsame area which gave birth a century earlier to the Paulician iconoclasts and a century later to the Sufism of Islam — three Magian tendencies whose inner relationship is unmistakable. The Qaraites, like the Puritans of all other Cultures, were combated by both orthodoxy and enlightenment. Rabbinical counterblasts appeared from Cordova and Fez to southern Arabia and Persia. But in that period appeared also — an outcome of "Jewish Sufism," and suggestive in places of Swedenborg — the *chef-d'œuvre* of rational mysticism, the Yesirah, germane in its Kabbalistic root-ideas to Byzantine image-symbolism and the contemporary magic of Greek "second-degree Christianity," and equally so to the folk-religion of Islam.

[1] See, for the following paragraphs, the articles "Jews," "Hebrew Religion," "Hebrew Literature," "Kabbalah," "Qaraites," etc., in *Ency. Brit.*, XI ed. — *Tr.*

[2] Strunz, *Gesch. der Naturwiss. im Mittelalter*, p. 89.

[3] Only with Nicolaus Cusanus was this state of things reversed.

But an entirely new situation was created when, from about the year 1000, the Western portion of the Consensus found itself suddenly in the field of the young Western Culture. The Jews, like the Parsees, the Byzantines, and the Moslems, had become by then civilized and cosmopolitan, whereas the German-Roman world lived in the townless land, and the settlements that had just come (or were coming) into existence around monasteries and market-places were still many generations short of possessing souls of their own. While the Jews were already almost fellaheen, the Western peoples were still almost primitives. The Jew could not comprehend the Gothic inwardness, the castle, the Cathedral; nor the Christian the Jew's superior, almost cynical, intelligence and his finished expertness in "money-thinking." There was mutual hate and contempt, due not to race-distinction, but to *difference of phase*. Into all the hamlets and country towns the Jewish Consensus built its essentially megalopolitan — proletarian — ghettos. The *Judengasse* is a thousand years in advance of the Gothic town. Just so, in Jesus's days, the Roman towns stood in the midst of the villages on the Lake of Genesareth.

But these young nations were, besides, bound up with the soil and the idea of a fatherland, and the landless "Consensus," which was cemented, not by deliberate organization, but by a wholly unconscious, wholly metaphysical impulse — an expression of the Magian world-feeling in its simplest and directest form — appeared to them as something uncanny and incomprehensible. It was in this period that the legend of the Wandering Jew arose. It meant a good deal for a Scottish monk to visit a Lombard monastery, and nostalgia soon took him home again, but when a rabbi of Mainz — in 1000 the seat of the most important Talmudic seminary of the West — or of Salerno betook himself to Cairo or Merv or Basra, he was at home in every ghetto. In this tacit cohesion lay the very idea of the Magian nation[1] — although the contemporary West was unaware of the fact, it was for the Jews, as for the Greeks of the period and the Parsees and Islam, State and Church and people all in one. This State had its own jurisprudence and (what Christians never perceived) its own public life,[2] and despised the surrounding world of the host-peoples as a sort of outland; and it was a veritable treason-trial that expelled Spinoza and Uriel Acosta — an event of which these host-peoples could not possibly grasp the under meaning. And in 1799 the leading thinker among the Eastern Hasidim, Senior Salman, was handed over by the rabbinical opposition to the Petersburg Government as though to a foreign state.

Jewry of the West-European group had entirely lost the relation to the open land which had still existed in the Moorish period of Spain. There were no more peasants. The smallest ghetto was a fragment, however miserable, of

---

[1] P. 174.

[2] The reader is recommended to study, in the light of all this, recent literature of the type of Hajim Bloch's *Golem* and the works of the brothers Tharaud. — *Tr.*

megalopolis, and its inhabitants (like those of hardened India and China) split into castes — the Rabbi is the Brahmin or Mandarin of the ghetto — and a coolie-mass characterized by civilized, cold, superior intelligence and an undeviating eye to business.   But this phenomenon, again, is not unique if our historical sense takes in the wider horizon, for *all* Magian nations have been in this condition since the Crusade period.   The Parsee in India possesses exactly the same business-power as the Jews in the European-American world and the Armenians and Greeks in southern Europe.   The same phenomenon occurs in every other Civilization, when it pushes into a younger *milieu* — witness the Chinese in California (where they are the targets of a true Anti-Semitism of western America), in Java, and in Singapore;   that of the Indian trader in East Africa;   and that of *the Romans in the Early Arabian World.*   In the last instance, indeed, the conditions were the exact reverse of those of to-day, for the "Jews" of those days were the Romans, and the Armæan felt for them an apocalyptic hatred that is very closely akin to our West-European Anti-Semitism.   The outbreak of 88, in which, at a sign from Mithridates, a hundred thousand Roman business-people were murdered by the exasperated population of Asia Minor, was a veritable *pogrom.*

Over and above these oppositions there was that of race, which passed from contempt into hate in proportion as the Western Culture itself caught up with the Civilization and the "difference of age," expressed in the way of life and the increasing primacy of intelligence, became smaller.   But all this has nothing to do with the silly catchwords "Aryan" and "Semite" that have been borrowed from philology.   The "Aryan" Persians and Armenians are in our eyes entirely indistinguishable from the Jews, and even in South Europe and the Balkans there is almost no bodily difference between the Christian and Jewish inhabitants.   The Jewish nation is, like every other nation of the Arabian Culture, the result of an immense *mission,* and up to well within the Crusades it was changed and changed again by accessions and secessions *en masse.*[1]   One part of Eastern Jewry conforms in bodily respects to the Christian inhabitants of the Caucasus, another to the South-Russian Tatars, and a large portion of Western Jewry to the North African Moors.   What has mattered in the West more than any other distinction is the difference *between the race-ideal of the Gothic springtime,*[2] which has bred its human type, and that of the Sephardic Jew, which first formed itself in the ghettos of the West and was likewise the product of a particular spiritual breeding and training under exceedingly hard external conditions — to which, doubtless, we must add the effectual spell of the land and people about him, and his metaphysical defensive reaction to that spell, especially after the loss of the Arabic language had made this part of the nation a self-contained world.   This feeling of being "different" is the more potent on both sides, the more breed the individual possesses.   It is *want* of race,

[1] See pp. 259, et seq.; 174, et seq.   [2] P. 127.

and nothing else, that makes intellectuals — philosophers, doctrinaires, Utopists — incapable of understanding the depth of this metaphysical hatred, which is the beat-difference of two currents of being manifested as an unbearable dissonance, a hatred that may become tragic for both, the same hatred as has dominated the Indian Culture in setting the Indian of race against the Sudra. During the Gothic age this difference is deep and religious, and the object of hatred is the Consensus as religion; only with the beginning of the Western Civilization does it become materialist, and begin to attack Jewry on its intellectual and business sides, on which the West suddenly finds itself confronted by an even challenger.

But the deepest element of separation and bitterness has been one of which the full tragedy has been least understood. While Western man, from the days of the Saxon emperors to the present, has (in the most significant sense of the words) *lived* his history, and lived it with a consciousness of it that no other Culture can parallel, the Jewish Consensus ceased to have a history at all.[1] Its problems were solved, its inner form was complete, conclusive, and unalterable. For it, as for Islam, the Greek Church, and the Parsees, centuries ceased to mean anything, and consequently no one belonging inwardly to the Consensus can even begin to comprehend the passion with which Faustians livingly experience the short crowded epochs in which their history and destiny take decisive turns — the beginning of the Crusades, the Reformation, the French Revolution, the German Wars of Liberation, and each and every turning-point in the existence of the several peoples. All this, for the Jew, lies thirty generations back. Outside him history on the grand style flowed on and past. Epochs succeeded to epochs, every century witnessed fundamental human changes, but in the ghetto and in the souls of its denizens all stood still. And even when he regarded himself as a member of the people amongst whom he sojourned and took part in their good and evil fortune — as happened in so many countries in 1914 — he lived these experiences, not really as something *his own*, but as a partisan, a supporter; he judged them as an interested spectator, and hence it is just the deepest meanings of the struggle that must ever remain hidden from him. A Jewish cavalry-general fought in the Thirty Years' War (he lies buried in the old Jewish cemetery at Prague[2]) — but what did the ideas of Luther or Loyola mean to him? What did the Byzantines — near relatives of the Jews — comprehend of the Crusades? Such things are among the tragic necessities of the higher history that consists in the life-courses of individual Cultures, and often have they repeated themselves. The Romans, then an ageing people, cannot possibly have understood what was at issue for the Jews in the trial of Jesus or the rising of Barcochebas.[3] The European-American

---

[1] P. 48.

[2] Prague contains a veritable corpus of commentary upon these pages. — *Tr.*

[3] A.D. 132. See *Ency. Brit.*, XI ed., Vol. XV, p. 402, and Vol. III, p. 395. — *Tr.*

world has displayed a complete incomprehension of the fellah-revolutions of Turkey (1908) and China (1911); the inner life and thought of these peoples, and consequently, even their notions of state and sovereignty (the Caliph in the one, the Son of Heaven in the other) being of an utterly different cast and, therefore, a sealed book, the course of events could neither be weighed up, nor even reckoned upon in advance. The member of an alien Culture can be a spectator, and therefore also a descriptive historian of the past, but he can never be a statesman, a man who feels the future working in him. If he does not possess the material power to enable him to act in the cadre of his own Culture, ignoring or manipulating those of the alien (which, of course, may occur, as with the Romans in the young East or Disraeli in England), he stands helpless in the midst of events. The Roman and the Greek always mentally projected the life-conditions of his Polis into the alien event; the modern European always regards alien Destinies in terms of constitution, parliament, and democracy, although the application of such ideas to other Cultures is ridiculous and meaningless; and the Jew of the Consensus follows the history of the present (which is nothing but that of the Faustian Civilization spread over continents and oceans) with the fundamental feelings of Magian mankind, even when he himself is firmly convinced of the Western character of his thought.

As every Magian Consensus is non-territorial and geographically unlimited, it involuntarily sees in all conflicts concerning the *Faustian* ideas of fatherland, mother tongue, ruling house, monarchy, constitution, a return from forms that are thoroughly alien (therefore burdensome and meaningless) to him towards forms matching with his own nature. Hence the word "international," whether it be coupled with socialism, pacifism, or capitalism, can excite him to enthusiasm, but what he hears in that word is *the essence of his landless and boundless Consensus.* While for the European-American democracy constitutional struggles and revolutions mean an evolution towards the Civilized ideal, for him they mean (as he almost never consciously realizes) the breaking-down of all that is of other build than himself. Even when the force of the Consensus in him is broken and the life of his host-people exercises an outward attraction upon him to the point of an induced patriotism, yet the party that he supports is always that of which the aims are most nearly comparable with the Magian essence. Hence in Germany he is a democrat and in England (like the Parsee in India) an imperialist. It is exactly the same misunderstanding as when West Europeans regard Young Turks and Chinese reformers as kindred spirits — that is, as "constitutionalists." If there is inward relationship, a man affirms even where he destroys; if inward alienness, his effect is negative even where his desire is to be constructive. What the Western Culture has destroyed, by reform-efforts of its own type where it has had power, hardly bears thinking of; and Jewry has been equally destructive where it has intervened.   The sense of the inevitableness of this reciprocal misunderstanding leads to the appalling hatred that settles deep in the blood and, fastening upon visible marks like race, mode of life, profession, speech, leads both sides to waste, ruin, and bloody excesses wherever these conditions occur.[1]

This applies also, and above all, to the religiousness of the Faustian world, which feels itself to be threatened, hated, and undermined by an alien metaphysic in its midst.   From the reforms of Hugh of Cluny and St. Bernard and the Lateran Council of 1215 to Luther, Calvin, and Puritanism and thence to the Age of Enlightenment, what a tide flowed through our waking-consciousness, when for the Jewish religion history had long ceased altogether!   Within the West-European Consensus we see Joseph Qaro in his *Schulehan Arukh* (1565) restating the Maimonides material in another form, and this could equally well have been done in 1400 or 1800, or for that matter not at all.   In the fixity of modern Islam of Byzantine Christianity since the Crusades (and, equally, of the life of Late China and of Late Egypt) all is formal and rolled even, not only the food-prohibitions, the prayer-runes, the phylacteries, but also the Talmudic casuistry, which is fundamentally the same as that applied for centuries to the Vendidad in Bombay and the Koran in Cairo.   The mysticism, too, of Jewry (which is *pure Sufism*) has remained, like that of Islam, unaltered since the Crusades; and in the last centuries it has produced three more saints in the sense of Oriental Sufism — though to recognize them as such we have to see through a colour-wash of Western thought-forms.   Spinoza, with his thinking in substances instead of forces and his thoroughly Magian dualism, is entirely comparable with the last stragglers of Islamic philosophy such as Murtada and Shirazi.   He makes use of the notions of his Western Baroque armoury, living himself into mode of imagination of that *milieu* so thoroughly as to deceive even himself, but below the surface movements of his soul he remains the unchanged descendant of Maimonides and Avicenna and Talmudic "*more geometrico*" methodology.   In Baal Shem, the founder of the Hasidim sect (born in Volhynia about 1698), a true Messiah arose.   His wanderings through the world of the Polish ghettos teaching and performing miracles are comparable only with the story of primitive Christianity; [2] here was a movement that had its sources in ancient currents of Magian, Kabbalistic mysticism, that gripped a large part of Eastern Jewry and was undoubtedly a potent fact in the religious history of the Arabian Culture; and yet, running its course as it did in the midst of an alien mankind, it passed practically unnoticed by it.   The peaceful battle that Baal Shem waged for God-immanent

[1] Instances — besides that of Mithradates and the Cyprus massacre (p. 198) quoted above — are the Sepoy Mutiny in India, the Boxer Rebellion in China, and the Bolshevist fury of Jews, Letts, and other alien peoples against Tsarist Russia.

[2] P. Levertoff, *Die religiöse Denkweise der Chassidim* (1918), pp. 128, et seq.; M. Buber, *Die Legende des Baalschem* (1907). [Brief account in J. and J. Tharaud, *Petite histoire des Juifs*, Ch. vii. — Tr.]

against the Talmudic pharisees of his time, his Christlike figure, the wealth of legends that were rapidly woven about his person and the persons of his disciples — all this is of the pure Magian spirit, and at bottom as alien to us of the West as primitive Christianity itself. The thought-processes of Hasidist writings are to non-Jews practically unintelligible, and so also is the ritual. In the excitement of the service some fall into convulsions and others begin to dance like the dervishes of Islam.[1] The original teaching of Baal Shem was developed by one of the disciples in Zaddikism, and this too, which was a belief in successive divine embassies of saints (Zaddiks), whose mere proximity brought salvation, has obvious kinship with Islamic Mahdism and still more with the Shiite doctrine of the imams in whom the "Light of the Prophet" takes up its abode. Another disciple, Solomon Maimon — of whom a remarkable autobiography exists — stepped from Baal Shem to Kant (whose abstract kind of thought has always possessed an immense attraction for Talmudic intellects). The third is Otto Weininger, whose moral dualism is a purely Magian conception and whose death in a spiritual struggle of essentially Magian experience is one of the noblest spectacles ever presented by a Late religiousness.[2] Something of the sort Russians may be able to experience, but neither the Classical nor the Faustian soul is capable of it.

In the "Enlightenment" of the eighteenth century the Western Culture in turn becomes megalopolitan and intellectual, and so, suddenly, accessible to the intelligentsia of the Consensus. And the latter, thus dumped into the middle of an epoch corresponding, for them, to the remote past of a long-expired Sephardic life-current, were inevitably stirred by echo-feelings, but these echoes were of the *critical and negative side only*, and the tragically unnatural outcome was that a cohesion already historically complete and incapable of organic progress was swept into the big movement of the host-peoples, which it shook, loosened, displaced, and vitiated to its depths. For, for the Faustian spirit, the Enlightenment was a step forward along its own road — a step over débris, no doubt, but still affirmative at bottom — whereas for Jewry it was destruction and nothing else, the demolition of an alien structure that it did not understand. And this is why we so often see the spectacle — paralleled by the case of the Parsees in India, of the Chinese and Japanese in a Christian *milieu*, and by modern Americans in China — of enlightenment, pushed to the point of cynicism and unqualified atheism, opposing an alien religion, while the fellah-practices of its own folk go on wholly unaffected. There are Socialists who superficially — and yet quite sincerely — combat every sort of religion, and yet in their own case follow the food-prohibitions and routine prayers and phylacteries with an anxious exactitude. More frequent actually is inward lapse from the Consensus qua creed — the spectacle that is presented to us by

[1] Levertoff, op. cit., p. 136.
[2] O. Weininger, *Taschenbuch* (1919), above all pp. 19, et seq.

the Indian student who, after an English university-training in Locke and Mill, acquires the same cynical contempt for Indian and Western faiths alike and must himself be crushed under the ruins of both. Since the Napoleonic era the old-civilized Consensus has mingled unwelcome with the new-civilized Western "society" of the cities and has taken their economic and scientific methods into use with the cool superiority of age. A few generations later, the Japanese, also a very old intellect, did the same, and probably with still greater success. Yet another example is afforded by the Carthaginians, a rear-guard of the Babylonian Civilization, who, already highly developed when the Classical Culture was still in the Etrusco-Doric infancy, ended by surrendering to Late Hellenism [1] — petrified in an end-state in all that concerned religion and art, but far superior to the Greeks and Romans as men of business, and hated accordingly.

To-day this Magian nation, with its ghetto and its religion, itself is in danger of disappearing — not because the metaphysics of the two Cultures come closer to one another (for that is impossible), but because the intellectualized upper stratum of each side is ceasing to be metaphysical at all. It has lost every kind of inward cohesion, and what remains is simply a cohesion for practical questions. The lead that this nation has enjoyed from its long habituation to thinking in business terms becomes ever less and less (*vis-à-vis* the American, it has already almost gone), and with the loss of it will go the last potent means of keeping up a Consensus that has fallen regionally into parts. In the moment when the civilized methods of the European-American world-cities shall have arrived at full maturity, the destiny of Jewry — at least of the Jewry in our midst (that of Russia is another problem) — will be accomplished.

Islam has *soil* under it. It has practically absorbed the Persian, Jewish, Nestorian, and Monophysite Consensus into itself.[2] The relic of the Byzantine nation, the modern Greeks, also occupy their own land. The relic of the Parsees in India dwells in the midst of the stiffened forms of a yet older and more fellahized Civilization and is thereby secured in its footing. But the West-European-American part of the Jewish Consensus, which has drawn to itself and bound to its destiny most of the other parts of Jewry, has now fallen into the machinery of a young Civilization. Detached from any land-footing since, centuries ago, it saved its life by shutting itself off in the ghetto, it is fragmented and faced with dissolution. But that is a Destiny, not *in* the Faustian Culture, but of the Magian.

---

[1] Their ship-building was in Roman times more Classical than Phœnician, their state was organized as a Polis, and their educated people, like Hannibal, were familiar with Greek.

[2] See p. 260, et seq.

CHAPTER X

THE STATE

(A)

THE PROBLEM OF THE ESTATES — NOBILITY AND PRIESTHOOD

THE STATE

(A)

THE PROBLEM OF THE ESTATES — NOBILITY AND PRIESTHOOD

I[1]

A FATHOMLESS secret of the cosmic flowings that we call Life is their separation into two sexes. Already in the earth-bound existence-streams of the plant world they are trying to part from one another, as the symbol of the flower tells us — into a something that *is* this existence and a something that keeps it going. Animals are free, little worlds in a big world — the cosmic — closed off as microcosms and set up against the macrocosm. And, more and more decisively as the animal kingdom unfolds its history, the dual direction of dual being, of the masculine and the feminine, manifests itself.

The feminine stands closer to the Cosmic. It is rooted deeper in the earth and it is immediately involved in the grand cyclic rhythms of Nature. The masculine is freer, more animal, more mobile — as to sensation and understanding as well as otherwise — more awake and more tense.

The male livingly experiences Destiny, and he *comprehends* Causality, the causal logic of the Become. The female, on the contrary, *is herself* Destiny and Time and the organic logic of the Becoming, and for that very reason the principle of Causality is for ever alien to her. Whenever Man has tried to give Destiny any tangible form, he has felt it as of feminine form, and he has called it Moirai, Parcæ, Norns. The supreme deity is never itself Destiny, but always either its representative or its master — just as man represents or controls woman. Primevally, too, woman is the seeress, and not because she knows the future, but because she *is* the future. The priest merely interprets the oracle; the woman is the oracle itself, and it is Time that speaks through her.

The man *makes* History, the woman *is* History. Here, strangely clear yet enigmatic still, we have a dual significance of all living happenings — on the one hand we sense cosmic flow as such, and on the other hand the chain and train of successive individuals brings us back to the microcosms themselves as the recipients, containers, and preservers of the flowing. It is this "second" history that is characteristically masculine — political, social, more conscious, freer, and more agitated than the other. It reaches back deep into the animal world, and receives highest symbolic and world-historical expression in the life-courses of the great Cultures. Feminine, on the contrary, is the primary,

[1] Cf. p. 3 and foot-note.

the eternal, the maternal, the plantlike (for the plant ever has something female in it), *the cultureless history of the generation-sequence,* which never alters, but uniformly and stilly passes through the being of all animal and human species, through all the short-lived individual Cultures. In retrospect, it is synonymous with Life itself. This history, too, is not without its battles and its tragedies. Woman in childbed wins through to her victory. The Aztecs — the Romans of the Mexican Culture — honoured the woman in labour as a battling warrior, and if she died, she was interred with the same formulæ as the fallen hero. Policy for Woman is eternally the conquest of the Man, through whom she can become mother of children, through whom she can become History and Destiny and Future. The target of her profound shyness, her tactical finesse, is ever the father of her son. The man, on the contrary, whose centre of gravity lies essentially in the other kind of History, wants that son as *his* son, as inheritor and carrier of his blood and historical tradition.

Here, in man and in woman, *the two kinds of History* are fighting for power. Woman is strong and wholly what she is, and she experiences the Man and the Sons only in relation to herself and her ordained rôle. In the masculine being, on the contrary, there is a certain contradiction; he is this man, and he is something else besides, which woman neither understands nor admits, which she feels as robbery and violence upon that which to her is holiest. This secret and fundamental war of the sexes has gone on ever since there were sexes, and will continue — silent, bitter, unforgiving, pitiless — while they continue. In it, too, there are policies, battles, alliances, treaties, treasons. Race-feeling of love and hate, which originate in depths of world-yearning and primary instincts of directedness, prevail between the sexes — and with a still more uncanny potency than in the other History that takes place between man and man. There are love-lyrics and war-lyrics, love-dances and weapon-dances, there are two kinds of tragedy — *Othello* and *Macbeth.* But nothing in the political world even begins to compare with the abysses of a Clytæmnestra's or a Kriemhild's vengeance.

And so woman despises that other History — man's politics — which she never comprehends, and of which all that she sees is that it takes her sons from her. What for her is a triumphant battle that annihilates the victories of a thousand childbeds? Man's history sacrifices woman's history to itself, and no doubt there is a female heroism too, that proudly brings the sons to the sacrifice (Catherine Sforza on the walls of Imola), but nevertheless there was and is and ever will be a secret politic of the woman — of the female of the animal world even — that seeks to draw away her male from his kind of history and to weave him body and soul into her own plantlike history of generic succession — that is, into herself. And yet all that is accomplished in the man-history is accomplished under the battle-cries of hearth and home, wives and children, race and the like, and its very object is the covering and upholding of this history of birth and death. The conflict of man and man is ever on account of the blood, of woman. *Woman, as Time, is that for which there is history at all.* The woman with race in her feels this even when she does not know it. She is Destiny, she plays Destiny. The play begins with the fight of men for the possession of her — Helen, and the tragedy of Carmen, and Catherine II, and the story of Napoleon and Désirée Clary, who in the end took Bernadotte over to the side of his enemies — and it is not a human play only, for this fight begins down in the animal world and fills the history of whole species. And it culminates in her swaying, as mother or wife or mistress, the Destiny of empires — Hallgerd in the Njal saga, the Frankish queen Brunhilde, Marozia who gave the Holy See to men of her choice. The man climbs up in *his* history until he has the future of a country in his hands — and then woman comes and forces him to his knees. Peoples and states may go down in ruin over it, but she in *her* history has conquered. This, in the last analysis, is always the aim of political ambition in a woman of race.[1]

Thus history has two meanings, neither to be blasphemed. It is cosmic or politic, it *is* being or it *preserves* being. There are two sorts of Destiny, two sorts of war, two sorts of tragedy — *public and private*. Nothing can eliminate this duality from the world. It is radical, founded in the essence of the animal that is both microcosm and participant in the cosmic. It appears at all significant conjunctures in the form of a conflict of duties, which exists only for the man, not for the woman, and in the course of a higher Culture it is never overcome, but only deepened. There are public life and private life, public law and private law, communal cults and domestic cults. As Estate,[2] Being is "in form" for the one history; as race, breed, it is in flow as *itself* the other history. This is the old German distinction between the "sword side" and the "spindle side" of blood-relationships. The double significance of directional Time finds its highest expression in the ideas of *the State* and *the Family*.

The ordering of the family is in living material what the form of the house is in dead.[3] A change in the structure and import of family life, and the plan

---

[1] And not until women cease to have race enough to have or to want children, not until they cease to *be* history, does it become possible for them to make or to copy the history of men. Conversely, it is deeply significant that we are in the habit of calling thinkers, doctrinaires, and humanity-enthusiasts of anti-political tendency "old women." They wish to imitate the other history, the history of woman, although they — cannot.

[2] No exact equivalent exists in common English for the German word "*Stand.*" "Aristocracy" is too narrow, as under most aspects the clergy and under some even the *Tiers* have to be reckoned in. "Class" fails because, for logical completeness, it has to be stretched so as to bring in the qualitatively unclassed as a distinct category. (A whole social history is contained in the use of these and similar words at different periods.) The word "Estate" itself is used nowadays for the "masses" ("Fourth Estate" = "Proletariat"), but this very use, by Socialists, is an assertion that the masses, as workers, possess a qualitative peculiarity and condition of their own, and the word thus continues to connote ideas of differentiation, specific constitution, and oriented outlook. It may, therefore, be employed here without fear of misunderstanding or reproach of pedantry. — Tr.

[3] Cf. pp. 120., et seq.

of the house changes also. To the Classical mode of housing corresponds the agnate family of Classical style. This is ever more sharply defined in Hellenic city-law than in the later Roman.[1] It refers entirely to the Estate as present in a Euclidean here-and-now, just as the Polis is conceived as an aggregate of bodies availably present. Blood-relationship, therefore, is neither necessary nor sufficient for it; it ceases at the limit of *patria potestas*, of the "house." The mother as such is not agnatically related to the offspring of her own body; only in so far as, like them, she is subject to the *patria potestas* of her living husband is she the agnatic sister of her children.[2] To the "Consensus," on the other hand, corresponds the Magian cognate family (Hebrew, "*Mishpasha*") which is representatively extended by both the paternal *and* the maternal blood-relationships, and possesses a "spirit," a little consensus, of its own, but no special head.[3] It is significant of the extinction of the Classical soul and the unfolding of the Magian that the "Roman" law of Imperial times gradually passes from *agnatio* to *cognatio*. Justinian's 118th and 127th novels reforming the law of inheritance affirm the victory of the Magian family-idea.[4]

On the other side, we see masses of individual beings streaming past, growing and passing, but *making* history. The purer, deeper, stronger, more taken-for-granted the common beat of these sequent generations is, the more blood, the more race they have. Out of the infinite they rise, every one with its soul,[5] bands that feel themselves in the common wave-beat of their being, as a whole — not mind-communities like orders, craft-guilds, or schools of learning, which are linked by common truths, but blood-confederates in the mêlée of fighting life.

There are streams of being which are "in form" in the same sense in which the term is used in sports. A field of steeplechasers is "in form" when the legs swing surely over the fences, and the hoofs beat firmly and rhythmically on the flat. When wrestlers, fencers, ball-players are "in form," the riskiest acts and moves come off easily and naturally. An art-period is in form when its tradition is second nature, as counterpoint was to Bach. An army is in form when it is like the army of Napoleon at Austerlitz and the army of Moltke at Sedan. Practically everything that has been achieved in world-history, in war and in that continuation of war by intellectual means [6] that we call politics;

---

[1] Mitteis, *Reichsrecht und Volksrecht* (1891), p. 63.

[2] Sohm, *Institutionen* (1911), p. 614. [*Ency. Brit.*, XI ed., Vol. XXIII, pp. 540-1. — *Tr.*]

[3] This principle formed the basis of the dynastic-idea of the Arabian world (Ommayads, Comneni, Sassanids), which is so hard for us to grasp. When a usurper had seized a throne, he hastened to marry one or another of the female members of the blood-community and so prolonged the dynasty; of law-made succession rights there was no question, nor under this idea could there be. (See also J. Wellhausen, *Ein Gemeinwesen ohne Obrigkeit*, (1900).

[4] See *Ency. Brit.*, XI ed., Vol. XXIII, p. 574. — *Tr.*

[5] See p. 18.

[6] An inversion of Clausewitz's famous expression that war is a continuation of policy by other means. (*On War*, I, i, § 24). — *Tr.*

in all successful diplomacy, tactics, strategy; in the competition of states or social classes or parties; has been the product of living unities that found themselves "in form."

The word for race- or breed-education is "training" (*Zucht, Züchtung*), as against the shaping (*Bildung*) which creates communities of waking-conciousness on a basis of uniform teachings or beliefs. Books, for example, are shaping agents, while the constant felt pulse and harmony of *milieu* into which one feels oneself, *lives* oneself — like a novice or a page of early Gothic times — are training influences. The "good form" and ceremonies of a given society are sense-presentations of the beat of a given species of Being, and to master them one must *have* the beat of them. Hence women, as more instinctive and nearer to cosmic rhythms, adapt themselves more readily than men to the forms of a new *milieu*. Women from the bottom strata move in elegant society with entire certainty after a few years — and sink again as quickly. But men alter slowly, because they are more awake and aware. The proletarian man never becomes wholly an aristocrat, the aristocrat never wholly a proletarian — only in the sons does the beat of the new *milieu* make its appearance.

The profounder the form, the stricter and more repellent it is. To the outsider, therefore, it appears to be a slavery; the member, on the contrary, has a perfect and easy command of it. The Prince de Ligne was, no less than Mozart, master of the form and not its slave; and the same holds good of *every* born aristocrat, statesman, and captain.

In all high Cultures, therefore, there is a *peasantry*, which is breed, stock, in the broad sense (and thus to a certain extent nature herself), and a *society* which is assertively and emphatically "in form." It is a set of classes or Estates, and no doubt artificial and transitory. But the history of these classes and estates is *world-history at highest potential*. It is only in relation to it that the peasant is seen as historyless. The whole broad and grand history of these six millennia has accomplished itself in the life-courses of the high Cultures, *because* these Cultures themselves placed their creative foci in Estates possessing breed and training, and so in the course of fulfilment became trained and bred. A Culture is Soul that has arrived at self-expression in sensible forms, but these forms are living and evolving.[1] Their matrix is in the intensified Being of individuals or groups — that is, in that which I have just called Being "in form." And when, and not until, this Being is sufficiently formed to that high rightness, it becomes representative of a representable Culture.[2]

This Culture is not only a grand thing, but wholly unlike any other thing in the organic world. It is the one point at which man lifts himself above the powers of Nature and becomes himself a Creator. Even as to race, breed,

---

[1] Not excluding art, although we are not *conscious* of them save through deduction from art-history.

[2] Original: "*Sie liegen im gesteigerten Dasein von Einzelnen und Kreisen, eben in dem, was soeben 'Dasein in Form' genannt worden ist, und durch diese Höhe des Geformtseins erst die Kultur repräsentirt.*"

he is Nature's creature — he *is* bred. But, as Estate, he breeds himself just as
he breeds the noble kinds of animal-plant with which he surrounds himself —
and that process, too, is in the deepest and most final sense "Culture." Culture
and class [1] are interchangeable expressions; they arise together and they vanish
together. The breeding of select types of wines or fruit or flowers, the breeding
of blood horses, *is* Culture, and the culture, in exactly the same sense, of the
human élite arises as the expression of a Being that has brought itself into high
"form."

For that very reason, there is found in every Culture a sharp sense of whether
this or that man belongs thereto or not. The Classical notion of the Barbarian, the Arabian of the Unbeliever (Amhaarez, Giaour), the Indian of the
Sudra — however differently the lines of cleavage were arrived at — are alike
in that the words do not primarily express contempt or hatred, but establish
that there are differences in pulse of Being which set an impassable barrier
against all contacts on the deeper levels. This perfectly clear and unambiguous
idea has been obscured by the Indian concept of a "fourth caste," which caste,
as we know now, has never existed at all.[2] The Code of Manu, with its celebrated regulations for the treatment of the Sudra, is the outcome of the fully
developed state of fellahdom in his India, and — irrespective of practical
actualities under either existing or even obtainable legislation — described the
misty idea of Brahmanism by the negative mode of dealing with its opposite,
very much as the Late Classical philosophy used the notion of the working
Banausos. The one has led us into misunderstanding caste as a specifically
Indian phenomenon, the other to a basically false idea of the attitude of Classical
man towards work.

In all such cases what really confronts us is the *residue* which does not count
for the inward life of the Culture and its symbolism, and is in principle left
out of every really significant classification, somewhat as the "outcast" is
ignored in the far East. The Gothic expression *"corpus christianum"* indicates
explicitly in its very terms that the Jewish Consensus does not belong to it.
In the Arabian Culture the other-believer is merely tolerated within the respective domains of the Jewish, the Persian, the Christian, and, above all, the
Islamic, nations, and contemptuously left to his own administration and his
own jurisdiction. In the Classical World it was not only barbarians that were
"outcasts" — so also in a measure were slaves, and especially the relics of the
autochthonous population like the Penestæ in Thessaly and the Helots of Sparta,
whom their masters treated in a way that reminds us of the conduct of the
Normans in Anglo-Saxon England and the Teutonic Knights in the Slavonic
East. The Code of Manu preserves, as designations of Sudra classes, the names

---

[1] So in the German, but see foot-note p. 329. "*Stand*" would have expressed the sense better. — *Tr.*

[2] R. Fick, *Die soziale Gliederung im nordöstlichen Indien zu Buddhas Zeit* (1897), p. 201; K. Hillebrandt, *Alt-Indien* (1899), p. 82. [Also the article "Brahmanism," *Ency. Brit.*, XI ed. — *Tr.*]

of ancient peoples of the "Colonial" region of the Lower Ganges. (As Magadha is amongst them, Buddha himself may have been a Sudra, like the "Cæsar" Asoka, whose grandfather Chandragupta was of the most humble origin.) Others are names of callings, and this again reminds us that also in the West and elsewhere certain callings were outcast — the beggars, for example (who in Homer are a class), smiths, singers, and the professional poor, who have been bred literally *en masse* by the *caritas* of the Church and the benevolence of laymen in the Early Gothic.

But, in sum, "caste" is a word that has been at least as much abused as it has been used. There were no castes in the Old and Middle Kingdoms of Egypt, nor in India before Buddha, nor in China before Han times. It is only in very Late conditions that they appear, and then we find them in all Cultures. From the XXIst Dynasty onwards (*c.* 1100 B.C.) Egypt was in the hands, now of the Theban priest-caste, now of the Libyan warrior-caste; and thereafter the hardening process went on steadily till the time of Herodotus — whose view of the conditions of his day as characteristically Egyptian is just as inaccurate as our view of those prevailing in India. *The distinction between Estate and Caste is that between earliest Culture and latest Civilization.* In the rise of the prime Estates — noble and priest — the Culture is unfolding itself, while the castes are the expression of its definitive fellah-state. The Estate is the most living of all, Culture launched on the path of fulfilment, "the form that living must itself unfold." [1] The caste is absolute finished-ness, the phase in which development has been succeeded by immutable fixation.

But the great Estates are something quite different from *occupation-groups* like those of artisans, officials, artists, which are professionally held together by technical tradition and the spirit of their work. They are, in fact, *emblems in flesh and blood*, whose entire being, as phenomenon, as attitude, and as mode of thought, possesses symbolic meaning. Within every Culture, moreover — while peasantry is a piece of pure nature and growth and, therefore, a completely *impersonal* manifestation — nobility and priesthood are the results of high breeding and forming and therefore express a *thoroughly personal Culture*, which, by the height of its form, rejects not merely barbarians, but presently also all who are not of their status, as a *residue* — regarded by the nobility as the "people" and by clergy as the "laity." And this *style of personality* is the material that, when the fellah-age arrives, petrifies into the type of a caste, which thereafter endures unaltered for centuries. As in the living Culture race and estate are in antithesis as the impersonal and the personal, in fellah-times *the mass and the caste*, the coolie and the Brahmin, *are in antithesis as the formless and the formal.* The living form has become formula, still possessing style, but possessing it as stylistic rigidity. This petrified style of the caste is of an extreme subtlety, dignity, and intellectuality, and feels itself infinitely superior

[1] See Vol. I, p. 157. — *Tr.*

to the developing mankind of a Culture — we can hardly form an idea of the lofty height from which the Mandarin or the Brahmin looks down upon European thoughts and actions, or how fundamentally the Egyptian priest must have despised a visiting Pythagoras or Plato. It moves impassive through time with the Byzantine dignity of a soul that has left all its problems and enigmas far behind it.

II

In the Carolingian pre-Culture men distinguished *Knechte*, *Freie*, and *Edle*. This is a primitive differentiation based merely on the facts of external life. But in Early Gothic times it runs:

> God hath shapen lives three,
> Boor and knight and priest they be.[1]

Here we have status-differences of a high Culture that has just awakened. And the stole and the sword stand together in face of the plough in strongest assertiveness as estates *vis-à-vis* the rest, the Non-Estate, that which, like themselves, is fact, but, unlike themselves, fact without deeper significance. The separation, inward and felt, is so destined, so potent, that no understanding can ignore it. Hatred wells up out of the villages, contempt flashes back from the castles. Neither possession nor power nor calling produced this abyss between the "lives." Logical justification for it there is none. It is metaphysical nature.

Later, with the cities, but younger than they, *burgherdom*, *bourgeoisie*, arises as the "Third Estate." The burgher, too, now looks with contempt upon the countryside, which lies about him dull, unaltered, and patient, and in contrast to which he feels himself more awake and freer and therefore further advanced on the road of the Culture. He despises also the primary estates, "squire and parson," as something lying intellectually below him and historically behind him. Yet, as compared with these two, the burgher is, as the boor was, a residue, a non-estate. In the minds of the "privileged" the peasant hardly now counts at all — the burgher counts, but as an opposite and a background. He is the foil against which the others become conscious of their own significance and of the fact that this significance is something lying outside all practical considerations. When we find that in all Cultures the same occurs in exactly the same form, and that, however different the symbolism of one Culture from that of another, their history fulfils itself everywhere in and by opposition of these groups — impulsive peasant wars in the Springtime, intellectually-based *civil* wars in the later period — then it is evident that the meaning of the facts must be looked for in the deepest foundations of Life itself.

---

[1] *Got hât driu leben geschaffen*
Gebûre, ritter, phaffen.
[Note the collective *ge-* attached to the first-named. — *Tr.*]

It is an *idea* that lies at the base of these two prime Estates, and only these. It gives them the potent feeling of a rank derived from a divine investiture and therefore beyond all criticism — a standing which imposes self-respect and self-consciousness, but the sternest self-discipline as well (and death itself if need be), as a duty and imbues both with the historical superiority, the soul-magic, that does not draw upon power but actually generates it. Those who — inwardly, and not merely nominally — belong to these Estates are *actually* something other than the residue; their lives, in contrast to those of burgher and peasant, are sustained in every part by a symbolic dignity. These lives do not exist in order to be merely lived, but to have meaning. It is the two sides of all freely moving life that come to expression in these Estates; *the one is wholly being, the other wholly waking-consciousness.*

Every nobility is a living symbol of *Time*, every priesthood of *Space*. Destiny and sacred Causality, History and Nature, the When and the Where, race and language, sex-life and feeling-life — all these attain in them to the highest possible expression. The noble lives in a world of facts, the priest in one of truths; the one has shrewdness, the other knowledge; the one is a doer, the other a thinker. Aristocratic world-feeling is essentially pulse-sense; priestly world-feeling proceeds entirely by tensions. Between the time of Charlemagne and that of Conrad II something formed itself in the time-stream that cannot be elucidated, but has to be felt if we are to understand the dawn of the new Culture. There had long been noblemen and ecclesiastics, but then first — and not for long — there were nobility and clergy, in the grand sense of the words and the full force of their symbolic significance.[1] So mighty is this onset of a symbolism that at first all other distinctions, such as those of country, people, and language, fall into the background. In all the lands from Ireland to Calabria the Gothic hierarchy was a single great community; the Early Classical chivalry before Troy, or the Early Gothic before Jerusalem, seems to us as of *one* great family. The old Egyptian nomes and the feudal states of the first Chóu times appear, in comparison with such Estates as these (and *because* of the comparison) just as colourless as Burgundy and Lorraine in the Hohenstaufen period. There is a cosmopolitan condition both at the beginning and at the end of every Culture, but in the first case it exists because the symbolic might of aristocratic-hierarchic forms still towers above those of nationality, and in the second because the formless mass sinks below them.

The two Estates in principle exclude one another. The prime opposition of

---

[1] The ease with which Bolshevism extinguished the four so-called estates or classes of Petrine Russia — nobles, merchants, small townspeople, and peasants — shows that these were mere imitations and administrative conveniences, and destitute of all symbolism — for symbolism no power on earth can choke. They correspond to the outward differences of rank and possessions that existed in the Visigothic and Frankish Kingdoms, and — as glimpses afforded by the earliest parts of the Iliad show — in Mycenæan times. It is reserved for the future to develop a true nobility and clergy in Russia.

cosmic and microcosmic, which pervades all being that moves freely in space, underlies this dual existence also. Each is possible and necessary only through the other. The Homeric world maintained a conspiracy of hostile silence towards the Orphic, and in turn (as we see from the Pre-Socratics) the former became an object of anger and contempt for the latter. In Gothic times the reforming spirits set themselves with a sacred enthusiasm across the path of the Renaissance-natures. State and Church have never really come to equilibrium, and in the conflict of Empire and Papacy their opposition rose to an intensity only possible for Faustian man.

Of the two, moreover, it is the nobility that is the true Estate, the sum of blood and race, being-stream in the fullest imaginable form. And therefore nobility is a higher peasantry. Even in 1250 the West had a widespread proverb: "One who ploughs in the forenoon jousts in the afternoon," and it was quite usual for a knight to marry the daughter of a peasant. In contrast to the cathedral, the castle was a development, by way of the country noble's house of Frankish times, from the peasant-dwelling. In the Icelandic sagas peasants' crofts are besieged and stormed like castles. Nobility and peasantry are plant-like and instinctive, deep-rooted in the ancestral land, propagating themselves in the family tree, breeding and bred. In comparison with them the priesthood is essentially the counter-estate, the estate of negation, of non-race, of detachment from earth — of free, timeless, and historyless waking-consciousness. In every peasant village, in every peasant family from the Stone Age to the peaks of the Culture, world-history plays itself out in little. Substitute for peoples families, and for lands farms — still the ultimate meaning of their strivings is the same — the maintenance of the blood, the succession of the generations, the cosmic, woman, power. *Macbeth* and *King Lear* might perfectly well have been thought out as village tragedies — and the fact is a proof of their tragic truth. In all Cultures nobility and peasantry appear in forms of *family descent*, and language itself connects them with the sexes, through which life propagates itself, has history, and is history. And as woman *is* history, the inward rank of peasant and noble families is determined by how much of race their women have in them, how far they *are* Destiny. And, therefore, there is deep meaning in the fact that the purer and more race-pervaded world-history is, the more the stream of its public life passes into and adapts itself to the private lives of individual great families. This, of course, is the basis of the dynastic principle, and not only that, but the basis of the idea of world-historical personality. The existence of entire states comes to depend on a few private destinies, vastly magnified. The history of Athens in the fifth century is in the main that of the Alcmæonidæ, the history of Rome is that of a few families of the type of the Fabii or the Claudii. The history of states in the Baroque is, broadly speaking, that of the operations of Habsburg and Bourbon family-politics, and its crises take form as marriages and wars of succession. The history of Napoleon's second marriage comprises also the burning of Moscow and the battle of Leipzig. The history of the Papacy is, right into the eighteenth century, that of a few noble families which competed for the tiara in order to found princely family-fortunes. This is true equally of Byzantine dignitaries and English premiers (witness the Cecils) and even, in numerous instances, of great revolution-leaders.

Of all this the priesthood (and philosophy so far as it is priesthood) is the direct negative. The Estate of pure waking-consciousness and eternal truths combats time and race and sex in every sense. Man as peasant or noble turns towards, man as priest turns away from, woman. Aristocracy runs the danger of dissipating and losing the broad being-stream of public life in the petty channels of its minor ancestors and relatives. The true priest, on the other hand, refuses in principle to recognize private life, sex, family, the "house." For the man of race death begins to be real and appalling only when it is death without heirs — Icelandic sagas no less than Chinese ancestor-worship teach us this. He does not entirely die who lives on in sons and nephews. But for the true priest *media vita in morte sumus;* what he shall bequeath is intellectual, and rejected woman bears no part in it. The phenomenal forms of this second Estate that occur again and again are celibacy, cloister, battlings with sex-impulse fought to the extreme of self-emasculation, and a contempt for mother-hood which expresses itself in orgiasm and hallowed prostitution, and not less in the intellectual devaluation of sexual life down to the level of Kant's vile definition of marriage.[1] Throughout the Classical world it was the rule that in the sacred precinct, the Temenos, no one must be born or die. The timeless must not come into contact with time. It is possible for the priest to have an intellectual recognition of the great moments of generation and birth, and to honour them sacramentally, but experience them he may not.

For while nobility *is* something, priesthood *signifies* something, and this alone would be enough to tell us that it is the opposite of all that is Destiny and Race and Estate. The castle, with its chambers and towers, walls and moats, tells of a strong-flowing life, but the cathedral, with its vaulting and pillars and choir, is, through and through, Meaning — that is to say, Orna-ment — and every venerable priesthood has developed itself up to that marvel-lous gravity and beauty of bearing in which every item, from facial expression and voice-inflection to costume and walk, is ornament, from which private life and even inward life have been eliminated as unessential — whereas that which a ripe aristocracy (such as that of eighteenth-century France) displays and parades is a finished living. It was Gothic thought that developed out of the priest-concept the *character indelebilis,* which makes the idea indestructible and wholly independent of the worthiness of its bearer's life in the world-as-

---

[1] As a treaty of reciprocal possession by the two parties which is made effective by the recipro-cal use of their sex-properties.

history — but every priesthood, and consequently also all philosophy (in the sense of the schools), contain it implicitly. If a priest has race, he leads an outward existence like peasant, knight, or prince. The Pope and cardinals of the Gothic period were feudal princes, leaders of armies, fond of the chase, connoisseurs and adepts in family politics. Among the Brahmins of the pre-Buddha "Baroque" were great landowners, well-groomed abbés, courtiers, spendthrifts, gourmets.[1] But it was the early period that had learned to distinguish the idea from the person — a notion diametrically opposed to the essence of nobility — and not until the Age of Enlightenment did the priest come to be judged, as priest, by his private life, and then not because that age had acquired sharper eyes, but because it had lost the idea.

The noble is the *man as history*, the priest is *the man as nature*. History of the high kind is always the expression and effect of the being of a noble society; and the criterion for the relative importance of its different events is always the pulse of this stream of being. That is why the battle of Cannæ matters much and the battles of Late Roman emperors matter not at all. The coming of a Springtime consistently coincides with the birth of a primary nobility, in whose sentiments the prince is merely "*primus inter pares*" and an object of mistrust. For not only does a strong race not need the big individual, but his existence is a reflection upon its worth; hence vassal-wars are pre-eminently the form in which the history of Early periods fulfils itself, and thenceforth the nobility has the fate of the Culture in hand. With a creative force that is all the more impressive because it is silent, Being is brought into form and "condition." The pulse in the blood is heightened and confirmed, *and for good*. For what this creative rise to living form is to the Spring — every Spring — the *might of tradition* is for the Late — every Late — period — namely, the old firm discipline, the life-beat, so sure that it outlives the extinction of all the old families and continually draws under its spell new men and new being-streams out of the deep. Beyond a shadow of doubt, all the history of Late periods, in respect of form and beat and tempo, is inherent (and irrevocably so) in the very earliest generations. Its successes are neither more nor less than the strength of the tradition in the blood. In politics, as in all other great and mature arts, success presupposes a being in high condition, a great stock of pristine experiences unconsciously and unquestioningly stored up as instincts and impulses. There is no other sort of political *maestria* but this. The big individual is only something better than an incident, only master of the future, in that he is effective (or is made effective), is Destiny (or has Destiny), in and through this form. This is what distinguishes necessary from superfluous art and therefore, also, *historically necessary from unnecessary politics*. It matters little if many of the big men come up out of the "people" (that is, the aggregate of the traditionless) into the governing stratum, or even if they are the

[1] Oldenberg, *Die Lehre der Upanishaden* (1915), p. 5.

only ones left to occupy it — the great tide of tradition takes charge of them, all unwitting, forms their intellectual and practical conduct, and rules their methods. And this tradition is nothing but the pulse of ancient and long-extinguished lines.

But Civilization, the real "return to Nature," is the extinction of nobility — not as physical stock (which would not matter), but as living tradition — and the supplanting of destiny-pulse by causal intelligence. With this, nobility becomes no more than a prefix. And, for that very reason, Civilized history is superficial history, directed disjointedly to obvious aims, and so become formless in the cosmic, dependent on the accident of great individuals, destitute of inward sureness, line, and meaning. With Cæsarism history relapses back into the historyless, the old beat of primitive life, with endless and meaningless battles for material power, such as those of the Roman soldier-emperors of the third century and the corresponding "Sixteen States" of China (265–420), which differ only in unessentials from the events of beast-life in a jungle.

III

It follows from this that true history is *not* "cultural" in the sense of anti-political, as the philosophers and doctrinaires of all commencing Civilizations assert. On the contrary, it is breed history, war history, diplomatic history, the history of being-streams in the form of man and woman, family, people, estate, state, reciprocally defensive and offensive in the wave-beat of grand facts. *Politics in the highest sense is life, and life is politics.* Every man is willy-nilly a member of this battle-drama, as subject or as object — there is no third alternative. The kingdom of the spirit is *not* of this world. True, but it presupposes it, as waking-being presupposes being. It is only possible as a consistent *saying* of "no" to the actuality that nevertheless exists and, indeed, must exist before it can be renounced. Race can dispense with language, but the very speaking of a language is an expression of antecedent race,[1] as are religions and arts and styles of thought and everything else that happens in the history of the spirit — and that there *is* such a history is shown by the power that blood possesses over feeling and reason. For all these are active waking-consciousness "in form," expressive, in their evolution and symbolism and passion, of the blood (again the blood) that courses through these forms in the waking-being of generation after generation. A hero does not need to know anything at all of this second world — he is life through and through — but a saint can only by the severest asceticism beat down the life that is in him and gain solitary communion with his spirit — and his strength for this again comes from life itself. The hero despises death and the saint life, but in the contrast between the heroism of great ascetics and martyrs and the piety of most (which is of

[1] P. 124.

the kind described in Revelation iii, 16 [1]) we discover that greatness, even in religion, presupposes Race, that life must be strong indeed to be worthy of such wrestlers. The rest is mere philosophy.

For this very reason nobility in the world-historical sense is much more than comfortable Late periods consider it; it is not a sum of titles and privileges and ceremonies, but an inward possession, hard to acquire, hard to retain — worth, indeed, for those who understand, the sacrifice of a whole life. An old family betokens not simply a set of ancestors (we all have ancestors), but ancestors who lived through whole generations on the heights of history; who not merely had Destiny, but were Destiny; in whose blood the form of happening was bred up to its perfection by the experience of centuries. As history in the grand sense begins with the Culture, it was mere panache for a Colonna to trace back his ancestry into Late Roman times. But it was not meaningless for the grandee of Late Byzantium to derive himself from Constantine, nor is it so for an American of to-day to trace his ancestry to a *Mayflower* immigrant of 1620. In actual fact Classical nobility begins with the Trojan period and not the Mycenæan, and the Western with the Gothic and not the Franks and Goths — in England with the Normans and not the Saxons. Only from these real starting-points is there History, and, therefore, only from then can there be an original aristocracy, as distinct from nobles and heroes. That which in the first chapter of this volume [2] I called cosmic beat or pulse receives in this aristocracy its fulfilment. For all that in riper times we call diplomatic and social "tact" — which includes strategic and business flair, the collector's eye for precious things, and the subtle insight of the judge of men — and generally all that which one has and does not learn; which arouses the impotent envy of the rest who cannot participate; which as "form" directs the course of events; is nothing but a particular case of the same cosmic and dreamlike sureness that is visibly expressed in the circlings of a flock of birds or the controlled movements of a thoroughbred horse.

The priest *circumscribes* the world-as-nature and deepens his picture of it by *thinking* into it. The noble *lives* in the world-as-history and deepens it by altering its picture. Both evolve towards the great tradition, but the evolution of the one comes of shaping and that of the other from training. This is a fundamental difference between the two Estates, and consequently only one of them is truly an Estate, and the other only *appears* to be such because of the completeness of the contrast. The field of effect of breed and training is the blood, and they pass on, therefore, from the fathers to the sons. Shaping (*Bildung*), on the other hand, presupposes talents, and consequently a true and strong priesthood is always a sum of individual gifts — a community of waking-

---

[1] "So, then, because thou art lukewarm, and neither cold nor hot, I will spue thee out of my mouth."

[2] P. 4, et seq.

consciousness — having no relation to origin in the race sense; and thus, in this respect as in others, it is a negation of Time and History. Intellectual affinity and blood-affinity — ponder and probe into the depths of these contrasted expressions! Heritable priesthood is a contradiction in terms. It existed indeed, in a sense, in Vedic India, but the basis of that existence was the fact that there was a second nobility, which reserved the privilege of priesthood to the gifted members of its own circle.[1] And elsewhere celibacy made an end even of this much infringement of principle. The "priest in the man" — whether the man be noble or not — stands for a focus of sacred Causality in the world. The priestly power is itself of a causal nature, brought about by higher causes and itself in turn an efficient cause. The priest is the *middleman* in the timeless extended that is stretched taut between the waking-consciousness and the ultimate secret; and, therefore, the importance of the clergy in each Culture is determined by its prime-symbol. The Classical soul denies Space and therefore needs no middleman for dealings with it, and so the Classical priesthood disappears in its very beginnings. Faustian man stands face to face with the Infinite, nothing *a priori* shields him from the crushing force of this aspect, and so the Gothic priesthood elevated itself to the heights of the Papal idea.

As two world-outlooks, two modes of blood-flow in the veins and of thought in the daily being and doing, are interwoven, there arise in the end (in every Culture) two sorts of moral, of which each looks down upon the other — namely, noble custom, and priestly askesis, reciprocally censured as worldly and as servile. It has been shown already [2] how the one proceeds from the castle and the other from the cloister and the minster, the one from full being in the flood of History and the other, aloof therefrom, out of pure waking-consciousness in the ambiance of a God-pervaded nature. The force with which these primary impressions act upon men is something that later periods will be unable even to imagine. The secular and the spiritual class-feeling are starting on their upward career, and cutting out for themselves an ethical *class-ideal* which is accessible only to the right people, and even to them only by way of long and strict schooling. The *great* being-stream *feels* itself as a unit as against the residue of dull, pulseless, and aimless blood. The *great* mind-community *knows* itself as a unit as against the residue of uninitiated. These units are the band of heroes and the community of saints.

It will always remain the great merit of Nietzsche that he was the first to recognize the dual nature of all moral.[3] His designations of "master-" and "slave-" moral were inexact, and his presentation of "Christianity" placed it much too definitely on the one side of the dividing line, but at the basis of all his opinions this lies strong and clear, that *good and bad are aristocratic, and good and*

---

[1] The case of Egypt is of course similar. — *Tr.*
[2] Pp. 272, et seq.
[3] *Jenseits von Gut und Böse*, § 260.

evil priestly, distinctions. Good and bad, which are Totemistic distinctions among primitive groups of men and tribes, describe, not dispositions, but men, and describe them comprehensively in respect of their living-being. The good are the powerful, the rich, the fortunate. Good means strong, brave, thorough-bred, in the idiom of every Springtime. Bad, cheap, wretched, common, in the original sense, are the powerless, propertyless, unfortunate, cowardly, negligible — the "sons of nobody" as ancient Egypt said.[1] Good and evil, Taboo concepts, assign value to a man according to his perceptions and reason — that is, his waking disposition and his *conscious* actions. To offend against love-ethic in the race sense is ungentle, to sin against the Church's love-command is wicked. The noble habit is the perfectly unconscious result of a long and continuous training. It is learned in intercourse and not from books. It is a felt rhythm, and not a notion. But the other moral is enunciated, ordered on the basis of cause and consequence, and therefore learnable and expressive of a *conviction.*

The one is historical through and through, and recognizes rank-distinctions and privileges as actual and axiomatic. Honour is always class-honour — there is no such thing as an "honour of humanity." The duel is not an obligation of unfree persons. Every man, be he Bedouin or Samurai or Corsican, peasant or workman, judge or bandit, has his own binding notions of honour, loyalty, courage, revenge, that do not apply to other kinds of life. Every life *has* custom-ethic — it is unthinkable without it. Children have it already in their play; they know at once, of themselves, what is fitting. No one has laid down these rules, but they exist. They arise, quite unconsciously, out of the "we" that has formed itself out of the uniform pulse of the group. Here, too, each being is "in form." Every crowd that, under one or another stimulus, has collected in the street has for the moment its own ethic, and anyone who does not absorb it and stand for it as self-evident — to say "follow it" would presume more rationality in the action than there is — is a poor, mean creature, an outsider. Uneducated people and children possess an astonishingly fine reactivity to this. Children, however, are also required to learn the Catechism, and in it they hear about the good and evil that are laid down — and are any thing rather than self-evident. Custom-ethic is not that which is *true,* but that which is *there;* it is a thing of birth and growth, feeling and organic logic. Moral, in contrast to this, is never actuality (for, if it were, all the world would be saintly), but an eternal demand hanging over the consciousness — and, *ex hypothesi,* over that of all men alike, irrespective of all differences of actual life and history. And, therefore, all moral is negative and all custom-ethic affirmative. In the latter "devoid of honour" is the worst, in the former "devoid of sin" is the highest, that can be said of anyone.

The basic concept of all living custom-ethic is honour. Everything else

---

[1] In contrast, the Spanish word "*Hidalgo*" means "son of somebody." — *Tr.*

— loyalty, modesty, bravery, chivalry, self-control, resolution — is comprised in it. And honour is a matter of the blood and not of the reason. One does not reflect on a point of honour — that is already dishonour. To lose honour means to be annulled so far as Life and Time and History are concerned. The honour of one's class, one's family, of man and woman, of one's people and one's country, the honour of peasant and soldier and even bandit — honour means that the life in a person is something that has worth, historical dignity, delicacy, nobility. It belongs to directional Time, as sin belongs to timeless Space. To have honour in one's body means about the same as to have race. The opposite sort are the Thersites-natures, the mud-souled, the riff-raff, the "kick-me-but-let-me-live's." To submit to insult, to forget a humiliation, to quail before an enemy — all these are signs of a life become worthless and superfluous. But this is not at all the same thing as priestly moral, for that moral does not cleave to life at any cost of degradation, but rather rejects and abstains from life as such, and therefore incidentally from honour. As has been said already, every moral action is, at the very bottom, a piece of askesis and a killing of being. And *eo ipso* it stands outside the field of life and the world of history.

IV

Here it is necessary to anticipate somewhat, and to consider whence it is that world-history (especially in the Late periods of the grand Cultures and the beginnings of the Civilizations) derives its rich variety of colour and the profound symbolism of its events. The primary Estates, nobility and clergy, are the purest expressions of the two sides of life, but they are not the only ones. In very early times — often, indeed, foreshadowed in the Primitive Age itself — yet other being-streams and waking-linkages break forth, in which the symbolism of Time and Space comes to living expression, and which, when (and not until) combined with these two, make up the whole fullness of what we call *social organization* or *society*.

While Priesthood is microcosmic and animal-like, Nobility is cosmic and plantlike (hence its profound connexion with the land). It is itself a plant, strongly rooted in the soil, established on the soil — in this, as in so many other respects, a supreme peasantry. It is from this kind of cosmic boundness that the idea of *property* arises, which to the microcosm as such, freely moving in space, is wholly alien. Property is a primary feeling and not a concept; it belongs to Time and History and Destiny, and not to Space and Causality. It cannot be logically based, but it is there.[1] "Having" begins with the plant, and propagates itself in the history of higher mankinds just to the precise extent that history contains plant-character and race. Hence property in the most genuine sense is always ground-property, and the impulse to convert

---

[1] Conversely, it can successfully be controverted — and often has been so in the Chinese and Classical, Indian and Western philosophies — but it does not get abolished.

other acquisitions into ground and soil is an evidence of sound stock. The plant *possesses* the ground in which it roots. It is its property,[1] which it defends to the utmost, with the desperate force of its whole being, against alien seeds, against overshadowing neighbour plants, against all nature. So, too, a bird defends the nest in which it is hatching. The bitterness fights over property occur — not in the Late periods of great Cultures, between rich and poor, and about movable goods — but here in the beginnings of the plant-world. When, in a wood, one feels all about one the silent, merciless battle for the soil that goes on day and night, one is appalled by the depth of an impulse that is almost identical with life itself. Here is a yearlong, tenacious, embittered wrestle, a hopeless resistance of the weak against the strong, that goes on to the point that the victor too is broken — such as is only paralleled in the most primitive of mankind when an old peasant-family is expelled from the clod, *from the nest,* or a family of noble stock is uprooted or, more truly, cut off from its roots, by money.[2] The far more conspicuous conflicts in the later cities have quite another meaning, for here — in communism of all kinds — it is not the experience of possessing, but the idea of property purely as material means that is fought for. The negation of property is never race-impulse, but the doctrinaire protest of the purely intellectual, urban, uprooted, anti-vegetal waking-consciousness of saints, philosophers, and idealists. The same reason actuates the monk of the hermitage and the scientific Socialist — be his name Moh-ti, Zeno, or Marx — to reject the plantlike; the same feeling impels men of race to defend it. Here, as ever, fact and truth are opposed. "Property is theft" is the ultra-materialistic form of the old thought: "What shall it profit a man if he shall gain the whole world and lose his own soul?" When the priest gives up property, he is giving up something dangerous and alien; when a noble does so, he is giving up himself.

This brings us to a duality of the property-idea feeling — *Having as power* and *Having as spoil.* Both, in primitive men of race, lie immediately together. Every Bedouin or Viking intends both. The sea-hero is always a sea-robber also; every war is concerned with possessions and, above all, possessions in land. But a step, and the knight becomes the robber-knight, the adventurer becomes conqueror and king, like Rurik the Norman in Russia and many an Achæan and Etruscan pirate in Homeric times. In all heroic poetry we find,

---

[1] The possession of movable things (food, equipment, arms) comes later, and is of much lower symbolic weight. It occurs widely in the animal world. The bird's nest, on the contrary, is a property of plantlike kind.

[2] Property in this most significant sense — the having grown up with something — refers therefore less to the particular person than to the family tree to which he belongs. In every quarrel within a peasant or even within a princely family, this is the deep and violent element. The master for the time being holds possession only in the name of the family line. Hence, too, the terror of death without heirs. *Property also is a Time-symbol,* and consequently it is closely related to marriage, which is a firm plantlike intergrowth and mutual possession of two human beings, so real as to be even reflected in an increasing facial similarity.

side by side with the strong and natural satisfaction of winning battles and power and women, and the unbridled outbursts of joy and grief, anger, and love, the immense delight of "having." When Odysseus lands at home, the first thing he does is to count the treasures in his boat, and when, in the Icelandic Saga, the peasants Hjalmar and Ölvarod perceive each that the other has no goods in his ship, they abandon their duel at once — he who fights from pride and for honour is a fool for his pains. In the Indian hero-epic, eagerness for battle means eagerness for cattle, and the "colonizing" Greeks of the tenth century were primarily corsairs like the Normans. On the high seas an alien ship is *a priori* good prize. But out of the feuds of South-Arabian and Persian Knights of A.D. 200, and the "private wars" of the Provençal barons of A.D. 1200 — which were hardly more than cattle-raids — there developed at the end of the feudal period the war proper, the great war with acquisition of land and people as its object. All this, in the end, brings the aristocratic Culture to the "top of its form," while, correspondingly, priests and philosophers despise it.

As the Culture rises to its height, these two primary urges trend widely apart, and hostility develops between them. *The history of this hostility is almost the same thing as world-history. From the feeling of power come conquest and politics and law; from that of spoil, trade and economy and money.* Law is the property of the powerful. Their law is the law of all. Money is the strongest weapon of the acquiring: with it he subdues the world. Economics likes and intends a state that is weak and subservient to it. Politics demands that economic life shall adapt itself to and within the State — Adam Smith and Friedrich List, Capitalism and Socialism. All Cultures exhibit at the outset a war- and a trade-nobility, then a land- and a money-nobility, and finally a military and an economic war-management and a ceaseless struggle of money against law.

Equally, on the other hand, *priesthood* and *learning* separate out. Both are directed towards, not the factual, but the true; both belong to the Taboo side of life and to Space. Fear before death is the source, not merely of all religion, but of all philosophy and natural science as well. Now, however, there develops a profane Causality in contrast to the sacred. "Profane" is the new counter-concept to "religious," which so far had tolerated learning only as a handmaiden. The whole of Late criticism, its spirit, its method, its aims, are profane — and the Late theology, even, is no exception to the rule. But invariably, nevertheless, the learning of all Cultures moves in the forms of the preceding priesthood — thus showing that it is merely a product of the contradiction itself, and how dependent it is and remains, in every particular, upon the primary image. Classical science, therefore, lives in cult-communities of the Orphic style, such as the school of Miletus, the Pythagorean society, the medical schools of Croton and Cos, the Attic schools of the Academy, the Peripatos, and the Stoa, every one of whose leaders belongs to the type of the sacrificial priest and seer, and even the Roman legal schools of the Sabiniani and Proculiani. The sacred book, the Canon is, scientifically as in other respects, Arabian — the scientific canon of Ptolemy (Almagest), the medical of Ibn Sina (Avicenna), and the philosophical corpus designated "Aristotle," but so largely spurious — so also the (mostly unwritten) laws and methods of quotation: [1] the Commentary as the form of thought-development; the universities as cloisters (Medrashim) which provided teachers and students with cell, food, and clothing; and tendencies in scholarship taking form as brotherhoods. The learned world of the West possesses unmistakably the form of the Catholic Church, and more particularly so in Protestant regions. The connecting link between the learned orders of the Gothic period and the order-like schools of the nineteenth century — the schools of Hegel, of Kant, of historical jurisprudence, and not a few of the English university colleges — is formed by the Maurists and Bollandists [2] of France, who from 1650 on mastered and largely created the ancillary "science" of history. In all the specialist sciences (medicine and lecture-room philosophy included) there are fully developed hierarchies leading up to school-popes, grades, and dignities (the doctor's degree as an ordination), sacraments and councils. The uninitiate is rigorously treated as the "layman," and the idea of a generalized priesthood residing in the believers themselves, which is manifested in "popular" science — for example, Darwinism — is passionately combated. The language of learning was originally Latin, but to-day all sorts of special languages have formed themselves which (in the domain of radioactivity, for example, or that of the law of contract) are unintelligible save to those who have received the higher initiation. There are founders of sects, such as many of Kant's and Hegel's disciples were; there are missionaries to the unbelievers, like the Monists. There are heretics, like Schopenhauer and Nietzsche, there is the weapon of the ban, and there is the Index in the form of the Conspiracy of Silence. There are ethical truths (for example, in Law the division of the objects into persons and things) and dogmas (like that of energy and mass, or the theory of inheritance), a ritual in the citation of orthodox writings, and even a scientific sort of beatification. [3]

More, the savant-type of the West (which in the nineteenth century reached its zenith, corresponding to the nadir of true priesthood) has brought to high perfection the study as the cell of a profane monachism that has its unconscious vows — of Poverty, in the shape of honourable disdain for fat living and wealth, and unfeigned contempt for the commercial professional and for all exploitation of scientific results for gain; of Chastity, which has evolved a veritable celibacy of science, with Kant as exemplar and culmination; and of Obedience, even to the point of sacrificing oneself to the standpoint of the

[1] See p. 248.

[2] See these headings in *Ency. Brit.*, XI. ed. — *Tr.*

[3] After death the teachers of error are excluded from the eternal bliss of the text-book and cast into the purgatorial fires of foot-notes, whence, purged by the intercession of the believer, they ascend into the paradise of the paragraphs.

School. Further, and lastly, there is a sort of estrangement from the world which is the profane echo of the Gothic flight from it, and leads to an almost complete disregard of the life in public and the forms of good society — little "breeding," much too much "shaping." Nobility, even in its later ramifications — the judge, the squire, the officer — still retains the old root-strong natural satisfaction in carrying on the stock, in possessions and honour, but the scientist counts these things as little beside the possession of a pure scientific conscience and the carrying on of a method or a view unimpaired by the commercialism of the world. The fact that the savant to-day has ceased to be remote from the world, and puts his science at the service of (not seldom, indeed, most shrewdly applies it to) technics and money-making, is a sign that the pure type is entering upon its decline and that the great age of intellectual optimism that is livingly expressed in him belongs already to the past.

In sum, we see that the Estates have a natural build which in its evolution and action forms the basic structure of every Culture's life-course. No specific decision made it; revolutions only alter it when they are forms of the evolution and not results of some private will. It never, in its full cosmic significance, enters the consciousness of men as doers and thinkers, because it lies too deep in human being to be other than a self-evident datum. It is merely from the surface that men take the catchwords and causes over which they fight on that side of history which theory regards as horizontally layered, but which in actuality is an aggregate of inseparable interpenetrations. First, nobility and priesthood arise out of the open landscape, and figure the pure symbolism of Being and Waking-Being, Time and Space. Then out of the one under the aspect of booty, and out of the other under the aspect of research, there develop doubled types of lower symbolic force, which in the urban Late periods rise to prepotency in the shapes of *economy* and *science*. In these two being-streams the ideas of Destiny and Causality are thought out to their limit, unrelentingly and anti-traditionally. Forces emerge which are separated by a deadly enmity from the old class-ideals of heroism and saintliness — these forces are *money and intellect*, and they are related to those ideals as the city to the country. Henceforward property is called riches, and world-outlook knowledge — a desanctified Destiny and a profane Causality. But science is in contradiction with Nobility too, for this does not prove or investigate, but *is*. "*De omnibus dubitandum*" is the attitude of a burgher and not of an aristocrat, while at the same time it contradicts the basic feeling of priesthood, for which the proper rôle of critique is that of a handmaid. Economy, too, finds an enemy here, in the shape of the ascetic moral which rejects money-getting, just as the genuine land-based nobility despises it. Even the old merchant-nobility has in many cases perished (e.g., Hanse Towns, Venice, Genoa), because with its traditions it could not and would not fall in with the business outlook of the big city. And, with all this, economy and science are themselves at enmity; once more, in the conflicts of money-getting and knowledge, *between counting-house and study*, business liberalism and doctrinaire liberalism, we meet the old great oppositions of action and contemplation, castle and cathedral. In one form or in another this order of things emerges in the structure of every Culture — hence the possibility of a comparative morphology in the social as in the other aspects of history.

Wholly outside the category of the true Estates are the calling-classes of the craftsmen, officials, artists, and labourers, whose organization in guilds (e.g., of smiths in China, of scribes in Egypt, and of singers in the Classical world) dates from pristine antiquity, and who because of their professional segregation (which sometimes goes as far as to cut off their *connubium* with others) actually develop into genuine tribes, as, for instance, the Falasha [1] of Abyssinia and some of the Sudra classes named in Manu's code. Their separation is due merely to their technical accomplishments and therefore not to their being vessels of the symbolism of Time and Space. Their tradition, likewise, is limited to their techniques and does not refer to a customary-ethic or a moral *of their own*, such as is always found in economy and science as such. As derived from a nobility, judges and officers are classes, whereas officials are a profession; as derived from priesthood, scholars are a class, while artists are a profession. Sense of honour, conscience, adhere in one case to the status, in the other to the achievement. There is something, slight though it may be, of symbolism in every category on the one side, and none in any category on the other. And consequently something of strangeness, irregularity, often disgrace, clings to them — consider, for example, executioners, actors, and strolling singers, or the Classical estimation of the artist. Their classes or guilds separate from general society, or seek the protection of other orders of society (or individual patrons and Mæcenases), but fit themselves in with that society they cannot, and their inability to do so finds expression in the guild-wars of the old cities and in uncouthness of every sort in the instincts and manners of artists.

v

A history of estates or classes, ignoring in principle that of profession-classes, is therefore a presentation of the metaphysical element in higher mankind, so far as this rises to grand symbolism in species of onflowing life, species in and along which the history of the Cultures moves to fulfilment.

At the very beginning, the sharply defined type of the peasant is something new. In Carolingian times, and under the Tsarist system of the "Mir" in Russia,[2] there were freemen and hinds cultivating the soil, *but no peasantry*.

---

[1] Black Jews, who are smiths to a man.

[2] The genuinely primitive Mir, contrary to the assertions of enthusiastic socialists and pan-slavists, dates only from after 1600, and has been abolished since 1861. Here the soil is *communal* soil, and the villagers are as far as possible held fast, in order to ensure that the tilling of this soil shall cover the demands of taxation.

Only when there emerges the feeling of being different from the two symbolic "lives" — Freidank's *Bescheidenheit* [1] comes into our minds — does this life become an Estate, the *nourishing* estate in the fullest sense of the word, the root of the great plant Culture, which has driven its fibres deep into Mother Earth and darkly, industriously, draws all juices into itself and sends them to the upper parts, where trunks and branches tower up in the light of history. It serves the great lives not merely by the nourishment that it wins out of the soil for them, but also with that other harvest of mother earth — its own blood; for blood flowed up for centuries from the villages into the high places, received there the high forms, and maintained the high lives. The relation is called (from the noble's point of view) *vassalage*, and we find it arising — whatever the superficial causes may be in each case — in the West between 1000 and 1400 and in the other Cultures at the "contemporary" periods. The Helotry of Sparta belongs with it, and equally so the old Roman *clientela*, from which after 471 the *rural* Plebs — that is, a free yeomanry — grew up. [2] Astonishing indeed is the force of this striving towards symbolic form in the Pseudomorphosis of the Late Roman East, where the caste system of the principate founded by Augustus (with its division into senatorial and equestrian officialdom) evolved backwards until, about 300, it had returned, wherever the Magian world-feeling prevailed, to a condition parallel to that of the Gothic in 1300 — the condition, in fact, of the Sassanid Empire of its own time. [3] Out of the official-dom of a highly Civilized administration came a minor nobility of decurions, village knights, and town politicians, who were responsible to the sovereign in body and goods for all outgoings — a feudalism formed backwards — and gradually made their positions heritable, just as happened under the Egyptian Vth dynasty and the first Chóu centuries [4] and the Europe of the Crusades. Military status, of officers and soldiers alike, became hereditary in the same way, [5] and service as a feudal obligation, and all the rest of what Diocletian presently reduced to formal law. The individual was firmly bound to the status (*corpori adnexus*), and the principle was extended as compulsory guild-membership to all trades, as in the Gothic or in old Egypt. But, above all, there necessarily arose from the ruins of the Late Classical slave-economy of "Latifundia" [6] the colonate of hereditary small farmers, while the great estates became administrative districts and the lord was made responsible for its taxes and its

[1] See *Ency. Brit.*, XI ed., Vol. XI, pp. 94, 786, or any histories of German literature. — *Tr.*

[2] See, further, below.

[3] Brentano, *Byzant. Volkswirtschaft* (1917), p. 15.

[4] Even I-wang (934–909) was obliged to leave conquered territories to his vassals, who put in counts and reeves of their own choice.

[5] See H. Delbrück, *Gesch. der Kriegskunst*, Vol. II, Book I, Ch. x; or C. W. C. Oman, *Art of War: Middle Ages*, Ch. i. — *Tr.*

[6] The slave in the Classical sense disappears automatically and completely in these centuries — one of the most significant indications that the Classical world-feeling, and with it its economic feeling, were extinct.

recruit-quota.[1] Between 250 and 300 the "colonus" became legally bound to the soil (*adscriptus glebæ*). And with that the differentiation of feudal lord and vassal *as class and class* [2] was reached.

Every new Culture has potentially its nobility and its priesthood. The apparent exceptions to this are due merely to the absence to tangible tradition. We know to-day that a real priesthood existed in ancient China [3] and we may assume as self-evident that there was a priest-estate in the beginnings of Orphism in the eleventh century B.C. — the more confidently as we have plain indications of it in the epic figures of Calchas and Tiresias. Similarly the development of the feudal constitution in Egypt presupposes a primitive nobility as early as the IIIrd Dynasty.[4] But the form in which, and the force with which, these Estates first realized themselves and then took charge of the course of history — shaped it, carried it, and even represented it in their own destinies — depend upon the Prime-symbol on which each individual Culture, with its entire form-language, is based.

The nobility, wholly plantlike, proceeds everywhere from the land, which is its primary property and with which it is fast bound. It possesses everywhere the basic form of the family, the gens (in which, therefore, the "other" gender of history, the feminine, is expressed also), and it manifests itself through the will-to-duration — duration, namely, of the blood — as the great symbol of Time and History. It will appear that the early officialdom of the vassal state, based on personal trustworthiness, everywhere — in China and Egypt, in the Classical and the Western World — [5] goes through the same development, first creating quasi-feudal court offices and dignities, then seeking hereditary connexion with the soil, and so finally becoming the origin of noble family-lines.

The Faustian will-to-infinity comes to expression in the *genealogical principle*, which — strange as it may seem — is peculiar to this Culture. And in this Culture, moreover, it intimately permeates and moulds all the historical forms, and supremely those of the states themselves. The historical sense that insists upon getting to know the destinies of its own blood backwards through the centuries and seeing *archival* proofs of dates and provenances up to the first

---

[1] Thus, later, under Justinian, Belisarius could furnish seven thousand cavalry from his own domains for the Gothic War. Very few German princes could have done so much in Charles V's time. [The last of such armies in Western history was the army of the House of Condé in the seventeenth century. These centuries of ours "correspond" with the period that set in with Justinian. — *Tr.*]

[2] Pöhlmann, *Röm. Kaiserzeit* (Pflugk-Harttungs *Weltgesch.*, I, pp. 200, et seq.).

[3] See p. 286.

[4] In spite of Ed. Meyer (*Gesch. d. Altertums*, I, § 243).

[5] Our marshal and the Chinese *sse-ma*, chamberlain and *Chen*, high steward and *ta-tsai*, high bailiff and *nan*, earl and *peh* (the Chinese ranks as in Schindler, *Das Priestertum im alten China*, p. 61, et seq.). Precisely corresponding Egyptian grades in Ed. Meyer, *Gesch. des Altertums*, I, § 222; Byzantine in the "*Notitia Dignitatum*" (derived in part from the Sassanid Court). In the Classical city-states certain official titles of ancient origin suggest court functions (Colacretæ, Prytanes, Consuls). See further below.

ancestors; the careful ordering of the genealogical tree, which is potent enough
to make present possession and inheritance dependent upon the fortunes of a
single marriage contracted perhaps five hundred years ago; the conceptions of
pure blood, birth-equivalence, *mésalliance* — all this is will-to-direction in time,
will towards Time's remote distances. There is no second example of it, save
perhaps in the Egyptian nobility, and there the comparable forms that were
attained were far weaker.

Nobility of the Classical style, on the contrary, relates to the present estate
of the agnatic family, and from it straight to a *mythical* origin, which does not
imply the historical sense in the least, but only a craving, sublimely regardless
of historic probability, for splendid backgrounds to the here and now of the
living. Only thus can we explain the otherwise baffling naïveté with which an
individual saw behind his grandfather Theseus and Heracles in one plane, and
fashioned himself a family tree (or several, perhaps, as Alexander did), and the
light-heartedness with which respectable Roman families would forge the
names of reputed ancestors into the old consular lists. At the funeral of a
Roman noble the wax masks of great forefathers were introduced into the
cortège, but it was only for the number and sound of the famous names and not
in the least on account of any genealogical connexion with the present. This
trait appears throughout the Classical nobility, which like the Gothic formed,
structurally and spiritually, one inward unit from Etruria to Asia Minor. On it
rested the power that, even at the beginning of the Late period, was still in
the possession of order-like family-groupings throughout the cities (phylæ,
phratriæ, tribus, and what not) which maintained a purely present membership
and unity by means of sacral forms — for example, the three Doric and the four
Ionic phylæ, and the three Etruscan tribes that appear in the earlier Roman history as Tities, Ramnes, and Luceres. In the Vedas the "father-" and the
"mother-"souls had claims to soul-rites only in respect of three nearer and three
further generations,[1] after which the past claimed them; and nowhere do we
find the Classical cult of souls reaching any further back than the Indian. It is
the very reverse of the ancestor-worship of the Chinese and the Egyptians,
which was by hypothesis without end, and therefore maintained the family in
a definite ordering even beyond bodily death. In China there still lives to-day
a duke, Kong, who is the descendant of Confucius and equally the descendant
of Lao-tse, of Chang-lu, and others. It is not a question of a many-branched
tree, but of carrying the line, the *tao* of being, straight on — if necessary, frankly
by adoption (the adopted member, pledged to the ancestor-cult, is thereby
spiritually incorporated in the family) or other expedients.

An unbridled joy of life streams through the flourishing centuries of this
estate, *the* Estate *par excellence*, which is direction and destiny and race through
and through. Love, because woman *is* history, and war because fighting *makes*

---

[1] Hardy, *Indische Religionsgesch.*, p. 260.

history, are the acknowledged foci of its thoughts and feelings. The Northern skald-poetry and the Southern *Minnesang* correspond to the old love-songs of the Chinese age of chivalry in the Shi-King,[1] which were sung in the Pi-Yung, the places of noble training (*hiao*). And the ceremonial public archery-displays, like the Early Classical agon, and the Gothic and the Persian-Byzantine [2] tourney, were manifestations of the life on its Homeric side.

In opposition to this side stands the *Orphic* — the expression of the space-experience of a Culture through the style of its priesthood. It was in accord with the Euclidean character of Classical extension — which needed no intermediaries for intercourse with near and corporeal gods — that in this case priesthood, from beginnings as an estate, rapidly degenerated into city-officialdom. Similarly, it was expressive of the Chinese *tao* that the place of the original hereditary priesthood came to be taken by professional classes of praying men, scribes, and oracle-priests, who could accompany the religious performances of the authorities and heads of families with the prescribed rites. It was in conformity, again, with the Indian world-feeling that lost itself in measureless infinity that the priest-class there became a second nobility, which with immense power, intruding upon every sort of life, planted itself between the people and its wilderness of gods. It is an expression, lastly, of the "cavern" feeling that the priest of true Magian cast is the monk and the hermit, and becomes more and more so, while the secular clergy steadily loses in symbolic significance.

In contrast to all these there is the Faustian priesthood, which, still without any profound import or dignity in 900, rose up thereafter to that sublime rôle of intermediary which placed it in principle between humanity (*all* humanity) and a macrocosm strained to all imaginable expanse by the Faustian passion of the third dimension. Excluded from history by celibacy and from time by its *character indelebilis*, it culminated in the Papacy, which represented the highest symbol of God's dynamic Space that it was possible to conceive; even the Protestant idea of a generalized priesthood has not destroyed it, but merely decentralized it from one point and one person into the heart of each individual believer.

The contradiction between being and waking-being that exists in every microcosm necessarily drives the two Estates against one another. Time seeks to absorb and subordinate Space, Space Time. Spiritual and worldly power are magnitudes so different in structure and tendency that any reconciliation, or even understanding, between them seems impossible. But this conflict has not in all Cultures come to world-historical expression. In China it promoted the *tao* idea that primacy should reside securely in an aristocracy. In

---

[1] M. Granet, *Coutumes matrimoniales de la Chine antique*, T'oung Pao (1912), pp. 517, et seq.

[2] The tournament was an institution in the other, western, half of the Magian world as well. — *Tr.*

India the conception of Space as infinite-indefinite required a primacy of the priesthood. In the Arabian Culture the Magian world-feeling involved in principle the inclusion of the worldly visible society of believers as a constituent in the grand consensus, and therefore the unity of spiritual and temporal polity, law, and sovereignty. Not that there was not friction between the two estates; far from it; in the Sassanid Empire there were bloody feuds between the country aristocracy of the Dikhans and the party of the Magi — even in some instances murders of sovereigns — and in Byzantium the whole fifth century is full of the struggles between the Imperial power and the clergy, which from an ever-present background to the Monophysite and Nestorian controversies.[1] But the basic interconnexion of the two orders was not in dispute.

In the Classical world, which abhorred the infinite in every sense, Time was reduced to the present and Extension to tangible unit-bodies; as the result, the grand symbolic estates became so voided of meaning that, as compared with the city-state, which expressed the Classical prime-symbol in the strongest imaginable form, they did not count as independent forces at all. In the history of Egyptian mankind, on the other hand, which is the history of striving with equal force towards distances of time and of space, the struggle of the two estates and their symbolisms is constantly recognizable right into the period of complete fellahdom. For the transition from the IVth to the Vth Dynasty is accompanied also by a visible triumph of the priestly over the knightly world-feeling; the Pharaoh, from being the body and vessel of the supreme deity, becomes its servant, and the Re sanctuary overpowers the tomb-temple of the ruler both in architectural and in suggestive force. The New Empire witnessed, immediately after its great Cæsars, the political autocracy of the Amen priesthood, Thebes, and then again the revolution of the "heretic" king Amenophis IV (Akhenaton) — in which one feels unmistakably a political as well as a religious side — and so on until after interminable conflicts between warrior- and priestly-castes, the Egyptian world ended in foreign domination.

In the Faustian Culture this battle between two high symbols of equal force has been waged in somewhat the same spirit, but with far greater passion still than in the Egyptian — so that, from the early Gothic onward, only armistice, never peace, has seemed possible between State and Church. But in this conflict the handicap against waking-being tells — it would shake off its dependence upon being, but it cannot. The mind needs the blood, but the blood does not need the mind. War belongs to the world of time and history — *intellectual battle is only a fight with reasons, only disputation* — and, therefore a *militant* Church must step from the world of truths into the world of facts — from the world of Jesus into that of Pilate. And so it becomes an element in race-history and subject to the formative powers of the *political* side of life. From early Feudalism to modern Democracy it fights with sword and cannon, poison and dagger,

[1] The life of John Chrysostom is an instance.

bribery and treason, all the weapons of party conflict in use at the time. It sacrifices articles of belief to worldly advantages, and allies itself with heretics and unbelievers against orthodox powers. The Papacy *as an idea* has a history of its own, but this bears no relation to the position of the popes in the sixth and seventh centuries as Byzantine viceroys of Syrian and Greek provenance; or to their later evolution into powerful landowners, with crowds of subject peasants; or to the Patrimonium Petri of the early Gothic — a sort of duchy in the possession of great families of the Campagna (Colonna, Orsini, Savelli, Frangipani), which alternately set up the popes, until finally the general Western feudalism prevailed here also, and the Holy See came to be an object of investiture within the families of the Roman baronage, so that each new pope, like a German or a French king, had to confirm the rights of his vassals. In 1032 the Counts of Tusculum nominated a twelve-year-old boy as pope. In those days eight hundred castle-towers stood up in the city area of Rome amongst and upon the Classical ruins. In 1045 three popes entrenched themselves in the Vatican, the Lateran, and Santa Maria Maggiore respectively, and were defended by their noble supporters.

Now supervened the city with its own soul, first emancipating itself from the soul of the countryside, then setting up as an equal to it, and finally seeking to suppress and extinguish it. But this evolution accomplished itself in *kinds of life*, and it also, therefore, is part of the history of the estates. The city-*life* as such emerges — through the inhabitants of these small settlements acquiring a common soul, and becoming conscious that the life within is something different from the life outside — and at once the spell of *personal freedom* begins to operate and to attract within the walls life-streams of more and more new kinds. There sets in a sort of passion for becoming urban and for propagating urban life. It is this, and not material considerations, that produced the fever of the colonization period in the Classical world, which is still recognizable to us in its last offshoots, and which it is not quite exact to speak of as colonization at all. For it was a creative enthusiasm in the man of the city that from the tenth century B.C. (and "contemporaneously" in other Cultures) drew generation after generation under the spell of a new life, with which there emerges for the first time in human history the idea of *freedom*. This idea is not of political (still less of abstract) origin, but is something bringing to expression the fact that within the city walls plantlike attachment to a soil has ceased, and that the threads that run through the whole life of the countryside have been snapped. And consequently the freedom-idea ever contains a negative; it looses, redeems, defends, always frees a man *from* something. Of *this* freedom the city is the expression; the city-spirit is understanding become free, and everything in the way of intellectual, social, and national movements that bursts forth in Late periods under the name of Freedom leads back to an origin *in this one prime fact of detachment from the land.*

But the city is older than the "citizen." It attracts first the calling-classes, which as such are outside the symbolic estates, and, when urban, take form as guilds. Then it draws in the primary estates themselves; the minor nobility moves its castles, the Franciscans their cloisters, within the contour. As yet, not much is inwardly altered. Not only Papal Rome, but all Italian cities of this time are filled with the fortified towers of the families, who issued thence to fight out their feuds in the streets. In a well-known fourteenth-century picture of Siena these towers stand up like factory chimneys round the market-place.[1] As for the Florentine palace of the Renaissance, if, in respect of the bright life within, it is the successor of Provençal courts, it is equally, with its "rusticated" façade, an offshoot of the Gothic castles that the French and German knights were still building on their hills. It was, in fact, only slowly that the new life separated out. Between 1250 and 1450, throughout the West, the immigrant families concentrated, *vis-à-vis* the guilds, into the patriciate, and in so doing detached themselves, spiritually as in other respects, from the country nobility. It was exactly the same in early China, Egypt, and the Byzantine Empire, and it is only in the light of this that we become able to understand the older Classical city-leagues (such as the Etruscan and, it may be, even the Latin) and the sacral connexions of colonial daughter-cities with their mother city. It was not the Polis as such, so far, that was the backbone of events, but the patriciate of phylæ and phratriæ within it. *The original Polis is identical with the nobility*, as Rome was up to 471, and Sparta and the Etruscan cities throughout. Synœcism grew out of it, and the city-state was formed by it. But here, as in other Cultures, the difference between country- and city-nobility was at first quite unimportant as compared with the strong and deep distinction between the nobility (in general) and the residue.

The burgher proper emerges when the fundamental distinction between town and country has brought the "families and the guilds," in spite of their otherwise implacable hostility to one another, to a sense of unity *vis-à-vis* the old nobility, the feudal system generally, and the feudal position of the Church. The notion of the "Third Estate" (to use the catchword of 1789) is essentially only a unit of *contradiction*, incapable of definition by positive content, and having neither customary-ethic of its own — for the higher bourgeois society took after the nobility, and the urban piety after the older priesthood — nor symbolism of its own — for the idea that life was not for the service of practical aims, but for the consistent expression of a symbolism of Time and Space, and could claim true dignity only to the extent that it was the worthy vessel of these, was necessarily repugnant to the urban reason as such. This reason, which dominates the entire political literature of the Late period, asserts a new grouping of estates as from the rise of cities — at first only in theory, but finally,

---

[1] Another example (beloved of artists) stands to this day in the town of San Gimigniano, which is almost nothing but a group of family towers ranging up to 150 ft. in height. — *Tr.*

when rationalism becomes omnipotent, in practice, even the bloody practice of revolutions. Nobility and clergy, so far as they are still extant, appear rather markedly as *privileged* classes, the tacit significance of the emphasis being that their claim to prescriptive rights on the ground of historical status is (from the point of view of timeless rational or "natural" law) obsolete nonsense. They now have their centre in the *capital city* (this also a Late-period idea) and now, and now only, develop aristocratic forms to that imposing combination of hauteur and elegance that we see, for example, in the portraits of Reynolds and Lawrence. In opposition to them stand the intellectual powers of the now supreme city, *economy and science*, which in conjunction with the mass of artisans, functionaries, and labourers feel themselves as a party, diverse in its constituents, but invariably solid at the call to battle for freedom — that is, for urban independence of the great old-time symbols and the rights that flowed from them. As components of the Third Estate, which counts by heads and not by rank, they are all, in all Late periods of all Cultures, "liberal" in one way or another — namely, free from the inward powers of non-urban life. Economy is freed to make money, science freed to criticize. And so in all the great decisions we perceive the intellect with its books and its meetings having the word ("Democracy"), and money obtaining the advantages ("Plutocracy") — and it is never ideas, but always capital, that wins. But this again is just the opposition of truths and facts, in the form in which it develops from the city-life.

Moreover, by way of protest against the ancient symbols of the soil-bound life, the city opposes to the aristocracy of birth the notion of an aristocracy of money and an aristocracy of intellect — the one not very explicit as a claim, but all the more effective as a fact; the other a truth, but nothing more than that and, as a spectacle for the eye, not very convincing. In every Late period there grows on to the ancient nobility — that in which some big bit of history (say, Crusades, or Norman conquest) has become stored as form and beat, but which often has inwardly decayed at the great courts — a genuine second crop. Thus in the fourth century B.C. the entry of great plebeian families as *conscripti* into the Roman Senate of *patres* produced within the senatorial order an aristocracy of "*nobiles*" — a nobility holding lands, but entitled by office. In just the same way a nobility of nepotism arose in Papal Rome; in 1650 there were scarcely fifty families of more than three centuries' status. In the Southern States of the American Union there grew up, from Baroque times onward, that planter-aristocracy which was annihilated by the money-powers of the North in the Civil War of 1861-5. The old merchant-nobility of the type of the Fugger, Welser, and Medici and the great Venetian and Genoese houses — to this type, too, must be assigned practically the whole of the patriciate of the Hellenic colonial cities of 800 — had always something of aristocracy in them,[1] race, tradition, high standards, and the nature-impulse to re-establish connexion

[1] Ambrogio Spinola is a case in point. — *Tr.*

with the soil by acquiring lands (although the old family house in town was no bad substitute). But the new money-aristocracy of deals and speculations rapidly acquired a taste for polite forms and at last forced its way into the birth-nobility — in Rome, as Equites, from the first Punic War, in France under Louis XIV [1] — which it disintegrated and corrupted, while the intellectual aristocracy of the Enlightenment, for its part, overwhelmed it with scorn. The Confucians took the old Chinese idea of *Shi* from the ethic of nobility and put it into the virtue of intellect, and made the Pi-Yung, from a centre of knightly battle-play, into an "intellectual wrestling-school," a gymnasium — quite in the spirit of our eighteenth century.

With the close of the Late period of every Culture the history of its estates also comes to a more or less violent end. The mere desire to live in rootless freedom prevails over the great imperative Culture-symbols, which a mankind now wholly dominated by the city no longer comprehends or tolerates. Finance sheds every trace of feeling for earth-bound immovable values, and scientific criticism every residue of piety. Another such victory also, in a measure, is the liberation of the peasant, which consists in relieving him from the pressure of servage, but hands him over to the power of money, which now proceeds to turn the land into movable property — which happened in our case in the eighteenth century; in Byzantium about 740 under the Nomos Georgikos of the legislator Leo III [2] (after which the colonate slowly disappeared); in Rome along with the founding of the Plebeian order in 471. In Sparta the simultaneous attempt of Pausanias to emancipate the Helots failed.

This Plebs is the Third Estate in the form in which it is constitutionally recognized as a unit; its representatives are the Tribunes, not officials, but trusted persons armed with a guaranteed immunity. The reform of 471,[3] which *inter alia* replaced the old three Etruscan tribes by four urban tribes or wards (a highly suggestive fact in itself), has been variously regarded as a pure emancipation of peasantry [4] or as an organization of the trading class.[5] But the Plebs, as Third Estate, as residue, is only susceptible of negative definition — as meaning everyone who does not belong to the land-nobility or is not the incumbent of a great priestly office. The picture is as variegated as that of the French "*Tiers État*" of 1789. Only the protest holds it together. In it are traders, craftsmen, day-labourers, clerks. The gens of the Claudii contained patrician *and* plebeian families — that is, great landlords and prosperous yeomen (for example, the Claudii Marcelli). The Plebs in the Classical city-state is what a combination of peasant and burgher is in a Baroque state of the West, when it protests in an

---

[1] The memoirs of the Duc de Saint Simon give a vivid picture of this evolution.
[2] P. 75.
[3] Corresponding to our seventeenth century.
[4] K. J. Neumann, *Die Grundherrschaft der römischen Republik* (1900); Ed. Meyer, *Kl. Schriften*, pp. 351, et. seq.
[5] A. Rosenberg, *Studien zur Entstehung der Plebs*, Herm. XLVIII (1913), pp. 359, et seq.

assembled states-general against the autocracy of a prince. Outside politics — that is, socially — the plebs, as a unit distinguished from nobility and priesthood, has no existence, but falls apart at once into special callings that are perfectly distinct in interests. It is a *Party*, and what it stands for as such is freedom in the urban sense of the word. The fact emerges still more distinctly from the success which the Roman land-nobility won immediately afterwards, in adding sixteen country tribes, designated by family names and unchallengeably controlled by themselves, to the four urban tribes that stood for bourgeoisie proper — namely, money and mind. Not until the great social conflict during the Samnite wars (contemporary with Alexander, and corresponding exactly to the French Revolution), which ended with the Lex Hortensia of 287, was the status-idea legally abolished and the history of the symbolic Estates closed. *The Plebs became the Populus Romanus* in the same way as in 1789 the "*Tiers État*" constituted itself the Nation. From this point on, in every Culture, it is something fundamentally different that happens under the label of social conflict.

The nobility of every Springtime had been *the* Estate in the most primary sense, history become flesh, race at highest potential. The priesthood was its *counter*-estate, saying no wherever nobility said yes and thus displaying the other side of life in a grand symbol.

The Third Estate, without proper inward unity, was the non-estate — the protest, in estate-form, against the existence of estates; not against this or that estate, but against the symbolic view of life in general. It rejects all differences not justified by reason or practically useful. And yet it does mean something itself, and means it very distinctly — *the city-life as estate* in contradistinction to that of the country, *freedom as a condition* in contrast to attachment. But, looked at from within its own field, it is by no means the unclassified residue that it appears in the eyes of the primary estates. The bourgeoisie has definite limits; it belongs to the Culture; it embraces, in the best sense, all who adhere to it, and under the name of people, *populus*, *demos*, rallies nobility and priesthood, money and mind, craftsman and wage-earner, as constituents of itself.

This is the idea that Civilization finds prevailing when it comes on the scene, and this is what it destroys by its notion of the Fourth Estate, *the Mass*, which rejects the Culture and its matured forms, lock, stock, and barrel. It is the absolute of formlessness, persecuting with its hate every sort of form, every distinction of rank, the orderliness of property, the orderliness of knowledge. It is the new nomadism of the Cosmopolis,[1] for which slaves and barbarians in the Classical world, Sudras in the Indian, and in general anything and everything that is merely human, provide an undifferentiated floating something that falls apart the moment it is born, that recognizes no past and possesses no future. Thus the Fourth Estate becomes the expression of the passing of a history over into the historyless. The mass is the end, the radical nullity.

[1] Pp. 102, et seq.

CHAPTER XI
THE STATE
(B)
STATE AND HISTORY

THE STATE

(B)

STATE AND HISTORY

I

WITHIN the world-as-history, in which we are so livingly woven that our perception and our reason constantly obey our feelings, the cosmic flowings appear as that which we call actuality, real life, being-streams in bodily form. Their common badge is Direction. But they can be grasped differently according as it is the *movement* or *the thing moved* that is looked at. The former aspect we call history and the latter family or stock or estate or people, but the one is only possible and existent through the other. History exists only as the history of something. If we are referring to the history of the great Cultures, then nation is the thing moved. State, *status*, means condition, and we obtain our impression of the State when, as a Being in moved Form flows past us, we fix in our eyes the Form as such, as something extended and timelessly standing fast, and entirely ignore direction and Destiny. State is history regarded as at the halt, history the State regarded as on the move. The State of actuality is the physiognomy of a historical unit of being; only the planned State of the theorist is a system.

A movement *has* form, and that which is moved is "*in form*," or, to use another sporting expression, when it is "going all out" it is in perfect condition. This is equally true for a racehorse or a wrestler and for an army or a people. The form abstracted from the life-stream of a people is the "condition" of that people with respect to its wrestle in and with history. But only the smallest part of this can be got at and identified by means of the reason. No real constitution, when taken by itself and brought down to paper as a system, is complete. The unwritten, the indescribable, the usual, the felt, the self-evident, so outweigh everything else that — though theorists never see it — the description of a state or its constitutional archives cannot give us even the silhouette of that which underlies the living actuality of a state as its essential form; an existence-unit of history is spoilt when we seriously subject its movement to the constraint of a written constitution.

The individual class or family is the smallest, the nation the largest unit in the stream of history.[1] Primitive peoples are subject to a movement that is not historical in the higher sense — the movement may be a jog-trot or may be a

---

[1] See pp. 159, et seq.

charge, but it has no organic character and no profound importance. Nevertheless, these primitive peoples are in motion through and through, to such an
extent, indeed, as to seem perfectly formless to the hasty observer. Fellaheen,
on the contrary, are the rigid objects of a movement that comes from outside
and impinges on them unmeaningly and fortuitously. The former includes the
"State" of the Mycenæan period; that of the Thinite period; that of the Shang
dynasty in China up to, say, the migration to Yin (1400); the Frankish realm
of Charlemagne; the Visigothic Kingdom to Eurich; and Petrine Russia —
state-forms often ample and efficient, but still destitute of symbolism and
necessity. To the latter belong the Roman, Chinese, and other Imperia, whose
form has ceased to have any expressive content whatever.

But between primitive and fellah lies the history of the great Culture.
A people in the style of a Culture — a historical people, that is — is called a
Nation.[1] A nation, as a living and battling thing, possesses a State not merely
as a condition of movement, but also (above all) *as an idea*. The State in the
simplest sense of the term may be as old as free-moving life itself. Swarms
and herds of even very lowly animal genera may have "constitutions" of some
sort — and those of the ants, of the bees, of many fish, or migrating birds, of
beavers, have reached an astounding degree of perfection — but the State of
the grand style is as old as and no older than its two prime Estates, nobility
and priesthood. These emerge *with* the Culture, they vanish into it, their
Destinies are to a high degree identical. Culture is the being of nations in
State-form.

A people is *as* State, a kindred is *as* family, "in form" — that is, as we have
seen, the difference between political and cosmic history, public and private
life, *res publica* and *res privata*. And both, moreover, are symbols of care.[2]
The woman *is* world-history. By conceiving and giving birth she cares for
the perpetuation of the blood. The mother with the child at her breast is the
grand emblem of cosmic life. Under this aspect, the life of man and woman
is "in form" as marriage. The man, however, *makes* history, which is an unending battle for the preservation of that other life. Maternal care is supple-
mented and paralleled by paternal. The man with weapon in hand is the other
grand emblem of the will-to-duration. A people "in condition" is originally
a band warriorhood, a deep and intimately felt community of men fit for arms.
State is the affair of man, it is Care for the preservation of the whole (including
the spiritual self-preservation called honour and self-respect), the thwarting of
attacks, the foreseeing of dangers, and, above all, the positive aggressiveness
which is natural and self-evident to every life that has begun to soar.

If all life were *one* uniform being-stream, the words "people," "state,"
"war," "policy," "constitution," would never have been heard of. But the

---

[1] Pp. 170, et seq.
[2] See Vol. I, pp. 136, et seq. — *Tr.*

eternal forceful *variety* of life, which the creative power of the Culture elevates to the highest intensities, is a fact, and historically we have no choice but to accept it as such, with all that flows therefrom. Plant-life is only plant-life in relation to animal life; nobility and priesthood reciprocally condition one another. *A people is only really such in relation to other peoples,* and the substance of this actuality comes out in natural and ineradicable oppositions, in attack and defence, hostility and war. War is the creator of all great things. All that is meaningful in the stream of life has emerged through victory and defeat.

A people shapes history inasmuch as it is "in condition" for the task of doing so. It livingly experiences an inward history — which gets it into this "condition," in which alone it becomes creative — and an outward history, which *consists* in this creation. Peoples as State, then, are the real forces of all human happening. In the world-as-history there is nothing beyond them. They *are* Destiny.

Res publica, the public life, the "sword side" of human being-currents, is in actuality invisible. The alien sees merely the men and not their inner connexion, for indeed this resides very deep in the stream of life, and even there is felt rather than understood. Similarly, we do not in actuality see the family, but only certain persons, whose cohesion in a perfectly definite sense we know and grasp by way of our own inward experience. But for each such mental picture there exists a group of constituent persons who are bound together as a life-unit by a like constitution of outer and inner being. This form in the flow of existence is called *customary ethic (Sitte)* when it arises of itself in the beat and march and is unconscious before it is conscious; and *law (Recht)* when it is *deliberately stated* and put forth for *acceptance*.

Law — irrespective of whether its authority derives from the feelings and impulse (unwritten law, customary law, English "equity") or has been abstracted by reflection, probed, and brought into system as Statute Law (*Gesetz*) — is the *willed* form of Being. The jural facts that it embraces are of the two kinds, though both possess time-symbolism — Care in two modes, prevision and provision — but, from the very difference in the proportions of consciousness that they respectively contain, it follows that throughout real history there must be two laws in opposition — the law of the fathers, of tradition, the inherited, grown, and well-tried law, sacrosanct because immemorially old, derived from the experience of the blood and therefore dependable; and the thought and planned law of reason, nature, and broad humanity, the product of reflection and therefore first cousin to mathematics, a law that may not be very workable, but is at any rate "just." It is in these two orders of law that the opposition between land-life and city-life, life-experience and study-experience, ripens till it bursts out in that revolutionary embitterment in which men take a law instead of being given it, and break a law that will not yield.

A law that has been laid down by a community expresses a *duty* for every member, but it is no proof of every member's *power*. On the contrary, it is a question of Destiny, who makes the law and for whom it is made. There are subjects and there are objects in the *making* of laws, although everyone is an object as to the validity thereof — and this holds good without distinction for the inner law of families, guilds, estates, and states. But for the State, which is the highest law-subject existing in historical actuality, there is, besides, an external law that it imposes upon aliens by hostilities. Ordinary civil law is a case of the first kind, a peace treaty of the second. But in all cases the law of the stronger is the law of the weaker also. To "have the right" is an expression of power. This is a historical fact that every moment confirms, but it is not acknowledged in the realm of truth, which is not of this world. In their conceptions of right, therefore, as in other things, being and waking-being, Destiny and Causality, stand implacably opposed. To the priestly and idealistic moral of good and evil belongs the *moral distinction of right and wrong*, but in the race-moral of good and bad the distinction is between those who give and those who receive the law. An abstract idea of justice pervades the minds and writings of all whose spirit is noble and strong and whose blood is weak, pervades all religions and all philosophies — but the fact-world of history knows only the *success* which turns the law of the stronger into the law of all. Over ideals it marches without pity, and if ever a man or a people renounces its power of the moment in order to remain righteous — then, certainly, his or its theoretical fame is assured in the second world of thought and truth, but assured also is the coming of a moment in which it will succumb to another life-power that has better understood realities.

So long as a historical power is so superior to its constituent units — as the State or the estate so often is to families and calling-classes, or the head of the family to its children — a just law *between* the weaker is possible as a gift from the all-powerful hand of the disinterested. But Estates seldom, and states almost never, feel a power of this magnitude over themselves, and consequently between them the law of the stronger acts with immediate force — as is seen in a victor's treaty, unilateral in terms and still more so in interpretation and observance. That is the difference between the *internal* and the *external* rights of historical life-units. In the first the will of an arbiter to be impartial and just can be effective — although we are apt to deceive ourselves badly as to the degree of effective impartiality even in the best codes of history, even in those which call themselves "civil" or "*bürgerlich*," for the very adjective indicates that *an estate* has possessed the superior force to impose them on everyone.[1] Internal laws are the result of strict logical-causal thought centring upon truths, but for that very reason their validity is ever dependent upon the material power of their author, be this Estate or State. A revolution that annihilates this

---

[1] Hence such codes throw out the privileges of nobility and clergy and sustain those of money and intellect, and display a frank preference for movable as against real property.

power annihilates also these laws — they remain true, but they are no longer actual. External laws on the other hand, such as all peace treaties, are essentially never true and always actual — indeed appallingly so. They set up no pretension whatever of being just — it is quite enough that they are valid. Out of them speaks *Life*, which possesses no causal and moral logic, but is organically all the more consistent and consequent for the lack of it. Its will is to possess validity *itself;* it feels with an inward certainty what is required to that end and, seeing that, knows what is law for itself and *has to be made* law for others. This logic is seen in every family, and particularly in old true-born peasant families as soon as authority is shattered and someone other than the head tries to determine "what is." It appears in every state, as soon as one party therein dominates the position. Every feudal age is filled with the contests between lords and vassals over the "right to rights." In the Classical world this conflict ended almost everywhere with the unconditional victory of the First Estate, which deprived the kingship of its legislative powers and made it an object of its own law-making — as the origin and significance of the Archons in Athens and the Ephors in Sparta prove beyond doubt. But the same happened in the Western field too — for a moment in France (institution of the States-General, 1302), and for good in England, where in 1215 the Norman baronage and the higher clergy imposed Magna Charta and thus sowed the seed that was to ripen into the effective sovereignty of Parliament. Hence it was that the old Norman law of the Estates here remained permanently valid. In Germany, on the contrary, the weak Imperial power, hard-pressed by the claims of the great feudatories, called in the "Roman" law of Justinian (that is, the law of the unlimited central power) to aid it against the early German land-laws.[1]

The Draconian Constitution, the πατρίος πολιτεία of the Oligarchs, was dictated by the nobility like the strictly patrician law of the Twelve Tables in Rome; [2] but by then the Late period of the Culture was well under way and the power of the city and of money were already fully developed, so that laws directed against these powers necessarily gave way very promptly to laws of the Third Estate (Solon, the Tribunate). Yet these, too, were estate-founded laws not less than their predecessors. The struggle between the two primary estates for the right of law-making has filled the entire history of the West, from the early Gothic conflict of secular and canon law for supremacy, to the controversy (not ended even to-day) concerning civil marriage.[3] And, for that matter, what are the constitutional conflicts that have occurred since the end of the

[1] Pp. 75, et seq. The corresponding attempt of the absolutist Stuarts to introduce Roman Law into England was defeated chiefly by the Puritan jurist Coke (d. 1634) — yet another proof that the spirit of laws is always a party-spirit.

[2] See pp. 65, et seq.

[3] Above all in connexion with divorce, in which the civil and the ecclesiastical views *both* hold good, literally side by side.

eighteenth century but the acquisition by the *Tiers État* (which, according to Sieyès's famous remark in 1789, "was nothing, but could be all") of the right to legislate bindingly upon all, producing a law that is just as much burghers' law as ever Gothic was nobles' law. The nakedest form in which right appears as the expression of might is (as I have already observed) in interstate treaty-making, in peace treaties, and in that Law of Nations of which already Mirabeau could say it is the law of the strong of which the observance is imposed upon the weak. A large part of the decisions of world-history is contained in laws of this kind. They are the constitution under which militant history progresses, so long as it does not revert to the original form of the armed conflict — original, and also basic; for every treaty that is valid and is meant to have real effects is an intellectual continuation thereof. If policy is war by other means,[1] the "right to give the law" is the spoil of the successful party.

II

It is clear, then, that on the heights of history two such life-forms, Estate and State, contend for supremacy, both being-streams of great inward form and symbolic force, each resolved to make its own destiny the Destiny of the whole. *That* — if we try to understand the matter in its depths and unreservedly put aside our everyday conceptions of people, economy, society, and politics — *is the meaning of the opposition between the social and the political conduct of events.* Social and political ideas do not begin to be differentiated till a great Culture has dawned, or even till feudalism is declining and the lord-vassal relation represents the social, and the king-people relation the political, side. But the social powers of the early time (nobility and priesthood) not less actively than those of the later (money and mind) — and the vocational groups of the craftsmen and officials and workers, too, as they were rising to their power in the growing cities — sought, each for itself, to subordinate the State-ideal to its own Estate-ideal, or more usually to its estate interests. And so there arose, at all planes from that of the national unit to that of the individual consciousness, a fight over the respective limits and claims of each — the result of which, in extreme cases, is that the one element succeeds so completely as to make the other its tool.[2]

[1] See p. 330. — *Tr.*

[2] Thus come about the much satirized forms of the "patrol-" or "barrack-state," as opponents call it with an unintelligent scorn. Similar points of view appear also in Chinese and Greek constitutional theories (O. Franke, *Studien zur Geschichte des konfuzianischen Dogmas* (1920), pp. 211, et seq.; Pöhlmann, *Geschichte der sozialen Frage und des Sozialismus in der antiken Welt* (1912). On the other hand, the political tastes of, for example, Wilhelm von Humboldt, who as a Classicist opposed the individual to the State, belong, not to political history at all, but to literature. For what he looked at was, not the capacity of the State to thrive in the real State-world around it, but its private existence within itself, without regard to the fact that such an ideal could not endure for an instant in the face of a neglected outer situation. It is a basic error of the ideologues that, in concentrating on the private life and referring to it the whole inner structure of the State, they entirely ignore the latter's position in point of outward power, though this in fact completely conditions its

In all cases, however, it is the State that determines the *external* position, and therefore the historical relations between peoples are always of *a political and not a social nature*. In domestic politics, on the contrary, the situation is so dominated by class-oppositions that at first sight social and political tactics appear inseparable, and indeed, in the thought of people who (as, for example, a bourgeoisie) equate their own class-ideal with historical actuality — and consequently cannot think in external politics at all — identical. In the external battle the State seeks alliances with other States, in the internal it is always in alliance with one or another Estate — the sixth-century Tyrannis, for instance, rested upon the combination of the State-idea with the interests of the Third Estate *vis-à-vis* the ancient noble oligarchy, and the French Revolution became inevitable from the moment that the *Tiers* — that is, intellect and money — left its friend the Crown in the lurch and joined the two other Estates (from the Assembly of Notables, 1787). We are thoroughly right therefore in feeling a distinction between State-history and class-history,[1] between political (horizontal) and social (vertical) history, war and revolution.[2] But it is a grave error of modern doctrinaires to regard the spirit of domestic history as that of history in general. *World history is, and always will be, State-history*. The inner constitution of a nation aims always at being "*in condition*" for the outer fight (diplomatic, military, or economic) and anyone who treats a nation's constitution as an aim and ideal in itself is merely ruining the nation's body. But, from the other point of view, it falls to the inner-political pulse-sense of a ruling stratum (whether belonging to the First or to the Fourth Estate) so to manage the internal class-oppositions that the focus and ideas of the nation are not tied up in party conflict, nor treason to the country thought of as an ace of trumps.

And here it becomes manifest that *the State and the first Estate* are cognate down to the roots — akin, not merely by reason of their symbolism of Time and Care, their common relation to race and the facts of genealogical succession, to the family and to the primary impulses of all peasantry (on which in the last analysis every State and every nobility is supported) — not merely in their relation to the soil, the clan-domain (be this heritable estate or fatherland), which even in nations of the Magian style is lowered in significance only because there the dignity of orthodoxy so completely surpasses everything else — but above all in high practice amidst all the facts of the historical world, in the

---

freedom for the inward development. The difference between the French and the German Revolutions, for example, consists in the fact that the one commanded the external situation and *therewith* the internal also, while the other commanded neither and was foredoomed to farce.

[1] Which is most definitely *not* identical with economic history in the sense of the materialist historian. More of this in the next chapter.

[2] It is to be noted that the author uses the terms "horizontal" and "vertical" here in the reverse sense to that in which they commonly figure in present-day *political* literature, although in *economic* works the usage is the same as that of the text. — *Tr.*

unforced unity of pulse and impulse, diplomacy, judgment of men, the art of command and masculine will to keep and extend power, which even in earliest times differentiated a nobility and a people out of the one and the same war-gathering; and, lastly, in the feeling for honour and bravery. Hence, right up to the latest phases, that State stands firmest in which the nobility or the tradition shaped by the nobility is wholly at the service of the common cause — as it was in Sparta as compared with Athens, in Rome *vis-à-vis* Carthage, in Tsin as against the *tao*-coloured state of Tsu.

The distinction is that a nobility self-contained as a class — or for that matter *any* Estate — experiences the residue of the nation only with reference to itself, and only desires to exercise power in that sense, whereas the very principle of the State is that it cares for all, and cares for the nobility as such only in relation to the major care. But a genuine old nobility *assimilates itself* to the State, and cares for all as though for a property. This care, in fact, is one of its grandest duties and one of which it is most deeply conscious; it feels it, indeed, an innate *privilege*, and regards service in the army and the administration as its special vocation.

It is, however, a distinction of quite another kind that holds as between the State-idea and the idea of any one of the other Estates. All these are inwardly alien to the State as such, and the State-ideals that they fashion out of their own lives have not grown up out of the spirit and the political forces of actual history — hence, indeed, the conscious emphasis with which they are labelled as social. And while in Early times the situation is simply that historical facts oppose the Church-community in its efforts to actualize *religious* ideals, in Late periods both the *business* ideal of the free economic life, and the *Utopian* ideal of the enthusiast who would actualize this or that abstraction, also come into the field.

But in the historical world there are no ideals, but only facts — no truths, but only facts. There is no reason, no honesty, no equity, no final aim, but only facts, and anyone who does not realize this should write books on politics — let him not try to *make* politics. In the real world there are no states built according to ideals, but only states that have *grown*, and these are nothing but living peoples "in form." No doubt it is "the form impressed that living doth itself unfold," but the impress has been that of the blood and beat of a *being*, wholly instinctive and involuntary; and as to the unfolding, if it is guided by the master of politics, it takes the direction inherent in the blood; if by the idealist, that dictated by his own convictions — in other words, the way to nullity.

But the destiny question, for States that exist in reality and not merely in intellectual schemes, is not that of their ideal task or structure, *but that of their inner authority*, which cannot in the long run be maintained by material means, but only by a belief — of friend *and* foe — in their effectiveness. The decisive problems lie, not in the working-out of constitutions, but in the organization of a sound working government; not in the distribution of political rights according to "just" principles (which at bottom are simply the idea that a *class* forms of its own legitimate claims), but in the efficient pulse of the whole (efficient in the sense that the play of muscle and sinew is efficient when an extended racehorse nears the winning-post), in that rhythm which attracts even strong genius into syntony; not, lastly, in any world-alien moral, but in the steadiness, sureness, and superiority of political leadership. The more self-evident all these things are, the less is said or argued about them; the more fully matured the State, the higher the standing, the historical capacity, and therefore the Destiny of the Nation. State-majesty, sovereignty, is a life-symbol of the first order. It distinguishes *subjects and objects* [1] in political events not only in inner, but also (which is far more important) in external, history. Strength of leadership, which comes to expression in the clear separation of these two factors, is the unmistakable sign of the life-force in a political unity — so much so that the shattering of existing authority (for example, by the supporters of an opposed constitutional ideal) almost always results not in this new party's making itself the subject of domestic policy, but in the whole nation's becoming the object of alien policy — and not seldom for ever.

For this reason, in every healthy State the letter of the written constitution is of small importance compared with the practice of the living constitution, the "form" (to use again the sporting term), which has developed of itself out of the experience of Time, the situation, and, above all, the race-properties of the Nation. The more powerfully the *natural* form of the body politic has built itself up, the more surely it works in unforeseen situations; indeed, in the limit, it does not matter whether the actual leader is called King or Minister or party-leader, or even (as in the case of Cecil Rhodes) that he has no defined relation to the State. The nobility which managed Roman politics in the period of the three Punic Wars had, from the point of view of constitutional law, no existence whatever.[2] The leader's responsibility is always to a minority that possesses the instincts of statesmanship and represents the rest of the nation in the struggle of history.

The fact, therefore, express and unequivocal, is that class-States — that is, States in which particular classes rule — are the *only* States. This must not be confused with the class-States to which the individual is merely *attached* in view of belonging to an estate, as in the case of the older Polis, the Norman States of England and Sicily, the France of the Constitution of 1791, and Soviet Russia to-day. The true class-State is an expression of the general historical experience

[1] Attention is drawn to this phrase, so as to avoid misconceptions as to the meaning of "subject" in the sequel. — *Tr.*

[2] Compare the position of the aristocratic families of the South in the history of the United States up to 1850–60. — *Tr.*

that it is always a single social stratum which, constitutionally or otherwise, provides the political leading. It is always a definite minority that represents the world-historical tendency of a State; and, within that again, it is a more or less self-contained minority that in virtue of its aptitudes (and often enough against the spirit of the Constitution) actually holds the reins. And, if we ignore, as exceptions proving the rule, revolutionary interregna and Cæsarian conditions, in which individuals and fortuitous groupings maintain their power merely by material means (and often without any aptitude for ruling), it is always the minority *within an Estate* that rules by tradition. In by far the greater number of cases this minority is one within the nobility — for example, the "gentry" which governed the Parliamentary style of England, the *nobiles* at the helm of Roman politics in Punic War times, the merchant-aristocracy of Venice, the Jesuit-trained (nobles who conducted the diplomacy of the Papal Curia in the Baroque).[1] Similarly, we find the political aptitude in self-contained groups within the religious Estate — not only in the Roman Catholic Church, but also in Egypt and India and still more in Byzantium and Sassanid Persia. In the Third Estate — though this seldom produces it, not being in itself a life-unit — there are cases such as those of third-century Rome, where a stratum of the plebs contains men trained in commerce, and France since 1789, where an element of the bourgeoisie has been trained in law; in these cases, it is ensured by a closed circle of persons possessing homogeneous practical gifts, which constantly recruits itself and preserves in its midst the whole sum of unwritten political tradition and experience.

That is the organization of *actual* states in contradistinction to those conceived on paper and in the minds of pedants. There is no best, or true, or right State that could possibly be actualized according to plan. Every State that emerges in history exists as it is but once and for a moment; the next moment it has, unperceived, become different, whatever the rigidity of its legal-constitutional crust. Therefore, words like "republic," "absolutism," "democracy," mean something different in every instance, and what turns them into catchwords is their use as definite concepts by philosophers and ideologues. A history of States is physiognomic and not systematic. Its business is not to show how "humanity" advances to the conquest of its eternal rights, to freedom and equality, to the evolving of a super-wise and super-just State, but to describe the political units that really exist in the fact-world, how they grow and flourish and fade, and how they are really nothing but actual life "in form." Let us make the attempt on this basis.

---

[1] For in those centuries the high dignities of the Church were invariably given to the nobility of Europe, who put the political qualities of the blood at her service. From this school in turn emanated statesmen like Richelieu, Mazarin, and Talleyrand, to name but a few.

III

History in the high style begins in every Culture with the feudal State, which is not a State in the coming sense of the word, but an ordering of the common life with reference to an *Estate*. The noblest fruit of the soil, its race in the proudest sense, here builds itself up in a rank-order from the simple knighthood to the *primus inter pares*, the feudal Overlord amongst his Peers. This sets in simultaneously with the architecture of the great cathedrals and the Pyramids — the stone and the blood elevated into symbols, the one *meaning*, the other *being*. The idea of feudalism, which has dominated all Springtimes, is the transition from the primitive, purely practical and factual, relationship of potentate to those who obey him (whether they have chosen him or have been subdued by him) into the *private-law* (and, therefore, deeply symbolical) relation of the lord to the vassal. This relation rests entirely upon the ethic of nobility, honour, and loyalty, and conjures up the cruellest conflicts between duty to one's lord and duty to one's own family. The decadence of Henry the Lion [1] is a tragic example of it.

The "State" exists here only to the extent of the limits of the feudal tie, and it expands its domain by the entry of alien vassals therein. Service to, and agency for, the ruler — originally personal and limited in time — very soon became the permanent fief which, if it escheated, *had* to be reassigned (already by 1000 the principle of the West was "No land without a lord"), and from that presently passed to the stage of being hereditary (law of Emperor Conrad II, 28th May 1037). Thereby the formerly immediate subjects of the ruler were mediatized, and henceforth they were only his subjects as being subjects of a vassal of his. Nothing but the strong social interbonding of the Estate ensured the cohesion of what must be called, even under these conditions, the State.

The idea of power and booty are seen here in classic union. When, in 1066, William and his Norman chivalry conquered England, the whole land was made King's property and fee, and it remains so in name to this day. Here is a true Viking delight in "having," the care of an Odysseus who begins by counting his treasure.[2] From this booty-sense of shrewd conquerors there came, quite suddenly, the famous exchequer-practice and officialdom of the early Cultures. It is well to distinguish these officials from the incumbents of the great confidential offices which had arisen out of the older personal agency;[3] they were *clerici* or clerks, and not *ministeriales* or ministers — "servants," but in a prouder sense now. The financial and clerical officialdom is an expression of Care, and it develops in exact proportion with the development of the dynastic idea. Thus in Egypt it reached an astonishingly high level at the very beginning of

[1] See p. 180.
[2] I.e., Domesday Book. — *Tr.*
[3] See p. 350.

the Old Kingdom.[1] The early Chinese official-State described in the *Tshou-li* is so comprehensive and complicated that the authenticity of the book has been doubted,[2] but in spirit and tendency it corresponds exactly with that of Diocletian, which enabled a feudal order to arise out of an immense fiscal machinery.[3] In the early Classical world it is markedly absent. *"Carpe diem"* was the motto of Classical economics from the first to last, and in this domain as in others Improvidence, the *autarkeia* of the Stoics, was elevated into a principle. Even the best calculators were no exception — thus Eubulus in Athens, 330 B.C., managed business with an eye to surpluses, but only to distribute them, when gained, amongst the citizens.

The extreme contrast to Eubulus's finance is afforded by the canny Vikings of the early West, who by the financial administration of their Norman states laid the foundations of the Faustian economics that extend to-day over the whole world. It is from the chequered table in the Norman counting-house of Robert the Devil (1028–35) that we have the name of the English "Exchequer" and hence the word "cheque." Here also originated the words "control," "quittance," "record."[4] Here it was that after 1066 England was organized as booty, with ruthless reduction of the Anglo-Saxons, to serfdom, and here too originated the Norman State of Sicily — for it was not upon nothing that Frederick II of Hohenstaufen later built; his most personal work, the constitutions of Melfi (1231) he did not create, but only (by methods borrowed from the money-economics of high Arabian Civilization) polished and perfected. From this centre the methodic and descriptive technique of finance spread into the business world of Lombardy and so into all the trading cities and administrations of the West.

But in Feudalism build-up and breakdown lie close together. When the primary estates were still in full bloom and vigour, the future nations, and with them the germ of the State-idea proper, were stirring into life. The opposition between temporal and spiritual power and that between crown and vassals was cut across again and again by oppositions of nationhood — German-French even from Otto the Great's times; German-Italian, which rent Italy between the Guelphs and Ghibellines and destroyed the German Empire; French-English, which brought about the English dominion over western France. Still, all this was far less important than the great decisions within the feudal order iself, where the idea of nationality was unknown. England was broken up into 60,251 fiefs, catalogued in the Domesday Book of 1084 (consulted even to-day upon occasion), and the strictly organized central power

---

[1] Ed. Meyer, *Gesch. d. Altertums*, I, § 244.

[2] Even by Chinese critics. See, however, Schindler, *Das Priestertum im alten China*, I, pp. 61, et seq.; Conrady, *China*, p. 533.

[3] See pp. 349, et seq.

[4] "*Compotus*," "*contrarotulus*" (the counter-roll retained for checking), "*quittancia*," "*recordatum*."

required allegiance to itself even from the sub-tenants of the peers, but all the same it was less than a hundred and fifty years later that Magna Charta was forced through (1215), and actual power transferred from the King to the Parliament of the vassals — made up of great barons and ecclesiastics in the Upper house, gentry and patricians in the Lower — which thenceforward became the support and champion of *national* development. In France the baronage, in conjunction with the clergy and the towns, forced the calling of the States-General in 1302; the General Privilege of Saragossa in 1283 made Aragon into a quasi-republic of nobles ruled by its Cortes, and in Germany a few decades earlier a group of great vassals made the election of the German Kingship dependent upon themselves as Electors.

The mightiest expression that the feudal idea found for itself — not merely in the West, but in any Culture — came out in the struggle between Empire and Papacy, both of which dreamed of a consummation in which the entire world was to become an immense feudal system, and so intimately enwove themselves into the dream that, with the decay of feudalism, both together fell from their heights in lamentable ruin.

The idea of a Ruler whose writ should run throughout the whole historical world, whose Destiny should be that of all mankind, has taken visible shape in, so far, three instances — firstly, in the conception of the Pharaoh as Horus; [1] secondly, in the great Chinese imagining of the Ruler of the Middle, whose domain is *tien-hia*, everything lying below the heavens; [2] and, thirdly, in early Gothic times. In 962 Otto the Great, answering to the deep mystical sense and yearning for historical and spatial infinity that was sweeping through the world of those days, conceived the idea of the "Holy Roman Empire, German by nation." But even earlier, Pope Nicolas I (860), still completely involved in Augustinian — that is, Magian — lines of thought, had dreamed of a Papal democracy which was to stand above the princes of this world, and from 1059 Gregory VII with all the prime force of his Faustian nature set out to actualize a papal world-dominion under the forms of a universal feudalism, with kings as vassals. The Papacy itself, indeed, under its domestic aspect, constituted the small feudal State of the Campagna, whose noble families controlled the election of popes, and which very rapidly converted the college of cardinals (to which the duty was entrusted from 1059 on) into a sort of noble oligarchy. But under the broader aspect of external policy Gregory VII actually *obtained* feudal supremacy over the Norman states of England and Sicily, both of which were created with his support, and actually awarded the Imperial crown as Otto

[1] See p. 279.

[2] "For the ruler of the Middle there is no foreign land" (Kung-yang). "The heaven speaks not; it causes its thoughts to be promulgated by a man" (Tung Chung-shu). His errors affect the whole Cosmos and bring about cataclysms in Nature (O. Franke, *Zur Geschichte des konfuzianischen Dogmas* (1920), pp. 212, et seq., 244, et seq.). Such mystic universalism was completely alien to Indian and Classical state-notions.

the Great had awarded the tiara. But a little later Henry VI of Hohenstaufen succeeded in the opposite sense; even Richard Cœur-de-Lion swore the vassal's oath to him for England, and the universal Empire was on the point of becoming a fact when the greatest of all popes, Innocent III (1198–1216) made the papal overlordship of the world real for a short time. England became a Papal fief in 1213; Aragon and Leon and Portugal, Denmark and Poland and Hungary, Armenia and the recently founded Latin Empire in Byzantium followed. But with Innocent's death disintegration set in within the Church itself, and the great spiritual dignitaries, whom their investitures turned into vassals of the Pope as overlord, soon followed the lay vassals' example and set about limiting him by means of representative institutions for their order.[1] The notion that a General Council stood higher than a pope was not of religious origin, but arose primarily out of the feudal principle. Its tendency corresponded precisely to that which the English magnates had made good in Magna Charta. In the councils of Constance (1414) and Basel (1431) the last attempts were made to turn the Church, under its temporal aspect, into a clerical feudalism, in which an oligarchy of cardinals would have become the representative of the whole Clerical Estate of the West and taken the place hitherto held by the Roman nobility. But by that time the feudal idea had long taken second place to that of the State, and so the Roman barons won the victory. The field of candidature for the Papacy was limited to the narrowest environs of Rome, and unlimited power over the organizations of the Church was *ipso facto* secured to the centre. As for the Empire, it had long ago become a venerated shadow, like the Egyptian and the Chinese.

In comparison with the immense dynamism of these decisions, the building-up of feudalism in the Classical world was slow, static, almost noiseless, so that it is hardly recognizable save from the traces of transition. In the Homeric epos as we have it now, every locality possesses its Basileus, who, it is fairly evident, was once a great vassal — we can see in the figure of Agamemnon the conditions in which the ruler of a wide region took the field with the train of his peers. But in the Greek world the dissolution of the feudal world was associated with the formation of the *city*-state, the political "point." In consequence, the hereditary court-offices, the *archai* and *timai*, the *prytaneis*, the Archons, and perhaps the original Prætor,[2] were all urban in nature; and the

---

[1] It must not be forgotten that the immense domains of the Church had become hereditary fiefs of the bishops and archbishops, who were no more disposed than the lay peers to permit interferences on the part of the overlord.

[2] After the overthrow of the Tyrannis, *c.* 500, the two regents of the Roman patriciate bear the title *prætor* or *judex*. But it seems to me probable that these go back beyond the Tyrannis and even the preceding oligarchic period into that of the kingship proper, and that as court-offices they have the same origin as our *Herzog*, duke (*præ-itor*); *Heerwart*, in Athens polemarch; and *Graf*, earl ("*Dinggraf*," hereditary arbiter, in Athens archon). The name "*consul*" (from 366) is philologically thoroughly archaic, and therefore implies no new creation, but the renascence of a title (king's adviser?) which oligarchic sentiment had long repudiated.

great families therefore developed, not separately in their counties, as in Egypt, China, and the West, but in the closest touch with the city, where they obtained possession of the rights of the King, one after the other, until nothing was left to the ruling house but that which could not be touched because of the gods — namely, the title attaching to its sacrificial function (hence the *rex sacrorum*). In the later parts of the Homeric epic (*c.* 800) it is the nobles who invite the king to take his seat, and even unseat him. The Odyssey really knows the kingship only as part of the saga — the actual Ithaca that it shows us is a city dominated by oligarchs.[1] The Spartiates, like the Roman partriciate of the Comitia Curiata, are the product of a feudal relation.[2] In the *phiditia*[3] there are evident remains of the old open table of the noble, but the power of the king has sunk to the shadowy dignity of the *rex sacrorum* of Rome, or the "kings" of Sparta, who were liable to be imprisoned or removed at any time by the Ephors. The essential similarity of these conditions forces us to presume that in Rome the Tarquinian Tyrannis of 500 was preceded by a period of oligarchical dominance, and this view is supported by the unquestionably genuine tradition of the *Interrex*, a person appointed by the council of the nobles (the Senate) from amongst its own members to act until it should please them to elect a king again.

Here, as elsewhere, there comes a time in which feudalism is falling into decay, but the coming State is not yet completed, the nation not yet "in form." This is the fearful crisis that emerges everywhere in the shape of the Interregnum, and forms the boundary *between the feudal union and the class-State*. In Egypt feudalism was fully developed by about the middle of the Vth Dynasty. The Pharaoh Asosi gave away his domains literally piece by piece to the vassals, and, further, the rich fiefs of the priesthood were (exactly as in the West) free of taxation and gradually became the permanent property ("mortmain," as we should say) of the great temples.[4] With the Vth Dynasty (*c.* 2530 B.C.) the "Hohenstaufen" age comes to an end. Under the shadow-kingship of the short-lived VIth Dynasty the princes (*rpati*) and counts (*hetio*) become independent; the high offices are all hereditary and the tomb-inscriptions show us more and more proud stress upon ancient lineage. That which later Egyptian historians have hidden under the reputed VIIth and VIIIth dynasties[5] is really half a century of anarchy and lawless conflicts between princes for each other's domains or for the Pharaoh-title. In China, even I-Wang (934–909) was obliged by his vassals to give out all conquered lands, and to do so to sub-tenants

---

[1] Beloch, *Griechische Geschichte*, I, 1, pp. 214, et seq.

[2] The Spartiates mustered in the best period of the sixth century some 4000 warriors, out of a total population of nearly 300,000, including Periœci and Helots (Ed. Meyer, *Gesch. d. Alt.*, III, § 264). The Roman families must at that time have been of about the same strength relatively to the *clientela* and the Latins.

[3] Men's messes. See the article Συσσίτια in Smith's *Dictionary of Classical Antiquities*. — Tr.

[4] Ed. Meyer, *Geschichte des Alt.*, I, § 264.

[5] Ed. Meyer, *Gesch. d. Alt.*, I, § 267, et seq.

nominated by them. In 842 Li-Wang was forced, with his heir, to flee, and the administration of the Empire was carried on by two individual princes. In this interregnum began the fall of the House of Chóu and the decline of the Imperial name into an honourable but meaningless title. It is the corresponding picture to that of the Interregnum in Germany, which began in 1254 and brought the Imperial power to its nadir of 1400 under Wenceslaus, simultaneously with the Renaissance-style of the *condottieri* and the complete decay of the Papal power. After the death of Boniface VIII, who in 1302 had once again asserted the feudal power of the Papacy in the Bull *Unam sanctam* and had consequently been arrested by the representatives of France, the Papacy experienced a century of banishment, anarchy, and impotence, while in the following century the Norman nobility of England for the most part perished in the contest of the houses of York and Lancaster for the throne.

IV

What this fall of Papacy and Empire meant was the victory of State over Estate. At the root of the feudal system there had been the feeling that the purpose of existence was that a "life" should be led in the light of what it meant. History was exhaustively comprised in the destinies of noble blood. But now the feeling sprang up that there was *something else* besides, something to which even nobility was subordinate, and which it shared with all other classes (whether of status or of vocation), something intangible, an idea. Events came to be viewed, no longer from a frankly private-law standpoint, but under a "public"-law aspect. The State might (and almost without exception did) remain aristocratic to its core; its outward appearance might be scarcely altered by the transition from the feudal group to the Class-State; the idea that those outside the Estates possessed rights as well as duties might be still unknown; *but* the feeling had become different, and the consciousness that Life existed to be lived on the heights of history had given way to the other sentiment, that it contained a *task*. The difference becomes very distinct when we contrast the policy of Rainald van Dassel (d. 1167) — one of the greatest German statesmen of all periods — with that of the Emperor Charles IV (d. 1378), and consider in parallel therewith the transition in Classical feeling from the "Themis" of the knightly age to the "Dike" of the growing Polis.[1] Themis involves only a claim, Dike implies a task as well.

The State-idea in its sturdy youth is always — and self-evidently, with a naturalness rooted deep in animality itself — bound up with the conception of an individual ruler. The same holds good, with the same self-evidence, for every roused crowd in every decisive situation — as every riotous assembly and every moment of sudden danger demonstrates afresh.[2] Such crowds are units

[1] See Ehrenberg, *Die Rechtsidee im frühen Griechentum* (1921), pp. 65, et seq.
[2] P. 18.

of feeling, but blind. They are "in form" for the onrush of events only when they are in the hands of the leader, who suddenly appears in their midst, is set at the head in a moment by that very unity of feeling, and finds an unconditional obedience. This process repeats itself in the formation of the great life-units that we call peoples and States, only more slowly and with surer meaning. In the high Cultures it is sometimes set aside or set back in favour of other modes of being "in form," for the sake of a great symbol and artificially; but even then under the mask of these forms we practically always find *de facto* an individual rulership, whether it be that of a King's adviser or a party leader; and in every revolutionary upheaval the original state of things reappears.

With this cosmic fact is bound up one of the most intimately inward traits of all directional life, the *inherited will*, which presents itself with the force of a natural phenomenon in every strong race and compellingly urges even the momentary leader (often quite unconsciously) to uphold his rank for the duration of his personal existence or, beyond it, for that of his blood streaming on through children and grandchildren. The same deep and plantlike trait inspires every real following, which feels in the continuance of the blood of leadership both a surety for and a symbol of the continuance of its own. It is precisely in revolutions that this primitive instinct comes out, full and strong and regardless of all principles. Precisely because of it the France of 1800 saw not only Napoleon, but also his hereditary position, as the true fulfilment of the Revolution. Theorists who, like Marx and Rousseau, start from conceptual ideals instead of from blood-facts have never grasped this immense force that dwells in the historical world, and have in consequence labelled its manifested effects as damnable and reactionary. But they are there, and with a force so insistent that even the symbolism of the high Cultures can only override them temporarily and artificially, as is shown in the engrossing of elective officers by particular families in the Classical, and the nepotism of the Baroque popes in our own case. Behind the fact that leadership is very often freely resigned, and the saying that "merit should rule," there is practically always the rivalry of magnates, who have no objection in principle to hereditary rulership, but prevent it in practice because each one of them secretly claims it for his own blood. This state of active, creative jealousy is the foundation on which the forms of Classical oligarchy are built up.

The combination of both elements produces the idea of Dynasty. This is so deeply rooted in the Cosmic and so closely interwoven into the factual web of historical life that the State-ideas of each and all the Cultures are *modifications of this one principle*, from the passionate affirmative of the Faustian to the resolute negative of the Classical Soul. The ripening of the State-idea of a Culture is associated with the city and even the adolescence of the city. Nations, historical peoples, are town-building peoples.[1] The *capital* takes the place of the

---

[1] Pp. 171, et seq.

castle and the palace as the centre of high history, and in it the feeling of the exercise of power, Themis, transforms itself into that of government, Dike. Here feudal unity is inwardly overcome by national, even in the consciousness of the First Estate itself, and here the bare fact of rulership elevates itself into the symbol of *Sovereignty*.

And so, with the sinking of feudalism, Faustian history becomes dynastic history. From little centres where princely families have their seats (whence they "spring," as the phrase goes, reminding us of plant and property), the shaping of nations proceeds — nations of strictly aristocratic constitution, but yet so that the State conditions the being of the Estate. The genealogical principle already ruling in the feudal nobility and the yeoman families, the expression of the feeling for expanse and the will-to-history, has become so powerful that the appearance of nations transcending the strong unities of language and landscape is dependent upon the destinies of ruling houses. Marriages and deaths sever or unite the blood of whole populations.[1] Where a Lotharingian and a Burgundian dynasty failed to take shape, there also nations already embryonic failed to develop. The doom that overhung the Hohenstaufen involved more than the imperial crown. For Germany and Italy it meant for centuries a deep unsatisfied longing for a united German-Italian nation, while the House of Habsburg, on the contrary, enabled, not a German, but an Austrian nation to develop.

In the Magian world, with its cavern-feeling, the dynastic principle was quite otherwise constituted. The Classical princeps, the legitimate successor of tyrants and tribunes, was the embodiment of the Demos. As Janus was the door and Vesta the hearth, so Cæsar was the people. He was the last creation of Orphic religiousness. The "Dominus et Deus," on the contrary, was Magian, a Shah participating in the divine Fire (the *hvareno* of the Mazdaist empire of the Sassanids, which becomes the aureole in Pagan and Christian Byzantium), which radiates about him and makes him *pius, felix, invictus* (the last-named, from Commodus's reign, his official title).[2] In Byzantium in the third century of our era the ruler-type underwent the same transition as was implied in the taking-down of Augustus's civil-service state to build Diocletian's feudalism. "The new creation begun by Aurelian and Probus and built up on the ruins by Diocletian and Constantine was about as alien to the Classical world and the principate as the empire of Charlemagne."[3] The Magian ruler governed the visible portion of the general Consensus of the orthodox, which was Church,

---

[1] P. 181, et seq.

[2] F. Cumont, *Mysterien der Mithra* (1910), pp. 74, et seq. The Sassanid government, which about A.D. 300 changed from the feudal union to the aristocratic State, was in all respects the pattern for Byzantium in ceremonial, in the knightly character of its Empire, in administrative management, and above all in the type of its Ruler. Cf. also A. Christensen, *L'Empire des Sassanides, le peuple, l'état, la cour* (Copenhagen, 1907).

[3] Ed. Meyer, *Kl. Schriften*, p. 146.

State, and Nation in one,[1] as Augustine described it in his *Civitas Dei*. The Western ruler is by the grace of God monarch in the *historical* world; his people is subordinated to him because God has invested him with it. But in matters of faith he is himself a subordinate — to God's Vicar on earth, or to his own conscience, as the case may be. That is the separation of State authority and Church authority, the great Faustian conflict between Time and Space. When, in 800, the Pope crowned the Emperor, he *chose* a new ruler for himself in order that he himself might thrive. Whereas the Emperor in Byzantium was, according to Magian world-feeling, his spiritual as well as his secular superior, an Emperor in the Frank lands was his *servant* in spiritual matters, besides being (perhaps) his arm in secular affairs. As an idea, the Papacy could arise only by separation from the Caliphate, for the Pope is *included* in the Caliph.

For this very reason, however, the choice of the Magian ruler cannot be bound down to a genealogical succession-law. It issues from the consensus of the ruling blood-kindred, out of whom the Holy Ghost speaks and designates the Chosen One. When Theodosius died, in 550, a relative, the nun Pulcheria, formally gave her hand to the old senator Marcianus, thereby incorporating this statesman in the family and securing the throne to him and continuance to the "dynasty"; [2] and this act, like many similar occurrences in the Sassanid and Abbassid houses, was taken as the outcome of a hint from above.

In China, the Emperor-idea of the early Chóu period, which was strictly bound up with feudalism, soon became a dream, which, rapidly and with increasing distinctness, came to reflect a whole preceding world in the form of three dynasties of Emperors and myth-Emperors more ancient still.[3] But, for the dynasties of the system of states that thereupon grew up (in which the title King, *Wang*, came at last into perfectly general use) strict rules came into force for royal successions, legitimacy — a notion quite alien to the early time — became a power to conjure with,[4] and extinction of lines, adoptions and *mésalliances* led, as in the Baroque of the West, to innumerable wars of succession.[5] Some principle of legitimacy, too, surely underlay the remarkable

---

[1] See p. 243.   [2] Krumbacher, *Byzant. Literaturegesch.*, p. 918.

[3] A bright light is thrown upon the formation of this picture by the fact that the descendants of the repeatedly overthrown dynasties of Hia and Shang reigned in the states of Ki-Sung throughout the Chóu period (Schindler, *Das Priestertum im alten China*, I, p. 30). This shows, firstly, that the picture of the Empire was mirrored back on some earlier or even perhaps a contemporary eminence of these states; and, secondly and above all, that here too "dynasty" was not what we currently mean by the name, but followed some quite different idea of the family. We may compare the fiction which made the German King, who was always chosen on Frankish territory and crowned in the sepulchral chapel of Charlemagne, into a "Frank," so that if circumstances had been different, there might have evolved the notion of a Frankish dynasty running from Charles to Conradin (see Amira, *German. Recht* in Herm. Paul, *Grundriss*, III, p. 147, note). From the Confucian age of enlightenment this picture became the basis of a State-theory, and later still it was turned to account by the Cæsars (p. 313).

[4] O. Franke, *Studien zur Gesch. d. Konfuz. Dogmas*, pp. 247, 251.

[5] An illuminating example is the "personal union" of the Ki and Tseng states, contested as contrary to law (Franke, op. cit., p. 251).

fact that the rulers of the Egyptian XIIth dynasty, with whom the late period of the Culture ended, had their sons crowned during their own lifetime.[1] The inward relationship between these three dynastic ideas is yet another proof that Being in these three Cultures was akin.

It requires a close insight into the political form-language of the Classical world to perceive that here also the course of things was exactly the same, and that it comprised not only the transition from feudal union to class-State, but even the dynastic principle as well. Classical being, indeed, said no to everything that might draw it into distances either of space or of time, and even in the fact-world of history ringed itself with creations that had something of the defensive in them. But all this narrowing and curtailing presupposes the thing against which it is striving to maintain itself. The Dionysiac squandering, and the Orphic negation, of the Classical body contained in the very *form* of their protest the Apollinian ideal of perfect bodily being.

Individual rulership and the will to transmit to heirs were unmistakably taken for granted in the oldest kingship.[2] But they had become questionable even by 800, as the rôle of Telemachus in the older parts of the Odyssey indicates. The royal title was frequently borne by great vassals and the most conspicuous of the nobles. In Sparta and in Lycia there were two of them, and in the Phæacian city of the epic and in many actual cities there were more. Next comes the splitting-off of offices from dignities. Lastly, the kingship itself becomes an office which the nobility confers (though at first, perhaps, only upon members of the old royal family); thus in Sparta the Ephors, as representing the First Estate, were in no wise limited in their choice by rule; and in Corinth from about 750 the royal clan of the Bacchiadæ abolished hereditary succession, and on each occasion set up a *prytaneus* with royal rank from within their own body. The great offices, which likewise were hereditary at first, came to be for one life only, then were limited to a term, and lastly became annual, and, further, were so arranged that there were more holders than offices, and the leadership was exercised by each in turn — the custom which, as is well known, led to the disaster of Cannæ. These annual offices, from the Etruscan annual dictature[3] to the Doric ephorate (which is found in Heraclea and Messene as well as Sparta) are firmly bound up with the essence of the Polis, and they reach their full structure about 650. Exactly at the corresponding date of the Western class-State (end of the fifteenth century), the hereditary power of dynasties was being secured by the Emperor Maximilian and his

---

[1] Ed. Meyer, *Gesch. d. Alt.*, I, § 281.

[2] G. Busolt, *Griech. Staatskunde* (1920), pp. 319, et. seq. U. von Wilamowitz (*Staat und Gesellschaft der Griechen*, 1910, p. 53), in disputing the existence of the patriarchal kingdom, misunderstands the immense difference between the conditions of the eighth century, indicated in the Odyssey, and those of the tenth.

[3] A. Rosenberg, *Der Staat der alten Italiker* (1913), pp. 75, et seq.

marriage-politics (against the claims of the Electors), by Ferdinand of Aragon, Henry VII of England, and Louis XI of France.[1]

But with the increasing emphasis upon the Classical here and now, the priesthood, which had the beginnings of an Estate in it, became *pari passu* a mere aggregate of city officials. The capital, so to call it, of the Homeric kingship, instead of being the centre for the radiation of State influence in all directions into the distance, contracted its magic circle until State and city became identical. Thereby, of course, the nobility was fused with the patriciate, and if even in the Gothic the representation of the young cities (for example, the English Commons or the French States-General) was exclusively by patricians, how much more so in the powerful city-state of the Classical! Not indeed in idea, *but in fact*, it was a pure kingless aristocratic State. The strictly Apollinian "form" of the growing Polis is called *oligarchy*.

And thus, at the close of the early periods of both these Cultures, we see two principles parallel and contrasted, the Faustian-genealogical and the Apollinian-oligarchic; two kinds of constitutional law, of Dike. The one is supported by an unmeasured sense of expanse, reaches back deep into the past with form-tradition, thinks forward with the same intense will-to-endure into the remotest future; but in the present, too, works for political effectiveness over broad expanses by well-considered dynastic marriages and by the truly Faustian, dynamic, and contrapuntal politics that we call *diplomacy*. The other, wholly corporeal and statuesque, is self-limited by its policy of *autarkeia* to the nearest and the most immediate present, and at every point stoutly denies that which Western being affirms.

Both the dynastic state and the city-state presuppose the city itself. But there is this difference, that a seat of government in the West, though it may be (and frequently is) far from being the greatest city of the land, is a force-centre in a field of political tensions such that every occurrence, in however remote a corner, vibrates generally throughout the whole — whereas in the Classical, life huddles closer and closer until it reaches the grotesque phenomenon of Synœcism — the very acme of the Euclidean will-to-form in the political world. It is impossible to imagine the State unless and until the nation sits physically concentrated in one heap, as one *body;* it must be *seen*, and even seen "at a glance." And while the Faustian tendency is more and more to diminish the number of dynastic centres — so that even Maximilian I could see

[1] Estate or Class was the basis, too, of the two great political associations in Byzantium, which are quite wrongly described as "Circus parties." These Blues and Greens called themselves "Demoi" and had their regular leaders. The circus was simply like the Palais Royal of 1789, the scene of public manifestations, and behind them were the class-associations of the Senate. When in 520 Anastasius I gave effect to the Monophysite tendency, the Greens sang orthodox hymns all day there, and so forced the Emperor publicly to cry off. The Western counterpart to this is formed by the Parisian parties under the "three Henries" (1580), the Guelphs and Ghibellines of Savonarola's Florence, and above all the insurgent faction in Rome under Pope Eugene IV. The suppression of the Nika Rebellion by Justinian in 532 was thus also the foundation of State-absolutism *vis-à-vis* the Estates.

looming in the distance a dynastically secure universal monarchy of his house — the Classical world fell apart into innumerable petty points, which, almost as soon as they came into existence, started to do that which for Classical mankind was almost a necessity of thought and the purest expression of *autarkeia* — to destroy one another.[1]

Synœcism with its consequence, the creation of the Polis-type proper, was exclusively the work of *aristocracy*. It was they that established the Classical city-state, and for themselves alone; it was the drawing-together of country nobility and patriciate that brought it into form. The vocational classes were already on the spot, and the peasantry ceased to count from the class point of view. And by the concentration of noble power at one point the kingship of the feudal period was shattered.

With these glimpses into Greece to go upon, we may venture, though under all reserves of course, to outline the history of primitive Rome. The Roman synœcism — the assembling of widely scattered noble families — is identical with the "founding" of the city, an Etruscan undertaking of the beginning of the seventh century.[2] Facing the royal stronghold of the Capitol, there had long been two other settlements on the Palatine and the Quirinal. To the first of these belonged the ancient goddess Diva Rumina [3] and the Etruscan Ruma clan; [4] the god of the second was Quirinus Pater. From these comes the dual name of Romans and "Quirites," and the dual priesthoods of the Salii and Luperci, which adhered to the two hills. Now, as the three blood-tribes named Ramnes, Tities, and Luceres are in all probability common to all Etruscan localities,[5] they must have existed in both of those which concern us here; and thus are explained, on the one hand, the number *six* of centuries of equites, of military tribunes, of aristocratic Vestals, and, on the other, the number *two* of the prætors (or consuls) who were, quite early, attached to the King as representatives of the nobles and gradually deprived him of all influence. Already by 600 the constitution of Rome must have been a strong oligarchy of "Patres" with a shadow-kingship [6] as figure-head. Thus both the older theory of an expulsion of the kings, and the newer of a slow disintegration of the royal power, can stand side by side after all, the former as referring to the fall of the Tarquinian Tyrannis, which (as everywhere else in the Classical world — Pisistratus in Athens, for example) had set itself up in opposition to the oli-

---

[1] This contrast gives rise to a corresponding contrast in idea of colonization. Whereas, e.g., the Prussian sovereigns invited settlers to their *land* (Salzburg Protestants, French Huguenots), Gelon forcibly transferred the populations of whole cities into Syracuse, which thus became the first megalopolis of the Classical world (*c.* 480).

[2] The Greek lecythi found in graves on the Esquiline date form this period.

[3] Wissowa, *Religion der Römer*, p. 242.

[4] W. Schulze, *Zur Geschichte lateinischen Eigennamen*, pp. 379, et. seq., 580, et seq.

[5] See p. 351.

[6] This is seen also in the relation of the *Pontifex Maximus* to the *Rex Sacrorum* — the latter with the three great Flamens to the kingship, the Pontifices and the Vestals to the aristocracy.

garchy about the middle of the sixth century; the latter as referring to the slow disintegration of the feudal power of the (may we say) Homeric kingship by the aristocratic city-state, *before* the "foundation," so-called — the crisis, probably, in which the prætors emerged, as the Archons and Ephors emerged elsewhere.

This Polis was no less strictly aristocratic than the Western class-State, with its nobility, clergy, and higher burgesses. The residue of the people belonging to it was merely its *object*, but — in the West the object of its political *care*, and in the Classical the object of its political *carelessness*. For here *"Carpe diem"* was the motto of the oligarchy as well as of others. It proclaims itself aloud in the poems of Theognis and the Song of Hybrias the Cretan. It made Classical finance till right into its latest phases — from the piracy practised by Polycrates upon his own people to the proscriptions of the Roman Triumvirs — into a more or less hand-to-mouth seizing of resources for the moment. In jurisprudence it emerges with unparalleled logic in the limitation of Roman edict-law to the term of office of the one-year prætor.[1] And, lastly, it is seen in the ever-growing practice of filling military, legal, and administrative offices (particularly the *more* important of them) by lot — a kind of homage to Tyche, the goddess of the Moment.

This was the Classical world's manner of being politically "in form" and, correspondingly, of thinking and feeling. There are no exceptions. The Etruscans were as much under its domination as the Dorians and the Macedonians.[2] When Alexander and his successors dotted the Orient far and wide with their Hellenistic cities, they did so without conscious choice, for they could not imagine any other form of political organization. Antioch was to be Syria, and Alexandria Egypt. The latter, under the Ptolemies and later under the Cæsars, was, not indeed legally, but certainly in practice, a Polis on a vast scale — for the country outside, long reverted to townless fellahdom and managed by immemorial precedents, stood at its gates like an alien frontier.[3] The Roman Imperium was nothing but the last and greatest Classical city-state standing on foundations of a colossal synœcism. Under Marcus Aurelius the rhetor Aristides could say with perfect justification that it had "brought together this world in the name of one city: wheresoever a man may be born in it, it is at its centre that he dwells." Even the conquered populations of the Empire — the wandering desert-tribes, the upland-valley communities of the Alps — were constituted as *civitates*. Livy thinks invariably in the forms of the city-state, and for Tacitus provincial history simply does not exist. When, in 49, Pompey, withdrawing before Cæsar, gave up Rome as militarily unimportant and betook himself to the East to create there a firm base of operations, he

[1] See p. 62, et seq.
[2] P. 173, et seq.
[3] This is clearly to be seen from Wilcken, *Grundzüge der Papyruskunde* (1912), pp. 1, et seq.

was doomed. Giving up the city, he had, in the eyes of the ruling classes, given up the State. To them Rome was all.[1]

These city-states were in principle inextensible. Their number could increase, but not their ambit. The notion that the transformation of the Roman *clientela* into a voting *plebs*, and the creation of the country tribes, meant a breach in the Polis-idea is incorrect. It was in Rome as in Attica — the whole life of the State remained as before limited to one point, which was the Agora, the Forum. However far away those to whom citizenship was granted might live — in Hannibal's day it might be anywhere in Italy, and later anywhere in the world — the *exercise* of his political right depended upon *personal presence* in the Forum. Hence the majority of the citizens were, not legally, but practically without influence in political business.[2] What citizenship meant for them, therefore, was simply the duty of military service and the enjoyment of the city's domestic law.[3] But even for the citizen coming to Rome, political power was limited by a second and *artificial* synœcism which came into existence after, and as the result of, enfranchisement of the peasant, and can only be understood as an unconscious effort to maintain the idea of the Polis strictly unimpaired; the new citizens were inscribed, regardless of their numbers, in a very few tribes (eight, under the Lex Julia), and were always, therefore, in a minority in the Comitia relatively to the citizens of the older franchise.

And naturally so, for this *civitas* was regarded through and through as one body, a σῶμα. That which did not belong to it was out of its law, *hostis*. The gods and the heroes stood above, the slave (not quite to be called human, according to Aristotle) below, this aggregate of persons.[4] But the individual was a ζῶον πολιτικόν in a sense that would be regarded by us, who think and live in our expanse-feeling, as an utter slavery; he existed *only* by reason of his membership of an individual Polis. Owing to this Euclidean feeling, the nobility as a self-contained body was at first synonymous with the Polis — to such an extent, indeed, that even in the Twelve Tables marriage between patricians and plebeians was forbidden and the Spartan Ephors began their

---

[1] Ed. Meyer, *Cæsars Monarchie* (1918), p. 308.

[2] Plutarch and Appian describe the masses of humanity that moved in by all the roads of Italy to vote on Tiberius Gracchus's land-bills. But this in itself shows that nothing of the sort had ever happened before; and immediately after his violence upon Octavius, Tiberius Gracchus saw downfall staring him in the face because the masses had streamed off home again and were not to be assembled a second time. In Cicero's day a Comitia often consisted only in speeches by a few politicians, without participation by others; but never did it occur to a Roman to transfer the place of voting to the residence of the individual voter — nor even to the Italians when they were fighting for citizenship in 90 B.C. So strong was the feeling of the Polis.

[3] In the Western dynasty-states the domestic law of each is valid for its *territory* and applies therefore to all persons present therein, irrespective of allegiance. In the city-state, on the contrary, the validity of its domestic law for a person arises from that person's possession of citizenship; *civitas*, therefore, means infinitely more than present-day nationality, for without it a man was without rights at all — as a "person," non-existent.

[4] See p. 60.

term of office, according to ancient custom, with a declaration of war against
the Helots. The relation was reversed whenever in consequence of a revolution
the non-noble became *the* Demos — but its meaning remained. As in inward,
so also in outward relationships, the *body* politic was the foundation of all
events throughout Classical history. The cities, hundreds of them, lay in wait
for each other, each as self-gathered, politically and economically, as it was
possible to make it, ready to bite, letting fly on the smallest excuse, and having
as its war-aim, not the extension of its own state, but the extinction of the
other side's. Wars ended with the destruction of the enemy's city and the
killing or enslavement of his citizens, just as revolutions ended with the massacre or expulsion of the losers and the confiscation of their property by the
victorious party. The natural interstate condition of the West is a close network of diplomatic relations, which may be broken through by wars; but the
Classical law of nations assumes war as a normal condition, interrupted from
time to time by peace treaties, and a declaration of war merely re-established the
natural state of policy. Only so do the forty- and fifty-year peace treaties,
spondai (such as the famous one of Nicias in 421), become intelligible, as temporary guarantee-treaties.

These two State-forms, with the styles of policy appropriate to each, are
assured by the close of the Early period. The State-idea has triumphed over
the feudal union, but it is the Estates that carry that idea, and the nation
has political existence only as their sum.

v

With the beginning of the Late period there is a decisive turn, where city
and country are in equilibrium and the powers proper to the city, money and
brains, have become so strong that they feel themselves, as non-estate, an equal
match for the old Estates. It is the moment when the State-idea finally rises
superior to the Estates and begins to set up *in their place* the concept of the Nation.

The State has fought and won to its rights along a line of advance from feudal
union to the aristocratic State. In the latter the Estates exist only with reference
to the State, instead of vice versa, but, on the other hand, the disposition of
things is such that the Government only meets the governed nation when and
in so far as the nation is class-ordered. Everyone belongs to the nation, but
only an élite to the classes, and these alone count politically.

But the nearer the State approaches its pure form, and the more it becomes
absolute — that is, independent of any other form-ideal — the more heavily the
concept of the nation tells against that of class, and there comes a moment when
the nation is governed *as such*, and distinctions of "standing" become purely
social. Against this evolution — which is one of the necessities of the Culture,
inevitable, irrevocable — the old noble and priestly classes make one more

effort of resistance. For them, now, *everything* is at stake — the heroic and the saintly, the old law, rank, blood — and, from their point of view, against what?

In the West this struggle of the old Estates against the State-power took the form of the *Fronde*. In the Classical world, where there was no dynasty to represent the future and the aristocracy alone had political existence, we find that a dynastic or quasi-dynastic embodiment of the State-idea actually *formed itself*, and, supported by the non-privileged part of the nation, raised this latter for the first time to power. That was the mission of the *Tyrannis*.

In this change from the class-State to the absolute State, which allowed no measures of validity but its own, the dynasties of the West — and those of Egypt and of China likewise — called the non-estate to their aid, *thereby recognizing it as a political quantity*. Herein lies the real importance of the struggle against the Fronde, in which, initially, the powers of the greater cities could not but see advantage to themselves, for here the ruler was standing forth in the name of the State, the care of all, and he was fighting the nobility because it wanted to uphold the *Estate* as a political magnitude.

In the Polis, on the contrary, where the State consisted exclusively in the form and embodied no hereditary head, the necessity of bringing out the unclassed on behalf of the State-idea produced the Tyrannis, in which a family or a faction of the nobility itself assumed the dynastic rôle, without which action on the part of the Third Estate would have been impossible. Late Classical historians were too remote from this process to seize its meaning, and dealt with it merely in terms of externals of private life. In reality, the Tyrannis was *the State*, and oligarchy opposed it under the banner of class. It rested, therefore, upon the support of peasants and burghers — in Athens (c. 580) the Diakrii and Paralii parties. Therefore, again, it backed the Dionysiac and Orphic cults against the Apollinian; thus in Attica Pisistratus forced the worship of Dionysus [1] on the peasantry, in Sicyon Clisthenes forbade the recital of the Homeric poems,[2] and in Rome it was almost certainly in the time of the Tarquins that the trinity Demeter (Ceres)-Dionysus-Kore was introduced.[3] Its temple was dedicated in 483 by Spurius Cassius, the same who perished later in an attempt to reintroduce the Tyrannis. The Ceres temple was the sanctuary of the Plebs, and its managers, the ædiles, were their trusted spokesmen before the tribunate was ever heard of.[4] The Tyrants, like the princes of the Western Baroque, were liberals in a broad sense of the word that ceased to be possible for them in the subsequent stage of bourgeois dominance. But the Classical also began at that time to pass round the word that

---

[1] Gercke-Norden, *Einl. i.d. Alt.-Wiss.*, II, p. 202.

[2] Busolt, *Griech. Geschichte*, II, pp. 346, et seq.

[3] Cf. pp. 282 and 305. Fronde and Tyrannis have as intimate a connexion with Puritanism — the same epochal phase, but in the religious instead of the political world — as the Reformation with the aristocratic State, and the "Second Religiousness" with Cæsarism.

[4] G. Wissowa, *Religion der Römer*, pp. 297, et seq.

"money makes the man (χρήματ' 'ανήρ)" [1] The sixth-century Tyrannis brought the Polis-idea to its conclusions and created the constitutional concept of the Citizen, the *Polites*, the *Civis*, the sum of these, irrespective of their class-provenance, forming the *soma* of the city-state. When, therefore, the oligarchy contrived to win after all — thanks once more to the Classical craving for the present, and the consequent fear and hatred evoked by the quasi-will-to-duration of the dynasts — the concept of the citizen was there, firmly established, and the non-patrician had learned to regard *himself* as an estate *vis-à-vis* a "rest." He had become a political party — the word "democracy" (in its specifically Classical sense) now acquired a really serious content — and what he set himself to do was, no longer to come to the aid of the State, but *to be himself the State* as the nobility had been before. He began to count — money and heads, for the money-census and the general franchise are alike bourgeois weapons — whereas an aristocracy does not count, but values, and votes not by heads, but by classes. As the absolute State came out of Fronde and First Tyrannis, so it perished in French Revolution and Second Tyrannis. In this second conflict, which is already one of defence, the dynasty returns to the side of the nobility in order to guard the State-idea against a new class-rule, that of the bourgeois.

In Egypt, too, the period between Fronde and Revolution is hall-marked. It is the Middle Kingdom. The XIIth Dynasty (2000–1788) — in particular Amenemhet I and Sesostris I — had established the absolute State in severe conflicts with the baronage. The first of these rulers, as a famous poem of the time relates, barely escaped from a court conspiracy, and the biography of Sinuhet [2] shows us that after his death, which was kept secret for a time, rebellion threatened. The third was murdered by palace officials. We learn from the inscriptions in the family grave of the earl Chmenotep [3] that the cities had become rich and almost independent, and warred with each other. Certainly they cannot have been smaller at that time than the Greek cities at the time of the Persian Wars. It was on them and on a certain number of loyal magnates that the dynasty rested.[4] Finally, Sesostris III (1887–1850) succeeded in completely abolishing feudal nobility. Thenceforward there was only a court-nobility and a single, admirably ordered bureau-State; [5] but already some lamented that people of standing were reduced to misery and that the "sons of nobodies" enjoyed rank and consideration.[6] Democracy was beginning and the great social evolution of the Hyksos period was brewing.

The corresponding place in China is that of the Ming- Chu (or Pa, 685–

---

[1] Beloch, *Griech. Geschichte*, I, 1, p. 354.
[2] Ed. Meyer, *Gesch. d. Alt.*, § 281.
[3] Ibid., §§ 280, et seq.
[4] On the means taken to secure the succession, cf. p. 379.
[5] Ed. Meyer, op. cit., § 286.
[6] Ibid., § 283. A. Erman, *Die Mahnworte eines ägyptischen Propheten* (*Sitz. Preuss. Akad.*, 1919, pp. 804, et seq.

591). These were Protectors of princely origin, who exercised an unconstitutional, but none the less real, power over a world of states weltering in anarchy, and called congresses of princes for the restoration of order and the recognition of stable political principles, even summoning the "Ruler of the Middle" himself (now become totally unimportant) out of the house of Chóu. The first was Hwang of Tsi (d. 645), who called the Diet of 659 and of whom Confucius wrote that he had rescued China from a reversion to barbarism. Their name Ming-dshu became later, like the word "tyrant," a term of obloquy, because later men were unwilling to see in the phenomenon anything but a power unauthorized by law — but it is beyond all question that these great diplomatists were an element working with a devoted care for the State and the historical future against the old Estates, and supported by the young classes of mind and money. It is a high Culture that speaks to us in the little that we so far know about them from Chinese sources. Some were writers; others selected philosphers to be their ministers. It is a matter of indifference whether we mentally parallel them with Richelieu or with Wallenstein or with Periander — in any case it is with them that the "people" first emerges as a political quantity.[1] It is the outlook and high diplomacy of genuine Baroque — the absolute State sets itself up in principle as the opponent of the aristocratic State, and wins through.

In this lies the close parallelism of these events with the Fronde of Western Europe. In France the Crown after 1614 ceased to summon the State-General, this body having shown itself to be too strong for the united forces of State and bourgeoisie. In England Charles I similarly tried to govern without Parliament after 1628. In Germany, at the same time, the Thirty Years' War broke out. The magnitude of its religious significance is apt to overshadow for us the other issue involved, and it must not be forgotten that it was also an effort to bring to a decision the struggle between imperial power and the Fronde of the *great* electors, and that between the individual princes and the lesser Frondes of their local estate-assemblies. But the centre of world-politics then lay in *Spain*. There, in conjunction with the high courtesies generally, the diplomatic style of the Baroque had evolved in the cabinet of Philip II; and the dynastic principle — which embodied the absolute State *vis-à-vis* the Cortes — had attained to its highest development in the course of the long struggle with the House of Bourbon. The attempt to align England also in the Spanish system had failed under Philip II, when Queen Mary, his wife, was disappointed of an heir already expected and announced. But now, under Philip IV, the idea of a universal monarchy spanning the oceans revived — no longer the mystic dream-monarchy of the early Gothic, the "Holy Roman Empire, German by nation," but the tangible ideal of a world-dominion in Habsburg hands, which

---

[1] S. Plath, *Verfassung und Verwaltung Chinas* (*Abh. Münch. Ak.*, 1864), p. 97, O. Franke, *Studien z. Gesch. d. Konfuz. Dogmas*, pp. 255, et seq.

was to centre in Madrid and to have the solid possession of India and America and the already sensible power of money as its foundations. It was at this time, too, that the Stuarts were tempted to secure their endangered position by marrying the heir of the English and Scottish thrones to a Spanish Infanta; but in the end Madrid preferred to link itself with its own collateral line in Vienna, and so James I readdressed his marriage-alliance proposals to the opposition party of the Bourbons. The futile complications of this family policy contributed more than anything else to bind the Puritan movement and the English Fronde into one great Revolution.

In these great decisions the actual occupants of the thrones were — as in "contemporary" China — only secondary figures compared with great individual statesmen, in whose hands the fate of the West rested for whole decades. Olivarez in Madrid and the Spanish Ambassador Oñate in Vienna were then the most powerful personages in Europe. Their opponents were Wallenstein, standing for the Empire-idea in Germany, and Richelieu, standing for the absolute State in France — and these were succeeded a little later by Mazarin in France, Cromwell in England, Oldenbarneveldt in Holland, Oxenstierna in Sweden. Not until the Great Elector of Brandenburg do we meet again a monarch having political importance of his own.

Wallenstein, unconsciously, began where the Hohenstaufen had stopped. Since the death of Frederick II, in 1250, the power of the Estates of the Empire had become unlimited, and it was against them, and as champion of an absolute emperor's state, that he fought during the first tenure of command. Had he been a greater diplomatist, had he been clearer and above all more resolute (for actually he was timid in the presence of decisive turnings), and had he, in particular, taken the trouble as Richelieu did to bring the person of the monarch under his influence — then probably it would have been all up with princedom within the Empire. He saw in these princes rebels, to be unseated and dispossessed of their lands; at the peak of his power (end of 1629), when militarily he held Germany in the hollow of his hand, he said aloud in conversation that the Emperor ought to be master in the Empire as the Kings of France and Spain were masters of their own. His army, which was "self-supporting" and by reason of its numbers also independent of the Estates, was the first instance in German history of an Imperial army of European significance; in comparison with it Tilly's army of the Fronde (for that was what the League really was) counted for little. When Wallenstein, in 1628, leaguered before Stralsund, visualizing a Habsburg sea-power in the Baltic wherewith to take the Bourbon system in the rear — and just then Richelieu was besieging La Rochelle, with better fortune — hostilities between himself and the League had become almost unavoidable. He absented himself from the Diet of Regensburg in 1630, saying that its seat "would presently be in Paris." This was the most serious political error of his life, for in his absence the Frondist Electors defeated the Emperor by threatening to displace him in favour of Louis XIII, and forced him to dismiss his general. And with that, though it did not realize the consequence of the step, the central power in Germany gave away its army. Henceforth Richelieu supported the greater Fronde in Germany with the object of breaking the Spanish power there, while on the other side Olivarez, and Wallenstein as soon as he regained his power, allied themselves with the French aristocrats, who thereupon took the offensive under the Queen-mother and Gaston of Orléans. But the Imperial power had missed its grand chance. The Cardinal won in both games. In 1632 he executed the last of the Montmorencys [1] and brought the Catholic Electors of Germany into open alliance with France. And thenceforward Wallenstein, becoming unsure of his own final purposes, learned more and more against the Spanish idea, thinking that he could keep the Empire-idea clear of it, and so *ipso facto* approached nearer and nearer to the standpoint of the Estates — like Marshal Turenne in the French Fronde a few years later. *This was the decisive turn in later German history.* With Wallenstein's secession the absolute emperor-state became impossible, and his murder in 1634 did not remedy matters, for the Emperor had no substitute to take his place.

And yet it was just then that the conjuncture was favourable once more. For in 1640 the decisive conflict between Crown and estates broke out simultaneously in Spain, France, and England. In almost every Spanish province the Cortes rose against Olivarez; Portugal, and with it India and Africa, fell away for ever, and it took years to regain even Catalonia and Naples. In England — just as in the Thirty Years' War — the constitutional conflict between the Crown and the gentry who dominated the Commons was carefully separated from the religious side of the Revolution, deep as was the interpenetration of the two. But the growing resistance that Cromwell encountered in the lower class in particular — which drove him, all unwillingly, into military dictatorship — and the later popularity of the restored monarchy show the extent to which, over and above all religious differences, aristocratic interest had been concerned in bringing about the fall of the dynasty.

At the very time of Charles I's trial and execution an insurrection in Paris was forcing the French Court to flee. Men shouted for a republic and built barricades. Had Cardinal de Retz been more of a Cromwell, victory of the Estates over Mazarin would have been at least a possibility. But the issue of this grand general crisis of the West was determined by the weight and the destinies of a few personalities, and took shape in such a way that it was in England *alone* that the Fronde (represented by Parliament) subjected the State and the kingship to its control — confirming this control, in the "glorious Revolution" of 1688, so permanently that even to-day essential parts of the old Norman State continue established. In France and Spain the kingship won unqualified

---

[1] After armed rebellion. — *Tr.*

victory. In Germany the Peace of Westphalia placed the Fronde of the greater princes in an English relation towards the Emperor and in the French relation towards the lesser Fronde of the local princes. In the Empire as such, the Estates ruled; in its provinces, the Dynasty. Thenceforth the Imperial dignity, like the English kingship, was a name, surrounded by relics of Spanish stateliness dating from the early Baroque; while the individual princes, like the leading families of the English aristocracy, succumbed to the model of Paris and their duodecimo absolutism was, politically and socially, bound in the Versailles style. So, in this field and in that, the decision fell in favour of the Bourbons and against the Habsburgs, a decision already visible to all men in the Peace of the Pyrenees of 1659.

With this epochal turn the State, which as a possibility is inherent in every Culture, was actualized and attained to such a height of "condition" as could neither be surpassed nor for long maintained. Already there is a quiet breath of autumn in the air when Frederick the Great is entertaining at Sans Souci. These are the years too, in which the great special arts attain to their last, most refined, and most intellectual maturity — side by side with the fine orators of the Athenian Agora there are Zeuxis and Praxiteles, side by side with the filigree of Cabinet-diplomacy the music of Bach and Mozart.

This cabinet-politics has itself become a high art, an artistic satisfaction to all who have a finger in it, marvellous in its subtlety and elegance, courtly, refined, working mysteriously at great distances — for already Russia, the North American colonies, even the Indian states are put into play in order by the mere weight of surprising combinations to bring about decisions at quite other points on the globe. It is a game with strict rules, a game of intercepted letters and secret confidants, of alliances and congresses within a system of governments which even then was called (with deep meaning) the "concert" of the powers — full of *noblesse* and *esprit*, to use the phrases of the period, a mode of keeping history "in form" never and nowhere else imagined, or even imaginable.

In the Western world, whose sphere of influence is already almost the sphere itself, the period of the absolutist State covers scarcely a century and a half — from 1660, when Bourbon triumphed over Habsburg in the Peace of the Pyrenees and the Stuarts returned to England, to the Coalition Wars directed against the French Revolution, in which London triumphed over Paris, or, if one prefers it so, over that Congress of Vienna in which the old diplomacy, that of blood and not money, gave the world its grand farewell performance. Corresponding periods are the Age of Pericles between the First and the Second Tyrannis, and the Tshun-tsiu, "Spring and Autumn," as the Chinese call the time, between the Protectors and the "Contending States."

In this last phase of dignified politics with forms traditional but not popular, familiar but not smiled at, the culminating points are marked by the extinction of the two Habsburg lines in quick succession and the diplomatic and warlike events that throng in 1700–10 round the Spanish, and in 1740–60 round the Austrian succession.[1] It is the climax also of the genealogical principle. *Bella gerant alii; tu, felix Austria, nube!* was indeed "an extension of war by other means." The phrase indeed was coined long before (in connexion with Maximilian I), but it was not until now that it reached its fullest effects. Fronde Wars pass over into Succession Wars, decided upon in cabinets and fought out chivalrously by small armies and according to strict conventions.[2] What was contended for was the heritage of half the world which the marriage-politics of early Baroque had brought together in Habsburg hands. The State is still "well up to form"; the nobility has become a loyal aristocracy of court and service, carrying on the wars of the Crown and organizing its administration. Side by side with the France of Louis XIV, there presently arose in Prussia a masterpiece of State organization. From the conflicts of the Great Elector with his Estates (1660) to the death of Frederick the Great (who received Mirabeau in audience three years before the Fall of the Bastille) Prussia's road is the same as France's, and the outcome in each case is a State which was in every point the opposite of the English order.

For the situation was otherwise in the Empire and in England. There the Frondes had won, and the nations were governed, not absolutely, but aristocratically. But between England and the Empire, again, there was the immense difference that England, as an island, could largely dispense with governmental watchfulness, and that her peers in the Upper House and her gentry in the Lower founded their actions on the self-evidentness of England's greatness;[3] whereas in the Empire the upper stratum of the land-princes — with the Diet at Regensburg as their Upper House — were chiefly concerned with educating into distinct "peoples" the fragments of the nation that had accidentally fallen to their respective hands, and with marking off their scattered bits of fatherland as strictly as possible from other "peoples'" bits. In place of the world-horizon that there had been in Gothic days, provincial horizon was cultivated by thought and deed. The idea of the Nation itself was aban-

---

[1] The fifty-year interval of these critical points, which is seen with special distinctness in the clear historical structure of the Baroque, but is recognizable also in the sequence of the three Punic Wars, is yet another hint that the Cosmic flowings in the form of human lives upon the surface of a minor star are not self-contained and independent, but stand in deep harmony with the unending movedness of the universe. In a small but noteworthy book, R. Mewes, *Die Kriegs- und Geistesperioden im Völkerleben unde Verkündigung des nächsten Weltkrieges* (1896), the relation of those war-periods with weather-periods, sun-spot cycles, and certain conjunctures of the planets is established, and a great war foretold accordingly for the period 1910–20. But these and numerous similar connexions that come within the reach of our senses (cf. pp. 5, et seq.) veil a secret that we have to respect and not to infringe with causal expositions or mystical brain-spectres.

[2] See C. von B(inder)-K(rieglstein), *Geist und Stoff im Kriege* (1896); F. N. Maude, *War and the World's Life* (1907), and other works by the same author; also, in more summary terms, the articles "Army" and "French Revolutionary Wars" by the present translator in *Ency. Brit.*, XI ed. — *Tr.*

[3] "Rule, Britannia" is an eighteenth-century product. — *Tr.*

doned to the realm of dreams — that *other* world which is not of race but of language, not of Destiny but of Causality. And in it arose the idea, and finally the fact, of the "people" as conceived by poets and thinkers, who founded themselves a republic in the clouds of verse and logic and at last came to believe that politics consisted in idealistic writing and reading and speaking, and not in deed and resolve — so that even to-day real deeds and resolves are confused with mere expressions of inclination.

In England the victory of the gentry and the Declaration of Rights (1689) in reality put an end to the State. Parliament put William III on his throne, just as later it prevented George I and George II from vacating theirs, in the interest of its class. The word "State," which had been current as early as the Tudors, fell into disuse — it has become impossible to translate into English either Louis XIV's "*L'état c'est moi*" or Frederick the Great's "*Ich bin der erste Diener meiner Staates.*" On the other hand, the word "society" established itself as the expression of the fact that the nation was "in form" under the class- and not under the state-régime; the same word that with a significant misunderstanding Rousseau and the Continental rationalists generally took over to express the hatred of the Third Estate for authority.[1] But in England authority as "the Government" was clear-cut and well understood. From George I onwards its centre was the Cabinet, a body which constitutionally did not exist at all [2] and factually was an executive committee of the faction of the nobility in command for the time being. Absolutism existed, but it was the absolutism of a class-delegation. The idea of "*lèse-majesté*" was transferred to Parliament, as the immunity of the Roman kings passed to the tribunes. The genealogical principle is there, too, but it is expressed in the family relations within the higher nobility and the influence of the same upon the parliamentary situation. Even in 1902 Lord Salisbury acted as a Cecil in proposing his nephew Balfour as his successor as against Joseph Chamberlain. The noble factions of Tory and Whig separated themselves more and more distinctly, very often, indeed, within the same family, according to whether the "power-" outweighed the "booty-" outlook — that is, according as land was valued above money [3] — or vice versa, a contrast that even in the eighteenth century was expressed within the higher bourgeoisie by the words "respectable" and "fashionable," standing for two opposed conceptions of the gentleman. The State's care for all is frankly replaced by class-interest. It is for this that the individual claims his freedom — that is what "freedom" means in English — but the insular existence and the build of "society" have created such relations that in the

---

[1] For this, and what follows, see my *Preussentum und Sozialismus*, pp. 31, et seq.

[2] Mr. Asquith (Lord Oxford) was the first British Prime Minister to be officially so styled. — *Tr.*

[3] "Landed" and "funded" interests (J. Hatschek, *Engl. Verfassungsgeschichte*, 1913, pp. 589, et seq. Walpole, the organizer of the Whig party after 1714, used to describe himself and Townshend as "the Firm;" and this "firm" with various changes of proprietorship governed without limitation till 1760.

last resort everyone *who belongs to it* (which is a matter of moment in a status-dictatorship) finds his interests represented by those of one or the other noble party.

This steadiness of last, deepest, and ripest form, which springs from the historical feeling of Western mankind, was denied to the Classical. Tyrannis vanished. Strict oligarchy vanished. The Demos which the politics of the sixth century had created as the sum of all men belonging to the Polis burst into factions and spasmodic shocks of noble *versus* non-noble, and conflicts began within states, *and between states*, in which each party tried to exterminate the other lest it should itself be exterminated. When in 511 — that is, still in the age of the Tyrants — Sybaris was annihilated by the Pythagoreans, the event, the first of its kind, shocked the entire Classical world; even in distant Miletus mourning was worn. But now the elimination of a Polis or a party was so usual that a regular form and choice of methods — corresponding to the typical peace-treaties of Western Baroque — arose for the disposal of the vanquished — for example, the inhabitants might be massacred or sold into slavery, the houses razed or divided as spoil. The will to absolutism is there — after the Persian Wars it is universal, in Rome and Sparta no less than in Athens — but the *willed* narrowness of the Polis, the point-politic, and the *willed* brevity of office-holding and immediacy of schemes made it impossible ever to reach a firm decision as to who should be "the State." [1] The high craft of diplomacy, which in the West was practised by cabinets inspired by a tradition, was here handicapped by an amateurism founded not on any accidental inadequacy of persons — the men were available — but solely in the political form itself. The course of this form from the First to the Second Tyrannis is unmistakable and corresponds to the same evolution in all other Late periods; but the specifically Classical style of it appears in the disorder and subjection to incidentals which naturally and inevitably followed from a life that could not and would not dissociate itself from the moment.

The most important example of this is the evolution of Rome during the fifth century — a period over which hitherto historians have wrangled, precisely because they have tried to find in it a consistency that can no more have existed there than anywhere else in the Classical State. A further source of misunderstanding is that the conditions of that development have been regarded as something quite primitive, whereas in fact even the city of the Tarquins must have already been in a very advanced state, and primitive Rome lay much further back. The relations of the fifth century are on a small scale in comparison with those of Cæsar's age, but they were not antiquated. Because written tradition is defective (as it was everywhere save in Athens), the literary movement which followed the Punic Wars set itself to fill the blanks with poetry and in particular (as was to be expected in the Hellenistic age)

---

[1] R. von Pöhlmann, *Griech. Gesch.* (1914), pp. 223-45.

with the evocation of an idyllic past, as, for example, in the story of Cincinnatus. And modern scholarship, though it has ceased to believe these legends, has nevertheless remained under the influence of the taste that inspired their invention, and continues to look at the conditions of the time through its eyes — the more readily as Greek and Roman history are treated as two separate worlds, and the evil practice of identifying the beginning of history with the beginning of sure documentation is followed as usual. In truth, the conditions of 500 B.C. are anything but Homeric. The trace of its walls shows that Rome under the Tarquins was, with Capua, the greatest city in Italy and bigger than the Athens of Themistocles.[1] A city that concludes commercial treaties with Carthage is no peasant commune. And it follows that the population in the four city tribes of 471 must have been very numerous, probably greater than the whole total of the sixteen country tribes scattered insignificantly in space.

The great success of the landowning nobility in overthrowing a Tyrannis that was almost certainly very popular, and establishing unrestricted senatorial rule, was nullified again by a series of violent events about 471 — the replacement of the family tribes by four great city-wards, the representation of these by tribunes (who were sacrosanct — i.e., who enjoyed a *royal* privilege that no single official of the aristocratic administration possessed) and lastly the liberation of the small peasantry from the *clientela* of the nobility.

The Tribunate was the happiest inspiration, not only of this period, but of the Classical Polis generally. It was *the Tyrannis raised to the position of an integral part of the Constitution*, and set in parallel, moreover, with the old oligarchical offices, all of which continued in being. This meant that the social revolution also was carried out in *legal forms*, so that what was elsewhere a wild discharge in shock and countershock became here a forum-contest, limited as a rule to debate and vote. There was no need to evoke the tyrant, for he was there already. The Tribune possessed rights inherent in position, not rights arising out of an office, and with his immunity he could carry out revolutionary acts that would have been inconceivable without street-fighting in any other Polis. This creation was an incident, but no other of its creations helped Rome to rise as this did. In Rome alone the transition from the First to the Second Tyrannis, and the further development therefrom till beyond the days of Zama,

[1] Ed. Meyer, *Gesch. d. Alt.* V § 809. If Latin became a literary language, only very late — after Alexander — the only deduction to be made from the fact is that under the Tarquins Greek and Etruscan must have been in general use — which, after all, goes without saying for a city that was of a size and position to have relations with Carthage; that waged war in alliance with Cyme and made use·of the Treasury of Massalia at Delphi; whose standard weights and measures were Dorian; whose mode of warfare was Sicilian; and whose walls contained a large foreign colony. Livy (IX, 36), following older statements, observes that about 300 the Roman boy was still brought upon Etruscan culture, as he was later on Greek. The ancient form "Ulixes" for Odysseus shows that the Homeric sagas were not only known, but popularly known here (cf. p. 284). The provisions of the Twelve Tables (c. 450) agree with the more or less contemporary law of Gortyn in Crete (cf. p. 63), not merely as to substance, but even stylistically — so exactly that the Roman patricians who drew them up must have been entirely at home with juristic Greek.

was accomplished, not indeed without shocks, but at any rate without catastrophe. The Tribune was the link between the Tarquins and Cæsar. With the Lex Hortensia of 287 he became all-powerful, *he is the Second Tyrannis in constitutional "form."* In the second century, tribunes caused consuls and censors to be arrested. The Gracchi were tribunes, Cæsar assumed the perpetual tribunate, and in the principate of Augustus the tribunician dignity was the essential element of his position, the only one in virtue of which he possessed sovereign rights.

The crisis of 471 was not unique but generically Classical. Its target was the oligarchy, which even now, within the Demos created by the Tyrannis, strove to be the impulsive force in affairs. It was no longer, as in Hesiod's day, the oligarchy as estate *versus* non-estate, but the *oligarchic party against a second party* — both in the cadre of the absolute state, which as such was not brought into the controversy. In Athens, 487 B.C., the archons were overthrown and their rights transferred to the college of strategi.[1] In 461 the Areopagus, the Athenian equivalent of the Senate, was overthrown. In Sicily (where relations with Rome were close) the democracy triumphed at Acragas (Agrigentum) in 471, at Syracuse in 465, at Rhegium and Messana in 461. In Sparta the kings Cleomenes (488) and Pausanias (470) tried in turn, without success, to free the Helots — in Roman terms, the Clientela — and thereby to acquire for the kingship, *vis-à-vis* the oligarchic Ephors, the importance of the tribunate in Rome. The missing element in this case, which was present (though overlooked by our scholars) in that of Rome, was the population-strength of the mercantile city that gives such movements both weight and leadership; it was on this that even the great Helot rising of 464 broke down (an event which probably inspired the Roman legends of a secession of the Plebs to the Mons Sacer).

In a Polis, the country nobility and the patriciate fuse (that is the object of synœcism, as we have seen), but not so the burgher and the peasant. So far as concerns their struggle with the oligarchy these are a single party — namely, the democratic — but otherwise they are *two*. This is what comes to expression in the next crisis. In this (*c.* 450) the Roman patriciate sought to re-establish its power *as a party* — for so we must interpret the introduction of the Decemvirs and the abolition of the Tribunate; the legislation of the Twelve Tables by which the plebs, which had recently attained political existence, was denied "Connubium" and "Commercium"; and above all the creation of the small country tribes in which the influence of the old families (not legally but in fact) predominated and which (in the Comitia Tributa now set up alongside the old Centuriata) enjoyed the unchallengeable majority of 16 to 4. This, of course, meant the disfranchisement of the townspeople by the peasantry, and there can be no doubt that it was a move of the Patrician party to make effective

---

[1] This measure — a usurpation of the administration by the "nation in arms" — corresponds to the setting-up of Consular Tribunes in Rome in the military disturbances of 438.

in one common blow the common antipathy of the countryside and themselves towards the money economics of the city.

The counterstroke came quickly; it is recognizable in the number *ten* of the tribunes who appear after the withdrawal of the Decemvirs,[1] but there were other events too that cannot but have belonged with it — the attempt of Sp. Mælius to set up a Tyrannis (439), the setting-up of Consular Tribunes by the army in place of the civil officials (438), and the Lex Canuleia (445) which made an end of the prohibition of connubium between patricians and plebeians.

There can be no doubt, of course, that there were factions within both the patrician and the plebeian parties which would have liked to upset this fundamental trait of the Roman Polis, the opposition of Senate and Tribunate, by abolishing the one or the other; but the form turned out to be so right that it was never seriously challenged. With the enforcement by the Army of plebeian eligibility to the highest offices (399) the contest took a quite different turn. The fifth century may be summed up, under the aspect of internal politics, as that of the struggle for lawful Tyrannis; thenceforward the polarity of the constitution was admitted, and the parties contended no longer for the abolition, but for the capture, of the great offices. This was the substance of the revolution that took place in the period of the Samnite Wars. From 287 the Plebes had the entrée to *all* offices, and the proposals of the tribunes, when approved by them, automatically became law; on the other hand, it was thenceforward always practicable for the Senate by corruption or otherwise to induce some one tribune to exercise his veto and thus to deprive the institution of its power. It was in the *struggle of two competent authorities* that the juristic subtlety of the Romans was developed. Elsewhere decisions were usually by way of fist and bludgeon — the technical word is "Cheirocracy" — but in this "best" period of Roman constitutional law, the fourth century, the habit was formed of using the weapons of thesis and interpretation, a mode of contest in which the slightest points of legal wording could be decisive.

But Rome was unique in all Classical history in this equilibrium of Senate and Tribunate. Everywhere else it was a matter not of swaying balance, but of sheer alternatives, namely Oligarchy *or* Ochlocracy. The absolute Polis and the Nation which was identical with it were accepted as given premises, but of the inward forms none possessed stability. The victory of one party meant the abolition of all the institutions of the other, and people became accustomed to regard nothing as either venerable enough or useful enough to be exempt from the chances of the day's battle. Sparta's "form," so to say, was senatorial, Athens's tribunician, and by the beginning of the Peloponnesian War,

---

[1] According to B. Niese. Modern investigators are right in the view that the Decemvirate was at first intended to be temporary; but the question is — what were the views of the party that backed them concerning the *new* constitutional order that was to follow. It was on that that a crisis had inevitably to come.

in 431, the idea that forms must be alternative was so firmly fixed that only radical solutions were henceforth possible.

With this, the future was set for Rome. It was the one state in which political passions had persons only, and no longer institutions, as their target; the only one which was firmly in "form." *Senatus Populusque Romanus* — that is, *Senate and Tribunate* — was the form of forged bronze that no party would henceforward batter, whereas all the rest, with the narrowness of their individual power-horizons in the world of Classical states, were only able to prove once more the fact that domestic politics exist simply in order that foreign politics may be possible.

VI

At this point, when the Culture is beginning to turn itself into the Civilization, the non-Estate intervenes in affairs decisively — and for the first time — as an independent force. Under the Tyrannis and the Fronde, the State has invoked its aid against the Estates proper, and it has for the first time learned to feel itself a power. Now it employs its strength *for itself*, and does so as a class standing for its freedom against the rest. It sees in the absolute State, in the Crown, in rooted institutions, the natural allies of the old Estates and the true and last representatives of symbolic tradition. This is the difference between the First and the Second Tyrannis, between Fronde and Bourgeois Revolution, between Cromwell and Robespierre.

The State, with its heavy demands on each individual in it, is felt by urban reason as a burden. So, in the same phase, the great forms of the Baroque arts begin to be felt as restrictive and become Classicist or Romanticist — that is, sickly or unformed; German literature from 1770 is one long revolt of strong individual personalities against strict poetry. The idea of the whole nation being "in training" or "in form" for anything becomes intolerable, for the individual himself inwardly is no longer in condition. This holds good in morals, in arts, and in modes of thought, but most of all in politics. Every bourgeois revolution has as its scene the great city, and as its hall-mark the incomprehension of old symbols, which it replaces by tangible interests and the craving (or even the mere wish) of enthusiastic thinkers and world-improvers to see their conceptions actualized. Nothing now has value but that which can be justified by reason. But, deprived thus of the exaltation of a form that is essentially symbolical and works metaphysically, the national life loses the power of keeping its head up in the being-streams of history. Follow the desperate attempts of the French Government — the handful of capable and farsighted men under the mediocre Louis XVI — to keep their country in "condition" when, after the death of Vergennes in 1787, the whole gravity of the external situation had become manifest. With the death of this diplomatist France disappeared for years from the political combinations of Europe;

at the same time the great reform that the Crown had carried through against all resistances — above all, the general administrative reform of that year, based on the freest self-management — remained completely ineffective, because in view of the pliancy of the State, the question of the moment for the Estates became, suddenly, the question of power.[1] As a century before and a century afterwards, European war was drawing visibly nearer with an inexorable necessity, but no one now took any notice of the external situation. The nobility as an Estate had rarely, but the bourgeoisie as an Estate had never, thought in terms of foreign policy and world-history. Whether the State in its new form would be able to hold its own at all amongst the other States, no one asked. All that mattered was whether it secured men's "rights."

But the bourgeoisie, the class of urban "freedom," strong as its class-feeling remained for generations (in West Europe even beyond 1848), was at no time wholly master of its actions. For, first of all, it became manifest in every critical situation that its unity was a *negative* unity, only really existent in moments of opposition to something, anything, else — "Tiers État" and "Opposition" are almost synonymous — and that when something constructive of its own had to be done, the interests of the various groups pulled all ways. To be free from something — that, all wanted. But the intellectual desired the State as an actualization of "justice" against the force of historical facts; or the "rights of man"; or freedom of criticism as against the dominant religion. And Money wanted a free path to business success. There were a good many who desired rest and renunciation of historical greatness, or wished this and that tradition and its embodiments, on which physically or spiritually they lived, to be spared. But there was another element, now and henceforth, that had not existed in the conflicts of the Fronde (the English Civil War included) or the first Tyrannis, but this time stood for a power — namely, that which is found in all Civilizations under different contemptuous labels — dregs, *canaille*, mob, *Pöbel* — but with the same tremendous connotation. In the great cities, which alone now spoke the decisive words — the open land can at most accept or reject *faits accomplis*, as our eighteenth century proves [2] — a mass of rootless fragments of population stands outside all social linkages. These do not feel themselves as attached either to an Estate or to a vocational class, nor even to the real working-class, although they are obliged to work.

[1] A. Wahl, *Vorgeschichte d. franz. Revolution*, II (1907); this work is the only presentation of the subject from the world-historical point of view. All Frenchmen, even the most modern, such as Aulard and Sorel, see things from one or another partisan angle. It is materialistic nonsense to talk of economic causes for a Revolution like this. Even the peasantry was better off than in most other countries, and in any case it was not among them that it began. It was amongst the *educated* that the catastrophe started, the educated of *all* the classes — in the high nobility and the clergy even sooner than in the higher bourgeoisie, because the course of the first assembly of Notables (1787) had disclosed the possibility of radically reshaping the form of government according to class-desires.

[2] Even the highly provincial March Revolution of 1848 in Germany was a purely urban matter; hence the vanishingly small proportion of the population involved as participants.

Elements drawn from all classes and conditions belong to it instinctively — uprooted peasantry, literates, ruined business men, and above all (as the age of Catiline shows with terrifying clarity) derailed nobles. Their power is far in excess of their numbers, for they are always on the spot, always on hand at the big decisions, ready for anything, devoid of all respect for orderliness, even the orderliness of a revolutionary party. It is from them that events acquire the destructive force which distinguishes the French Revolution from the English, and the Second Tyrannis from the First. The bourgeoisie looks at these masses with real uneasiness, defensively, and seeks to separate itself from them — it was to a defensive act of this category, the 13th Vendémiaire, that Napoleon owed his rise.[1] But in the pressure of facts the separating frontier cannot be drawn; wherever the bourgeoisie throws into the scale against the older orders its feeble weight of aggressiveness — feeble in relative numbers and feeble because its inner cohesion is risked at every moment — this mass has forced itself into their ranks, pushed to the front, imparted most of the drive that wins the victory, and very often managed to secure the conquered position for itself — not seldom with the continued idealistic support of the educated who are intellectually captivated, or the material backing of the money powers, which seek to divert the danger from themselves on to the nobility and the clergy.

There is another aspect, too, under which this epoch has its importance — in it for the first time abstract truths seek to intervene in the world of facts. The capital cities have become so great, and urban man so superior and influential over the waking-consciousness of the whole Culture (*this influence is what we call Public Opinion*) that the powers of the blood and the tradition inherent in the blood are shaken in their hitherto unassailable position. For it must be remembered that the Baroque State and the absolute Polis in their final development of form are thoroughly living expressions of a *breed*, and that history, so far as it accomplishes itself in these forms, possesses the full pulse of that breed. Any theory of the State that may be fashioned here is one that is deduced from the facts, that bows to the greatness of the facts. The idea of the State had finally mastered the blood of the first Estate, and put it wholly and without reserve at the State's service. "Absolute" means that the great being-stream is *as a unit* in form, possesses *one* kind of pulse and instinct, whether the manifestations of that pulse be diplomatic or strategic flair, dignity of moral and manners, or fastidious taste in arts and thoughts.

As the contradictory to this grand fact, now, Rationalism appears and spreads, that which has been described above [2] as the *community of waking-consciousness in the educated*, whose religion is criticism and whose numina are

---

[1] Hence also the exclusive bourgeois character of the National Guard in France from 1815 to 1851, the period between two phases of popular Tyrannis. In the *coup d'état* by which Napoleon III seized the throne, Paris was filled with regular troops, and the National Guard was forbidden to assemble on pain of death. — *Tr.*

[2] Pp. 97, and 305.

not deities but concepts. Now begins the influence of books and general theories upon politics — in the China of Lao-tse as in the Athens of the Sophists and the Europe of Montesquieu — and the public opinion formed by them plants itself in the path of diplomacy as a political magnitude of quite a new sort. It would be absurd to suppose that Pisistratus or Richelieu or even Cromwell determined their actions under the influence of abstract systems, but after the victory of "Enlightenment" that is what actually happens.

Nevertheless the historical rôle of the great concepts of the Civilization is very different from the complexion that they presented in the minds of the ideologues who conceived them. The effect of a truth is always quite different from its tendency. In the world of facts, truths are simply *means*, effective in so far as they dominate spirits and therefore determine actions. Their historical position is determined not by whether they are deep, correct, or even merely logical, but by whether they *tell*. We see this in the phrase "catchword," "*Schlagwort.*" What certain symbols, livingly experienced, are for the Spring-time religions — the Holy Sepulchre for the Crusader, the Substance of Christ for the times of the Council of Nicæa — that two or three inspiriting word-sounds are for every Civilized revolution. It is only the catchwords that are facts — the residue of the philosophical or sociological system whence they come does not matter to history. But, *as* catchwords, they are for about two centuries powers of the first rank, stronger even than the pulse of the blood, which in the petrifying world of the outspread cities is beginning to be dulled.

But — the critical spirit is only one of the two tendencies which emerge out of the chaotic mass of the Non-Estate. Along with abstract concepts abstract Money, — money divorced from the prime values of the land — along with the study the counting-house, appear as political forces. The two are in-wardly cognate and inseparable — the old opposition between priest and noble continued, acute as ever, in the bourgeois atmosphere and the city framework.[1] Of the two, moreover, it is the Money that, as pure fact, shows itself un-conditionally superior to the ideal truths, which so far as the fact-world is concerned exist (as I have just said) only as catchwords, as means. If by "democracy" we mean the form which the Third Estate as such wishes to impart to public life as a whole, it must be concluded that democracy and plutocracy are the same thing under the two aspects of wish and actuality, theory and practice, knowing and doing. It is the tragic comedy of the world-improvers' and freedom-teachers' desperate fight against money that they are *ipso facto* assisting money to be effective. Respect for the big number — ex-pressed in the principles of equality for all, natural rights, and universal suf-frage — is just as much a class-ideal of the unclassed as freedom of public opinion (and more particularly freedom of the press) is so. These are ideals, but in actuality the feedom of public opinion involves the preparation of public

[1] See pp. 348.

opinion, which costs money; and the freedom of the press brings with it the question of possession of the press, which again is a matter of money; and with the franchise comes electioneering, in which he who pays the piper calls the tune. The representatives of the ideas look at one side only, while the representatives of money operate with the other. The concepts of Liberalism and Socialism are set in effective motion only by money. It was the Equites, the big-money party, which made Tiberius Gracchus's popular movement possible at all; and as soon as that part of the reforms that was advantageous to themselves had been successfully legalized, they withdrew and the movement collapsed. Cæsar and Crassus financed the Catilinarian movement, and so directed it against the Senatorial party instead of against property. In England politicians of eminence laid it down as early as 1700 that "on 'Change one deals in votes as well as in stocks, and the price of a vote is as well known as the price of an acre of land." [1] When the news of Waterloo reached Paris, the price of French government stock rose [2] — the Jacobins had destroyed the old obligations of the blood and so had emancipated money; now it stepped forward as lord of the land.[3] There is no proletarian, not even a Communist, movement that has not operated in the interest of money, in the directions indicated by money, and for the time permitted by money — and that, without the idealist amongst its leaders having the slightest suspicion of the fact.[4] Intellect rejects, money directs — so it runs in every last act of a Culture-drama, when the megalopolis has become master over the rest. And, in the limit, intellect has no cause of complaint. For, after all, it *has* won its victory — namely, in its own realm of truths, the realm of books and ideals that is not of this world. Its conceptions have become venerabilia of the beginning Civilization. But Money wins, through these very concepts, in *its* realm, which is *only* of this world.

In the Western world of States, it was in England that both sides of Third-Estate politics, the ideal and the real, graduated. Here alone it was possible for the Third Estate to avoid the necessity of marching against an absolute State in order to destroy it and set up its own dominion on the ruins. For here it could grow up into the strong form of the First Estate, where it found a fully developed form of interest-politics, and from whose methods it could borrow for its own purposes a traditional tactic such as it could hardly wish to improve

---

[1] J. Hatschek, *Engl. Verfassungsgesch.*, p. 588.

[2] On the other side of the Channel, it is well known that the Rothschild fortune was founded in a dramatic play upon the varying news from the front in Belgium.

In the second phase of the Franco-German War of 1870-1 the bankers of Frankfurt took up holdings in the loans floated by the French Government of National Defence. — *Tr.*

[3] But even during the Reign of Terror in the middle of Paris, there flourished the establishment of Dr. Belhomme, in which members of the highest aristocracy ate and drank and danced out of all danger for so long as they could pay (G. Lenôtre, *Das revolutionäre Paris*, p. 409).

[4] The great movement which makes use of the catchwords of Marx has not delivered the entrepreneur into the power of the worker, but both into that of the Bourse.

upon. Here was the home of Parliamentarism, genuine and quite inimitable, which had insular position instead of the state as its starting-point, and the habits of the First and not the Third Estate as its background. Further, there was the circumstance that this form had grown up in the full bloom of Baroque and, therefore, had Music in it. The Parliamentary style was completely identical with that of cabinet-diplomacy;[1] and in this *anti-democratic* origin lay the secret of its successes.

But it was on British soil, too, that the rationalistic catchwords had, one and all, sprung up, and their relation to the principles of the Manchester School was intimate — Hume was the teacher of Adam Smith. "Liberty" self-evidently meant intellectual *and* trade freedom. An opposition between fact-politics and enthusiasm for abstract truths was as impossible in the England of George III as it was inevitable in the France of Louis XVI. Later, Edmund Burke could retort upon Mirabeau that "we demand our liberties, not as rights of man, but as rights of Englishmen." France received her revolutionary ideas without exception from England, as she had received the style of her absolute monarchy from Spain. To both she imparted a brilliant and irresistible shape that was taken as a model far and wide over the Continent, but of the practical employment of either she had no idea. The successful utilization of the bourgeois catchwords [2] in politics presupposes the shrewd eye of a ruling class for the intellectual constitution of the stratum which intends to attain power, but will not be capable of wielding it when attained. Hence in England it was successful. But it was in England too that money was most unhesitatingly used in politics — not the bribery of individual high personages which had been customary in the Spanish or Venetian style, but the "nursing" of the democratic forces themselves. In eighteenth-century England, first the Parliamentary elections and then the decisions of the elected Commons were systematically managed by money;[3] England, too, discovered the ideal of a Free Press, and discovered along with it that the press serves him who owns it. It does not spread "free" opinion — it generates it.

Both *together* constitute liberalism (in the broad sense); that is, freedom from the restrictions of the soil-bound life, be these privileges, forms, or feelings — freedom of the intellect for every kind of criticism, freedom of money for every kind of business. But both, too, unhesitatingly aim at the domination

---

[1] Both the old parties possessed clear lines of tradition back to 1680.

[2] The moral and political "Enlightenment" movement was in England also a product of the Third Estate (Priestley and Paley, Paine, Godwin), and for that reason was unable to grasp things with the fine discrimination of a Shaftesbury.

[3] Pelham, the successor of Walpole, paid to members of the Commons, through his secretary, £500 to £800 at the end of each session according to the value of the services rendered by each recipient to the Government — i.e., the Whig party. The party agent Dodington described his parliamentary activities in these words: "I never attended a debate if I could help it, and I never missed a division that I could possibly take part in. I heard many arguments that convinced me, but never one that influenced my vote."

of a *class*, a domination which recognizes no overriding supremacy of the State. Mind and money, being both inorganic, want the State, not as a matured form of high symbolism to be venerated, but as an engine to serve a purpose. Thus the difference between these forces and those of Frondism is fundamental, for the latter's reaction had been a defence of the old Gothic against the intrusive Baroque way of living and being "in form," — and now both these are on the defensive together and almost indistinguishable. Only in England (it must be emphasized again and again) the Fronde had disarmed, not only the State in open battle, but also the Third Estate by its inward superiority, and so attained to the one kind of first-class form that democracy is capable of working up to, a form neither planned nor aped, but naturally matured, the expression of an old breed and an unbroken sure tact that can adapt itself to the use of every new means that the changes of Time put into its hands. Thus it came about that the English Parliament, while taking part in the Succession-Wars of the Absolute States, handled them as economic wars with business aims. The mistrust felt for high form by the inwardly formless Non-Estate is so deep that everywhere and always it is ready to rescue its freedom — *from* all form — by means of a dictatorship, which acknowledges no rules and is, therefore, hostile to all that has grown up, which, moreover, in virtue of its mechanizing tendency, is acceptable to the taste both of intellect and of money — consider, for example, the structure of the state-machine of France which Robespierre began and Napoleon completed. Dictatorship in the interests of a class-ideal appealed to Rousseau, Saint-Simon, Rodbertus, and Lassalle as it had to the Classical ideologues of the fourth century — Xenophon in the Cyropædia and Isocrates in the Nicocles.[1]

But the well-known saying of Robespierre that "the Government of the Revolution is the despotism of freedom against tyranny" expresses more than this. It lets out the deep fear that shakes every multitude which, in the presence of grave conjunctures, feels itself "not up to form." A regiment that is shaken in its discipline will readily concede to accidental leaders of the moment powers of an extent and a kind which the legitimate command could never acquire, and which *if* legitimate would be utterly intolerable. But this, on a larger scale, is the position of every commencing Civilization. Nothing reveals more tellingly the decline of political form than that upspringing of formless powers which we may conveniently designate, from its most conspicuous example, *Napoleonism*. How completely the being of Richelieu or of Wallenstein was involved in the unshakable antecedents of their period! And how instinct with form, under all its outer unform, was the English Revolution! Here, just the reverse; the Fronde fights *about* the form, the absolute State *in* the form,

---

[1] Here it was actually the interest of bourgeois and "enlightenment" ideals that the personal régime of dictatorship was thought to favour, for the opposition to these ideas lay in the strict state-ideal of the Polis, which according to Isocrates was marked with the curse of inability to die.

but the bourgeoisie *against* the form. The mere abolition of an order that had become obsolete was no novelty — Cromwell and the heads of the First Tyrannis had done that. But, that behind the ruins of the visible there is no longer the substance of an invisible form; that Robespierre and Napoleon find nothing either around or in them to provide the *self-evident* basis essential to any new creation; that for a government of high tradition and experience they have no choice but to substitute an accidental régime, whose future no longer rests secure on the qualities of a slowly and thoroughly trained minority, but depends entirely on the chance of the adequate successor turning up — such are the distinguishing marks of this turning of the times, and hence comes the immense superiority that is enjoyed for generations still by those states which manage to retain a tradition longer than others.

The First Tyrannis had completed the Polis with the aid of the non-noble; the latter now destroyed it with the aid of the Second Tyrannis. As an idea, it perishes in the bourgeois revolutions of the fourth century, for all that it may persist as an arrangement or a habit or an instrument of the momentary powers that be. Classical man never ceased, in fact, to think and live politically in its form. But never more was it for the multitude a symbol to be respected and venerated, any more than the Divine Right of Kings was venerated in the West after Napoleon had almost succeeded in making his own dynasty "the oldest in Europe."

Further, in these revolutions too, as ever in Classical history, there were only local and temporary solutions — nothing resembling the splendid sweep of the French Revolution from the Bastille to Waterloo — and the scenes in them were more atrocious still, for the reason that in this Culture, with its basically Euclidean feeling, the only possible way seemed to be that of physical collision of party against party, and the only possible end for the loser, not functional incorporation in the victor's system as in the West, but destruction root and branch. At Corcyra (427) and Argos (370) the possessing classes were slaughtered *en masse;* in Leontini (422) they were expelled from the city by the lower classes, which carried on affairs for a while with slaves until, in fear of an avenging return, they evacuated altogether and migrated to Syracuse. The refugees from hundreds of these revolutions inundated the cities, recruited the mercenary armies of the Second Tyrannis, and infested the routes by land and sea. The readmission of such exiled fractions is a standing feature in the peace-terms offered by the Diadochi and later by the Romans. But the Second Tyrannis itself secured its positions by acts of this kind. Dionysius I (407–367) secured his hegemony over Syracuse — the city in whose higher society, along with that of Athens, centred the ripest culture of Hellas, the city where Æschylus had produced his Persian trilogy in 470 — by wholesale executions of educated people and confiscations of their property; this he followed up by entirely rebuilding the population, in the upper levels by granting large properties to his adherents, and in the lower by raising masses of slaves to the citizenship and distributing amongst them (as was not uncommon) the wives and daughters of the victims.[1]

After the characteristically Classical fashion, the type of these revolutions was such as to produce always an increase of number, never of extent. Multitudes of them happened, but each proceeded purely for itself and at one point of its own, and it is only the fact that they were contemporary with one another that gives them the character of a collective phenomenon, which marks an epoch. Similarly with Napoleonism; here again, a formless regimen for the first time raised itself above the framework of the State, yet without being able to attain to complete inward detachment therefrom. It supported itself on the Army, which, *vis-à-vis* the nation that had lost its "form," began to feel itself as an independent power. That is the brief road from Robespierre to Bonaparte — with the fall of the Jacobins the centre of gravity passed from the administration to the ambitious generals. How deeply this new tendency implanted itself in the West may be seen from the example of Bernadotte and Wellington, and even more from the story of Frederick William III's "call to my People" in 1813 — in this case the continuance of the dynasty would have been challenged by the military had not the King stiffened himself to break with Napoleon.[2]

This anti-constitutionality of the Second Tyrannis declared itself also in the position taken by Alcibiades and Lysander in the armed forces of their respective cities during the latter stages of the Peloponnesian War, a position incompatible with the basic form of the Polis. The first-named, destitute as an exile of official position, and against the will of the home authorities, exercised from 411 the *de facto* command of the Athenian Navy; the second, though not even a Spartiate, felt himself entirely independent at the head of an army devoted to his person. In the year 408 the contest of the two powers for the supremacy over the Ægean world took the form of a contest between these two individuals.[3] Shortly after this, Dionysius of Syracuse built up the first large-scale professional army and introduced engines of war (artillery)[4] — a new form which served as a model for the Diadochi and Rome also. Thereafter the spirit of the army was a political power on its own account, and it became a serious question how far the State was master, and how far tool, of its army.

[1] Diodorus XIV, 7. The drama was repeated in 317, when Agathocles the ex-potter let loose his mercenary bands and the mob upon the new upper classes. After the massacre the "people" of the "purified city" assembled and conferred the dictature upon the "saviour of true and genuine freedom" (Deodorus XIX, 6, et seq.). On the whole movement see Busolt, *Griech. Staatskunde*, pp. 396, et seq., and Pöhlmann, *Gesch. d. soz Frage*, I, pp. 416, et seq.

[2] Already that part of the Prussian army which had been in Russia had declared against Napoleon — and that, though its general, Yorck, was no liberal, but the old strict type of the Frederician officer. — Tr.

[3] Ed. Meyer, *Gesch. d. Alt.*, IV, §§ 626, 630.

[4] H. Delbrück, *Gesch. d. Kriegskunst* (1908), I, p. 142.

The fact that the government of Rome was exclusively in the hands of a military committee [1] from 390 to 367 [2] reveals pretty clearly that the army had a policy of its own. It is well known that Alexander, the Romanticist of the Second Tyrannis, fell more and more under the influence of his generals, who not only compelled the retreat from India but also disposed of his inheritance amongst themselves as a matter of course.

This is essentially Napoleonism, and so is the extension of *personal* rule over regions united by ties neither national nor jural, but merely military and administrative. But extension was just what was essentially incompatible with the Polis. The Classical State is the one State that was incapable of any organic widening, and the conquests of the Second Tyrannis therefore resolved themselves into a *juxtaposition of two political units*, the Polis and the subjugated territory, the cohesion of which was initially accidental and perpetually in danger. Thus arose that strange picture of the Hellenistic-Roman world, the true significance of which is not even yet recognized — *a circle of border-regions*, and within them a congeries of Poleis to which, small as they were, the conception of the State proper, the *res publica*, continued to be bound as exclusively as ever. In this middle (indeed, so far as concerned each individual, hegemony was in one point) was the theatre of all real politics. The "*orbis terrarum*" — a significant expression — was merely a means or object to it. The Roman notions of "*imperium*" — dictatorial powers of administration outside the city moat (which were automatically extinguished when its holder entered the Pomœrium) — and of "*provincia*" as the opposite of "*res publica*," express the common Classical instinct, which knew only the city's body as the State and political subject, and the "outside" only in relation to it, as object to it. Dionysius made his city of Syracuse into a fortress surrounded by a "scrap-heap of states," and extended his field of power thence, over Upper Italy and the Dalmatian coast, into the northern Adriatic, where he possessed Ancona and Hatria at the mouth of the Po. Philip of Macedon, following the example of his teacher Jason of Pheræ (murdered in 370), adopted the reverse plan, placing his centre of gravity in the periphery (that is, practically in the army) and thence exercising a hegemony over the Hellenic world of States. Thus Macedonia came to extend to the Danube, and after Alexander's death there were added to this outer circle the empires of the Seleucids and the Ptolemies —

---

[1] Three to six "*tribuni militares consulari protestate*" instead of the Consuls. Just at this juncture, as the result of the introduction of pay and longer duration of service with the colours, there must have come into being a nucleus of true professional soldiers, who would have the election of centurions in their own hands and by whom the spirit of the army was determined. It is entirely erroneous to speak of a peasant-levy at this stage, quite apart from the fact that the four great city-tribes contributed a considerable part of the rank and file and a part, too, whose influence was even greater than its numerical strength. Even in the "good old days" picture presented to us by Livy and others we can clearly perceive the influence exerted by the standing formations upon the contests of parties.

[2] It is perhaps not a mere coincidence that 367 is the year of Dionysius's death.

each governed from a Polis (Antioch, Alexandria), but through the intermediary of existing native machinery, which, be it said, was at its lowest better
than any Classical administration of it could have been. Rome herself in the
same period (*c.* 326–265) built up her Middle-Italian territory as a *border state*,
secured in all directions by a system of colonies, allies, and settlements with
Latin right. Then, from 237, we find Hamilcar Barca winning for Carthage, a
city old established in the Classical way of life, an empire in Spain; C. Flaminius
(225) conquering the Po Valley for Rome; and finally Cæsar making his Gallic
empire. These were the foundations upon which rested, first, the Napoleonic
struggles of the Diadochi in the East, then those of Scipio and Hannibal in the
West — the limits of the Polis outgrown in both cases — and lastly the Cæsarian struggles of the Triumvirs, who supported themselves on the total of *all*
the border states and used their means, in order to be — "the first in Rome."

VII

In Rome the strong and happily conceived form of the State that was
reached about 340 kept the social revolution within constitutional limits.
A Napoleonic figure like Appius Claudius the Censor of 310, who built the first
aqueduct and the Appian Way, and ruled in Rome almost as a tyrant, very
soon failed when he tried to eliminate the peasantry by means of the great-city
masses and so to impart the one-sided Athenian direction to politics — for
that was his aim in taking up the sons of slaves into the Senate, in reorganizing
the Centuries on a money instead of a land-assessment basis,[1] and in distributing
freedmen and landless men amongst the country tribes, so that they might
outvote the rustics (as they were always able to do, since the latter rarely attended). But his successors in the censorship lost no time in reversing this, and
relegated the landless to the great city-tribes again. The non-estate itself, well
led by a minority of distinguished families, saw its aim (as has been said before)
not in the destruction, but in the acquisition, of the senatorial organs of
administration. In the end, it forced its way into all offices (even, by the Lex
Ogulnia, of 300, into the politically important priesthoods of the Pontifices
and Augurs), and by the outbreak of 287 it secured force of law for *plebiscita*
even without the Senate's approval.

The practical result of this freedom-movement was precisely the reverse of
that which ideologues would have expected — there were no idealogues in
Rome. The greatness of its success robbed the non-estate of its object and
thereby deprived it of its driving force, for positively, when not "in opposition," it was null. After 287 the state-form existed for the purpose of being
politically *used*, and used, too, in a world in which only the states of the great
fringe — Rome, Carthage, Macedonia, Syria, and Egypt — really counted.
It had ceased to be in any danger of becoming the passive of "peoples'-rights"

---

[1] According to K. J. Neumann, this goes back to the great Censor.

activities. And it was precisely this security that formed the basis on which the one people that had remained "in form" rose to its grandeur.

On the one hand, it had developed within the Plebs, formless and long weakened in its race-impulses by the mass-intake of freedmen,[1] an upper stratum distinguished by great practical aptitudes, rank, and wealth, which joined forces with a corresponding stratum within the patriciate. Hence there came into existence a very narrow circle of men of the strongest race-quality, dignified life, and broad political outlook, in whom the whole stock of experience in governing and generalship and negotiation was concentrated and transmitted; who regarded the direction of the State as the one profession worthy of their status, considered themselves as inheritors of a privilege to exercise it, and educated their children solely in the art of ruling and the convictions of a measurelessly proud tradition. This nobility, which as such had no constitutional existence, found its constitutional engine in the Senate, which had originally been a body representing the interests of the patricians (that is, the "Homeric" aristocracy), but in which from the middle of the fourth century ex-consuls — men who had both ruled and commanded — sat as life-members, forming a close group of eminent talents that dominated the assembly and, through it, the State. Even by 279 the Senate appeared to Cineas, the ambassador of Pyrrhus, like a council of kings, and finally its kernel was a small group of leading men, holding the titles "*princeps*" and "*clarissimus*," men in every respect — rank, power, and public dignity — the peers of those who reigned over the empires of the Diadochi.[2] There came into being a government such as no megalopolis in any other Culture whatsoever has possessed, and a tradition to which it would be impossible to find parallels save perhaps in the Venice and the Papal Curia of the Baroque, and there under a wholly different set of conditions. Here were no theories such as had been the ruin of Athens, none of the provincialism that had made Sparta in the long run contemptible, but simply a praxis in the grand style. If "Rome" is a perfectly unique and marvellous phenomenon in world-history, it is due, not to the Ro-

[1] According to Roman law, the freed slave at once acquired citizenship, with some few limitations. As the slave-material came from all over the Mediterranean region and most of all from the East, it was a vast rootless mass that collected in the four urban tribes, alien from all the tendencies of the old Roman blood; and it quickly destroyed these when, after the Gracchan movement, it had succeeded in bringing its weight of numbers to bear with effect.

[2] From the end of the fourth century the nobility developed into a closed circle of families that had, or claimed to have, consuls among their ancestors. The more strictly this condition was enforced, the more frequent were the falsifications of the old consul-lists in order to "legitimize" rising families of strong race and talent. The first (and truly revolutionary) outburst of forgery occurs in the epoch of Appius Claudius the Censor, when the curule ædile C. Flavius, the son of a slave, put the list in order — that was the time when even royal cognomina were discovered amongst plebeian families. The second was in the days of the battle of Pydna (168), when the dominance of the nobility began to assume Cæsarian forms (E. Kornemann, *Der Priesterkodex in der Regia*, 1912, pp. 56, et seq.). Of the 200 Consulates between 232 and 133, 159 fell to 26 families, and thereafter — blood-quality being exhausted, but the form as such being all the more studiously preserved in consequence — the rise of *novi homines* like Cato and Cicero became a rare phenomenon.

man "people," which in itself, like any other, was raw material without form, but to this class which brought Rome into condition and kept her so, willy-nilly — with the result that this particular stream of being, which in 350 was still without importance save to middle Italy, gradually drew into its bed the entire history of the Classical, and made the last great period of that history a *Roman* period.

It was the very perfection of political *flair* that was displayed by this small circle (which possessed no sort of public rights) in managing the democratic forms created by the Revolution — forms that here as elsewhere derive all value from the use that is made of them. The only factor in them that if mishandled would have been dangerous in an instant — namely, the inter-penetration of two mutually exclusive powers — was handled so superbly *and so quietly* that it was always the higher experience that gave the note, while the people remained throughout convinced that decisions were made by, and in the sense desired by, itself. *To be popular, and yet historically successful in the highest degree* — here is the secret of this policy, and for that matter the only possibility of policy existing at all in such times, an art in which the Roman régime has remained unequalled to this day.

Nevertheless, on the other side of the picture, the result of the Revolution was the *emancipation of Money*. Thenceforward money was master in the Comitia Centuriata. That which called itself "*populus*" there became more and more a tool in the hands of big money, and it required all the tactical superiority of the ruling circles to maintain a counterpoise in the Plebs, and to keep effective a representation of the yeomanry, under the leadership of the noble families, in the thirty-one country tribes from which the great city mass continued to be excluded. Hence the drastic energy with which the arrangements made by Appius Claudius were revoked. The natural alliance between high finance and the mass, though we see it actually at work later (under the Gracchi and Marius) for the destruction of the tradition of the blood,[1] was at any rate made impossible for many generations. Bourgeoisie and yeomanry, money and landowning, maintained a reciprocal equilibrium of separate organisms, and were held together and made efficient by the State-idea (of which the nobility was the incarnation) until this inward form fell to pieces, and the two tendencies broke apart in enmity. The First Punic War was a traders' war and directed against the agrarian interest, and, therefore, the consul Appius Claudius (a descendant of the great Censor) laid the decision of the matter in 284 before the Comitia Centuriata. The conquest of the Po plain, on the other hand, was in the interests of the peasantry and it was, therefore, in the Comita Tributa that it was carried by the Tribune C. Flaminius — the first genuinely Cæsarian type in Roman history, builder of the Via Flaminia and the Circus Flaminius. But when in pursuance of his policy he (as Censor in 220) forbade the Senators

---

[1] Another instance, among many, is its rôle in preparing the German crash of 1918.

to engage in trade, and also at the same time made the old noble centuries accessible to plebeians, he was practically benefiting only the new financial nobility of the First Punic War period, and thus (entirely in spite of himself) he became the creator of *high finance organized as an Estate* — that is, that of the Equites, who a century later put an end to the great age of the nobility. Henceforth, when Hannibal (before whom Flaminius had fallen on the field of battle) had been disposed of, money steadily became, even for the government as such, the *"ultima ratio"* in the accomplishment of its policy — the last true State-policy that the Classical world was to know.

When the Scipios and their circle had ceased to be the governing influence, nothing remained but the private policies of individuals, who followed their own interests without scruple, and looked upon the *"orbis terrarum"* as passive booty. The historian Polybius (who belonged to that circle) regarded Flaminius as a mere demagogue and traced to him all the misfortunes of the Gracchan period. He was wholly in error as to Flaminius's intentions, but he was right as to his effect. Flaminius — like the elder Cato, who with the blind zeal of the agrarian overthrew the great Scipio on account of his world-policy — achieved the reverse of what he intended. Money stepped into the place of blood-leadership, and money took less than three generations to exterminate the yeomanry.

If it was an improbable piece of good luck in the destinies of the Classical peoples that Rome was the only city-state to survive the Revolution with an unimpaired constitution, it was, on the contrary, almost a miracle that in our West — with its genealogical forms deep-rooted in the idea of duration — violent revolution broke out at all, even in one place — namely, Paris. It was not the strength, but the weakness of French Absolutism which brought the English ideas, in combination with the power of money, to the point of an explosion which gave living form to the catchwords of the "Enlightenment," which bound together virtue and terror, freedom and despotism, and which echoed still even in the minor catastrophes of 1830 and 1848 and the more recent Socialistic longing for catastrophe.[1] In England itself, when the aristoc-

---

[1] And even in France, where the judicial class in the parlements openly scorned the Government, and with impunity tore down royal proclamations from the walls and put up their own *arrêts* instead (R. Holtzmann, *Französ. Verfassungsgesch.* (*1910*), *p. 353*); where "orders were given, but not obeyed, laws enacted, but not executed" (A. Wahl, *Vorgesch. d. franz. Revolution*, I, 29 and passim); where high finance could overthrow Turgot and anyone else whose reform-schemes disquieted it; where the whole educated world, headed by princes and nobles, prelates and generals, was Anglomaniac and applauded opposition in any shape or form — even there nothing would have happened but for the sudden concurrence of a set of incidents — the fashion which set in amongst French officers of aiding the American republicans in their struggle with the English King; the diplomatic reverse in Holland (27 Oct. 1787) in the middle of the reforming activity of the Government; and the perpetual change of ministers under pressure from irresponsible quarters. In the British Empire, the falling-away of the Colonies was the result of attempts of high-Tory circles (in collusion with George III, but in reality of course in their own interests) to strengthen the Royal power. This party possessed in the Colonies a strong contingent of royalists, notably in the

racy ruled more absolutely than ever in France, there was certainly a small circle round Fox and Sheridan which was enthusiastic for the ideas of the Revolution — all of which were of English provenance — and men talked of universal suffrage and Parliamentary reform.[1] But that was quite enough to induce both parties, under the leadership of a Whig (the younger Pitt), to take the sharpest measures to defeat any and every attempt to interfere in the slightest degree with the aristocratic régime for the benefit of the bourgeoisie. The English nobility let loose the twenty-year war against France, and mobilized all the monarchs of Europe to bring about in the end, not the fall of Napoleon, but the fall of the Revolution — the Revolution that had had the naïve daring to introduce the opinions of private English thinkers into practical politics, and so to give a position to the Tiers État of which the consequences were all the better foreseen in the English lobbies for having been overlooked in the Paris salons.[2]

What was called "Opposition" in England was — the attitude of one aristocratic party while the other was running the Government. It did not mean there, as it meant all over the Continent, professional criticism of the work which it was someone else's profession to do, but the practical endeavour to force the activity of Government into a form in which the opposition was ready and fit at any moment to take it over. But this Opposition was at once — and in complete ignorance of its social presuppositions — taken as a model for that which the educated in France and elsewhere aimed at creating, namely, a class-domination of the Tiers État under the eyes of a dynasty, no very clear idea being formed as to the latter's future. The English dispositions were, from Montesquieu onwards, lauded with enthusiastic misunderstanding — although these Continental countries, not being islands, lacked the first condition precedent for an "English" evolution. Only in one point was England really a model. When the bourgeoisie had got so far as to turn the absolute state back again into an Estate-state, they found over there a picture which in fact had never been other than it was. True, it was the aristocracy alone who ruled in it — but at least it was not the Crown.

The result of the turn, and the basic form of the Continental States at the

---

South: these elements, fighting on the British side, decided the battle of Camden, and after the final victory of the rebels mostly emigrated to Canada, which had remained loyal.

[1] In 1793 there were 306 members of the House of Commons who were elected by 160 persons in all. Old Sarum, the constituency of the elder Pitt, consisted of one tenement, returning two members.

[2] Afterwards — from 1832 — the English nobility itself, through a series of prudent measures, drew the bourgeoisie into *co-operation* with it, but under its continued guidance and, above all, in the framework of tradition, within which consequently the young talent grew up. Democracy thus actualized itself here so that the Government remained strictly "in form" — the old aristocratic form — while the individual was free to practise politics according to his bent. This transition, in a peasantless society dominated by business interests, was the most remarkable achievement of inner politics in the nineteenth century.

beginning of the Civilization, is "Constitutional Monarchy," the extremest possibility of which appears as what we call nowadays a Republic. It is necessary to get clear, once and for all, of the mumblings of the doctrinaires who think in timeless and therefore unreal concepts and for whom "Republic" is a form-in-itself. The republican ideal of the nineteenth century has no more resemblance to the Classical *res publica*, or even to Venice or the original Swiss cantons, than the English constitution to a "constitution" in the Continental sense. That which *we* call republic is a *negation*, which of inward necessity postulates that the thing denied is an ever-present possibility. It is non-monarchy in forms borrowed from the monarchy. The genealogical feeling is immensely strong in Western mankind; it strains its conscience so far as to pretend that Dynasty determines its political conduct even when Dynasty no longer exists at all. The historical is embodied therein, and unhistorically we cannot live. It makes a great difference whether, as in the case of the Classical world, the dynastic principle conveys absolutely nothing to the inner feelings of a man, or, as in the case of the West, it is real enough to need six generations of educated people to fight it down in themselves. Feeling is the secret enemy of all constitutions that are plans and not growths; they are in last analysis nothing but defensive measures born of fear and mistrust. The urban conception of freedom — freedom *from* something — narrows itself to a merely anti-dynastic significance, and republican enthusiasm lives only on this feeling.

Such a negation inevitably involves a preponderance of theory. While Dynasty and its close congener Diplomacy conserve the old tradition and pulse, Constitutions contain an overweight of systems, bookishness, and framed concepts — such as is entirely unthinkable in England, where nothing negative and defensive adheres to the form of government. It is not for nothing that the Faustian is *par excellence* the reading and writing Culture. The printed book is an emblem of temporal, the Press of spatial, infinity. In contrast with the immense power and tyranny of these symbols, even the Chinese Civilization seems almost empty of writing. In Constitutions, literature is put into the field against knowledge of men and things, language against race, abstract right against successful tradition — regardless of whether a nation involved in the tide of events is still capable of work and "maintaining its form." Mirabeau was quite alone and unsuccessful in combating the Assembly, which "confused politics with fiction." Not only the three doctrinaire constitutions of the age — the French of 1791, the German of 1848 and 1919 — but practically all such attempts shut their eyes to the great Destiny in the fact-world and imagine that that is the same as defeating it. In lieu of unforeseen happenings, the incidents of strong personality and imperious circumstances, it is Causality that is to rule — timeless, just, unvarying, rational cohesion of cause and effect. It is symptomatic that no written constitution knows of money as a political force. It is pure theory that they contain, one and all.

This rift in the essence of constitutional monarchy is irremediable. Here actual and conceptual, work and critique, are frontally opposed, and it is their mutual attrition that constitutes what the average educated man calls internal politics.   Apart from the cases of Prussia-Germany and Austria — where constitutions did come into existence at first,[1] but in the presence of the older political traditions were never very influential — it was only in England that the practice of government kept itself homogeneous. Here, race held its own against principle. Men had more than an inkling that real politics, politics aiming at historical success, is a matter of training and not of shaping. This was no aristocratic prejudice, but a cosmic fact that emerges much more distinctly in the experience of any English racehorse-trainer than in all the philosophical systems in the world. Shaping can refine training, but not replace it. And thus the higher society of England, Eton and Balliol, became training-trounds where politicians were worked up with a consistent sureness the like of which is only to be found in the training of the Prussian officer-corps — trained, that is, as connoisseurs and masters of the underlying pulse of things (not excluding the hidden course of opinions and ideas). Thus prepared, they were able, in the great flood of bourgeois-revolutionary principles that swept over the years after 1832, to preserve and control the being-stream which they directed. They possessed "training," the suppleness and collectedness of the rider who, with a good horse under him, feels victory coming nearer and nearer. They allowed the great principles to move the mass because they knew well that it is money that is the "wherewithal" by which motion is imparted to these great principles, and they substituted, for the brutal methods of the eighteenth century, methods more refined and not less effective — one of the simpler of these being to threaten their opponents with the cost of a new election. The doctrinaire constitutions of the Continent saw only the one side of the fact democracy. Here, where there was no constitution, but men were in "condition," it was seen as a whole.

A vague feeling of all this was never quite lost on the Continent. For the absolute State of the Baroque there had been a perfectly clear form, but for "constitutional monarchy" there were only unsteady compromises, and Conservative and Liberal parties were distinguished — not, as in England after Canning, by the possession of different but well-tested modes of government, applied turn-and-turn-about to the actual work of governing — but according to the direction in which they respectively desired to alter the constitution — namely, towards tradition or towards theory. Should the Parliament serve the Dynasty, or vice versa? — that was the bone of contention, and in disputing over it it was forgotten that *foreign* policy was the final aim. The "Spanish" and the misnamed "English" sides of a constitution would not and could not grow together, and thus it befell that during the nineteenth century the diplo-

---

[1] Early, that is, in the post-revolutionary era here considered. — *Tr.*

matic service outwards and the Parliamentary activity inwards developed in two divergent directions. Each became in fundamental feeling alien to, and contemptuous of, the other. Life fretted itself to soreness in a form that it had not developed out of itself. After Thermidor, France succumbed to the rule of the Bourse, mitigated from time to time by the setting up of a military dictature (1800, 1851, 1871, 1918). Bismarck's creation was in fundamentals of a dynastic nature, with a parliamentary component of decidedly subordinate importance, and in it the inner friction was so strong as to monopolize the available political energy, and finally, after 1916, to exhaust the organism itself. The Army had its own history, with a great tradition going back to Frederick William I,[1] and so also had the administration. In them was the source of Socialism as one kind of true political "training," diametrically opposed to the English[2] but, like it, a full expression of strong race-quality. The officer and the official were trained high. But the necessity of breeding up a corresponding political type was not recognized. Higher policy was handled "administratively" and minor policy was hopeless squabbling. And so army and administration finally became aims in themselves, after Bismarck's disappearance had removed the one man who even without a supply of real politicians to back him (this tradition alone could have produced) was big enough to treat both as tools of policy. When the issue of the World War removed the upper layers, nothing remained but parties educated for opposition only, and these brought the activity of Government down to a level hitherto unknown in any Civilization.

But to-day Parliamentarism is in full decay. It was a *continuation of the Bourgeois Revolution by other means*, the revolution of the Third Estate of 1789 brought into legal form and joined with its opponent the Dynasty as one governmental unit. Every modern election, in fact, is a civil war carried on by ballot-box and every sort of spoken and written stimulus, and every great party-leader is a sort of Napoleon. In this form, meant to remain infinitely valid, which is peculiar to the Western Culture and would be nonsensical and impossible in any other, we discern once more our characteristic tendency to infinity, historical foresight[3] and forethought, and *will to order the distant future*, in this case according to bourgeois standards of the present.

All the same, Parliamentarism is not a summit as the absolute Polis and the Baroque State were summits, but a brief transition — namely, between the

---

[1] The reassertion of this tradition after the emergency-army of the Wars of Liberation (1812–15) had dispersed into the body of the community is a remarkable story, in which military and political standpoints cannot be separated. See Vidal de la Blache, *La Régéneration de l'Armée Prusse* (1910), Ch. vi. — Tr.

[2] See *Preussentum und Sozialismus*, pp. 40, et seq.

[3] The genesis of the Roman Tribunate was a blind incident, the happy consequences of which no one really foresaw. Western Constitutions, on the contrary, have been thoroughly thought out and their effects precisely calculated — whether the calculation proved to be correct or incorrect, the care is undeniable.

Late-Culture period with its mature forms and the age of great individuals in a formless world. It contains, like the houses and furniture of the first half of the nineteenth century, a residue of good Baroque. The parliamentary habit is English Rococo — but, no longer un-self-conscious and in the blood, but superficial-initiative and at the mercy of goodwill. Only in the brief periods of first enthusiasms has it an appearance of depth and duration, and then only because in the flush of victory respect for one's newly-won status makes it incumbent to adopt the high manners of the defeated class. To preserve the form, even when it contradicts the advantage, is the convention which makes parliamentarism *possible*. But when this convention comes to be fully observed, *the very fact that it is so means that the essence of parliamentarism has already been evaporated*. The Non-Estate falls apart again into its natural interest-groups, and the passion of stubborn and victorious defence is over. And as soon as the form ceases to possess the attractiveness of a young ideal that will summon men to the barricades, unparliamentary methods of attaining an object without (and even in spite of) the ballot-box will make their appearance — such as money, economic pressure, and, above all, the strike. Neither the megalopolitan masses nor the strong individuals have any real respect for this form without depth or past, and when the discovery is made that it is *only* a form, it has already become a mark and shadow. With the beginning of the twentieth century Parliamentarism (even English) is tending rapidly towards taking up itself the rôle that it once assigned to the kingship. It is becoming an impressive spectacle for the multitude of the Orthodox, while the centre of gravity of big policy, already *de jure* transferred from the Crown to the people's representatives, is passing *de facto* from the latter to unofficial groups and the will of unofficial personages. The World War almost completed this development. There is no way back to the old parliamentarism from the domination of Lloyd George and the Napoleonism of the French militarists. And for America, hitherto lying apart and self-contained, rather a region than a State, the parallelism of President and Congress which she derived from a theory of Montesquieu has, with her entry into world politics, become untenable, and must in times of real danger make way for formless powers such as those with which Mexico and South America have long been familiar.

VIII

With this enters the age of gigantic conflicts, in which we find ourselves to-day. It is the *transition from Napoleonism to Cæsarism*, a general phase of evolution, which occupies at least two centuries and can be shown to exist in all the Cultures. The Chinese call it Shan-Kwo, the "period of the Contending States" (480–230, corresponding to the Classical 300–50.[1] At the beginning

---

[1] From the few European works that concern themselves with questions of ancient Chinese history, it emerges that Chinese literature contains a very great amount of material bearing on this

are reckoned seven great powers, which, first planlessly, but later with clearer and clearer purpose, tend to the inevitable final result of this close succession of vast wars and revolutions. A century later there are still five. In 441 the ruler of the Chóu dynasty became a state-pensioner of the "Eastern Duke," and the remains of territory that he possessed ceased accordingly to figure in later history. Simultaneously began in the unphilosophical north-west [1] the swift rise of the "Roman" state of Tsin, which extended its influence westward and southward over Tibet and Yunnan and enclosed the other states in a great arc. The focus of the opposition was in the kingdom of Tsu in the Taoist south,[2] whence the Chinese Civilization pressed slowly outwards into the still little-known lands south of the great river. Here we have in fact the opposition of Rome and the Hellenistic — on the one side, hard, clear will-to-power; on the other, the tendency to dreaming and world-improvement. In 368–320 (corresponding to the Second Punic War) the contest intensified itself into an uninterrupted struggle of the whole Chinese world, fought with mass armies, for which the population was strained to the extreme limit. "The allies, whose lands were ten times as great as those of Tsin, in vain rolled up a million men — Tsin had ever reserves in hand still. From first to last a million men fell," writes Sze-ma-tsien. Su-tsin, who began by being Chancellor of Tsin, but later became a supporter of the League of Nations (*hoh-tsung*) idea and went over to the Opposition, worked up two great coalitions (333 and 321), which, however, collapsed from inward disunity at the first battles. His great adversary, the Chancellor Chang-I, resolutely Imperialist, was in 311 on the point of bringing the Chinese world to voluntary subjection when a change of occupancy of the throne caused his combination to miscarry. In 294 began the campaigns of Pe-Ki.[3] It was in the prestige of his victories that the King of Tsin took the mystic Emperor-title of the legendary age,[4] which openly expressed the claim to world-rule, and was at once imitated by the ruler of Tsi in the east.[5] With this began the second maximum phase of the decisive struggles. The number

period, which corresponds in innumerable parallels to our own present time. But there is a total lack of any political treatment of it that can be taken seriously. References: Hübotter, *Aus den Plänen der Kämpfenden Reiche* (1912); Piton, "The Six Great Chancellors of Tsin," *China Review*, XIII, 202, 255, 365, XIV, 3; Ed. Chavannes, *Mém. hist. de Se-ma-tsien* (1895 and following); Pfizmair, *Sitz. Wien Akad.*, XLIII (1863) ("Tsin"), XLIV ("Tsu"); A. Tschepe, *Histoire du royaume de Ou* (1896), and *de Tchou* (1903).

[1] Corresponding more or less to the province of Shen-si.

[2] On the middle Yang-tse-kiang.

[3] Biography 13 of Sze-ma-tsien. So far as the translated evidences allow us to judge, the preparation and dispositions of these campaigns, the boldness of the operations by which he drove the enemy on to ground where he could beat him, and the novel tactical execution of the separate battles, stamp Pe-Ki as one of the greatest military geniuses of all time, a figure worthy indeed of adequate treatment by a military expert. It is from this period that we have the authoritative work of Sun-tse on War: Giles, *Sun-Tse on the Art of War* (1910). [Or Capt. F. R. Calthrop, *The Book of War — Sun and Wu* (1908). — *Tr.*]

[4] See pp. 312, et seq.

[5] Now approximately Shan-tung and Pe-chi-li.

of independent states grew steadily less. In 255 even the home state of Confucius, Lu, vanished, and in 249 the Chóu dynasty came to an end. In 246 the mighty Wang-Cheng became, at the age of thirteen, Emperor of Tsin, and in 241, with the aid of his Chancellor Lui-Shi (the Chinese Mæcenas [1]), he fought out to victory the last bout that the last opponent, the Empire of Tsu, ventured to challenge. In 221, sole ruler in actual fact, he assumed the title Shi (Augustus). This is the beginning of the Imperial age in China.

No era confronts its mankind so distinctly with the alternative of *great form* or *great individual powers* as this "Period of the Contending States." In the degree in which the nations cease to be politically in "condition," in that degree possibilities open up for the energetic private person who means to be politically creative, who will have power at any price, and who as a phenomenon of force becomes the Destiny of an entire people or Culture. Events have become unpredictable on the basis of form. Instead of the given tradition that can dispense with genius (because it is itself cosmic force at highest capacity), we have now the accident of great fact-men. The accident of their rise brings a weak people (for example, the Macedonians), to the peak of events overnight, and the accident of their death (for example, Cæsar's) can immediately plunge a world from personally secured order into chaos.

This indeed had been manifested earlier in critical times of transition. The epoch of the Fronde, the Ming-shu, the First Tyrannis, when men were not in form, but fought about form, has always thrown up a number of great figures who grew too big for definition and limitation in terms of office. The change from Culture to Civilization, with its typical Napoleonism, does so too. But with this, which is the preface to unredeemed historical formlessness, dawns the real day of the great individual. For us this period attained almost to its climax in the World War; in the Classical World it began with Hannibal, who challenged Rome in the name of Hellenism (to which inwardly he belonged), but went under because the Hellenistic East, in true Classical fashion, apprehended the meaning of the hour too late, or not at all. With his downfall began that proud sequence that runs from the Scipios through Æmilius Paullus, Flamininus, the Catos, the Gracchi, Marius, and Sulla to Pompey, Cæsar, and Augustus. In China, correspondingly, during the period of the "Contending States," a like chain of statesmen and generals centred on Tsin as the Classical figures centred on Rome. In accordance with the complete want of understanding of the political side of Chinese history that prevails, these men are usually described as Sophists.[2] They were so, but only in the same sense as leading

---

[1] Piton "Lu-puh-Weih," *China Rev.* XIII. pp. 365 et seq.

[2] Even if the Chinese authors themselves misunderstood the expression in the same, or anything like the same, way as their Western translators, the fact would only prove that the appreciation of political problems vanished as rapidly in the Chinese Imperial Age as in fact it did in the Roman — because they were no longer personally and livingly experienced. The much-admired Sze-ma-tsien is after all a compiler of the same rank as Plutarch (with whom he corresponds in

Romans of the same period were Stoics — that is, as having been educated in the philosophy and rhetoric of the Greek East. All were finished orators and all from time to time wrote on philosophy, Cæsar and Brutus no less than Cato and Cicero, but they did so not as professional philosophers, but because *otium cum dignitate* was the habit of cultivated gentlemen. In business hours they were masters of fact, whether on battle-field or in high politics, and precisely the same is true of the Chancellors Chang-I and Su-tsin; [1] the dreaded diplomatist Fan-Sui who overthrew Pe-Ki, the general; Wei-Yang the legislator of Tsin; Lui-Shi, the first Emperor's Mæcenas, and others.

The Culture had bound up all its forces in strict form. Now they were released, and "Nature" — that is, the cosmic — broke forth immediate. The change from the absolute State to the battling Society of nations that marks the beginning of every Civilization may mean for idealists and ideologues what they like — in the world of facts it means the transition from government in the style and pulse of a strict tradition to the *sic volo, sic jubeo* of the unbridled personal régime. The maximum of symbolic and *super*-personal form coincides with that of the Late period of the Culture — in China about 600, in the Classical about 450, for ourselves about 1700. The minimum in the Classical lies in the time of Sulla and Pompey, and for us will be reached (and possibly passed) in the next hundred years. Great interstate and internal conflicts, revolutions of a fearful kind, interpenetrate increasingly, but the questions at issue in all of them without exception are (consciously and frankly or not) questions of unofficial, and eventually purely personal, power. It is historically of no importance what they themselves aimed at theoretically, and we need not know the catchwords under which the Chinese and Arabian revolutions of this stage broke out, nor even whether there were such catchwords. None of the innumerable revolutions of this era — which more and more become blind outbreaks of uprooted megalopolitan masses — has ever attained, or ever had the possibility of attaining, an aim. What stands is only the *historical fact* of an accelerated demolition of ancient forms that leaves the path clear for Cæsarism.

But the same is true also of the wars, in which the armies and their tactical

---

date also). The high point of historical comprehension, *which presumes an equivalent experience in life*, must for China have lain in the period of the Contending States, as it lies for us in the nineteenth century and after.

[1] Both, like most of the leading statesmen of the time, were pupils of Kwei-ku-tse, whose knowledge of men, deep sense of the historically possible, and command of the diplomatic technique of the age (the "Art of the vertical and the horizontal") must have made him one of the most influential personalities of the period. Another figure of the same sort of weight after him was the thinker and war-theorist above alluded to, Sun-tse, who amongst others was the tutor of the Chancellor Lui-Si.

[Sun-Tse's book of war, as presented in Calthrop's translation, is comparable to nothing in Western military literature short of Clausewitz's *Vom Kriege*. Clausewitz was a contemporary and product of the Napoleonic epoch, and the glow of Romanticism has not yet passed from him; Sun, on the other hand, came "later," and his atmosphere is the shrewd factual atmosphere of pre-Cæsarism. — *Tr.*]

methods become more and more the creation, not of the epoch, but of un-controlled individual captains, who in many cases discovered their genius very late and by accident. While in 300 there were *Roman* armies, in 100 there were the armies of Marius and Sulla and Cæsar; and Octavian's army, which was composed of Cæsar's veterans, led its general much more than it was led by him. But with this the methods of war, its means, and its aims assumed raw-natural and ferocious forms,[1] very different from those prevailing before. Their duels were not eighteenth-century Trianon duels, encounters in knightly forms with fixed rules to determine when a man might declare himself exhausted, what maximum of force might be employed, and what conditions the chivalry permitted a victor to impose. They were ring-battles of infuriated men with fists and teeth, fought to the bodily collapse of one and exploited without reserve or restraint by the victor. The first great example of this "return to Nature" is afforded by the French Revolutionary and Napoleonic armies, which, instead of artificial manœuvres with small bodies, practised the mass-onset without regard to losses and thereby shattered to atoms the refined strategy of the Rococo. To bring the whole muscular force of a nation on to the battle-fields by the universal-service system was an idea utterly alien to the age of Frederick the Great.[2]

Similarly, in every Culture, the technique of war hesitatingly followed the advance of craftsmanship, until at the beginning of the Civilization it suddenly takes the lead, presses all mechanical possibilities of the time relentlessly into its service, and under pressure of military necessity even opens up new domains hitherto unexploited — but at the same time renders largely ineffectual the personal heroism of the thoroughbred, the ethos of the noble, and the subtle intellect of the Late Culture. In the Classical world, where the Polis made mass-armies essentially impossible — for relatively to the general smallness of Classical forms, tactical included, the numbers of Cannæ, Philippi, and Actium were enormous and exceptional — the second Tyrannis (Dionysius of Syracuse leading) introduced mechanical technique into warfare, and on a large scale.[3]

---

[1] A story is told of Sun, that when for a jest (or a demonstration of tactics) opposed forces were made up from the court ladies, one of the commanders, the sovereign's favourite wife, was executed by Sun's command for disobeying an order. — *Tr.*

[2] Frederick's "conscripts" (*Landeskinder*) were a long-service element, small in proportion to the population, and of serf status. Only the relative poverty of Prussia compelled this much of departure from the then normal procedure of recruiting volunteers, to which the Prussian army reverted as soon as its treasury could afford to do so. Maurice de Saxe is the one outstanding soldier of the period who advocated universal citizen service. But the famous "*Rêveries*" were written ("in thirteen sleepless nights") in 1732, before he had held high command. The military works of Leibniz touch upon the subject, but he was a practical man as well as a philosopher, and his detailed proposals are in the spirit of the time. On the contrary, the pure philosopher Spinoza definitely advocated universal service. — *Tr.*

[3] Large, that is, relatively to the general development of Classical technics in other fields, which was of the slightest — not in any way outstanding if judged by, say, Assyrian or Egyptian standards.

Then for the first time it became possible to carry out sieges like those of Rhodes (305), Syracuse (213), Carthage (146), and Alesia (52), in which also the increasing importance of rapidity, even for Classical strategy, became evident. It was in line with this tendency that the Roman legion, the characteristic structure of which developed only in the Hellenistic age, worked like a machine as compared with the Athenian and Spartan militias of the fifth century. In China, correspondingly, iron was worked up for cutting and thrusting weapons from 474, light cavalry of the Mongolian model displaced the heavy war-chariot, and fortress warfare suddenly acquired outstanding importance.[1] The fundamental craving of Civilized mankind for speed, mobility, and mass-effects finally combined, in the world of Europe and America, with the Faustian will to domination over Nature and produced dynamic methods of war that even to Frederick the Great would have seemed like lunacy, but to us of to-day, in close proximity to our technics of transportation and industry, are perfectly natural. Napoleon horsed his artillery and thereby made it highly mobile (just as he broke up the mass army of the Revolution into a system of self-contained and easily moved corps), and already at Wagram and Borodino it had augmented its purely physical effectiveness to the point of what we should call rapid-fire and drum fire.[2] The second stage is — most significantly — marked by the American Civil War of 1861-5 — which even in the numbers of troops it involved far surpassed the order of magnitude of the Napoleonic Wars [3] and in which for the first time the railway was used for large troop-movements, the telegraph-network for messages, and a steam fleet, keeping the sea for months on end, for blockade, and in which armoured ships, the torpedo, rifled weapons, and monster artillery of extraordinary range were discovered.[4, 5] The third stage is that of the World War, preluded by the Russo-Japanese conflict; [6] here submarine and aircraft were set to work, speed of invention became

[1] The book of the Socialist Moh-ti, of this period, treats of universal love of mankind in its first part, of fortress artillery in its second — a singular example of contraposition of truths and facts. Forke in *Ostasiat. Ztschr.*, VIII (Hirth number).

[2] A whole literature exists for Napoleon's "case-shot attack," which was closely studied in the years before 1914 with the definite aim of finding a key to victories that the mechanical developments in the defensive rifle had made doubtful. — *Tr.*

[3] On the side of the North, more than 1½ million men out of barely 20 million inhabitants.
[The total of men of military age in the North was 4,600,000, of whom 2,780,000 actually enlisted. The figure of 1,700,000 is a reduction to a three-year level — i.e., men who served throughout the war counting as 1⅓ each and men who served for one year as ⅓ each. The Southern states put into the field, on the same three-years' basis, 900,000 out of 1,065,000 men of military age. (Dodge, *Birds Eye View of our Civil War*.) — *Tr.*]

[4] To which should be added, though on a small scale, the first serious attempts at submarines, machine-guns, and magazine rifles. — *Tr.*

[5] Amongst the wholly new problems was that of rapidly restoring railways and bridges; the bridge at Chattanooga, for the heaviest military trains, 240 metres long and 30 metres high, was built in 4½ days.

[6] Modern Japan belongs to the Western Civilization no less than "modern" Carthage of the third century to the Classical.

a new arm in itself, and the extent (though most certainly not the intensity) of the means used attained a maximum. But to this expenditure of force there corresponds everywhere the ruthlessness of the decisions. At the very outset of the Chinese Shan-Kwo period we find the utter annihilation of the State of Wu — an act which in the preceding Chun-tsiu period chivalry would have made impossible. Even in the peace of Campo Formio Napoleon outraged the *convenances* of the eighteenth century, and after Austerlitz he introduced the practice of exploiting military success without regard to any but material restrictions. The last step still possible is being taken in the peace treaty of the Versailles type, which deliberately avoids finality and settlement, and keeps open the possibility of setting up new conditions at every change in the situation. The same evolution is seen in the chain of the three Punic Wars. The idea of wiping out one of the leading great powers of the world — which eventually became familiar to everyone through Cato's deliberately dry insistence on his *"Ceterum censeo Carthaginem esse delendam"* — never crossed the mind of the victor of Zama and, for all the wild war-ethics of the Classical Poleis, it would have seemed to Lysander, as he stood victorious in Athens, an impiety towards every god.

The Period of the Contending States begins for the Classical world with the battle of Ipsus (301) which established the trinity of Eastern great powers, and the Roman victory over the Etruscans and Samnites at Sentinum (295), which created a mid-Italian great power by the side of Carthage. Then, however, the characteristic Classical preference for things near and in the present resulted in eyes' being shut while Rome won, first the Italian south in the Pyrrhic adventure, then the sea in the first Punic War, and then the Celtic north through C. Flaminius. The significance even of Hannibal (probably the only man of his time who clearly saw the trend of events) was ignored by all, the Romans themselves not excepted. It was at *Zama*, and not merely later at Magnesia and Pydna, that the Hellenistic Eastern powers were defeated. All in vain the great Scipio, truly anxious in the presence of the destiny to which a Polis overloaded with the tasks of a world-dominion was marching, sought thereafter to avoid all conquest. In vain his entourage forced through the Macedonian War, against the will of every party, merely in order that the East could thenceforth be ignored as harmless. Imperialism is so necessary a product of any Civilization that when a people refuses to assume the rôle of master, it is seized and pushed into it. The Roman Empire was *not* conquered — the *"orbis terrarum"* condensed itself into that form and forced the Romans to give it their name. It is all very Classical. While the Chinese states defended even the mere remnants of their independence with the last bitterness, Rome after 146 only took upon herself to transform the Eastern land-masses into provinces because there was no other resource against anarchy left. And even this much resulted in the inward form of Rome — the last which had remained upright — melting in the Gracchan disorders. And (what is unparalleled elsewhere) it was not between states that the final rounds of the battle for Imperium were fought, but between the parties of a city — the form of the Polis allowed of no other outcome. Of old it had been Sparta *versus* Athens, now it was Optimate *versus* Popular Party. In the Gracchan revolution, which was already (134) heralded by a first Servile War, the younger Scipio was secretly murdered and C. Gracchus openly slain — the first who as Princeps and the first who as Tribune were political centres in themselves amidst a world become formless. When, in 104, the urban masses of Rome for the first time lawlessly and tumultuously invested a private person, Marius, with Imperium, the deeper importance of the drama then enacted is comparable with that of the assumption of the mythic Emperor-title by the ruler of Tsin in 288. The inevitable product of the age, Cæsarism, suddenly outlines itself on the horizon.

The heir of the Tribune was Marius, who like him linked mob and high finance and in 87 murdered off the old aristocracy in masses. The heir of the Princeps was Sulla, who in 82 annihilated the class of the great merchants by his proscriptions. Thereafter the final decisions press on rapidly, as in China after the emergence of Wang Cheng. Pompey the Princeps and Cæsar the Tribune — tribune not in office, but in attitude — were still party-leaders, but nevertheless, already at Lucca, they were arranging with Crassus and each other for the first partition of the world amongst themselves. When the heirs of Cæsar fought his murderers at Philippi, both had ceased to be more than groups. By Actium the issue was between individuals, and Cæsarism will out, even in such a process as this.

In the corresponding evolution within the Arabian world it is, of course, the Magian Consensus that takes the place of the bodily Polis as the basic form in and through which the facts accomplish themselves; and this form, as we have seen, excluded any separation of political and religious tendencies to such an extent that even the urban bourgeois urge towards freedom (marking, here as elsewhere, the beginning of the Period of Contending States) presents itself in orthodox disguise, and so has hitherto almost escaped notice.[1] It appeared as a will to break loose from the Caliphate, which the Sassanids, and Diocletian following them, had created in the forms of the feudal state. From the times of Justinian and Chosroes Nushirvan this had had to meet the onset of Frondeurs — led by the heads of the Greek and Mazdaist Churches, the nobility, both Persian-Mazdaist (above all Irak) and Greek (particularly the Asiatic), and the high chivalry of Armenia, which was divided into two parts by the difference of religion. The absolutism almost attained in the seventh

---

[1] For the politico-social history of the Arabian World there is the same lack of deep and penetrating research as for the Chinese. Only the political evolution of the Western margin up to Diocletian, regarded hitherto as within the Classical pale, is an exception.

century was then suddenly destroyed by the attack of Islam. In its *political* beginnings Islam was strictly aristocratic; the handful of Arabian families [1] who everywhere kept the leading in their hands, very soon formed in the conquered territories a new higher nobility of strong breed and immense self-sufficingness which thrust the dynasty down to the same level as its English "contemporaries" thrust theirs. The Civil War between Othman and Ali (656–661) was the expression of a true Fronde, and its movements were all in the interests of two clans and their respective adherents. The Islamic Whigs and Tories of the eighth century, like the English of the eighteenth, *alone* practised high politics, and their coteries and family quarrels are more important to the history of the time than any events in the reigning house of the Ommaiyads (661–750).

But with the fall of the gay and enlightened dynasty that has resided in Damascus — that is, West-Aramæan and Monophysite Syria — the natural centre of gravity of the Arabian Culture reappeared; it was the East-Aramæan region. Once the basis of Sassanid and now of Abbassid power, but always — irrespective of whether its shaping was Persian or Arabian, or its religion Mazdaist, Nestorian, or Islamic — it expressed one and the same grand line of development and was the exemplar for Syria as for Byzantium alike. From Kufa the movement started which led to the downfall of the Ommaiyads and their *ancien régime*, and the character of this movement — of which the whole extent has never to this day been observed — was that *of a social revolution directed against the primary orders of society and the aristocratic tradition.*[2] It began among the Mavali, the small bourgeoisie in the East, and directed itself with bitter hostility against the Arabs, not *qua* champions of Islam but *qua* new nobility. The recently converted Mavali, almost all former Mazdaists, took Islam more seriously than the Arabs themselves, who represented also a class-ideal. Even in the army of Ali the wholly democratic and Puritan Qaraites had split off,[3] and in their ranks we see for the first time the combination of fanatic sectarianism and Jacobinism. Here and now there emerged not only the Shiite tendency, but also the first impulses towards the Communistic Karramiyya movement, which can be traced to Mazdak[4] and later produced the vast outbreaks under Babek. The Abbassids were anything but favourites with the insurgents of Kufa, and it was only owing to their great diplomatic skill that they were first allowed a footing as officers and then — almost like Napoleon — were able to enter into the heritage of a Revolution that had spread over the whole

---

[1] It was a few thousands only that accompanied the first conquerors and spread themselves from Tunis to Turkestan, and these everywhere constituted themselves a self-contained and close Estate in the entourage of the new potentates. An "Arabian *Völkerwanderung*" is out of the question.

[2] J. Wellhausen, *Das arabische Reich und sein Sturz* (1902), pp. 309, et seq.

[3] Compare the inner divisions of the English Parliamentary army in and after the Civil Wars. — *Tr.*

[4] See p. 261.

East. After their victory they built Baghdad — a resurrected Ctesiphon, symbol of the downfall of feudal Arabism — and this first world-city of the new Civilization became from 800 to 1050 the theatre of the events which led from Napoleonism to Cæsarism, *from the Caliphate to the Sultanate*, which, in Baghdad no less than in Byzantium, is the Magian type of power without form — here also the only kind of power still possible.

We have to recognize quite clearly, then, that in the Arabian world as elsewhere democracy was a class-ideal — the outlook of townsmen and the expression of their will to be free from the old linkages with land, be it a desert or plough-land. The "no" which answered the Caliph-tradition could disguise itself in very numerous forms, and neith r free-thought nor constitutionalism in our sense was necessary to it. *Magian mind and Magian money are "free" in quite a different way.* The Byzantine monkhood was liberal to the point of turbulence, not only against court and nobility, but also against the higher ecclesiastical powers, which had developed a hierarchy (corresponding to the Gothic) even before the Council of Nicæa. The consensus of the Faithful, the "people" in the most daring sense, was looked upon as willed by God ("Nature," Rousseau would have said), as *equal* and free from all powers of the blood. The celebrated scene in which the Abbot Theodore of Studion adjured the Emperor Leo V to obey (813) is a Storming of the Bastille in Magian forms.[1] Not long afterwards there began the revolt of the Paulicians, very pious and in social matters wholly radical,[2] who set up a state of their own beyond the Taurus, ravaged all Asia Minor, defeated one Imperial levy after another, and were not subjugated till 874. This corresponds in every way to the communistic-religious movement of the Karramiyya, which extended from the Tigris to Merv and whose leader Babek succumbed only after a twenty years' struggle (817–837);[3] and the other like outbreak of the Carmathians[4] in the West (890–904), whose liaisons reached from Arabia into all the Syrian cities and who propagated rebellion as far as the Persian coast. But, besides these, there were still other disguises of the political party-battle. When now we are told that the Byzantine army was Iconoclast and that the military party was consequently opposed by an Iconodule monkish party, we begin to see the passions of the century of the image-controversy (740–840) in quite a new light, and to understand that the end of the crisis (843) — the final defeat of the Iconoclasts and *simultaneously* of the free-church monkish policy — signifies a Restoration in the 1815 sense of the word.[5] And, lastly, this period is the time of the

---

[1] K. Dieterich, *Byz. Charakterköpfe*, p. 54: "Since thou wilt have an answer from us, receive it then! Paul has said some in the Church are ordained by God to be Apostles, some prophets, but he said nothing about Emperors — we will not follow though it were an angel that bade us; how much less if thou!"

[2] Cf. p. 316.   [3] Huart, *Gesch. d. Araber* (1914), I, p. 299.

[4] See *Ency. Brit.*, XI ed., art. "Carmathians." — *Tr.*

[5] Krumbacher, *Byz. Lit.-Gesch.*, p. 969.

fearful slave-rebellion in Irak — the kernel of the Abbassids' realm — which throws sudden light upon a series of other social upheavals. Ali, the Spartacus of Islam, founded in 869, south of Baghdad, a veritable Negro state out of the masses of runaways, built himself a capital, Muktara, and extended his power far in the directions of Arabia and Persia alike, where he gained the support of whole tribes. In 871 Basra, the first great port of the Islamic world, inhabited by nearly a million souls, was taken, deluged in massacre, and burnt. Not till 883 was this slave-state destroyed.

Thus slowly the Sassanid-Byzantine forms were hollowed out, and in the place of the ancient traditions of the higher officialdom and nobility there arose the inconsequent and wholly personal power of incidental geniuses — *the Sultanate.* For this is the specifically Arabian form, and it appears simultaneously in Byzantium and Baghdad and takes its steady course from the Napoleonic beginnings about 800 to the completed Cæsarism of the Seljuk Turks about 1050. This form is purely Magian, belongs only to that Culture, and is incomprehensible without the most fundamental axioms of its soul. The Caliphate, a synthesis of political (not to say cosmic) beat and style, was not abolished — for the Caliph as the representative of God recognized by the Consensus of the elect is sacred — but he was deprived of all powers that Cæsarism needed to possess, just as Pompey and Augustus in fact, and Sulla and Cæsar in fact and in name, abstracted these powers from the old constitutional forms of Rome. In the end there remained to the Caliph about as much power as the Senate and the Comitias had under Tiberius. The whole richness of being in high form — in law, costume, ethic — that had once been a symbol, was now mere trappings covering a formless and purely factual régime.

So we find by the side of Michael III (842–867) Bardas, and by Constantine VII (912–959) Romanos — the latter even formally Co-Emperor.[1] In 867 the ex-groom Basileios, a Napoleonic figure, overthrew Bardas and founded the sword-dynasty of the Armenians (to 1081), in which generals instead of Emperors mostly ruled — force-men like Romanos, Nicephorus, and Bardas Phocas. The greatest amongst them was John Tzimisces (969–976) in Armenian Kiur Zan. In Baghdad it was the *Turks* who played the Armenian rôle; in 842 the Caliph Vathek invested one of their leaders for the first time with the title of Sultan. From 862 the Turkish prætorians held the ruler in tutelage, and in 945 Achmed, the founder of the Sultan-dynasty of the Buyids, formally restricted the Abbassid Caliph to his religious dignities. And then there set in, in both the world-cities, an unrestrained competition between the mighty provincial families for possession of the supreme power. In the case of the Christian we find, indeed, Basileios II and others challenging the great latifundia lords, but this does not in the least mean social purposes in the legis-

---

[1] For all this see Krumbacher, op. cit., pp. 969–90; C. Neumann, *Die Weltstellung des Byz. Reiches vor den Kreuzzügen* (1894), pp. 21, et seq.

lator. It was an act of self-defence on the part of the momentary potentate against possible heirs, and closely analogous, therefore, to the proscriptions of Sulla and the Triumvirs. Half Asia Minor belonged to the Dukas, Phocas, and Skleros connexions; the Chancellor Basileios, who could keep an army on pay out of his own fabulous resources, has long ago been compared with Crassus.[1] But the imperial age proper begins only with the Seljuk Turks.[2] Their leader Togrulbek won Irak in 1043 and Armenia in 1049, and in 1055 forced the Caliph to grant him the *hereditary* Sultanate. His son Alp Arslan conquered Syria and, by the victory of Manzikert, gained eastern Asia Minor. The remnant of the Byzantine Empire thenceforward possessed no importance to, or influence on, the further destinies of the Turkish Islamic Imperium.

This is the phase, too, which in Egypt is concealed under the name of the "Hyksos." Between the XIIth and the XVIIIth Dynasties lay two centuries,[3] which began with the collapse of the *ancien régime* which had culminated with Sesostris III,[4] and ended with the beginning of the New Empire. The numbering of the dynasties itself suffices to disclose something catastrophic. In the lists of kings the names appear successive or parallel, usurpers of obscurest origin, generals, people with strange titles, often reigning only a few days. With the very first king of the XIIIth Dynasty the high-Nile records at Semne break off, and with his successor the archives at Kahun come to an end. It is the time out of which the Leiden Papyrus portrays the great social revolution.[5]

[1] Krumbacher, op. cit., 993.

[2] And perhaps not in Baghdad alone, for the gifted Maniakes, who was hailed by the army in Sicily as Emperor and fell in 1043 in his march on Byzantium, must have been a Turk.

[3] 1785–1580. See, for the following, Ed. Meyer, *Gesch. d. Alt.* §§ 298, et seq.; Weill, *La Fin du moyen empire égyptien* (1918). That Ed. Meyer's assignment is correct as compared with the 1670 years of Petrie has long been proved by the thickness of the strata in which objects have been found and the tempo of the style-evolution (Minoan included). Here it is demonstrated afresh by comparison with corresponding sections in the other Cultures.

[4] P. 387.

[5] Erman, "*Mahnworte eines äg ypt. Propheten*" (*Sitz. Preuss. Akad.*, 1919, pp. 804, et seq.): "The higher officials are displaced, the land robbed of its royalty by a few madmen, and the counsellors of the old state pay their court to upstarts; administration has ceased, documents are destroyed, all social differences abolished, the courts fallen into the hands of the mob. The noble classes go hungry and in rags, their children are battered on the wall, and their mummies torn from the grave. Mean fellows become rich and swagger in the palaces on the strength of the herds and ships that they have taken from their rightful owners. Former slave-girls become insolent and aliens lord it. Robbery and murder rule, cities are laid waste, public buildings burned down. The harvest diminishes, no one thinks now of cleanliness, births are few — and oh, that mankind might cease!" Here is the very picture of the megalopolitan and Late revolution, as it was enacted in the Hellenistic (p. 405) and in 1789 and 1871 in Paris. It is the world-city masses, will-less tools of the ambition of leaders who demolish every remnant of order, who desire to see in the outer world the same chaos as reigns within their own selves. Whether these cynical and hopeless attempts start from alien intruders like the Hyksos or the Turks, or from slaves as in the case of Spartacus and Ail; whether the division of property is shouted for as at Syracuse or has a book for banner like Marxism — all this is superficial. It is wholly immaterial what slogans scream to the wind while the gates and the skulls are being beaten in. Destruction is the true and only impulse, and Cæsarism the only issue. The world-city, the land-devouring demon, has set its rootless and futureless men in motion; and in destroying they die.

The fall of the Government and the victory of the mass is followed by outbreaks of the army and the rise of ambitious soldiers. In Egypt from about 1680 appears the name of the "Hyksos,"[1] a designation with which the historians of the New Empire, who no longer understood or wished to understand the meaning of the epoch, covered up the shame of these years. These Hyksos, there can be no doubt whatever, played the part that the Armenians played in Byzantium; and in the Classical world too, the destinies of the Cimbri and Teutones, would have gone the same way had they defeated Marius and his legions of city *canaille;* they would have filled the armies of the Triumvirs again and again, and in the end probably set up barbarian chieftains in their place — for the case of Jugurtha shows the lengths to which foreigners dared to go with the Rome of those days. The provenance or constitution of the intruders does not matter — they might be body-guards, insurgent slaves, Jacobins, or purely alien tribes. What does matter is what they were for the Egyptian world in that century of theirs. In the end they set up a state in the Western Delta and built a capital, Auaris, for it.[2] One of their leaders, Khyan by name, who styled himself, not Pharaoh, but "Embracer of the Country" and "prince of the young men" (names as essentially revolutionary as the *Consul sine collega* or *dictator prepetuus* of Cæsar's time) a man probably of the stamp of John Tzimisces, ruled over all Egypt and spread his renown as far as Crete and the Euphrates. But after him began a fight of all the districts for the Imperium, and out of that fight Amasis and the Theban dynasty eventually emerged victorious.

For us this time of Contending States began with Napoleon and his violent-arbitrary government by order. His head was the first in our world to make effective the notion of a military and at the same time popular world-domination — something altogether different from the Empire of Charles V and even the British Colonial Empire of his own day. If the nineteenth century has been relatively poor in great wars — and revolutions — and has overcome its worst crises diplomatically by means of congresses, this has been due precisely to the continuous and terrific war-preparedness which has made disputants, fearful at the eleventh hour of the consequences, postpone the definitive decision again and again, and led to the substitution of chess-moves for war. For this is the century of gigantic permanent armies and universal compulsory service. We ourselves are too near to it to see it under this terrifying aspect. In all world-history there is no parallel. Ever since Napoleon, hundreds of thousands, and

---

[1] The Papyrus says: "the archer-folk from without" — that is, the barbarian mercenary troops. To these the native youth attached itself.

[2] Glance also at the Negro-state in Irak and the "contemporary" attempts of Spartacus, Sertorius, and Sextus Pompey, and we get a fair idea of the variety of the possibilities. Weill assumes, 1785-1765, the collapse of the Kingdom, a usurper (a general); 1765-1675, numerous small potentates, in the Delta wholly independent; 1675-1633, struggle for unity, especially the rulers of Thebes, with an ever-increasing retinue of dependent rulers, including the Hyksos; 1633, victory of the Hyksos and defeat of the Thebans; 1591-1571, final triumph of the Thebans.

latterly millions, of men have stood ready to march, and mighty fleets renewed every ten years have filled the harbours.   It is a war without war, a war of overbidding in equipment and preparedness, a war of figures and tempo and technics, and the diplomatic dealings have been not of court with court, but of headquarters with headquarters.   The longer the discharge was delayed, the more huge became the means and the more intolerable the tension.   This is the Faustian, the dynamic, form of "the Contending States" during the first century of that period, but it ended with the explosion of the World War.   For the demand of these four years has been altogether too much for the principle of universal service — child of the French Revolution, revolutionary through and through, as it is in this form — and for all tactical methods evolved from it.[1] The place of the permanent armies as we know them will gradually be taken by professional forces of volunteer war-keen soldiers; and from millions we shall revert to hundreds of thousands.   But *ipso facto* this second century will be one of *actually* Contending States.   *These* armies are not substitutes for war — they are *for* war, and they want war.   Within two generations it will be they whose will prevails over that of all the comfortables put together.   In these wars of theirs for the heritage of the whole world, continents will be staked, India, China, South Africa, Russia, Islam called out, new technics and tactics played and counterplayed.   The great cosmopolitan foci of power will dispose at their pleasure of smaller states — their territory, their economy and their men alike — all that is now merely province, passive object, means to end, and its destinies are without importance to the great march of things. We ourselves, in a very few years, have learned to take little or no notice of events that before the War would have horrified the world; who to-day seriously thinks about the millions that perish in Russia?

Again and again between these catastrophes of blood and terror the cry rises up for reconciliation of the peoples and for peace on earth.   It is but the background and the echo of the grand happening, but, as such, so necessary that we have to assume its existence even if, as in Hyksos Egypt, in Baghdad and Byzantium, no tradition tells of it.   Esteem as we may the wish towards all this, we must have the courage to face facts as they are — that is the hallmark of men of race-quality and it is by the being of these men that *alone* history is.   Life if it would be great, is hard; it lets choose *only* between victory and ruin, not between war and peace, and to the victory belong the sacrifices of victory.   For that which shuffles querulously and jealously by the side of the events is only literature, — written or thought or lived literature — mere truths that lose themselves in the moving crush of facts.   History has never deigned to take notice of these propositions.   In the Chinese world Hiang-Sui tried, as early as 535, to found a peace league.   In the period of the Contending States, imperialism (*Lien-heng*) was opposed by the League of Nations idea

---

[1] As an inspiriting idea it may be retained; translated into actuality it will never be again.

(*Hoh-tsung*),[1] particularly in the southern regions, but it was foredoomed like every half-measure that steps into the path of a whole, and it had vanished even before the victory of the North. But both tendencies alike rejected the political taste of the Taoists, who, in those fearful centuries, elected for intellectual self-disarmament, thereby reducing themselves to the level of mere material to be used up by others and for others in the grand decisions. Even Roman politics — deliberately improvident as the Classical spirit was in all other respects — at least made one attempt to bring the whole world into one system of equal co-ordinated forces which should do away with all necessity for further wars — that is, when at the fall of Hannibal Rome forwent the chance of incorporating the East. But reluctance was useless; the party of the younger Scipio went over to frank Imperialism in order to make an end of chaos, although its clear-sighted leader foresaw therein the doom of his city, which possessed (and in a high degree) the native Classical incapacity for organizing anything whatever. The way from Alexander to Cæsar is unambiguous and unavoidable, and the strongest nation of any and every Culture, consciously or unconsciously, willing or unwilling, has had to tread it.

From the rigour of these facts there is no refuge. The Hague Conference of 1907 was the prelude of the World War; the Washington Conference of 1921 will have been that of other wars. The history of these times is no longer an intellectual match of wits in elegant forms for pluses and minuses, from which either side can withdraw when it pleases. The alternatives now are to stand fast or to go under — there is no middle course. The only moral that the logic of things permits to us now is that of the climber on the face of the crag — a moment's weakness and all is over. To-day all "philosophy" is nothing but an inward abdication and resignation, or a craven hope of escaping realities by means of mysticisms. It was just the same in Roman times. Tacitus tells us [2] how the famous Musonius Rufus tried, by exhortations on the blessings of peace and the evils of war, to influence the legions that in 70 stood before the gates of Rome, and barely escaped alive from their blows. The military commander Avidius Cassius called the Emperor Marcus Aurelius a "philosophical old woman."

In these conditions so much of old and great traditions as remains, so much of historical "fitness" and experience as has got into the blood of the twentieth-century nations, acquires an unequalled potency. For us *creative* piety, or (to use a more fundamental term) the pulse that has come down to us from first origins, adheres only to forms that are older than the Revolution and Napoleon,[3] forms which grew and were not made. Every remnant of them, however tiny, that has kept itself alive in the being of any self-contained minority whatever

[1] Piton, op. cit., p. 521.
[2] *Hist.*, III, 1.
[3] Including the constitution of the United States of America. Only thus can we account for the reverence that the American cherishes for it, even where he clearly sees its insufficiency.

will before long rise to incalculable values and bring about historical effects which no one yet imagines to be possible. The traditions of an old monarchy, of an old aristocracy, of an old polite society, in so much as they are still healthy enough to keep clear of professional or professorial politics, in so far as they possess honour, abnegation, discipline, the genuine sense of a great mission (*race-quality*, that is, and training), sense of duty and sacrifice — can become a centre which holds together the being-stream of an entire people and enables it to outlast this time and make its landfall in the future. To be "in condition" is everything. It falls to us to live in the most trying times known to the history of a great Culture. The last race to keep its form, the last living tradition, the last leaders who have both at their back, will pass through and onward, victors.

x

By the term "Cæsarism" I mean that kind of government which, irrespective of any constitutional formulation that it may have, is in its inward self a return to thorough formlessness. It does not matter that Augustus in Rome, and Hwang-ti in China, Amasis in Egypt and Alp Arslan in Baghdad disguised their position under antique forms. The spirit of these forms was dead,[1] and so all institutions, however carefully maintained, were thenceforth destitute of all meaning and weight. Real importance centred in the wholly personal power exercised by the Cæsar, or by anybody else capable of exercising it in his place. It is the *récidive* of a form-fulfilled world into primitivism, into the cosmic-historyless. Biological stretches of time once more take the place vacated by historical periods.[2]

At the beginning, where the Civilization is developing to full bloom (today), there stands the miracle of the Cosmopolis, the great petrifact, a symbol of the formless — vast, splendid, spreading in insolence. It draws within itself the being-streams of the now impotent countryside, human masses that are wafted as dunes from one to another or flow like loose sand into the chinks of the stone. Here money and intellect celebrate their greatest and their last triumphs. It is the most artificial, the cleverest phenomenon manifested in the light-world of human eyes — uncanny, "too good to be true," standing already almost beyond the possibilities of cosmic formation.

Presently, however, the idea-less facts come forward again, naked and gigantic. The eternal-cosmic pulse has finally overcome the intellectual tensions of a few centuries. In the form of democracy, money has won. There has been a period in which politics were almost its preserve. But as soon as it has destroyed the old orders of the Culture, the chaos gives forth a new and

---

[1] Cæsar recognized this clearly. "*Nihil esse rem publicam, appellationem modo sine corpore ac specie*" (Suetonius, *Cæsar*, 77).

[2] See p. 48.

overpowering factor that penetrates to the very elementals of Becoming — the Cæsar-men. Before them the money collapses. *The Imperial Age, in every Culture alike, signifies the end of the politics of mind and money.* The powers of the blood, unbroken bodily forces, resume their ancient lordship. "Race" springs forth, pure and irresistible — the strongest win and the residue is their spoil. They seize the management of the world, and the realm of books and problems petrifies or vanishes from memory. From now on, new destinies in the style of the pre-Culture time are possible afresh, and visible to the consciousness without cloaks of causality. There is no inward difference more between the lives of Septimius Severus and Gallienus and those of Alaric and Odoacer. Rameses, Trajan, Wu-ti belong together in a uniform up-and-down of history-less time-stretches.[1]

Once the Imperial Age has arrived, there are no more political problems. People manage with the situation as it is and the powers that be. In the period of Contending States, torrents of blood had reddened the pavements of all world-cities, so that the great truths of Democracy might be turned into actualities, and for the winning of rights without which life seemed not worth the living. Now these rights are won, but the grandchildren cannot be moved, even by punishment, to make use of them. A hundred years more, and even the historians will no longer understand the old controversies. Already by Cæsar's time reputable people had almost ceased to take part in the elections.[2] It embittered the life of the great Tiberius that the most capable men of his time held aloof from politics, and Nero could not even by threats compel the Equites to come to Rome in order to exercise their rights. This is the end of the great politics. The conflict of intelligences that had served as substitute for war must give place to war itself in its most primitive form.

It is, therefore, a complete misunderstanding of the meaning of the period to presume, as Mommsen did,[3] a deep design of subdivision in the "dyarchy" fashioned by Augustus, with its partition of powers between Princeps and Senate. A century earlier this constitution would have been a real thing, but that would in itself suffice to make it impossible for such an idea to have entered the heads of the present force-men. Now it meant nothing but the attempt of a weak personality to deceive itself as to inexorable facts by mantling them in empty forms. Cæsar saw things as they were and was guided in the exercise of his rulership by definite and unsentimental practical considerations. The legislation of his last months was concerned wholly with transitional provi-

[1] See p. 48.

[2] Cicero, in his *Pro Sestio*, draws attention to the fact that five people for each tribe attended plebiscites, and these really belonged to tribes other than that which they were representing. But these five were present only in order to have themselves bought by the possessors of the real power. Yet it was hardly fifty years since the Italians had died in masses for this franchise.

[3] And, strangely, Ed. Meyer also, in his masterpiece *Cæsars Monarchie*, the one work of statesman-like quality yet written about this epoch — and previously in his essay on Augustus (*Kleine Schriften*, pp. 441, et seq.).

sions, none of which were intended to be permanent. This precisely is what has generally been overlooked. He was far too deep a judge of things to anticipate development or to settle its definitive forms at this moment, with the Parthian War impending. But Augustus, like Pompey before him, was not the master of his following, but thoroughly dependent upon it and its views of things. The form of the Principate was not at all his discovery, but the doctrinaire execution of an obsolete party-ideal that Cicero — another weakling — had formulated.[1] When, on the 13th January 27, Augustus gave back the state-power to the "Senate and People" of Rome — a scene all the more meaningless because of its sincerity — he kept the Tribunate for himself. In fact, this was the one element of the polity that could manifest itself in actuality. The Tribune was the legitimate successor of the Tyrant,[2] and as long ago as 122 B.C. Caius Gracchus had put into the title a connotation limited no longer by the legal bounds of the office, but only by the personal talents of the incumbent. From him it is a direct line through Marius and Cæsar to the young Nero, who set himself to defeat the political purposes of his mother Agrippina. The Princeps,[3] on the other hand, was thenceforth only a costume, a rank — very likely a fact in society, certainly not a fact in politics. And this, precisely, was the conception invested with light and glamour by the theory of Cicero, and *already* — and by him of all people — associated with the Divus-idea.[4] The "co-operation" of the Senate and People, on the contrary, was an antiquated ceremonial, with about as much life in it as the rites of the Fratres Arvales — also restored by Augustus. The great parties of the Gracchan age had long become retinues — Cæsarians and Pompeians — and finally there only remained on the one side the formless omnipotence, the plain brutal "fact," the Cæsar — or whoever managed to get the Cæsar under his influence — and on the other side the handful of narrow ideologues who concealed dissatisfaction under philosophy and thenceforward sought to advance their ideals by conspiracy. What these Stoics were in Rome, the Confucians were in China — and, seen thus, the episode of the "Burning of the Books," decreed by the Chinese Augustus in 212, begins to be intelligible through the reproach of immense vandalism that the minds of later literates fastened upon it. But, after all, these Stoic enthusiasts for an ideal that had become impossible had killed Cæsar:[5] to the

---

[1] *De Re Publica*, 54 B.C., a monograph intended for Pompey.

[2] See p. 395.

[3] See p. 409.

[4] In *Somnium Scipionis*, VI, 26, he is a god who so rules the State *quam hunc mundum ille princeps deus*.

[5] It was with every justification that, in the presence of the corpse, Brutus called out the name of Cicero, while Antony, on his side, denounced him as the intellectual author of the deed. But this "freedom" meant nothing but the oligarchy of a few families, for the masses had long ago become tired of their rights. Nor is it in the least surprising that Money was behind Intellect in the murder, for the great fortunes of Rome saw in Cæsarism the beginning of the end of their power.

Divus-cult they opposed a Cato- and Brutus-cult; the philosophers in the Senate (which by then was only a noble club) never wearied of lamenting the downfall of "freedom" and fomenting conspiracies such as Piso's in 65. Had this been the state of things at Nero's death, it would have been Sulla over again; and that is why Nero put to death the Stoic Thrasea Pætus, why Vespasian executed Helvidius Priscus, and why copies of the history of Cremutius Cordus, which lauded Brutus as the last of the Romans, were collected and burnt in Rome. These were acts of defensive State necessity *vis-à-vis* blind ideology — acts such as those we know of Cromwell and Robespierre — and it was in exactly the same position that the Chinese Cæsars found themselves *vis-à-vis* the school of Confucius, which had formerly worked out their ideal of a state-constitution and now had no notion of enduring the actuality. This great Burning of the Books was nothing but the destruction of one part of the politico-philosophical literature and the abolition of propaganda and secret organizations.[1] This defensive lasted in both Imperia for a century, and then even reminiscences of party-political passions faded out and the two philosophies became the ruling world-outlook of the Imperial age in its maturity.[2] But the world was now the theatre of *tragic family-histories* into which state-histories were dissolved; the Julian-Claudian house destroyed Roman history, and the house of Shi-hwang-ti (even from 206 B.C.) destroyed Chinese, and we darkly discern something of the same kind in the destinies of the Egyptian Queen Hatshepsut and her brothers (1501–1447). It is the last step to the definitive. With world-peace — *the peace of high policies* — the "sword side"[3] of being retreats and the "spindle side" rules again; henceforth there are only *private* histories, private destinies, private ambitions, from top to bottom, from the miserable troubles of fellaheen to the dreary feuds of Cæsars for the private possession of the world. The wars of the age of world-peace are private wars, more fearful than any State wars because they are formless.

For world-peace — which has often existed in fact — involves the private renunciation of war on the part of the immense majority, but along with this it involves an unavowed readiness to submit to being the booty of others who do *not* renounce it. It begins with the State-destroying wish for universal reconciliation, and it ends in nobody's moving a finger so long as misfortune only touches his neighbour. Already under Marcus Aurelius each city and each land-patch was thinking of itself, and the activities of the ruler were his

---

[1] Taoism, on the other hand, was supported, as preaching the entire renunciation of politics. Said Shakespeare's Cæsar:

> "Let me have men about me that are fat,
> Sleek-headed men and such as sleep o'nights."

[2] Tacitus, even, failed to understand. He hated these first Cæsars, because they defended themselves by every imaginable means against a stealthy opposition — in *his own* circles — an opposition that from Trajan's time no longer existed. (Yet a little longer, and the Emperor Marcus Aurelius could himself be a Stoic. *Tr.*)

[3] P. 329.

private affair as other men's were theirs. The remoter peoples were as indifferent to him and his troops and his aims as they were to the projects of Germanic war-bands. On this *spiritual* premiss a second Vikingism develops. The state of being "in form" passes from nations to bands and retinues of adventurers, self-styled Cæsars, seceding generals, barbarian kings, and what not — in whose eyes the population becomes in the end merely a part of the landscape. There is a deep relation between the heroes of the Mycenæan primitive age and the soldier-emperors of Rome, and between, say, Menes and Rameses II. In our Germanic world the spirits of Alaric and Theodoric will come again — there is a first hint of them in Cecil Rhodes — and the alien executioners of the Russian preface, from Jenghiz Khan to Trotski (with the episode of Petrine Tsarism between them) are, when all is said and done, very little different from most of the pretenders of the Latin-American republics, whose private struggles have long since put an end to the form-rich age of the Spanish Baroque.

With the formed state, high history also lays itself down weary to sleep. Man becomes a plant again, adhering to the soil, dumb and enduring. The timeless village and the "eternal" peasant [1] reappear, begetting children and burying seed in Mother Earth — a busy, not inadequate swarm, over which the tempest of soldier-emperors passingly blows. In the midst of the land lie the old world-cities, empty receptacles of an extinguished soul, in which a historyless mankind slowly nests itself. Men live from hand to mouth, with petty thrifts and petty fortunes, and endure. Masses are trampled on in the conflicts of the conquerors who contend for the power and the spoil of this world, but the survivors fill up the gaps with a primitive fertility and suffer on. And while in high places there is eternal alternance of victory and defeat, those in the depths pray, pray with that mighty piety of the Second Religiousness that has overcome all doubts for ever.[2] There, in the souls, world-peace, the peace of God, the bliss of grey-haired monks and hermits, is become actual — and there alone. It has awakened that depth in the endurance of suffering which the historical man in the thousand years of his development has never known. Only with the end of grand History does holy, still Being reappear. It is a drama noble in its aimlessness, noble and aimless as the course of the stars, the rotation of the earth, and alternance of land and sea, of ice and virgin forest upon its face. We may marvel at it or we may lament it — but it is there.

[1] Pp. 89 and 349.
[2] P. 310

CHAPTER XII

THE STATE

(C)

PHILOSOPHY OF POLITICS

THE STATE

(C)

PHILOSOPHY OF POLITICS

I

To POLITICS as an idea we have given more thought than has been good for us, since, correspondingly, we have understood all the less about the observation of Politics as a reality. The great statesmen are accustomed to act immediately and on the basis of a sure flair for facts. This is so self-evident, to them, that it simply never enters their heads to reflect upon the basic general principles of their action — supposing indeed that such exist. In all ages they have known what they had to do, and any theory of this knowledge has been foreign to both their capacities and their tastes. But the professional thinkers who have turned their attention to the *faits accomplis* of men have been so remote, inwardly, from these actions that they have just spun for themselves a web of abstractions — for preference, abstraction-myths like justice, virtue, freedom — and then applied them as criteria to past and, especially, future historical happening. Thus in the end they have forgotten that concepts are only concepts, and brought themselves to the conclusion that there is a political science whereby we can form the course of the world according to an ideal recipe. As nothing of the kind has ever or anywhere happened, political doing has come to be considered as so trivial in comparison with abstract thinking that they debate in their books whether there is a "genius of action" at all.

Here, on the contrary, the attempt will be made to give, instead of an ideological system, a *physiognomy* of politics as it has actually been practised in the course of general history, and not as it might or ought to have been practised. The problem was, and is, to penetrate to the final meaning of great events, to "see" them, to feel and to transcribe the symbolically important in them. The projects of world-improvers and the actuality of History have nothing to do with one another.[1]

The being-streams of humanity are called History when we regard them as movement, and family, estate, people, nation, when we regard them as the

---

[1] "Empires perish, but a good verse stands," said W. von Humboldt on the field of Waterloo. But, all the same, the personality of Napoleon preformed the history of the next century. Good verses! — he should have questioned a peasant by the way-side. They "stand" — for literary teaching. Plato is eternal — for philologists. But Napoleon inwardly rules *us*, all of *us*, our states and our armies, our public opinion, the whole of our political outlook, and the more effectually the less we are conscious of it.

object moved.[1] Politics is the way in which this fluent Being maintains itself, *grows*, triumphs over other life-streams. *All living is politics*, in every trait of instinct, in the inmost marrow.[2] That which we nowadays like to call life-energy (vitality), the "it" in us that at all costs strives forward and upward, the blind cosmic drive to validity and power that at the same time remains plantwise and racewise, bound up with the earth, the "home"-land; the directedness, the need to actualize — it is this that appears in every higher mankind, as its political life, seeking naturally and inevitably the great decisions that determine whether it shall be, or shall suffer, a Destiny. For it grows or *it dies out;* there is no third possibility.

For this reason the nobility, as expression of a strong race-quality, is the truly political Order, and training and not shaping is the truly political sort of education. Every great politician, a centre of forces in the stream of happening, has something of the noble in his feeling of self-vocation and inward obligation. On the other hand, all that is microcosmic and "intellect" is unpolitical, and so there is a something of priestliness in all program-politics and ideology. The best diplomats are the children; in their play, or when they want something, a cosmic "it" that is bound up in the individual being breaks out immediately and with the sure tread of the sleep-walker. They do not learn, but unlearn, this art of early years as they grow older — hence the rarity in the world of adults of the Statesman.

It is only in and between these being-streams that fill the field of the high Culture that high policy exists. They are only possible, therefore, in the plural. A people *is*, really, only in relation to peoples.[3] But the natural, "race," relation between them is for that very reason a relation of war — this is a fact that no truths avail to alter. War is the primary politics of *everything* that lives, and so much so that in the deeps battle and life are one, and being and will-to-battle expire together. Old Germanic words for this, like "*orrusta*" and "*orlog*," mean seriousness and destiny in contrast to jest and play — and the contrast is one of intensity, not of qualitative difference. And even though all high politics tries to be a substitution of more intellectual weapons for the sword and though it is the ambition of the statesman at the culminations of all the Cultures to feel able to dispense with war, yet the primary relationship between diplomacy and the war-art endures. The character of battle is common to both, and the tactics and stratagems, and the necessity of material forces in the background to give weight to the operations. The aim, too, remains the same — namely, the growth of one's own life-unit (class or nation) at the cost of the other's. And every attempt to eliminate the "race" element only leads to its transfer to other ground; instead of the conflict of states we have that of

[1] P. 361.
[2] P. 116 and 339.
[3] P. 363.

parties, or that of areas, or (if there also the will to growth is extinct) that of the adventurers' retinues, to whose doings the rest of the population unresistingly adjusts itself.

In every war between life-powers the question at issue is which is to govern the whole. It is always a life, never a system, law, or program that gives the beat in the stream of happening.[1] To be the centre of action and effective focus of a multitude,[2] to make the inward form of one's own personality into that of whole peoples and periods, to be history's commanding officer, with the aim of bringing one's own people or family or purposes to the top of events — that is the scarce-conscious but irresistible impulse in every individual being that has a historical vocation in it. There is only *personal* history, and consequently only *personal* politics. The struggle of, not principles but men, not ideals but race-qualities, for executive power is the alpha and omega. Even revolutions are no exception, for the "sovereignty of the people" only expresses the fact that the ruling power has assumed the title of people's leader instead of that of king. The method of governing is scarcely altered thereby, and the position of the governed not at all. And even world-peace, in every case where it has existed, has been nothing but the slavery of an entire humanity under the regimen imposed by a few strong natures determined to rule.

The conception of executive power implies that the life-unit — even in the case of the animals — is subdivided into subjects and objects of government. This is so self-evident that no mass-unit has ever for a moment, even in the severest crises (such as 1789), lost the sense of this inner structure of itself. Only the incumbent vanishes, not the office, and if a people does actually, in the tide of events, lose all leadership and float on haphazard, it only means that control has passed to outside hands, that it has become *in its entirety* the mere object.

Politically gifted *peoples* do not exist. Those which are supposed to be so are simply peoples that are firmly in the hands of a ruling minority and in consequence feel themselves to be in good form. The English as a people are just as unthinking, narrow, and unpractical in political matters as any other nation, but they possess — for all their liking for public debate — a *tradition of confidence*. The difference is simply that the Englishman is the object of a regimen of very old and successful habits, in which he acquiesces because experience has shown him their advantage. From an acquiescence that has the outward appearance of agreement, it is only one step to the conviction that this government depends upon his will, although paradoxically it is the government that, for technical reasons of its own, unceasingly hammers the notion into his head. The ruling class in England has developed its aims and methods

[1] This is what is expressed in the English proverb: "Men, not measures," which is the very key to the secrets of all political achievement.

[2] Pp. 18 and 364.

quite independently of the "people," and it works with and within an unwritten constitution of which the refinements — which have arisen from practice and are wholly innocent of theory — are to the uninitiated as opaque as they are unintelligible. But the courage of a troop depends on its confidence in the leadership, and confidence means involuntary abstention from criticism. It is the officer who makes cowards into heroes, or heroes into cowards, and this holds good equally for armies, peoples, classes, and parties. *Political talent in a people* is nothing but confidence in its leading. But that confidence has to be acquired; it will ripen only in its own good time, and success will stabilize it and make it into a tradition. What appears as a lack of the feeling of certainty in the ruled is really lack of leadership-talent in the ruling classes, which generates that sort of uninstinctive and meddlesome criticism which by its very existence shows that a people has got "out of condition."

II

How is politics *done?* The born statesman is above all a valuer — a valuer of men, situations, and things. He has the "eye" which unhesitatingly and inflexibly embraces the round of possibilities. The judge of horses takes in an animal with one glance and knows what prospects it will have in a race. To do the correct thing without "knowing" it, to have the hands that imperceptibly tighten or ease the bit — his talent is the very opposite to that of the man of theory. The secret pulse of all being is one and the same in him and in the things of history. They sense one another, they exist for one another. The fact-man is immune from the risk of practising sentimental or program politics. He does not believe in the big words. Pilate's question is constantly on his lips — truths? The born statesman stands beyond true and false. He does not confuse the logic of events with the logic of systems. "Truths" or "errors" — which here amount to the same — only concern him as intellectual currents, and in respect of *workings*. He surveys their potency, durability, and direction, and duly books them in his calculations for the destiny of the power that he directs. He has convictions, certainly, that are dear to him, but he has them as a private person; no real politician ever felt himself tied to them when in action. "The doer is always conscienceless; no one has a conscience except the spectator," said Goethe, and it is equally true of Sulla and Robespierre as it is of Bismarck and Pitt. The great Popes and the English party-leaders, so long as they had still to strive for the mastery of things, acted on the same principles as the conquerors and upstarts of all ages. Take the dealings of Innocent III, who very nearly succeeded in creating a world-dominion of the Church, and deduce therefrom the catechism of success; it will be found to be in the extremest contradiction with all religious moral. Yet without it there could have been no bearable existence for any Church, not to mention English Colonies, American fortunes, victorious revolutions, or, for that matter, states or parties or peoples in general. It is *life*, not the individual, that is conscienceless.

The essential, therefore, is to understand the time *for* which one is born. He who does not sense and understand its most secret forces, who does not feel in himself something cognate that drives him forward on a path neither hedged nor defined by concepts, who believes in the surface, public opinion, large phrases and ideals of the day — he is not of the stature for its events. He is in their power, not they in his. Look not back to the past for measuring-rods! Still less sideways for some system or other! There are times, like our own present and the Gracchan age, in which there are two most deadly kinds of idealism, the reactionary and the democratic. The one believes in the reversibility of history, the other in a teleology of history. But it makes no difference to the inevitable failure with which both burden a nation over whose destiny they have power, whether it is to a memory or to a concèpt that they sacrifice it. The genuine statesman is incarnate history, its directedness expressed as individual will and its organic logic as character.

But the true statesman must also be, in a large sense of the word, an educator — not the representative of a moral or a doctrine, but an exemplar in doing.[1] It is a patent fact that a religion has never yet altered the style of an existence. It penetrated the waking-consciousness, the *intellectual* man, it threw new light on another world, it created an immense happiness by way of humanity, resignation, and patience unto death, but over the forces of life it possessed no power. In the sphere of the living only the great personality — the "it," the race, the cosmic force bound up in that personality — has been creative (not shaping, but breeding and training) and has effectively modified the type of entire classes and peoples. It is not "the" truth or "the" good or "the" upright, but "the" Roman or "the" Puritan or "the" Prussian that is a fact. The sum of honour and duty, discipline, resolution, is a thing not learned from books, but *awakened* in the stream of being by a living exemplar; and that is why Frederick William I was one of those educators, great for all time, whose personal race-forming conduct does not vanish in the course of the generations. The genuine statesman is distinguished from the "mere politician" — the player who plays for the pleasure of the game, the *arriviste* on the heights of history, the seeker after wealth and rank — as also from the schoolmaster of an ideal, by the fact that he dares to demand sacrifices — *and* obtains them, because his feeling that he is necessary to the time and the nation is shared by thousands, transforms them to the core, and renders them capable of deeds to which otherwise they could never have risen.[2]

[1] See p. 341.

[2] The same, too, holds good of the Churches, which are different in kind from the Religion — namely, elements of the world of facts and, therefore, political and not religious in the type of their leadership. It was not the Christian evangel, but the Christian martyr, who conquered the world, and that which gave him his strength was not the doctrine, but the example, of the Man on the Cross.

Highest of all, however, is not action, but the *ability to command*. It is this that takes the individual up out of himself and makes him the centre of a world of action. There is one kind of commanding that makes obedience a proud, free, and noble habit. That kind Napoleon, for example, did *not* possess. A residue of subaltern outlook in him prevented him from training men to be men and not bureau-personnel, and led him to govern through edicts instead of through personalities; as he did not understand this subtlest tact of command and, therefore, was obliged to do everything really decisive himself, he slowly collapsed from inability to reconcile the demands of his position with the limit of human capabilities. But one who, like Cæsar or Frederick the Great, possesses this last and highest gift of complete humanity feels — on a battle-evening when operations are sweeping to the willed conclusion, and the victory is turning out to be conclusive of the campaign; or when the last signature is written that rounds off a historical epoch — a wondrous sense of power that the man of truths can never know. There are moments — and they indicate the maxima of cosmic flowings — when the individual feels himself to be identical with Destiny, the centre of the world, and his own personality seems to him almost as a covering in which the history of the future is about to clothe itself.

The first problem is to make oneself somebody; the second — less obvious, but harder and greater in its ultimate effects — *to create a tradition*, to bring on others so that one's work may be continued with one's own pulse and spirit, to release a current of like activity that does not need the original leader to maintain it in form. And here the statesman rises to something that in the Classical world would doubtless have been called divinity. He becomes the creator of a new life, the *spirit*-ancestor of a young race. He himself, as a unit, vanishes from the stream after a few years. But a minority called into being by him takes up his course and maintains it indefinitely. This cosmic something, this soul of a ruling stratum, an individual *can* generate and leave as a heritage, and throughout history it is this that has produced the durable effects. The great statesman is rare. Whether he comes, or wins through, too soon or too late, incident determines. Great individuals often destroy more than they have built up — by the gap that their death makes in the flow of happening. But *the creation of tradition means the elimination of the incident*. A tradition breeds a high average, with which the future can reckon — no Cæsar, but a Senate, no Napoleon, but an incomparable officer-corps. A strong tradition attracts talents from all quarters, and out of small gifts produces great results. The schools of painting of Italy and Holland are proof of this, no less than the Prussian army and the diplomacy of the Roman Curia. It was the great flaw in Bismarck, as compared with Frederick William I, that he could achieve, but could not form a tradition; that he did not parallel Moltke's officer-corps by a corresponding race of politicians who would identify themselves in feeling with his State and its new tasks, would constantly take up good men from below and so provide for the continuance of the Bismarckian action-pulse for ever. If this creation of a tradition does not come off, then instead of a homogeneous ruling stratum we have a congeries of heads that are helpless when confronted by the unforeseen. If it does, we have a *Sovereign People* in the one sense of the phrase that is worthy of a people and possible in the world of fact — a highly trained, self-replenishing minority with sure and slowly ripened traditions, which attracts every talent into the charmed circle and uses it to the full, and *ipso facto* keeps itself in harmony with the remainder of the nation that it rules. Such a minority slowly develops into a true "breed," even when it had begun merely as a party, and the sureness of its decisions comes to be that of blood, not of reason. But this means that what happens in it happens "of itself" and does not need the Genius. *Great politics*, so to put it, *takes the place of the great politician.*

What, then, *is* politics? It is the art of the possible — an old saying, and almost an all-inclusive saying. The gardener can obtain a plant from the seed, or he can improve its stock. He can bring to bloom, or let languish, the dispositions hidden in it, its growths and colour, its flower and fruit. On his eye for possibilities — and, therefore, necessities — depends its fulfilment, its strength, its whole Destiny. But the basic form and direction of its being, the stages and tempo and direction thereof, are *not* in his power. It must accomplish them or it decays, and the same is true of the immense plant that we call a "Culture" and the being-streams of human families that are bound up in its form-world. The great statesman is the gardener of a people.

Every doer is born in a time and for a time, and thereby the ambit of *his* attainable achievement is fixed. For his grandfather, for his grandson, the data, and therefore the task and the object, are not the same. The circle is further narrowed by the limits of his personality, the properties of his people, the situation, and the men with whom he has to work. It is the hall-mark of the high politician that he is rarely caught out in a misappreciation of this limit, and equally rarely overlooks anything realizable within it. With this — one cannot too often repeat, especially to Germans — goes a sure discrimination between what "ought" to be and what *will* be. The basic forms of the state and of political life, the direction and the degree of their evolution, are given values unalterably dependent on the given time. They are the track of political success and not its goal. On the other hand the worshippers of political ideals create out of nothing. Their intellectual freedom is astounding, but their castles of the mind, built of airy concepts like wisdom and righteousness, liberty and equality, are in the end all the same; they are built from the top storey downwards. The master of fact, for his part, is content to direct imperceptibly that which he sees and accepts as plain reality. This does not seem very much, yet it is the very starting-point of freedom, in a grand sense of the word. The knack lies in the little things, the last careful touch of the helm, the fine sensing of the most delicate oscillations of collective and individual souls. The art of the statesman consists not only in a clear idea of the main lines drawn undeviably before him, *but also* in the sure handling of the single occurrences and the single persons, encountered along those lines, which can turn an impending disaster into a decisive success. The secret of all victory lies in the organization of the non-obvious. An adept in the game can, like Talleyrand, go to Vienna as ambassador of the vanquished party and make himself master of the victor. At the Lucca meeting, Cæsar, whose position was wellnigh desperate, not only made Pompey's power serviceable to his own ends, but undermined it at the same time, and without his opponent's becoming aware of the fact. But the domain of the possible has dangerous edges, and if the finished tact of the great Baroque diplomatists almost always managed to keep clear, it is the very privilege of the ideologues to be always stumbling over it. There have been turns in history in which the statescraftman has let himself drift with the current awhile, in order not to lose the leadership. Every situation has its elastic limit, and in the estimation of that limit not the smallest error is permissible. A revolution that reaches explosion-point is always a proof of lack of the political pulse in the governors *and* in their opponents.

Further, the necessary must be done *opportunely* — namely, while it is a present wherewith the governing power can buy confidence in itself, whereas if it has to be conceded as a sacrifice, it discloses a weakness and excites contempt. Political forms are living forms whose changes inexorably follow a definite direction, and to attempt to prevent this course or to divert it towards some ideal is to confess oneself "out of condition." The Roman nobility possessed this congruence of pulse, the Spartan did not. In the period of mounting democracy we find again and again (as in France before 1789 and Germany before 1918) the arrival of a fatal moment when it is too late for the necessary reform to be given as a free gift; *then* that which should be refused with the sternest energy is given as a *sacrifice*, and so becomes the sign of dissolution. But those who fail to detect the first necessity in good time will all the more certainly fail to misunderstand the second situation. Even a journey to Canossa can be made too soon or too late — the timing may settle the future of whole peoples, whether they shall be Destiny for others, or themselves the objects of another's Destiny. But the declining democracy also repeats the same error of trying to hold what was the ideal of yesterday. This is the danger of our twentieth century. On the path towards Cæsarism there is ever a Cato to be found.

The influence that a statesman — even one in an exceptionally strong position — possesses over the *methods* of politics is very small, and it is one of the characteristics of the high-grade statesman that he does not deceive himself on this matter. His task is to work in and with the historical form that he finds in existence; it is only the theorist who enthusiastically searches for more ideal forms. But to be politically "in form" means necessarily, amongst other things, an unconditional *command of the most modern means*. There is no choice about it. The means and methods are premisses pertaining to the time and belong to the inner form of the time — and one who grasps at the inapposite, who permits his taste or his feelings to overpower the pulse in him, loses at once his grip of realities. The danger of an aristocracy is that of being conservative in its means, the danger of a democracy is the confusion of formula and form. The means of the present are, and will be for many years, parliamentary — elections and the press. He may think what he pleases about them, he may respect them or despise them, but he *must command them*. Bach and Mozart *commanded* the musical means of their times. This is the hall-mark of mastery in any and every field, and statecraft is no exception. Now, the publicly visible outer form thereof is not the essential but merely the disguise, and consequently it may be altered, rationalized, and brought down to constitutional texts — without its actualities being necessarily affected in the slightest — and hence the ambitions of all revolutionaries expend themselves in playing the game of rights, principles, and franchises on the surface of history. But the statesman knows that the extension of a franchise is quite unimportant in comparison with the technique — Athenian or Roman, Jacobin or American or present-day German — of *operating* the votes. How the English constitution reads is a matter of small import compared with the fact that it is managed by a small stratum of high families, so that an Edward VII is simply a minister of his Ministry. And as for the modern Press, the sentimentalist may beam with contentment when it is constitutionally "free" — but the realist merely asks at whose disposal it is.

Politics, lastly, is the form in which is accomplished the history of a nation within a plurality of nations. The great art is to maintain one's own nation inwardly "in form" for events outside; this is the natural relation of home and foreign politics, holding not only for Peoples and States and Estates, but for living units of every kind, down to the simplest animal swarms and down into the individual bodies. And, as between the two, *the first exists exclusively for the second and not vice versa*. The true democrat is accustomed to treat home politics as an end in itself; the rank and file of diplomats think solely of foreign affairs; but just because of this the individual successes of either "cut no ice." No doubt, the political master exhibits his powers most obviously in the tactics of home reform; in his economic and social activities; in his cleverness in maintaining the public form of the whole, the "rights and liberties," both in tune with the tastes of the period and *at the same time* effective; and in the education of the feelings without which it is impossible for a people to be "in condition" — namely, trust, respect for the leading, consciousness of power, contentment, and (when necessary) enthusiasm. But the value of all this depends upon its relation to this basic fact of higher history — that a people is not alone in the world, and that its future will be decided by its force-relationships towards other peoples and powers and not by its mere internal ordering. And, since the ordinary man is not so long-sighted, it is the ruling minority that must possess this quality on behalf of the rest, and not unless there is such a minority does the statesman find the instrument wherewith he can carry his purposes into effect.[1]

III

In the early politics of all Cultures the governing powers are pre-established and unquestioned. The whole being is strictly in patriarchal and symbolic form. The connexions with the mother soil are so strong, the feudal tie, and even its successor the aristocratic state, so self-evident to the life held in their spell, that politics in a Homeric or Gothic age is limited to plain action within the cadre of the given forms. In so far as these forms change, they do so more or less spontaneously, and the idea that it is a *task* of politics to bring about the changes never definitely emerges into anyone's mind, even if a kingdom be overthrown or a nobility reduced to subjection. There is only class-politics, Imperial- or Papal- or vassal-politics. Blood and race speak in actions undertaken instinctively or half-consciously — even the priest behaves, *qua* politician, as the man of race. The "problems" of the State are not yet awakened. The sovereignty, the primary orders, the entire early form-world, are God-given, and it is on them as premises, not about them as objects of dispute, that the organic minorities fight their battles. These minorities we call *Factions*.

It is of the essence of the Faction that it is wholly inaccessible to the idea that the order of things can be changed to a plan. Its object is to win for itself status, power, or possessions within this order — like all growing things in a growing world. There are groups in which relationships of houses, honour and loyalty, bonds of union of almost mythic inwardness, play a part, and from which abstract ideas are totally excluded. Such were the factions of the Homeric and Gothic periods, Telemachus and the suitors in Ithaca, the Blues and Greens under Justinian, the Guelphs and Ghibellines, the Houses of Lancaster and York, the Protestants,[2] the Huguenots, and even later the motive forces of Fronde and First Tyrannis. Machiavelli's book rests entirely on this spirit.

The change sets in as soon as, with the great city, the Non-Estate, the bourgeoisie, takes over the leading rôle.[3] Now it is the reverse, the political *form* becomes the object of conflict, the problem. Heretofore it was ripened,

---

[1] It should scarcely need to be emphasized that this is the basic principle, not of an aristocratic régime, but of government itself. Cleon, Robespierre, Lenin, every gifted mass-leader, has treated his office thus. Anyone who genuinely felt himself as the delegate of the multitude, instead of as the regent of such as do not know what they want, would not remain master of his house for one day. The only question is whether the great popular leaders apply their powers for their own benefit or for that of others; and on that much might be said.

[2] Originally an assembly of nineteen princes and free cities (1529).   [3] See pp. 355, 398, et seq.

now it must needs be shaped. Politics becomes awake, not merely comprehended, but reduced to comprehensible ideas. The powers of intellect and money set themselves up against blood and tradition. In place of the organic we have the organized; *in place of the Estate, the Party*. A party is not a growth of race, but an aggregate of heads, and therefore as superior to the old estates in intellect as it is poorer in instinct. It is the mortal enemy of naturally matured class-ordering, the mere existence of which is in contradiction with its essence. Consequently, the notion of party is always bound up with the unreservedly negative, disruptive, and socially levelling notion of *equality*. Noble ideals are no longer recognized, but only vocational interests.[1] It is the same with the freedom-idea, which is likewise a negative.[2] *Parties are a purely urban phenomenon.* With the emancipation of the city from the country, everywhere (whether we happen to know it evidentially or not) Estate politics gives way to party politics — in Egypt at the end of the Middle Kingdom, in China with the Contending States, in Baghdad and Byzantium with the Abbassid period. In the capitals of the West the parties form in the parliamentary style, in the city-states of the Classical they are forum-parties, and we recognize parties of the Magian style in the Mavali and the monks of Theodore of Studion.[3]

But always it is the Non-Estate, the unit of protest against the essence of Estate, whose leading minority — "educated" and "well-to-do" — comes forward as a party with a program, consisting of aims that are not felt but defined, and of the rejection of everything that cannot be rationally grasped. *At bottom, therefore, there is only one party*, that of the bourgeoisie, the liberal, and it is perfectly conscious of its position as such. It looks on itself as coextensive with "the people." Its opponents (above all, the genuine Estates — namely, "squire and parson") are enemies and traitors to "the people," and its opinions are the "voice of the people" — which is inoculated by all the expedients of party-political nursing, oratory in the Forum, press in the West, until these opinions do fairly represent it.

The prime Estates are nobility and priesthood. The prime Party is that of money and mind, the liberal, the megalopolitan. Herein lies the profound justification, in *all* Cultures, of the ideas of Aristocracy and Democracy. Aristocracy despises the mind of the cities, Democracy despises the boor and hates the countryside.[4] It is the difference between Estate politics and party politics,

[1] Hence it is that on the soil of burgher equality the possession of money immediately takes the place of genealogical rank.

[2] See p. 354.

[3] Pp. 424, et seq. Compare also Wellhausen, *Die relig.-polit. Oppositionsparteien im alten Islam* (1901).

[4] It is an important factor in the democracy of England and America that in the first the yeomanry had died out and in the second has never existed. The "farmer" is spiritually a suburban and in practice carries on his farming as an industry. Instead of villages, there are only fragments of megalopolis.

class-consciousness and party inclination, race and intellect, growth and construction. Aristocracy in the completed Culture, and Democracy in the incipient cosmopolitan Civilization, stand opposed till both are submerged in Cæsarism. As surely as the nobility is *the* Estate (and the Tiers État never manages to get itself into real form in this fashion), so surely the nobility fails to feel as a party, though it may organize itself as one.

It has in fact no choice but to do so. All modern constitutions repudiate the Estates and are built on the Party as self-evidently the basic form of politics. The nineteenth century — correspondingly, therefore, the third century B.C. — is the heyday of party politics. Its democratic character compels the formation counter-parties, and whereas formerly, as late even as the eighteenth century, the "Tiers" constituted itself in imitation of the nobility as an Estate, now there arises the *defensive* figure of the Conservative party, copied from the Liberal,[1] dominated completely by the latter's forms, bourgeois-ized without being bourgeois, and obliged to fight with rules and methods that liberalism has laid down. It has the choice of handling these means better than its adversary[2] or of perishing; but it is of the intimate structure of an Estate that it does not understand the situation and challenges the form instead of the foe, and is thus involved in that use of extreme methods which we see dominating the inner politics of whole states in the early phases of every Civilization, and delivering them helpless into the hands of the enemy. The compulsion that there is upon every party to be bourgeois, at any rate in appearance, turns to sheer caricature when below the bourgeoisie of education and possessions the Residue also organizes itself as a party. Marxism, for example, is in theory a negation of bourgeoisie, but as a party it is in attitude and leadership essentially middle-class. There is a continuous conflict between its will — which necessarily steps outside the bounds of party politics and therefore of constitutionalism (both being exclusively liberal phenomena), and can in honesty only be called civil war — and the appearances which it feels obliged, in justice to itself, to keep up. But for Marxism, again, these appearances are indispensable, at this particular period, if durable success is to be attained. A noble party in a parliament is inwardly just as spurious as a proletarian. Only the bourgeoisie is in its natural place there.

In Rome, from the introduction of the Tribunes, in 471, to the recognition of their legislative omnipotence, in the revolution of 287,[3] patricians and plebeians had fought their fight essentially as Estates, classes. But thereafter these opposite terms possessed hardly more than genealogical significance, and there developed instead parties, to which the terms liberal and conservative

---

[1] And wherever, as in Egypt, India, and the West, there exists a *political* opposition between the two primary Estates, there is also a clerical party — the party, so to speak, of the Church as distinct from religion and of the priest as distinct from the believer.

[2] And with its content of race-strength it has an excellent chance of successfully doing so.

[3] P. 409.

respectively may quite reasonably be applied — namely, the Populus,[1] supreme in the forum, and the nobility, with its fulcrum in the Senate. The latter had transformed itself (about 287) from a family council of the old clans into a state council of the administrative aristocracy. The associations of the Populus are with the property-graded Comitia Centuriata and the big-money group of the Equites, those of the nobility with the yeomanry that was influential in the Comitia Tributa. Think on the one hand of the Gracchi and Marius, and on the other of C. Flaminius, and a little penetration will disclose the complete change in the position of the Consuls and the Tribunes. They are no longer the chosen trustees of the first and third Estates, with lines of conduct determined by that fact, but they represent party, and on occasion change it. There were "liberal" consuls like the Elder Cato and "conservative" Tribunes like the Octavius who opposed Ti. Gracchus. Both parties put up candidates at elections, and used every sort of demagogic operation to get them in — and when money had failed to win an election, it got to work afterwards with (increasing) success upon the person elected.

In England Tories and Whigs constituted themselves, from the beginning of the nineteenth century, as parties, both becoming in form bourgeois and both taking up the liberal program literally, whereby public opinion as usual was completely convinced and set at rest.[2] This was a master-stroke, delivered at the correct moment, and prevented the formation of a party hostile to the Estate-principle such as arose in France in 1789. The members of the lower House, hitherto emissaries of the ruling stratum, became popular representatives, but still continued to depend financially upon it. The leading remained in the same hands, and the opposition of the parties, which from 1830 assumed the titles of Liberal and Conservative almost as a matter of course, was always one of pluses and minuses, never of blank alternatives. In these same years the literary freedom-movement of "young Germany" changed into a party-movement, and in America under Andrew Jackson the National-Whig and Democratic parties organized themselves as opposites, and open recognition was given to the principle that elections were a business, and state offices from top to bottom the "spoils of the victors."[3]

---

[1] *Plebs* corresponds to the "Tiers" (burghers and yeomen) of the eighteenth century, *populus* to the megalopolitan masses of the nineteenth. The difference manifested itself in their respective attitudes towards the freed slaves, mostly of non-Italian origin. These the Plebs, as an order, sought to thrust away into as few tribes as possible, but in the Populus as a party they very soon came to play the decisive rôle.

[2] P. 412.

[3] Simultaneously, too, the Roman Catholic Church quietly changed the basis of its politics from a class to a party, and did so with a strategic sureness that cannot be too much admired. In the eighteenth century it had been, as regards the style of its diplomacy, the allocation of its offices and the spirit of its higher circles, aristocratic through and through. Think of the type of the abbé, and of the prince-prelates who became ministers and ambassadors, like the young Cardinal Rohan. Now, in the true liberal fashion, opinions took the place of origins, working-power that of taste, and the great weapons of democracy — press, elections, money — were handled with a skill that liberalism proper rarely equalled and never surpassed.

But the form of the governing minority *develops steadily from that of the Estate,* *through that of the Party, towards that of the Individual's following.* The outward sign of the end of Democracy and its transition into Cæsarism is not, for example, the disappearance of the party of the Tiers État, the Liberal, but the disappearance of party itself as a form. The sentiments, the popular aim, the abstract ideals that characterize all genuine party politics, dissolve and are supplanted by *private* politics, the unchecked will-to-power of the race-strong few. An Estate has instincts, a party has a program, but a following has a master. That was the course of events from Patricians and Plebeians, through Optimates and Populares, to Pompeians and Cæsarians. The period of real party government covers scarcely two centuries, and in our own case is, since the World War, well on the decline. That the entire mass of the electorate, actuated by a common impulse, should send up men who are capable of managing their affairs — which is the naïve assumption in all constitutions — is a possibility only in the first rush, and presupposes that not even the rudiments of organization by definite groups exists. So it was in France in 1789 and in 1848. An assembly has only to *be*, and tactical units will form at once within it, whose cohesion depends upon the will to *maintain* the dominant position once won, and which, so far from regarding themselves as the mouthpieces of their constituents, set about making all the expedients of agitation amenable to their influence and usable for their purposes. A tendency that has organized itself in the people, has already *ipso facto* become the *tool* of the organization, and continues steadily along the same path until the organization also becomes in turn the tool of the leader. The will-to-power is stronger than any theory. In the beginning the leading and the apparatus come into existence for the sake of the program. Then they are held on to defensively by their incumbents for the sake of power and booty — as is already universally the case to-day, for thousands in every country live on the party and the offices and functions that it distributes. Lastly the program vanishes from memory, and the organization works for its own sake alone.

With the elder Scipio or Quinctius Flamininus comradeship on campaign is still the implication when we speak of their "friends." But the younger Scipio went further and his "Cohors Amicorum" was no doubt the first example of an organized following whose activity extended to the law-courts and the elections.[1] In the same way the old purely *patriarchal and aristocratic relation of loyalty* between patron and client evolved into a community of interest based on very material foundations, and even before Cæsar there were written compacts between candidates and electors with specific provisions as to payment and performances. On the other side, just as in present-day America,[2] clubs and

[1] For what follows see M. Gelzer, *Die Nobilität d. röm. Republik* (1912), pp. 43, et seq.; A. Rosenberg, *Untersuchungen zur röm. Centurienverfassung* (1911), pp. 62, et seq.

[2] The reputation of Tammany Hall in New York is universal, but the relations approximate to this condition in all countries ruled by parties. The American Caucus, which first distributes the

election committees were formed, which so controlled or frightened the mass of the electors of their wards as to be able to do election business with the great leaders, the pre-Cæsars, as one power with another. Far from this being the shipwreck of democracy, it is its very meaning and necessary issue, and the lamentations of unworldly idealists over this destruction of their hopes only show their blind ignorance of the inexorable duality of truths and facts and of the intimate linkage of intellect and money.

Politico-social theory is only one of the bases of party politics, but it is a necessary one. The proud series that runs from Rousseau to Marx has its anti-type in the line of the Classical Sophists up to Plato and Zeno. In the case of China the characteristics of the corresponding doctrines have still to be ex-tracted from Confucian and Taoist literature; it suffices to name the Socialist Moh-ti. In the Byzantine and Arabian literature of the Abbassid period — in which radicalism, like everything else, is orthodox-religious in constitution — they hold a large place, and they were driving forces in all the crises of the ninth century. That they existed in Egypt and in India also is proved by the spirit of events in the Hyksos time and in Buddha's. Literary form is not essential to them — they are just as effectively disseminated by word of mouth, by sermon and propaganda in sects and associations, which indeed is the standard method at the close of the Puritan movements (Islam and Anglo-American Christianity amongst them).

Whether these doctrines are "true" or "false" is — we must reiterate and emphasize — a question without meaning for political history. The refutation of, say, Marxism belongs to the realm of academic dissertation and public debates, in which everyone is always right and his opponent always wrong. But whether they are *effective* — from when, and for how long, the belief that actuality can be ameliorated by a system of concepts is a real force that politics must reckon with — that does matter. We of to-day find ourselves in a period of boundless confidence in the omnipotence of reason. Great general ideas of freedom, Justice, humanity, progress are sacrosanct. The great theories are gospels. Their power to convince does not rest upon logical premises, for the mass of a party possesses neither the critical energy nor the detachment seriously to test them, but upon the sacramental hypostasis in their keywords. At the same time, the spell is limited to the populations of the great cities and the period of Rationalism as the "educated man's religion." [1] On a peasantry it has no hold, and even on the city masses its effect lasts only for a certain time. But *for* that time it has all the irresistibleness of a new revelation. They are converted to it, hang fervently upon the words and the preachers thereof, go to

---

offices of State amongst its members and then forces their names upon the mass-electorate, was introduced into England by Joseph Chamberlain in his "National Liberal Federation," and in Germany its advances have been rapid since 1919.

[1] P. 305.

martyrdom on barricades and battle-field and gallows; their gaze is set upon a political and social other-world, and dry sober criticism seems base, impious, worthy of death.

But for this very reason documents like the *Contrat Social* and the *Communist Manifesto* are engines of highest power in the hands of forceful men who have come to the top in party life and know how to form and to use the convictions of the dominated masses.[1]

The power that these abstract ideals possess, however, scarcely extends in time beyond the two centuries that belong to party politics, and their end comes not from refutation, but from boredom — which has killed Rousseau long since and will shortly kill Marx. Men finally give up, not this or that theory, but the belief in theory of any kind and with it the sentimental optimism of an eighteenth century that imagined that unsatisfactory actualities could be improved by the application of concepts. When Plato, Aristotle, and their contemporaries defined and blended the various kinds of Classical constitution so as to obtain a wise and beautiful resultant, all the world listened, and Plato himself tried to transform Syracuse in accordance with an ideological recipe — and sent the city downhill to its ruin.[2] It appears to me equally certain that it was philosophical experimentation of this kind that put the Chinese southern states out of condition and delivered them up to the imperialism of Tsin.[3] The Jacobin fanatics of liberty and equality delivered France, from the Directory onward, into the hands of Army and Bourse for ever, and every Socialistic oubreak only blazes new paths for Capitalism. But when Cicero wrote his *De re publica* for Pompey, and Sallust his two comminations for Cæsar, nobody any longer paid attention. In Tiberius Gracchus we may discover perhaps an influence derived from the Stoic enthusiast Blossius, who later committed suicide after having similarly brought Aristonicus of Pergamum to ruin;[4] but in the first century b.c. theories had become a threadbare school-exercise, and thenceforward power and power alone mattered.

For us, too — let there be no mistake about it — the age of theory is drawing to its end. The great systems of Liberalism and Socialism all arose between about 1750 and 1850. That of Marx is already half a century old, and it has had no successor. Inwardly it means, with its materialist view of history, that Nationalism has reached its extreme logical conclusion; it is therefore an end-term. But, as belief in Rousseau's Rights of Man lost its force from (say)

[1] P. 18, et seq.

[2] For the story of this tragic experiment, see Ed. Meyer, *Gesch. d. Alt.*, § 987, et seq.

[3] See p. 417. The "plans of the Contending States," the Tchun-tsiu-fan-lu, and the biographies of Sze-ma-tsien are full of examples of the pedagogic in interventions of "wisdom" into the province of politics.

[4] For this "Sun-state" formed of slaves and day-labourers see Pauly-Wissowa, *Realencyel.*, 2, 961. Similarly, the revolutionary King Cleomenes III of Sparta was likewise under the influence of a Stoic, Sphærus. One can understand why "philosophers and rhetors" — i.e., professional politicians, fantastics and subverters — were expelled again and again by the Roman Senate.

1848, so belief in Marx lost its force from the World War. When one contrasts the devotion unto death that Rousseau's ideas found in the French Revolution with the attitude of the Socialists of 1918, who had to keep up before and in their adherents a conviction that they themselves no longer possessed — for the sake, not of the idea, but of the power that depended on it — one discerns also the stretches of the road ahead, where what still remains of program is doomed to fall by the way as being henceforth a mere handicap in the struggle for power. Belief in program was the mark and the *glory* of our grandfathers — in our grandsons it will be a proof of provincialism. In its place is developing even now the seed of a new resigned piety, sprung from tortured conscience and spiritual hunger, whose task will be to found a new Hither-side that looks for secrets instead of steel-bright concepts and in the end will find them in the deeps of the "Second Religiousness." [1]

IV

This is the one side, the verbal side, of the great fact Democracy. It remains now to consider the other, the decisive side, that of race. [2] Democracy would have remained in minds and on paper had there not been amongst its champions true master-natures for whom — unconscious though they may be, and often have been, of the fact — the people is nothing but an object and the ideal nothing but a means. All, even the most irresponsible, methods of demagogy — which inwardly is exactly the same as the diplomacy of the *ancien régime*, but designed for application to masses instead of to princes and ambassadors, to wild opinions and sentiments and will-outbursts instead of to choice spirits, an orchestra of brass instead of old chamber-music — have been worked out by honest but practical democrats, and it was from them that the parties of tradition learnt them.

It is characteristic, however, of the course of democracy, that the authors of popular constitutions have never had any idea of the actual workings of their schemes — neither the authors of the "Servian" Constitution in Rome nor the National Assembly in Paris. Since these forms of theirs are not, like feudalism, the result of growth, but of thought (and based, moreover, not on deep knowledge of men and things, but on abstract ideas of right and justice), a gulf opens between the intellectual side of the laws and — the practical habits that silently form under the pressure of them, and either adapt them to, or fend them off from, the rhythm of actual life. Only experience has ever taught the lesson, and only at the end of the whole development has it been assimilated, that the rights of the people and the influence of the people are two different things. The more nearly universal a franchise is, the *less* becomes the power of the electorate.

[1] P. 310.
[2] P. 114.

In the beginning of a democracy the field belongs to intellect alone. History has nothing nobler and purer to show than the night session of the 4th August 1789 and the Tennis-Court Oath, or the assembly in the Frankfurt Paulskirche on the 18th May 1848 — when men, with power in their very hands, debated general truths so long that the forces of actuality were able to rally and thrust the dreamers aside. But, meantime, that other democratic quantity lost no time in making its appearance and reminding men of the fact that one can make use of constitutional rights only when one has money.[1] That a franchise should work even approximately as the idealist supposes it to work presumes the absence of any organized leadership operating on the electors (in *its* interest) to the extent that its available money permits. As soon as such leadership does appear, the vote ceases to possess anything more than the significance of a censure applied by the multitude to the individual organizations, over whose structure it possesses in the end not the slightest positive influence. So also with the ideal thesis of Western constitutions, the fundamental right of the mass to choose its own representatives — it remains pure theory, for in actuality every developed organization recruits itself.[2] Finally the feeling emerges that the universal franchise contains no effective rights at all, not even that of choosing between parties. For the powerful figures that have grown up on their soil control, through money, all the intellectual machinery of speech and script, and are able, on the one hand, to guide the individual's opinions as they please *above* the parties, and, on the other, through their patronage, influence, and legislation, to create a firm body of whole-hearted supporters (the "Caucus") which excludes the rest and induces in it a vote-apathy which at the last it cannot shake off even for the great crises.

In appearance, there are vast differences between the Western, parliamentary, democracy and the democracies of the Egyptian, Chinese, and Arabian Civilizations, to which the idea of a universal popular franchise is wholly alien. But in reality, for us in this age of ours, the mass is "in form" as an *electorate* in exactly the same sense as it used to be "in form" as a collectivity of obedience — namely, as an *object for a subject* — as it was "in form" in Baghdad as the sects, and in Byzantium in its monks, and elsewhere again as a dominant army or a secret society or a "state within a state." Freedom is, as always, purely *negative*.[3] It consists in the repudiation of tradition, dynasty, Caliphate; but the executive power passes, at once and undiminished, from these institutions to new forces — party leaders, dictators, presidents, prophets, and their

---

[1] The early democracy, which in our case reaches up to Lincoln, Bismarck, and Gladstone, has to learn this by *experience*. The later democracy, in our case mature parliamentarism, starts out from it; here truths and facts finally separate out in the form of party ideals and party funds. It is the money that gives the real parliamentarian his sense of being freed from the dependence which is implicit in the naïve idea that the elector has of his delegate.

[2] P. 452.

[3] P. 354.

adherents — towards which the multitude continues to be unconditionally the passive object.[1] "Popular self-determination" is a courteous figure of speech — in reality, under a universal-inorganic franchise, election has soon ceased to possess its original meaning. The more radical the political elimination of the matured old order of Estates and callings, the more formless and feckless the electoral mass, the more completely is it delivered into the hands of the new powers, the party leaders, who dictate their will to the people through all the machinery of intellectual compulsion; fence with each other for primacy by methods which in the end the multitude can neither perceive nor comprehend; and treat public opinion merely as a weapon to be forged and used for blows at each other. But this very process, viewed from another angle, is seen as an irresistible tendency driving every democracy further and further on the road to suicide.[2]

The fundamental rights of a Classical people (demos, populus) extended to the holding of the highest state and judicial offices.[3] For the exercise of these the people was "in form" in its Forum, where the Euclidean point-mass was corporeally assembled, and there it was the object of an influencing process in the Classical style; namely, by bodily, near, and sensuous means — by a rhetoric that worked upon every ear *and eye;* by devices many of which to us would be repellent and almost intolerable, such as rehearsed sob-effects and the rending of garments;[4] by shameless flattery of the audience, fantastic lies about opponents; by the employment of brilliant phrases and resounding cadenzas (of which there came to be a perfect repertory for this place and purpose) by games and presents; by threats and blows; but, above all, by money. We have its beginnings in the Athens of 400,[5] and its appalling culmination

[1] That the mass all the same *feels* itself as freed is simply another outcome of the profound incompatibility between megalopolitan spirit and mature tradition. Its *acts*, so far from being independent, are in inward relation with its subjection to money-rule.

[2] The German Constitution of 1919 — standing by virtue of its date on the verge of the *decline* of democracy — most naïvely admits a dictatorship of the party machines, which have attracted all rights into themselves and are seriously responsible to no one. The notorious system of proportional election and the Reichslist [see *Ency. Brit.*, 1922 Supplement, II, 249. — *Tr.*] secures their self-recruitment. In place of the "people's" rights, which were axiomatic in the Frankfurt Constitution of 1848, there is now only the right of parties, which, harmless as it sounds, really nurses within itself a Cæsarism of the organizations. It must be allowed, however, that in this respect it is the most advanced of all the constitutions. Its issue is visible already. A few quite small alterations and it confers unrestricted power upon individuals.

[3] And *legislation*, too, was bound up with an office. Even when, as a formality, acceptance or rejection by an assembly was requisite, the law in question could be brought in only by an official; for example, a Tribune. The constitutional demands of the masses, therefore (which in any case were mostly instigated by the real power-holders), expressed themselves in the issue of the elections to office, as the Gracchan period shows.

[4] Even Cæsar, at fifty years of age, was obliged to play this comedy at the Rubicon for his soldiers because they were used to it and expected it when anything was asked of them. It corresponds to the "chest-tones of deep conviction" of our political assemblies.

[5] But the Cleon type must obviously have existed also in contemporary Sparta, and in Rome at the time of the Consular Tribunes.

in the Rome of Cæsar and Cicero. As everywhere, the elections, from being nominations of class-representatives, have become the battle-ground of party candidates, an arena ready for the intervention of money, and, from Zama onwards, of ever bigger and bigger money. "The greater became the wealth which was capable of concentration in the hands of individuals, the more the fight for political power developed into a question of money." [1] It is unnecessary to say more. And yet, in a deeper sense, it would be wrong to speak of corruption. It is not a matter of degeneracy, it is the democratic ethos itself that is foredoomed of necessity to take such forms when it reaches maturity. In the reforms of the Censor Appius Claudius (310), who was beyond doubt a true Hellenist and constitutional ideologue of the type of Madame Roland's circle, there was certainly no question but that of the franchise as such, and not at all of the arts of gerrymandering — but the effect was simply to prepare the way for those arts. Not in the scheme as such, but from the first applications of it, race-quality emerged, and very rapidly it forced its way to complete dominance. And, after all, in a dictatorship of money it is hardly fair to describe the employment of money as a sign of decadence.

The career of office in Rome from the time when its course took form as a series of elections, required so large a capital that every politician was the debtor of his entire entourage. Especially was this so in the case of the ædileship, in which the incumbent had to outbid his predecessors in the magnificence of his public games, in order later to have the votes of the spectators. (Sulla failed in his first attempt on the prætorship precisely because he had not previously been ædile.) Then again, to flatter the crowd of loafers it was necessary to show oneself in the Forum daily with a brilliant following. A law forbade the maintenance of paid retainers, but the acquisition of persons in high society by lending them money, recommending them for official and commercial employments, and covering their litigation expenses, in return for their company in the Forum and their attendance at the daily levee, was more expensive still. Pompey was *patronus* to half the world. From the peasant of Picenum to the kings of the Orient, he represented and protected them all, and this was his political capital which he could stake against the non-interest-bearing loans of Crassus and the "gilding" [2] of every ambitious fellow by the conqueror of Gaul. Dinners were offered to the electors of whole wards, [3] or free seats for the gladiatorial shows, or even (as in the case of Milo) actual cash, delivered at home — out of respect, Cicero says, for traditional morals. Election-capital rose to American dimensions, sometimes hundreds of millions of sesterces; vast as was the stock of cash available in Rome, the elections of 54 locked up so much of it that the rate of interest rose from four to eight per cent. Cæsar

[1] Gelzer, *Nobilität*, p. 94; along with Ed. Meyer's *Cæsar* this book gives the best survey of Roman democratic methods.

[2] "*Inaurari,*" to which end Cicero recommended his friend Trebatius to Cæsar.

[3] "*Tributim ad prandium vocare,*" Cicero, *Pro Murena*, 72.

paid out so much as ædile that Crassus had to underwrite him for twenty millions before his creditors would allow him to depart to his province, and in his candidature for the office of Pontifex Maximus he so overstrained his credit that failure would have ruined him, and his opponent Catulus could seriously offer to buy him off. But the conquest and exploitation of Gaul — this also an undertaking motived by finance — made him the richest man in the world. In truth, Pharsalus was won there in advance.[1] For it was for *power* that Cæsar amassed these milliards, like Cecil Rhodes, and not because he delighted in wealth like Verres or even like Crassus, who was first and foremost a financier and only secondarily a politician. Cæsar grasped the fact that on the soil of a democracy constitutional rights signify nothing without money and everything with it. When Pompey was still dreaming that he could evoke legions by stamping on the ground, Cæsar had long since condensed the dream to reality with his money. It must be clearly understood, however, that he did not introduce these methods but found them in existence, that he made himself master of them but never identified himself with them. For practically a century parties grouped on principles had been dissolving into personal followings grouped upon men who pursued private political aims and were expert in handling the political weapons of their time.

Amongst these means, besides money, was influence upon the courts. Since Classical assemblies voted, but did not debate, the trial before the rostra was *a form of party battle* and the school of schools for political persuasiveness. The young politician began his career by indicting and if possible annihilating some great personage,[2] as the nineteen-year-old Crassus annihilated the renowned Papirius Carbo, the friend of the Gracchi, who had later gone over to the Optimates. This was why Cato was tried no less than forty-four times, though acquitted in every case. The legal side of the question was entirely subordinate in these affairs.[3] The decisive factors were the party affinities

---

[1] For from that time sesterces flowed through his hands by the million. The votive treasures of the Gallic temples which he put up for sale in Italy sent down the value of gold with a rush. From King Ptolemy he and Pompey extorted 144,000,000 (and Gabinius another 240,000,000) as the price of recognition. The Consul Æmilius Paullus (50) was bought for 36,000,000, Curio for 60,000,000. We can guess from such figures how enviable was the position of his closer associates. At the triumph of 46 every soldier in an army of well over 100,000 men received 24,000 sesterces, officers and other leaders much more. Yet at his death the state treasury was still full enough to secure Antony's position.

[2] Gelzer, op. cit., p. 68.

[3] Extortion and corruption were the usual charges. As in those days these things were identical with politics, and the judges and plaintiffs had acted precisely in the same way as the defendants, the art consisted in using the forms of a well-acted ethical passion to cover a party speech, of which the real import was only comprehensible to the initiated. This corresponds entirely with the modern parliamentary usage. The "people" would be very much astonished to see party opponents, after delivering wild speeches in the chamber (for the reporters) chatting together in the lobbies, or to be told how a party passionately champions a proposal after it has made certain by agreement with the other side that it will not be passed. In Rome, too, the judgment was not the important thing in these "trials"; it was enough if a defendant voluntarily left the city and so retired from the occupancy of, or candidature for, office.

of the judges, the number of patrons, and the size of the crowd of backers — the number of the witnesses was really only paraded in order to bring the financial and political power of the plaintiff into the limelight. The intention in all Cicero's oratory against Verres was to convince the judges, under the veil of fine ethical passion, that the condemnation of the accused was *in the interests of their order*. Given the general outlook of the Classical, the courts self-evidently existed to serve private and party interests. Democratic complainants in Athens were accustomed at the end of their speeches to remind the jurymen from the people that they would forfeit their fees by acquitting the wealthy defendant.[1] The tremendous power of the Roman Senate consisted mainly in their occupancy of every seat of the judicial (jurors') bench, which placed the destinies of every citizen at their mercy; hence the far-reachingness of the Gracchan law of 122 which handed over the judicature to the Equites and delivered over the nobility — that is, the official class — to the financial world.[2] In 83 Sulla, simultaneously with his proscription of the financial magnates, restored the judicature to the Senate, *as political weapon*, of course, and the final duel of the potentates finds one more expression in the ceaseless changing of the judges selected.

Now, whereas the Classical, and supremely the Forum of Rome, drew the mass of the people together as a visible body in order to compel it to make that use of its rights which was desired of it, the "contemporary" English-American politics have created *through the press* a force-field of world-wide intellectual and financial tensions in which every individual unconsciously takes up the place allotted to him, so that he must think, will, and act as a ruling personality somewhere or other in the distance thinks fit. This is dynamics against statics, Faustian against Apollinian world-feeling, the passion of the third dimension against the pure sensible present. Man does not speak to man;[3] the press and its associate, the electrical news-service, keep the waking-consciousness of whole peoples and continents under a deafening drum-fire of theses, catchwords, standpoints, scenes, feelings, day by day and year by year, so that every Ego becomes a mere function of a monstrous intellectual Something. Money does not pass, politically, from one hand to the other. It does not turn itself into cards and wine. It is turned into *force*, and its quantity determines the intensity of its working influence.

Gunpowder and printing belong together — both discovered at the culmination of the Gothic, both arising out of Germanic technical thought — as *the two grand means* of Faustian distance-tactics. The Reformation in the beginning of

---

[1] See Pöhlmann, *Griech. Gesch.* (1914), pp. 236, et seq. [Cf. Aristophanes, *Wasps.* — Tr.]

[2] Thus it was possible for Rutilius Rufus to be condemned in the notorious case of 93, because as proconsul he had in accordance with his duty proceeded against the extortions of the concessionnaire associations.

[3] Radio broadcasting has now emerged to enable the leader to make personal conquests of the million, and no one can foretell the changes in political tactic that may ensue therefrom. — Tr.

the Late period witnessed the first flysheets and the first field-guns, the French Revolution in the beginning of the Civilization witnessed the first tempest of pamphlets of the autumn of 1788 and the first mass-fire of artillery at Valmy. But with this the printed word, produced in vast quantity and distributed over enormous areas, became an uncanny weapon in the hands of him who knew how to use it. In France it was still in 1788 a matter of expressing private convictions, but England was already past that, and deliberately seeking to produce impressions on the reader. The war of articles, flysheets, spurious memoirs, that was waged from London on French soil against Napoleon is the first great example. The scattered sheets of the Age of Enlightenment transformed themselves into "the Press" — a term of most significant anonymity. Now the *press campaign* appears as the prolongation — or the preparation — of war by other means, and in the course of the nineteenth century the strategy of outpost fights, feints, surprises, assaults, is developed to such a degree that a war may be lost ere the first shot is fired — because the Press has won it meantime.

To-day we live so cowed under the bombardment of this intellectual artillery that hardly anyone can attain to the inward detachment that is required for a clear view of the monstrous drama. The will-to-power operating under a pure democratic disguise has finished off its masterpiece so well that the object's sense of freedom is actually flattered by the most thorough-going enslavement that has ever existed. The liberal bourgeois mind is *proud* of the abolition of censorship, the last restraint, while the dictator of the press — Northcliffe! — keeps the slave-gang of his readers under the whip of his leading articles, telegrams, and pictures. *Democracy has by its newspaper completely expelled the book from the mental life of the people.* The book-world, with its profusion of standpoints that compelled thought to select and criticize, is now a real possession only for a few. The people reads the *one* paper, "its" paper, which forces itself through the front doors by millions daily, spellbinds the intellect from morning to night, drives the book into oblivion by its more engaging layout, and if one or another specimen of a book does emerge into visibility, forestalls and eliminates its possible effects by "reviewing" it.

What is truth? For the multitude, that which it continually reads and hears. A forlorn little drop may settle somewhere and collect grounds on which to determine "the truth" — but what it obtains is just *its* truth. The other, the public truth of the moment, which alone matters for effects and successes in the fact-world, is to-day a product of the Press. What the Press wills, is true. Its commanders evoke, transform, interchange truths. Three weeks of press work, and the truth is acknowledged by everybody.[1] Its bases are irrefutable for

---

[1] The most striking example of this for future generations will be the "War-guilt" question, which is the question — *who* possesses the power, through control of press and cable in all parts of the world, to establish in world-opinion that truth which he needs for his political ends and to maintain it for so long as he needs it? An altogether different question (which only in Germany is confused with the first) is the purely scientific one — to *whose* interest was it that an event about which there was already a whole literature should occur in the summer of 1914 in particular?

just so long as money is available to maintain them intact. The Classical rhetoric, too, was designed for effect and not content — as Shakespeare brilliantly demonstrates in Antony's funeral oration — but it did limit itself to the bodily audience and the moment. What the dynamism of our Press wants is *permanent* effectiveness. It must keep men's minds continuously under its influence. Its arguments are overthrown as soon as the advantage of financial power passes over to the counter-arguments and brings these still oftener to men's eyes and ears. At that moment the needle of public opinion swings round to the stronger pole. Everybody convinces himself at once of the new truth, and regards himself awakened out of error.

With the political press is bound up the need of universal school-education, which in the Classical world was completely lacking. In this demand there is an element — quite unconscious — of desiring to shepherd the masses, as the object of party politics, into the newspaper's power-area. The idealist of the early democracy regarded popular education, without *arrière pensée*, as enlightenment pure and simple, and even to-day one finds here and there weak heads that become enthusiastic on the Freedom of the Press — but it is precisely this that smooths the path for the coming Cæsars of the world-press. Those who have learnt to read succumb to their power, and the visionary self-determination of Late democracy issues in a thorough-going determination of the people by the powers whom the printed word obeys.

In the contests of to-day tactics consists in depriving the opponent of this weapon. In the unsophisticated infancy of its power the newspaper suffered from official censorship which the champions of tradition wielded in self-defence, and the bourgeoisie cried out that the freedom of the spirit was in danger. Now the multitude placidly goes its way; it has definitively won for itself this freedom. But in the background, unseen, the new forces are fighting one another by buying the press. Without the reader's observing it, the paper, *and himself with it*, changes masters.[1] Here also money triumphs and forces the free spirits into its service. No tamer has his animals more under his power. Unleash the people as reader-mass and it will storm through the streets and hurl itself upon the target indicated, terrifying and breaking windows; a hint to the press-staff and it will become quiet and go home. The Press to-day is an army with carefully organized arms and branches, with journalists as officers, and readers as soldiers. But here, as in every army, the soldier obeys blindly, and war-aims and operation-plans change without his knowledge. The reader

---

[1] In preparation for the World War the press of whole countries was brought financially under the command of London and Paris, and the peoples belonging to them reduced to an unqualified intellectual slavery. The more democratic the inner form of a nation is, the more readily and completely it succumbs to this danger. This is the style of the twentieth century. To-day a democrat of the old school would demand, not freedom for the press, but freedom from the press; but meantime the leaders have changed themselves into parvenus who have to secure their postion *vis-à-vis* the masses.

neither knows, nor is allowed to know, the purposes for which he is used, nor even the rôle that he is to play. A more appalling caricature of freedom of thought cannot be imagined. Formerly a man did not dare to think freely. Now he dares, but cannot; his will to think is only a willingness to think to order, and this is what he feels as *his* liberty.

And the other side of this belated freedom — it is permitted to everyone to say what he pleases, *but* the Press is free to take notice of what he says or not. It can condemn any "truth" to death simply by not undertaking its communication to the world — a terrible censorship of silence, which is all the more potent in that the masses of newspaper readers are absolutely unaware that it exists.[1] Here, as ever in the birth-pangs of Cæsarism, emerges a trait of the buried springtime.[2] The arc of happening is about to close on itself. Just as in the concrete and steel buildings the expression-will of early Gothic once more bursts forth, but cold, controlled, and Civilized, so the iron will of the Gothic Church to power over souls reappears as — the "freedom of democracy." The age of the "book" is flanked on either hand by that of the sermon and that of the newspaper. Books are a personal expression, sermon and newspaper obey an impersonal *purpose*. The years of Scholasticism afford the only example in world-history of an intellectual discipline that was applied universally and permitted no writing, no speech, no thought to come forth that contradicted the *willed* unity. This is spiritual dynamics. Classical, Indian, or Chinese mankind would have been horrified at this spectacle. But the same things recur, and as a *necessary* result of the European-American liberalism — "the despotism of freedom against tyranny," as Robespierre put it. In lieu of stake and faggots there is the great silence. The dictature of party leaders supports itself upon that of the Press. The competitors strive by means of money to detach readers — nay, peoples — *en masse* from the hostile allegiance and to bring them under their own mind-training. And all that they learn in this mind-training, is what it is considered that they should know — a higher will puts together the picture of their world for them. There is no need now, as there was for Baroque princes, to impose military-service liability on the subject — one whips their souls with articles, telegrams, and pictures (Northcliffe!) until they *clamour* for weapons and force their leaders into a conflict to which they *willed* to be forced.

This is the end of Democracy. If in the world of truths it is *proof* that decides all, in that of facts it is *success*. Success means that one being triumphs over the others. Life has won through, and the dreams of the world-improvers have turned out to be but the tools of *master*-natures. In the Late Democracy, *race* bursts forth and either makes ideals its slaves or throws them scornfully into the pit. It was so, too, in Egyptian Thebes, in Rome, in China — but in no

[1] The great Burning of the Books in China (p. 433) was innocuous by comparison.
[2] P. 434.

other Civilization has the will-to-power manifested itself in so inexorable a form as in this of ours. The thought, and consequently the action, of the mass are kept under iron pressure — for which reason, and for which reason only, men are permitted to be readers and voters — that is, in a dual slavery — while the parties become the obedient retinues of a few, and the shadow of coming Cæsarism already touches them. As the English kingship became in the nineteenth century, so parliaments will become in the twentieth, a solemn and empty pageantry. As then sceptre and crown, so now peoples' rights are paraded for the multitude, and all the more punctiliously the less they really signify — it was for this reason that the *cautious* Augustus never let pass an opportunity of emphasizing old and venerated customs of Roman freedom. But the power is migrating even to-day, and correspondingly elections are degenerating for us into the farce that they were in Rome. Money organizes the process in the interests of those who possess it,[1] and election affairs become a preconcerted game that is staged as popular self-determination. If election was originally *revolution in legitimate forms*,[2] it has exhausted those forms, and what takes place is that mankind "elects" its Destiny again by the primitive methods of bloody violence when the politics of money become intolerable.

Through money, democracy becomes its own destroyer, after money has destroyed intellect. But, just *because* the illusion that actuality can allow itself to be improved by the ideas of any Zeno or Marx has fled away; because men have learned that in the realm of reality one power-will *can be overthrown only by another* (for that is the great human experience of Contending States periods); there wakes at last a deep yearning for all old and worthy tradition that still lingers alive. Men are tired to disgust of money-economy. They hope for salvation from somewhere or other, for some real thing of honour and chivalry, of inward nobility, of unselfishness and duty. And now dawns the time when the form-filled powers of the blood, which the rationalism of the Megalopolis has suppressed, reawaken in the depths. Everything in the order of dynastic tradition and old nobility that has saved itself up for the future, everything that there is of high money-disdaining ethic, everything that is intrinsically sound enough to be, in Frederick the Great's words, the *servant* — the hard-working, self-sacrificing, caring *servant* — of the State, all that I have described elsewhere in one word as Socialism in contrast to Capitalism [3] — all this becomes suddenly the focus of immense life-forces. Cæsarism *grows* on the soil of Democracy, but its roots thread deeply into the underground of blood tradition. The Classical

---

[1] Herein lies the secret of why all radical (i e., poor) parties necessarily become the tools of the money-powers, the Equites, the Bourse. Theoretically their enemy is capital, but practically they attack, not the Bourse, but Tradition on behalf of the Bourse. This is as true of to-day as it was for the Gracchan age, and in all countries. Fifty per cent of mass-leaders are procurable by money, office, or opportunities to "come in on the ground-floor," and with them they bring their whole party.

[2] P. 415.

[3] See *Preussentum und Sozialismus*, p. 41, et seq.

Cæsar derived his power from the Tribunate, and his dignity and therewith his permanency from his being the Princeps. Here too the soul of old Gothic wakens anew. The spirit of the knightly orders overpowers plunderous Viking-ism. The mighty ones of the future may possess the earth as their private property — for the great political form of the Culture is irremediably in ruin — but it matters not, for, formless and limitless as their power may be, it has a task. And this task is the unwearying care for this world as it is, which is the very opposite of the interestedness of the money-power age, and demands high honour and conscientiousness. But for this very reason there now sets in the final battle between Democracy and Cæsarism, between the leading forces of dictatorial money-economics and the *purely political* will-to-order of the Cæsars. And in order to understand this *final battle between Economics and Politics*, in which the latter *reconquers* its realm, we must now turn our glance upon the physiognomy of economic history.

CHAPTER XIII

THE FORM-WORLD OF ECONOMIC LIFE

(A)

MONEY

THE FORM–WORLD OF ECONOMIC LIFE

(A)

MONEY

I

THE standpoint from which to comprehend the economic history of great Cultures is not to be looked for on economic ground. Economic thought and action are a side of life that acquires a false appearance when regarded as a self-contained *kind* of life. Least of all is the secure standpoint to be had on the basis of the present-day world-economics, which for the last 150 years has been mounting fantastically, perilously, and in the end almost desperately — an economics, moreover, that is exclusively Western-dynamic, anything but common-human.

That which we call national economy to-day is built up on premises that are openly and specifically English. The industry of machines, which is unknown to all other Cultures, stands in the centre as though it were a matter of course and, without men being conscious of the fact, completely dominates the formulation of ideas and the deduction of so-called laws. Credit-money, in the special form imparted to it by the relations of world-trade and export-industry in a peasantless England, serves as the foundation whereupon to define words like capital, value, price, property — and the definitions are then transferred without more ado to other Culture-stages and life-cycles. The insular position of England has determined a conception of politics, and of its relation to economics, that rules in all economic theories. The creators of this economic *picture* were David Hume [1] and Adam Smith.[2] Everything that has since been written about them or against them always presupposes the critical structure and methods of their systems. This is as true of Carey and List as it is of Fourier and Lassalle. As for Smith's greatest adversary, Marx, it matters little how loudly one protests against English capitalism when one is thoroughly imbued with its images; the protest is itself a recognition, and its only aim is, through a new kind of accounting, to confer upon objects the advantage of being subjects.

From Adam Smith to Marx it is nothing but self-analysis of the economic thinking of a single Culture on a particular development-level. Rationalistic through and through, it starts from Material and its conditions, needs, and

---

[1] *Political Discourses*, 1752.
[2] The celebrated *Wealth of Nations*, 1776.

motives, instead of from the *Soul* — of generations, Estates, and peoples — and its creative power. It looks upon men as constituent parts of situations, and knows nothing of the big personality and history-shaping will, of individuals or of groups, the will that sees in the facts of economics not ends but means. It takes economic life to be something that can be accounted for without remainder by visible causes and effects, something of which the structure is quite mechanical and completely self-contained and even, finally, something that stands in some sort of causal relation to religion and politics — these again being considered as individual self-contained domains. As this outlook is the systematic and not the historical, the timeless and universal validity of its concepts and rules is an article of faith, and its ambition is to establish the one and only correct method of applying "the" science of management. And accordingly, wherever its truths have come into contact with the facts, it has experienced a complete fiasco — as was the case with the prophecies of bourgeois theorists concerning the World War,[1] and with those of proletarian theorists on the induction of the Soviet economy.

Up to now, therefore, there has been no national economy, in the sense of a morphology of the economic *side* of life and more particularly of that side in the life of the high Cultures, with their formations — concordant as to stage, tempo, and duration — of economic styles. Economics has no system, but a physiognomy. To fathom the secret of its inner form, its *soul*, demands the physiognomic flair. To succeed in it it is necessary to be a "judge" of it as one is a "judge" of men or of horses, and requires even less "knowledge" than that which a horseman needs to have of zoölogy. But this faculty of "judgment" can be awakened, and the way to awaken it is through the sympathetic outlook on history which gives a shrewd idea of the race-instincts, which are at work in the economic as in other constituents of active existence, symbolically shaping the external position — the economic "stuff," the need — in harmony with their own inner character. *All economic life is the expression of a soul-life.*

This is a new, a German, outlook upon economics, an outlook from beyond all Capitalism and Socialism — both of which were products of the jejune rationality of the eighteenth century, and aimed at nothing but a material analysis and subsequent synthesis of the economic surface. All that has been taught hitherto is no more than preparatory. Economic thought, like legal,[2] stands now on the verge of its true and proper development, which (for us, as for the Hellenistic-Roman age) sets in only where art and philosophy have irrevocably passed away.

The attempt which follows is meant only as a flying survey of the possibilities here available.

---

[1] It was the opinion of the expert, almost everywhere, that the economic consequences of general mobilization would compel the breaking-up of hostilities within a few weeks.

[2] P. 81.

Economics and politics are sides of the *one* livingly flowing current of being, and not of the waking-consciousness, the intellect.[1] In each of them is manifested the pulse of the cosmic flowings that are occluded in the sequent generations of individual existences. They may be said, not to *have* history, but to *be* history. Irreversible Time, the When, rules in them. They belong, both of them, to race and not, as religion and science belong, to language with its spatial-causal tensions; they regard facts, not truths. There are economic *Destinies* as there are political, whereas in scientific doctrines, as in religious, there is *timeless connexion of cause and effect.*

Life, therefore, has a political and an economic kind of "condition" of fitness for history. They overlie, they support, they oppose each other, but the political is unconditionally the first. Life's will is to preserve itself and to prevail, or, rather, to make itself stronger in order that it may prevail. But in the economic state of fitness the being-streams are fit as *self*-regarding, whereas in a political they are fit as *other*-regarding. And this holds good all along the series, from the simplest unicellular plant to swarms and to peoples of the highest free mobility in space. Nourishment and winning-through — the difference of dignity between the two sides of life is recognizable in their relation to death. There is no contrast so profound as that between *hunger-death and hero-death.* Economically life is in the widest sense threatened, dishonoured, and *debased* by hunger — with which is to be included stunting of possibilities, straitened circumstances, darkness, and pressure not less than starvation in the literal sense. Whole peoples have lost the tense force of their race through the gnawing wretchedness of their living. Here men die *of* something and not *for* something. Politics sacrifices men for an idea; they fall for an idea; but economy merely wastes them away. *War is the creator, hunger the destroyer, of all great things.* In war life is elevated by death, often to that point of irresistible force whose mere existence guarantees victory, but in the economic life hunger awakens the ugly, vulgar, and wholly unmetaphysical sort of fearfulness for one's life under which the higher form-world of a Culture miserably collapses and the naked struggle for existence of the human beasts begins.

The double sense of all history that is manifested in man and woman has been discussed in an earlier chapter.[2] There is a private history which *represents* "life in space" as a procreation-series of the generations, and a public history that *defends and secures it* as a political "in-form"-ness — the "spindle side" and the "sword side" of being. They find expression in the ideas of Family and of State, but also in the primary form of the house [3] wherein the good spirits of the marriage-bed — the Genius and the Juno of every old Roman dwelling — were protected by that of the door, the Janus. To this private history of the family

---

[1] Pp. 1, et seq., and 335.
[2] P. 327, et seq.
[3] Pp. 95, 120, et seq.

the economic now attached itself. The duration of a flourishing life is inseparable from its strength; its secret of begetting and conceiving is seen at its purest in the being of breed-strong peasant stock that is rooted, healthy and fruitful, in its soil. And as in the form of the body the organ of sex is bound up with that of the circulation,[1] so the middle of the house in *another* sense is formed by the sacred hearths, the Vesta.

For this very reason the significance of economic history is something quite different from that of political. In the latter the foreground is taken up by the great individual destinies, which fulfil themselves indeed in the binding forms of their epoch, but are nevertheless, each in itself, strictly personal. The concern of the former, and of family history, is the course of development of the form-*language;* everything once-occurring and personal is an unimportant private-destiny, and only the basic form common to the million cases matters. But even so economics is only a foundation, for Being that is in any way meaningful. What really signifies is not *that* an individual or a people is "in condition," well nourished and fruitful, but *for what* he or it is so; and the higher man climbs historically, the more conspicuously his political and religious will to inward symbolism and force of expression towers above everything in the way of form and depth that the economic life as such possesses. It is only with the coming of the Civilization, when the whole form-world begins to ebb, that mere life-preserving begins to outline itself, nakedly and insistently — this is the time when the banal assertion that "hunger and love" are the driving forces of life ceases to be ashamed of itself; when life comes to mean, not a waxing in strength for the task, but a matter of "happiness of the greatest number," of comfort and ease, of "*panem et circenses*"; and when, in the place of grand politics, we have economic politics as an end in itself.

Since economics belongs to the race side of life, it possesses, like politics, a customary ethic and not a moral — yet again the distinction of nobility and priesthood, facts and truths. A vocation-class, like an Estate, possesses a *matter-of-course.* feeling for (not good and evil, but) good and bad. Not to have this feeling is to be void of honour, law. For those engaged *in* the economic life, too, honour stands as central criterion, with its tact and fine flair for what is "the right thing" — something quite separate from the sin-idea underlying the religious contemplation *of* the world. There exist, not only a very definite vocational honour amongst merchants, craftsmen, and peasants, but equally definite gradations downward for the shopkeeper, the exporter, the banker, the contractor, and even, as we all know, for thieves and beggars, in so far as two or three of them feel themselves as fellow practitioners. No one has stated or written out these customary-ethics, but they exist, and, like class-ethics everywhere and always, they are binding only within the circle of membership. Along with the noble virtues of loyalty and courage, chivalry and

[1] P. 5.

comradeship, which are found in every vocational society, there appear clean-cut notions of the ethical value of industry, of success, of work, and an astonishing sense of distinction and apartness. This sort of thing a man *has* — and without knowing much about it, for custom is evidenced to consciousness only when it is infringed — while, on the contrary, the prohibitions of religion which are timeless, universally valid, but never realizable ideals, must be, learned before a man can know or attempt to follow them.

Religious-ascetic fundamentals such as "selfless," "sinless," are without meaning in the economic life. For the true saint economics in itself is sinful,[1] and not merely taking of interest or pleasure in riches or the envy of the poor. The saying concerning the "lilies of the field" is for deeply religious (and philosophical) natures unreservedly true. The whole weight of their being lies outside economics and politics and all other facts of "this world." We see it in Jesus's times and St. Bernard's and in the Russian soul of to-day; we see it too in the way of life of a Diogenes and a Kant. For its sake men choose voluntary poverty and itinerancy and hide themselves in cells and studies. Economic activity is *never* found in a religion or a philosophy, always only in the political organism of a *church* or the social organism of a theorizing fellowship; it is ever a compromise with "this world" and an index of the presence of a will-to-power.[2]

II

That which may be called the economic life of the plant is accomplished on and in it without its being itself anything but the theatre and will-less object of a natural process.[3] This element underlies the economy of the human body also, still unalterably vegetal and dreamy, pursuing its will-less (in this respect almost alien) existence in the shape of the circulatory organs. But when we come to the animal body freely mobile in space, being is not alone — it is accompanied by waking-being, the comprehending apprehension, and, therefore, the compulsion to *provide by independent* thought for the preservation of life. Here begins

---

[1] "*Negotium*" (by which is meant every form of gainful activity; business is *commercium*) "*negat otium neque quærit veram quietem quæ est deus*," are the words of the *Decretum Gratiani* (cf. p. 77).

[2] Pilate's question settles also the relation of economy to science. The religious man will always try in vain, catechism in hand, to improve the instincts of his political environment. But it goes on its way undisturbed and leaves him to his thoughts. The saint can only choose between adapting himself to this environment — and then he becomes a Church politician and conscienceless — and fleeing from it into a hermitage or even into the Beyond. But the same happens also — and here not without a comic side to it — in the intellectualism of the city. The philosopher who has built up an ethical-social system that is replete with virtue and (of course) the only true one, may enlighten the economic life as to how it should behave and at what it should aim. It is even the same spectacle, whether labelled liberal, anarchistic, or socialistic, or derived from Plato, Proudhon, or Marx. Here, too, economy carries on undisturbed and leaves the thinker to choose between withdrawing to pour out on paper his lamentations of this world, and entering it as an economic politician, in which case he either makes himself ridiculous, or else promptly throws his theory to the devil and starts to win himself a leading place.

[3] See pp. 1, et seq.

life-anxiety, leading to touch and scent, sight and hearing with ever-sharper senses; and presently to movements in space for the purpose of searching, gathering, pursuing, tricking, stealing, which develop in many species of animals (such as beavers, ants, bees, numerous birds and beasts of prey) into a rudimentary economy-technique which presupposes a process of reflection and, therefore, a certain emancipation of understanding from sensation. Man is genuinely man inasmuch as his understanding has freed itself from sensation and, as thought, intervened creatively in the relations between microcosm and macrocosm.[1] Quite animal still is the trickery of woman towards man, and equally so the peasant's shrewdness in obtaining small advantages — both differing in no wise from the slyness of the fox, both consisting in the ability to see into the secret of the victim at *one glance*. But on the top of this there supervenes, now, the economic *thought* that sows a field, tames animals, changes and appreciates and exchanges things, and finds a thousand ways and means of better preserving life and transforming a dependence upon the environment into a mastery over it. That is the underlayer of all Cultures. Race makes use of an economic thought that can become so powerful as to detach itself from given purposes, build up castles of abstraction, and finally lose itself in Utopian expanses.

All higher economic life develops itself on and over a peasantry. Peasantry, *per se*, does not presuppose any basis but itself.[2] It is, so to say, race-in-itself, plantlike and historyless,[3] producing and using wholly for itself, with an outlook on the world that sweepingly regards every other economic existence as incidental and contemptible. To this *producing* kind of economy there is presently opposed an *acquisitive* kind, which makes use of the former as an object — as a source of nourishment, tribute, or plunder. Politics and trade are in their beginnings quite inseparable, both being masterful, personal, warlike, both with a hunger for power and booty that produces quite another outlook upon the world — an outlook not from an angle into it, but from above down on its tempting disorder, an outlook which is pretty candidly expressed in the choice of the lion and the bear, the hawk and the falcon, as armorial badges. Primitive war is always also booty-war, and primitive trade intimately related to plunder and piracy. The Icelandic sagas narrate how, often, the Vikings would agree with a town population for a market-peace of a fortnight, after which weapons were drawn and booty-making started.

Politics and trade in developed form — the art of achieving material successes over an opponent by means of intellectual superiority — are both a replacement of war by other means. Every kind of diplomacy is of a business

---

[1] See p. 6.

[2] Exactly the same is true of wandering bands of hunters and pastorals. But the economic foundation of the great Culture is always a mankind that adheres fast to the soil, and nourishes and supports the higher economic forms.

[3] See p. 331.

nature, every business of a diplomatic, and both are based upon penetrative judgment of men and physiognomic tact. The adventure-spirit in great seafarers like the Phœnicians, Etruscans, Normans, Venetians, Hanseatics, the spirit of shrewd banking-lords like the Fugger and the Medici and of mighty financiers like Crassus and the mining and trust magnates of our own day, must possess the strategic talent of the *general* if its operations are to succeed. Pride in the clan-house, the paternal heritage, the family tradition, develops and counts in the economic sphere as in the political; the great fortunes are like the kingdoms and have their history,[1] and Polycrates and Solon, Lorenzo de' Medici and Jürgen Wullenweber are far from being the only examples of political ambitions developing out of commercial.

But the genuine prince and statesman wants to rule, and the genuine merchant only wants to be wealthy, and here the acquisitive economy divides to pursue aim and means separately.[2] One may aim at booty for the sake of power, or at power for the sake of booty. The great ruler, too, the Hwang-ti, the Tiberius, the Frederick II — has the will to wealth, the will to be "rich in land and subjects," but it is with and under a sense of high responsibilities. A man may lay hands on the treasurers of the whole world with a good conscience, not to say as a matter of course: he may lead a life of radiant splendour or even dissipation — if only he feels himself (Napoleon, Cecil Rhodes, the Roman Senate of the third century) to be the engine of a mission. When he feels so, the idea of private property can scarcely be said to exist so far as he is concerned.

He who is out for purely economic advantages — as the Carthaginians were in Roman times and, in a far greater degree still, the Americans in ours — is correspondingly incapable of purely political *thinking*. In the decisions of high politics he is ever deceived and made a tool of, as the case of Wilson shows — especially when the absence of statesmanlike instinct leaves a chair vacant for moral sentiments. This is why the great economic groupings of the present day (for example, employers' and employees' unions) pile one political failure on another, unless indeed they find a real political politician as leader, and he — makes use of them. Economic and political thinking, in spite of a high degree of consonance of form, are in direction (and therefore in all tactical details) basically different. Great business successes[3] awaken an unbridled sense of *public* power — in the very word "capital" one catches an unmistakable undertone of this. But it is only in a few individuals that the colour and direction of their willing and their criteria of situations of things undergo change. Only

---

[1] Undershaft in Shaw's *Major Barbara* is a true ruler-figure of this realm.

[2] P. 344. As a means for governments it is called finance-economy (financial policy). Here the whole nation is the object of a levy of tribute, in the forms of taxes and customs, of which the purpose is not to make, so to say, the upkeep of its life more comfortable, but to secure its historical position and to enhance its power.

[3] Using the phrase widely, as including, for instance, the rise of workmen, journalists, and men of learning to positions of leadership.

when a man has really ceased to feel his enterprise as "his own business," and its aim as the simple amassing of property, does it become possible for the captain of industry to become the statesman, the Cecil Rhodes. But, conversely, the men of the political world are exposed to the danger of their will and thought for historical tasks degenerating into mere provision for their private life-upkeep; then a nobility can become a robber-order, and we see emerging the familiar types of princes and ministers, demagogues and revolution-heroes, whose zeal exhausts itself in lazy comfortableness and the piling-up of immense riches — there is little to choose in this respect between Versailles and the Jacobin Club, business bosses and trade-union leaders, Russian governors and Bolshevists. And in the maturity of democracy the politics of those who have "got there" is identical, not merely with business, but with speculative business of the dirtiest great-city sort.

All this, however, is the very manifestation of the hidden course of a high Culture. In the beginning appear the primary orders, nobility and priesthood, with their symbolism of Time and Space. The political life, like the religious experience, has its fixed place, its ordained adepts, and its allotted aims for facts and truths alike, in a well-ordered society,[1] and down below, the economic life moves unconscious along a sure path. Then the stream of being becomes entangled in the stone structures of the town, and intellect and money thenceforward take over its historical guidance. The heroic and the saintly with their youthful symbolic force become rarer, and withdraw into narrower and narrower circles. Cool bourgeois clarity takes their place. At bottom, the concluding of a system and the concluding of a deal call for one and the same kind of professional intelligence. Scarcely differentiated now by any measure of symbolic force, political and economic life, religious and scientific experience make each other's acquaintance, jostle one another, commingle. In the frictions of the city the stream of being loses its strict rich form. Elementary economic factors come to the surface and interplay with the remains of form-imbued politics, just as sovereign science at the same time adds religion to its stock of objects. Over a life of economics political self-satisfaction spreads a critical-edifying world-sentiment. But out of it all emerge, in place of the decayed Estates, the individual life-courses, big with true political or religious force, that are to become destiny for the whole.

And thus we begin to discern the morphology of economic history. First there is a *primitive economy* of "man," which — like that of plants and animals — follows a biological [2] time-scale in the development of its forms. It completely dominates the primitive age, and it continues to move on, infinitely slowly and confusedly, underneath and between the high Cultures. Animals and plants are brought into it and transformed by taming and breeding, selection

---

[1] P. 331.
[2] P. 31.

and sowing; fire and metals are exploited, and the properties of inorganic nature made by technical processes serviceable for the conduct of life. All this is perfused with political-religious ethic and meaning, without its being possible distinctly to separate Totem and Taboo, hunger, soul-fear, sex-love, art, war, sacrificial rites, belief, and experience.

Wholly different from this, both in idea and in evolution, and sharply marked off in tempo and duration, are the *economic histories of the high Cultures*, each of which has its own economic style. To feudalism belongs the economy of the townless countryside. With the State ruled radially from cities appears the urban economy of money, and this rises, with the oncoming of the Civilization, into the dictature of money, simultaneously with the victory of world-city democracy. Every Culture has its own independently developed form-world. Bodily money of the Apollinian style (that is, the stamped coin) is as antithetical to relational money of the Faustian-dynamic style (that is, the booking of credit-units) as the Polis is to the State of Charles V. But the economic life, just like the social, forms itself pyramidally.[1] In the rustic underground a thoroughly primitive condition maintains itself almost unaffected by the Culture. The Late urban economy, which is already the activity of a resolute minority, looks down with steady contempt upon the pristine land-economy that continues all around it, while the latter in turn glares sulkily at the intellectualized style that prevails within the walls. Finally the cosmopolis brings in a Civilized world-economy, which radiates from very small nuclei within a few centres, and subjects the rest to itself as a provincial economy, while in the remoter landscapes thoroughly primitive ("patriarchal") custom often prevails still. With the growth of the cities the way of life becomes ever more artificial, subtle and complex. The great-city worker of Cæsar's Rome, of Haroun-al-Raschid's Baghdad, and of the present-day Berlin feels as self-evidently necessary much that the richest yeoman deep in the country regards as silly luxury, but this self-evident standard is hard to reach and hard to maintain. In every Culture the quantum of work grows bigger and bigger till at the beginning of every Civilization we find an intensity of economic life, of which the tensions are even excessive and dangerous, and which it is impossible to maintain for a long period. In the end a rigid, permanent-set condition is reached, a strange hotch-potch of refined-intellectual and crude-primitive factors, such as the Greeks found in Egypt and we have found in modern India and China — unless, of course, the crust is being disintegrated from below by the pressure of a young Culture, like the Classical in Diocletian's time.

Relatively to this economic movement, men are economically "in form" as an economic *class*, just as they are in form for world-history as a political Estate. Each individual has an economic position *within the economic order* just as he has a grade of some sort in the *society*. Now, both these kinds of allegiances

---

[1] See pp. 172 and 280.

make claims upon the feelings, thoughts, and relations all at once. A life insists on being, and on meaning something as well, and the confusion of our ideas is made worse confounded by the fact that, to-day, as in Hellenistic times, political parties, in their desire to ameliorate the *upkeep*-standards of certain economic groups, have elevated these groups to the dignity of a political Estate, as Marx, for instance, elevated the class of factory-workers.

Confusion — for the first and genuine Estate is nobility. From it the officer and the judge and all concerned in the highest duties of government and administration are direct derivatives. They are Estate-like formations that *mean* something. So, too, the body of scholars and scientists belongs to the priesthood [1] and has a very sharply definite kind of class-exclusiveness. But the grand symbolism of the Estates goes out with castle and cathedral. The *Tiers*, already, is the Non-Estate, the remainder, a miscellaneous and manifold congeries, which means very little as such save in the moments of political protest, so that the importance it creates *for itself* is a party importance. The individual is conscious of himself not *as* a bourgeois, but *because* he is a "liberal" and thus part and parcel of a great thing, not indeed as representing it in his person, but as *adhering* to it from conviction. In consequence of this weakness of its social "form," the economic "form" of the bourgeoisie becomes all the more relatively conspicuous in its callings, guilds and unions. In the cities, at any rate, a man is primarily designated according to the way in which he makes his living.

Economically, the first (and anciently almost the only) mode of life is that of the peasant,[2] which is pure *production*, and therefore the pre-condition of every other mode. Even the primary Estates, too, in early times, base their way of life entirely upon hunting, stock-keeping, and agricultural landowning, and even in Late periods land is regarded by nobles and priests as the only truly honourable kind of property. In opposition to it stands trade, the mode of the acquisitive *middleman* or intervener,[3] powerful out of all proportion to its numbers, already indispensable even in quite early conditions — a refined parasitism, completely unproductive and, therefore, land-alien and far-ranging, "free," and unhampered spiritually, too, by the ethic and the practice of the countryside, a life sustaining itself on another life. Between the two, now, a third kind of economy, the *preparatory* economy of technics, grows up in numberless crafts, industries, and callings, which creatively apply reflections upon

---

[1] Including the medical profession, which indeed is indistinguishable in primitive times from the priests and magicians.

[2] Herdsmen, fishermen, and hunters included. There is, moreover, a strange and very profound relation between peasant and miner, evidenced in ancient sagas and rites. The metals are coaxed out of the shaft as the corn out of the earth, and the game out of the thicket. And for the real miner even metal is something that *lives* and grows.

[3] This is true from the earliest sea-voyaging to the Bourse of the world-city, and all traffic, whether by river, road, or rail belongs with it.

nature and whose honour and conscience are bound up in achievement.[1] Its oldest guild, which reaches back into the sheer primitive and fills the picture of this primitive with its dark sagas and rites and notions, is the guild of the smiths, who — as the result of their proud aloofness from the peasantry and the fear that hangs about them, and leads to their being venerated and banned by turns — have often become true tribes with a race of their own, as in the case of the Abyssinian Falasha or "Black Jews."[2]

In these three economics of production, preparation, and distribution, as in everything else belonging to politics and life at large, there are *the subjects and objects of leading* — in this case, whole groups that dispose, decide, organize, discover; and other whole groups whose function is simply to execute. The grading may be hard and definite or it may be scarcely perceptible,[3] promotion may be impossible or unimpeded, the relative dignity of the task may be almost equal throughout a long scale of slow transitions or different beyond comparison. Tradition and law, talent and possessions, population numbers, cultural level, and economic situation may effectively override this basic antithesis of subjects and objects — but it exists, it is as much a premiss as life itself, and it is unalterable. Nevertheless, economically *there is no worker-class;* that is an invention of theorists who have fixed their eyes on the position of factory-workers in England — an industrial, peasantless land in a transitional phase — and then extended the resultant scheme so confidently over all the Cultures and all the ages that the politicians have taken it up and used it as a means of building themselves parties. In actuality there is an almost uncountable number of purely serving activities in workshop and counting-houses, office and cargo-deck, roads, mine-shafts, fields, and meadows. This counting-up, portering, running of errands, hammering, serving, and minding often enough lacks that element which elevates life above mere upkeep and invests work with the dignity and the delight attaching, for example, to the status-duties of the officer and the savant, or the personal triumphs of the engineer, the manager, and the merchant — but, even apart from that, all these things are quite

---

[1] With this belong the machine industry, with its purely Western type of the inventor and engineer, and practically, also, a great part of the modern agronomy, as, for instance, in America.

[2] Even to-day the mining and metal industries are felt to be somehow nobler than, for example, the chemical and electrical. They possess the most ancient patent of nobility in the technical world, and a relic of cult-mystery lies over them.

[3] That is, up to the limit of servage and slavery, although very often — as in the present-day East and as in Rome in the case of "vernæ" — slavery itself may be nothing but a form of compulsory-labour contract and, apart from that, hardly sensible. The free employee often lives in far stricter subjection and enjoys far less respect, and his formal right to "give notice" is in many cases practically valueless to him.

[British readers will recall in this connexion the "Chinese slavery" controversy in South Africa in 1904, and the questions of indentured labour that come to the surface not infrequently in Australian politics. And in an older generation defenders of slavery as practised in the sugar islands of the West Indies are still to be found — not to mention the survivors and tradition-bearers of the "Old South" in the United States. — Tr.]

incapable of being compared amongst themselves. The brain or brawn of the work, its situation in village or in megalopolis, the duration and intensity of the doing of it, bring it to pass that farm-labourers, bank clerks, and tailors' hands live in perfectly different economic worlds, and it is only, I repeat, the party politics of quite Late phases that lures them by means of catchwords into a protest-combination, with the intention of making use of its aggregate mass. The classical slave, on the contrary, is such chiefly in terms of constitutional law — that is, so far as the body-Polis was concerned, he simply did not exist [1] — but economically he might be land-worker or craftsman, or even director or wholesale merchant with a huge capital (*peculium*), with palaces and country villas and a host of subordinates — freemen included. And what he could become, over and above this, in late Roman times will appear in the sequel.

III

With the oncoming of Spring there begins in every Culture an economic life of settled form.[2] The life of the population is entirely that of the peasant on the open land. The experience of the town has not yet come. All that elevates itself from amongst the villages, castles, palaces, monasteries, temple-closes, is not a city, but a *market*, a mere meeting-point of yeomen's interests, which also acquired, and at once, a certain religious and political meaning, but certainly cannot be said to have had a special life of its own. The inhabitants, even though they might be artisans or traders, would still *feel* as peasants, and even in one way or another work as such.

That which separates out from a life in which everyone is alike producer and consumer is *goods*, and traffic in goods is the mark of all early intercourse, whether the object be brought from the far distance or merely shifted about within the limits of the village or even the farm. A piece of goods is that which adheres by some quiet threads of its essence to the life that has produced it or the life that uses it. A peasant drives "his" cow to market, a woman puts away "her" finery in the cupboard. We say that a man is endowed with this world's "goods"; the word "pos*session*" takes us back right into the plantlike origin of property, into which this particular being — no other — has grown, from the roots up.[3] Exchange in these periods is a process whereby goods pass from one circle of life into another. They are valued with reference to life, according to a sliding-scale of *felt* relation to the moment. There is neither a conception of value nor a kind or amount of goods that constitutes a general measure —

---

[1] P. 60.

[2] We know this accurately for the Egyptian and the Gothic beginnings, and in general terms for the Chinese and the Classical; as for the *economic pseudomorphosis* of the Arabian (see pp. 189, et seq., 349) it may be summarized, after Hadrian, as a process of disintegration of the highly civilized Classical money-economy culminating in the appearance, under Diocletian, of a Springtime barter-economy with, in the East, the true Magian element of bargaining visibly superposed.

[3] P. 343.

for gold and coin are goods too, whose rarity and indestructibility causes them to be highly prized.[1]

Into the rhythm and course of this barter the dealer only comes as an intervener.[2] In the market the acquisitive and the creative economics encounter one another, but even at places where fleets and caravans unload, trade only appears as the *organ* of countryside traffic.[3] It is the "eternal" form of economy, and is even to-day seen in the immemorially ancient figure of the pedlar of the country districts remote from towns, and in out-of-the-way suburban lanes where small barter-circles form naturally, and in the private economy of savants, officials, and in general everyone not actively part of the daily economic life of the great city.

With the soul of the town a quite other kind of life awakens.[4] As soon as the market has become the town, it is not longer a question of mere centres for goods-streams traversing a purely peasant landscape, but of a second world within the walls, for which the merely producing life "out there" is nothing but object and means, and out of which another stream begins to circle. The decisive point is this — the true urban man is *not* a producer in the prime terrene sense. He has not the inward linkage with soil or with the goods that pass through his hands. He does not live with these, but looks at them from outside and appraises them in relation to his own life-upkeep.

With this goods become wares, exchange turnover, *and in place of thinking in goods we have thinking in money*.

With this a purely extensional something, a form of limit-defining, is abstracted from the visible objects of economics just as mathematical thought abstracts something from the mechanistically conceived environment. Abstract

[1] Neither the copper pieces of the Italian Villanova-graves of early Homeric times (Willers *Gesch. d. röm. Kupferprägung*, p. 18) nor the early Chinese bronze coins in the form of women's drapery (*pu*), bells, rings, or knives (*tsien*, Conrady, *China*, p. 504) are described as money, but quite distinctly symbols of goods. And the coins struck by the governments of early Gothic times (in imitation of the Classical) as signs of sovereignty figured in economic life only as wares; a piece of gold is worth as much as a cow, *but not vice versa*.

[2] Hence it is that so often he is not an outcome of the fixed and self-contained life of the country-side, but an alien appearing in it, an alien having neither importance nor antecedents. This is the rôle of the Phœnicians in the earliest period of the Classical; of the Romans in the East in Mithradates's time; of the Jews, and with them Byzantines, Persians, and Armenians, in the Gothic West; of the Arabs in the Sudan; of the Indians in East Africa; and of the West-Europeans in present-day Russia.

[3] And, consequently, on a very small scale. As foreign trade was in those days highly adventurous and appealed to the imagination, it was as a rule immensely exaggerated. The "great" merchants of Venice and the Hansa about 1300 were hardly the equals of the more distinguished craftsmen. The turnover of even the Medici or the Fugger about 1400 was equivalent to that of a shop-business in a small town to-day. The largest merchant vessels, in which usually several traders held part shares, were much smaller than modern German river-barges, and made only *one* considerable voyage each year. The celebrated wool-export of England, a main element of Hanseatic trade, amounted about 1270 to hardly as much as the contents of two modern goods-trains (Sombart, *Der moderne Kapitalismus*, (I, pp. 280, et seq.).

[4] P. 91.

money corresponds exactly to abstract number.[1] Both are entirely inorganic. The economic picture is reduced exclusively to quantities, whereas the important point about "goods" had been their quality. For the early-period peasant "his" cow is, first of all, just what it is, a unit being, and only secondarily an object of exchange; but for the economic outlook of the true townsman the only thing that exists is an abstract money-value which at the moment happens to be in the shape of a cow that can always be transformed into that of, say, a bank-note. Even so the genuine engineer sees in a famous waterfall not a unique natural spectacle, but just a calculable quantum of unexploited energy.

It is an error of all modern money-theories that they start from the value-token or even the material of the payment-medium instead of from the form of economic thought.[2] In reality, money, like number and law, is a *category of thought*. There is a monetary, just as there is a juristic and a mathematical and a technical, thinking of the world-around. From the sense-experience of a house we obtain quite different abstracts, according as we are mentally appraising it from the point of view of a merchant, a judge, or an engineer, and with reference to a balance-sheet, a lawsuit, or a danger of collapse. Next of kin to thinking in money, however, is mathematics. To think in terms of business is to calculate. The money-value is a numerical value measured by a unit of reckoning.[3] This exact "value-in-itself," like number-in-itself, the man of the town, the man without roots, is the first to imagine; for peasants there are only ephemeral felt values in relation to now this and now that object of exchange. What he does not use, or does not want to possess, has "no value" for him. Only in the economy-picture of the real townsman are there objective values and kinds of values which have an existence apart from his private needs, as thought-elements of a generalized validity, although in actuality every individual has his proper system of values and his proper stock of the most varied kinds of value, and feels the ruling prices of the market as "cheap" or "dear" with reference to these.[4]

Whereas the earlier mankind *compares* goods, and does so not by means of the reason only, the later *reckons* the values of wares, and does so by rigid un-

[1] Cf. Vol. I, Ch. II.

[2] Marks and dollars are no more "money" than metres and grammes are "forces." *Pieces* of money are real values. It is only our ignorance of Classical physics that has saved us from confusing gravitation with a pound-weight — in our mathematics, with its Classical basis, we still mix number with magnitude, and our imitation of Classical coinage has brought about the same confusion between money and pieces of money.

[3] Conversely, therefore, we can call the metric system (cm., g.) a valuation, and in fact all money-measures proceed from the weight theories of physics.

[4] Similarly all value-theories, however objective they are meant to be, are developed — and inevitably so — out of a subjective principle. That of Marx, for example, defines value in the way that promotes the interest of the manual worker, the effort of the discoverer or the organizer seeming to him, therefore, valueless. But it would be wrong to describe this as "erroneous." All these theories are "right" for their supporters and "wrong" for their opponents, and it is not reasons but *life* that settles whether one is a supporter or an opponent.

qualitative measures. Now gold is no longer measured against the cow, but the cow against the gold, and the result is expressed by an abstract number, the price. Whether and how this measure of value finds symbolic expression in a value-sign — as the written, spoken, or represented number-sign is, in a sense, number — depends on the economic style of the particular Culture, each of which produces a different sort of money. The common condition for the appearance of this is the existence of an urban population that thinks economically in terms of it, and it is its particular character that settles whether the value-token shall serve also as payment-medium; thus the Classical coin and *probably* the Babylonian silver did so serve, whereas the Egyptian *deben* (raw copper weighed out in pounds) was a measure of exchange, but neither token nor payment-medium. The Western and the "contemporary" Chinese banknote,[1] again, is a medium, but not a measure. In fact we are accustomed to deceive ourselves thoroughly as to the rôle played by coins of precious metal in *our* sort of economy; they are just wares fashioned in imitation of the Classical custom, and hence, measured against book-values of credit money, they have a "price."

The outcome of this way of thinking is that the old *possession*, bound up with life and the soil, gives way to the *fortune*, which is essentially mobile and qualitatively undefined: it does not *consist in* goods, but it is *laid out in* them. Considered by itself, it is a purely numerical quantum of money-value.[2]

As the seat of this thinking, the city becomes the money-market, the centre of values, and a stream of money-values begins to infuse, intellectualize, and command the stream of goods. *And with this the trader, from being an organ of economic life, becomes its master.* Thinking in money is always, in one way or another, trade or business thinking. It presupposes the productive economy of the land, and, therefore, is always primarily acquisitive, for there is no third course. The very words "acquisition," "gain," "speculation," point to a profit tricked off from the goods *en route* to the consumer — an *intellectual plunder* — and for that reason are inapplicable to the early peasantry. Only by attuning ourselves exactly to the spirit and economic outlook of the true townsman can we realize what they mean. He works not for needs, but for sales, for "money." The business view gradually infuses itself into every kind of activity. The countryman, inwardly bound up with traffic in goods, was at once giver and taker, and even the trader of the primitive market was hardly an exception to this rule. But with money-traffic there appears between producer and consumer, as though between two separate worlds, the third party, the *middleman*, whose thought is dominated *a priori* by the business side of life. He forces the producer to offer, and the consumer to inquire of him. He elevates mediation

---

[1] The Western introduced (on a very modest scale) by the Bank of England from the end of the eighteenth century, the Chinese dating from the period of the Contending States.

[2] And is thought of as "amount," whereas we speak of the "extent" of a property in goods.

to a monopoly and thereafter to economic primacy, and forces the other two to be "in form" in *his* interest, to prepare the wares according to *his* reckonings, and to cheapen them under the pressure of *his* offers.

He who commands this mode of thinking is the master of money.[1] In all the Cultures evolution takes this road. Lysias informs us in his oration against the corn-merchants that the speculators at the Piræus frequently spread reports of the wreck of a grain-fleet or of the outbreak of war, in order to produce a panic. In Hellenistic-Roman times it was a widespread practice to arrange for land to go out of cultivation, or for imports to be held in bond, in order to force up prices. In the Egyptian New Empire wheat-corners in the American style were made possible by a bill-discounting that is fully comparable with the banking operations of the West.[2] Cleomenes, Alexander the Great's administrator for Egypt, was able by book transactions to get the whole corn-supply into his own hands, thereby producing a famine far and wide in Greece and raking in immense gains for himself. To think economically on any terms but these is simply to become a mere pawn in the money-operations of the great city. This style of thought soon gets hold of the waking-consciousness of the entire urban population and, therefore, of everyone who plays any serious part in the conduct of economic history. "Peasant" and "burgher" stand not only for the difference of country and city, but for that of possessions and money as well. The splendid Culture of Homeric and Provençal princely courts was something that waxed and waned with the men themselves — we can often, even to-day, see it in the life of old families in their country-seats — but the more refined culture of the bourgeoisie, its "comfort," is something coming from outside, something that can be paid for.[3] All highly developed economy is urban economy. World-economy itself, the characteristic economy of all Civilizations, ought properly to be called world-city-economy. The destinies even of this world-economy are now decided in a few places, the "money-markets of the world[4] — in Babylon, Thebes, and Rome, in Byzantium and Baghdad, in London, New York, Berlin, and Paris. The residue is a starveling provincial economy that runs on in its narrow circles without being conscious of its utter dependence. Finally, money is the form of intellectual energy in which the ruler-will, the political and social, technical and mental, creative power, the craving for a full-sized life, are concentrated. Shaw is entirely right when he says: "The universal regard for money is the one hopeful fact

[1] Even to the modern pirates of the money-market who intervene amongst the interveners and gamble with money as "wares."

[2] Preisigke, *Girowesen im griechischen Ægypten* (1910). These trading forms of the Ptolemaic period were already in vogue, and at the same high level, under the XVIIIth Dynasty.

[3] So also with the bourgeois ideal of freedom. In theory and, therefore, constitutionally, a man may be free *in principle*, but *actually*, in the economic private-life of the cities, he is made free only by money.

[4] The name "bourse" can be applied even in other Cultures, if by that word we mean the thought-organ of a developed money-economy.

in our civilization . . . the two things [money and life] are inseparable: money is the counter that enables life to be distributed socially: it *is* life. . . ."[1] What is here described as Civilization, then, is the stage of a Culture at which tradition and personality have lost their immediate effectiveness, and every idea, to be actualized, has to be put into terms of money. At the beginning a man was wealthy because he was powerful — now he is powerful because he has money. Intellect reaches the throne only when money puts it there. Democracy is the completed equating of money with political power.

Through the economic history of every Culture there runs a desperate conflict waged by the soil-rooted tradition of a race, by its *soul*, against the spirit of money. The peasant-wars of the beginning of a Late period (in the Classical, 700–500; in the Western, 1450–1650; in the Egyptian, end of Old Kingdom) are the first reaction of the blood against the money that is stretching forth its hand from the waxing cities over the soil.[2] Stein's warning that "he who mobilizes the soil dissolves it into dust" points to a danger common to *all* Cultures; if money is unable to attack possession, it insinuates itself into the thoughts of the noble and peasant possessors, until the inherited possession that has grown with the family's growth begins to seem like resources merely "put into" land and soil and, so far as their essence is concerned, mobile.[3] Money aims at mobilizing *all* things. World-economy is the actualized economy of values that are completely detached in thought from the land, and made fluid.[4] The Classical money-thinking, from Hannibal's day, transformed whole cities into coin and whole populations into slaves and thereby converted both into money that could be brought from everywhere to Rome, and used outwards from Rome as a power.

The Faustian money-thinking "opens up" whole continents, the water-

---

[1] Preface to *Major Barbara* (Constable, London 1909).

[2] P. 343.

[3] The "farmer" is the man whose connexion with the piece of land is no longer anything more than practical.

[4] The increasing intensity of this thinking appears in the economic picture as a *growth of the available money-mass*, which is abstract and imagined and has nothing to do with the visible supply of gold as a ware. The "stiffening" of the money-market, for example, is a purely intellectual process played out in the hands of a small handful of men. The increasing energy of money-thinking consequently awakens, in every Culture, the feeling that the "value of money is going down" — enormously so, for example, in the time between Solon and Alexander — with reference, namely, to the unit of calculation. What actually happens is that the mercantile units of value have become artificial and no longer comparable with the primary and livingly experiential values of the peasant economy. In the end it ceases to matter in what figures the Attic treasure of the Delian League (454) or the sums involved in the peace-treaties of 241 and 201, or the booty of Pompey in 64 are reckoned, and whether we ourselves shall pass in a few decades from the milliards — still unknown in 1850, but commonplace to-day — to the billions. There is no common standard for the value of a talent in 430 and in 30 B.C., for gold, like cattle and corn, has continually altered not only its own numeration, but its significance within an ever-advancing urban economy. The only steady element is the fact that quantity of money — not to be confused with the stock of tokens and the means of payment — is an *alter ego* mirroring thought in money.

power of gigantic river-basins, the muscular power of the peoples of broad regions, the coal measures, the virgin forests, the laws of Nature, and transforms them all into financial energy, which is laid out in one way or in another — in the shape of press, or elections, or budgets, or armies — for the realization of masters' plans.   Ever new values are abstracted from whatever world-stock is still, from the business point of view, unclaimed, "the slumbering spirits of gold," as John Gabriel Borkman says; and what the things themselves are, apart from this, is of no economic significance at all.

IV

As every Culture has its own mode of thinking in money, so also it has its proper money-symbol through which it brings to visible expression its principle of valuation in the economic field.   This something, a sense-actualizing of the thought, is in importance fully the equal of the spoken, written, or drawn figures and other symbols of the mathematic.   Here lies a deep and fruitful domain of inquiry, so far almost unexplored.   Not even the basic notions have been correctly enunciated, and it is therefore quite impossible to-day to translate intelligibly the money-idea that underlay the barter and the bill business of Egypt, the banking of Babylonia, the book-keeping of China, and the capitalism of the Jews, Parsees, Greeks, and Arabs from Haroun-al-Raschid's day.   All that is possible is to set forth the essential opposition of Apollinian and Faustian money — the one, *money as magnitude*, and the other, *money as function*.[1]

Economically, as in other ways, Classical man saw his world-around as a sum of bodies that changed their place, travelled, drove or hit or annihilated one another, as in Democritus's description of Nature.   Man was a body among bodies, and the Polis as sum thereof a body of higher order.   All the needs of life consisted in corporeal quantities, and money, too, therefore represented such a body, in the same way as an Apollo-statue represented a god.   About 650, simultaneously with the stone body of the Doric temple and the free statue true-modelled in the round, appeared the *coin*, a metal weight of beautiful impressed form.   Value as a magnitude had long existed — in fact as long as this Culture itself.   In Homer, a talent is a little aggregate of gold, in bullion and decorative objects, of a definite total weight.   The Shield of Achilles represents "two talents" of gold, and even as late as Roman times it was usual to specify silver and gold vessels by weight.[2]

The discovery of the Classically formed money-body, however, is so extraordinary that we have not even yet grasped it in its deep and purely Classical significance.   We regard it as one of the "achievements of humanity," and so we strike these coinages everywhere, just as we put statues in our streets and squares.   So much and no more it is within our power to do; we can imitate

[1] Cf. Vol. I, Ch. II.
[2] Friedländer, *Röm. Sittengesch.*, IV (1921), p. 301.

the shape, but we cannot impart the same economic significance thereto. The coin *as money* is a purely Classical phenomenon — only possible in an environment conceived wholly on Euclidean ideas, but there creatively dominant over all economic life. Notions like income, resources, debt, capital, meant in the Classical cities something quite different from what they mean to us. They meant, not economic energy radiating from a point, but a sum of valuable objects in hand. Wealth was always a mobile *cash-supply*, which was altered by addition and subtraction of valuable objects and had nothing at all to do with possessions in land — for in Classical thinking the two were completely separate. Credit consisted in the lending of cash in the expectation that the loan would be repaid in cash. Catiline was poor because, in spite of his wide estates,[1] he could find nobody to lend him the cash that he needed for his political aims; and the immense debts of Roman politicians [2] had for their ultimate security, not their equivalent in land, but the definite prospect of a province to be plundered of its movable assets.[3]

In the light of this, and only in the light of this, we begin to understand certain phenomena such as the mass-execution of the wealthy under the Second Tyrannis, and the Roman proscriptions (with the object of seizing a large part of the cash current in the community), and the melting down of the Delphian temple-treasure by the Phocians in the Sacred War, of the art-treasures of Corinth by Mummius, and of the last votive offerings in Rome by Cæsar, in Greece by Sulla, in Asia Minor by Brutus and Cassius, without regard to artistic value when the noble stuffs and metals and ivory were needed.[4] The captured statues and the vessels borne in the triumphs were, in the eyes of the spectators, sheer cash, and Mommsen [5] could attempt to determine the site of Varus's disaster by the places in which coin-hoards were unearthed — for the Roman veteran carried his whole property in precious metal on his person. Classical wealth does not consist in having possessions, but piling money; a Classical money-market was not a centre of credit like the bourses of our world and of

[1] Sallust, *Catilina*, 35, 3.

[2] P. 458.

[3] How difficult it was for Classical man to figure to himself the transformation of a physically indefinable asset like land into bodily money is shown by the stone posts (ὅροι) on land in Greece, which were meant to *represent* the mortgages on it, and by the Roman method of sale *per æs et libram*, in which a clod of earth was handed over for a coin in the presence of witnesses. Consequently, trade in goods (properly so called) never existed, nor anything like, for example, a current price for arable land. A regular relation between land-value and money-value was as unthinkable to the Classical mind as such a relation between artistic value and money-value. Intellectual — i.e., incorporeal — products like dramas and frescoes possessed economically no value at all. For the Classical idea of law, cf. p. 81.

[4] Not very much can have been left of Classical art-treasures even by Augustus's time. The refined Athenians themselves thought far too unhistorically to be moved to spare a chryselephantine statue merely because it was the work of Phidias. It is worth remembering that the gold parts of the famous Athene-figure of the Parthenon cella were made removable and tested for weight from time to time. Economic use of them, therefore, was provided for from the outset.

[5] *Ges. Schriften*, IV, 200, et seq.

ancient Thebes, but a city in which an important part of the world's cash was actually collected. It may be taken that in Cæsar's time much more than half of the Classical world's gold was in Rome.

But when, from about Hannibal's time, this world advanced into the state of unlimited plutocracy, the naturally limited mass of precious metals and materially valuable works of art in its sphere of control became hopelessly inadequate to cover needs, and a veritable craving set in for new bodies capable of being used as money. Then it was that men's eyes fell upon the slave, who was another sort of body, but a thing and not a person [1] and capable, therefore, of being thought of as money. From that point Classical slavery became unique of its kind in all economic history. The properties of the coin were extended to apply to living objects, and the stock of men in the regions "opened up" to the plunderings of proconsuls and tax-farmers became as interesting as the stock of metal. A curious sort of double valuation developed. The slave had a market price, although ground and soil had not. He served for the accumulation of great uninvested fortunes, and hence the enormous slave-masses of the Roman period, which are entirely inexplicable by any other sort of necessity. So long as man needed only as many slaves as he could gainfully employ, their number was small and easily covered by the prisoners of war and judgment-debtors.[2] It was in the sixth century that Chios made a beginning with the importation of bought slaves (Argyronetes). The difference between these and the far more numerous paid labourers was originally of a political and legal, not an economic kind. As the Classical economy was static and not dynamic, and was ignorant of the systematic opening-up of energy-sources, the slaves of the Roman age did not exist to be exploited in work, but were employed — more or less — so that the greatest possible number of them could be maintained. Specially presentable slaves possessing particular qualifications of one sort or another were preferred, because for equal cost of maintenance they represented a better asset; they were loaned as cash was loaned; and they were allowed to have businesses on their account, so that they could become rich; [3] free labour was undersold — all this so as to cover at any rate the upkeep of this capital.[4] The bulk of them cannot have been employed at all. They answered their purpose by simply existing, as a stock of money in hand which was not bound up to a natural limit

[1] P. 600.

[2] The belief that slaves ever constituted, even in Athens or Ægina, as much as a third of the population is a complete delusion. On the contrary, the revolutions of the period after 400 presuppose an enormous surplus of free paupers.

[3] P. 480.

[4] Herein lies the difference between this slavery and the sugar-slavery of our own Baroque. The latter represents a threshold phase of our *machine industry*, an organization of "living" energy, which began with man-fuel, but presently passed over to coal-fuel; and slavery came to be considered immoral only when coal had established itself. Looked at from this angle, the victory of the North in the American Civil War (1865) meant the economic victory of the concentrated energy of coal over the simple energy of the muscles.

like the stock of metal available in those days. And through that very fact the need of slaves grew and grew indefinitely and led, not only to wars that were undertaken simply for slave-getting, but to slave-hunting by private entrepreneurs all along the Mediterranean coasts (which Rome winked at) and to a new way of making the proconsuls' fortunes, which consisted in bleeding the population of a region and then selling it into slavery for debt. The market of Delos must have dealt with ten thousand slaves a day. When Cæsar went to Britain, the disappointment caused in Rome by the money-poverty of the Britons was compensated by the prospect of rich booty in slaves. When, for example, Corinth was destroyed, the melting-down of the statues for coinage and the auctioning of the inhabitants at the slave-mart were, for Classical minds, one and the same operation — the transformation of corporeal objects into money.

In extremest contrast to this stands the symbol of Faustian money — money as Function, the value of which lies in its effect and not its mere existence. The specific style of this economic thinking appears already in the way in which the Normans of A.D. 1000 organized their spoils of men and land into an economic force.[1] Compare the pure book-valuation of these ducal officials (commemorated in our words "cheque," "account," and "checking")[2] with the "contemporary" gold talent of the Iliad, one meets at the very outset of the Culture the rudiments of its modern credit-system, which is the outcome of confidence in the force and durability of its economic mode, and with which the idea of money in our sense is almost identical. These financial methods, transplanted to the Roman Kingdom of Sicily by Roger II, were developed by the Hohenstaufen Emperor Frederick II (about 1230) into a powerful system far surpassing the original in dynamism and making him the "first capitalist power of the world";[3] and while this fraternization of mathematical thinking-power and royal will-to-power made its way from Normandy into France and was applied on the grand scale to the exploitation of conquered England (to this day English soil is nominally royal demesne) its Sicilian side was imitated by the Italian city-republics, and (as their ruling patricians soon took the methods of the civic economy into use for their private book-keeping,) spread over the commercial thought and practice of the whole Western world. Little later, the Sicilian methods were adopted by the Order of the Teutonic Knights and by the dynasty of Aragon, and it is probably to these origins that we should assign the model accountancy of Spain in the days of Philip II, and of Prussia in those of Frederick William I.

[1] Pp. 371, et seq. The resemblance with the Egyptian administration under the Old Kingdom and the Chinese in the earliest Chóu period is unmistakable.

[2] The *clerici* of these exchequer offices were the archetype of the modern bank-clerk. Cf. p. 371.

[3] Hampe, *Deutsche Kaisergeschichte*, p. 246. Leonardo Pisano, whose *Liber Abaci* (1202) was authoritative in accountancy till well beyond the Renaissance, and who introduced, besides the Arabian system of numerals, negative numbers to indicate debit, was promoted by the great Hohenstaufen.

The decisive event, however, was the invention — "contemporary" with that of the Classical coin about 650 — of double-entry book-keeping by Fra Luca Pacioli in 1494. Goethe calls this in *Wilhelm Meister* "one of the finest discoveries of the human intellect," and indeed its author may without hesitation be ranked with his contemporaries Columbus and Copernicus. To the Normans we owe our modes of reckoning and to the Lombards our book-keeping. These, be it observed, were the same two Germanic stocks which created the two most suggestive juristic works of the early Gothic,[1] and whose longing into distant seas gave the impulses for the two discoveries of America. "Double-entry book-keeping is born of the same spirit as the system of Galileo and Newton. . . . With the same means as these, it orders the phenomenon into an elegant system, and it may be called the first Cosmos built up on the basis of a mechanistic thought. Double-entry book-keeping discloses to us the Cosmos of the economic world by the same method as later the Cosmos of the stellar universe was unveiled by the great investigation of natural philosophy. . . . Double-entry book-keeping rests on the basic principle, logically carried out, of comprehending all phenomena purely as quantities." [2]

Double-entry book-keeping is a pure Analysis of the space of values, referred to a co-ordinate system, of which the origin is the "Firm." The coinage of the Classical world had only permitted of arithmetical compilations with value-*magnitudes*. Here, as ever, Pythagoras and Descartes stand opposed. It is legitimate for us to talk of the "integration" of an undertaking, and the graphic curve is the same optical auxiliary to economics as it is to science. The Classical economy-world was ordered, like the cosmos of Democritus, according to *stuff and form*. A stuff, in the form of a coin, carries the economic movement and presses against the demand-unit of equal value-quantity at the place of use. *Our* economy-world is ordered by *force and mass*. A field of money-tensions lies in space and assigns to every object, irrespective of its specific kind, a positive or negative effect-value,[3] which is represented by a book-entry. "*Quod non est in libris, non est in mundo.*" But the symbol of the functional money thus imagined, that which *alone* may be compared with the Classical coin, is not the actual book-entry, nor yet the share-voucher, cheque, or note, *but the act by which the function is fulfilled in writing*, and the rôle of the value-paper is merely to be the *generalized historical evidence* of this act.

Yet side by side with this the West, in its unquestioning admiration of the Classical, has gone on striking coins, not merely as tokens of sovereignty, but in the belief that this evidenced money was money corresponding in reality to

---

[1] P. 75.

[2] Sombart, *Der moderne Kapitalismus*, II, p. 119.

[3] There is a close relation between our picture of the nature of electricity and the process of the "clearing-house," in which the positive and negative money-positions of several firms (centres of tension) are equated amongst themselves by a purely mental act and the true position made presentable by a booking. Cf. Vol. I, Ch. XI.

the economics in thought. In just the same way, even within the Gothic age, we took over Roman law with its equating of things to bodily magnitudes, and the Euclidean mathematic, which was built upon the concept of number as magnitude. And so it befell that the evolution of these three intellectual form-worlds of ours proceeded, not like the Faustian music in a pure and flowerlike unfolding, but in the shape of a *progressive emancipation from the notion of magnitude.* The mathematic had already achieved this by the close of the Baroque age.[1] The jurisprudence, on the other hand, has not yet even recognized its coming task,[2] but this century is going to set it, and to demand that which for Roman jurists was the self-evident basis of law, namely, the inward congruence of economic and legal thought and an equal practical familiarity with both. The conception of money that was symbolized in the coin agreed precisely with the Classical thing-law, but with us there is nothing remotely like such an agreement. Our whole life is disposed dynamically, not statically and Stoically; therefore our essentials are forces and performances, relations and capacities — organizing talents and intuitive intellects, credit, ideas, methods, energy-sources — and not mere existence of corporeal things. The "Romanist" thing-thought of our jurists, and the theory of money that consciously or unconsciously starts from the coin, are equally alien to our life. The vast metallic hoard to which, in imitation of the Classical, we were continually adding till the World War came, has indeed made a rôle for itself off the main road, but with the inner form, tasks, and aims of modern economy it has *nothing* to do; and if as the result of the war it were to disappear from currency altogether, nothing would be altered thereby.[3]

Unhappily, the modern national economics were founded in the age of Classicism. Just as statues and vases and stiff dramas alone counted as true art, so also finely stamped coins alone counted as true money. What Josiah Wedgwood (1758) aimed at with his delicately toned reliefs and cups, that also, at bottom, Adam Smith aimed at in his theory of value — namely, the pure present of tangible magnitudes. For it is entirely consonant with the illusion that money

---

[1] Vol. I, Ch. II.

[2] P. 81.

[3] In our Culture the credit of a country rests upon its economic capacity and the political organization thereof — which imparts to the operations and bookings of finance the character of real money-creations — and not on any quantity of gold that may be put into this or that. It is the Classicist superstition that raises the gold reserve to the status of an actual measure of credit — actual in that the level of credit is thereby made dependent, not upon " will," but upon " can." But the current coins are *wares*, which, relatively to national credit, possess a *price* — the poorer the credit, the higher the price of gold — so that thenceforth it can only be upheld against that of *other* wares. Thus gold is measured like other wares against the unit of book-reckoning, and not vice versa as the term "gold standard" suggests. It serves also as means of payment in minor transactions, as for that matter a postage-stamp does. In old Egypt (whose money-thought is astoundingly like the Western) there was nothing resembling the coin even under the New Empire. The written transfer was entirely sufficient, and the Classical coins that filtered in from 650 to the founding of Alexandria and the Hellenistic régime were usually cut to pieces and reckoned by weight as a ware.

and pieces of money are the same, to measure the value of a thing against the magnitude of a quantity of work. Here work is no longer an *effecting* in a world of effects, a working which can differ infinitely from case to case as to inward worth and intensity and range, which propagates itself in wider and wider circles and like an electric field may be measured but not marked off — but the *result* of the effecting, considered entirely materially, *that which is worked-up*, a tangible thing showing nothing noteworthy about it except just its extent.

In reality, the economy of the European-American Civilization is built up on work of a kind in which distinctions go entirely according to the inner quality — more so than ever in China or Egypt, let alone the Classical World. It is not for nothing that we live in a world of economic dynamism, where the works of the individual are not additive in the Euclidean way, but functionally related to one another. The purely executive work (which alone Marx takes into account) is in reality nothing but the function of an inventive, ordering, and organizing work; it is from this that the other derives its meaning, relative value, and even possibility of being done at all. The whole world-economy since the discovery of the steam-engine has been the creation of a quite small number of superior heads, without whose high-grade work everything else would never have come into being. But this achievement is of creative thinking, not a quantum,[1] and its value is not to be weighed against a certain number of coins. Rather it *is* itself money — Faustian money, namely, which is not minted, but *thought of as an efficient centre* coming up out of a life — and it is the inward quality of that life which elevates the thought to the significance of a fact. *Thinking in money generates money* — that is the secret of the world-economy. When an organizing magnate writes down a million on paper, that million exists, for the personality as an economic centre vouches for a corresponding heightening of the economic energy of his field. This, and nothing else, is the meaning of the word "Credit" for us. But all the gold pieces in the world would not suffice to invest the actions of the manual worker with a meaning, and therefore a value, if the famous "expropriation of the expropriators" were to eliminate the superior capacities from their creations; were this to happen, these would become soulless, will-less, empty shells. Thus, in fact, Marx is just as much a Classical, just as truly a product of the Romanist law-thought as Adam Smith; he sees only the completed magnitude, not the function, and he would like to separate the means of production from those whose minds, by the discovery of methods, the organization of efficient industries, and the acquisition of outlet-markets, alone turn a mass of bricks and steel into a factory, and who, if their forces find no field of play, do not occur.[2]

---

[1] That is why it does not exist for our (present) jurisprudence.

[2] All this equally holds good for the case of "workers" taking over the leadership of the works. Either they are incapable of management, and the business collapses, or they are capable of something, and then they themselves become inwardly entrepreneurs and think thenceforward only of maintaining their power. No theory can eliminate this fact from the world, for so life *is*.

If anyone seeks to enunciate a theory of modern work, let him begin by thinking of this basic trait of all life. There are subjects and objects in every kind of life as lived, and the more important, the more rich in form, the life is, the clearer the distinction between them. As every stream of Being consists of a minority of leaders and a huge majority of led, so *every sort of economy consists in leader-work and executive work.* The frog's perspective of Marx and the social-ethical ideologues shows only the aggregate of last small things, but these only exist at all in virtue of the first things, and the spirit of this world of work can be grasped only through a grasp of its highest possibilities. The inventor of the steam-engine and not its stoker is the determinant. The *thought* is what matters.

And, similarly, thinking in money has subjects and objects: those who by force of their personality generate and guide money, and those who are maintained by money. Money of the Faustian brand is the *force* distilled from economy-dynamics of the Faustian brand, and it appertains to the destiny of the individual (on the economic side of his life-destiny) that he is inwardly constituted to represent a part of this force, or that he is, on the contrary, nothing but mass to it.

V

The word "Capital" signifies the centre of this thought — not the aggregate of values, but that which *keeps them in movement as such.* Capitalism comes into existence only with the world-city existence of a Civilization, and it is confined to the very small ring of those who represent this existence by their persons and intelligence; its opposite is the provincial economy. It was the unconditional supremacy achieved by the coin in Classical life (including the political side of that life) that generated the static capital, the ἀφορμή or starting-point, that by its existence drew to itself, in a sort of magnetic attraction, things and again things *en masse.* It was the supremacy of book-values, whose abstract system was quickly detached from personality by double-entry book-keeping and worked forward by virtue of its own inward dynamism, that produced the modern capital that spans the whole earth with its field of force.[1]

Under the influence of its own sort of capital the economic life of the Classical world took the form of a gold-stream that flowed from the provinces to Rome and back, and was ever seeking new areas whose stock of worked-up gold had not yet been "opened up." Brutus and Cassius carried the gold of

[1] Thus it is only since 1770 that the banks have become centres of an economic power which made its first intervention with politics at the Congress of Vienna. Till then the banker had in the main concerned himself with bill business. The Chinese, and even the Egyptian, banks had a different significance, and the Classical banks, even in the Rome of Cæsar's day, may best be described as cash-tills. They collected the yield of taxes in cash, and lent cash against replacement; thus the temples, with their stock of precious metal in the form of votive offerings, became "banks." The temple of Delos, through several centuries, lent at ten per cent.

Asia Minor on long mule-trains to the battle-field of Philippi — one can imagine what sort of an economic operation the plunder of a camp after a battle must have been — and even C. Gracchus, almost a century earlier, alluded to the amphoræ that went out from Rome to the provinces full of wine and came back full of gold. This hunt for the gold possessions of alien peoples corresponds exactly to the present-day hunt for coal, which in its deeper meaning is not a thing, but a store of energy.

But, equally, the Classical craving for the near and present could not but match the Polis-ideal with an *economic ideal of Autarkeia*, an economic atomization corresponding to the political. Each of these tiny life-units desired to have an economic stream wholly of its own, wholly self-contained, circling independently of all others and *within the radius of visibility*. The polar opposite of this is the Western notion of the *Firm*, which is thought of as an entirely impersonal and incorporeal centre of force, from which activity streams out in all directions to an indefinite distance, and which the proprietor by his ability to think in money does not *represent*, but *possesses and directs* — that is, has in his power — like a little cosmos. The duality of firm and proprietor would have been utterly unimaginable for the Classical mind.[1]

Consequently, as the Western Culture presents a maximum, so the Classical shows a minimum, of *organization*. For this was completely absent even as an idea from Classical man. His finance was one of provisional expedients made rule and habit. The wealthy burgher of Athens and Rome could be burdened with the equipment of war-ships. The political power of the Roman ædile (and his debts) rested on the fact that he not only produced the games and the streets and the buildings, but paid for them too — of course, he could recoup himself later by plundering his province. Sources of income were thought of only when the need of income presented itself, and then drawn upon, without any regard for the future, as the moment required — even at the cost of entirely destroying them. Plunder of the treasures of one's own temples, sea-piracy against one's own city, confiscation of the wealth of one's own fellow-citizens were everyday methods of finance. If surpluses were available, they were distributed to the citizens — a proceeding to which plenty of people besides Eubulus of Athens owed their popularity.[2] Budgets were as unknown as any other part of financial policy. The "economic management" of Roman provinces was a system of robbery, public and private, practised by senators and financiers without the slightest consideration as to whether the exported values could be replaced. Never did Classical man think of systematically intensifying his economic life, but ever looked to the result of the moment, the tangible quantum of cash. Imperial Rome would have gone down in ruin had it not

---

[1] The idea of the Firm took shape even in Late Gothic times as "*ratio*" [hence the modern French phrase "*raison sociale*" Tr.] or "*negotiatio*." It is impossible to render it exactly in a Classical language. *Negotium* meant for the Romans a concrete process, a "deal" and not a "business."

[2] Pöhlmann, *griech. Geschichte* (1914), p. 216, et seq.

been fortunate enough to possess in old Egypt a Civilization that had for a thousand years thought of *nothing* but the organization of its economy. The Roman neither comprehended nor was capable of copying this style of life,[1] but the accident that Egypt provided the political possessor of this fellah-world with an inexhaustible source of gold rendered it unnecessary for him to make a *settled habit* of proscription at home; the last of these financial operations in massacre-form was that of 43, shortly before the incorporation of Egypt.[2] The amassed gold of Asia Minor that Brutus and Cassius were then bringing up, which meant an army and the dominion of the world, made it necessary to put to the ban some two thousand of the richest inhabitants of Italy, whose heads were brought to the Forum in sacks for the offered rewards. It was no longer possible to spare even relatives, children, and grey-heads, or people who had never concerned themselves with politics. It was enough that they possessed a stock of cash and that the yield would otherwise have been too small.

But with the extinction of the Classical world-feeling in the early Imperial age, this mode of thinking in money disappeared also. *Coins again became wares* — because men were again living the peasant life [3] — and this explains the

[1] Gercke-Norden, *Einl. in der Altertumswissensch.*, III, p. 291.

[2] Kromayer, in Hartmann's *Röm. Gesch.*, p. 150.

[3] The "Jews" of those times were the Romans (p. 318), and the Jews themselves were peasants and artizans and small traders (Parván, *Die Nationalität der Kaufleute in röm. Kaiserreich*, 1909; also Mommsen, *Röm. Gesch.*, V, p. 471); that is, they followed the very callings that in the Gothic period became the *object* of their merchant activity. Present-day "Europe" is in exactly the same position *vis-à-vis* the Russians whose profoundly mystical inner life feels "thinking in money" *as a sin*. (The Pilgrim in Gorki's *Night-asylum*, and Tolstoi's thought generally; pp. 194, 278.) Here to-day as in the Syria of Jesus's time we have two economic worlds juxtaposed (pp. 192, et seq.): an upper, alien, and civilized world intruded from the West (the Bolshevism of the first years, totally Western and un-Russian, is the lees of this infiltration), and a townless barter-life that goes on deep below, uncalculating and exchanging only for immediate needs. We have to think of the catchwords of the surface as a voice, in which the Russian, simple and busied wholly with his soul, hears resignedly the will of God. Marxism amongst Russians is based on an inward misunderstanding. They bore with the higher economic life of Petrinism, but they neither created it nor recognized it. The Russian does not fight Capital, but he does not *comprehend* it. Anyone who understands Dostoyevski will sense in these people a young humanity *for which as yet no money exists*, but only goods in relation to a life whose centre of gravity does *not* lie on the economical side. The horror of values supervening from nowhere which before the war drove many to suicide is a misconstrued literary disguise of the fact that, for a townless barter-thinking, money-getting by means of money is an impiety, and (from the view-point of the coming Russian religion) a sin. To-day, with the towns of Tsarism in ruin and the mankind in them living the village life under the crust (temporarily) of urban-thinking Bolshevism, he has freed himself from the Western economy. His apocalyptic hatred — the same that the simple Jew of Jesus's day bore to the Roman — is directed against Petersburg, as a city and the seat of a political power of Western stamp, but also as the centre of a thinking in Western money that has poisoned and misdirected the whole life. The Russian of the deeps to-day is bringing into being a third kind of Christianity, still priestless, and built *on the John Gospel* — a Christianity that stands much nearer to the Magian than to the Faustian and, consequently, rests upon a new symbolism of baptism, and looks neither at Rome nor at Wittenberg, but past Byzantium towards Jerusalem, with premonitions of coming crusades. This is the *only* thing that this new Russia really cares about. And it will no doubt let itself fall once again under the economy of the West, as the primitive Christian submitted to the Romans and the Gothic Christian to the Jews. But inwardly it has no part nor lot therein. (Cf. pp. 192, 226, 278, 293, 295.)

immense outflow of gold into the farther East after Hadrian's reign, which has hithero been unaccountable. And as economic life in forms of gold-streams was extinguished in the upheaval of a young Culture, so also the slave ceased to be money, and the ebb of the gold was paralleled by that mass-emancipation of the slaves which numerous Imperial laws, from Augustus's reign onwards, tried in vain to check — till under Diocletian, in whose famous maximum tariff [1] money-economy was no longer the standpoint, the type of the Classical slave had ceased to exist.

[1] See the article "Diocletian, Edict of," *Ency. Brit.*, XI ed. — *Tr.*

CHAPTER XIV

THE FORM-WORLD OF ECONOMIC LIFE

(B)

THE MACHINE

THE FORM-WORLD OF ECONOMIC LIFE

(B)

THE MACHINE

I

TECHNIQUE is as old as free-moving life itself. Only the plant — so far as we can see into Nature — is the mere theatre of technical processes. The animal, in that it moves, has a technique of movement so that it may nourish and protect itself.

The original relation between a waking-microcosm and its macrocosm — "Nature" — consists in a touch through the senses [1] which rises from mere sense-*impressions* to sense-*judgment*, so that already it works critically (that is, separatingly) or, what comes to the same thing, *causal-analytically*.[2] The stock of what has been determined then is enlarged into a system, as complete as may be, of the most primary experiences — identifying marks[3] — a spontaneous method by which one is enabled to feel at home in one's world; in the case of many animals this has led to an amazing richness of experience that no human science has transcended. But the primary waking-being is always an *active* one, remote from mere theory of all sorts, and thus it is in the minor technique of everyday life, and upon things *in so far as they are dead*,[4] that these experiences are involuntarily acquired. This is the difference between Cult and Myth,[5] for at this level there is no boundary line between religion and the profane — all waking-consciousness *is* religion.

The decisive turn in the history of the higher life occurs when the *determination* of Nature (in order to be guided by it) changes into a *fixation* — that is, a purposed alteration of Nature. With this, technique becomes more or less sovereign and the instinctive prime-experience changes into a definitely "conscious" prime-*knowing*. Thought has emancipated itself from sensation. It is the *language of words* that brings about this epochal change. The liberation of speech from speaking [6] gives rise to a stock of signs for communication-speech which are much more than identification-marks — they are *names* bound up with a sense of meaning, whereby man has the secret of numina (deities, nature-forces) in his power, and *number* (formulæ, simple laws), whereby the inner form of the actual is abstracted form the accidental-sensuous.[7]

---

[1] P. 6. [2] Pp. 9 et seq. [3] P. 25 [4] P. 25
[5] P. 268. [6] P. 134. [7] Pp. 25, et seq.; 267, et seq.

With that, the system of identification-marks develops into a theory, a *picture* which detaches itself from the technique of the day [1] — whether this be a day of high-level Civilized technics or a day of simplest beginnings — by way of *abstraction*, as a piece of waking-consciousness uncommitted to activity. One "knows" what one wants, but much must have happened for one to have that knowledge, and we must make no mistake as to its character. By numerical experience man is enabled to switch the secret on and off, but he has not discovered it. The figure of the modern sorcerer — a switchboard with levers and labels at which the workman calls mighty effects into play by the pressure of a finger without possessing the slightest notion of their essence — is only the symbol of human technique in general. The picture of the light-world around us — in so far as we have developed it critically, analytically, as theory, as picture — is nothing but a switchboard of the kind, on which particular things are so labelled that by (so to say) pressing the appropriate button particular effects follow with certainty. The secret itself remains none the less oppressive on that account.[2] But through this technique the waking-consciousness does, all the same, intervene masterfully in the fact-world. Life *makes use* of thought as an "open sesame," and at the peak of many a Civilization, in its great cities, there arrives finally the moment when technical critique becomes tired of being life's servant and makes itself tyrant. The Western Culture is even now experiencing an orgy of this unbridled thought, and on a tragic scale.

Man has listened-in to the march of Nature and made notes of its indices. He begins to imitate it by means and methods that utilize the laws of the cosmic pulse. He is emboldened to play the part of God, and it is easy to understand how the earliest preparers and experts of these artificial things — for it was here that art came to be, *as counter-concept to nature* — and how in particular the guardians of the smith's art, appeared to those around them as something uncanny and were regarded with awe or horror as the case might be. The stock of such discoveries grew and grew. Often they were made and forgotten and made again, were imitated, shunned, improved. But in the end they constituted for whole continents a store of *self-evident* means — fire, metal-working, instruments, arms, ploughs, boats, houses, animal-taming, and husbandry. Above all, the metals, to whose site in the earth primitive man is led by some uncannily mystical trait in him. Immemoriably old trade-routes lead to ore-deposits that are kept secret, through the life of the settled countryside and over frequented seas, and along these, later, travel cults and ornaments and

---

[1] And not vice versa. Cf. p. 268.

[2] The "correctness" of physical data (i.e., their applicability never disproved up to date, and therefore ranking as an *interpretation*) is wholly independent of their technical value. An undoubtedly wrong, and even self-contradictory, theory may be more valuable for practical purposes than a "correct" and profound one, and physical science has long been careful to avoid applying the words "right" and "wrong" in the popular sense, and to regard their syntheses as images rather than flat formulæ.

persistent legends of islands of tin and lands of gold. The primary trade of all is the metal trade, and with it the economics of production and of work are joined intrusively by a third — alien, venturesome, free-ranging over the lands.

On this foundation, now, arises the technique of the higher Cultures, expressive in quality and colour and passion of the whole soul of these major entities. It need hardly be said that Classical man, who felt himself and his environment alike Euclidean, set himself *a priori* in hostile opposition to the very idea of technique. If by "Classical" technique we mean something that (along with the rest that we comprehend in the adjective) rose with determined effort above the universal dead perfection of the Mycenæan age, then there was no Classical technique.[1] Its triremes were glorified row-boats, its catapults and onagers mere substitutes for arms and fists — not to be named in the same breath with the war-engines of Assyria and China — and as for Hero and his like, it was flukes and not discoveries that they achieved. They lacked the inner weight, the fatedness of their moment, the deep necessity. Here and there men played with data (and why not?) that probably came from the East, but no one devoted serious attention to them and, above all, no one made a real effort to introduce them into the ensemble-picture of life.

Very different is the Faustian technics, which with all its passion of the third dimension, and from earliest Gothic days, thrusts itself upon Nature, with the firm resolve to *be its master*. Here, and only here, is the connexion of insight and utilization a matter of course.[2] Theory is working hypothesis [3] from the outset. The Classical investigator "contemplated" like Aristotle's deity, the Arabian sought as alchemist for magical means (such as the Philosophers' Stone) whereby to possess himself of Nature's treasures *without effort*,[4] but the Western strives to *direct* the world according to his will.

The Faustian inventor and discoverer is a unique type. The primitive force of his will, the brilliance of his visions, the steely energy of his practical ponderings, must appear queer and incomprehensible to anyone at the standpoint of another Culture, but for us they are in the blood. Our whole Culture has a discoverer's soul. To *dis*-cover that which is not seen, to draw it into the light-world of the inner eye so as to master it — that was its stubborn passion from the first days on. All its great inventions slowly ripened in the deeps,

[1] What Diels has managed to assemble in his work *Antike Technik* amounts to a comprehensive nullity. If we take away from it what belongs to the older Babylonian Civilization (such as water clocks and sun-dials) and to the younger Arabian Springtime (such as chemistry or the wonder-clock of Gaza), there is nothing left but devices, such as door-locks of a sort, that it would be an insult to attribute to any other Culture.

[2] The Chinese Culture, too, made almost all these European discoveries on its own account — including compass, telescope, printing, gunpowder, paper, porcelain — but the Chinese did not wrest, but *wheedled*, things out of Nature. No doubt he felt the advantages of his knowledge and turned it to account, but he did not hurl himself upon it to exploit it.

[3] P. 301.

[4] It is the same spirit that distinguishes the Jewish, Parsee, Armenian, Greek, and Arab ideas of business from that of the Western peoples.

to emerge at last with the necessity of a Destiny. All of them were very nearly approached by the high-hearted, happy research of the early Gothic monks.[1] Here, if anywhere, the religious origins of all technical thought are manifested.[2] These meditative discoverers in their cells, who with prayers and fastings *wrung* God's secret out of him, felt that they were *serving* God thereby. Here is the Faust-figure, the grand symbol of a true discovering Culture. The *Scientia experimentalis*, as Roger Bacon was the first to call nature-research, the *insistent* questioning of Nature with levers and screws, began that of which the issue lies under our eyes as a countryside sprouting factory-chimneys and conveyor-towers. But for all of them, too, there was the truly Faustian danger of the Devil's having a hand in the game,[3] the risk that he was leading them in spirit to that mountain on which he promises all the power of the earth. This is the significance of the *perpetuum mobile* dreamed of by those strange Dominicans like Petrus Peregrinus, which would wrest the almightiness from God. Again and again they succumbed to this ambition; they forced this secret out of God in order themselves to be God. They listened for the laws of the cosmic pulse in order to overpower it. And so they created the *idea of the machine* as a small cosmos obeying the will of man alone. But with that they overpassed the slender border-line whereat the reverent piety of others saw the beginning of sin, and on it, from Roger Bacon to Giordano Bruno, they came to grief. Ever and ever again, true belief has regarded the machine as of the Devil.

The passion of discovery declares itself as early as the Gothic architecture — compare with this the deliberate form-poverty of the Doric! — and is manifest throughout our music. Book-printing appeared, and the long-range weapon.[4] On the heels of Columbus and Copernicus come the telescope, the microscope, the chemical elements, and lastly the immense technological corpus of the early Baroque.

Then followed, however, simultaneously with Rationalism, the discovery of the steam-engine, which upset everything and transformed economic life from the foundations up. Till then nature had rendered services, but now she was tied to the yoke as *a slave*, and her work was as though in contempt measured by a standard of horse-power. We advanced from the muscle-force of the

[1] P. 301. Albertus Magnus lived on in legend as the great magician. Roger Bacon meditated upon steam-engines, steamships, and aircraft. (F. Strunz, *Gesch. d. Naturwiss. in Mittelalter*, 1910, p. 88.)

[2] P. 268. According to Roger Bacon the "third rôle of science," which is not relative to the other sciences, consists in the power that makes it to search the secrets of nature, to discover past and future, and to produce so many marvellous results that power is assured to those who possess it. . . . The Church should take it into consideration in order to spare Christian blood in the struggle with the infidel and above all in preparation for the perils that will menace us in the days of Antichrist (E. Gilson, *Philosophie du Moyen Age*, p. 218). *Tr.*

[3] P. 288.

[4] Greek fire was only to terrify and to ignite, but here the tense force of the gases of explosion are converted into energy of motion. Anyone who seriously compares the two does not understand the spirit of the Western technique.

Negro, which was set to work in organized routines, to the organic reserves of the Earth's crust, where the life-forces of millennia lay stored as coal; and to-day we cast our eyes on inorganic nature, where water-forces are already being brought in to supplement coal. As the horse-powers run to millions and milliards, the numbers of the population increase and increase, on a scale that no other Culture ever thought possible. This growth is a *product of the Machine,* which insists on being used and directed, and to that end centuples the forces of each individual. For the sake of the machine, human life becomes precious. *Work* becomes the great word of ethical thinking; in the eighteenth century it loses its derogatory implication in all languages. The machine works and forces the man to co-operate. The entire Culture reaches a degree of activity such that the earth trembles under it.

And what now develops, in the space of hardly a century, is a drama of such greatness that the men of a future Culture, with other soul and other passions, will hardly be able to resist the conviction that "in those days" nature herself was tottering. The politics stride over cities and peoples; even the economics, deeply as they bite into the destinies of the plant and animal worlds, merely touch the fringe of life and efface themselves. But this technique will leave traces of its heyday behind it when all else is lost and forgotten. For this Faustian passion has altered the Face of the Earth.

This is the outward- and upward-straining life-feeling — true descendant, therefore, of the Gothic — as expressed in Goethe's Faust monologue when the steam-engine was yet young. The intoxicated soul wills to fly above space and Time. An ineffable longing tempts him to indefinable horizons. Man would free himself from the earth, rise into the infinite, leave the bonds of the body, and circle in the universe of space amongst the stars. That which the glowing and soaring inwardness of St. Bernard sought at the beginning, that which Grünewald and Rembrandt conceived in their backgrounds, and Beethoven in the trans-earthly tones of his last quartets, comes back now in the intellectual intoxication of the inventions that crowd one upon another. Hence the fantastic traffic that crosses the continents in a few days, that puts itself across oceans in floating cities, that bores through mountains, rushes about in subterranean labyrinths, uses the steam-engine till its last possibilities have been exhausted, and then passes on to the gas-engine, and finally raises itself above the roads and railways and flies in the air; hence it is that the spoken word is sent in one moment over all the oceans; hence comes the ambition to break all records and beat all dimensions, to build giant halls for giant machines, vast ships and bridge-spans, buildings that deliriously scrape the clouds, fabulous forces pressed together to a focus to obey the hand of a child, stamping and quivering and droning works of steel and glass in which tiny man moves as unlimited monarch and, at the last, feels nature as beneath him.

And these machines become in their forms less and ever less human, more ascetic, mystic, esoteric. They weave the earth over with an infinite web of subtle forces, currents, and tensions. Their bodies become ever more and more immaterial, ever less noisy. The wheels, rollers, and levers are vocal no more. All that matters withdraws itself into the interior. Man has felt the machine to be devilish, and rightly. It signifies in the eyes of the believer the deposition of God. It delivers sacred Causality over to man and by him, with a sort of foreseeing omniscience is set in motion, silent and irresistible.

II

Never save here has a microcosm felt itself superior to its macrocosm, but here the little life-units have by the sheer force of their intellect made the unliving dependent upon themselves. It is a triumph, so far as we can see, unparalleled. Only this our Culture has achieved it, and perhaps only for a few centuries.

But for that very reason Faustian man has become *the slave of his creation*. His number, and the arrangement of life as he lives it, have been driven by the machine on to a path where there is no standing still and no turning back. The peasant, the hand-worker, even the merchant, appear suddenly as inessential in comparison with the *three great figures that the Machine has bred and trained up in the cause of its development: the entrepreneur, the engineer, and the factory-worker*. Out of a quite small branch of manual work — namely, the preparation-economy — there has grown up (*in this one Culture alone*) a mighty tree that casts its shadow over all the other vocations — namely, *the economy of the machine-industry*.[1] It forces the entrepreneur not less than the workman to obedience. *Both* become slaves, and not masters, of the machine, that now for the first time develops its devilish and occult power. But although the Socialistic theory of the present day has insisted upon looking only at the latter's contribution and has claimed the word "work" for him alone, it has all become possible only through the sovereign and decisive achievement of the former. The famous phrase concerning the "strong arm" that bids every wheel cease from running is a piece of wrong-headedness. To stop them — yes! but it does not need a worker to do that. To keep them running — no! The centre of this

---

[1] Marx is quite right; it is one of the creations (and what is more, the proudest creation) of the bourgeoisie. But, spellbound as he is by the ancient-mediæval-modern scheme, he has failed to note that it is only the bourgeoisie of this one single Culture that is master of the destiny of the Machine. So long as it dominates the earth, every non-European tries and will try to fathom the secret of this terrible weapon. Nevertheless, inwardly he abhors it, be he Indian or Japanese, Russian or Arab. It is something fundamental in the essence of the Magian soul that leads the Jew, as entrepreneur and engineer, to stand aside from the creation proper of machines and devote himself to the business side of their production. But so also the Russian looks with fear and hatred at this tyranny of wheels, cables, and rails, and if he adapts himself for to-day and to-morrow to the inevitable, yet there will come a time when he will *blot out the whole thing from his memory and his environment*, and create about himself a wholly new world, in which nothing of this Devil's technique is left.

artificial and complicated realm of the Machine is the organizer and manager. The mind, not the hand, holds it together. But, for that very reason, to preserve the ever endangered structure, *one* figure is even more important than all the energy of enterprising master-men that make cities to grow out of the ground and alter the picture of the landscape; it is a figure that is apt to be forgotten in this conflict of politics — the *engineer*, the priest of the machine, the man who knows it. Not merely the importance, but the very existence of the industry depends upon the existence of the hundred thousand talented, rigorously schooled brains that command the technique and develop it onward and onward. The quiet engineer it is who is the machine's master and destiny. His thought is as possibility what the machine is as actuality. There have been fears, thoroughly materialistic fears, of the exhaustion of the coal-fields. But so long as there are worthy technical path-finders, dangers of this sort have no existence. When, and only when, the crop of recruits for this army fails — this army whose thought-work forms one inward unit with the work of the machine — the industry must flicker out in spite of all that managerial energy and the workers can do. Suppose that, in future generations, the most gifted minds were to find their soul's health more important than all the powers of this world; suppose that, under the influence of the metaphysic and mysticism that is taking the place of rationalism to-day, the very élite of intellect that is now concerned with the machine comes to be overpowered by a growing sense of its *Satanism* (it is the step from Roger Bacon to Bernard of Clairvaux) — then nothing can hinder the end of this grand drama that has been a play of intellects, with hands as mere auxiliaries.

The Western industry has diverted the ancient traditions of the other Cultures. The streams of economic life move towards the seats of King Coal and the great regions of raw material. Nature becomes exhausted, the globe sacrificed to Faustian thinking in energies. The *working* earth is the Faustian aspect of her, the aspect contemplated by the Faust of Part II, the supreme transfiguration of enterprising work — and contemplating, he dies. Nothing is so utterly antipodal to the motionless satiate being of the Classical Empire. It is the engineer who is remotest from the Classical law-thought, and he will see to it that his economy has *its own* law, wherein forces and efficiencies will take the place of Person and Thing.

III

But titanic, too, is the onslaught of money upon this intellectual force. Industry, too, is earth-bound like the yeoman. It has its station, and its materials stream up out of the earth. Only high finance is *wholly* free, wholly intangible. Since 1789 the banks, and with them the bourses, have developed themselves on the credit-needs of an industry growing ever more enormous, as a power on their own account, and they will (as money wills in every Civilization) to be the only power. The ancient wrestle between the productive and the acquisitive economies intensifies now into a silent gigantomachy of intellects, fought out in the lists of the world-cities. This battle is the despairing struggle of technical thought to maintain its liberty against money-thought.[1]

The dictature of money marches on, tending to its material peak, in the Faustian Civilization as in every other. And now something happens that is intelligible only to one who has penetrated to the essence of money. If it were anything tangible, then its existence would be for ever — but, as it is a form of thought, *it fades out as soon as it has thought its economic world to finality*, and has no more material upon which to feed. It thrust into the life of the yeoman's countryside and set the earth a-moving; its thought transformed every sort of handicraft; to-day it presses victoriously upon industry to make the productive work of entrepreneur and engineer and labourer alike its spoil. The machine with its human retinue, the real queen of this century, is in danger of succumbing to a stronger power. But with this, money, too, is at the end of its success, and the last conflict is at hand in which the Civilization receives its conclusive form — the conflict *between* money and blood.

The coming of Cæsarism breaks the dictature of money and its political weapon democracy. After a long triumph of world-city economy and its interests over political creative force, the political side of life manifests itself after all as the stronger of the two. The sword is victorious over the money, the master-will subdues again the plunderer-will. If we call these money-powers "Capitalism," [2] then we may designate as Socialism the will to call into life a mighty politico-economic order that transcends all class interests, a system of *lofty* thoughtfulness and duty-sense that keeps the whole in fine condition for the decisive battle of its history, and this battle is also the battle of money and law.[3] The *private* powers of the economy want free paths for their acquisition of great resources. No legislation must stand in their way. They want to make the laws themselves, in their interests, and to that end they make use of the tool they have made for themselves, democracy, the subsidized party. Law needs, in order to resist this onslaught, a high tradition and an ambition of strong families that finds its satisfaction not in the heaping-up of riches, but in the tasks of true rulership, above and beyond all money-advantage. *A power can be overthrown only by another power*, not by a principle, and no power that can confront

---

[1] Compared with this mighty contest between the two handfuls of steel-hard men of race and of immense intellect — which the simple citizen neither observes nor comprehends — the battle of mere interests between the employing class and the workers' Socialism sinks into insignificance when regarded from the distant world-historical view-point. The working-class movement is what its leaders *make* of it, and hatred of the owner has long enlisted itself in the service of the bourse. Practical communism with its "class-war" — to-day a long obsolete and adulterated phrase — is nothing but the trusty henchman of big Capital, which knows perfectly well how to make use of it.

[2] In this sense the interest-politics of the workers' movements also belong to it, in that their object is not to overcome the money-values, but to possess them.

[3] P. 345.

money is left but this one. Money is overthrown and abolished only by blood. *Life* is alpha and omega, the cosmic onflow in microcosmic form. It is *the* fact of facts within the world-as-history. Before the irresistible rhythm of the generation-sequence, everything built up by the waking-consciousness in its intellectual world vanishes at the last. Ever in History it is life and life only — race-quality, the triumph of the will-to-power — and not the victory of truths, discoveries, or money that signifies. *World-history is the world court,* and it has ever decided in favour of the stronger, fuller, and more self-assured life — decreed to it, namely, the right to exist, regardless of whether its right would hold before a tribunal of waking-consciousness. Always it has sacrificed truth and justice to might and race, and passed doom of death upon men and peoples in whom truth was more than deeds, and justice than power. And so the drama of a high Culture — that wondrous world of deities, arts, thoughts, battles, cities — closes with the return of the pristine facts of the blood eternal that is one and the same as the ever-circling cosmic flow. The bright imaginative Waking-Being submerges itself into the silent service of Being, as the Chinese and Roman empires tell us. Time triumphs over Space, and it is Time whose inexorable movement embeds the ephemeral incident of the Culture, on this planet, in the incident of Man — a form wherein the incident life flows on for a time, while behind it all the streaming horizons of geological and stellar histories pile up in the light-world of our eyes.

For us, however, whom a Destiny has placed in this Culture and at this moment of its development — the moment when money is celebrating its last victories, and the Cæsarism that is to succeed approaches with quiet, firm step — our direction, willed and obligatory at once, is set for us within narrow limits, and on any other terms life is not worth the living. We have not the freedom to reach to this or to that, but the freedom to do the necessary or to do nothing. And a task that historic necessity has set *will* be accomplished with the individual or against him.

Ducunt Fata volentem, nolentem trahunt.

INDEX

Prepared by DAVID M. MATTESON

i

A NOTE ON THE TYPE
in which this book is set

The type in which this book has been set (on the Monotype) is Garamont, a Monotype modernization of a type first cut by Claude Garamond (1510–61). Of his life very few facts are known. He was a pupil of Geofrey Tory, one of the ablest of early French type-designers, and seems to have been the first to devote himself entirely to designing and casting types apart from a printing establishment. He carried out many of the reforms proposed by Tory, and his letters, which were greatly admired, were bought by printers throughout Europe. They won him the patronage of the French king, Francis I, who commissioned him in 1541 to design Greek types in various sizes for the Royal Printer. In 1545 he enlarged his business to include printing and publishing. After his death his type-foundry was sold to Guillaume Le Blé and continued to operate from then (1561) until the French Revolution. Garamond gave to his types a certain elegance, a feeling of movement, and a general effect of lightness, clearness, and symmetry. To him we owe the letters known as "Old Style." In particular he improved the italics by inclining the capital letters and filling in with flourishes the gaps caused by the inclination—the result being what are known as "swash letters." In 1640 Cardinal Richelieu acquired for the French nation original steel punches and copper matrices made and used by Garamond. They and the types cast by means of them are still the property of the nation; they are kept in the Imprimerie Nationale, Paris, and are still used.